Articles on American Slavery

An eighteen–volume set collecting nearly four hundred of the most important articles on slavery in the United States

Edited with Introductions by
Paul Finkelman

State University of New York,
Binghamton

A Garland Series

Contents of the Series

Vol. 13

Rebellions, Resistance, and Runaways Within the Slave South

Edited with an Introduction
by Paul Finkelman

Garland Publishing, Inc.
New York & London
1989

Library of Congress Cataloging-in-Publication Data

Rebellions, resistance, and runaways within the slave
South/ edited with an introduction
by Paul Finkelman.

p. cm.—(Articles on American slavery; vol. 13)
Includes bibliographical references.
ISBN 0–8240–6793–2 (alk. paper)
1. Slavery—Southern States—Insurrections, etc.
2. Fugitive slaves—Southern States—History—
1775–1865. I. Finkelman, Paul. II. Series.

E447.R43	1989
975'.03—dc20	89–23597

Printed on acid-free, 250-year-life paper
Manufactured in the United States of America

Design by Julie Threlkeld

General Introduction

Few subjects in American history have been as compelling as slavery. This should not surprise us. Slavery affected millions of Americans, north and south. Afro-Americans, Euro-Americans, and Native Americans were involved in the system. All antebellum Americans were affected, directly or indirectly, by slavery. Slavery especially affected Americans from 1861 until well after Reconstruction. As Lincoln noted in his famous second inaugural address: "The slaves constituted a peculiar and powerful interest. All knew that this interest was somehow the cause of the war."

The goal of this series is to reprint the key articles that have influenced our understanding of slavery. This series includes pioneering articles in the history of slavery, important breakthroughs in research and methodology, and articles that offer major historiographical interpretations. I have attempted to cover all major subtopics of slavery, to offer wide geographic representation and methodological diversity. At the same time, I have resisted the temptation to reprint highly technical articles that will make sense only to specialists in certain fields. For example, I have not included a number of important slavery related articles on economics, law, theology, and literary criticism (to offer just a few examples) because they appeared to be beyond the interest of most generalists.

I have used articles from a wide variety of scholarly journals. I have also used essays and articles in edited volumes, as long as the main focus of those volumes was not slavery, abolition, or black studies. It is my hope that such books are readily available to scholars and students and will show up through card catalogues or on-line catalogue searches. For the same reason I have not reprinted chapters from books about slavery, which are often found in anthologies. With a few exceptions, I have not reprinted articles that later became chapters of books on the same subject. In a few cases I have strayed from this general rule of thumb. I have also generally avoided essay reviews of books, unless the essays go well beyond the common book review or even essay review format. I have also tried to avoid certain famous historiographical controversies that resulted in large numbers of essays being collected and published. With some exceptions, therefore, I have not included the many articles attacking the "Elkins" thesis or Fogel and Engerman's Time on the Cross. Students and scholars interested in these two enormously important scholarly works, and the criticism of them, will find a great deal on both in their card catalogues. Finally, I have also excluded articles from Encyclopedias and dictionaries. These editorial decisions mean that many famous essays and articles will not be found in these volumes. Indeed, a few very important scholars are not represented because all of their work has been in books that are directly on the subject of slavery. Finally, some important articles were left out because we were unable to secure permission from the copyright holders to reprint them in this series.

This project was made easier by the hard work and dedication of Carole Puccino and Leo Balk at Garland Publishing, Inc. A project of this magnitude would not be possible without the help of a number of other scholars, who read lists of proposed articles and discussed the whole problem of slavery with me. I am especially grateful for the help and suggestions of Catherine Clinton, Robert Cottrol, Jill DuPont, Seymour Drescher, Linda Evans, Ronald Formasano, John Hope Franklin, Kermit L. Hall, Robert Hall, Graham Hodges, Michael P. Johnson, Charles Joyner, Alan Kulikoff, Greg Lind, David McBride, Randall Miller, Alfred Moss, James Oakes, Albert J. Raboteau, Judith Schafer, Robert Sikorski, John David Smith, Jean Soderlund, Margaret Washington, William M. Wiecek, Julie Winch, Betty Wood, and Bertram Wyatt-Brown. Two SUNY-Binghamton students, Marci Silverman and Beth Borchers, helped me with much of the bibliographic work on this project. Carol A. Clemente and the inter-library loan staff at SUNY-Binghamton were absolutely wonderful. Without their patience, skills, and resourcefulness, I would have been unable to complete these volumes.

—Paul Finkelman

Contents

Introduction

Slaves were, as Kenneth Stampp has noted, "a troublesome property."[1] Afro-Americans were enslaved by force and kept in that status by force. The whip was the symbol of the master; the chain was the symbol of bondage. Anyone forced to labor, even by the threat of violence, is likely to resist. Slaves resisted in countless ways, from secretly breaking farm equipment or feigning illness to openly assaulting their masters, overseers, or any white they might run into. Slave resistance took the form of individual actions that could be passive or violent, as well as the form of collective action under the leadership of a Nat Turner or a Denmark Vesey.

Whenever possible slaves sought freedom. Some chose to escape to the North.[2] More common were slaves who "ran off" for short periods of time, only to be captured or returned. Such runaways disrupted the routine of farms and plantations all across the South. Runaways "effectively deprived the master of the slave's labor" and also challenged the rules of the masters.[3] Runaways often disappeared for short periods of time. The most common reasons for running off were to visit family on other plantations (usually spouses, children, or parents) or to avoid the wrath of an angry master.

Even more common than running off were small acts of disobedience and rebellion, as slaves "protested by shirking their duties, injuring the crops, feigning illness, and disrupting the routine. These acts were, in part, an unspectacular kind of 'day-to-day resistance to slavery.'"[4]

Far more spectacular were slave revolts. There were few large ones, and relatively few small ones. Individual acts of violent rebellion—the killing of a master or overseer—were also rare, but common enough to make all whites in the South have some fears of their slaves. However few the revolts were, each one undermined the self-confidence of the South's ruling race and left many whites shaken and fearful.

In 1822, a resident of Charleston, South Carolina wrote: "Let it never be forgotten, that 'our NEGROES are truly the *Jacobins* of the country; that they are the *anarchists* and the *domestic enemy*; the *common enemy of civilized society*, the barbarians who would, IF THEY COULD, become the DESTROYERS *of our race.*"[5]

These sentiments were expressed in the aftermath of the abortive Denmark Vesey revolt, a carefully planned conspiracy that may have involved as many as 9,000 slaves in Charleston and the surrounding area. Although Vesey was hanged, along with more than 130 other consipirators, residents of the city remained fearful. Four years later another Charlestonian wrote that it was "vain to conceal, what every trifling incident brings to our notice, that there are many who dread the scenes of 1822."[6]

The reaction in South Carolina to the Vesey conspiracy was only a prelude to the entire South's reaction to the Nat Turner rebellion of 1831, which led to the death of nearly sixty and more than one hundred slaves. Everywhere southerners trembled in fear of slave revolts. As far away as Louisiana, panic ensued.[7]

But, even when times were calm, southerners could not afford to relax. In 1833 Governor Robert Hayne told the South Carolina legislature that "A state of military preparation must always be with us a state of perfect domestic security. A period of profound peace and consequent apathy may expose us to the danger of domestic insurrection."[8] As the southern historian John Hope Franklin has concluded: "The slave was never so completely subjugated as to allay all fears that he would make a desperate, bloody attempt to destroy the institution which bound him. Slaveholders could never be quite certain that they had established unquestioned control; fear and apprehension were always present."[9] The essays in this volume elaborate on this problem.

—*Paul Finkelman*

Notes

1. Kenneth Stampp, *The Peculiar Institution* (New York: Random House, 1956) Chap.   3.

2. See Volume 6 of this series on Fugitive Slaves.

3. James Oakes, *The Ruling Race* (New York: Alfred A. Knopf, 1982) 188.

4. Stampp, *The Peculiar Institution*, 108–09.

5. Quoted in William W. Freehling, *Prelude to Civil War: The Nullification Controversy in South Carolina, 1816–1836* (New York: Harper and Row, 1965) 59.

6. Quoted in Freehling, *Prelude to Civil War*, 61.

7. Judith K. Schafer, "The Immediate Impact of Nat Turner's Insurrection on New Orleans," *Louisiana History* 21 (Fall, 1980) 361–76.

8. Quoted in John Hope Franklin, *The Militant South, 1800–1861* (Cambridge: Harvard University Press, 1956) 78.

9. Franklin, *The Militant South*, 70–71.

Further Reading

Aptheker, Herbert.   *American Negro Slave Revolts*. (New York: Columbia University Press, 1943).

Blassingame, John.   *The Slave Community*. (New York: Oxford University Press, 1972).

Davis, T.J.   *A Rumor of Revolt*. (New York: The Free Press, 1985).

Franklin, John Hope.   *The Militant South, 1800–1861*. Cambridge: Harvard University Press, 1956.

Freehling, William W.   *Prelude to Civil War: The Nullification Controversy in South Carolina, 1816–1836.* (New York: Harper and Row, 1965).

Killens, John O.   *Great Gettin' Up Morning: A Biography of Denmark Vesey*. (New York: Doubleday, 1972).

Kilson, Marion D.   "Towards Freedom: An Analysis of Slave Revolts in the United States," *Phylon* 25 (Summer, 1964) 175–87.

Littlefield, Daniel, and Lonnie E. Underhill.   "Slave 'Revolt' in the Cherokee Nation, 1842," *American Indian Quarterly* 3 (Summer, 1977) 121–33.

Mullin, Gerald W.   *Flight and Rebellion: Slave Resistance in Eighteenth Century Virginia*. (New York: Oxford University Press, 1972).

Oakes, James.   *The Ruling Race*. (New York: Alfred A. Knopf, 1982).

Oates, Stephen.   *The Fires of Jubilee: Nat Turner's Fierce Rebellion* (New York: Harper & Row, 1975).

Schafer, Judith K.   "The Immediate Impact of Nat Turner's Insurrection on New Orleans," *Louisiana History* 21 (Fall, 1980) 361–76.

Stampp, Kenneth.   *The Peculiar Institution.* New York: Random House, 1956).

Wood, Peter.   *Black Majority: Negroes in Colonial South Carolina, 1670 to the Stono Rebellion.* (New York: Alfred A. Knopf, 1974).

Rebellions, Resistance, and Runaways Within the Slave South

"Our slaves are the happiest three millions of human beings on whom the sun shines," declared a pamphlet[1] circulated in ten thousand copies by the Committee on Slaves and Slavery of the Texas House of Representatives in 1857.

The delightful picture of the slave system presented in the pamphlet is somewhat marred, however, by frequent references to the wave of slave rebellions which had swept the South and Texas the year before. The happy and contented slaves, it seems, had unaccountably risen up to overthrow the benign masters—to burn their mansions, poison their wells, defy their bloodhounds and whipping-posts, ignore their preachments of meekness, and challenge the very foundation of their benevolent system.

This curious contradiction has little worried the slave-owners and their spiritual descendants whose version of life in the slave South dominates respectable historical thinking to this day. But it has been seized by others, notably the Negro scholars, such as Carter G. Woodson and W. E. B. DuBois, and the Marxists, such as James S. Allen and Herbert Aptheker, as a lever to pry loose the truth about slavery in America.

A study of slave insurrections in Texas helps give the lie to the Bourbon thesis that slavery was a pleasant idyll and that, at any rate, the Negroes accepted their position with docility if not actual gratification.

Resistance to the slave system on the part of the slaves took many forms, including individual flight, sabotage, slow-down, self-mutilation, suicide, and, rarely, purchase of freedom.[2] Here we are concerned only with the most serious and fundamental act of resistance—insurrection.

[1] Committee on Slaves and Slavery, Texas House of Representatives, *A Report and Treatise on Slavery and the Slavery Agitation*, Austin, 1857, p. 50.
[2] *Cf.* Herbert Aptheker, *American Negro Slave Revolts*, New York, 1943, Ch. VI.

408

We can be guided in general by the definition of the act offered in an 1858 statute of Texas: "By 'insurrection of slaves' is meant an assemblage of three or more, with arms, with intent to obtain their liberty by force."[3] In nearly every case, however, the insurrection cited will be seen to involve considerably more than three persons, as the smaller rebellions were seldom reported.

Indeed, concerning insurrections of any size, accurate reporting apparently almost never occurred. Normally such news would be suppressed, minimized, or alluded to indirectly and belatedly by the Southern press. For example, a New Orleans newspaper which followed Texas affairs closely and is one of the most valuable contemporary sources admitted in 1856 that "we have refrained from publishing a great deal which we receive by the mails, going to show that there is a spirit of turbulence abroad in various quarters."[4] One student refers to the "habitual reserve maintained on the topic by the Southern press."[5] The overriding consideration was no doubt the well-founded fear that such news would reach the ears of the slaves wherever the newspaper was circulated. An additional consideration is brought to light in an interesting letter in another issue of this New Orleans newspaper, in which the writer warns prospective buyers not to pay high prices for the slaves from Northeastern Texas, as he has personally witnessed their contamination with ideas of rebellion.[6] Here obviously is an economic motive of no little importance to local papers for suppressing news of slave unrest.

[3] Act of February 12, 1859, *General Laws of the 7th Legislature of the State of Texas*, Austin, 1858, p. 175.

[4] New Orleans *Daily Picayune*, December 9, 1856, quoted in Aptheker, *op. cit.*, p. 159.

[5] Harvey Wish, "The Slave Insurrection Panic of 1865," *Journal of Southern History*, V, p. 206.

[6] New Orleans *Daily Picayune*, August 19, 1860, quoted in William W. White, "The Texas Slave Insurrection of 1860," *Southwestern Historical Quarterly*, LII, p. 283.

On the other hand, as we shall see, it suited the interests of the slaveowners on certain occasions to exaggerate reports of insurrection. This distorted contemporary reportage has its counterpart in the treatment of the subject in today's histories, where, for the most part, it is simply ignored.

The slaveowners had more success in hiding the actual outbreaks than in concealing the fact that they were haunted by what one researcher has called "the ubiquitous fear of rebellion."[7] This fear, in fact, played a significant role in the separation of Texas from Mexico. Stephen F. Austin, in a letter to his sister, wrote that *"Texas must be a slave country. It is no longer a matter of doubt.* The interest of Louisiana requires that it should be, a population of fanatical abolitionists in Texas would have a very pernicious and dangerous influence on the overgrown population of that state.'"[8]

The slaveowner, like members of other ruling classes, created his spectres in his own image. A Southern newspaper could ascribe the cause of a Texas insurrection thus: "Doubtless the uppermost idea was that of unrestrained riot, the luxury of unbounded license in the immediate gratification of every animal appetite, the orgies of idleness, gluttony, and lust.'"[9]

Obviously we must look elsewhere to discover the real precipitants of revolt. Frederick Law Olmsted, whose Southern journeys are recorded with unusual insight and compassion, remarked[10] that "any great event having the slightest bearing upon the question of emancipation" produced unrest among the slave population. This is certainly

[7] Harold Schoen, "The Free Negro in the Republic of Texas," *Southwestern Historical Quarterly*, XL, p. 186.

[8] Eugene C. Barker, ed., *The Austin Papers*, vol. III, Austin, 1926. Stephen F. Austin to Mrs. Mary Austin Holley, August 2, 1835. Emphasis in original.

[9] New Orleans *Daily Picayune*, August 19, 1860, quoted in White, *loc. cit.*

[10] Frederick Law Olmsted, *Journey in the Back Country*, London, 1860, p. 475, quoted in Aptheker, *op. cit.*, p. 79.

the case in Texas, with the major insurrections coinciding with national elections or military actions of some nature. Another time for rebellion was during economic depression, when the slave's condition deteriorated, his work load increased, and he and his family faced sale. The ever-present and most important cause of revolt was the inhuman cruelty which indeed is almost synonymous with slavery and which Herbert Aptheker has proved beyond doubt or apology was "characteristic of the institution of American Negro slavery."[11]

Some writers[12] have alleged that slaves in Texas were treated better than in other Southern states. Available evidence seems to indicate otherwise. Olmsted, in his trip to Texas, found whipping, branding, cropping, and more refined tortures no less common than in the rest of the South.[13] One of the earliest reports on Texas slavery indicates that the proximity to Mexico led to increased cruelty. In a letter to the President of Mexico General Manuel Mier y Teran wrote on June 30, 1828, that "these slaves are beginning to learn the favorable intent of the Mexican law toward their unfortunate condition and are becoming restless under their yoke, and the masters, in the effort to retain them, are making that yoke even heavier; they extract their teeth, set on the dogs to tear them in pieces, the most lenient being he who but flogs his slaves until they are flayed."[14]

The first slave insurrection of consequence in Texas occurred during the Texas Revolution. The Texas leaders had been apprehensive of such a development, generally

[11] Aptheker, op. cit., p. 131.

[12] E.g., R. N. Richardson, Texas the Lone Star State, New York, 1941, p. 222; Abigail Curlee, A Study of Texas Slave Plantations, 1822 to 1865, unpublished thesis, Austin, 1932, pp. 89ff.

[13] Frederick Law Olmsted, A Journey Through Texas, New York, 1857, passim.

[14] Quoted in Alleine Howren, "Causes and Origins of the Decree of April 6, 1830," Southwestern Historical Quarterly, XVI, p. 376.

feeling that the danger came from Mexican designs to stir up the slaves. Benjamin Milam warned in a letter in July, 1835, that Santa Anna planned "if possible, to get the slaves to revolt."[15] In August, Horatio Allsberry issued an open letter in which he repeated the warning.[16] Thomas J. Pilgrim recognized that the danger lay less in Mexican actions than in the opportunity afforded the Negro slaves themselves by the conflict. In a letter to Austin, he reported that military action was to be expected along the Brazos, and asks, "Would there not be great danger from the Negroes should a large Mexican force come so near?"[17]

A few days after actual fighting began, B. J. White wrote to the new Commander-in-Chief, Austin, reporting on the military situation. He then goes on, "I now have some unpleasant news to communicate. The negroes on Brazos made an attempt to rise. Majr Sutherland came on here for a few men to take back, he told me—John Davis returned from Brazoria bringing the news that near 100 had been taken up many whipped nearly to death some hung etc R. H. Williams had nearly Kild one of his. . . ." White adds this highly interesting postscript, "The negroes above alluded to had devided all the cotton farms. and they intended to ship the cotton to New Orleans and make the white men serve them in turn."[18]

After this revolt, considerable fear of insurrection seems to have spread among the Texas slaveowners. Henry Austin wrote James F. Perry advising flight from the large Peach Point Plantation because, among other reasons, of "the apprehension of a possible rising of the negroes."[19] One of the reasons given for the mass exodus known as the "runaway scrape" is that "there was also undoubtedly

[15] Barker, op. cit., p. 82.
[16] Ibid., p. 190.
[17] Ibid., p. 162.
[18] Ibid., p. 108.
[19] Ibid., p. 318.

some apprehension due to the presence of so many negroes."[20]

There are reports during 1841 which indicate considerable unrest among the slaves. In July, a Negro man and woman were hanged in San Augustine after having confessed to poisoning their masters, the Hyde family. The tortures to which any Negro suspects were subjected as a matter of course made confessions of doubtful significance, however. There were several other slaves executed around this same period, but the causes are not clear.[21]

In the fall of the same year, vague reports of the type which not infrequently indicated that genuine insurrectionary events had occurred appeared in various newspapers. We give the report from the Houston *Telegraph and Texas Register*:[22]

NEGROES—The citizens of several of the eastern counties of the republic, have lately been thrown into some alarm on accounts of the suspicious movements of many of their slaves. In San Augustine, several slaves have run-away from their masters; and circumstances indicate that they have been decoyed away by some lurking scoundrels . . . either abolitionists or negro thieves. In Nacodoches, the conduct of the slaves has been such as to excite fears that an insurrection was contemplated by the slave population. Negroes might be seen at all hours of night, coming in and going out of town, and going from one plantation to another, on their master's saddle or perhaps plough horse, after his having been worked in the plough all day; negro dances were regular once and sometimes thrice a week. In order to put a stop to this evil, the citizens of Nacogdoches and the surrounding settlements held several meetings; and at a very large meeting held in that town, resolved themselves into patrol companies, their vigilance has been increasing, and it has had, so far, a most salutary effect.

Flight from slavery was easier in the settlements to the West and reports of individual runaways were very fre-

---

[20] Carolyn Callaway, *The Runaway Scrape: An Episode of the Texas Revolution,* unpublished thesis, Austin, 1942, p. 36.

[21] Harriet Smither, ed., "The Diary of Adolphus Sterne," *Southwestern Historical Quarterly,* XXXII.

[22] Houston *Telegraph and Texas Register,* September 15, 1841.

quent. From a Houston newspaper of January 15, 1845, we take this account of a daring group rebellion and flight:[23]

RUNAWAY NEGROES.—A party of twenty-five negroes ran away from Bastrop on the night of the 27th ult. They were mounted on some of the best horses that could be found, and several of them were well armed. It is supposed that some Mexican has enticed them to flee to the Mexican settlements west of the Rio Grande. Several of the citizens of Bastrop have gone in pursuit of them; but fears are entertained that, they will not be overtaken.

A week later we learn that the insurrection was only partly successful:[24]

RUNAWAY NEGROES CAPTURED.—We learn from the LaGrange *Intelligencer,* that seventeen of the Slaves who lately eloped from Bastrop, were captured on the Guadalupe on the 3rd inst., above Seguin, by Mr. H. McCullough, Sheriff of Gonzales County. Seven or eight Slaves are still missing, and it is feared they have escaped to the Mexican settlement on the Rio Grande.

A few months later, the slaveowner statesmen of Texas wrote into the constitution of what was about to be the newest state of the Union a provision that anyone killing or dismembering a slave would be punished just as if the crime had been committed against a free white person. "Except," they add, " in case of insurrection of such slave."[25]

The year 1856 was one of tremendous slave unrest in Texas as in the rest of the South. In September, the Columbus County slaveowners' Vigilance Committee sent the following letter, published under the heading, "Contemplated Servile Rising in Texas," to the Galveston *News:*[26]

COLUMBUS, Colorado Co., Sept. 9, 1856
The object of this communication is to state to you all the facts of any importance connected with a recent intended insurrection.
Our suspicions were aroused about two weeks ago, when a meeting of the citizens of the county was called, and a committee of

---

[23] Houston *Telegraph,* January 15, 1845.
[24] *Ibid.,* January 22, 1845.
[25] Sec. 3, Art. VIII, Texas Constitution of 1845.
[26] Galveston *News,* September 11, 1865, quoted in Olmsted, *op. cit.,* p. 503f.

investigation appointed to ferret out the whole matter, and lay the facts before the people of the county for their consideration. The committee entered upon their duties, and, in a short time, they were in full possession of the facts of a well-organized and systematized plan for the murder of our entire white population, with the exception of the young ladies, who were to be taken captives, and made the wives of the diabolical murderers of their parents and friends. The committee found in their possession a number of pistols, bowie-knives, guns, and ammunition. Their passwords of organization were adopted, and their motto, "Leave not a shadow behind."

Last Saturday, the 6th Inst., was the time agreed upon for the execution of their damning designs. At a late hour at night, all were to make one simultaneous, desperate effort, with from two to ten apportioned to nearly every house in the county, kill all the whites, save the above exception, plunder their homes, take their horses and arms, and fight their way on to a "free State" [Mexico].

Notwithstanding the intense excitement which moved every member of our community, and the desperate measures to which men are liable to be led on by such impending danger to which we have been exposed by our indulgence and lenity to our slaves, we must say the people acted with more caution and deliberation than ever before characterized the action of any people under similar circumstances.

More than two hundred negroes had violated the law, the penalty of which is death. But, by unanimous consent, the law was withheld, and their lives spared, with the exception of three of the ringleaders, who were, on last Friday, the 5th inst., at 2 o'clock P. M., hung, in compliance with the unanimous voice of the citizens of the county.

Without exception, every Mexican in the county was implicated. They were arrested, and ordered to leave the county within five days, and never again to return, under the penalty of death. There is one, however, by the name of Frank, who is proven to be one of the prime movers of the affair, that was not arrested; but we hope that he may yet be, and have meted out to him such reward as his black deed demands.

We are satisfied that the lower class of the Mexican population are incendiaries in any country where slaves are held, and should be dealt with accordingly. And, for the benefit of the Mexican population, we would here state, that a resolution was passed by the unanimous voice of the county, forever forbidding any Mexican from coming within the limits of the county.

Peace, quiet, and good order are again restored, and, by the watchful care of our Vigilance Committee, a well-organized patrol, and good discipline among our planters, we are persuaded that

9

there will never again occur the necessity of a communication of the character of this.

Yours respectfully,
John H. Robson,
H. A. Tatum, —Cor. Com.
J. H. Hicks.

The same issue of the Galveston *News* has also the following paragraph :[27]

We learn, from the Columbian *Planter*, of the 9th, that two of the negroes engaged in the insurrection at Columbus were whipped to death; three more were hung last Friday, and the Mexicans who were implicated were ordered to leave the country. There was no proof against these last beyond surmises. The band had a deposit of arms and ammunition in the bottom. They had quite a number of guns, and a large lot of knives, manufactured by one of their number. It was their intention to fight their way to Mexico.

The LaGrange *True Issue* of September 5 reported[28] that the Columbus County slaves "had organized into companies of various sizes, had adopted secret signs and passwords, sworn never to divulge the plot under penalty of death, and had elected captains and subordinate officers to command the respective companies." The LaGrange newspaper suggests rather unconvincingly that the insurrection was " for the purpose of not fleeing to Mexico, but of murdering the inhabitants—men, women, and children promiscuously."

The Austin *State Gazette,* after commenting on the "great clemency" shown the slaves involved, reports[29] that "a white man named William Mehrmann has been adjudged guilty of being connected with the insurrectionists, and sentenced to leave the county," a penalty which the newspaper judges to be "exceedingly mild." The same issue of the *State Gazette* contains an advertisement—"which," the editors gracefully state, "we insert gratuitously"—in which the Vigilance Committee of Colorado County mi-

[27] *Ibid.*, p. 504.
[28] Quoted in *ibid.*
[29] Austin *State Gazette*, September 27, 1856.

nutely describes Mehrmann, warns of the thirty-nine lashes which await his return to the county, and thoughtfully adds, for the benefit of "the various newspapers," that "Mehrmann said when he was leaving this place that he wanted to go to Fayette County."

The next month, October, witnessed another large-scale revolt, concerning which we unfortunately have few details. The postmaster at Halletsville, in Lavaca County, reported[30] that the slaves in the area planned to rise up on October 31, killing their masters where necessary, seizing all arms and ammunition for flight to Mexico. Three white men were said to be implicated, one of whom, Davidson, was captured. He allegedly confessed, and was given one hundred lashes. The Austin *Southern Intelligencer* reported[31] this punishment with satisfaction and invited Davidson to "shed lugubrious tears at the first abolition meeting which he shall attend." Its report of this insurrection closes with the interesting notation, "No Mexicans have been implicated this time."

In November still another "extensive scheme of negro insurrection" was uncovered, this time in Lavaca, DeWitt, and Victoria counties. A letter from Victoria on November 7 declared[32] that the "negroes had killed off all the dogs in the neighborhood, and were preparing for a general attack" when their plans were betrayed. Several white men were again implicated, one being "severely horsewhipped" and the others banished. The punishment given the slaves is not recorded.

Also during November, the Clarksville *Standard* reported[33] rumors of insurrection in Rusk county and in its own area. A few weeks later it was compelled to record[34]

---

[30] Harvey Wish, *op. cit.*, p. 207.

[31] Austin *Southern Intelligencer*, November 19, 1856.

[32] Herbert Aptheker, *Essays in the History of the American Negro*, New York, 1945, p. 56.

[33] Clarksville *Standard*, November 1, 1856.

[34] *Ibid.*, December 20, 1856.

that "It seems that the seeds of a plot have been germinating in our midst." It urged that the Negroes involved be "severely dealt with" and the whites hanged.

At about this same time, an Arkansas newspaper reported[35] an elaborate plot by slaves and free Negroes aimed at capturing the army arsenal at Little Rock. "It appears," the newspaper says, "that the plot at Little Rock is a part of the same conspiracy which was detected recently in Texas, and in Union County in this state." Without details, as usual, it goes on to say that the movement covered parts of Louisiana as well, and was headed by a Louisiana Negro. Elaborate plans were said to have been made, including passwords and signs for the whole area.

At the beginning of 1857, the Cherokee County *Texas Enquirer* summed up the situation by saying that "Servile insurrections seem to be the order of the day in this State."[36] The Galveston *News* had the following to say :[37]

"Never has there been a time in our recollection when so many insurrections, or attempts at insurrection, have transpired in rapid succession as during the past six months. The evidence in regard to some of these has indeed proved very unsatisfactory, showing nothing but that the negroes had got hold of some indistinct and vague ideas about obtaining their freedom. . . . In other cases the plans have been more matured, and in some instances, arms have been provided, and all the necessary arrangements made not only to effect their own escape, but to slaughter their owners."

The *News* speaks of the efforts of white Abolitionists throughout the South and then touches upon the effect of the presidential campaign during the fall in which the new Republican Party's first candidate, John C. Frémont, was violently attacked as an Abolitionist by the Southern press. Olmsted says[38] that if the Democrats did not themselves believe that Frémont planned emancipation, they at least

---

[35] Fort Smith *Herald*, quoted in *ibid.*, November 22, 1856.

[36] Cherokee County *Texas Inquirer*, January 12, 1857.

[37] Galveston *News*, n.d., quoted in Clarksville *Standard*, January 17, 1857.

[38] Olmsted, *op. cit.*, introduction.

convinced their slaves, a contention which the *News* would seem to bear out:

"These attempted insurrections have transpired almost simultaneously in different States of the South, and all of them since it became known that Mr. Fremont was brought out by Northern Abolitionists as their candidate. . . . It was the general impression among the negroes that his election would, in some way, result in setting them all free."

Abraham Lincoln has also commented upon this fact, remarking to John Hay that "As soon as the news of Fremont's defeat came to the plantations the disappointment of the slaves flashed into insurrection."[39]

The legislative pamphlet, *A Report and Treatise on Slavery and the Slavery Agitation,* tells us what was in the siaveowners' minds at this time. It approvingly quotes Senator J. H. Hammond:[40]

"We have to rely more and more on the power of fear. We must, in all our intercouse with them, assert and maintain strict mastery, and impress it on them that they are slaves. . . . We are determined to continue masters, and to do so, we have to draw the rein tighter and tighter day by day, to be assured that we hold them in complete check."

The greatest wave of slave revolts was still to come. It was during the year 1860 that the slavocracy was to be shown that it could not continue to rule in the old way. No other factor was more important in laying bare the impending doom of the slave system, and in bringing the slaveowners to attempt a counter-revolutionary coup by force of arms, than the tremendous upsurge of revolt in 1860 by the Negro people aided, in almost every case, by white allies.

The difficulty in obtaining an accurate picture of the insurrectionary movement arises at this point not from suppression by the Southern press, but rather from wild exaggeration. Reports of slave revolts involving whites

[39] Carl Sandburg, *Abraham Lincoln: The War Years,* New York, 1939, vol. II, p. 27.

[40] Committee on Slaves and Slavery, *op. cit.,* p. 45.

could now be put to several uses by the ruling class. Hysterical support could be whipped up for the slavocracy's approaching military gamble. All voices of dissent—Union Democrats as well as Republicans, moderate slaveowners as well as Abolitionists—could be silenced. The fateful election could be held in an atmosphere of terror and repression. Back of the exaggeration, however, can be discerned unmistakably an uprising of vast proportions against the slave system.

The coming tempest was presaged only slightly early in the year. In Marshall, a meeting of slaveowners convicted a local man, E. C. Palmer, of being an Abolitionist, and asked Congress to make abolitionism treason.[41] In Fannin County, in May, three slaves named Jess, Ruben, and Emma were hanged for killing their masters. "They confessed," reports the Matagorda *Gazette*, "that a general uprising of the negroes of the neighborhood had been planned, and that a white man was at the head of it."[42]

In July the storm broke: a wave of fires attributed to Negro and Abolitionist incendiarism swept across North Texas.[43] In a few days, there were fires reported in Dallas, Denton, Ladonia, Black Grove, Millwood, and elsewhere. Fires of little damage were reported from Milford, Honey Grove, Waxahachie, Jefferson, and Austin. The Marshall *Republican* later reported that over one million dollars' worth of damage had been done.[44]

A letter to the *State Gazette* from Dr. Pryor of the Dallas *Herald* on July 12 reported[45] that the Crill Miller plantation house near there had been burned. The Negroes on the plantation had been arrested and allegedly confessed

[41] Matagorda *Gazette*, January 4, 1860.
[42] *Ibid.*, July 4, 1860.
[43] A compilation of these reports may be found in White, *op. cit.*; others occur in the Matagorda *Gazette*, and in Aptheker, *American Negro Slave Revolts*.
[44] Cited in Curlee, *op. cit.*, p. 130.
[45] Austin *State Gazette*, July 12, 1860.

that "Abolition preachers" planned to "devastate" North Texas, after which, the letter continues,

general revolt of the slaves, aided by the white men of the North in our midst was to come off on the day of election in August. Each county has a special superintendent—a white man—and each laid off into districts under the supervision of a white man. . . . Arms have been discovered in the possession of negroes and the whole plot of insurrection revealed for a general civil war at the August election. I write in haste; we sleep upon our arms; and the whole county is deeply excited.

A letter to the *State Gazette* on July 25 relates[46] that similar plots had been uncovered in Lancaster and Waxahachie. In the latter town, where the insurrectionists' plans had progressed to the point of a tentative division of the land, over one hundred slaves were arrested, questioned, and, in varying degrees, punished. A large mob was assembled, led by the Committee of Vigilance consisting, we are assured, of the "most respectable and responsible men of this county," to execute the three leaders of the insurrection, the Negro slaves Sam Smith, Cato, and Patrick. This last man calmly assured his torturers that the actions of himself and the others were "just the beginning of the good work." All three met their fate "with a composure worthy," in the opinion of the correspondent, "of a better cause."

On July 17 a white man, William H. Crawford, was lynched in Fort Worth, with the approbation of civic leaders, on suspicion of being an Abolitionist.[47] Another man was hanged for allegedly distributing pistols to slaves in the area. The offices of the Jacksboro newspaper, *The White Man*, were reportedly burned on July 29.[48]

On August 5, the town of Henderson was set on fire, "beyond doubt," said the Vigilance Committee, "by an incendiary." The damage was reported at $200,000. A local

[46] *Ibid.*, July 23, 1860.
[47] Fort Worth *Chief*, July 25, 1860.
[48] Matagorda *Gazette*, August 22, 1860.

man, Green Herndon, and a slave of his were hanged.[49] A Henderson resident signing himself "S" wrote as follows to the Austin *State Gazette:*[50]

A committee of fifty-two of the best citizens of the town and county, have been selected, have been in close session and correspondence with the neighboring counties since the first excitement occasioned by the fire and loss subsided. ... They believe that emissaries are throughout the state, directly under the control of the Abolition Aid Society of the North, and furnished by that organization with any requisite amount of means and money. That their object is to produce a well digested plan, which by fire and assassination will finally render life and property insecure, and the slave by constant rebellion a curse to the master. ... That there exists great uncertainty as to whether the August or November election day was the one fixed upon for the assassination. That Ammunition, fire-arms and poison had been plentifully supplied to the negroes in many neighborhoods and others probably yet were to be supplied. That the whole county was divided into districts, under the captaincy or control of chosen white men of their number; and those sub-divided among the leading or most reliable negroes, and that days were set for burning particular towns, to destroy ammunition, produce consternation, etc.

Another Henderson citizen writes to the Marshall *Republican* in part as follows:[51]

"Authenticated statements were made, that in several places poison had been found with negroes, and confessions made that on the day of election this poison was to be administered in the food at breakfast, and deposited in the wells and springs, and that a general plot had been made for an indiscriminate, wholesale destruction by poison and arms on that day."

The Washington County Vigilance Committee arrested several Negroes who were charged with planning, along with several whites, a "general insurrection" to take place August 6. There is no indication of their fate.[52]

The Nacogdoches *Chronicle* reported[53] on August 7 that a young druggist in Waxahachie had been hanged for giv-

[49] *Ibid.*
[50] Austin *State Gazette,* September 15, 1860.
[51] Marshall *Republican,* n.d., quoted in *ibid.,* August 18, 1860.
[52] Brenham *Enquirer,* August 11, 1860, quoted in *ibid.,* August 25, 1860.
[53] Quoted in White, *op. cit.,* p. 271.

ing strychnine to slaves to put in wells, that a white man suspected of incendiarism had been shot in Tyler, and that J. E. Lemon had been banished from Wood County as a suspected Abolitionist.

It was reported[54] on August 9 that two white men had been hanged in Anderson County. Anthony Wyrick and Alford Cable, both blacksmiths, were judged guilty of the usual charge, supplying the Negro slaves with poison and firearms.

The Rusk *Enquirer* of August 11 reported[55] a planned revolt on the Timmons plantation. The slaves were to arm themselves, fire the buildings, poison the wells, and kill the masters as they returned from the election. "Some of the white men implicated," we are told, "live in the county, others live out of the State."

A Waxahachie merchant wrote[56] on August 11 of a plot "similar to the Dallas affair," for which two white men had been hanged and twenty-odd Negroes were to be hanged the next week. From Round Top came a report[57] of the firing of a house by several Negro runaways accompanied by a white man.

Also on August 11 came the news[58] of a meeting in Denton which set up a Committee of Safety with practically unlimited powers after reaching "the inevitable conclusion that there exists in our midst a regular organized band of abolitionists . . . committing outrages . . . inciting our slave population . . ." and receiving mail, reported the postal authorities, who had apparently looked to see, from Northern Abolitionists.

The last bit of news on this eventful day informs us[59] that a slaveowner meeting in Matagorda which imposed

[54] Fairfield *Pioneer*, quoted in *ibid.*, p. 272.
[55] Quoted in Matagorda *Gazette*, August 29, 1860.
[56] Austin *State Gazette*, August 11, 1860.
[57] Houston *Telegraph*, August 11, 1860.
[58] Austin *State Gazette*, August 11, 1860.
[59] *Ibid.*

new restrictions on the population of that area also offered
to raise a company to send to the aid of the Northeastern
counties, which had been reduced "to the condition of
revolution, which we are forced to regard as a repetition
of the horrors enacted at Harper's Ferry, only upon a
broader field, and in all probability with far greater resources.''

In Gilmer a mob of nearly five hundred people, apparently organized by the pillars of local society, hanged a
white man named Morrison on August 14. He was "charged
with having endeavored to incite the slaves of Wood, Titus,
and Hopkins counties to an insurrection."[60]

Two map salesmen, Parker and Hughes, were arrested
in Richmond, Fort Bend County, on suspicion of being
Abolitionists. There seems to have been little evidence, but
one was horsewhipped and both ordered out of the state.[61]

Congressman John H. Reagan wrote his brother on
August 18 a letter interesting both for its contents and for
the prominence of its author. He says, in part:[62]

> A plot has been discovered in Tennessee colony, and extend-
> ing out from there, between some white men and negroes, similar to
> that in Dallas, Ellis and Tarrant counties. Indeed, it is regarded
> as a part of the same plot—to poison as many people as they could
> on Sunday Night before the election, and on the day of the elec-
> tion to burn the houses and kill as many of the women and children
> as they could while the men were gone to the election, and then
> kill the men as they returned home.
>
> On last Sunday two white men, who lived up near Catfish
> Bayou, were hung as the ringleaders of the plot in this county.
> Our vigilance committees and patrol have been active here in
> guarding against other dangers and in investigating this matter.
>
> One negro has been hung in Henderson and one in Cherokee
> County, and we are informed that the town of Henderson has
> been burned—supposed by incendiaries—but no particulars yet.
>
> I am strongly persuaded, from all I can learn, that these things

[60] Matagorda *Gazette*, September 12, 1860.

[61] *Ibid.*, August 15, 1860.

[62] John H. Reagan to Morris Reagan, August 18, 1860, quoted in John
Townsend, *The Doom of Slavery in the Union: Its Safety Out of It*, Charleston, S.C., 1860. p. 34f.

must be the result of an abolition plot arranged elsewhere than in Texas, and that its execution has been committed to the desperate set of Kansas outlaws or similar men. And I do not think one of them ought to be permitted to leave the State alive where his complicity can be clearly shown.

The South Carolina pamphlet urging secession which reprinted this letter has two more letters[63] from Texas which shed an interesting light on the slaveholders' state of mind at this time. One declares that ''it is better for us to hang ninety-nine innocent men than to let one guilty one pass.'' The other reveals the fact, not elsewhere mentioned, that many of the Negroes and ''Lincolnites'' killed at this time were executed by burning. This jolly note is then added:

Unless the churches send out new recruits of John Browns, I fear the boys will have nothing to do this winter, (as they have hung all that can be found,) the school boys have become so excited by the sport in hanging Abolitionists, that the schools are completely deserted, they having formed companies, and will go seventy-five or one hundred miles on horseback to participate in a single execution of the sentence of Judge Lynch's Court.

The Matagorda *Gazette* of August 22 reported[64] that ''the woods around Bastrop seem to be alive with runaway slaves.'' New incendiary attempts at Jefferson, Galveston, Houston, and Indianola were spoken of, and the conclusion reached that ''incendiarism is at work in all parts of the state.''

The *State Gazette* of August 25 tells of new incidents.[65] The town of Belleview, in Rusk County, has been burned. A Negro has been hanged in Athens and others punished for possessing poison. A meeting in Guadalupe County orders certain residents to leave the county at once, being suspected of implication in a ''deep and diabolical scheme . . . for insurrection.'' And a Georgetown Negro has been hanged after confessing—''without whipping,'' we are

---

[63] *Ibid.*, p. 36f.
[64] Matagorda *Gazette*, August 22, 1860.
[65] Austin *State Gazette*, August 25, 1860.

proudly informed—to burning a stable. He had two white accomplices, apparently not captured.

The San Antonio *Ledger* of the same date reports[66] that an insurrection has been frustrated in Bastrop and Cauldwell Counties. Negro cabins along Walnut Creek were said to be filled with guns and powder.

A New Orleans newspaper reported[67] on August 29 that Mount Vernon, Texas, had been burned completely and one "incendiary" hanged. Other suspects were being driven from the state.

A New York salesman was hanged and his wife imprisoned in Chapel Hill, according to a letter to the Goliad *Messenger*,[68] after he had confessed to supplying guns to slaves in the area. A somewhat curious item in a New Orleans newspaper related[69] that three Abolitionists arrested in Chapel Hill confessed that there were three thousand Abolitionists in Texas. The report added darkly that they "had been seen to take negroes privately to their rooms."

The store and post office at Lavernia were burned, in what was, said the *State Gazette,* "clearly the work of an incendiary."[70] Two whites, both named Boardwright, were hanged in Robertson County for "tampering with slaves."[71] There was serious unrest in Halletsville and Cedar Creek at about this same time. And in lower Fayette County about two hundred Negroes were involved in a widespread insurrectionary plan. At LaGrange they were to meet other slaves who were to fight their way to freedom, and to head with them for Mexico. It was reported that over twenty-

---

[66] San Antonio *Ledger*, August 25, 1860, quoted in White, *op. cit.*, p. 271.

[67] New Orleans *Daily Crescent*, August 29, 1860, quoted in *ibid.*, p. 275.

[68] Quoted in *ibid.*

[69] New Orleans *Daily Picayune*, n.d., quoted in *ibid.*, p. 278.

[70] Austin *State Gazette*, September 8, 1860.

[71] *Northern Standard*, September 22, 1860, quoted in White, *op. cit.*, p. 276.

five whites and fifty Negroes had been hanged in Fayette County since July.[72]

As the date of election drew near, the "Bailey letter" appeared, creating a sensation in the slaveowner press. This letter was widely used in the election campaign to demonstrate the depravity of the Abolitionists. We give the text of this curious document below. It is addressed to Reverend William Buley.[73]

Denton Creek, July 3rd, 1860

Dear Sir: A painful abscess in my right thumb is my apology for not writing at Anderson. Our glorious cause is progressing finely as far South as Brenham. There I parted with Bro. Wampler; he went still further South. He will do good wherever he goes. I have traveled up through the frontier counties, part of the time under a fictitious name. I found many friends who had been initiated and understood the mystic red. I met with a good number of our friends at Georgetown. We held a consultation, and were unanimous of opinion that we should be cautious of our new associates: most of them are desperate characters, and may betray us, as there are slaveholders among them, and value a poor negro much more than a horse. The only good they will do will be destroying towns, mills, &c., which is our only hope in Texas at present. If we can break Southern merchants and millers, and have their places filled by honest Republicans, Texas will be an easy prey if we will only do our duty. All we want for the time being is control of trade. Trade, assisted by preaching and teaching, will soon control public opinion, (public opinion is mighty and will prevail.) Lincoln will certainly be elected, we will then have the Indian Nation, cost what it will. Squatter sovereignty will prevail there as it has in Kansas. That accomplished, we have but one more step to take, but one more struggle to make, that is, free Texas. We will then have a connected link from the Lakes to the Gulf. Slavery will then be surrounded by land and water, and soon sting itself to death. I repeat, Texas we must have, and our only chance is to break up the PRESENT INHABITANTS in whatever way we can, and it must be done. Some of us will most assuredly suffer in accomplishing our object, but our Heavenly Father will reward us for assisting him in blotting out the greatest curse on earth. It would be impossible for any of us to do an act that is as blasphemous in the sight of God as holding slaves. We must have frequent consultations with our colored friends; (let your meetings be in the night;) impress upon their clouded intellects the

[72] New Orleans *Picayune*, September 13, 1860, quoted in *ibid.*
[73] Copied from photostat in Curlee, *op. cit.*, appendix E.

21

blessings of freedom. Induce all to leave you can.—our arrangements for their accommodation to go north are better than they have been, but not as good as I would like. We will need more agents, both local and traveling. I will send out traveling agents when I get home. You must appoint a local agent in every neighborhood in your district. I will recommend a few (who) I think will do to rely upon, to-wit: Brothers Leake, Wood, Ives, Evans, McDaniel, Vickery, Cole, Nugent, Shaw, White, Gilford, Ashley, Drake, Meeks, Shults and Newman.

Brother Leake, the bearer of this, will take a circuitous route, and see as many of our colored friends as he can. He also recommends a different match to be used about towns, &c. Our friends sent a very inferior article. They emit too much smoke and do not contain enough camphene. They are calculated to get some of our friends hurt. I will send a supply when I get home. I will have to reprove you and your co-workers for your negligence in sending funds for our agents. But few have been compensated for (their) trouble. Correspondent and industrious agent, brother Webber, has received but a trifle—not so much as apprentices' wages. Neither has brother Willet, Mungen (or Munger)* and others. You must call upon our colored friends for more money. They must not expect us to do all. They certainly will give every cent if they know how soon their shackles will be broken. My hand is very painful and I must close.

Yours, truly,
Wm. H. Bailey

N.B.—Brother Leake will give you what few numbers of "Impending Crisis" I have. Also Brother Sumner's speech, and Brother Beecher's Letter, etc, Farewell.

On August 19, a copy of this letter, duly certified as correct by the Tarrant County Clerk, was mailed to slave-owners throughout the state by John Henry Brown, editor and historian (!) of Belton. He adds this interesting exhortation to those whom he addressed "in the bonds of country, of patriotism, of home:"[74]

The above hellish document came into our hands from the most reliable and undoubted source. That it is authentic and true, there is not the shadow of doubt. The events at and near Brenham and in Georgetown, since the date of the letter, and before the finder could possibly have heard of those events, are alone sufficient to prove the truth of the statements in it. To make it public, would destroy all plans to entrap the conspirators. To avoid that and yet profit by its revelations, we print privately suffi-

[74] *Ibid.*

cient copies to forward one to at least one tried, true and discreet friend in each of the principal counties. To you, as one such, we confide it. Our plan is, to communicate it to a few of the most cool, discreet and unflinching men in our county, and advise the same course to you. There are twenty abolition names in the letter. Traps may be set for them through true and discreet postmasters. Exercise your best judgment—we will do the same. Our advice is, (as a general rule,) whip no abolitionist, drive off no abolitionist—*hang them,* or let them alone. There may be exceptions—but not many.

The letter was made public at a meeting in Fort Worth on September 11 at which the following resolutions were passed:[75]

(1) Committees should be set up throughout the state and prepare lists of "Black Republicans, abolitionists, or higher-law" men of every class, and make accurate lists in every county; List No. 1, all suspected persons; No. 2, black list, to be exterminated by immediate hanging. . . .

(2) That we look upon the course of the Austin Intelligencer, and other papers and persons who attribute the late fires to accident, and who assert that the hue and cry about abolition incendiarism has been raised for political effect, as insulting to the intelligence of Texas, and as justly subjecting the editor of the Austin Intelligencer, or any other papers or persons guilty of the like offense, to be placed at once on the list of persons whose future course is to be carefully watched by the proper committee.

Reverend Buley, to whom the letter allegedly was addressed, was arrested in Arkansas, returned to Tarrant County, and hanged. He reportedly[76] confessed that the letter was his, but to nothing else, "as he was to be hanged anyway."

The Bailey letter must have been the basis of the speech by Texas' influential Louis T. Wigfall in the Senate in December, the climax of which charged Lincoln himself with being a professional Abolitionist agitator and a member of "the mystic red."[77]

Senator Wigfall may not have been very convincing in

[75] Austin *State Gazette,* September 22, 1860.
[76] White, *op. cit.,* p. 266.
[77] Quoted in Aptheker, *op. cit.,* p. 112f.

his charges that the Republican Party was to blame, but a chill nevertheless struck the hearts of his Southern listeners at any mention of the very real danger of Negro insurrection. In fact, the Senator's wife turned out to be among those who seemed unwilling to return to the South after secession, fearing a slave revolt.[78]

There is evidence that this fear was well-founded, although there was apparently no large-scale insurrection in Texas during the war. In the New York *Daily Tribune* of May 11, 1861, a "Voice from the Under Current" rose from Texas to tell of seething restlessness and mass flights among the slaves, and to urge their being armed as the quickest way to end the war.[79]

A Texas slaveowner reported[80] in 1863 that his "black wretches" were sabotaging plantation activity constantly, even after his new overseer began shooting them when unmerciful beatings seemed ineffectual. The distraught master even considered, in his extremity, selling his slaves and working "with my hands!"

Obviously insurrection was made impossible as the slave states became one vast armed camp. Flight by individual slaves or small groups became the most effective means of resistance. Particularly as there was now a liberating army to flee to! Many Texas slaves made their way to Lincoln's army, to march with the two hundred thousand Negro troops who provided the Union with the decisive balance of military power—and who dealt the final shattering blow to the slavocracy's morale.

In a gesture of supreme historic irony, the Confederacy in the end attempted to enlist Negroes in its armed forces. Negro volunteers were to receive the greatest gift a slave-

[78] *Ibid.*, p. 27.

[79] Herbert Aptheker, *To Be Free: Studies in American Negro History,* New York, 1948, p. 71.

[80] Aptheker, *Essays in the History of the American Negro*, p. 176f.

owner could bestow—emancipation. Needless to say, the scheme was a failure.[81]

As our narrative has shown, the Negro slaves were not without allies in their inexorable struggle against the South's ruling class. Their unremitting resistance at the actual point of enslavement, flaring sporadically into open assault on the system itself, acted as a magnet drawing into motion other groups oppressed by the slavocracy. These allies were to be found, in Texas, among the free Negroes, the Mexican people, some Indians, and the poor whites.

Free Negroes were everywhere feared by the slaveowners. An emergency act was passed by the provisional government shortly after the outbreak of the Texas Revolution forbidding the entry of free Negroes into the state. The act was obviously based on the fear of insurrection. After the Republic was established, the Beaumont Committee of Safety reported its conviction that the presence of free Negroes inevitably would lead to "the infusion of dissatisfaction and disobedience into the brain of the honest and contented slave." The Mayor of Houston warned that where there were free Negroes, one might look for "dissatisfaction, insubordination, and finally insurrection among the slaves." The Harrisburg Grand Jury made a similar warning in June, 1839.[82]

The slave revolts of the 1850's frequently involved free Negroes, as we have seen. One Negro-chaser told Olmsted of the hazards to be encountered by the escaped slave he was pursuing, then added, "but then every nigger or Mexican he could find would help him,"[83] obviously referring to free Negroes as well as to slaves. As the Civil War approached, the restrictions became even more severe upon the freemen, so that they were actually "free" only in the most limited sense. Some were fully re-enslaved.

[81] Cf. ibid., pp. 200-203.
[82] Schoen, op. cit., pp. 171f, 183, 185.
[83] Olmsted, op. cit., p. 106.

At the very first house Olmsted visited in Texas, he was told that the Mexican population aided the slaves "in all their bad habits, married them . . . and ran them off every day to Mexico."[84] We have already seen how Mexicans were involved in many of the major slave insurrections in the state, and how they were banished *en masse* from many areas. As Olmsted wrote:[58]

> Wherever slavery in Texas has been carried in a wholesale way into the neighborhood of Mexicans it has been found necessary to treat them as outlaws . . . the whole native population of county after county has been driven, by the formal proceedings of substantial planters, from its homes, and forbidden, on pain of no less punishment than instant death, to return to the vicinity of the plantations.

Meetings were sometimes held by the slaveowners to consider the problem of the Mexican people's opposition to slavery. One such meeting was held at Gonzales in 1845 with planters from several counties participating. "Before the convention met," a student briskly reports, "citizens were administering one hundred and fifty lashes to the bare back of a peon and branding the letter T on his forehead."[86]

The objective in most Texas insurrections, as we have seen, was to escape to the haven of Mexico. The Austin *State Times* estimated[87] in 1854 that there were upwards of two hundred thousand escaped slaves in Mexico, a figure which seems difficult to believe. It is clear, however, that the number was large.

In Piedras Negras, observed the shocked Mrs. W. L. Cazneau in 1851,[88] "the hundreds of runaway slaves . . . have all the social rights and honors of the most esteemed citizen." As the purpose of her book was to plead that the unfortunate condition of the peons of Mexico be alleviated

[84] *Ibid.*, p. 64.
[85] *Ibid.*, p. 456.
[86] Curlee, *op. cit.*, p. 134.
[87] Quoted in *ibid.*
[88] Mrs. W. L. Cazneau (pseudonym: Cora Montgomery); *Eagle Pass*, New York, 1852, p. 138.

by extending into that country the beneficent system of slavery, she is somewhat dismayed by the "great allurement" that "this equality of caste and color" seems to have.

Some Indian tribes apparently furnished help to insurgent Negroes. In 1850 the Houston *Telegraph* reported[89] that some fifteen hundred former American slaves were fighting alongside of the Comanche Indians. Mrs. Cazneau, the next year, tells[90] of the hundreds of Negroes who migrated with the famous Seminole chief, Wild Cat, from Florida to West Texas. Wild Cat's interpreter was an escaped slave of some fame called Gopher John.

Whites were frequently involved in slave revolts, though the slaveowner habit of always ascribing the role of leader to any white man involved in an insurrection was assuredly not correct. The slaveowners tended to attribute unrest to the machinations of white Abolitionists, Lincolnites, Northern fanatics, and Black Republicans (the color of the soul rather than the skin is apparently referred to).

"Into [the slaves'] Garden of Eden is coming Satan in the guise of an Abolitionist," wailed the Texas legislature's committee on slavery in 1857.[91] The fact is, of course, that rather than slave insurrections being a product of the Abolitionist movement, the exact reverse is true. In any event, the greatest Abolitionists—Frederick Douglass, Sojourner Truth, Harriet Tubman—were themselves Negroes.

The frequent white support to slave revolts in Texas seems to have come from local farmers and artisans—the poor whites who were also oppressed by the slavocracy. Special mention should be made of the Germans in Texas, almost none of whom held slaves and who were themselves refugees from Prussian tyranny. When asked by Olmsted about their attitude toward rebellious Negroes, one de-

---

[89] Quoted in Aptheker, *American Negro Slave Revolts*, p. 343.
[90] Cazneau, *op. cit.*, p. 140.
[91] Committee on Slaves and Slavery, *op. cit.*, p. 50.

clared, "That German would be a Judas who would do aught to hinder a man fleeing toward liberty."[92]

His allies were important to the American Negro in his revolts against slavery. But it is to his own indomitable resistance to enslavement that we must look, in the last analysis, for the explanation of his emancipation.

WENDELL G. ADDINGTON

University of Texas

[92] Olmsted, *op. cit.*, p. 324.

AMERICAN NEGRO SLAVE REVOLTS

HERBERT APTHEKER

THE persistent and desperate struggles of the American Negro against slavery took eight forms, none of which have yet received anything like the treatment they deserve: (1) The purchase of freedom; (2) strikes; (3) sabotage; (4) suicide and self-mutilation; (5) flight—to communities of runaways, to the French, Indians, Canadians, Dutch, Spanish, Mexicans, British armies; (6) enlistment in federal forces—Negroes were with Prescott at Bunker Hill, with Perry at Lake Erie, with Jackson at New Orleans; (7) anti-slavery agitation—talking, writing— (Douglass, Tubman, Walker, Still, Steward and a host of others) ; (8) revolts.

Nothing in American historiography has been more neglected, nor, when treated, more distorted, than the story of these revolts. Out of Channing's thousands of pages, about five touch this subject and his treatment is, among the standard histories cf Beard, McMaster, Rhodes, Hildreth, Schouler, Osgood, Bancroft, the most extensive. Sectional historians, with rare exceptions,[1] are worse, and Negro writers [2] are hardly better. The score of pages devoted to slave revolts by U. B. Phillips still remain the most complete record of this important chapter in American history. But his pretentiously "objective" account is actually a subtle apology for the Southern Bourbons.[3]

During the period of slavery the subject was taboo, and clear examples [4] of censorship may be found. Yet sources yield enough evidence to demonstrate conclusively that the fear of slave revolts [5] and

---

[1] Exceptions are R. Scarborough, *Opposition to Slavery in Georgia;* and H. S. Cooley, *A Study of Slavery in New Jersey.*

[2] See *Journal of Negro History,* VII, p. 361; XV, p. 112.

[3] At times not so subtle, as in one dedication "to the dominant class of the south . . .", *A History of Transportation in the Eastern Cotton Belt to 1860* (New York, 1908).

[4] C. H. Ambler, *Thomas Ritchie,* p. 25; *Writings of Monroe* (Hamilton Edition), III, p. 208-209; compare letter from Camden, South Carolina, in New York *Post* of July 18, 1816 and in Richmond *Enquirer,* July 20; *Niles' Register,* XLI, p. 180; dispatch of December 16, 1856 to New York *Weekly Tribune;* New Orleans *Picayune,* December 7 and December 24, 1856.

[5] *Virginia Historical Register,* IV, p. 63; J. Ballagh, *History of Slavery in Virginia,* p. 91, note; *American Historical Review,* I, p. 89; *Writings of Jefferson* (Ford), VI, p. 349; H. M. M'Call, *History of Georgia,* I, p. 125; (E. C. Holland) *A Refutation of Calumnies . . .* p. 61;

512

30

AMERICAN NEGRO SLAVE REVOLTS 513

the panic that ensued upon the discovery, or supposed discovery, of plots, or the suppression of revolts, were factors of prime importance in the social, political and economic life of the United States. This panic was no rare phenomenon. Indeed it was occasioned at least one hundred thirty times between 1670 and 1865.

An examination of the laws and customs regulating slavery, as reference to the footnotes will establish, substantiate the existence of this fear of revolt. These laws and customs at least deserve mention, for they indicate something of what the Negro slaves faced in conspiring and rebelling. Laws or customs provided for abysmal ignorance, patrols, passes, no arms to slaves, no resistance to whites, no anti-slavery agitation, and a policy of divide and rule: division between poor whites and slaves, domestic and field slaves and the drivers and mass of Negro slaves. Spying [6] and the "Christian doctrine of resignation" reinforced these instruments of class rule in America's slave system.

There is no evidence of Negro slave revolts until well into the seventeenth century, and those that did occur in that century generally centered in Virginia. Moreover, it was not until the second decade of the next century that the outbreaks lost their character of mass flights and sporadic raids by outlaw bands and became organized revolts. It is important to observe that there were very few Negroes until about 1680 (three hundred in Virginia in 1649, only two thousand in 1670— about five percent of the colony's population).[7] It was not until 1660 that they were legally declared slaves.[8] Tobacco, mostly in Virginia, was the only staple crop, and it was mainly raised by indentured white servants until about 1675.[9] There was no other staple crop and thus no plantation system in the other southern colonies until about 1730 when rice and indigo were introduced, and there was as yet little use anywhere in the country of Negro labor and little concentration of Negroes.

By 1715 one-third of the population of Virginia, the Carolinas, and Maryland (Georgia had no slavery until 1750) were slaves (46,700

E. P. Burke, *Reminiscences of Georgia*, p. 158; H. A. Herbert, *Abolition Crusade*, p. 11; F. L. Olmsted, *A Journey in the Back Country*, p. 30, 376-7, 474; R. Ogden, *Life and Letters of E. L. Godkin*, I, p. 124, 136-37.

[6] *Life and Times of F. Douglass* (1882), p. 70.

[7] L. C. Gray, *History of Agriculture in Southern U. S. . . . .*, II, p. 1025, table 39.

[8] Henning, *Statutes at Large*, I, p. 540, II, p. 26; H. Catterall, *Judicial Cases Concerning Slavery*, I, p. 50.

[9] Gray, I, p. 308-09; P. A. Bruce, *Economic History of Virginia . . .* , II, p. 57; U. Phillips, *American Negro Slavery*, p. 75.

out of 123,510).[10] Within five years Negro importation became important in Louisiana also,[11] and by 1754, when the plantation system, based principally on crops of tobacco, rice and indigo,[12] was well established, over thirty-six percent of the population of the four colonies mentioned above as well as Georgia, were slaves (222,000 out of 609,000).[13] This was the proper setting for the real slave revolts, and from about 1720 to 1865, they occurred regularly.

Two conditions seem to have been important in precipitating these revolts. There was either economic depression or some unusual excitement concerning slavery, or, as was true in four great upheavals, (South Carolina 1737-40, Virginia 1800-02, South Carolina 1822, Virginia 1831), a combination of both.

In 1720 and 1737-40, South Carolina suffered from many conspiracies and revolts. The former period was marked by a drought and the beginning of the latter by a famine costing the lives of several slaves.[14] There were revolts in Louisiana in 1730 and 1732 in which the mortality of the slaves was enormous. Although within the dozen years preceding 1731 about seven thousand slaves had been imported, in that year there were less than thirty-five hundred living.[15] The Negro agitation in New York in 1741 came after the terrible winter of 1740-41, when the suffering of the exploited was acute and many starved or froze to death.[16] From about 1794 to 1804 depression gripped the South causing a period of tremendous revolutionary activity, particularly in Virginia where the depression was worst.[17] Precisely the same is true of the period 1820-31. During 1840-42 there were frequent plots and one important revolt in Louisiana and Mississippi, at a time when both these states were very hard hit by a depression following a disastrous fall in the prices of land, cotton and sugar.[18]

Temporary excitement seems also to have been at least partly responsible for many uprisings. The landing of Spotswood in Virginia started rumors among the Negroes that he had orders to free them

[10] Gray, II, p. 1025.
[11] Gray, I, p. 335.
[12] Cotton and sugar became important in 1795.
[13] Gray, II, p. 1025 (figures in text on Maryland, I, p. 348, do not agree with those in this table).
[14] Virginia *Gazette*, August 19-26, 1737; Gray, I, p. 176.
[15] Gray, I, p. 335.
[16] W. Dunlap, *History of New Netherlands*, II, p. clxvi.
[17] *Writings of Washington* (Ford), XIV, p. 196; Gray, II, p. 616-17.
[18] *Mississippi Historical Society Publications*, X, p. 317-18; Gray, II, p. 643, 744, 1033.

and these led to the revolt of 1730.[19] The Spanish offer of freedom and good treatment during the war between England and Spain in 1739 helped provoke the troubles of 1737-40 in South Carolina.[20] Many of the plots and revolts during the Revolution and the War of 1812 were stimulated by Tory and British offers of aid as well as by a growth of anti-slavery discussion during the former period. The West Indian uprisings starting in 1792 were probably important in causing risings in Virginia and Louisiana. The Missouri debates influenced the Vesey attempt of 1822,[21] and there were further exciting incidents in the period 1826-31. The last troubles, starting in 1854 and going through the War, were no doubt affected by the Nebraska debate, the Kansas War, and the campaigns of 1856 and 1860. Large and sudden additions to the slave population is a factor of some weight in explaining some of the revolts, like those in South Carolina in 1730 and in Hinds and Madison counties, Mississippi, in 1835.[22]

These three factors, then, or a combination of them, appear to be the driving forces behind the history of American Negro slave revolts.

Within the limits of this paper we can outline only the most important of these plots and revolts. It is worthy of note that they are all the main outbreaks which were recorded within definite periods of rebellious activity.

A conspiracy was formed by slaves in the city of New York on the first day of 1712, the plotters ". . . tying themselves to secrecy by Sucking ye blood of each Others hand. . . ." It matured very early in the morning of April 8, when about twenty-five of them set fire to a house and, armed with a few guns, clubs, and knives, waited for the whites to approach. About nine were killed and five or six seriously wounded. The alarm soon spread and soldiers hastened from the fort. In about one day most of the rebels were captured. Six were not, for "one shot first his wife and then himself and some who had hid themselves in Town when they went to Apprehend them Cut their own throats." [23] A reporter, who had stated that the outbreak "has put us into no small consternation the whole Town being under Arms," later remarked, "We have about seventy Negro's in Custody.

[19] *Virginia Magazine of History and Biography*, XXXII, p. 322-23.
[20] R. Scarborough, p. 4, 14; *Collections of South Carolina Historical Society*, I, p. 185
[21] L. Kennedy and T. Parker, *An Official Report of the Trials*, p. 64.
[22] D. Rowland, *History of Mississippi*, II, p. 783; Gray, I, p. 94; II, p. 903, table 34.
[23] *New York Genealogical and Biographical Record*, XXI, p. 162-63.

and 'tis fear'd that most of the Negro's here (who are very numerous) [24] knew of the late conspiracy to murder the Christians." [25]

Twenty-seven slaves were condemned, but six, including a pregnant woman, were pardoned. Twenty-one, then, were executed, and since the law passed in 1708 [26] permitted any type of punishment,[27] the Governor was able to describe the modes of execution as follows: ". . . some were burnt others hanged, one broke on the wheele, and one hung a live in chains in the town, so that there has been the most exemplary punishment inflicted that could be possibly thought of. . . ." [28] This outbreak, in part, influenced Massachusetts to forbid further importation of slaves in 1713, and led Pennsylvania, in August, 1712, to place a high duty on slaves which effectively discouraged their importation.[29]

Among the main causes of the rebelliousness of the South Carolina slaves in 1737-40, acute economic hardship and Spanish persuasion have been mentioned. In addition, Negroes outnumbered whites four to one; many of them had been captured in Angola and thus were Catholics who were naturally drawn to the Spaniards.[30]

Sunday, September 9, 1739, the Negroes on a plantation at Stono, some twenty miles west of Charleston, South Carolina, revolted and killed the two guards of a magazine. Arming themselves, they set out for the Edisto river, whose mouth is directly north of St. Augustine, Florida (then held by Spain). "Several Negroes joyned them, they called out liberty, marched on with colours displayed, and two drums beating," killing and burning all in their path in their bid for freedom, so that "the Country thereabout was full of flames." [31] About twenty-five whites were killed, but not indiscriminately, for one, "a good man and kind to his slaves," was spared.[32] On their march the Negroes met and almost captured Lieutenant-Governor Bull, who fled

[24] At this time there were about 1,800 Negroes and over 10,000 whites in New York. A. J. Northrup, *Slavery in New York*, p. 268.
[25] Boston *Weekly News-Letter*, April 7-14, April 14-21, 1712.
[26] This followed an uprising causing the death of seven whites and the execution of four slaves, including an Indian. *Documents Relative to Colonial History of New York*, V, p. 39.
[27] *Loc. cit.* [24], p. 266.
[28] *Loc. cit.* [26], p. 341-42.
[29] New York *Weekly Tribune*, September 22, 1855; A. W. Lauber, *Indian Slavery*, p. 290; C. P. Keith, *Chronicles of Pennsylvania*, II, p. 505.
[30] *Colonial Records of Georgia*, XXII, part 2, p. 233.
[31] *Ibid.*, p. 234-35; IV, p. 412-13.
[32] *Ibid.*, XXII, part 2, p. 234.

and helped spread the alarm. A gentleman, appropriately named Golightly, observed the slaves, and ran to the nearby town of Wilton where the Presbyterian minister, Archibald Stobo, was holding services. The good Christians, being armed as usual, and learning that their slaves had left the services of their earthly masters, set out in pursuit.[33] The Negroes, numbering from eighty to one hundred, who had by this time marched over ten miles, stopped to rest and refresh themselves. They were surprised by the whites, but, says a letter, "behaved boldly." [34] One account reads: [35]

They gave 2 Fires, but without any damage. We return'd the Fire and bro't down 14 on the spot; and pursuing after them, within 2 Days kill'd twenty odd more, and took about 40; who were immediately some shot, some hang'd, and some Gibbeted alive. A Number came in and were seized and discharged; and some are out yet, but we hope will soon be taken.

About twenty escaped and ten were overtaken thirty miles to the south. They "fought stoutly for some time and were killed on the Spot." [36]

Early in June, 1740, a plot of slaves involving about two hundred Negroes in and about Charleston was discovered a short time before the uprising was to have broken out. On the day set about one hundred fifty Negroes had gathered, but while yet unarmed, were attacked by the whites. Fifty were captured and hanged, ten a day.[37] In this same month, a terrific fire swept the city doing well over a million pounds damage and necessitating aid from other colonies. Although it was first ascribed to the slaves, this charge was later denied. The cause is not definitely known, but it is certain that in the summer of 1741 at least two Negroes were burnt here for incendiary acts.[38]

It is this revolutionary activity, together with the Negro's persistent attempts to run away, that were given prominent places in the arguments of leading statesmen connected with the Georgia enterprise, like Oglethorpe, Stephens, Martyn, Egmont, for instituting a

[33] *South Carolina History and Genealogy Magazine*, x, p. 28; D. D. Wallace's account, *History of South Carolina*, I, p. 373 f. differs.
[34] *Cf.* footnote [30].
[35] Boston *News-Letter*, November 1-8, 1739.
[36] *Cf.* footnote [34].
[37] *Collections Georgia Historical Society*, I, p. 173; Boston *News-Letter*, July 3-10, 1740.
[38] *Ibid.*, January 15-22, April 30-May 7, 1740; July 7, August 15, August 27-September 3, September 24-October 1, 1741.

prohibition of Negroes in that colony, which lasted until 1750.[39] South Carolina itself passed laws in 1740 for the purpose of lessening the danger. Slave importations were taxed, and the funds so raised were designated for the importation of white Protestant settlers. At the same time rather vague laws were passed requiring better food and clothing for slaves and providing that they should not be worked over fourteen hours a day in winter or fifteen hours in summer.[40]

The Negro agitation in New York City in 1741 has been both interpreted by historians as a bona-fide conspiracy and dismissed as a complete frame-up.[41] A combination of the two attitudes is probably the correct one. The winter had been unusually severe, discontent had been expressed at the trials, and there had been many fires (in Hackensack, New Jersey,[42] where two Negroes were burnt, as well as in New York). On the other hand, some contemporaries doubted the existence of a plot, and the testimony shows that the star witness was a liar. The discontent and the war with Spain may also have been the reasons for a frame-up, and rewards or tortures vitiate many of the confessions. Furthermore, the one full contemporary record was written by one of the judges, Horsmanden, who was, obviously, out to prove a serious plot.

From these facts, one may logically decide that there was trouble but that it was not so serious as Horsmanden would have us believe in his volume and certainly not so serious as to warrant, from the slave owner's viewpoint, the terrible punishments inflicted. Concerning the terror there is no question. Altogether about one hundred fifty Negroes and twenty-five whites, including seventeen soldiers, were arrested. Four whites and thirteen or fourteen Negroes were burnt. Eighteen Negroes were hanged, two in chains. Seven who were indicted were never found, and about seventy were banished.[43]

The struggle of the American Negro against slavery during the revolutionary period, and during the War of 1812, took mainly the forms of flight and enlistment. This may account for the small number

[39] Cf. Colonial Records of Georgia. I, p. 50; Scarborough, p. 9, 12, 37, 73.

[40] D. D. Wallace, Henry Laurens, p. 82; Annual Report of American Historical Association, 1895, p. 657; E. Channing, History of United States, II, p. 391.

[41] Beard, Rise of American Civilization (1936), I, p. 81; Magazine of American History, XI, p. 414.

[42] H. S. Cooley, p. 43; New Jersey Historical Society Proceedings, 1874, p. 179.

[43] D. Horsmanden, The Negro Conspiracy . . . , New York, 1744, reprinted 1810, 1851

of revolts during these periods,[44] though conspiracies and rumors of conspiracies abounded. Two fairly serious outbreaks did, however, mark the first period, one, notwithstanding Bassett's denial, in North Carolina in 1775, the other in Georgia in 1776.[45]

The factors making for the many revolts of the 1790s and the early 1800s, the depression and the West Indian slave outbreaks, have already been pointed out. The most important instances will now be sketched.

A plan for revolt in Pointe Coupée Parish, Louisiana, in April, 1795,[46] never was carried out because of betrayal after disagreement as to method. It appears certain that whites were implicated and three were banished. A group of Negroes attempted to rescue their imprisoned comrades but failed, twenty-five of their number being killed. Twenty-three Negroes were hung and their bodies displayed from New Orleans to Pointe Coupée, some one hundred and fifty miles away. In consequence, Carondelet, the governor, forbade by proclamation continuance of the slave trade, a prohibition which lasted until the territory came under the jurisdiction of our own free nation.[47]

The year 1800 is the most important one in the history of American Negro slave revolts. It is the birth year of John Brown and Nat Turner, the year in which Denmark Vesey bought his freedom, and the year of Gabriel's attempt.

The Governor of Virginia, Monroe, and the military authorities of Richmond had been warned of rumors of revolt as early as August 10, but Monroe heard nothing definite until two o'clock in the afternoon of August 30, the day set for its outbreak. At that time Mr. Mosby Sheppard told him that his slaves, Tom, and, ironically enough, Pharoah, had said that a Negro uprising was to occur that very evening.[48] Military precautions were immediately taken, Monroe even appointing three aides for himself. Although Sheppard's information

44 H. B. Stowe, in her novel, *Dred* (II, p. 302, Boston, 1856), and W. H. Siebert in his *The Underground Railroad* (p. 340, New York, 1899), suggested that the fact that many Negroes always fled served as a safety-valve and diminished the number of slave revolts.

45 J. S. Bassett, *Slavery . . . Colony of North Carolina*, p. 62; but see, *Colonial Records of North Carolina*, X, p. xxiii; S. Ashe, *History of North Carolina*, I, p. 435-36; F. Martin, *History of North Carolina*, II, p. 353; *South Carolina History and Genealogical Magazine*, IV, p. 205.

46 Phillips puts it in 1796. His account distorts as usual; it is a thorough understatement. (*American Negro Slavery*, p. 474, New York, 1918.)

47 A. Phelps, *Louisiana . . .*, p. 171-72.

48 *Calendar of Virginia State Papers*, IX, p. 128, 134; see A. Bontemps' recent novel, *Black Thunder*.

was correct and on that night about one thousand slaves, armed with clubs and swords which they had "been making ever since last harvest," had gathered some six miles outside of Richmond, these precautions were unnecessary, for there occurred a tremendous rainstorm flooding rivers, tearing down bridges and making military operations impossible.[49]

The chosen general of these Negroes was Gabriel, slave of Thomas Prosser of Henrico, a twenty-four-year-old giant of six feet two, who had intended "to purchase a piece of silk for a flag, on which they would have written 'death or liberty.' " Another leader was Jack Bowler, four years older and three inches taller than Gabriel, who felt that "we had as much right to fight for our liberty as any men." Solomon and Martin, brothers of Gabriel, were prominent too. The former conducted the sword making, the latter bitterly opposed delaying the revolt: "Before he would any longer bear what he had borne, he would turn out and fight with his stick." [50]

Scores of Negroes were arrested, every county captain in the state was warned, and over six hundred fifty soldiers guarded Richmond.[51] Gabriel was captured in Norfolk on September 25 and sent to Richmond. He was tried and condemned but his execution was postponed for three days until October 7, in the hope that he would talk. Monroe himself interviewed him, but reported that "From what he said to me, he seemed to have made up his mind to die, and to have resolved to say but little on the subject of the conspiracy." About thirty-five Negroes were executed. Two condemned slaves escaped from the Westmoreland jail.[52]

Jefferson pointed out [53] to Monroe that "The other states & the world at large will forever condemn us if we indulge a principle of revenge, or go one step beyond absolute necessity. They cannot lose sight of the rights of the two parties, & the object of the unsuccessful one." Ten were reprieved and banished.

It is not known how many Negroes were involved. One witness said two thousand, another six thousand, and one ten thousand.[54] Monroe stated: [55]

[49] *Works of Monroe*, III, p. 234; *Calendar of Virginia State Papers*, IX, p. 141.
[50] *Ibid.*, IX, p. 151, 160, 165.
[51] Monroe, III, p. 242.
[52] Monroe, III, p. 213; *Calendar of Virginia State Papers*, IX, p. 160.
[53] Jefferson, VII, p. 457-58.
[54] *Calendar of Virginia State Papers*, IX. p. 141, 164, 165.
[55] Monroe, III, p. 239, 216-18.

38

It was distinctly seen that it embraced most of the slaves in this city
[Richmond] and neighbourhood, and that the combination extended to
several of the adjacent counties, Hanover, Caroline, Louisa, Chesterfield,
and to the neighbourhood of the Point of the Fork; and there was good
cause to believe that the knowledge of such a project pervaded other parts,
if not the whole of the State.

He did not, however, believe that it extended "to any State South
of us," yet there were conspiracies and panic in North Carolina. A
new ordinance (passed in July) requiring hired slaves to wear badges
and masters to pay fees for the privilege of hiring out their slaves
in Charleston, indicated the restlessness there.[56] The nation, from
Massachusetts to Mississippi, was terror-stricken; the former state provided for the removal of many free Negroes and the governor of the
latter state issued a hundred circulars to the leading planters urging
vigilance, while its lower house passed, in 1802, a bill which was killed
in council, prohibiting importation of male Negroes.[57] Gabriel's conspiracy was followed by the establishment of a guard of sixty-eight
men for the capital at Richmond together with a night watch for
each of its wards. Resolutions favoring federal aid in colonizing "bad"
Negroes were passed and Monroe earnestly but vainly pressed the
matter.[58] The colonization society was finally formed in 1817, following a year of considerable unrest on the part of the slaves.

An interesting feature of Gabriel's attempt was that the Negroes
expected, or, at least, hoped that the poorer whites would join them.[59]
Moreover, they had intended to spare Frenchmen, Quakers, and Methodists,[60] and, indeed, testimony directly implicating two Frenchmen

[56] S. Ashe, p. 185; Charleston *City Gazette,* July 18, 1800. Rumors of a great conspiracy, as the Hartford *American Mercury,* October 16, 1800, said, were "wholly false"
and probably originated in the desire of the Federalists to discredit Jefferson and lay the
blame for the unrest upon his "wild, anarchistic" ideas.

[57] G. H. Moore, *Notes on Slavery in Massachusetts,* p. 231-37; D. Rowland, *History of
Mississippi,* II, p. 631-32; *Mississippi Territorial Archives,* I, p. 311-312, 373-78; Gray, II,
p. 688.

[58] *Atlantic Monthly,* X, p. 337-45; M. N. Stanard, *Richmond,* p. 85; Monroe, III, p.
292-95, 336-38.

[59] *Calendar of Virginia State Papers,* IX, p. 141, 164.

[60] One witness added poor white women and one said young women, intimating that
the last exception did not have the purest motives. This was mentioned but once, and implicitly contradicted many times, yet most writers on this have made rape one of the
certain and prime purposes of the Negroes. This is the most flagrant kind of distortion.
Most contemporary reports of plots and almost all later accounts of them put rape down
as one of the aims. *Yet there is no case of an attack on a white woman in the history of
Negro revolts.* The chauvinistic historians may storm or, as is frequent, resort to false-

39

was offered.[61] These exceptions are easily explained. The current slogan of the French Revolution, "liberty, equality, fraternity," was enough to win the respect of these slaves, while the consistent opposition of the Quakers to slavery won the Negroes' friendship. Methodists, members of an essentially frontier church, were strongly democratic and equalitarian, and gave trouble to the slavocracy until abolition.

Evidence concerning the plots in Virginia and North Carolina in 1801-02 is not as full as that for 1800, but an informed contemporary, the editor of the Norfolk *Herald*, felt [62] that the latter threat was "not near so formidable" as that of 1802. Certainly hundreds of Negroes were arrested, particularly in Norfolk, Petersburg, and Richmond, and in Martin and Bertie counties, North Carolina. About ten to fifteen slaves were executed in Virginia and fifteen or twenty in North Carolina. Some were transported, others cropped, and many lashed.[63] These plots were betrayed by confidential slaves.[64] But there is quite convincing evidence that the poor whites were allied with the Negroes. It appears in a letter of John B. Scott and in the testimony of a slave, Lewis, on two different occasions that whites, "the common run of poor white people," were to aid the slaves.[65] A slave, Arthur (probably Arthur Farrar, to whom Lewis refers), is reported as having made the following recruiting speech: [66]

I have taken it on myself to let the country be at liberty this lies upon my mind for a long time. Mind men I have told you a great deal I have joined with both black and white which is the common men or poor white people, mulattoes will join with me to help free the country, although they are free already. I have got 8 or 10 white men to lead me in the fight on the magazine, they will be before me and hand out guns, powder, pistols, shot and other things that will answer the purpose . . . black men I mean to lose my life in this if they will take it.

What actually did happen to this "docile, contented" Negro slave is not known.

hood, but nevertheless this remains a fact. *Ibid.*, IX, p. 152, 171; *cf.* Howison, *Virginia*, II, p. 391; Ballagh, p. 92.
[61] *Loc. cit.* [60], p. 152, 165.
[62] Quoted in New York *Evening Post*, June 21, 1802.
[63] *Calendar of Virginia State Papers*, IX, p. 270-72; 274-75, 279, 293-310; *Post*, June 18, 21, 23, 25, 28, July 10, 1802, December 1, 1801; Bassett, state . . . , p. 94; Ashe, II, p. 186; Wertenbaker, *Norfolk*, p. 140; Monroe, III, p. 344-45, 346, 348-49.
[64] *Calendar of Virginia State Papers*, X, p. 82.
[65] *Ibid.*, IX, p. 294, 298, 300.
[66] *Journal of Negro History*, XVI, p. 161.

On the afternoon of January 9, 1811,[67] the people of New Orleans were thrown into the "utmost dismay and confusion" on discovering wagons and carts straggling into the city filled with people whose faces "wore the masks of consternation" and who told of having just escaped from a "miniature representation of the horrors of St. Domingo." Governor Claiborne ordered out all patrols, forbade male Negroes from "going at large" and, though the "day was rainy and cold and the roads uncommonly deep," soldiers were immediately dispatched to the center of the trouble, thirty-five miles away. General Hampton, leading four hundred militia and sixty regular United States troops, left from New Orleans, and Major Milton, with two hundred soldiers, left Baton Rouge, and by forced marches arrived at the scene of action at about midnight of the ninth. Here were to be seen about four hundred Negroes, "the most active, prime slaves," armed with scythes and cane-knives, and a few guns. To this number had grown the band, led by a mulatto, Charles, which had revolted from a Mr. Andry and had since marched some fifteen miles, devastating and killing [68] all in its path, with drums beating and flags flying, "determined no longer to submit to the hardships of their situation."

General Hampton did not order his four hundred sixty men to attack until about 4:30 A.M., when he thought the Negroes were surrounded. But they rang "the alarm bell, and with a degree of extraordinary silence for such a rabble, commenced and affected their retreat up the river." They were then met by Major Milton's force of two hundred men and soon "the whole of the banditti [a favorite term] were routed, killed, wounded, and dispersed." Sixty-six were shot or executed on the spot, seventeen were later reported missing and "are supposed generally to be dead in the woods, as many bodies have been seen by the patrols." Sixteen were taken prisoners and sent to New Orleans for trial. They were executed and their heads strung on poles at intervals from the city to Andry's plantation. What more occurred there in 1811 [69] cannot be definitely stated but this paragraph from a New Orleans paper is suggestive: [70]

[67] This account and all quotations are from letters and reprints in the New York *Evening Post*, January 15, February 19, 20, 26, 27, 1811.

[68] How many were killed is not known. The governor said "several."

[69] Gayarre is his account of this (*History of Louisiana*, fourth edition, New Orleans, 1903, IV, p. 267-68) tells of one well-armed white who successfully held off the "cowardly" Negroes. His citation is F. X. Martin and nothing like that is to be found there; and it has been found nowhere else. Accounts are in F. Martin, *History of Louisiana*, II, p. 300-01; A. Fortier, III, p. 78-79; A. Phelps, p. 249-50.

[70] Paper's name not given. In New York *Evening Post*, February 27, 1811.

41

We are sorry to learn that a ferocious sanguinary disposition marked the character of some of the inhabitants. Civilized man ought to remember well his standing, and never let himself sink down to a level with a savage; our laws are summary enough and let them govern.

Early in 1816 Virginia was rocked by an indigenous John Brown, one George Boxley. In appearance he was anything but like Brown, but in ideas he was well nigh identical. Boxley was between thirty and forty years of age, six feet one or two inches tall, with a "thin visage, of a sallow complexion, thin make, his hair light or yellowish, (thin on top of his head, and tied behind)—he stoops a little in his shoulders, has large whiskers, blue or grey eyes, pretends to be very religious, is fond of talking and speaks quick." [71] Contemporaries were in doubt as to "whether he is insane or not" since he openly "declared that the distinction between the rich and the poor was too great; that offices were given rather to wealth than to merit; and seemed to be an advocate for a more leveling system of government. For many years he had avowed his disapprobation of the slavery of the negroes, and wished they were free." [72]

Late in 1815 Boxley formed a conspiracy in Spotsylvania, Louisa and Orange counties, but it was betrayed by a slave woman. Early in 1816 about thirty Negroes were arrested. Boxley, after vainly trying to organize a rescue party, fled. He finally surrendered, but with the flame of a candle and a file smuggled to him by his wife, he escaped in May, and was never recaptured, though a $1,000 reward was offered. About six Negroes were executed and the same number transported.[73] A month after his escape a considerable plot was uncovered by a confidential slave whose identity was never revealed, in Camden, South Carolina. It is interesting that the rising was to have taken place on July fourth. Many were implicated, and six were hanged. The state purchased the informer's freedom for $1,100 and enacted a law granting him fifty dollars a year for life.[74]

Two considerable expeditions against communities of runaways who [75] harassed slaveowners were carried through in 1816, one near

[71] Governor's reward notice in Richmond *Enquirer*, May 22, 1816.
[72] *Calendar of Virginia State Papers*, x, p. 433-35.
[73] *Ibid.*; Phillips, *American Negro Slavery*, p. 476; *Journal Negro History*, xvi, p. 166-67; New York Post, April 16, 1816; Richmond *Enquirer*, May 22, 29, 1816.
[74] New York *Evening Post*, July 18, 1816; (E. C. Holland), *A Refutation*, p. 74-77; H. T. Cook, *Life of D. R. Williams*, p. 130; H. M. Henry, *Police Control . . . South Carolina*, p. 151.
[75] H. T. Cook, *op. cit.*, p. 130.

Ashepoo, South Carolina, and the other against the abandoned British fort, called Negro Fort, at Appalachicola Bay, Florida. The Milledge-ville (Georgia) *Journal* of June 26, 1816, had complained against the latter "establishment so pernicious to the Southern States" and demanded: "How long shall this evil, requiring immediate remedy, be permitted to exist?" A short time, indeed, it turned out to be. In July, United States troops accompanied by Indians set out for the fort. It withstood a siege for about two weeks, but surrendered on July 27, after a direct hit from a cannon had killed two hundred seventy men, women and children. Out of the original three hundred thirty occupants only forty survived.[76] This haven for fugitive slaves and base for their attacks on American slaveholders was eliminated by the annexation of Florida in 1819, after the first Seminole War.

A free Negro, Moses, betrayed a slave plot in Goochland County,[77] Virginia, in 1822, but that same year, in Charleston, another free Negro, Denmark Vesey, attempted to be a real Moses. He read to the slaves "from the bible how *the children of Israel were delivered out of Egypt from bondage.*" If his companion were to bow "to a white person he would rebuke him, and observe that all men were born equal, and that he was surprised that any one would degrade himself by such conduct; that he would never cringe to the whites, nor ought any who had the feelings of a man." One slave stated that "Vesey said the negroes were living such an abominable life, they ought to rise. I said I was living well—he said though I was others were not. . . ." He had not heeded the urgings of the slaveowners for free Negroes to go to Africa, "*because he had not the will, he wanted to stay and see what he could do* for his fellow-creatures," including his own children, who were slaves.[78] Most of the other Negroes felt as Vesey did. Two of the rebels said, "They never spoke to any person of color on the subject, or knew of any one who had been spoken to by the other leaders, who had withheld his assent." Nevertheless the leaders feared exposure, and it came. One of them, Peter Poyas, had warned an agent, "Take care and don't mention it to those waiting men who receive presents of old coats, etc., from their masters, or

[76] C. M. Brevard, *A History of Florida*, I, p. 42-45.
[77] J. Russell, *Free Negro in Virginia*, p. 169.
[78] J. Hamilton, *Negro Plot*, p. 36; L. H. Kennedy and T. Parker, *Official Report* . . . , p. III, 20, 87-88. Emphasis as in original.

they'll betray us. . . ." The traitor was Devany, slave of Colonel Prioleau.[79]

Vesey had set the date for the second Sunday in July. Sunday was selected because on that day it was customary for slaves to enter the city, and July, because many whites would then be away. The betrayal led him to put the date ahead one month, but Vesey could not communicate with his country confederates, some of whom were eighty miles outside the city.[80] Peter Poyas and Mingo Harth, who were the two leaders first arrested, behaved "with so much composure and coolness" that "the wardens were completely deceived." Both were freed on May 31 although spies were put on their trails. Another slave, William, gave further testimony and more arrests followed, the most damaging of which was that of Charles Drayton, who agreed to act as a spy. This led to complete disclosure.[81] One hundred thirty-one Negroes were arrested in Charleston and forty-seven condemned. Twelve were pardoned and transported, but thirty-five were hanged. Twenty were banished and twenty-six acquitted, although the owners were asked to transport eleven of these. Thirty-eight were discharged by the court. Four white men, American, Scottish, Spanish, and German, were fined and imprisoned for aiding the Negroes despite the fact that their aid appeared to be only verbal.[82] Although the leaders had kept lists of their comrades, only one list and part of another was found. Moreover, most of them followed the admonition of Poyas, "Die silent, as you shall see me do," and so it is difficult to say how many Negroes were involved.[83] One witness said 6,600 outside of Charleston, another said nine thousand altogether were involved. The plan of revolt, comprising simultaneous attacks from five points and a sixth force on horseback to patrol the streets, further indicated a very considerable number of conspirators.[84] The preparations had been thorough. By the middle of June the Negroes had made about two hundred fifty pike heads and bayonets and over three hundred daggers. They had noted every store containing any arms and had given instructions to all slaves who tended or could easily get horses

[79] Kennedy and Parker, p. 26, 21-22.
[80] Ibid., p. 34-35.
[81] Ibid., p. 48 ff.; see also Atlantic Monthly, VII, p. 728-44.
[82] Kennedy and Parker, p. 188 and appendix.
[83] Ibid., p. 25, 42; see also A. Grimké, Right on the Scaffold. . . .
[84] Ibid., p. 27, 38; (Hamilton), p. 30, 38.

as to when and where to bring the animals. Even a barber had assisted by making wigs for the slaves. Vesey also had twice written to St. Domingo, telling of his plans and asking aid. All who opposed were to be killed, for "'he that is not with me is against me' was their creed." [85] There was certainly also a plan to rescue the leaders; [86] and, according to one source,[87] on the day of Vesey's execution "Another attempt at insurrection was made but the State troops held the slaves in check. So determined, however, were they to strike a blow for liberty that it was found necessary for the federal government to send soldiers to maintain order." Contemporary evidence in only the second point has been found.[88]

There was trouble outside Charleston this same year. It might have been in part the work of the Negroes whom Vesey had enlisted for the revolt in July and could not warn of the change. The *National Intelligencer* of July 23 told of the execution of three Negroes in Jacksonboro, forty miles west of Charleston. An item of August 24 gave notice of the Governor's reward of $200 for the killing or capturing of fifteen or twenty armed Negroes harassing the planters.[89] *Niles' Weekly Register* of September 28 said: "It appears that an insurrection of the blacks was contemplated at Beaufort, South Carolina, and that ten Negroes belonging to the most respectable families were arrested. The town council was in secret session. Particulars had not transpired." They rarely did. Tighten restrictive laws, get rid of as many free Negroes as possible, keep the slaves ignorant, hang the leaders, banish others, whip, crop, scourge scores, and above all keep it secret, or if you must talk, speak of the slaves' contentedness and docility: Such was the attitude of the ruling class. On this particular occasion one ingenious pamphleteer [90] suggested that Negro slaves be strictly forbidden to attend fourth of July celebrations!

We must know the circumstances surrounding the revolt led by Nat Turner in Virginia in 1831 to understand the panic that fol-

[85] Kennedy and Parker, p. 32-33; 37-40.
[86] *Ibid.*, p. 49.
[87] *Harper's Encyclopedia of United States History*, 1902, x, p. 53-54.
[88] Richmond *Enquirer*, August 3, 1822, quoting Charleston *Courier* (n. d.) and August 23, 1822, quoting Charleston City *Gazette* (n. d.).
[89] *National Intelligencer* (Washington), August 24; Richmond *Enquirer*, August 30, 1822.
[90] (E. C. Holland), *Practical Considerations . . . Relative to the Slave Population of South Carolina*, 1823, p. 33, note.

lowed.[91] The ten preceding years had been marked by a severe depression. In 1825-30, the prices of cotton and slaves reached the lowest point they were to touch until the Civil War. Slave trading, a very important industry in Virginia, dwindled and to the local consternation the Negro population grew more rapidly than did the white. British anti-slavery agitation increased, Mexico abolished slavery in 1829, and attempts were made by Mexico and Colombia (apparently backed by England and France), to acquire Puerto Rico and Cuba and wipe out slavery there. Moreover, from 1825 to 1832 there were slave revolts and plots in Venezuela, Brazil, Cuba, Martinique, and the British West Indies (Tortola, Antigua, and Jamaica), as well as in Delaware, Maryland, Virginia, North Carolina, South Carolina, Georgia, Alabama, Mississippi, Kentucky, Tennessee and Louisiana. (See Table on p. 538. It was due to the urging of some of these states that additional federal troops were sent into Louisiana and Virginia in the spring of 1831. They soon saw service in the Nat Turner revolt.

Nat Turner was born October 2, 1800, and at the time of the revolt was described as follows:

5 feet 6 or 8 inches high, weighs between 150 and 160 pounds rather bright complexion, but not a mulatto, broad shoulders, large flat nose, large eyes, broad flat feet, rather knock-kneed, walks brisk and active, hair on the top of the head very thin, no beard, except on the upper lip and the top of the chin, a scar on one of his temples, also one on the back of his neck, a large knot on one of the bones of his right arm, near the wrist, produced by a blow.

Turner was an intelligent and gifted man who could not reconcile himself to the status quo. His religion offered him a rationalization for his rebellious feelings and, knowing how to read, he immersed himself in the stories of the Bible. In 1826 or 1827 he ran away, as his father had done successfully, and stayed away for one month. He then returned for ". . . the Spirit appeared to me and said I had my wishes directed to the things of this world, and not to the kingdom of Heaven, and that I should return to the service of my earthly master. . . ." But the other Negroes ". . . found fault, and murmured against me, saying that if they had my sense they would not serve any master in the world."

[91] Substantiation and amplification of everything said in connection with this will be found in the writer's master thesis, Columbia, February, 1937. Footnotes are therefore omitted.

May 12, 1828, while working in the fields, Turner
heard a loud noise in the heavens, and the Spirit instantly appeared to me
and said the Serpent was loosened, and Christ had laid down the yoke he
had borne for the sins of men, and that I should take it on and fight against
the Serpent, for the time was fast approaching when the first should be
last and the last should be first.

Ques. Do you not find yourself mistaken now? Ans. Was not Christ
crucified. . . .[92]

The solar eclipse of February 12, 1831, was his sign. This fact permits
J. C. Ballagh to refer to the superstitious character of the "negro intelligence." As a matter of fact a contemporary (white) newspaper
tells of a sermon which claimed that "during the eclipse the whole city
(New York) South of Canal-Street would sink. Some persons actually
went to the upper part of the City."

Turner then told four slaves that it was time to prepare the revolt.
July fourth was selected. This leads another writer, W. H. Parker, to
cry, "Shame! shame!" for he believes that Negroes in fighting for
freedom would "pervert that sacred day"! But Turner was ill on the
"sacred day" and he waited for another sign. This came on August 13,
in the peculiar greenish blue color of the sun. A meeting was called
for Sunday, August 21. Turner arrived last and noticed a newcomer.
"I saluted them on coming up, and asked Will how came he there, he
answered, his life was worth no more than others, and his liberty as
dear to him. I asked him if he meant to obtain it? He said he would,
or lose his life. This was enough to put him in full confidence." Such
were the "bandits," as the governor and press called them, that Turner
led. In the evening of that Sunday this group of six slaves started on
their crusade against slavery by killing Turner's master, Joseph
Travis, together with his family. Within twenty-four hours, some
seventy Negroes, several mounted, had covered an area of twenty miles
and had killed about sixty men, women and children.[93] When within
three miles of the Southampton county seat, Jerusalem (now called

[92] The questioner was T. R. Gray, Turner's counsel, who published 50,000 copies of
the Confessions. The pamphlet was not permitted in the South and, so far as is known,
only two exist, one in the 135th street branch of the New York Library, one in
Virginia State Library, Richmond.

[93] Writers who apologize for slavery and glance over the slaughter of Negroes that followed this revolt, dilate at length upon this "horrible" killing. Yes, it was terrible, but
it was a revolt, and as Steffens remarked to Debs, who objected to bloodshed in the
Russian Revolution, "True, 'Gene. That's all true that you say. A revolution is no gentleman."

Courtland), there was, against Turner's advice, a fatal delay, and the Negroes, whose guns, said the Richmond *Compiler* of August 29, were not "fit for use" were overwhelmed by volunteer and state troops. Soon hundreds of soldiers, including United States troops and cavalry, swarmed over the county and, together with the inhabitants, killed more than one hundred slaves. Some of these "in the aggonies of Death declared that they was going happy fore that God had a hand in what they had been doing . . ." The slaughter ended when the commanding officer, General Eppes, threatened martial law.

Though he never left the county, Turner was not caught until October 30. By November 5, after pleading not guilty, for, as he said, he did not feel *guilty*, Jeremiah Cobb had sentenced him to "be hung by the neck until you are dead! dead! dead!" on November 11. Turner went calmly to his death, the seventeenth slave to be legally executed (three free Negroes also were hanged). Other slaves were arrested, tortured or executed in Virginia, North Carolina, Delaware, Maryland, South Carolina, Georgia, Alabama, Tennessee, Kentucky, Louisiana and Mississippi. The revolt and the panic and terror that followed were the first important overt events fostering an open and decisive break between the North and the South, leading to severe repressive laws in every one of the border and southern states, the disappearance of southern anti-slavery societies, the appearance of scores in the North, the temporary strengthening of the colonization movement, a growth in Virginia sectionalism, clearly shown in the debates of 1831-32, and minor population movements, particularly of free Negroes, out of the slave states. As a tradition the Turner revolt has had and continues to have influence, the most important instance of this being its influence on John Brown.

There is evidence [94] that, in North Carolina and Virginia, the rebellious spirit extended to whites in common with Negroes. Nothing so frightened the rulers of the South as the possibility of the effective unity of the exploited, white and black, and the hints of it at this time furthered the policy of complete control and very strict censorship of all opposition to slavery within the South that prevailed from 1832 to the end of the Civil War.

The slaveholders of Madison and Hinds counties, in the center of Mississippi became uneasy in June, 1835, due to rumors of an im-

[94] *Cf.* Niles *Weekly Register*, XVI, p. 180 (October 15, 1831). Governor Floyd in his legislative message of December 6, 1831, stated that the unrest was "not confined to the

pending uprising. In that month a lady of the former county reported to her neighbors that she had overheard the following alarming statements of one of her slaves: "she wished to God it was all over and done with; that she was tired of waiting on the *white folks,* and wanted to be her own mistress the balance of her days, and clean up her own house." [95] A favorite slave was sent among the others as a spy and soon accused one Negro. This Negro "after receiving a most severe chastisement" confessed that a plot for a revolt had been formed and implicated a Mr. Blake and his slaves. One of that gentleman's slaves "was severely whipped by order of the (Vigilance) committee, but refused to confess anything—alleging all the time, that if they wanted to know what his master had told him, they might whip on until they killed him; that he had promised him that he would never divulge it." [96] Other slaves were tortured and it was finally discovered that there was a general plot of the slaves and that a number of white men were implicated. During July about fifteen slaves and six white men were hanged, the latter including two steam doctors,[97] Joshua Cotton and William Saunders, who appear to have been members of the gang of the notorious John Murrell. This last-named individual was the leader of a band of desperadoes operating in many of the slave states. They would help a Negro escape, then kidnap him and sell him back into slavery. According to the reported confession of Cotton, "Our object in undertaking to excite the negroes to rebellion, was not for the purpose of liberating them, but for plunder." It appears, however, that two of the whites, A. L. Donovan and R. Blake, actually hated slavery.[98]

In 1840 there was intense excitement in the central and south central parts of Louisiana. The New Orleans *Picayune* of September 1 states, "Four hundred slaves living in the parish of Iberville, Louisiana, were induced on the 25th ultimo, to rise against their masters, but they were easily put down, forty were placed in confinement and

slaves." (Henry Wilson, *History of the Rise and Fall of Slave Power in America),* I, p. 191; *J. Negro Hist.,* xvi, p. 163.

[95] H. R. Howard, *The History of V. A. Stewert* . . . appendix to this is "proceedings . . . Madison County . . . 1835 . . ." Quotation is from p. 224.

[96] *Ibid.,* p. 226-27.

[97] Medical treatment by steam was, at this time, almost as common, though not as reputable, as bleeding.

[98] *Loc. cit.* [96], p. 232-33; *Memoir of S. S. Prentiss,* I, p. 161-62; Sydmor, *Slavery in Mississippi,* p. 246, 251. The activities of Murrell are described in the body of Howard's book.

twenty sentenced to be hung." A letter of August 26 remarks that twenty-nine slaves were to be hung in Rapides and Avoyelles parishes. "A negro man . . . confessed, after being taken up, that he had intended, if successful, to whip his master to death. The whole country was constantly patroled by citizens." [99] According to Solomon Northup,[100] a free Negro who was kidnaped in Washington and arrived in this region in 1841, the Negroes had planned a mass flight, presumably to Mexico, but when all preparations had been made, the leader, Lew Cheney, "In order to curry favor with his master" betrayed the plot. "The fugitives were surrounded . . . carried in chains to Alexandria (in Rapides) and hung by the populace. Not only those, but many who were suspected, though entirely innocent, were taken from the field and from the cabin, and without the shadow of process or form of trial hurried to the scaffold." A regiment of soldiers was required to stop the slaughter. "Lew Cheney escaped, and was even rewarded for his treachery . . . his name is despised and execrated by all his race throughout the parishes of Rapides and Avoyelles."

During the six years preceding the Civil War there were reports of slave conspiracies and revolts in Maryland, Virginia, the Carolinas, Georgia, Florida, Arkansas, Alabama, Louisiana, Texas, Kentucky, Missouri, and Tennessee. The greatest excitement was during the presidential campaign years of 1856 and 1860 and some reports are of doubtful validity. But enough remains to warrant the statement that Negro restlessness was characteristic. The excitement in 1856 started in Texas in September, ran through Arkansas, Louisiana, Florida, Georgia, South Carolina, Virginia, and reached its height in December, especially in Kentucky and Tennessee. Probably thousands were arrested, certainly hundreds were lashed and tortured, and at least sixty were killed.[101]

99 Printed in New York *Evening Post*, September 11, 12, 14, 1840.

100 *Twelve Years a Slave*, p. 246 ff.

101 For references to this see: F. L. Olmsted, *A Journey through Texas*, p. 503-04; his *Journey in the Back Country*, p. 475; *Calendar of Virginia State Papers*, XI, p. 50, 343-344; New Orleans *Picayune* from September, 1856, to February, 1857; New York *Weekly Tribune* for November and December, 1856; Phillips, *Plantation and Frontier*, II, p. 116; *Annual Report of the American Anti-slavery Society, 1857-58*, p. 78; Catterall, II, p. 565-66; *Journal of Southern History*, I, p. 43-44; S. Ellis, *Solitary Horseman*, p. 209. Typical errors and distortion by understatement are in C. Patterson, *Negro in Tennessee*, p. 50; I. E. Mc-Dougle, *Slavery in Kentucky*, p. 43.

Preceding, during and following the John Brown raid the excitement was extraordinary.[102] The facts pertinent to this paper, concerning that raid, may be briefly stated. While his biographers [103] have pointed out that Nat Turner was one of the immortal old man's heroes, none has mentioned the later risings of the slaves, particularly those of 1856, as having influenced him. But there is evidence that one of Brown's most trusted followers, Charles P. Tidd, had received a letter [104] at Tabor, Iowa, from E. W. Clarke, dated December 25, 1856, in which this occurred: "The slaves are in a state of insurrection all over the country. Every paper brings us accounts of their plots for a general uprising."

It is likely that this in part explains Brown's feelings, expressed August, 1857, that the Negroes would immediately respond to his efforts though no preparatory notice had been given them. He told W. A. Phillips (who felt that the Negroes were a "peaceful, domestic, inoffensive race . . . incapable of reprisal"), that "You have not studied them right, and you have not studied them long enough." [105] We must also remember that Brown's most famous exploit before Harper's Ferry was his forcible freeing of eleven slaves in Missouri in 1858 and guiding them to Canada. This was undertaken at the request of one of the Negroes and could not have been carried out had it not been for the fighting spirit of these men and women.

The raid would not have been possible without the counsel of such Negroes as Douglass, Gloucester, Smith, Still, Garnett,[106] who also raised funds. The raiding party itself contained five Negroes, four escaped slaves returning to slave territory, Copeland, Leary, Anderson, Green, and one free Negro, Newby, who was spurred on by the desire to free his own children and wife, who had but recently written him, —"come this fall without fail, money or no money I want to see you so much; that is one bright hope I have before me." [107]

102 See Missouri *Democrat*, December 29, 1859; *Principia* (New York) for 1860; Flanders, *Plantation Slavery in Georgia*, p. 275; New York *Weekly Tribune* for 1860; *Journal of Southern History*, I, p. 47; *American Historical Review*, XXXVI, p. 763; A. C. Cole, *The Irrepressible Conflict*, p. 77-78; *Congressional Globe*, 36th Congress, 2nd session, p. 74. Typical understatements are in Phillips, *American Negro Slavery*, p. 487-88; J. H. Brown, *History of Texas*, I, p. 385.
103 Redpath, p. 38, 145; Du Bois, p. 87; Wilson, p. 357.
104 *Calendar of Virginia State Papers*, XI, p. 343-44.
105 O. G. Villard, *John Brown*, p. 313, 362.
106 *Ibid.*, p. 323.
107 Warren, *John Brown*, p. 343-44.

Dallas was destroyed by fire in July, 1860, and this was attributed to the slaves. Three Negroes, Sam, Cato, and Patrick, were executed: [108]

As they passed through the town they surveyed with composure the ruins of the once flourishing town that now lay a blackened mass before them . . . They met their fate with a composure worthy of a better cause. Patrick, with unparalleled nonchalance, died with a chew of tobacco in his mouth, and refused to make any statement whatever.

The story of four years ago was repeated and literally thousands of slaves were tortured, lashed, banished, murdered. Every plot or revolt or supposed conspiracy was blamed upon the Black Republican Party. The Senator from Texas, Wigfall, said (December 12, 1860) : [109]

We say to those States that you shall not . . . permit men to go there [south] and excite your citizens to make John Brown raids or bring fire and strychnine within the limits of the State to which I owe allegiance. You shall not publish newspapers and pamphlets to excite our slaves to insurrection. . . . We will have peace . . . (or) withdraw from the Union."

But some Southerners, as well as Northerners, doubted the existence of such a plot. Thus a letter from Lamar County, Texas, of September, 1860, declared: [110]

It is the opinion of many of our citizens, after mature deliberation, and thorough investigation . . . that these reports had their origin in the minds of scheming politicians, and are a part of that great plan concocted and being put in execution to nerve the Southern arms and excite the Southern mind, preparatory to precipitating the cotton States into a revolution.

When it is remembered that many of those arms and minds, belonging to the southern poor whites were becoming increasingly opposed [111] to slavery the need of such a concoction is clearer. Northerners, however, began to wonder whether the South might not require their aid in putting down the revolts. Senator Doolittle of Wisconsin thought the Constitution required this, but Congressman Giddings of Ohio replied that if liberation would most effectively *protect* the inhabitants, the slaves should be freed. This he called a "remedy" for

108 *Principia*, August 11, 1860.
109 *Congressional Globe*, 36th Congress, 2nd session, p. 73.
110 Louisville *Democrat* (n. d.), quoted in *Principia*, November 10.
111 Olmsted, *Journey in the Back Country*, p. 180.

slave revolts; but it was not a remedy calculated to increase the slave-holder's love for the Union.[112] Greeley in the New York *Weekly Tribune* of December 13, 1856, had stated, "They ask for more territory to be subject to the taskmaster and his cruelties, to the slave and his insurrections . . . what claim will the South have on the North when insurrections do come?"

Moreover, the insecurity of its labor supply was a major factor in reducing the profitableness of the slave system. And it was to raise this profitableness that the South clung to its policy of expansion. And expansion diffused the slave population, and thus decreased the danger of revolt. After secession a completely unashamed and unmitigated policy of suppressing all opposition to slavery might be instituted free from the annoying criticism of the abolitionists. If there should be a greater possibility of escape for fugitive slaves into a nearby foreign land, this would be compensated by a renewal of the African slave trade which, in the fifties, was increasingly demanded.

Although there are evidences of revolts of slaves during the Civil War in Kentucky and Arkansas (1861), Virginia and South Carolina (1862), Georgia (1864), and suspicious fires in Charleston (1861), Richmond (1864), Columbia (1865),[113] probably the main forms of the Negro's struggle against slavery at this period were flight and enlistment in the federal army. Hundreds of thousands of slaves ran away in the years 1861-65, although for more than the first year the Union army acted as a huge slave-catching organization. Though Negroes were not accepted into the Union forces until almost two years of the war had gone by (and then under disadvantageous conditions), still by the end of the war there were over 186,000 Negroes fighting in the Union army, more than 104,000 of whom were recruited in Confederate territory.[114] We have the word of Lincoln himself that if it were not for these thousands of dark hands that eagerly grasped guns and heroically [115] wielded them, the North might not have won.

Indeed, John Brown's idea that slavery was war had considerable

112 New York *Evening Post*, September 27, 1860; *Principia*, November 3, 1860.
113 *Principia*, May 18, June 1, December 21, 1861; S. J. Ravenal, *Charleston*, p. 496; *Calendar of Virginia State Papers*, XI, p. 233-36; Flanders . . . *Georgia*, p. 275; A. C. Cole, *op. cit.*, p. 399; J. Rhodes, *Historical Essays*, p. 301-13; *Georgia Historical Quarterly*, VIII, p. 195-214; *The War of the Rebellion*, Series I, XIV, p. 291, 306.
114 *Journal of Negro History*, XI, p. 575-76; Du Bois, *Black Reconstruction, passim;* H. A. Trexler, *Slavery in Missouri*, p. 206.
115 See *The War of the Rebellion*, Series I, XIV, p. 190, 194, 198, 226.

concrete justification. During slavery the South was a dictatorial oligarchy [116] which terrorized the slaves and suppressed their frequent insubordination and revolts. The fear of such rebelliousness was a persistent factor in the life of the South which has too long been overlooked by social historians. The facts presented here certainly refute the stereotype of a docile Negro slave; [117] the American Negro consistently and courageously struggled against slavery in every possible way and he must continue in this tradition if he is to break down the barriers of discrimination today.

REPORTED AMERICAN NEGRO SLAVE CONSPIRACIES AND REVOLTS

(Those treated in the text are denoted by asterisk; references are selective, not exhaustive.)

Date		Locality	Date		Locality
1663		Va.	1710		Va.
1672		Va.	1711		S. C.
1680s		Va., N. Y.	1712*	120	N. Y.
1687	118	Va.	1713		S. C.
to 1688		Md.	1720		Mass., S. C.
1690s		Va., Mass.	1722	121	Va.
1694		Va.	1723		Mass., Conn., Va.
			1730		Va., S. C., La.
1702		N. Y.	1732		La.
1705	119	Md.	1734	122	S. C., Pa., N. J.
1708*		N. Y.	1737		Pa., S. C.
1709		Va.	1738		S. C.

[116] Olmsted, . . . *Back Country*, p. 62, 264, 444.

[117] Among recent works, Catterall (I, p. 54, note 7) explicitly denies docility; Bancroft (*Slave Trading* . . . , p. 17, 41, 277, 283-84) implicitly.

[118] Hening, *Statutes*, II, p. 204, 299; Ballagh, p. 79; Phillips, *American Negro Slavery*, p. 472; H. Henry, *Police Control*, p. 148; *William and Mary College Quarterly*, X, p. 177-78; Brackett, *Negro in Maryland*, p. 92; J. Coffin, . . . *Newbury* . . . , p. 153; P. A. Bruce, *Economic History*, II, p. 116, 118.

[119] A. Northrup, *Slavery in New York*, p. 260-61; J. Scharf, *Maryland*, I, 375; *Calendar of Virginia State Papers*, I, p. 129.

[120] *Executive journals . . . council . . . colony of Virginia*, III, p. 236; Hening, III, p. 537-38; H. L. Osgood, *American Colony in Eighteenth Century*, II, p. 218; (E. C. Holland), *A Refutation* . . . , p. 28-29, 63; *Journal of Southern History*, I, p. 458; D. Wallace, *South Carolina*, I, p. 372.

[121] *Doc. rel. col. hist.*, *N. Y.*, v, p. 610; *Coll. S. C. Hist. Soc.*, I, p. 252; Wallace, I, p. 372; J. Coffin, *An Account* . . . , p. 9; *Va. Hist. Register*, IV, p. 63; Hening, IV, p. 126 ff.; *Boston Weekly News-Letter*, April 4-11, May 2-9, 9-16, July 4-11, August 8-15, October 10-18, November 14-21, 1723; Ballagh, p. 72 note.

[122] Gayarre, *op. cit.*, I, p. 440; *Va. Mag. of Hist. and Biog.*, XXXII, p. 323; XXXVI, p. 345-46; *Boston Gazette*, October 19-26, 1730; La Roy Sunderland, *Anti-slavery Manual* (1837), p. 84; Coffin, *An Account* . . . , p. 14; Martin, *La.*, I, p. 295-96; *Archives of New Jersey*, 1st Series, XI, p. 335-37, 340-42; Wallace, I, p. 372; *Minutes of Provincial Council of Pennsylvania*, IV, p. 259; Flanders, *op. cit.*, p. 24, 273.

REPORTED AMERICAN NEGRO SLAVE CONSPIRACIES AND REVOLTS

(Those treated in the text are denoted by an asterisk; references are selective, not exhaustive.)

Date		Locality	Date		Locality
1739	} 123	*S. C., Md.	1792	} 129	Va.
1740*		S. C.	1793		Va.
1741*		N. Y., N. J.	1795*		La.
1747	} 124	S. C.	1796	} 130	N. J., N. Y.
1755-6		Va.	1797		Va., S. C.
1759		S. C.	1799		Va.
1760	} 125	S. C.	1800*		Va., N. C., S. C.
1761		S. C.	1801-2*		Va., N. C.
1765		S. C.			
1766		S. C.	1803	} 131	Pa.
1767		Va.	1804		Pa., Ga., La.
1768		Mass.	1805-6	132	N. C., S. C., Va.
1771-2	} 126	Ga., N. J.			
1774		Ga., Mass.	1807	} 133	Miss.
1775		*N. C., S. C.	1808		Va.
1776*		Ga.	1809		Va.
			1810		Va., Ga.
1778	} 127	N. Y.	1811*		La.
1779		Ga., N. J.			
1782	} 128	Va.	1812	} 134	Va.
1786		Ga., Va.	1813		Va.
1787		S. C.	1814		Va.

123 H. Catterall, *Judicial Cases* . . . , IV, p. 35; J. Brackett, *Negro in Maryland*, p. 93-94.

124 *South Carolina Historical and Genealogical Magazine*, XXXI, p. 219; *Official Records of Dinwiddie*, II, p. 101-03, 474; W. Schaper, *Sectionalism . . . S. C.*, p. 310; Coffin, p. 15.

125 Wallace, *South Carolina*, I, p. 374, III, p. 509; *State Records of North Carolina*, XI, p. 226; Boston *Chronicle*, January 11-18, 1768; G. Moore . . . *Mass.*, p. 129.

126 Cooley, p. 43-44; *Letters of Mrs. Adams*, I, p. 24; *Plantation and Frontier*, II, p. 118-19; *Colonial Records of Georgia*, XII, p. 146-47, 325-26; Wallace, *Laurens*, p. 120, note 2.

127 *South Carolina Historical and Genealogical Magazine*, VIII, p. 6-7; W. B. Stevens, *Georgia*, II, p. 317; E. F. Hatfield, *History of Elizabeth, New Jersey*, p. 476.

128 *Calendar of Virginia State Papers*, III, p. 149; Stevens, *op. cit.*, II, p. 376-78; *Calendar of Virginia State Papers*, IV, p. 132; Wallace, *South Carolina*, II, p. 415.

129 *Calendar of Virginia State Papers*, V, p. 488-89, 534-35, 540, 512, 546-47, 552, 555, 624-25, 651; *William and Mary Quarterly* (1st Series), XX, p. 275.

130 J. Atkinson, *Newark*, p. 171; H. M. Henry, *op. cit.*, 150; A. Steward, *Twenty-two Years a Slave*, p. 34-38; *Calendar of Virginia State Papers*, VI, p. 51-52; Phillips, *American Negro Slavery*, p. 188-89.

131 E. R. Turner, *Negro in Pennsylvania*, p: 152-53; Channing, *United States*, V, p. 134; Phillips, *op. cit.*, p. 476; *Louisiana Historical Quarterly*, VII, p. 224.

132 J. Bassett, *Slavery in State of North Carolina*, p. 95-96; *Annual Report Am. Historical Association, 1896*, I, p. 881-82; Ballagh, *Virginia*, p. 109; *William and Mary College Quarterly* (1), VIII, p. 219; *Calendar of Virginia State Papers*, VII, p. 437.

133 D. Rowland, *Mississippi*, II, p. 634; *Calendar of Virginia State Papers*, X, p. 31, 62-63; Flanders, *Georgia*, p. 274.

134 *Calendar of Virginia State Papers*, X, p. 120-23, 217, 223, 241, 279, 367, 387-88; G. P. Coleman, *Virginia Silhouettes*, p. 21.

REPORTED AMERICAN NEGRO SLAVE CONSPIRACIES AND REVOLTS

(Those treated in the text are denoted by an asterisk; references are selective, not exhaustive.)

Date		Locality	Date		Locality
1816*		Va., Fla., S. C.	1836	} 140	Ga., Tenn.
1819	135	Ga., S. C.	1837		La.
1820	} 136	Fla.	1840	141	* La., D. C., N. C., Va.
1821		N. C.	1841-3		La., Ga., Miss.
1822*		S. C., Va.	1845	} 142	Md.
1824	} 137	Va.	1851		Ga.
1826		Miss., N. C.	1854	} 143	Ala.
1827		Ga.	1855		Md., La., Mo., Ga., S. C.
1829	} 138	Ky., Va., S. C., N. C.	1856*		all over
1830		Miss., Md., N. C., La., Tenn.	1857		Md.
1831*		all over	1859	} 144	John Brown
1833	} 139	Va.	1860*		all over
1835		*Miss., S. C., Ga., La.	1861-65*		

There were also many uprisings on boats. Only fairly successful ones appear to have been reported—as in 1730, 1731, 1732, 1747, 1761, 1826, 1830, 1839, 1841.[145]

[135] Phillips, *American Negro Slavery*, p. 477, 510; *Plantation and Frontier*, II, p. 91.

[136] Catterall, II, p. 327-28; Bassett, *op. cit.*, p. 96; Ashe, *North Carolina*, II, p. 281-82.

[137] J. Russell, *Free Negro*, p. 169; Sydnor, *Slavery in Mississippi*, p. 149; *Niles' Register*, XXXI, p. 192; *African Repository*, III, p. 157.

[138] *Calendar of Virginia State Papers*, x, p. 567-69; *Tyler's Quarterly History Magazine*, I, p. 14; *Niles' Register*, XXXVI, p. 53; XXXVII, p. 18-19, 277; XXXVIII, p. 157; Catterall, II, p. 340-41; *American Slavery as It Is*, p. 51; Hart, *Slavery and Abolition*, p. 116; *The Liberator* (Boston), January 1, 15, March 19, 1831; Sydnor, p. 116; Scarborough, p. 89; *Senate Document 209*, 57th Congress, 2nd session, p. 56, 261-64.

[139] *Calendar of Virginia State Papers*, x, p. 587; *Niles' Register*, XLVIII, p. 149; XLIX, p. 331; E. P. Burke, *Reminiscences of Georgia*, p. 156-58.

[140] Phillips, *American Negro Slavery*, p. 485; *Louisiana Historical Quarterly*, VII, p. 223, and for January, 1937; *Niles' National Register*, LIII, p. 129.

[141] New York *Post*, August 27, September 8, 1840; *Van Buren Manuscripts*, letter of September 11, 1840, Library of Congress.

[142] R. B. Flanders, *op. cit.*, p. 275; Phillips, *American Negro Slavery*, p. 486; Brackett, *Maryland*, p. 96; *Niles' National Register*, LX, p. 368, 384; LXIII, p. 212; LXVIII, p. 293.

[143] New York *Weekly Tribune*, September 16, 1854; Trexler, *op. cit.*, p. 72-73; *Plantation and Frontier*, II, p. 120; Brackett, *op. cit.*, p. 97; Catterall, III, p. 648-49.

[144] Brackett, *Negro in Maryland*, p. 97.

[145] Boston *Gazette*, April 26-May 3, 1731; Boston *Weekly News-Letter*, October 27-November 2, 1732; Coffin, *An Account . . .*, p. 14, 15, 34; F. Bancroft, *Slavetrading*, p. 41, 277; *Niles' Register*, XXXVIII, p. 328; a bibliography of the *Creole* (1841) is in G. H. Barnes & D. Dumond, *Letters . . . Weld . . . Grimké*, II, p. 886 note.

The article by Dr. Paul Radin on "Economic Factors in Primitive Religion," published in the Spring issue, is a chapter from his book, *Primitive Religion*, published by Viking Press.

MORE ON AMERICAN NEGRO SLAVE REVOLTS

Since the publication of the present writer's "American Negro Slave Revolts" (SCIENCE & SOCIETY, I, no. 4) he has come across about thirty more plots and uprisings. It is therefore proper to revise the previous approximation of one hundred and thirty, and to declare that there were at least one hundred and sixty reported[1] American Negro slave conspiracies and revolts between 1663 and 1865.

Some of these new conspiracies have features worthy of particular notice. Thus it is clear that slaves of different states jointly planned an uprising in the Spring of 1810, and that they had considered the scheme for several months. In about March, 1810, two letters[2] were found on a road in Halifax county, North Carolina. One was from a slave in Greene county, Georgia, to another slave, Cornell Lucas, of Martin county, North Carolina; another, likewise from and to slaves, had been sent from Tennessee and was intended for Brunswick county, Virginia. The contents of both letters, even as to details, were similar, and one, that to Cornell Lucas, may be quoted in full:

Dear Sir—I received your letter to the fourteenth of June, 1809 with great freedom and joy to hear and understand what great proceedance you have made, and the resolu-

[44] *Life in Letters of W. D. Howells,* II, p. 104.
[45] *Ibid.,* p. 121.
[46] Carl Van Doren, *The American Novel,* p. 139.
[1] Censorship was strong and this word "reported" is an important qualification. Thus Fanny Kemble (*Journal of a residence on a Georgia plantation in 1838-1839,* London, 1863, p. 300-01, 359) refers to a hushed-up slave conspiracy which she does not date. And a gentleman in South Carolina, reminiscing in 1888, refers to a reported plot in Abbeville, but gives no date. (J. B. O'Neall and J. A. Chapman, *Annuals of Newberry,* Newberry, 1892, Part II, p. 501.)
[2] N. Y. *Evening Post,* April 30, 1810.

tion you have in proceeding on in business as we have undertook, and hope you will still continue in the same mind. We have spread the sense nearly over the continent in our part of the country, and have the day when we are to fall to work, and you must be sure not to fail on that day, and that is the 22d April, to begin about midnight, and do the work at home first, and then take the armes of them you slay first, and that will strengthen us more in armes—for freedom we want and will have, for we have served this cruel land long enuff, & be as secret convaing your nuse as possabel, and be sure to send it by some cearfull hand, and if it happens to be discovered, fail not in the day, for we are full abel to conquer by any means. Sir, I am your Captain James, living in the state of Jorgy, in Green county—so no more at present, but remaining your sincer friend and captain until death.

These letters were given to General T. Blount, a North Carolina congressman, and he, in turn, forwarded them to J. Milledge, Governor of Georgia. This probably explains the passage in the latter's message to the legislature referring[3] to information he had received "from a source so respectable as to admit but little doubt of the existence of a plan of an insurrection being formed among our domesticks and particularly in Greene county." A resident of Augusta, Georgia, wrote[4] to a friend in Salem, Massachusetts, on April 9, 1810, that

The letter from "Captain James" is but a small part of the evidence of the disposition of the Blacks in this part of the country. The most vigorous measures are taking to defeat their infernal designs. May God preserve us from the fate of St. Domingo. The papers here will, for obvious reasons, observe total silence on this business; and the mail near closing, I can say no more on the subject at present.

And, so far as Georgia is concerned, "no more on the subject at present" is known.

A letter of May 30, 1810, from no less an individual than Richard W. Byrd of Smithfield, Virginia, to Governor John Tyler affords evidence of repercussions in that state. He wrote,[5] in part:

An insurrection of the blacks, on the Saturday night, preceding Whit-Sunday, is much feared. As to myself, I am not satisfied that their plans are perfectly matured; but that such a scheme has been in contemplation, is beyond all doubt. Our unremitted vigilance may probably frustrate their designs in this neighborhood—but unless similar exertions are *generally* used, the consequences may be extremely fatal. A report, that such an attempt would be made about Whit-Sunday, in North Carolina, has been very prevalent here for eight or ten days.

One "negro boy," after "receiving twenty lashes" stated "that the operations were to commence in Carolina . . . that they were to fight with clubs, spikes and axes, and, if necessary, they (the Carolina negroes) would immediately come on here to help the Virginia negroes." Mr. Byrd felt that the

[3] R. B. Flanders, *Plantation Slavery in Georgia*, Chapel Hill, 1933, p. 274.

[4] N. Y. *Evening Post*, April 30, 1810.

[5] *Broadsides*: Virginia, May 30, 1810. Ac 5225, Mss. room, Library of Congress. Similar fears were expressed at this time in Norfolk—see *Calendar of Virginia State Papers*, x, p. 83.

slave preachers used their religious meetings as veils for revolutionary schemes and referred particularly to a "General Peter" of Isle of Wight, who had been in communication with slaves of North Carolina.

In their letters the slaves referred to the planned revolt as an earthquake, and one Virginia slave had been heard to say "that there would be an earthquake here [as well as in North Carolina] on the same night, that he was entitled to his freedom, and he would be damned, if he did not have it in a fortnight." Mr. Byrd concluded by remarking that "We have taken up many of these fellows, and expect to go on in the same way. This course may possibly avert the dreadful calamity with which we are threatened," since he thought "it probable that we have broken the chain by which they were linked."

As a matter of fact there were reports of an actual slave outbreak with several casualties near Richmond in June, 1810, but these were later denied.[6] Nothing concerning this, either of confirmation or refutation, is in the Richmond papers, and the truth about it is not clear. Certainly, at the end of November of this same year, "a dangerous conspiracy among the negroes was discovered" in Lexington, Kentucky, and a "great many" slaves were arrested, but their fate is unknown.[7]

A New Orleans plot of 1812 involved whites as well as slaves.[8] It was discovered August 18. "The militia were ordered out which has completely frustrated their intentions. Some white men who were at their head are in prison; however a strong guard of the militia are still ordered out every night." One of these white men, Joseph Wood, was executed in New Orleans on September 13. "All the militia of the city were under arms— strong patrols were detailed for the night." It appears[9] that another of the whites implicated was named Macarty, but what became of him, or the Negroes involved, is not known.

A secondary source[10] refers to secret revolutionary organizations of

---

[6] Philadelphia *General Advertiser*, July 2, 1810; Boston *Columbian Sentinel*, July 4, 1810.

[7] Entry of December 1, 1810, in diary of William L. Brown, Mss. room, New York Public Library.

[8] N. Y. *Evening Post*, September 21, October 20, 1812.

[9] H. T. Catterall, *Judicial Cases Concerning American Slavery and the Negro*, Washington, 1932, III, p. 449.

[10] B. J. Lossing, *The Pictorial Field Book of the War of 1812* (New York, 1869), p. 690. Lossing states he is "indebted to an accomplished American scholar and professor in one of our colleges" for this material. A glance at the table in this communication and that in the writer's previous article will show that the years of the War of 1812 were marked by considerable concerted slave rebelliousness. A letter detailing extreme fears of slaves in South Carolina in 1812 will be found in the New York *Evening Post*, August 4, 1812.

slaves in South Carolina in 1813. And this is of particular interest for it publishes a song, written by a slave, and said to have been sung at the meetings of these groups. It parodied "Hail, Columbia," and was as follows:

Hail! all hail! ye Afric clan!
Hail! ye oppressed, ye Afric band
Who toil and sweat in slavery bound,
And when your health and strength are gone,
Are left to hunger and to mourn.
Let *independence* be your aim,
Ever mindful what 'tis worth,
Pledge your bodies for the prize,
Pile them even to the skies!

CHORUS:

Firm, united let us be,
Resolved on death or liberty!
As a band of patriots joined,
Peace and plenty we shall find.

Look to heaven with manly trust,
And swear by Him that's always just
That no white foe, with impious hand
Shall slave your wives and daughters more,
Or rob them of their virtue dear!
Be armed with valor firm and true,
Their hopes are fixed on Heaven and you,
That Truth and Justice will prevail.

CHORUS:

Firm, united, etc.

Arise! arise! shake off your chains!
Your cause is just, so Heaven ordains;
To you shall freedom be proclaimed!
Raise your arms and bare your breasts,
Almighty God will do the rest.
Blow the clarion's warlike blast;
Call every negro from his task;
Wrest the scourge from Buckra's hand,
And drive each tyrant from the land!

CHORUS:

Firm, united, etc.

A good deal has been written about the Maroons, or outlying pugnacious fugitive slaves, of the West Indies and Central and South America,

61

but the existence of such groups in the United States is rarely mentioned. They did, however, exist, and while the material on them is highly dispersed, it is very impressive.

One interesting camp of slaves caused alarm in Alabama in 1827. This runaway camp, situated in the fork of the Alabama and Tombigbee rivers, was attacked[11] in June by a body of armed slaveholders. In the engagement one white was wounded, three slaves killed, several wounded and captured, while some escaped. The slaves, men and women, had lived for years in cabins they had erected and carried on marauding expeditions against nearby plantations. They were, before the attack, about to build a fort, after which " . . . a great number of negroes in the secret were to join them, and it is thought that in that event they could not be taken without bringing cannon to bear upon them." One of the whites in the attack declared:

This much I can say that old Hal [a leader of the slaves] and his men fought like Spartans, not one gave an inch of ground, but stood, was shot dead or wounded and fell on the spot. The negro man Pompey, who is now living, tried to get his gun fresh primed after he was shot through the thigh.

Other recently discovered slave plots and revolts are:

1721	S. C.	} [12]		1795	La., N. C.	} [14]
1747	N. Y.			1796	N. C., S. C., Ga.	
1791	La.	} [13]		1802	Va.	} [15]
1792	La., N. C.			1803	N. C.	
1793	S. C.					

[11] Mobile *Register*, June 20, 21, 1827, quoted in N. Y. *Evening Post*, July 11, 12, 1827. Louisiana was troubled by two runaway camps the same year (see N. Y. *Evening Post*, December 4, 1827).

[12] C. Headlam, ed., *Calendar of State Papers, America and West Indies*, March, 1720, to December, 1721, p. 425; *The Letters and Papers of Cadwalleder Colden*, New York, 1937, VIII, p. 345.

[13] R. R. Hill, *Descriptive Catalogue of the Documents Relating to the History of the United States . . . deposited in the Archivo General de Indias at Seville*, Washington, 1916, p. 402, 100; The Boston *Gazette*, September 3, 1792; M. Treudley in *Journal of Race Development*, VII, p. 124.

[14] R. R. Hill, *op. cit.*, p. 16; Charleston *City Gazette*, July 18, 23, 1795; R. H. Taylor in *North Carolina Hist. Rev.*, V, p. 23-24; N. Y. *Minerva*, June 11, July 16, August 4, 12, 26, November 21, and for December, 1796; W. Priest, *Travels in the United States*, London, 1802, VIII, p. 171.

[15] C. W. Janson, *The Stranger in America*, London, 1807, p. 395-98; N. Y. *Evening Post*, June 2, 1803.

1805	Md., Ga., La.	
1811	Va., La.	16

1825	N. C.	
1829	Ga.	19

1812	Va., Ky.	
1813	D. C.	17

1830	La.	
1840	Ala.	20

1814	Md., Va.	
1818	N. C.	18

The conventional attitude on the behavior of the American Negro as a slave may be illustrated by excerpts from a few very recent works: Maury Maverick[21]—"Slaves, counted by the millions, were quite complacent"; Professor J. D. Hicks[22]—"Attempts at insurrection were extremely rare"; Professor J. G. Randall[23]—"Surprisingly few instances of slave insurrections"; the late Professor U. B. Phillips[24]—"Slave revolts and plots were very seldom in the United States." A minimum of one hundred and sixty reported cases of plots or revolts certainly does not indicate complacency, nor that organized efforts for freedom were a rarity. It does demonstrate a consistent, courageous, and, ultimately, decisive struggle[25] against enslavement on the part of the American Negro people.

HERBERT APTHEKER

[16] N. Y. *Evening Post*, August 12, September 3, November 2, 1805; D. Rowland, *Official Letter Books of W. C. C. Claiborne*, Jackson, 1917, VI, p. 20; *Calendar of Virginia State Papers*, x, p. 97-98; E. G. Swem, *A Bibliography of Virginia*, II, Richmond, 1917, p. 124.

[17] N. Y. *Evening Post*, February 11, June 12, 1812; C. G. Bowers, ed., *The Diary of E. Gerry, Jr.*, N. Y., 1927, p. 198-99; John Graham to James Monroe, Washington, July 19, 1813; *Monroe Correspondence*, Library of Congress.

[18] Richmond *Enquirer*, August 27, 1814; Norfolk *Herald*, March 29, April 8, 1814; see also letter from Philip Stuart to James Madison, July 29, 1814, in *Madison Papers;* and John Smith to Edward Tiffin, August 28, 1814; Walter Jones to James Monroe, December 10, 1814, in *Monroe Papers*, Library of Congress; *North Carolina Hist. Rev.*, v, p. 24.

[19] G. G. Johnson, *Ante-bellum North Carolina*, Chapel Hill, 1937, p. 515; *Southern Advocate* (Huntsville, Ala.), April 24, May 8, 1829; James Stuart, *Three Years in North America*, Edinburgh, 1833, p. 123; *Journal of Southern History*, II, p. 325-26.

[20] *Southern Advocate*, January 29, 1830; Richmond *Enquirer*, February 6, 1830; S. A. Ferrall, *A Ramble of Six Thousand Miles . . .* , London, 1832, p. 196; K. E. R. Pickard, *The Kidnapped and the Ransomed*, N. Y., 1856, p. 159-61.

[21] *A Maverick American* (New York, 1937), p. 315.

[22] *The Federal Union* (Boston, 1937), p. 496.

[23] *The Civil War and Reconstruction* (New York, 1937), p. 53.

[24] *Georgia Historical Quarterly* (December, 1937), XXI, p. 311.

[25] Appreciation of this fact is given in Harvey Wish, *Journal of Negro History* (July, 1937), XXII, p. 320.

NOTE—In some cases similar dates and places are here listed as in the table in SCIENCE & SOCIETY, I, no. 4, 536-38. But the plots are distinct.

MAROONS WITHIN THE PRESENT LIMITS OF THE UNITED STATES

An ever-present feature of ante-bellum southern life was the existence of camps of runaway Negro slaves, often called maroons, when they all but established themselves independently on the frontier. These were seriously annoying, for they were sources of insubordination. They offered havens for fugitives, served as bases for marauding expeditions against nearby plantations and, at times, supplied the nucleus of leadership for planned uprisings. Some contemporary writers and a few later historians have noticed,[1] in a general and meager way, the existence of this feature of American slavery. It merits, however, detailed treatment.

It appears that notice of these maroon communities was taken only when they were accidentally uncovered or when their activities became so obnoxious or dangerous to the slavocracy that their destruction was felt to be necessary. Evidence of the existence of at least fifty such communities in various places and at various times, from 1672 to 1864, has been found. The mountainous, forested, or swampy regions of South Carolina, North Carolina, Virginia, Louisiana, Florida, Georgia, Mississippi, and Alabama (in order of importance) appear to have been the favorite haunts for these black Robin Hoods. At times a settled life, rather than a pugnacious

[1] Charles W. Janson, *The Stranger in America*, London, 1807, pp. 328-30; William H. Russell, *My Diary North and South*, Boston, 1863, pp. 88-89; Frederick L. Olmsted, *Journey in Seaboard Slave States*, London, 1904, II, pp. 177-78; Olmsted, *Journey in the Back Country*, London, 1860, pp. 30, 55; T. W. Higginson, *Army Life in a Black Regiment*, Boston, 1870, p. 248; James Parton, *Life of Andrew Jackson*, Boston, 1860, II, pp. 397-98; W. H. Siebert, *The Underground Railroad*, N. Y., 1899, p. 25; S. M. Ellis, *The Solitary Horseman*, Kensington, 1927, p. 169; V. A. Moody in *Louisiana Historical Quarterly* (1924) VII, pp. 224-25; R. H. Taylor in *North Carolina Historical Review* (1928), V, pp. 23-24; U. B. Phillips in *The South in the Building of the Nation*, Richmond, 1909, IV, p. 229.

167

and migratory one, was aimed at, as is evidenced by the fact that these maroons built homes, maintained families, raised cattle, and pursued agriculture, but this all but settled life appears to have been exceptional.

The most noted of such communities was that located in the Dismal Swamp between Virginia and North Carolina.[2] It seems likely that about two thousand Negroes, fugitives, or the descendants of fugitives, lived in this area. They carried on a regular, if illegal, trade with white people living on the borders of the swamp. Such settlements may have been more numerous than available evidence would indicate, for their occupants aroused less excitement and less resentment than the guerrilla outlaws.

The activities of maroons in Virginia in 1672 approached a point of rebellion so that a law was passed[3] urging and rewarding the hunting down and killing of these outlaws. An item[4] of November 9, 1691, notices the depredations caused by a slave, Mingoe, from Middlesex county, Virginia, and his unspecified number of followers in Rappahannock county. These Negroes not only took cattle and hogs, but, what was more important, they had recently stolen "two guns, a Carbyne & other things."

In June, 1711, the inhabitants of the colony of South Carolina were kept[5] "in great fear and terror" by the activities of "several Negroes [who] keep out, armed, and robbing and plundering houses and plantations."

[2] See references in note 1, and an article by Edmund Jackson in *The Pennsylvania Freeman*, January 1, 1852; Harriet B. Stowe, *Dred*, 2 vols., Boston, 1856; Margaret Davis in *South Atlantic Quarterly* (1934), XXXIII, pp. 171-184.

[3] W. Hening, *Statutes at Large of Virginia*, II, p. 299; P. A. Bruce, *Economic History of Virginia in 17th Century*, N. Y., 1896, II, p. 115.

[4] *Order Book*, Middlesex County, 1680-1694, pp. 526-27 (Virginia State Library); Bruce, *op. cit.*, II, p. 116.

[5] E. C. Holland, *A Refutation of the Calumnies*, Charleston, 1823, p. 63; D. D. Wallace, *The History of South Carolina*, N. Y., 1934, I, p. 372.

These men were led by a slave named Sebastian, who was finally tracked down and killed by an Indian hunter. Lieutenant Governor Gooch of Virginia wrote[6] to the Lords of Trade, June 29, 1729, "of some runaway Negroes beginning a settlement in the Mountains & of their being reclaimed by their Master." He assured the Lords that the militia was being trained to "prevent this for the future."

In September, 1733, the Governor of South Carolina offered a reward of £20 alive and £10 dead for "Several Run away Negroes who are near the Congerees, & have robbed several of the Inhabitants thereabouts." The Notchee Indians offered, April, 1744, to aid the government of South Carolina in maintaining the subordination of its slave population. Three months later, July 5, 1774, Governor James Glen applied "for the assistance of some Notchee Indians in order to apprehend some runaway Negroes, who had sheltered themselves in the Woods, and being armed, had committed disorders. . ."[7]

The number of runaways in South Carolina in 1765 was exceedingly large. This led to fears of a general rebellion.[8] At least one considerable camp of maroons was destroyed that year by military force. A letter from Charleston of August 16, 1768, told[9] of a battle with a body of maroons, "a numerous collection of outcast mullattoes, mustees, and free negroes."

Governor James Habersham of Georgia learned[10] in December, 1771, "that a great number of fugitive Negroes had Committed many Robberies and insults between this

[6] Virginia Manuscripts from British Record Office. Sainsbury, IX, p. 462, Virginia State Library.

[7] Council Journal (MS.) V, pp. 487, 494; XI, pp. 187, 383, South Carolina Historical Commission, Columbia, S. C.

[8] D. D. Wallace, op. cit. I, p. 373.

[9] The Boston Chronicle, October 3-10, 1768.

[10] The Colonial Records of Georgia, ed., A. D. Candler, Atlanta, 1907, XII, pp. 146-47, 325-26.

town [Savannah] and Ebenezer and that their Numbers (which) were now Considerable might be expected to increase daily." Indian hunters and militiamen were employed to blot out this menace. Yet the same danger was present in Georgia in the summer of 1772. Depredations, piracy and arson, were frequent, and again the militia saw service. A letter[11] from Edmund Randolph to James Madison of August 30, 1782, discloses somewhat similar trouble in Virginia. At this time it appears that "a notorious robber," a white man, had gathered together a group of about fifty men, Negro and white, and was terrorizing the community.

The British had combatted the revolutionists' siege of Savannah with the aid of a numerous body of Negro slaves who served under the inspiration of a promised freedom. The defeat of the British crushed the hopes of these Negroes. They fled, with their arms, called themselves soldiers of the King of England, and carried on a guerrilla warfare for years along the Savannah river. Militia from Georgia and South Carolina, together with Indian allies, successfully attacked the Negro settlement in May, 1786, with resulting heavy casualties.[12] Governor Thomas Pinckney of South Carolina referred[13] in his legislative message of 1787 to the serious depredations of a group of armed fugitive slaves in the southern part of the state.

Chesterfield and Charles City counties, Virginia, were troubled[14] by maroons in November, 1792. At least one

[11] M. D. Conway, *Omitted Chapters in History Disclosed in the Life and Papers of Edmund Randolph*, N. Y., 1888, pp. 50-51.

[12] W. B. Stevens, *A History of Georgia*, Philadelphia, 1859, II, pp. 376-78; C. G. Woodson, *The Negro in Our History*, Washington, 1928, p. 123; *Historical Manuscripts Commission, Report on American Manuscripts*, London, 1904, II, p. 544.

[13] C. C. Pinckney, *Life of General Thomas Pinckney*, Boston, 1895, p. 95; D. D. Wallace, *op. cit.*, II, p. 415.

[14] Letter dated Richmond, November 19 in Boston *Gazette*, December 17, 1792.

white man was killed while tracking them down. Ten of the runaways were finally captured, with the aid of dogs. The neighborhood of Wilmington, North Carolina, was harassed[15] in June and July, 1795, by "a number of runaway Negroes, who in the daytime secrete themselves in the swamps and woods . . . . at night committed various depredations on the neighbouring plantations." They killed at least one white man, an overseer, and severely wounded another. About five of these maroons, including the leader, known as the General of the Swamps, were killed by hunting parties. It was hoped that "these well-timed severities" would "totally break up this nest of miscreants—At all events, this town has nothing to apprehend as the citizens keep a strong and vigilant night guard." Within two weeks of this first report, of July 3, the capture and execution of four more runaways was reported. On July 17 it was believed that only one leader and a "few deluded followers" were still at large.

The existence of a maroon camp in the neighborhood of Elizabeth City, North Carolina, in May, 1802, is indicated by the fact that the plots and insubordination uncovered among the servile population at that time were attributed[16] to the agitation of an outlawed Negro, Tom Copper, who "has got a camp in one of the swamps." In March, 1811, a runaway community in a swamp in Cabarrus county, North Carolina, was wiped out. These maroons[17] "had bid defiance to any force whatever, and were resolved to stand their ground." In the attack two Negro women were captured, two Negro men killed and another wounded.

[15] Wilmington *Chronicle* (photostat, Library of Congress), July 3, 10, 17, 1795; Charleston *City Gazette*, July 18, 23, 1795; R. H. Taylor in *North Carolina Historical Review* (1928), V, pp. 23-24.

[16] Raleigh *Register* (State Library, Raleigh), June 1, 1802; N. Y. *Herald*, June 2, 1802.

[17] Edenton *Gazette*, March 22, 1811; G. G. Johnson, *Ante-bellum North Carolina*, Chapel Hill, 1937, p. 514.

The close proximity of the weakly governed Spanish territory of East Florida persistently disturbed the equanimity of American slaveholders. Many of the settlers in that region, moreover, were Americans, and they, aided by volunteers from the United States, raised the standard of revolt in 1810, the aim being American annexation.[18] In the correspondence of Lieutenant Colonel Thomas Smith and Major Flournoy, both of the United States Army and both actively on the side of the rebels or "patriots" in the Florida fighting, and of Governor Mitchell of Georgia, there are frequent references to the fleeing of American slaves into Florida, where they helped the Indians in their struggle against the Americans and the "patriots." A few examples may be cited.

Smith told Gen. Pinckney, July 30, 1812, of fresh Indian depredations in Georgia and of the escape of about eighty slaves. He planned to send troops against them, for "The safety of our frontier I conceive requires this course. They have, I am informed, several hundred fugitive slaves from the Carolinas and Georgia at present in their Towns & unless they are checked soon they will be so strengthened by desertions from Georgia & Florida that it will be found troublesome to reduce them." And it was troublesome. In a letter to Governor Mitchell of August 21, 1812, Smith declared, "The blacks assisted by the Indians have become very daring." In September further slave escapes were reported from Georgia. On September 11, a baggage train under Captain Williams and twenty men, going to the support of Colonel Smith, was attacked and routed, Williams himself being killed by Indians and maroons. In January, 1813, further escapes were reported, and in February, Smith wrote of battles with Negroes and Indians and the destruction of a Negro fort. One Georgian participant in this fighting,

---

[18] J. W. Pratt, *Expansionists of 1812*, N. Y., 1925, pp. 92, 116, 192-95, 212.

Colonel Daniel Newnan, declared the maroon allies of the Indians were "their best soldiers."[19]

The refusal of the Senate of the United States, at the moment, to sanction occupation of East Florida, finally led to a lull in the fighting. By 1816, however, the annoyance and danger from runaway slaves again served as justification for American intervention. With southern complaints[20] ringing in its ears the administration dispatched, in July, United States troops with Indian allies under Col. Duncan Clinch against the main stronghold of the maroons, the well-stocked Negro fort on Appalachicola Bay. After a seige of ten days a lucky cannon shot totally destroyed the fort and annihilated two hundred and seventy men, women and children. But forty souls survived.[21]

Another major expedition against a maroon community was carried out in 1816. This occurred near Ashepoo, South Carolina. Governor David R. Williams's remarks concerning this in his message of December, 1816, merit quotation:[22]

A few runaway negroes, concealing themselves in the swamps and marshes contiguous to Combahee and Ashepoo rivers, not having been interrupted in their petty plunderings for a long time, formed the nucleus, round which all the ill-disposed and audacious near them gathered, until at length their robberies became too serious to be suffered with impunity. Attempts were then made to disperse them, which either from insufficiency of numbers or bad arrangement, served by their failure only to encourage a wanton destruction of property. Their forces now became alarming, not less from its numbers than from its arms and ammunition with which it was supplied.

[19] T. F. Davis in *Florida Historical Quarterly* (1930), IX, pp. 106-07, 111, 138; *Niles' Weekly Register*, December 12, 1812, III, pp. 235-37.

[20] See, for example, Richmond *Enquirer*, July 10, 1816.

[21] *Connecticut Courant*, September 10, 24, 1816; *State Papers*, 2d sess., 15 cong., vol. IV; J. B. McMaster, *History*, IV, p. 431; McMaster's account is practically copied by H. B. Fuller, *The Purchase of Florida*, Cleveland, 1906, p. 228.

[22] H. T. Cook, *Life and Legacy of David R. Williams*, N. Y., 1916, p. 130.

The peculiar situation of the whole of that portion of our coast, rendered access to them difficult, while the numerous creeks and water courses through the marshes around the islands, furnished them easy opportunities to plunder, not only the planters in open day, but the inland coasting trade also without leaving a trace of their movements by which they could be pursued. . . I therefore ordered Major-General Young-blood to take the necessary measures for suppressing them, and authorized him to incur the necessary expenses of such an expedition. This was immediately executed. By a judicious employment of the militia under his command, he either captured or destroyed the whole body.

The Norfolk *Herald* of June 29, 1818, referred[23] to the serious damages occasioned by a group of some thirty runaway slaves, acting together with white men, in Princess Anne county, Virginia. It reported, too, the recent capture of a leader and "an old woman" member of the outlaws. In November of that year maroon activities in Wake county, North Carolina, became serious enough to evoke notice from the local press[24] which advised "the patrol to keep a strict look out." Later an attack upon a store "by a maroon banditti of negroes" led by "the noted Andey, alias Billy James, better known here by the name of Abaellino," was repulsed by armed citizens. The paper believed that the death of at least one white man, if not more, might accurately be placed at their hands. The Raleigh *Register* of December 18, 1818, printed Governor Branch's proclamation offering $250 reward for the capture of seven specified outlaws and $100 for Billy James alone. There is evidence[25] that, in this same year, maroons were active in Johnston county, in that state, and one expedition against them resulted in the killing of at least one Negro.

Expeditions against maroons took place[26] in Williams-

[23] Quoted in N. Y. *Evening Post*, July 7, 1818.
[24] Raleigh *Register*, November 13, 27, 1818.
[25] G. G. Johnson, *op. cit.*, p. 514.
[26] U. B. Phillips, *Plantation and Frontier Documents*, Cleveland, 1909, II. p. 91.

burg county, South Carolina, in the summer of 1819. Three slaves were killed, several captured and one white was wounded. Similar activities occurred in May, 1820, in Gates county, North Carolina. A slave outlaw, Harry, whose head had been assessed at $200, was killed by four armed whites. "It is expected that the balance of Harry's company [which had killed at least one white man] will very soon be taken."[27]

Twelve months later there was similar difficulty near Georgetown, South Carolina, resulting[28] in the death of one slaveholder and the capture of three outlaws. The activities of considerable maroon groups in Onslow, Carteret, and Bladen counties, North Carolina, aided by some free Negroes, assumed the proportions of rebellion in the summer of 1821. There were plans for joint action between these outlaws and the field slaves against the slaveholders. Approximately three hundred members of the militia of the three counties saw service for about twenty-five days in August and September. About twelve of these men were wounded when two companies of militia accidentally fired upon each other. The situation was under control by the middle of September, "although the said militia (sic) did not succeed in apprehending all the runaways & fugitives, they did good by arresting some, and driving others off, and suppressing the spirit of insurrection."[29] A newspaper item of 1824 discloses[30] that the "prime mover" of the trouble mentioned above, Isam, "alias General Jackson," was among those who escaped at the time, for he is there reported as dying from lashes publicly inflicted at Cape Fear, North Carolina.

[27] Edenton *Gazette*, May 12, 1820, quoted by N. Y. *Evening Post*, May 17, 1820.

[28] N. Y. *Evening Post*, June 11, 1821.

[29] See petition of John H. Hill, Colonel Commandant of the Carteret Militia, dated December, 1825, and accompanying memoranda in Legislative Papers, 1824-1825 (No. 366), North Carolina Historical Commission, Raleigh; R. H. Taylor, *op. cit.*, V, p. 24; G. G. Johnson, *op. cit.*, p. 514.

[30] N. Y. *Evening Post*, May 11, 1824.

In the summer of 1822 activity among armed runaway slaves was reported[31] from Jacksonborough (now Jacksonboro) South Carolina. Three were executed on July 19. In August Governor Bennett offered a reward of two hundred dollars for the capture of about twenty maroons in the same region. It is possible that these Negroes had been enlisted in the far-flung conspiracy of Denmark Vesey, uncovered and crushed in June, 1822.

The Norfolk *Herald* of May 12, 1823, contains[32] an unusually full account of maroons under the heading "A Serious Subject." It declares that the citizens of the southern part of Norfolk county, Virginia,

have for some time been kept in a state of mind peculiarly harrassing and painful, from the too apparent fact that their lives are at the mercy of a band of lurking assassins, against whose fell designs neither the power of the law, or vigilance, or personal strength and intrepidity, can avail. These desperadoes are runaway negroes, (commonly called outlyers). . . . Their first object is to obtain a gun and ammunition, as well to procure game for subsistence as to defend themselves from attack, or accomplish objects of vengeance.

Several men had already been killed by these former slaves, one, a Mr. William Walker, very recently. This aroused great fear, "No individual after this can consider his life safe from the murdering aim of these monsters in human shape. Every one who has haply rendered himself obnoxious to their vengeance, must, indeed, calculate on sooner or later falling a victim" to them. Indeed, one slaveholder had received a note from these amazing fellows suggesting it would be healthier for him to remain indoors at night—and he did.

A large body of militia was ordered out to exterminate these outcasts and "thus relieve the neighbouring inhabitants from a state of perpetual anxiety and apprehension, than which nothing can be more painful." Dur-

[31] Washington *National Intelligencer*, July 23, August 24, 1822.
[32] Quoted in N. Y. *Evening Post*, May 15, 1823.

ing the next few weeks there were occasional reports[33] of the killing or capturing of outlaws, culminating June 25 in the capture of the leader himself, Bob Ferebee, who, it was declared, had been an outlaw for six years. He was executed July 25. In October of this year runaway Negroes near Pineville, South Carolina, were attacked.[34] Several were captured, and at least two, a woman and a child, were killed. One of the maroons was decapitated, and his head stuck on a pole and publicly exposed as "a warning to vicious slaves."

A maroon community consisting of men, women, and children was broken up by a three-day attack made by armed slaveholders of Mobile county, Alabama, in June, 1827. The Negroes had been outlaws for years and lived entirely by plundering neighboring plantations.[35] At the time of the attacks the Negroes were constructing a stockade fort. Had this been finished it was believed that field slaves thus informed would have joined them. Cannon would then have been necessary for their destruction. The maroons made a desperate resistance, "fighting like Spartans." Three were killed, others wounded, and several escaped. Because of the poor arms of the Negroes but one white was slightly wounded.

In November, 1827, a Negro woman returned to her master in New Orleans after an absence of sixteen years. She told[36] of a maroon settlement some eight miles north of the city containing about sixty people. A drought prevailed at the moment so it was felt that "the uncommon dryness . . . has made those retreats attainable . . .

[33] *Ibid.*, May 29, June 5, June 30, 1823.

[34] Charleston *City Gazette* quoted in N. Y. *Evening Post*, October 24, 1823; *Niles' Weekly Register*, October 18, 1823, XXV, p. 112; T. J. Kirkland and R. M. Kennedy, *Historic Camden*, Columbia, 1926, part two, p. 190.

[35] Mobile *Register*, June 20, 21, 1827, quoted in N. Y. *Evening Post*, July 11, 12, 1827; U. B. Phillips in *The South in the Building of the Nation*, Richmond, 1909, IV, p. 229.

[36] N. Y. *Evening Post*, December 4, 1827.

and we are told there is another camp about the head of the bayou Bienvenu. Policy imperiously calls for a thorough search, and the destruction of all such repairs, wherever found to exist.''

In the summer of 1829 ''a large gang of runaway negroes, who have infested the Parishes of Christ Church and St. James, [S. C.] for several months, and committed serious depredations on the properties of the planters'' was accidentally discovered[37] by a party of deer hunters. One of the Negroes was wounded and four others were captured. Several others escaped, but the Charleston *Mercury* hoped the citizens would ''not cease their exertions until the evil shall be effectually removed.''

Maroons were important factors in causing slave insubordination in Sampson, Bladen, Onslow, Jones, New Hanover, and Dublin counties, North Carolina, from September through December, 1830. Citizens complained[38] that their ''slaves are become almost uncontrollable. They go and come and when and where they please, and if an attempt is made to correct them they immediately fly to the woods and there continue for months and years Committing grievous depredations on our Cattle, hogs and Sheep.'' One of these fugitive slaves, Moses, who had been out for two years, was captured in November. From him one elicited[39] the information that an uprising was imminent, that the conspirators ''had arms & ammunition secreted, that they had runners or messengers to go between Wilmington, Newbern & Elizabeth City to 'carry word' & report to them, that there was a camp in Dover Swamp of 30 or 40—another about Gastons Island, on Price's Creek, several on Newport River, several near

[37] *Ibid.*, August 10, 1829.
[38] G. G. Johnson, *op. cit.*, pp. 515, 517; R. H. Taylor, *op. cit.*, V, p. 31.
[39] See letter dated November 15, 1830, Newbern, from J. Turgwyn to Governor John Owen in Governor's *Letter Book*, Vol. XXVIII, pp. 247-49, and letter from J. I. Pasteur to Governor Owen also dated Newbern, Nov. 15, 1830, in Governor's Papers No. 60, Historical Commission, Raleigh.

Wilmington.'' Arms were found in the place named by Moses

> in possession of a white woman living in a very retired situation—also some meat, hid away & could not be accounted for—a child whom the party [of citizens] found a little way from the house, said that his mamy dressed victuals every day for 4 or 5 runaways, & shewed the spot . . . where the meat was then hid & where it was found—the place or camp in Dover was found, a party of neighbours discovered the camp, burnt 11 houses, and made such discoveries, as convinced them it was a place of rendezvous for numbers (it is supposed they killed several of the negroes).

Newspaper accounts referred to the wholesale shooting of fugitives. In 1830 the Roanoke *Advertiser* stated:[40] ''The inhabitants of Newbern being advised of the assemblage of sixty armed slaves in a swamp in their vicinity, the military were called out, and surrounding the swamp, killed the whole party.'' A later item dated Wilmington, January 7, 1831, declared,[41] ''There has been much shooting of negroes in this neighborhood recently, in consequence of symptoms of liberty having been discovered among them.'' It is of interest to note that Richmond papers, on receiving the first reports of Nat Turner's revolt of August, 1831, asked[42] concerning the rebels, ''Were they connected with the desperadoes who harrassed (sic) N. Carolina last year?''

In June, 1836, there is mention[43] that ''a band of runaway negroes in the Cypress Swamp'' near New Orleans ''had been committing depredations.'' The next year, in July, was reported[44] the killing of an outlaw slave leader, Squire, near New Orleans, whose band, it was felt, was responsible for the deaths of several white men. Squire's career had lasted for three years. A guard of

[40] Quoted in *The Liberator* (Boston), January 8, 1831.
[41] N. Y. *Sentinel*, quoted in *Liberator*, March 19, 1831.
[42] Richmond *Enquirer*, August 30, 1831.
[43] *Louisiana Advertiser*, June 8, 1836, quoted by *Liberator*, July 2, 1836.
[44] New Orleans *Picayune*, July 19, 1837.

soldiers was sent to the swamp for his body, which was exhibited for several days in the public square of the city.

The year 1837 also saw the start of the Florida or Seminole War which was destined to drag on until 1843. This war, "conducted largely as a slave catching enterprise for the benefit of the citizens of Georgia and Florida," was, before its termination, to take an unknown number of Indian and Negro lives together with the lives of fifteen hundred white soldiers and the expenditure of twenty million dollars.[45]   The Indians had, at the beginning of hostilities, about 1,650 warriors and 250 Negro fighters. The latter were "the most formidable foe, more blood-thirsty, active, and revengeful, than the Indian."[46]

Armed runaways repulsed an attack near Wilmington, North Carolina, in January, 1841, after killing one of the whites. A posse captured three of the Negroes and lodged them in the city jail. One escaped, but two were taken from the prison by some twenty-five whites and lynched.[47] Late in September two companies of militia were despatched in search of a body of maroons some 45 miles north of Mobile, Alabama.[48] "It is believed that these fellows have for a long time been in the practice of theft and arson, both in town and country. . . A force from above was scouring down, with bloodhounds, &c to meet the Mobile party." A month later frequent attacks upon white men by runaway Negroes were reported[49] from Terrebonne Parish, Louisiana.

Several armed planters near Hanesville, Mississippi,

[45] Grant Foreman, *Indian Removal*, Norman, 1932, pp. 366, 383; see also *The Liberator*, March 18, 1837.

[46] John T. Sprague, *The Origin, Progress, and Conclusion of the Florida War*, N. Y., 1848, p. 309; J. R. Giddings, *The Exiles of Florida*, Columbus, 1858, pp. 121, 139.

[47] Wilmington *Chronicle* January 6, 1841, in *Liberator*, January 22, 1841.

[48] New Orleans *Bee*, October 4, 1841.

[49] Lafourche (La.) *Patriot* in *Liberator*, November 12, 1841.

in February, 1844, set an ambush for maroons who had been exceedingly troublesome. Six Negroes, "part of the gang," were trapped, but three escaped. Two were wounded, and one was killed.[50] In November, 1846, about a dozen armed slaveholders surprised "a considerable gang of runaway negroes" in St. Landry Parish, Louisiana. The maroons refused to surrender and fled. Two Negroes, a man and a woman, were killed, and two Negro women were "badly wounded." The others escaped.[51]

Joshua R. Giddings referred[52] to the flight in September, 1850, of some three hundred former Florida maroons from their abode in present Oklahoma to Mexico. This was accomplished after driving off Creek Indians sent to oppose their exodus. The *Pennsylvania Freeman* of October 30, 1851, citing the Houston *Telegraph* (n.d.), states that fifteen hundred former American slaves were aiding the Comanchee Indians of Mexico in their fighting. Five hundred of these Negroes were from Texas. Giddings also referred to unsuccessful expeditions by slaveholders of Texas in 1853 into Mexico to recover fugitive Negroes, and declared that at the time he was writing (1858), maroons in southern Florida were again causing trouble. F. L. Olmsted gave[53] evidence of maroon troubles in the 1850's in Virginia, Louisiana, and northern Alabama.

A letter of August 25, 1856, to Governor Thomas Bragg of North Carolina, signed by Richard A. Lewis and twenty-one other citizens, informed[54] him of a "very secure retreat for runaway negroes" in a large swamp between Bladen and Robeson counties. There "for many years past, and at this time, there are several runaways of bad and daring character—destructive to all kinds of Stock

---

[50] Hanesville *Free Press*, March 1, 1844, cited by *Liberator*, April 5, 1844.
[51] New Orleans *Picayune*, quoted in *Liberator*, December 4, 1846.
[52] Giddings, *op. cit.*, pp. 316, 334, 337.
[53] Olmsted, *Seaboard, op. cit.*, p. 177; *Back Country, op. cit.*, pp. 30, 55.
[54] Governor's *Letter Book*, No. 43, pp. 514-515, Historical Commission, Raleigh.

and dangerous to all persons living by or near said swamp." Slaveholders attacked these Negroes August 1, 1856, but accomplished nothing and saw one of their own number killed. "The negroes ran off cursing and swearing and telling them to come on, they were ready for them again." The Wilmington *Journal* of August 14 mentioned that these runaways "had cleared a place for a garden, had cows, &c in the swamp." Mr. Lewis and his friends were "unable to offer sufficient inducement for negro hunters to come with their dogs unless aided from other sources." The Governor suggested that magistrates be requested to call for the militia, but whether this was done or not is unknown.

A runaway camp was destroyed,[55] and four Negroes, including a woman, captured near Bovina, Mississippi, in March, 1857. A similar event, resulting in the wounding of three maroons occurred in October, 1859, in Nash county, North Carolina.[56] An "organized camp of white men and negroes" was held responsible for a servile conspiracy, involving whites, which was uncovered[57] in Talladega county, Alabama, in August, 1860.

The years of the Civil War witnessed a considerable accentuation in the struggle of the Negro people against enslavement. This was as true of maroon activity as it was generally. There were reports[58] of depredations committed by "a gang of runaway slaves" acting together with two whites along the Comite river, Louisiana, early in 1861. An expedition was set "on foot to capture the whole party." A runaway community near Marion, South Carolina, was attacked[59] in June, 1861. There were no

[55] Vicksburg *Whig*, cited by *Liberator*, April 3, 1857.
[56] *The Day Book*, Norfolk, October 13, 1859.
[57] Laura White, in *Journal of Southern History*, I (1935), p. 47.
[58] N. Y. *Daily Tribune*, March 11, 1861.
[59] H. M. Henry, *Police Control of the Slave in South Carolina*, Emory, 1914, p. 121.

casualties, however, the slave hunters capturing but two
Negro children, twelve guns and one axe.

Confederate Brigadier-General R. F. Floyd asked[60] Governor Milton of Florida on April 11, 1862, to declare martial law in Nassau, Duval, Clay, Putnam, St. John's, and
Volusia counties "as a measure of absolute necessity, as
they contain a nest of traitors and lawless negroes." In
October, 1862, a scouting party of three armed whites, investigating a maroon camp containing one hundred men,
women, and children in Surry county, Virginia, were
killed[61] by these fugitives. Governor Shorter of Alabama
commissioned[62] J. H. Clayton in January, 1863, to destroy
the nests in the southeastern part of the state of "deserters, traitors, and runaway Negroes."

Colonel Hatch of the Union army reported[63] in August, 1864, that "500 Union men, deserters, and negroes
were . . . raiding towards Gainesville," Florida. The same
month a Confederate officer, John K. Jackson, declared
that[64]

> Many deserters . . . are collected in the swamps and fastnesses
> of Taylor, La Fayette, Levy and other counties, [in Florida]
> and have organized, with runaway negroes, bands for the
> purpose of committing depredations upon the plantations and
> crops of loyal citizens and running off their slaves. These
> depredatory bands have even threatened the cities of Tallahassee, Madison, and Marianna.

A Confederate newspaper noticed[65] similar activities in
North Carolina in 1864. It reported it

> difficult to find words of description . . . of the wild and terrible consequences of the negro raids in this obscure . . .
> theatre of the war. . . In the two counties of Currituck and

[60] *Official Records of the Rebellion*, Ser. I, Vol. LIII, p. 233.
[61] *Calendar of Virginia State Papers*, XI, pp. 233-36.
[62] *Official Records of the Rebellion*, Ser. I, Vol. XV, p. 947; Georgia Lee
Tatum, *Disloyalty in the Confederacy*, Chapel Hill, 1934, p. 63.
[63] Tatum, *op. cit.*, p. 88.
[64] *Official Records of the Rebellion*, Ser. I, Vol. XXV, Part II, p. 607.
[65] *Daily Richmond Examiner*, January 14, 1864.

Camden, there are said to be from five to six hundred negroes, who are not in the regular military organization of the
Yankees, but who, outlawed and disowned by their masters,
lead the lives of banditti, roving the country with fire and
committing all sorts of horrible crimes upon the inhabitants.
This present theatre of guerrilla warfare has, at this time,
a most important interest for our authorities. It is described
as a rich country, . . . and one of the most important sources
of meat supplies that is now accessible to our armies. . . .

The account ends with a broad hint that white deserters
from the Confederate army were fighting shoulder to
shoulder with the self-emancipated Negroes.

The story of the American maroons is of interest not
only because it forms a fairly important part of the history of the South and of the Negro, but also because of
the evidence it affords to show that the conventional picture of slavery as a more or less delightful, patriarchal
system is fallacious. The corollary of this fallacious picture—docile, contented slaves—is also, of course, seriously
questioned. Indeed, taking this material on maroons in
conjunction with that recently presented on servile revolts,[66] leads one to assert that American slavery was a
horrid form of tyrannical rule which often found it necessary to suppress ruthlessly the desperate expressions of
discontent on the party of its outraged victims.

HERBERT APTHEKER

[66] Harvey Wish, *Journal of Negro History* (1937) XXII, pp. 302-320;
present writer, *Science and Society* (1937), I, pp. 512-538; II (1938), pp.
386-391.

DAY TO DAY RESISTANCE TO SLAVERY[1]

The tradition that has grown up about Negro slavery is that the slaves were docile, well adapted to slavery, and reasonably content with their lot. A standard work on the Negro problem in the United States says:

"The Negroes brought into the New World situation and presently reduced to a perpetual servitude became very rapidly accommodated to the environment and status. The explanation of the comparative ease with which this was brought about doubtless lies in the peculiar racial traits of the Negro peoples themselves. They are strong and robust in physique and so everywhere sought after as laborers. In disposition they are cheerful, kindly and sociable: in character they are characteristically extrovert, so readily obedient and easily contented. More than most other social groups they are patiently tolerant under abuse and oppression and little inclined to struggle against difficulties. These facts of racial temperament and disposition make the Negroes more amenable to the condition of slavery than perhaps any other racial group."[2]

This concept is gradually being changed as the study of slave revolts, and of the social tension caused by the constant threat of revolt progresses.[3] In answer to the question, " 'Are the masters afraid of insurrection?' (a slave) says, 'They live in constant fear upon this subject. The least unusual noise at night alarms them greatly. They cry out, 'What is that?' 'Are the boys all in'?"[4]

The purpose of this paper is to study a less spectacular aspect of slavery—the day to day resistance to slavery, since it is felt that such a study will throw some further

[1] We wish to express our appreciation to Professor M. J. Herskovits, under whose direction this research has been carried on.

[2] Reuter, E. B., *The American Race Problem*, New York, 1927, p. 7.

[3] Cf. Aptheker, Herbert, "American Negro Slave Revolts," *Science and Society*, 1:512-538, 1937; Wish, Harvey, "American Slave Insurrections before 1861," *Journal of Negro History*, 23:435-450, 1938; Wish, Harvey, "The Slave Insurrection Panic of 1856," *Journal of Southern History*, 5:206-222, 1939; see also Herskovits, M. J., *The Myth of the Negro Past*, pp. 99-105.

[4] Clarke, Lewis, *Narratives of the Sufferings of Lewis and Milton Clarke*, Boston, 1846, p. 123.

388

light on the nature of the Negro's reaction to slavery. Our investigation has made it apparent that the Negroes not only were very discontented, but that they developed effective protest techniques in the form of indirect retaliation for their enslavement. Since this conclusion differs sharply from commonly accepted belief, it would perhaps be of value if a brief preliminary statement were made of how belief so at variance with the available documentary materials could gain such acceptance.

The picture of the docile, contented Negro slave grew out of two lines of argument used in ante-bellum times. The pro-slavery faction contended that the slaves came of an inferior race, and that they were happy and contented in their subordinate position, and that the dancing and singing Negro exemplified their assumption. Abolitionists, on the other hand, tended to depict the Negro slave as a passive instrument, a good and faithful worker exploited and beaten by a cruel master. As one reads the controversial literature on the slavery question, it soon becomes apparent that both sides presented the Negro as a docile creature; one side because it wished to prove that he was contented, the other because it wished to prove that he was grossly mistreated. Both conceptions have persisted to the present time. Writers who romanticize the "Old South" idealize the condition of the slaves, and make of them happy, willing servitors, while those who are concerned with furthering the interests of the Negroes are careful to avoid mention of any aggressive tendencies which might be used as a pretext for further suppressing the Negroes.

Many travelers in the South have accepted the overt behavior of the slaves at its face value. The "yas suh, Cap'n," the smiling, bowing, and scraping of the Negroes have been taken as tokens of contentment. Redpath's conversations with slaves indicated how deep seated this behavior was.[5]

[5] Redpath, James, *The Roving Editor: or, Talks with Slaves in the Southern States*, New York, 1859.

This point of view, however, neglects the fact that the whites have always insisted on certain forms of behavior as a token of acceptance of inferior status by the Negro. The following quotation from Dollard is pertinent:

"An informant already cited has referred to the Negro as a 'Dr. Jekyll and Mr. Hyde.' He was making an observation that is well understood among Negroes—that he has a kind of dual personality, two rôles, one that he is forced to play with white people and one the 'real Negro' as he appears in his dealings with his own people. What the white southern people see who 'know their Negroes' is the rôle that they have forced the Negro to accept, his caste rôle."[6]

The conceptual framework within which this paper is written is that the Negro slaves were forced into certain outward forms of compliance to slavery; that, except for the few who were able to escape to the North, the Negroes had to accept the institution of slavery and make their adjustments to that institution. The patterns of adjustment which we have found operative are: slowing up of work, destruction of property, malingering and self-mutilation.

The sources of our material are: (1) general works on slavery, labor, and the Negro; (2) the journals and the travel accounts of southerners and of visitors to the slave territory; and (3) the biographies and autobiographies of slaves. Most of the secondary sources take some cognizance of the fact that slaves slowed up their work, feigned illness, and the like, but this behavior is regarded as a curiosity. There has been no attempt by those writers who set down such facts to understand their social and economic significance. The journals and travel-books vary greatly in the amount of information they contain. This, of course, is due to the authors' variations in interest and acuteness. Olmsted's *Seaboard Slave States,* for instance, abounds in anecdotes, and in expressions of opinion as to the extent of loaf-

[6] Dollard, John, *Caste and Class in a Southern Town*, New Haven, 1937, pp. 255, 256.

ing and malingering. Susan Smedes' *Memorials of a Southern Planter*, on the other hand, contains just one foot-noted reference to any such behavior. Life stories of ex-slaves emphasizes running away, forms of punishment, and other aspects of slavery that would make interesting reading. Yet while references to slowing up work, or feigning illness, are thus few in number, where they are made they are stated in such a way that they leave no doubt that there was a persistent pattern of such behavior.

Slaveholders ever underate the intelligence with which they have to grapple. I really understood the old man's mutterings, attitudes and gestures, about as well as he did himself. But slaveholders never encourage that kind of communication, with the slaves, by which they might learn to measure the depths of his knowledge. Ignorance is a high virtue in a human chattel; and as the master studies to keep the slave ignorant, the slave is cunning enough to make the master think he succeeds. The slave fully appreciates the saying, 'where ignorance is bliss 'tis folly to be wise'.["]

We have felt it wise to quote extensively. Much of the meaning of incidents and interpretations lies in the phrasing of the author—in sensing his own emphasis on what he says. Methodologically, in attempting to analyze an existing stereotype, as we are trying to do here, it would seem wisest to present the picture as it appeared to contemporaries, and thus as given in their own words.

II

The Negroes were well aware that the work they did benefited only the master. "The slaves work and the planter gets the benefit of it."[8] "The conversation among the slaves was that they worked hard and got no benefit, that the masters got it all."[9] It is thus not surprising that one

[7] Douglass, Frederick, *Life and Times of Frederick Douglass*, p. 8.

[8] Wm. Brown, an escaped slave; in: Benjamin Drew, *The Refugee*, Boston, 1856, p. 281.

[9] Thomas Hedgebeth, a free Negro, in: Benjamin Drew, *The Refugee*, Boston, 1856, p. 276.

finds many recurring comments that a slave did not do half
a good day's work in a day. A northerner whom Lyell met
in the South said:

"Half the population of the south is employed in seeing that
the other half do their work, and they who do work, accomplish half
what they might do under a better system."[10]

An English visitor, with a very strong pro-slavery bias
corroborates this:

"The amount of work expected of the field hand will not be
more than one half of what would be demanded of a white man;
and even that will not be properly done unless he be constantly
overlooked."[11]

Statements of other writers are to the same effect:

"It is a common remark of those persons acquainted with slave-
labour, that their proportion is as one to two. This is not too
great an estimate in favour of the free-labourer; and the circumstances of their situation produce a still greater disparity."[12]

"A capitalist was having a building erected in Petersburg, and
his slaves were employed in carrying up the brick and mortar for
the masons on their heads: a Northerner, standing near, remarked
to him that they moved so indolently that it seemed as if they were
trying to see how long they could be in mounting the ladder without actually stopping. The builder started to reprove them, but
after moving a step turned back and said: 'It would only make
them move more slowly still when I am not looking at them, if I
should hurry now. *And what motive have they to do better?* It's
no concern of theirs how long the masons wait. I am sure if I was
in their place, I shouldn't move as fast as they do.'"[13]

A well-informed capitalist and slave-holder remarked,

"In working niggers, we always calculate that they will not
labor at all except to avoid punishment, and they will never do

[10] Lyell, Sir Charles, *A Second Visit to the United States of America*,
New York, 1849, II, 72.

[11] Ozanne, T. D., *The South as It Is*, London, 1863, pp. 165, 166.

[12] Anon., *An Inquiry Into the Condition and Prospects of the African
Race*, Philadelphia, 1839, p. 83.

[13] Olmsted, F. L., *A Journey in the Seaboard Slave States,* New York,
1863, p. 210.

more than just enough to save themselves from being punished, and no amount of punishment will prevent their working carelessly or indifferently. It always seems on the plantations as if they took pains to break all the tools and spoil all the cattle that they possibly can, even when they know they'll be directly punished for it."[14]

Just how much of this was due to indifference and how much due to deliberate slowing up is hard to determine. Both factors most probably entered. A worker who had to devote himself to a dull task from which he can hope to gain nothing by exercising initiative soon slips into such a frame of mind that he does nothing more than go through the motions. His chief concern is to escape from the realities of his task and put it in the back of his mind as much as possible.

There is, indeed, a strong possibility that this behavior was a form of indirect aggression. While such an hypothesis cannot be demonstrated on the basis of the available contemporary data, it is supported by Dollard's interpretation of similar behavior which he found in Southern towns.

"If the reader has ever seen Stepin Fetchit in the movies, he can picture this type of character. Fetchit always plays the part of a well-accommodated lower-class Negro, whining, vacillating, shambling, stupid, and moved by very simple cravings. There is probably an element of resistance to white society in the shambling, sullenly slow pace of the Negro; it is the gesture of a man who is forced to work for ends not his own and who expresses his reluctance to perform under these circumstances."[15]

Certainly description after description emphasizes the mechanical plodding of the slave workers:

"John Lamar wrote, 'My man Ned the carpenter is idle, or nearly so at the plantation. He is fixing gates and, like the idle groom in Pickwick, trying to fool himself into the belief that he is doing something—He is an eye servant.' "[16]

[14] Ibid., p. 104.
[15] Dollard, op. cit., p. 257.
[16] Phillips, U. B., American Negro Slavery, New York, 1918, p. 192.

"'Those I saw at work appeared to me to move very slowly and awkwardly, as did those engaged in the stables. These also were very stupid and dilatory in executing any orders given them, so that Mr. C. would frequently take the duty off their hands into his own, rather than wait for them, or make them correct their blunders; they were much, in these respects, what our farmers call *dumb Paddees*—that is, Irishmen who do not readily understand the English language, and who are still weak and stiff from the effects of the emigrating voyage. At the entrance gate was a porter's lodge, and, as I approached I saw a black face peeping at me from it, but both when I entered and left, I was obliged to dismount and open the gate myself.

"'Altogether, it struck me—slaves coming here as they naturally did in comparison with free laborers, as commonly employed on my own and my neighbors' farms, in exactly similar duties—that they must have been difficult to direct efficiently, and that it must be irksome and trying to one's patience, to have to superintend their labor.'"[17]

To what extent this reluctant labor was the rule may be appreciated when it is pointed out that a southern doctor classified it under the name *Dysaethesia Aethiopica* as a mental disease peculiar to Negroes. Olmsted quotes this Dr. Cartwright as follows:

"'From the careless movements of the individual affected with this complaint, they are apt to do much mischief, which appears as if intentional, but it is mostly owing to the stupidness of mind and insensibility of the nerves induced by the disease. Thus, they break, waste, and destroy everything they handle—abuse horses and cattle —tear, burn, or rend their own clothing, and, paying no attention to the rights of property, steal others to replace what they have destroyed. They wander about at night, and keep in a half nodding state by day. They slight their work—cut up corn, cotton and tobacco, when hoeing it, as if for pure mischief. They raise disturbances with their overseers, and among their fellow servants, without cause or motive, and seem to be insensible to pain when subjected to punishment.

"'. . . The term "rascality" given to this disease by overseers,

[17] Olmsted, *op. cit.*, p. 11.

is founded on an erroneous hypothesis, and leads to an incorrect empirical treatment, which seldom or never cures it.' "[18]

There are only two possible interpretations of the doctor's statement. Either the slaves were so extraordinarily lazy that they gave the appearance of being mentally diseased, or the doctor was describing cases of hebephrenic schizophrenia. Either situation is startling. The phenomenon was obviously widespread, and if it was actually a mental disease it certainly would indicate that Negroes did not become "easily adjusted to slavery."

Whatever the case, it is certain that the slaves consciously saved their energy. Olmsted, who always had his eye open for such incidents, reported:

"The overseer rode among them, on a horse, carrying in his hand a raw-hide whip, constantly directing and encouraging them; but, as my companion and I, both, several times noticed, as often as he visited one line of the operations, the hands at the other end would discontinue their labor, until he turned to ride toward them again."[19]

The few statements on this point we have by ex-slaves seem to indicate that the slaves as a group made a general policy of not letting the master get the upper hand.

"I had become large and strong; and had begun to take pride in the fact that I could do as much hard work as some of the older men. There is much rivalry among slaves, at times, as to which can do the most work, and masters generally seek to promote such rivalry. But some of us were too wise to race with each other very long. Such racing, we had the sagacity to see, was not likely to pay. We had times out for measuring each other's strength, but we knew too much to keep up the competition so long as to produce an extraordinary day's work. We knew that if, by extraordinary exertion, a large quantity of work was done in one day, the fact, becoming known to the master, might lead him to require the same amount every day. This thought was enough to bring us to a dead halt whenever so much excited for the race."[20]

[18] Olmsted, op. cit., pp. 192, 193.
[19] Ibid., p. 388.
[20] Douglass, op. cit., p. 261.

Writer after writer, describing incidents in which slaves were compelled to assist in punishing other slaves states that they did so with the greatest of reluctance.

"The hands stood still;—they knew Randall—and they knew him also take a powerful man, and were afraid to grapple with him. As soon as Cook had ordered the men to seize him, Randall turned to them, and said—'Boys, you all know me; you know that I can handle any three of you, and the man that lays hands on me shall die. This white man can't whip me himself, and therefore he has called you to help him.' The overseer was unable to prevail upon them to seize and secure Randall, and finally ordered them all to go to their work together.'"[21]

In some cases it was noted that the slave resisting punishment took pains not to treat his fellows with any more than the absolute minimum of violence.

With such demonstrations of solidarity among the slaves it is not surprising to find a slave telling of how he and his fellows "captured" the institution of the driver. The slave Solomon Northrup was such a driver. His task was to whip the other slaves in order to make them work.

" 'Practice makes perfect,' truly; and during eight years' experience as a driver I learned to handle the whip with marvelous dexterity and precision, throwing the lash within a hair's breadth of the back, the ear, the nose without, however, touching either of them. If Epps was observed at a distance, or we had reason to apprehend he was sneaking somewhere in the vicinity, I would commence plying the lash vigorously, when, according to arrangement, they would squirm and screech as if in agony, although not one of them had in fact been grazed. Patsey would take occasion, if he made his appearance presently, to mumble in his hearing some complaints that Platt was whipping them the whole time, and Uncle Abram, with an appearance of honesty peculiar to himself would declare roundly I had just whipped them worse than General Jackson whipped the enemy at New Orleans.'"[22]

[21] Brown, W. W., *Life of Williams Welles Brown, A Fugitive Slave*, Boston, 1848, p. 18. See also Williams, James, *Narratives of James Williams*, Boston, 1838, pp. 56, 62, 65.

[22] Northup, Solomon, *Twelve Years a Slave*, 1853, pp. 226, 227.

Williams, another slave whose task was to drive his fellows, said:

"He was at these periods terribly severe to his hands, and would order me to use up the cracker of my whip every day upon the poor creatures who were toiling in the field; and in order to satisfy him, I used to tear it off when returning home at night. He would then praise me for a good fellow and invite me to drink with him."[23]

The amount of slowing up of labor by the slaves must, in the aggregate, have caused a tremendous financial loss to plantation owners. The only way we have of estimating it quantitatively is through comparison of the work done in different plantations and under different systems of labor. The statement is frequently made that production on a plantation varied more than 100% from time to time. Comparison in the output of slaves in different parts of the South also showed variations of over 100%. Most significant is the improvement in output obtained under the task, whereby the slaves were given a specific task to fulfill for their day's work, any time left over being their own. Olmsted gives us our best information on this point:

"These tasks certainly would not be considered excessively hard by a northern laborer; and, in point of fact, the more industrious and active hands finished them often by two o'clock. I saw one or two leaving the field soon after one o'clock, several about two; and between three and four, I met a dozen women and several men coming home to their cabins, having finished their day's work.

"Under this 'Organization of Labor' most of the slaves work rapidly and well. In nearly all ordinary work, custom has settled the extent of the task, and it is difficult to increase it. The driver who marks it out, has to remain on the ground until it is finished, and has no interest in overmeasuring it; and if it should be systematically increased very much, there is danger of a general stampede to the swamp, a danger the slave can always hold before his master's cupidity."[24]

[23] Williams, James, *Narratives of James Williams*, Boston, 1838, p. 43.
[24] Olmsted, *op. cit.*, pp. 435, 436.

"It is the custom of tobacco manufacturers to hire slaves and free negroes at a certain rate of wages each year. A task of 45 pounds per day is given them to work up, and all they choose to do more than this, they are paid for—payment being made once a fortnight; and invariably this over-wages is used by the slave for himself, and is usually spent in drinking, licentiousness, and gambling. The man was grumbling that he had saved but $20 to spend at the holidays. One of the manufacturers offered to show me by his books, that nearly all gained by over-work $5 a month, many $20 and some as much as $28.[25]

"He (the speaker) was executor of an estate in which, among other negroes, there was one very smart man, who, he knew perfectly well, ought to be earning for the estate $150 a year, and who could if he chose, yet whose wages for a year being let out by the day or job, had amounted to but $18, while he had paid for medical attendance upon him $45."[26]

The executor of the estate finally arranged for this man to work out his freedom, which he readily accomplished.

A quantitative estimate can be made from another situation which Olmsted observed. Rain during a previous day had made certain parts of the work more difficult than others. The slaves were therefore put on day work, since it would not be possible to lay out equitable tasks.

"Ordinarily it is done by tasks—a certain number of the small divisions of the field being given to each hand to burn in a day; but owing to a more than usual amount of rain having fallen lately, and some other causes, making the work harder in some places than in others, the women were now working by the day, under the direction of a 'driver,' a negro man, who walked about among them, taking care they had left nothing unburned. Mr. X inspected the ground they had gone over, to see whether the driver had done his duty. It had been sufficiently well burned, but not more than a quarter as much ground had been gone over, he said, as was usually burned in tasked work,—and he thought they had been very lazy, and reprimanded them for it."[27]

[25] *Ibid*, p. 103.
[26] *Ibid*, p. 103.
[27] *Ibid*, p. 430.

Most revealing of all is this statement:

"'Well, now, old man,' said I, 'you go and cut me two cords today!' 'Oh, massa! two cords! Nobody could do dat. Oh! massa, dat is too hard! Neber heard o' nobody's cuttin' more 'n a cord o' wood in a day, round heah. No nigger couldn't do it.' 'Well, old man, you have two cords of wood cut to-night or to-morrow morning you shall get two hundred lashes—that's all there is about it. So look sharp.' And he did it and ever since no negro ever cut less than two cords a day for me, though my neighbors never get but one cord. It was just so with a great many other things—mauling rails —I always have two hundred rails mauled in a day; just twice what it is the custom of the country to expect of a negro, and just twice as many as my negroes had been made to do before I managed them myself."

"These estimates, let it be recollected in conclusion, are all deliberately and carefully made by gentlemen of liberal education, who have had unusual facilities of observing both at the North and the South."[28]

The slaves were well aware of their economic value, and used it to good advantage. The skilled laborers among the slaves knew their worth, and frequently rebelled against unsatisfactory work situations. Slaves who were hired out would run away from the masters who had hired them, and then either return home, or remain in hiding until they felt like returning to work.

"The slave, if he is indisposed to work, and especially if he is not treated well, or does not like the master who has hired him, will sham sickness—even make himself sick or lame—that he need not work. But a more serious loss frequently arises, when the slave, thinking he is worked too hard, or being angered by punishment or unkind treatment, 'getting the sulks,' takes to 'the swamp,' and comes back when he has a mind to. Often this will not be till the year is up for which he is engaged, when he will return to his owner, who, glad to find his property safe, and that it has not died in the swamp, or gone to Canada, forgets to punish him, and immediately sends him for another year to a new master.

"'But, meanwhile, how does the negro support life in the swamp?' I asked.

[28] *Ibid*, p. 207.

" 'Oh, he gets sheep and pigs and calves, and fowls and turkey; sometimes they will kill a small cow. We have often seen the fires, where they were cooking them, through the woods in the swamp yonder. If it is cold, he will crawl under a fodder stack, or go into the cabins with some of the other negroes, and in the same way, you see, he can get all the corn, or almost anything else he wants.

" 'He steals them from his master?'

" 'From anyone: frequently from me. I have had many a sheep taken by them.'[29]

" 'It is a common thing, then?'

" 'Certainly it is, very common, and the loss is sometimes exceedingly provoking. One of my neighbors here was going to build, and hired two mechanics for a year. Just as he was ready to put his house up, the two men, taking offense at something, both ran away, and did not come back at all, till their year was out, and then their owner immediately hired them out again to another man.' '[30]

One plantation overseer wrote to the plantation owner concerning a carpenter he had hired out to one G. Moore:

"Not long before Jim run away G More (sic.) wanted him to make some gates and I sent him theireselves (sic.) and he run away from him and cum home and then he left me withow (sic.) a cause."[31]

Even the threat of a whipping did not deter such slaves from running off for a time when they were displeased. The quotation from Olmsted below is typical of a constantly recurring pattern of statements:

"The manager told me that the people often ran away after they have been whipped or something else had happened to make them angry. They hide in the swamp and come into the cabins at night to get food. They seldom remain away more than a fortnight and when they come in they are whipped."[32]

Some of the resistance took on the aspects of organized strikes:

"Occasionally, however, a squad would strike in a body as a protest against severities. An episode of this sort was recounted

[29] The speaker had freed his slaves.

[30] Olmsted, op. cit., pp. 100, 101.

[31] Bassett, J. S., The Southern Plantation Overseer as Revealed in His Letters, Northampton, Mass., 1925, p. 66.

[32] Olmsted, F. L., A Journey in the Back Country, New York, 1863, p. 79.

in a letter of a Georgia overseer to his absent employer: 'Sir: I write you a few lines in order to let you know that six of your hands has left the plantation—every man but Jack. They displeased me with their work and I give some of them a few lashes, Tom with the rest. On Wednesday morning they were missing. I think they are lying out until they can see you or your Uncle Jack.' The slaves could not negotiate directly at such a time, but while they lay in the woods they might make overtures to the overseer through slaves on a neighboring plantation as to terms upon which they would return to work, or they might await their master's posthaste arrival and appeal to him for a redress of grievances. Humble as their demeanor might be, their power of renewing the pressure by repeating their act could not be ignored.''[33]

John Holmes, an escaped slave, told how he ran off and hid in the swamp after an overseer attempted to whip him.

"At last they told all the neighbors if I would come home, they wouldn't whip me. I was a great hand to work and made a great deal of money for our folks.''[34]

The same overseer had further trouble with the slaves.

"She (a slave) was better with her fists, and beat him, but he was better at wrestling and threw her down. He then called the men to help him, but all hid from him in the brush where we were working. . . . Then (later) the calculation was to whip us every one, because we did not help the overseer. . . . That night every one of us went away into the woods. . . . We went back, but after a while (the overseer) came back too, and stayed the year out. He whipped the women but he did not whip the men, of fear they would run away.''[35]

III

The indifference of the slaves to the welfare of the masters extended itself to a complete contempt for property values. The slaves were so careless with tools that they were equipped with special tools, and more clumsy than ordinary ones:

[33] Phillips, U. B., *American Negro Slavery*, pp. 303, 304.
[34] Drew, B., *The Refugee*, p. 164.
[35] *Ibid.*, p. 167.

"*The 'nigger hoe'* was first introduced into Virginia as a substitute for the plow, in breaking up the soil. The law fixes its weight at four pounds,—as heavy as the woodman's axe. It is still used, not only in Virginia, but in Georgia and the Carolinas. The planters tell us, as the reason for its use, that the negroes would break a Yankee hoe in pieces on the first root, or stone that might be in their way. An instructive commentary on the difference between free and slave labor!"[36]

"The absence of motive, and the consequent want of mental energy to give vigor to the arm of the slave is the source of another great drawback upon the usefulness of his labour. His implements or tools are at least one-third (in some instances more than twofold) heavier and stronger than the northern man's to counteract his want of skill and interest in his work. A Negro hoe or scythe would be a curiosity to a New England farmer."[37]

Not only tools but live stock suffered from the mistreatment by the slaves. Olmsted found not only the "nigger hoe" but even discovered that mules were substituted for horses because horses could not stand up under the treatment of the slaves.

.... "I am shown tools that no man in his senses, with us, would allow a laborer, to whom he was paying wages, to be encumbered with; and the excessive weight and clumsiness of which, I would judge, would make work at least ten per cent greater than those ordinarily used with us. And I am assured that, in the careless and clumsy way they must be used by the slaves, anything lighter or less crude could not be furnished them with good economy, and that such tools as we constantly give our laborers and find profit in giving them, would not last out a day in a Virginia corn-field —much lighter and more free from stones though it be than ours.

"So, too, when I ask why mules are so universally substituted for horses on the farm, the first reason given, and confessedly the most conclusive one, is, that horses cannot bear the treatment they always must get from negroes; horses are always soon foundered or crippled by them but mules will bear cudgeling, and lose a meal

[36] Parson, C. G., *Inside View of Slavery*, Boston, 1853, p. 94.
[37] Anon. *An Inquiry Into the Condition and Prospects of the African Race*. Philadelphia, 1839, p. 83.

or two now and then, and not be materially injured, and they do not take cold or get sick if neglected or overworked. But I do not need to go further than to the window of the room in which I am writing, to see, at almost any time, treatment of cattle that would insure the immediate discharge of the driver, by almost any farmer owning them in the North.''[38]

Redpath verifies Olmsted's statement—by telling how he saw slaves treat stock. It is important to note that Redpath was a strong abolitionist and most sympathetic toward the slaves.

''He rode the near horse, and held a heavy cowhide in his hand, with which from time to time he lashed the leaders, as barbarous drivers lash oxen when at work. Whenever we came to a hill, especially if it was very steep, he dismounted, lashed the horses with all his strength, varying his performances by picking up stones, none of them smaller than half a brick, and throwing them with all his force, at the horses' legs. He seldom missed.

''The wagon was laden with two tons of plaster in sacks.

''This is a fair specimen of the style in which Negroes treat stock.''[39]

The indifference to live-stock is well illustrated by an incident which Olmsted recounts:

''I came, one afternoon, upon a herd of uncommonly fine cattle as they were being turned out of a field by a negro woman. She had given herself the trouble to let down but two of the seven bars of the fence, and they were obliged to leap over a barrier at least four feet high. Last of all came, very unwillingly, a handsome heifer, heavy with calf; the woman urged her with a cudgel and she jumped, but lodging on her belly, as I came up she lay bent, and, as it seemed, helplessly hung upon the top bar. . . . The woman struck her severely and with a painful effort she boggled over.''[40]

In the Sea Islands off the coast of Georgia, Kemble reported that the slaves started immense fires, destroying large sections of woods through careless or maliciousness.

[38] Olmsted, F. L., *A Journey in the Seaboard Slave States*, pp. 46, 47.
[39] Redpath, *op. cit.*, p. 241.
[40] Olmsted, F. L., *A Journey in the Back Country*, p. 227.

"The 'field hands' make fires to cook their midday food wherever they happen to be working, and sometimes through their careless neglect, but sometimes, too, undoubtedly on purpose, the woods are set fire to by these means. One benefit they consider . . . is the destruction of the dreaded rattlesnakes.''[41]

The slaves on Lewis' West Indies plantation let cattle get into one of his best cane-pieces because they neglected to guard them, being more interested in a dance which was going on. They were fully aware that the cattle were ruining the sugar cane, but kept right on singing and dancing. Lewis was able to get only a handful of house servants to drive the cattle out of the cane, and that not until the cane-piece was ruined.[42]

One tobacco planter complained that his slaves would cut the young plants indiscriminately unless they were watched. When it became late in the season and there was need of haste to avoid frost they would work only the thickest leaving the sparser ones untouched.[43] Another planter said that he could cultivate only the poorer grades of tobacco because the slaves would not give necessary attention to the finer sort of plants.[44] An English visitor said:

"The kitchens and out-offices are always at the distance of several yards from the principal dwelling. This is done as well to guard against the house-Negroes through carelessness setting the houses on fire, for they generally sit over it half the night, as to keep out their noise." (sic.)[45]

The full import of these practices strikes home fully only when they are read in the words of the original observers. Olmsted's comments, and the ease with which he found incidents to illustrate them, are most valuable. So

[41] Kemble, F. A., *Journal of a Residence on a Georgian Plantation in 1838-1839*, New York, 1863, p. 242.
[42] Lewis, M. G., *Journal of a West Indian Proprietor, 1815-1817*, London, 1929, p. 267.
[43] Phillips, U. B., *Plantation and Frontier Documents, 1649-1863*, Cleveland, 1909, p. 34.
[44] Olmsted, F. L., *A Journey in the Seaboard Slave States*, p. 91.
[45] Hanson, C. W., *The Stranger in America*, London, 1807, p. 357.

important is his testimony that we must once more quote him at some length.

"Incidents, trifling in themselves, constantly betray to a stranger the bad economy of using enslaved servants. The catastrophe of one such occurred since I began to write this letter. I ordered a fire to be made in my room, as I was going out this morning. On my return, I found a grand fire—the room door having been closed and locked upon it 'out of order.' Just now, while I was writing, down tumbled upon the floor, and rolled away close to the valance of the bed, half a hod-full of ignited coal, which had been so piled upon the diminutive grate, and left without a fender or any guard, that this result was almost inevitable. If I had not returned at the time I did, the house would have been fired."[46]

"On the rice plantation which I have particularly described, the slaves were, I judge, treated with at least as much discretion and judicious consideration of economy, consistently with humane regard to their health, comfort, and morals, as on any other in all the Slave States; yet I could not avoid observing—and I certainly took no pains to do so, nor were any special facilities offered me for it—repeated instances of that waste and misapplication of labor which it can never be possible to guard against, when the agents of industry are slaves. Many such evidences of waste it would not be easy to specify; and others, which remain in my memory after some weeks, do not adequately account for the general impression that all I saw gave me; but there were, for instance, under my observation gates left open and bars left down, against standing orders; rails removed from fences by the negroes (as was conjectured, to kindle their fires with, mules lamed, and implements broken, by careless usage; a flat boat, carelessly secured, going adrift on the river; men ordered to cart rails for a new fence depositing them so that a double expense of labor would be required to lay them, more than would have needed if they had been placed, as they might have almost as easily been, by a slight exercise of forethought . . . making statements which their owner was obliged to receive as sufficient excuse, though, he told me, he felt assured they were false—all going to show habitual carelessness, indolence, and mere eye-service."[47]

[46] Olmsted, F. L., *A Journey in the Seaboard Slave States*, p. 145.
[47] *Ibid.*, p. 480.

But not only did the Negro slaves refuse to work, and not only did they destroy property, but they even made it impossible for planters to introduce new work techniques by feigning clumsiness. They prevented the introduction of the plow in this way on many plantations.[48] Olmsted here cites many instances. Lewis, quoted in *Plantation Documents*, found the same thing to be true in Jamaica.

"It appears to me that nothing could afford so much relief to the negroes, under the existing system of Jamaica, as the substituting of labor of animals for that of slaves in agriculture wherever such a measure is practicable. On leaving the island, I impressed this wish of mine upon the mind of my agents with all my power; but the only result has been the creating a very considerable expense in the purchase of ploughs, oxen and farming implements; the awkwardness and still more the obstinacy of the few negroes, whose services were indispensable, was not to be overcome: they broke plough after plough, and ruined beast after beast, till the attempt was abandoned in despair."[49]

IV

Malingering was a well-known phenomenon throughout the slave states.[50] The purpose of feigning illness was generally to avoid work, although occasionally a slave who was being sold would feign a disability either to avoid being sold to an undesirable master, or to lower his purchase price so as to obtain revenge on a former master. The women occasionally pretended to be pregnant, because preg-

[48] *Ibid.*, pp. 481-484.

[49] Phillips, U. B., *Plantation and Frontier Documents, 1694-1863*, p. 137.

[50] Since this paper was written a significant contribution has appeared which throws a new light on the subject of slave illness. (Felice Swados, "Negro Health on the Ante Bellum Plantations," *Bulletin of the History of Medicine*, vol. x, no. 3, October, 1941.) Though Swados demonstrated that the rate of actual sickness among the Negroes was very high, she leaves some doubt as to what proportion of sickness was feigned. For instance, in a footnote (p. 472) she refers to Sydnor's compilations of the records of sickness on several plantations as indications of the extent of actual sickness, even going so far as to note that on one plantation most of the sickness occurred during the picking season. Sydnor, himself, indicates that he believes that these records demonstrate that a great deal of the sickness was feigned.

nant women were given lighter work assignments and were allowed extra rations of food.

In a situation such as this in which physical disability was an advantage, one would expect much malingering. One might also expect to find functional mental disorders, hysterical disorders which would get one out of work. There is some evidence that many had such functional disorders.

"There are many complaints described in Dr. Cartwright's treatise, to which the Negroes, in slavery, seem to be peculiarly subject.

" 'Negro-consumption, a disease almost unknown to medical men of the Northern States and of Europe, is also sometimes fearfully prevalent among the slaves. 'It is of importance,' says the Doctor, to know the pathognomic signs in its early stages, not only in regard to its treatment but to detect impositions, as negroes, afflicted with this complaint are often for sale; the acceleration of the pulse, on exercise, incapacitates them for labor, as they quickly give out, and have to leave their work. This induces their owners to sell them, although they may not know the cause of their inability to labor. Many of the negroes brought South, for sale, are in the incipient stages of this disease; they are found to be inefficient laborers, and sold in consequence thereof. The effect of superstition —a firm belief that he is poisoned or conjured—upon the patient's mind, already in a morbid state (dyaesthesia), and his health affected from hard usage, overtasking or exposure, want of wholesome food, good clothing, warm, comfortable lodging, with the distressing idea (sometimes) that he is an object of hatred or dislike, both to his master or fellow-servants, and has no one to befriend him, tends directly to generate that erythism of mind which is the essential cause of negro consumption' " . . . 'Remedies should be assisted by removing the *original cause*[51] of the dissatisfaction or trouble of mind, and by using every means to make the patient comfortable, satisfied and happy.' "[52]

Of course it is impossible to determine the extent of these disorders. Assuming that Dr. Cartwright's assumption was correct, very few observers would be qualified to make an adequate diagnosis, and a very small proportion of

[51] Cartwright's italics.
[52] Olmsted, F. L., *A Journey in the Seaboard Slave States*, p. 193.

these would be inclined to accept his interpretation. After all, functional disorders are in many cases almost impossible to tell from real disorders or from feigning, and since the behavior which Cartwright describes could very easily be interpreted on another, and easier, level by a less acute observer.

Of the extent to which illness was feigned there can, however, be little doubt. Some of the feigning was quite obvious, and one might wonder why such flagrant abuses were tolerated. The important thing to remember is that a slave was an important economic investment. Most slave owners sooner or later found out that it was more profitable to give the slave the benefit of the doubt. A sick slave driven to work might very well die.

"But the same gentleman admitted that he had sometimes been mistaken and had made men go to work when they afterwards proved to be really ill; therefore, when one of his people told him he was not able to work, he usually thought, 'very likely he'll be all the better for a day's rest, whether he's really ill or not,' and would let him off without being very particular in his examination. Lately he had been getting a new overseer, and when he was engaging him he told him that this was his way. The observer replied, 'It's my way too, now; it didn't used to be, but I had a lesson. There was a nigger one day at Mr. ———'s who was sulky and complaining; he said he couldn't work. I looked at his tongue, and it was right clean, and I thought it was nothing but damned sulkiness so I paddled him, and made him go to work; but, two days after, he was under ground. He was a good eight hundred dollar nigger, and it was a lesson to me about taming possums, that I ain't going to forget in a hurry.' "[53]

So one might find situations like this:

"At one, which was evidently the 'sick house' or hospital, there were several negroes, of both sexes, wrapped in blankets, and reclining on the door steps or on the ground, basking in sunshine. Some of them looked ill, but all were chatting and laughing as I rode up to make inquiry."[54]

[53] *Ibid.*, p. 189.
[54] *Ibid.*, pp. 416, 417.

The situation turned in on itself. The masters were always suspicious of the sick slaves, so that slaves who were moderately sick accentuated their symptoms in order to make out a convincing case.

"It is said to be nearly as difficult to form a satisfactory diagnosis of negroes' disorders, as it is of infants', because their imagination of symptoms is so vivid, and because not the smallest reliance is to be placed on their accounts of what they have felt or done. If a man is really ill, he fears lest he should be thought to be simulating, and therefore exaggerates all his pains, and locates them in whatever he supposes to be the most vital parts of his system.

"Frequently the invalid slaves will neglect or refuse to use the remedies prescribed for their recovery. They will conceal pills, for instance, under their tongue, and declare they have swallowed them, when, from their producing no effect, it will be afterwards evident that they have not. This general custom I heard ascribed to habit acquired when they were not very disagreeably ill and were loth to be made quite well enough to have to go to work again."[55]

Fortunately in this field we have some quantitative estimates which enable us to appreciate fully the extent of these practices. Sydnor has digested the records of sickness on various plantations. From the Wheeles plantation records he found that of 1,429 working days 179 were lost on account of sickness, a ratio of almost one to seven. On the Bowles' plantation, in one year 159½ days were missed on account of sickness but only five days were on Sundays This is a recurrent pattern, everybody sick on Saturday, and scarcely anybody sick on Sunday. On the Leigh plantation, where thirty persons were working there were 398 days of sickness. In examining this record Sydnor discovered that the rate of sickness was greatest at the times of the year when there was the most work to be done.[56] Olmsted says that he never visited a plantation on which twenty Negroes were employed where he did not find one or more not at work on some trivial pretext.[57]

[55] Ibid., p. 187.
[56] Sydnor, C. S., Slavery in Mississippi, New York, 1933, pp. 45ff.
[57] Olmsted, F. L., A Journey in the Seaboard Slave States, p. 187.

Lewis' anecdote is typical:

"On Saturday morning there were no fewer than forty-five persons (not including children) in the hospital; which makes nearly a fifth of my whole gang. Of these the medical people assured me that not above seven had anything whatever the matter with them. . . . And sure enough on Sunday morning they all walked away from the hospital to amuse themselves, except about seven or eight."[58]

Sometimes the feigning did not work, as is shown by two incidents that Olmsted relates:

A Mr. X asked if there were any sick people.

" 'Nobody, oney dat boy Sam, sar.'

" 'What Sam is that?'

" 'Dat little Sam, sar; Tom's Sue's Sam, sar.'

" 'What's the matter with him?'

" 'Don' spec der's nothing much de matter wid him nof, sar. He came in Sa'dy, complaining he had de stomach-ache, an' I give him some ile, sar, 'spec he mus' be well dis time, but he din go out dis mornin'.'

" 'Well, I see to him.

"Mr. X went to Tom's Sue's cabin, looked at the boy and concluded that he was well, though he lay abed, and pretended to cry with pain, ordered him to go out to work."[59]

A planter asked the nurse if anyone else was sick.

" 'Oney dat woman Caroline.'

" 'What do you think is the matter with her?'

" 'Well, I don't think there is anything de matter wid her, masser; I mus answer you for true, I don't tink anything de matter wid her, oney she's a little sore from dat whipping she got.' "

The manager found the woman groaning on a dirty bed and after examining her, scolded her and sent her to work.[60]

The prevalence of malingering may be better appreciated when one realizes that despite the fact that Olmsted

[58] Lewis, M. G., *Journal of a West Indian Proprietor, 1815-1817*, London. 1929, p. 168.

[59] Olmsted, F. L., *A Journey in the Seaboard Slave States*, pp. 423, 424.

[60] Olmsted, F. L., *A Journey in the Back Country*, p. 77.

refers to it throughout four volumes of his works, in one place he has five whole pages of anecdotes concerning it.[61]

Pretending to be pregnant was a type of escape in a class by itself, since the fraud must inevitably have been discovered. This in itself may give us some insight into the Negroes' attitude toward the relative advantages of escaping work and of escaping punishment. Just as the slave who ran off into the woods for a temporary relief from work, the pseudo-pregnant woman must have realized in advance that she would inevitably be punished.

"I will tell you of a most comical account Mr. ——— has given me of the prolonged and still protracted pseudo-pregnancy of a woman called Markie, who for many more months than are generally required for the process of continuing the human species, pretended to be what the Germans pathetically and poetically call 'in good hope' and continued to reap increased rations as the reward of her expectation, till she finally had to disappoint the estate and receive a flogging.[62]

One woman sought to escape from the consequences of her fraud. The results were quite tragic:

"A young slave woman, Becky by name, had given pregnancy as the reason for a continued slackness in her work. Her master became skeptical and gave notice that she was to be examined and might expect the whip in case her excuse were not substantiated. Two days afterwards a Negro midwife announced that Becky's baby had been born; but at the same time a neighboring planter began search for a child nine months old which was missing from his quarter. This child was found in Becky's cabin, with its two teeth pulled and the tip of its navel cut off. It died; and Becky was convicted only of manslaughter."[63]

An outstanding example of malingering is given by Smedes, a writer who insisted so emphatically on the devotion of the slaves to their masters.

[61] Olmsted, F. L., *A Journey in the Seaboard Slave States*, pp. 187-191.
[62] Kemble, F. A., *op. cit.*, p. 235.
[63] Phillips, U. B., *American Negro Slavery*, p. 436.

"The cook's husband, who for years had looked on himself as nearly blind; and therefore unable to do more than work about her, and put her wood on the fire, sometimes cutting a stick or two, made no less than eighteen good crops for himself when the war was over. He was one of the best farmers in the country.''[64]

The most effective means of retaliation against an unpopular master which the slave had at his command was by feigning disability on the auction block. How often this was done we do not know, but Phillips accepts it as a recognized pattern.

"Those on the block often times praised their own strength and talents, for it was a matter of pride to fetch high prices. On the other hand if a slave should bear a grudge against his seller, or should hope to be bought only by someone who would expect but light service he might pretend a disability though he had it not.''[65]

Coleman offers the same opinion:

"Similar actions were not unknown in slave sales. Frequently on such occasions there is a strong indisposition in such creatures to be sold, and that by stratagem to avoid sale, they may frequently feign sickness, or magnify any particular complaint with which they are affected.[66]

"As was customary at a public auction of slaves, the auctioneer announced that Mr. Anderson, the master, would give a bill of sale for his slave with the usual guarantee—'sound of mind and body and a slave for life.' While there began a lively bidding among the Negro traders, George suddenly assumed a strange appearance— his head was thrown back, his eyes rolled wildly, his body and limbs began to twitch and jerk in an unheard of manner.

" 'What's the matter with your boy, Mr. Anderson?' one of the traders asked the owner, who, astonished and puzzled, drew nearer the block. But Mr. Anderson did not answer the question. George was now foaming at the mouth, and the violent twitching and jerking increased precipitously.

[64] Smedes, S., *Memorials of a Southern Planter*, Baltimore, 1887, p. 80.
[65] Phillips, U. B., *American Negro Slavery*, p. 199.
[66] Coleman, J. W., *Slavery Times in Kentucky*, Chapel Hill, N. C., 1940, p. 130.

" 'What's the matter with you, boy?' gruffly demanded the trader. 'O, I 'es fits I has!' exclaimed George, whereupon his body doubled up and rolled off the block.

"Of course the auction was hastily terminated. George was hustled off to jail, and a doctor sent for, but, after a careful examination; the medical man was somewhat mystified as to the slaves's actual condition. He advised the master to leave George in the jailer's custody for a while, promising to look in on him the next morning. Under his master's instruction, the wily slave was put to bed in the debtor's room, where he soon sank, apparently, into a sound sleep.

"Next morning when the jailer brought in breakfast, he found the bed empty. George was gone, and nothing was heard of him again until word came, several weeks later, that he was safe in Canada.'"[67]

Or, again, we read:

"A young girl, of twenty years or thereabouts, was the next commodity put up. Her right hand was entirely useless—'dead,' as she aptly called it. One finger had been cut off by a doctor, and the auctioneer stated that she herself chopped off the other finger— her forefinger—because it hurt her, and she thought that to cut it off would cure it.

" 'Didn't you cut your finger off?' asked a man, 'kase you was mad?'

"She looked at him quietly, but with a glance of contempt, and said:

" 'No, you see it was a sort o' sore, and I thought it would be better to cut it off than be plagued with it.'

"Several persons around me expressed the opinion that she had done it willfully, to spite her master or mistress, or to keep her from being sold down South.'"[68]

Another instance is described as follows:

"As I came up, a second-rate plantation hand of the name of Noah, but whom the crier persisted in calling 'Noey,' was being offered, it being an administrator's sale. Noey, on mounting the steps, had assumed a most drooping aspect, hanging his head and

[67] *Ibid.*, pp. 129-130.
[68] Redpath, *op. cit.*, pp. 253-254.

affecting the feebleness of old age. He had probably hoped to have
avoided sale by a dodge, which is very common in such cases. But
the first bid—$1,000—startled him, and he looked eagerly to the
quarter whence it proceeded. 'Never mind who he is, he has got
the money. Now, gentlemen, just go on; who will say fifty.' And
so the crier proceeds with his monotonous calling. 'I ain't worth all
that, mass'r; I ain't much count no how,' cried Noey energetically
to the first bidder. 'Yes you are, Noey—ah, $1,000, thank you, sir.'
replies the crier.''[69]

The strength of Negro resistance to slavery becomes
apparent in the extent to which the slaves mutilated themselves in their efforts to escape work. A girl on Lewis'
plantation who had been injured tied pack thread around
her wounds when they started to heal and then rubbed dirt
in them. In her anxiety to avoid work she gave herself a
very serious infection.[70] But this action was mild compared
to that of others.

"General Leslie Coombs, of Lexington, owned a man named
Ennis, a house carpenter. He had bargained with a slave-trader
to take him and carry him down the river. Ennis was determined
not to go. He took a broadaxe and cut one hand off; then contrived
to lift the axe, with his arm pressing it to his body, and let it fall
upon the other, cutting off the ends of the fingers.''[71]

" 'But some on 'em would rather be shot then be took, sir,' he
added simply.

"A farmer living near a swamp confirmed this account, and
said he knew of three or four being shot on one day.''[72]

Planters had much trouble with slaves fresh from Africa, the new slaves committing suicide in great numbers.
Ebo landing in the Sea Islands was the site of the mass
suicide of Ebo slaves who simply walked in a body into the
ocean and drowned themselves. A planter writing on the
handling of slaves mentions the difficulty of adjusting the

69 Pollard, E. A., The Southern Spy, Washington, 1859, pp. 13-14.
70 Lewis, op. cit., p. 168.
71 Clarke, op. cit., p. 125.
72 Olmsted, F. L., A Journey in the Seaboard Slave States, p. 160.

Africans to slavery. He advocates mixing them in with seasoned slaves.

"It too often happens that poor masters, who have no other slaves or are too greedy, require hard labor of these fresh negroes, exhaust them quickly, lose them by sickness and more often by grief. Often they hasten their own death; some wound themselves, others stifle themselves by drawing in the tongue so as to close the breathing passage, others take poison, or flee and perish of misery and hunger."[73]

The one problem of Negro resistance to slavery which is most enticing is that of the attitude of slave mothers toward their children. There are frequent references in the literature to Negro women who boasted about the number of "niggers they hade for the massah," but breeding was probably quite secondary to sex activity. It would be interesting to discover the motives behind this apparent pleasure in presenting babies to the master. Some of the women may have been sincere in their pride. What makes this problem peculiarly important is the presence of much indirect evidence that, the Negro mothers either had no affection for their children, or did not want them to be raised as slaves.

We know quite well that African Negroes are (at least reasonably) able to take care of their children, and that the slave women efficiently tended the children of the plantation mistress. Yet one runs across comment after comment that the Negro mothers were ignorant, and careless, and did not know how to care for their own offspring. Typical of such statements is this:

"The Negro mothers are often so ignorant and indolent, that they cannot be trusted to keep awake and administer medicine to their own children; so that the mistress has often to sit up all night with a sick Negro child."[74]

Gnion Johnson states that plantation owners in the Sea Islands offered the mothers rewards to take good care of

[73] Phillips, U. B., *Plantation and Frontier Documents*, II, p. 31.
[74] Lyell, *op. cit.*, p. 264.

their children. They were paid for those who survived the first year! This at least would indicate that there was something to be desired in their attitude toward their children.

Occasionally one runs across a reference to a slave mother killing her child, but the statements are almost invariably incomplete. For instance, Catterall[75] has a record of a trial, the details of which are: "The prisoner was indicted for murder of her own child," no more. Or a plantation overseer writes, "Elizabeth's child died last night. She smothered it somehow."[76] There is no indication as to whether or not the smothering was deliberate.

Several cases, where it was certain that parents killed their children to keep them from slavery, have been described. They are important enough to be given in detail.

"Of all the cases of slave rendition, the saddest and probably the most circulated at the time was that of Margaret Garner. Winter was the best time for flight across the Ohio River, for when it was frozen over the difficulties of crossing were fewer. Simeon Garner, with his wife Margaret and two children, fled from slavery in Kentucky during the cold winter of 1856 and, after crossing the frozen stream at night, made their ways to the house of a free Negro in Cincinnati.

"Quickly tracing the fugitive Negroes to their hideout in Cincinnati, the armed pursuers, after some resistance, broke down the door and entered the house. There they found Margaret, the mother, who, preferring death to slavery for her children, had striven to take their lives, and one child lay dead on the floor. The case was immediately brought into court, where despite the efforts made by sympathetic whites, rendition was ordered. On their return to slavery, Margaret in despair attempted to drown herself and child by jumping into the river but even the deliverance of death was denied her, for she was recovered and soon thereafter sold to a trader who took her to the cotton fields of the Far South.'"[77]

[75] Catterall, H. H., (ed.), *Judicial Cases Concerning American Slavery and the Negro*, Washington, D. C., 1926-1937, Vol. II, p. 59.

[76] Bassett, *op. cit.*, p. 59.

[77] Coleman, J. W., *op. cit.*, p. 208.

"Not only were slaves known to take the lives of their masters or overseers, but they were now and then charged with the murder of their own children, sometimes to prevent them from growing up in bondage. In Covington a father and mother, shut up in a slave baracoon and doomed to the southern market, 'when there was no eye to pity them and no arm to save,' did by mutual agreement 'send the souls of their children to Heaven rather than have them descend to the hell of slavery,' and then both parents committed suicide."[78]

" 'Take off your shoes, Sylva,' said Mrs. A., 'and let this gentleman see your feet.'

" 'I don't want to,' said Sylva.

" 'But I want you to,' said her mistress.

" 'I don't care if you do,' replied Sylva sullenly.

" 'You must,' said the mistress firmly.

"The fear of punishment impelled her to remove the shoes. Four toes on one foot, and two on the other were wanting! 'There!' said the mistress, 'my husband, who learned the blacksmith's trade for the purpose of teaching it to the slaves, to increase their market value, has, with his own hands, pounded off and wrung off all those toes, when insane with passion. And it was only last week that he thought Sylva was saucy to me, and he gave her thirty lashes with the horse whip. She was so old that I could not bear to see it, and I left the house.

" 'Sylva says,' Mrs. A. continued, 'that she has been the mother of thirteen children, every one of whom she has destroyed with her own hands, in their infancy, rather than have them suffer slavery'!"[79]

V

The patterns of resistance to slavery studied in this paper are: (1) deliberate slowing up of work; (2) destruction of property, and indifferent work (3) feigning illness and pregnancy; (4) injuring one's self; (5) suicide; (6) a possibility that a significant number of slave mothers killed their children.

[78] *Ibid.*, p. 269.
[79] Parson, C. G., *op. cit.*, p. 212.

The motivation behind these acts was undoubtedly complex. The most obvious of the motives was a desire to avoid work. It has been demonstrated that the slaves were acutely conscious of the fact that they had nothing to gain by hard work except in those instances where they were working under the task system. The destruction of property and the poor quality of the slaves' work was mainly due to their indifference to their tasks. There is enough evidence that they could, and did, work hard and well when sufficiently motivated to refute any contention that the Negro slaves were congenitally poor workers.

Many of the slaves reacted to the institution of slavery in a far more drastic fashion than could be manifested by a mere desire to avoid work. Some of these slaves committed suicide; others killed members of their families, usually their children, in order that they might not grow up as slaves.

Possibly the most significant aspect of these patterns of resistance is the aggression against the white masters they imply. Unfortunately, however, though this aspect may be the most significant, it is the least subject to proof. On the plane of logic, there is every reason to believe that a people held in bondage would devise techniques such as have been described above as an indirect means of retaliation. The statement of Dollard, previously quoted,[80] indicates that such techniques (slowness, inefficiency, etc.) are used at the present time as a means of indirect aggression.

The material presented here suggests the need for a reconsideration of the concept of the Negro's easy adjust-ment to slavery. He was not a cheerful, efficient worker, as has been assumed. Rather, he was frequently rebellious, and almost always sullen, as any person faced with a disagreeable situation from which he cannot escape will normally be. Nor, can the belief that racial inferiority is re-

[80] See above, p. 393.

sponsible for inefficient workmanship on his part be supported. For such deficiencies of his workmanship as he manifested, or, indeed, may still be manifested, are seen to be explainable in terms that are in no sense to be couched in the conventional mold of inherent racial differences.

RAYMOND A. BAUER
ALICE H. BAUER

Department of Anthropology
Northwestern University

Slave Rebelliousness and Social Conflict in North Carolina, 1775 to 1802

Jeffrey J. Crow

Q UILLO, a slave of James Hunt of Granville County, North Carolina, has not been remembered as a Revolutionary patriot or prominent political figure, but to local whites he must surely have seemed a troublesome symbol of the American Revolution gone awry. In April 1794, Granville County authorities accused Quillo of plotting a slave insurrection. Slaves who testified against him disclosed some striking attitudes and ideas among blacks. Quillo, they said, had "intended to give a large treat at Craggs Branch to the black people." While serving cider and brandy, he planned to hold an "election" in which slaves would choose burgesses, justices of the peace, and sheriffs "in order to have equal Justice distributed so that a weak person might collect his debts, as well as a Strong one." Not only had Quillo asked several slaves to stand as candidates, but the bondsmen expected these black representatives to employ force "in collecting the monies due them." In his defense Quillo asserted that the idea for an election had come from Tom, a mulatto slave. The election had been called off or postponed because someone had broken into a white man's cellar and stolen liquor. If the election had been held, the slaves who attended could have been charged with the theft of that liquor. According to the slave deponents, Quillo had also been in touch with a Negro in neighboring Person County who had heard that a band of Negroes intended to march toward Granville. One slave charged that after the election Quillo and "his associates were to proceed to inlist what forces they could to join the said party from Person and with them to force their way wherever they choosed, and to murder all who stood in their way, or opposed them." Quillo had supposedly vowed to "clear . . . out" the whites if they tried to interfere.[1]

Quillo's "election" may have been a ruse for some deeper scheme, but

Mr. Crow is head of the General Publications Branch, Historical Publications Section, of the North Carolina Division of Archives and History, Raleigh. He wishes to thank Robert M. Calhoon, Robert F. Durden, Paul D. Escott, Raymond Gavins, Marvin L. Michael Kay, Marc W. Kruman, William S. Price, Jr., and Peter H. Wood for their many helpful suggestions during the preparation of this article. Mr. Crow and Mr. Kay plan to analyze the evolution of class and caste structures in North Carolina, 1740-1810, in a future study.

[1] Trial of Quillo, Apr. 1794, Granville County Papers, North Carolina Division of Archives and History, Raleigh.

the manner in which he organized his polls with a "treat," like a country squire, could not have escaped Granville County whites. Something unsettling to whites was happening when slaves could speak of "equal justice" and contemplate the democratic election of a shadow government. The contagion of liberty that had been released by the American Revolution was dangerously spreading to the "wrong" people.

Slave rebelliousness was a familiar reality in eighteenth-century America. This may explain why most historians who have studied blacks in the colonial and Revolutionary periods have never been drawn into the debate over the creation of docile Sambos that absorbed scholars of nineteenth-century slavery for so long.[2] Students of the subject now agree that most slaves were never reconciled to, or broken by, the system. Though few organized or participated in rebellions, many engaged in other acts of resistance such as running away, arson, poisoning, destruction of property, sabotage, and assault.[3] Benjamin Quarles's classic study of the Negro in the Revolution provided the first comprehensive view of black engagement in and response to the War for Independence. Quarles found that blacks were far from passive; they fought for both sides, provided significant manpower to the British and American armies, and took active steps to achieve their freedom. Since the appearance of Quarles's book, Winthrop D. Jordan, Gerald (Michael) W. Mullin, and Peter H. Wood have added to our knowledge of slave rebelliousness in the eighteenth century with their perceptive and sensitive treatments of black life and white attitudes.[4]

Yet the link connecting slave rebelliousness to the Revolution or to the social turmoil that attended the Revolutionary War remains tenuous. The bondsmen's attitudes toward the Revolution are not revealed directly in a corpus of writings but must be inferred from their behavior in response to social, political, cultural, and military pressures. The American Revolution provides dramatic evidence to suggest that those pressures were immense.

[2]Stanley M. Elkins, *Slavery: A Problem in American Institutional and Intellectual Life* (Chicago, 1959); Ann J. Lane, ed., *The Debate over Slavery: Stanley Elkins and His Critics* (Urbana, Ill., 1971).

[3]See especially Kenneth M. Stampp, "Rebels and Sambos: The Search for the Negro's Personality in Slavery," *Journal of Southern History*, XXXVII (1971), 367-392; John W. Blassingame, *The Slave Community: Plantation Life in the Antebellum South* (New York, 1972), 184-216; and Paul D. Escott, *Slavery Remembered: A Record of Twentieth-Century Slave Narratives* (Chapel Hill, N.C., 1979), 71-94.

[4]Benjamin Quarles, *The Negro in the American Revolution* (Chapel Hill, N.C., 1961); Winthrop D. Jordan, *White over Black: American Attitudes toward the Negro, 1550-1812* (Chapel Hill, N.C., 1968); Gerald W. Mullin, *Flight and Rebellion: Slave Resistance in Eighteenth-Century Virginia* (New York, 1972); Peter H. Wood, *Black Majority: Negroes in Colonial South Carolina from 1670 through the Stono Rebellion* (New York, 1974). See also Wood's excellent historiographical analysis, " 'I Did the Best I Could for My Day': The Study of Early Black History during the Second Reconstruction, 1960 to 1976," *William and Mary Quarterly*, 3d Ser., XXXV (1978), 185-225.

118

As John Shy has argued, the Revolutionary War was a "political education conducted by military means" for thousands of Americans—black as well as white, he might have added.[5] In the South, that education took place amidst great social chaos, approaching anarchy, that had been set off by the war but continued long after hostilities ended in 1783.

North Carolina was particularly vulnerable to the devastating effects of the war. Cherokee raids in the west, British raids along the coast, and a loyalist uprising of Scottish Highlanders at the Battle of Moore's Creek Bridge confronted the North Carolinians at the outset of the conflict. Though the British did not invade North Carolina until 1780, loyalism plagued the new state government, and a major tory plot was uncovered and quashed in 1777. In the later stages of the war North Carolina became the battleground of Nathanael Greene and Lord Cornwallis, spawning a fierce internecine warfare between whigs and tories that lasted well into 1782. War-weary North Carolinians learned to their sorrow that the patriot militia treated them no better than marauding loyalists did.[6]

The peace treaty of 1783 did not magically restore order to North Carolina's social, economic, and political life. Commerce was at a standstill and the currency was virtually worthless. Not one newspaper was being published in the state. Courts met sporadically. In the wake of British occupation and the "Tory War," needy families in the lower Cape Fear counties were even exempted from paying taxes. Bitter antagonisms still divided the people, and loyalists continued to suffer social ostracism, legal sanctions, and political discrimination.[7] Such distressed circumstances greatly affected public and private life. When William Hooper, one of North Carolina's signers of the Declaration of Independence, was elected to the General Assembly in 1782, he spoke of contributing his "mite towards relief of this wretched state from its present anarchy and gloomy expectations."[8] More than a year later Moravian leader Friedric Wilhelm Marshall still found North Carolina's prognosis poor: "It cannot be denied that this country is in the condition of a patient convalescing from fever, who begins to be conscious of his weakness and still needs medicine and care. The land itself, the people of property, commerce, public and private credit, the currency in circulation, all are laid waste and ruined."[9]

It is the thesis of this article that the Revolution generated powerful

[5]John Shy, "The American Revolution: The Military Conflict Considered as a Revolutionary War," in Stephen G. Kurtz and James H. Hutson, eds., *Essays on the American Revolution* (Chapel Hill, N.C., 1973), 121-156, quotation on p. 147.

[6]Jeffrey J. Crow, "Tory Plots and Anglican Loyalty: The Llewelyn Conspiracy of 1777," *North Carolina Historical Review*, LV (1978), 1-17; Carole Watterson Troxler, *The Loyalist Experience in North Carolina* (Raleigh, 1976); Robert O. DeMond, *The Loyalists in North Carolina during the Revolution* (Durham, 1940).

[7]Samuel A'Court Ashe, *History of North Carolina*, II (Raleigh, 1925), 1-22.

[8]William Hooper to James Iredell, Apr. 8, 1782, in Don Higginbotham, ed., *The Papers of James Iredell* (Raleigh, N.C., 1976), II, 336.

[9]F. W. Marshall to Unity's Vorsteher Collegium, Oct. 28, 1783, in Adelaide L. Fries, ed., *Records of the Moravians in North Carolina*, IV (Raleigh, 1930), 1921.

internal tensions that racially destabilized southern society, particularly in North Carolina. The social conflict and disorder endemic to the Revolutionary War and its aftermath weakened stratified systems of caste. It has often been noted that clashes between ethnic groups intensify when the social structure lacks definition. Disorders occur in precisely those situations that are characterized by uncertainty over the color line and its breakdown. Demographic changes that disrupt old social patterns, major catastrophes such as war, and the transformation of values when new ideas are introduced generate tension and misunderstanding.[10] Between the outbreak of the Revolution and the turn of the nineteenth century acute tensions, which frequently erupted into violence, existed between blacks and whites in the South. Racial conflict polarized both groups but also promoted collective responses from each. For Afro-Americans, unstable racial patterns forged new hopes of freedom and a growing sense of cohesiveness that helped mold a black community. For whites, fluid racial patterns produced unsettling fears and a lack of social cohesiveness as blacks became increasingly assertive and white dissenters attempted to ameliorate slavery or abolish it completely. White fears of slave insurrection, heightened by instances of black unrest, culiminated in the widespread slave revolt scares of 1800-1802. The brutal subjugation of a small number of slave conspirators and the terrorization of countless other bondsmen restored white solidarity. The reassertion of the dominant white group's authority erased questions about caste and about the social position of blacks that had vexed southern whites since the Revolution. The color line was once more powerfully reinforced.

In focusing on North Carolina in the crucial years between 1775 and 1802, the present analysis pursues three lines of inquiry: how the actions of Afro-Americans contributed to the social trauma of the Revolution; how whites responded to the realization that their movement for Independence was unavoidably affecting the institution of slavery and the behavior of their black bondsmen; and, finally, how the conflicting perceptions of blacks and whites collided to produce the slave insurrection scares of 1800-1802.

The tremendous upheaval in the South that the Revolution brought about is only beginning to be explored. The Revolution occasioned a breakdown of the normal cohesive elements in southern society that sanctioned existing power relationships, thereby allowing economically and politically dispossessed groups to challenge the authority of the ruling class. This challenge came not only from tories and the "disaffected," but

---

[10]Lewis A. Coser, *Continuities in the Study of Social Conflict* (New York, 1967), 59, 96; Coser, "Some Sociological Aspects of Conflict," in Gary T. Marx, ed., *Racial Conflict: Tension and Change in American Society* (Boston, 1971), 14-16; Tamotsu Shibutani and Kian M. Kwan, "Changes in Life Conditions Conducive to Interracial Conflict," *ibid.*, 135, 138-141; Joseph S. Himes, "The Functions of Racial Conflict," *ibid.*, 456-460.

also from slaves.[11] Slave rebelliousness manifested itself in two ways: open revolt by force of arms, and defection to the British. Southern Revolutionaries accused the British crown of stirring up the slaves with promises of freedom. The North Carolina whig James Iredell, writing in 1776, cited Britain's "diabolical purpose of exciting our own Domestics (Domestics they forced upon us) to cut our throats, and involve Men, Women, and Children in one universal Massacre."[12] But the slave unrest that accompanied the opening stages of the war was too widespread to have been the work of a single British conspiracy, though royal governors and military observers had often commented on the potential for a massive slave insurrection in the southern colonies. From the Chesapeake to the Georgia coast, black insurgents sprang into action even before the British tendered their help. Mindful of that threat, North Carolina whigs had been closely monitoring their slaves long before Lord Dunmore of Virginia offered freedom to slaves who enlisted in the service of the crown.

The town of Wilmington was especially sensitive to the danger of insurrection because of its large black populace. Located at the mouth of the Cape Fear River, Wilmington was the chief entrepôt for North Carolina's growing naval stores industry and for the rice that the province's coastal planters produced. Consequently, surrounding New Hanover County had one of the largest and most concentrated Negro populations in the colony. Negroes constituted over 60 percent of the taxables in the county.[13] In June 1775 the Wilmington Committee of Safety, enforcing a 1753 statute that ostensibly limited the bearing of arms to those slaves whose masters had posted bond for them, disarmed all blacks to keep them "in order." It also instituted "Patroles to search & take from Negroes all kinds of Arms whatsoever." The situation, warned Wilmington Revolutionaries on July 13, was "truly alarming, the Governor collecting men, provisions, warlike stores of every kind, spiriting up the back counties, & perhaps the Slaves." The Revolutionaries charged that the British commander of Fort Johnston, guarding the entrance to Cape Fear, "had given Encouragement

[11]Three recent essays that explore slave unrest and social disorder during the Revolution are Ronald Hoffman, "The 'Disaffected' in the Revolutionary South," in Alfred F. Young, ed., *The American Revolution: Explorations in the History of American Radicalism* (DeKalb, Ill., 1976), 273-316; Michael Mullin, "British Caribbean and North American Slaves in an Era of War and Revolution, 1775-1807," in Jeffrey J. Crow and Larry E. Tise, eds., *The Southern Experience in the American Revolution* (Chapel Hill, N.C., 1978), 235-267; and Peter H. Wood, " 'Taking Care of Business' in Revolutionary South Carolina: Republicanism and the Slave Society," *ibid.*, 268-293.
[12]["Causes of the American Revolution"], June 1776, in Higginbotham, ed., *Iredell Papers*, I, 409.
[13]H. Roy Merrens, *Colonial North Carolina in the Eighteenth Century: A Study in Historical Geography* (Chapel Hill, 1964), 77-79; James M. Clifton, "Golden Grains of White: Rice Planting on the Lower Cape Fear," *N.C. Hist. Rev.*, L (1973), 365-369. The General Assembly of 1715 defined all slaves over 12 years of age as taxables.

to Negroes to Elope from their Masters & they [the British] promised to protect them."[14]

Janet Schaw, a Scottish gentlewoman then visiting the lower Cape Fear, observed the mounting hysteria. The Revolutionaries, she wrote, claimed that the crown had promised "every Negro that would murder his Master and family that he should have his Master's plantation. This last Artifice they may pay for, as the Negroes have got it amongst them and believe it to be true. Tis ten to one they may try the experiment, and in that case friends and foes will be all one."[15] When Schaw traveled to Wilmington in July 1775, the slaves accompanying her "were seized and taken into custody till I was ready to return with them." An insurrection was expected hourly. "There had been a great number of them [blacks] discovered in the adjoining woods the night before," she explained, "most of them with arms, and a fellow belonging to Doctor [Thomas] Cobham was actually killed. All parties are now united against the common enemies." Patrols regularly searched Negro houses, and authorities imposed a curfew on all blacks. Decidedly loyalist in her views, Schaw talked to the commander of the midnight patrol and found that he thought the Revolutionaries' agitation about a slave revolt "a trick intended in the first place to inflame the minds of the populace, and in the next place to get those who had not before taken up arms to do it now and form an association for the safety of the town." In other words, the commander was convinced that the Wilmington patriots were preying upon white fears of slave rebellion to unite the white populace behind the Revolutionary cause. He believed the death of Cobham's slave an unconscionable act because "it was a fact well known" that the slave regularly met his black "Mistress every night in the opposite wood." The slave "wench" was forced "to carry on the intrigue with her black lover with great secrecy" because her master was so strict. Plotting a tryst, not an insurrection, had cost the slave his life. Even so, Schaw concluded, "My hypothesis is . . . the Negroes will revolt."[16]

Schaw's assessment of the situation proved correct, for the rumors of a slave insurrection that spread across the Carolinas in the summer of 1775 were not unfounded.[17] The alarm first sounded across the Tar River basin—Beaufort, Pitt, and Craven counties—in July 1775. On July 1 the Pitt

[14]Committee Minutes, June 21, 1775, Leora H. McEachern and Isabel M. Williams, eds., *Wilmington—New Hanover Safety Committee Minutes, 1774-1776* (Wilmington, N.C., 1974), 30; Wilmington Safety Committee to Samuel Johnston, July 13, 1775, *ibid.*, 43; Committee Minutes, July 21, 1775, *ibid.*, 45, 47. See also Proceedings of the Safety Committee at Wilmington, July 7, 1775, in William L. Saunders, Walter Clark, and Stephen B. Weeks, eds., *The Colonial Records of North Carolina* (Raleigh, Winston, Goldsboro, and Charlotte, 1886-1914), X, 72, hereafter cited as *N.C. Recs.*

[15]Janet Schaw, *Journal of a Lady of Quality* . . . , ed. Evangeline Walker Andrews and Charles M. Andrews (New Haven, Conn., 1921), 199.

[16]*Ibid.*, 199-200, 201.

[17]In South Carolina a Charles Town merchant, Josiah Smith, Jr., stated that "our Province at present is in a ticklish Situation, on account of our numerous Domesticks, who have been unhappily deluded by some villainous Persons into the no-

County Committee of Safety, acting on a tip from a slave informant, alerted patrollers to the possibility of an insurrection. One week later the committee ordered the patrollers to "shoot one or any number of Negroes who are armed and doth not willingly surrender their arms," and gave them "Discretionary Power, to shoot any Number of Negroes above four, who are off their Masters Plantations, and will not submit." The insurrection was termed a "deep laid Horrid Tragick Plan laid for destroying the inhabitants of this province without respect of persons, age or sex." A posse of some one hundred men apprehended the "suspected heads" of the plot until over forty blacks had been jailed. The movers behind the scheme were said to be a white sea captain and "Merrick, a negro man slave who formerly Belonged to Major Clark a Pilot at Okacock but now to Capt[ain] Nath Blinn of Bath Town." For two days the safety committee sat in judgment of the suspected conspirators and ordered approximately ten (the exact number is indeterminable) to be whipped with "80 lashes each." Several others had their ears cropped, but the remainder were evidently released.[18]

No sooner had these blacks been punished than word came of other Negroes "being in arms on the line of Craven and Pitt." To meet this threat whites "posted guards upon the roads for several miles that night." Another report alleged that a band of 250 slaves had been pursued for several days "but none taken nor seen tho' they were several times fired

---

tion of being all set free on the Arrival of . . . new Gov[erno]r Lord W[illia]m Campbell[;] it is their common Talk throughout the Province, and has occasioned impertinent behaviour in many of them, insomuch that our Provincial Congress now sitting hath voted the immediate raising of Two Thousand Men Horse and food, to keep those mistaken creatures in awe, as well as to oppose any Troops that may be sent among us with coercive Orders" (Smith to James Poyas, May 18, 1775, and to George Appleby, June 16, 1775, in Josiah Smith, Jr., Letter Book, Southern Historical Collection, University of North Carolina at Chapel Hill).

[18]Proceedings of the Safety Committee in Pitt County, July 8, 1775, N.C. Recs., X, 87; John Simpson to Richard Cogdell, July 15, 1775, ibid., 94-95. Merrick's role in the plot raises interesting questions about the activities of Negro pilots at the beginning of the Revolution. Tensions between Negro and white pilots had erupted in 1773 when white watermen petitioned the legislature to deny licenses to free Negroes and slaves who were guiding vessels up and down the province's rivers "to the Great prejudice and Injury of your Petitioners." The white pilots also condemned "the Insolent and Turbilent disposition and behaviour of such Free negroes and Slaves" (To His Excellency Josiah Martin . . . , N.C. Recs., IX, 803-804). In Charles Town in Aug. 1775, Revolutionaries executed Thomas Jeremiah, a free Negro pilot and reputed loyalist who had allegedly incited slaves to revolt. On this episode see Wood, " 'Taking Care of Business,' " in Crow and Tise, eds., Southern Experience, 282-287. A Negro pilot steered Sir Peter Parker's fleet into Charles Town harbor for the British assault in June 1776 (Virginia Gazette [Purdie], July 12, 1776). Such well-traveled slaves as pilots may have been the first to join the British and offer their especially valuable skills. The relative freedom they enjoyed by performing such a critical function in the coastal trade appears to have made them a rebellious lot, particularly resistant to white control.

at." Negroes who were captured revealed that a group of slaves planned to rise on the night of July 8 and "to fall on and destroy the family where they lived, then to proceed from House to House (Burning as they went) until they arrived in the Back Country where they were to be received with open arms by a number of Persons there appointed and armed by Government for their Protection, and as a further reward they were to be settled in a free government of their own." Unlike the purported plot in Wilmington, the Tar River conspiracy seems to have been a genuine threat. The chairman of the Pitt County safety committee noted that "in disarming the negroes we found considerable ammunition."[19]

Violence between master and slave was only one measure of the tensions afflicting southern society. Defection to the British was a powerful political statement in itself, and those slaves who chose this course vastly outnumbered those who took up arms. In North Carolina numerous slaves from as far inland as 150 miles escaped to the British fleet as soon as the warships dropped anchor off the mouth of the Cape Fear River in March 1776. Captain George Martin, under Sir Henry Clinton's command, organized the runaways into a company of Black Pioneers, support troops who relieved British soldiers of such onerous duties as building fortifications, laundering clothes, cooking, and managing horses and wagons. The Negro unit, numbering fifty-four at the outset, provided valuable intelligence on the roads and waterways of North Carolina, South Carolina, and Georgia. One ex-slave, for example, was from Town Creek, North Carolina, and knew the road as far as Cross Creek (present-day Fayetteville) "and above that the road from Virg[inia] to Charlestown." Another worked on the Wilmington ferry and was familiar with the road as far north as New Bern and as far south as Georgia. One runaway, named River, had fled from Charles Town. His owner was Arthur Middleton, who would soon sign the Declaration of Independence for South Carolina.[20] River had already declared his own independence.

The admiralty muster rolls of the ships off Cape Fear in the spring of 1776 frequently recorded the names of Negroes who "deserted from the Rebels" or "fled for Protection." H.M.S. *Scorpion*, for instance, listed thirty-six defectors on March 3, 1776. At least eleven and probably twelve women were among this group. Fifteen of these blacks, including one woman, joined Sir Peter Parker's fleet on May 21 for service in the Royal Navy.[21] Some of these runaways may have been refugees from a grisly

---

[19]Simpson to Cogdell, July 15, 1775, *N.C. Recs.*, X, 94-95.

[20]"List of the Names of the Negroes belonging to Capt. Martin's Company, who they belonged to and the respective places they lived at," copy from the Sir Henry Clinton Papers, Clements Library, University of Michigan–Ann Arbor, held by the N.C. St. Arch.

[21]North Carolina Colonial Records Project, British Records Collection, Adm. 36/8377, N.C. St. Arch. Several black refugees who boarded H.M.S. *St. Lawrence* in Apr. 1776 later joined the British army at Staten Island in New York (*ibid.*, Adm. 36/8434).

mission that South Carolina Revolutionaries had conducted against Sullivan's Island in Charles Town harbor in December 1775. Many slaves had fled to the island, and the Council of Safety ordered William Moultrie to destroy their encampment. Under cover of darkness Moultrie and fifty or sixty raiders "early in the Morning sett Fire to the Pest house, took some Negroes & Sailors Prisoners, killed 50 of the former that would not be taken, and unfortunately lost near 20 that were unseen by them till taken off the Beach by the Men Warrs Boats."[22]

Slaves defected from tories as well as from whigs. Lieutenant Isaac DuBois, submitting a loyalist claim for compensation after the war, declared that his slave London, a baker, had "joined the Kings Troops at Cape Fear in North Carolina, was taken into the Service by Order of Sir Henry Clinton, and inrolled in a Company of Black Pioneers under the command of Captain George Martin, by which Service the said Slave became intitled to his Freedom."[23] Similarly, John Provey, a free black, evidently had no trouble deciding which side proffered the best hope of freedom. He gave up his small North Carolina farm "at the Commencement of the late unfortunate Troubles in North America" and "took the first Opportunity of joining His Majesty's troops under the Command of Sir Henry Clinton at Cape Fear, leaving all his Property behind him, and remained with the Army till its arrival at New York in 1776, when he was regularly Inlisted into a Company stiled the Black Pioneers, with which he bore arms until the End of the War."[24]

Throughout the war, blacks capitalized on the unsettled conditions brought on by civil strife, roving armies, and the weakened mechanisms of control to seek their freedom. Wherever the British army marched, slaves followed. What had been a trickle of runaways in 1775-1776 became a flood after the British inaugurated their southern offensive in late 1778. Charles Stedman, Cornwallis's commissary, recalled simply that "the negroes in general followed the British army." Whitmel Hill, one of North Carolina's largest slave owners and a leading Revolutionary, excoriated the British for "carrying off large droves of Slaves," but blacks needed no encouragement from the redcoats to flee their masters. Despite misgivings on Clinton's part, Cornwallis was forced to devise careful plans to utilize the bonanza of manpower available to him. In 1780 he appointed John Cruden, a Wilmington loyalist and merchant, commissioner of sequestered estates in South Carolina and subsequently in North Carolina. Cruden was eventually responsible for over 5,000 blacks on an estimated 400

[22]Josiah Smith, Jr., to James Poyas, Jan. 10, 1776, in Josiah Smith, Jr., Letter Book; "Journal of the Council of Safety," Dec. 7, 9, 10, 1775, South Carolina Historical Society, *Collections*, III (Charleston [1859]), 64-65, 73, 75. Smith reported that the *Scorpion*, cruising the coastal waters with North Carolina royal Gov. Josiah Martin in Jan. 1776, had on board "Forty of our Negros." These may have been survivors of the Sullivan's Island raid.
[23]Loyalist Claim by Isaac DuBois, 1789, Brit. Recs. Coll., A.O. 12/73.
[24]Loyalist Claim by John Provey, 1784, *ibid.*, A.O. 13/123.

whig plantations, where provisions for the British army were to be grown.[25]

Many runaway slaves accompanied Cornwallis's army as it drove through North Carolina. The British general turned these camp followers into an army of foragers despite "great Complaints . . . of Negroes Stragling from the Line of March, plund[e]r[in]g & Using Violence to the Inhabitants[.] It is Lord Cornwallis possitive Orders that no Negroe shall be Suffred to Carry Arms on any pretence." In time he ordered an end to the "Shameful Marauding" and "Scandalous Crimes" of his Negro legions, but he never ceased using them.[26]

A stronger image of social revolution could hardly have existed in the South than a band of black foragers swooping down on a small farm and stripping it of foodstuffs and livestock. Some fear-struck North Carolina slaveholders fled to Virginia "with their Negroes and Effects."[27] Black Carolinians, meanwhile, closely observed the progress of the British army, hung on rumors, generated a few themselves, and waited for the right moment to bolt for freedom. Mrs. Jean Blair, who had moved her household inland from Edenton to Windsor as the war had drawn closer, wrote in January 1781 that "the Negroes bring Strange storys. They say people are getting ready to run again and the English are to be in Edenton by Saturday." Once Cornwallis came near, the flight began. "All my Brothers Negroes at Booth except two fellows are determined to go to them, even old Affra," Mrs. Blair sadly conceded. "W[hitmel] Hill lost twenty in two nights." Mrs. Blair also feared the black foragers. "It is said they have no Arms," she declared, "but what they find in the houses they plunder. When they applyed for arms they were told they had no occasion for any as they were not to go any place where any number of Rebels were collected. It is said there are two thousand of them out in different Partys."[28] Another slaveholder reported the loss of "60 prime slaves," while one

[25]Stedman, The History Of The Origin, Progress, And Termination Of The American War, II (London, 1794), 217n.; N.C. Recs., XIV, 2. Lt. Col. Hardy Murfree informed North Carolina republican Gov. Abner Nash in 1780 that "a great many Negroes goes to the Enemy" (Murfree to Nash, Nov. 1, 1780, ibid., XV, 138). On Cruden's activities see Loyalist Claim by James Cruden (brother of the late John Cruden), 1788, Brit. Recs. Coll., A.O. 12/37, A.O. 13/28; Franklin and Mary Wickwire, Cornwallis: The American Adventure (Boston, 1970), 142-143; and Sylvia R. Frey, "The British and the Black: A New Perspective," The Historian, XXXVIII (1976), 229-230, 232.

[26]A. R. Newsome, ed., "A British Orderly Book, 1780-1781," N.C. Hist. Rev., LX (1932), 276, 280, 287, 296, 297, 370, quotation on p. 296.

[27]Turnbull to Lord Rawdon, Oct. 23, 1780, Cornwallis Papers, P.R.O. 30/11/3, 263-264, Library of Congress.

[28]Jean Blair to Helen Blair, Jan. 4, 1781, in Higginbotham, ed., Iredell Papers, II, 203; Blair to Hannah Iredell, May 10, 19, June 5, 1781, ibid., 239, 245, 257; Blair to James Iredell, July 21, 1781, ibid., 266.

whig predicted that if Cornwallis could arm them, he could raise an Army of "500 Negroes" in Wilmington alone.[29]

The chaos of the war forced Afro-Americans to make difficult decisions. William Hooper identified the personal conflicts, created by the war, that made one slave a rebel and another a loyal servant. During the British evacuation of Wilmington in November 1781, three of Hooper's bondsmen went "off with the British"; another was seized by the patriot militia; and five others died of smallpox. His house servant John, however, resisted British bribes. He was offered everything—clothes, money, freedom—"to attach him to the service of the British. . . . He pretended to acquiesce, and affected a perfect satisfaction at this change of situation; but in the evening of the day after Mrs. Hooper left the town, he stole through the British sentries, and without a pass, accompanied by a wench of Mrs. Allen's, he followed Mrs. Hooper seventy miles on foot, and overtook her, to the great joy of himself and my family." John's sister Lavinia "pursued a different conduct. She went on board the fleet after the evacuation of the town, and much against her will was forced ashore by some of my friends and returned to me."[30]

Lavinia's actions symbolized Afro-Americans' rising expectations, which were swelled by the war. Her freedom ship had sailed away, but the desire for freedom burned hotter than ever among slaves who, like her, stayed behind. The Revolution was a great liberating experience for thousands of slaves. Contemporaries estimated that the South lost as many as 55,000 bondsmen. Many evacuated with the British or were emancipated. Others simply attempted to pass as free blacks.[31] But the whites who forced Lavinia to return to bondage also symbolized an inescapable truth about postwar southern society: the white community would not give up slavery. Thus the racial conflict that the tumultuous events of 1775 had sharpened did not subside in the war's aftermath but deepened as the opposing interests of blacks and whites collided.

The South's weakened social structure after the war made the region fertile ground for racial conflict. Free blacks were no longer predominantly light-skinned mulattoes, and this change made caste distinctions based on color difficult to enforce. Slaves had learned during the war that collective action, particularly defection to the British, offered the chance for freedom. In postwar North Carolina, collective resistance to slavery became more prevalent and purposive. Bands of runaways in the

[29]Nathan Bryan to Gov. Thomas Burke, Sept. 6, 1781, *N.C. Recs.*, XV, 634-635; William Caswell to Burke, Sept. 4, 1781, *ibid.*, XXII, 593. See also Loyalist Claim by Samuel Marshall, 1789, Brit. Recs. Coll., A.O. 12/74.

[30]Hooper to James Iredell, Feb. 17, 1782, in Higginbotham, ed., *Iredell Papers*, II, 328, 329.

[31]Historian David Ramsay estimated that South Carolina alone lost 25,000 slaves in the Revolution (*Ramsay's History of South Carolina, from its First Settlement*

Great Dismal Swamp or near towns such as New Bern and Wilmington had occasionally sent tremors through colonial North Carolina, to be sure, but those rebels were often African newcomers, unlikely candidates to organize a full-scale slave revolt. They had been content to remain isolated and insulated in their lowland fastnesses.[32] Rebel slaves after the war had decidedly different objectives. At the same time whites had to contend with a bewildering maze of social conditions in which slaves agitated for freedom, free blacks proliferated, and troublesome dissenters raised questions about slavery and its humanity. This instability fostered deep anxieties, social stress, and mounting tensions.

Among those North Carolinians who sought to ameliorate slavery was William Hooper. Born and educated in Boston, Hooper had led a successful fight in 1773-1774 to pass a law that made it a crime to kill a slave.[33] In 1784 he introduced a bill in the state's House of Commons that might be termed a "slave bill of rights." The bill passed one reading in the lower house before being sent to the Senate, where it was evidently buried. It would have provided slaves with limited protection from arbitrary treatment by their masters. Hooper's bill stated that slaves constituted "a very large part of the property of the good Citizens of this State" and were needed as a labor force. Thus for reasons of "humanity and the policy and interest" of the slave owners, slavery must be rendered "as little burdensome and distressing as possible." Declaring that "justice should be duly administered to those of our fellow Creatures who are consigned to

---

in 1670 to the year 1808, I [Newberry, 1858], 178-179, 270-272). See also Mary Beth Norton, " 'What an Alarming Crisis Is This': Southern Women and the American Revolution," in Crow and Tise, eds., *Southern Experience*, 215, 223, 233, n. 38, and Ira Berlin, *Slaves without Masters: The Free Negro in the Antebellum South* (New York, 1974), 15-50.

[32]During the constitutional convention of 1835, William Gaston, justice of the North Carolina Supreme Court, noted "that previous to the Revolution there were scarcely any emancipated Slaves in this State; and that the few free men of color that were here at that time, were chiefly Mulattoes, the children of white women, and therefore unquestionably free, because their mothers were so" (*Proceedings and Debates of the Convention of North-Carolina Called to Amend the Constitution of the State* [Raleigh, 1836], 351). Ira Berlin substantiates the large number of mixed bloods among free Negroes (as early as 1755 in Maryland) in *Slaves without Masters*, 3-4, 6-7, 177-181. Marvin L. Michael Kay and Lorin Lee Cary in their paper "Albion's Fatal Tree Transplanted: Crime, Society, and Slavery in North Carolina, 1748-1772," delivered at the 1978 meeting of the Southern Historical Association in St. Louis, Mo., estimate that at least 25% of the runaways they surveyed were "unmistakably African." See also Jeffrey J. Crow, *The Black Experience in Revolutionary North Carolina* (Raleigh, 1977), 41-45, and Alan D. Watson, "Impulse toward Independence: Resistance and Rebellion among North Carolina Slaves, 1750-1775," *Journal of Negro History*, LXIII (1978), 317-328.

[33]Crow, *Black Experience in North Carolina*, 25; Don Higginbotham and William S. Price, Jr., "Was It Murder for a White Man to Kill a Slave?: Chief Justice Martin Howard Condemns North Carolina's Peculiar Institution," *WMQ*, 3d Ser., XXXVI (1979), 593-601.

such servitude," the bill enjoined slaveholders to provide "wholesome and competent diet and Cloathing," and limited whippings to twenty-five lashes, since "immoderate correction is a dishonour to a free Country and a disgrace to humanity." It also promised slaves the same punishments as whites. For example, a slave who committed a crime for which a white man would hang could not be put to death in any other manner.[34]

The humanitarian movement to ameliorate slavery, like Hooper's bill, made little headway in North Carolina. North Carolina Quakers took a determined stand against slavery, but their efforts were only modestly successful. In 1775 the Standing Committee of the Yearly Meeting in North Carolina debated the issue of slavery and the following year advised Friends "to Cleanse their Hands" of slave ownership. By 1777 Quakers had manumitted at least forty slaves in North Carolina, prompting a troubled General Assembly to enact a law to "prevent domestic Insurrections." The lawmakers denounced the "evil and pernicious Practice of freeing Slaves .... at this alarming and critical Time." They authorized county sheriffs to apprehend and auction off any slaves freed illegally. This same law was reenacted in 1788 and again in 1796.[35]

During the war and until the nineteenth century sheriffs rounded up recently freed blacks and sold them at public auctions. Quaker attorneys attempted various defenses to prevent reenslavement. They argued, for example, that the 1777 statute was an ex post facto law. When that failed, they turned to the natural rights philosophy that had been so central to the Revolution's ideology. A lawyer defending the Negro Judy before the Perquimans County court during the 1790s asserted that "the taking, apprehending and dragging of Negroes (as confessedly done in the Case) living quietly and peaceably with their masters from their houses, is arbitrary and illegal." He contended that such action was "unjust & incompatible with liberty," that it violated the Bill of Rights, and that "all

<hr/>

[34]Legislative Papers (House of Commons), Box 52, May-June 1784, N.C. St. Arch.; Journal of the House of Commons, May 1784, *N.C. Recs.*, XIX, 637. For other forms of social control and punishment of blacks, including castration and burning, see Marvin L. Michael Kay and Lorin Lee Cary, " 'The Planters Suffer Little or Nothing': North Carolina Compensations for Executed Slaves, 1748-1772," *Science and Society*, XL (1976), 288-306, and Crow, *Black Experience in Revolutionary North Carolina*, 19-33, 38-39.
[35]Manuscript Minutes of the Yearly Meeting of Friends in North Carolina, Quaker Collection, I, 132, Guilford College Library, quoted in Peter Kent Opper, "North Carolina Quakers: Reluctant Slaveholders," *N.C. Hist. Rev.*, LII (1975), 37; Laws of North Carolina, 1777, *N.C. Recs.*, XXIV, 14-15, quotations on p. 14; David Brion Davis, *The Problem of Slavery in the Age of Revolution, 1770-1823* (Ithaca, N.Y., 1975), 198-199. Documents illustrating Quaker antislavery convictions are printed in Robert M. Calhoon, *Religion and the American Revolution in North Carolina* (Raleigh, 1976), 41-49.
[36]Case of Negro Judy, n.d., Perquimans County Slave Papers, 1759-1864, N.C. St. Arch. See also Case of Harry, Dinah, and Patt, Apr. 5, 1785, and Account of sales of Negroes, Oct. 1788, *ibid.*

Men possess certain natural & unalienable rights to life Liberty & property," even Negroes.[36]

The Quakers' activities greatly alarmed other whites and magnified their
anxieties. In 1795 a Pasquotank County grand jury bitterly chided the
Friends for promoting slave unrest and endangering the white populace.
The grand jurors asserted that Quakers were subjecting the state to "great
perril." The "idea of emancipation, amonghts Slaves is publicly held out to
them, and incouraged by the Conduct of the Quakers," the jurors charged.
"The Minds of the Slaves, are not only greatly corrupted and allienated
from the Service of Their Masters . . . But runaways are protected, harbored, and incourag'd by them—Arsons are even committed, without a
possibility of discovery." The Quakers persisted in this behavior, the jurors complained, despite the "miserable havock and massacres which have
taken place in the West Indies, in consequence of emancipation; Knowing
the opinion of the Northern States; of the many thousand Slaves around
them; and of the infatuated enthusiasm of Men calling themselves religious."[37]

The white backlash against manumission—invariably led by slaveholders—overwhelmed the humanitarian gestures of the Quakers and other freethinkers. This opposition manifested itself in several ways. When a
Nova Scotian ship, manned by Negro seamen and auxiliaries, sailed into
New Bern in 1785, the legislature urged the governor to seize the black
crew as the property of United States citizens. The blacks, nine men and
two women, had allegedly left with the British at the end of the war. Their
freedom was short-lived, for Governor Richard Caswell complied with the
lawmakers' request.[38] Similarly, the General Assembly overturned the
will of Mark Newby, who had intended that his slaves be freed at age
twenty-one. Only six of the assemblymen protested the reenslavement of
the blacks as "tyrannic and unconstitutional."[39] By 1790 North Carolina
was the only southern state in which manumission was not the prerogative
of the slave owner. A 1741 act stipulated that only the county court could
free slaves after determining their worthiness by virtue of "meritorious
services."[40]

Why was this so? North Carolina had a reputation during the eighteenth
century as a haven for fugitive slaves, and Tar Heel slaveholders were not
eager to embellish that reputation. The Great Dismal Swamp, trackless
and virtually impenetrable, in particular served as a sanctuary for runa-

[37]Grand Jury Presentment, Dec. 1795, Pasquotank County Slave Papers, 1734-
1860, N.C. St. Arch.
[38]Jour. House of Commons, Dec. 1785, N.C. Recs., XVII, 385, 389; Caswell to
John C. Bryan, Dec. 30, 1785, Mar. 12, May 24, 27, June 23, July 10, 1786, ibid.,
595-596, XVIII, 571-572, 623, 625, 663, 680-681; Caswell to John W. Stanley,
May 27, 1786, ibid., XVIII, 624-625; Caswell to Abner Neale, June 23, 1786,
ibid., 662-663.
[39]Journal of the State Senate, Nov. 1790, ibid., XXI, 762-763; Jour. House of
Commons, Dec. 1790, ibid., 1004, 1019-1020, quotation on p. 1020.
[40]Berlin, Slaves without Masters, 29.

ways.[41] North Carolina's repressive laws reflected the unstable conditions
that alarmed slaveholders; easing manumission would only flood society
with more free blacks. Because skin color was no longer strictly emblem-
atic of caste, the General Assembly in 1785 finally resorted to badges to
distinguish free Negroes from slaves. Henceforth, free blacks in Wilmington, Washington, Edenton, and Fayetteville had to register with the town
commissioners, pay a fee, and wear a "badge of cloth . . . to be fixed on the
left shoulder, and to have thereon wrought in legible capital letters the
word FREE."[42]

In spite of such repressive strictures the white community could not
maintain absolute control over the bondsmen's lives or eradicate their
hopes for freedom. Black assertiveness in postwar North Carolina revealed a greater collective consciousness among slaves and an increasing
willingness to use violence to liberate not only individuals but groups of
slaves. In 1783 the Chowan County court tried the slave Grainge for the
"atrocious Crime of endeavouring to Stir up Slaves for the Diabolical purpose of Murdering their Masters and Mistresses." He was found guilty and
sentenced to "have Both his Ears Cut off & have two hundred Stripes well
Laid on his Bare Back." William Bryan of Craven County received £50
from the General Assembly in 1783 "for a negro man slave killed in suppressing of Rebel Slaves." Two years later the Chowan County court
found the Negro Titus guilty of "breaking open the Public Goal (sic) . . . and
letting out several [black?] Prisoners therein Confined."[43]
Fears of collective resistance to slavery proliferated during the 1790s
after news arrived of major slave revolts in the West Indies, especially
Saint Domingue. A report from New Bern in 1792 asserted that "the
negroes in this town and neighbourhood, have stirred a rumour of their
having in contemplation to rise against their masters and to procure themselves their liberty; the inhabitants have been alarmed and keep a strict
watch to prevent their procuring arms; should it become serious, which I
don't think, the worst that could befal us, would be their setting the town
on fire. It is very absurd of the blacks, to suppose they could accomplish
their views." In the summer of 1795 Wilmington suffered sporadic attacks
by a "number of runaway Negroes, who in the daytime secrete themselves
in the swamps and woods" and at night commit "various depredations on
the neighboring plantations." They fatally ambushed at least one white
overseer and wounded another. Posses eventually killed five of the rene-

[41]Mullin, *Flight and Rebellion*, 110-112.
[42]Laws of North Carolina, 1785, *N.C. Recs.*, XXIV, 725-730, quotation on p.
728. Statutes should not be mistaken for actual behavior; they reflected instead the
type of ideal behavior the legislators hoped to elicit. In effect, laws were a response
to a perceived social disorder. On this point see Jordan, *White over Black*, 587-588,
and William M. Wiecek, "The Statutory Law of Slavery and Race in the Thirteen
Mainland Colonies of British America," *WMQ*, 3d Ser., XXXIV (1977), 258-280.
[43]The Chowan County court cases are in C.R.X. (County Records X), Box 4,
N.C. St. Arch. For Bryan's compensation claim see *N.C. Recs.*, XIX, 258.

gades, including their leader, the "General of the Swamps."[44] In Bertie County in 1798 three black men were accused of heading a conspiracy of 150 slaves, armed with "Guns, clubs, Swords, and Knives." Evidently, the blacks "did attack, pursue, knock down and lay prostrate the patrollers," but the only casualty was a horse. Consequently, the three leaders were convicted of a high misdemeanor against "the laws and dignity of the state," instead of rebellion, and were punished with thirty-nine lashes and cropped ears.[45]

The fear that slave insurrections might spread from the West Indies to North America enveloped the South. In 1795, North Carolina barred the entry of all West Indian slaves over the age of fifteen, traditionally the age at which white boys were considered fit for military service. Later that year, when French refugees fleeing the racial wars of the Caribbean sailed into Wilmington with thirty or forty of their slaves, residents prevented their landing for fear that the blacks might incite revolt. In 1798, Governor Samuel Ashe went so far as to issue a proclamation that urged citizens to block the landing of any Negroes from the islands, slave or free. Ashe called on all civil and military officers on the coast to enforce the slave trade laws stringently.[46]

The conflict between master and slave, the anxieties of whites caused by slave restiveness, the frustration of blacks as avenues to freedom were continually blocked, and the crisscrossing social tensions among various groups, white and black, in post-Revolutionary North Carolina society culminated in a major slave insurrection scare in 1802. This event came in the midst of the Second Great Awakening and in the wake of the Gabriel Prosser revolt in Richmond two years earlier. Quakers continued to agitate for emancipation and flout the manumission laws, and the bitter presidential campaign of 1800 had just been fought. These conflicts fragmented the white community severely, and slaves displayed acumen and shrewd political judgment in seizing such a moment to revolt.[47]

[44]The New Bern situation was reported in the *Boston Gazette, and the Country Journal*, Sept. 3, 1792, and reports about Wilmington in 1795 appeared in the *Wilmington Chronicle: and North-Carolina Weekly Advertiser*, July 3, 10, 17, 1795, and the *City Gazette & Daily Advertiser* (Charleston), July 18, 23, 1795, all as quoted in Herbert Aptheker, *American Negro Slave Revolts* (New York, 1943), 213, 217.

[45]Trial of three Negro men, May 31, 1798, Bertie County Slave Papers, 1744-1815, N.C. St. Arch.

[46]P. Manyeon to Benjamin Smith, Dec. 2, 1795, Slavery Papers, Miscellaneous Collection, N.C. St. Arch.; R. H. Taylor, "Slave Conspiracies in North Carolina," *N.C. Hist. Rev.*, V (1928), 25. A petition from citizens of Wilmington to Congress in 1803 precipitated a national debate on the importation of blacks and mulattoes from the West Indies and the passage of legislation to counter the menace (Jordan, *White over Black*, 382-383).

[47]Particularly trenchant discussions linking social tensions among whites with slave rebelliousness are Jordan, *White over Black*, 115-121; Wood, " 'Taking Care of Business,' " in Crow and Tise, eds., *Southern Experience*, 268-293; and Eugene

The Great Revival in particular produced new tensions in the social order. The interracial camp meetings, the democratic appeal of the Methodist and Baptist services, the abolitionist impulse of Methodism in its fledgling years, and the phenomenon of black preachers exhorting racially mixed congregations differed sharply from previous modes of religious expression and custom.[48] These conditions helped nurture the flowering of the black church, which quickly became a locus of collective resistance to slavery. As an institution independent of the ruling elite, the black church attracted the loyalty of an oppressed group, selected its own leadership, and—to the extent that it provided a structure for social solidarity—served a fundamental political purpose in challenging the elite's power.[49]

When translated into political terms, black religion and the egalitarianism of evangelical Protestantism had explosive results. Indeed, the fear that conversion might foster rebellion greatly exercised the slaveholding South in the eighteenth century.[50] After Prosser's revolt in 1800, St. George Tucker, one of the nation's most perceptive opponents of slavery, concluded that the "love of freedom" among Negroes was ineluctable. "Fanaticism is spreading fast among the Negroes of this country," he cautioned, "and may form in time the connecting link between the black religionists and the white. . . . It certainly would not be a novelty, in the history of the world, if Religion were made to sanctify plots and conspiracies."[51] The specter of black jacobinism infused with religion, raised by Federalists against Jeffersonians in 1800, led a Virginian to observe after

---

D. Genovese, *Roll, Jordan, Roll: The World the Slaves Made* (New York, 1974), 587-597. See also David Barry Gaspar, "The Antigua Slave Conspiracy of 1736: A Case Study of the Origins of Collective Resistance," *WMQ*, 3d Ser., XXXV (1978), 308-323.

[48]Rhys Isaac, "Evangelical Revolt: The Nature of the Baptists' Challenge to the Traditional Order in Virginia, 1765 to 1775," *WMQ*, 3d Ser., XXXI (1974), 345-368; Donald G. Mathews, *Slavery and Methodism: A Chapter in American Morality, 1780-1845* (Princeton, N.J., 1965), 3-29; W. Harrison Daniel, "Virginia Baptists and the Negro in the Early Republic," *Virginia Magazine of History and Biography*, LXXX (1972), 60-69.

[49]Donald G. Mathews, *Religion in the Old South* (Chicago, 1977), 185-236; Vincent Harding, "Religion and Resistance among Antebellum Negroes, 1800-1860," in August Meier and Elliott Rudwick, eds., *The Making of Black America: Essays in Negro Life and History*, I (New York, 1969), 179-197.

[50]During the first Great Awakening, George Whitefield was blamed for inciting Negro plots in places such as New York and South Carolina (Jordan, *White over Black*, 181). Landon Carter commented that his slaves had "grown so much worse" since the quickening of the religious pulse (Jack P. Greene, ed., *The Diary of Colonel Landon Carter Sabine Hall, 1752-1778*, I [Charlottesville, Va., 1965], 378).

[51][St. George Tucker], *Letter To A Member Of The General Assembly Of Virginia On The Subject Of The Late Conspiracy Of The Slaves; With A Proposal For Their Colonization* (Baltimore, 1801), 11-12.

the near-cataclysm at Richmond, "This doctrine, in this country, and in every country like this (as the horrors of St. Domingo have already proved) cannot fail of producing either a general insurrection, or a general emancipation. It has been most imprudently propagated at many of our tables, while our servants have been standing behind our chairs, for several years past. It has been, and is still preached by the Methodists, Baptists and others, from the pulpit, without any sort of reserve. What else then could we expect than what has happened?"[52]

Beginning in Kentucky, the Great Revival swept eastward and arrived in North Carolina in the fall of 1801.[53] By early 1802 blacks and whites were attending camp meetings, where impassioned religious services often induced hysterical responses. The Reverend Samuel McCorkle described how "as if by an electric shock, a large number in every direction, men, women, children, white and black, fell and cried for mercy."[54] But more than religious conversion was taking place at these gatherings. The revival offered an opportunity for, and was an instrument of, Negro rebellion. At the same time that religion stirred the souls of North Carolinians, not coincidentally rumors of a black slave insurrection spread through the eastern counties of Camden, Bertie, Currituck, Martin, Halifax, Pasquotank, Hertford, Washington, and Warren.

Former Governor William R. Davie raised the initial alarm in February 1802. Writing to Governor Benjamin Williams from Halifax County, Davie reported a suspected Negro plot originating in Southampton County, Virginia, and extending down the Roanoke River valley into North Carolina. A Negro organizing the revolt had allegedly written a letter addressed to the "Representative of the Roanoak Company." In language reminiscent of both the political and spiritual revolutions of the eighteenth century this letter stated that once the "conflagration" began, whites would "acknowledge liberty & equality" and be "glad to purchase their lives at any price." Whites must learn that "the breath of liberty is as free for us as for themselves." The letter was signed a "true friend in liberty or death." Davie nervously compared the situation with Saint Domingue, where the murder of several thousand whites had stained "the whole Colony."[55]

[52]*Virginia Herald* (Fredericksburg), Sept. 23, 1800, as quoted in Jordan, *White over Black,* 396.

[53]The standard work on this social phenomenon, though it does not pay much attention to Afro-Americans, is John B. Boles, *The Great Revival, 1787-1805: The Origins of the Southern Evangelical Mind* (Lexington, Ky., 1972).

[54]Samuel McCorkle to John Langdon, Jan. 8, June 4-8, 1802, in William Henry Foote, *Sketches of North Carolina, Historical and Biographical* ... (New York, 1846), 392, 402-403.

[55]Correspondence between William R. Davie and Benajmin Williams, Feb. 1802, is in the Governor's Letter Book [Benjamin Williams], 542, 552, 556, 560, 565, N.C. St. Arch. Other correspondents in the letter book discussed rumors of slave unrest in other counties but generally discounted the existence of any plot, especially in Camden County. From Halifax County came a petition to pardon the

The fires of slave rebellion ignited not in Halifax County, however, but in an area farther down the Roanoke River, near its confluence with Albemarle Sound. As in Prosser's conspiracy, a few of the plotters in North Carolina could read and write and thus pass information and messages. They were acculturated slaves with freedom of movement that enabled them to reach numerous bondsmen on the widely scattered plantations. The interconnecting waterways of eastern North Carolina evidently made the transmission of information not only feasible but unstoppable. The insurgents used social occasions in the slave quarters—in one instance a dance or "Ball"—to map out their strategy. But at the core of the plot may have been the black preacher.

Dr. Joe, a slave preacher, apparently served the North Carolina conspiracy in much the same way that Martin Prosser, a preacher, served his brother Gabriel's plot in Richmond. In May 1802 the Pasquotank County court tried Dr. Joe for conspiring with Tom Copper "to Rebel and make insurrections." Tom Copper was a black guerrilla whose camp was hidden in the swamps near Elizabeth City. Styling himself the "General to command this county in a plot to kill the white people," Copper staged a daring raid on Elizabeth City's jail with "six stout negroes, mounted on horseback" to liberate the slaves held there on a conspiracy charge. Four of the marauders were captured, but two escaped.[56] The Pasquotank County court found Dr. Joe innocent of any complicity with Copper, but his master had to post a bond of £200 for his release plus two sureties of £250 each to guarantee his good behavior. Moreover, the court enjoined the preacher not to "Assemble or hold any Meeting, Congregation or other Assembly of Slaves or other people of Colour upon or under any pretence Whatsoever."[57]

Suspicions about the activities of Dr. Joe and other slave preachers were well founded. The black conspirators used religious meetings to plot their uprising. At one sermon the slave Charles angrily told another slave that "there were a great many whites there . . . [and] that they ought to be killed." One slaveholder, a Baptist elder, gave his slave Virginia permission "to hold a night Meeting on Monday Night," that is, a religious service, at which plans for the revolt were subsequently discussed. The slave Moses admitted that "Joe preached with a pistol in his pocket." Another slave had observed several conspirators "talking low" and "while at preaching saw [a] number of Negroes standing talking two & two during the sermon." The slave Frank, one of the ringleaders ultimately executed, had been seen at a "quarterly Meeting at Wiccacon." The conspirators

---

slave Toney, who had been convicted of plotting an insurrection. Williams pardoned him.

[56]*Raleigh Register and North-Carolina State Gazette*, June 1, 1802; Aptheker, *Slave Revolts*, 231-232.

[57]Trial of Dr. Joe, May 22, 1802, Pasquotank County Court Minutes, 1799-1802, N.C. St. Arch.; Calhoon, *Religion and the Revolution*, 66-68.

planned to coordinate the rising on June 10, 1802, to coincide with the quarterly meetings of several Kehukee Baptist associations, when the whites would be most vulnerable. One insurgent stated succinctly that "they were to begin at the Quarterly Meeting."[58]

Accumulated tensions, unbearable grievances and frustrations, and the example of Prosser's revolt helped propel these blacks toward rebellion. A few conspirators apparently associated the plot with a class revolt, for they anticipated reinforcements from Tuscarora Indians and from "a number of poor people (white which they expected would Join them)." Caesar, one of the leaders or "captains" of the cabal, told Moses that he foresaw "a Warm Winter, a dry Spring & a Bloody Summer, & that he expected the Negroes were going to Rise." Dave, another leader ultimately executed, confided to Sam that he was "very tired & weary" because "the Damn'd White people plagued him so bad they ought all to be killed & shall . . . if he could get a great many to join him." Peter "had fallen out with his overseer & had been whipped & Damn him he ought to be killed & all the rest." Peter had also attended "a logg roling & the Overseer had been whipping two of the negroes," which reinforced his determination to re- volt. Sam told Harry "that them guns we heard was in Virginia & that the Negroes was then fighting the White people." Indeed, Dave insisted that the conspirators "could get encouragement from Virginia. The head negroes in Virginia lives about Richmond." These men spoke not as solitary rebels who sought personal liberty but as individuals who identified with an oppressed group and were willing to use violence against the system that enslaved them.

In May, patrollers in Bertie County had been unable to uncover any evidence of the slave plot. Then on June 2, 1802, while searching Negro houses in Colerain, they found a small piece of paper that listed the names of fourteen black men. The Negro woman in whose house the paper was discovered confessed that the slave Fed had left it with her that morning and said that he was carrying it from Sumner's Frank to Brown's King. The communication began, *"Captain Frank Sumner is to command* (and then names of the men and the 10th of June was the time) *you are to get as many men as you can—To Capt. King, Brown, &c."*[59] During the ensuing week the Negroes named in the letter were apprehended and confined at Windsor. On June 10 the Bertie County court convened. The court consisted of some of the county's most prominent slaveholders, including United States Senator David Stone. The justices grimly undertook the business of trying the suspected conspirators. Six plotters, including Sumner's Frank

---

[58]The sources for this plot, especially depositions, are too numerous to cite for each quotation. The information, unless specified, has been culled from the Slavery Papers, Misc. Coll.; Perquimans County Slave Papers, 1759-1864; Bertie County Slave Papers, 1744-1815; and the *Raleigh Reg.*, May-Aug. 1802. The bulk of the depositions relating to the slave plot is in the Bertie County Slave Papers.

[59]*Raleigh Reg.*, July 6, 1802. See also Guion Griffis Johnson, *Ante-Bellum North Carolina: A Social History* (Chapel Hill, 1937), 510-513.

and Senator Stone's Bob, were hanged with ruthless dispatch. Though the court prescribed the punishments and performed the executions, the whole process had the aspect of lynch law. The Bertie court hanged eleven blacks, deported six more who offered testimony, and whipped and cropped perhaps two dozen others.

The Colerain letter had evidently circulated through several northeastern counties. The Negro Dennis, owned by Thomas Fitts of Bertie County, confessed that Jacob of Perquimans County "gave a letter to Mr. Browns Frank[.] They all knew of This letter, he saw Jacob of Edenton [Chowan County] & he told his depon[en]t he Gave a letter to Frank, to be Carried to King who was to Carry it to Dave, Mr. Browns Hestor read the letter, & Said to Dave, Mr. Fitt & Mr. Brown was To be first Killed, as they were Supposed to be the head Men on The river."[60] The imprisoned slaves testified that the plot had been in the works for several weeks, and its leaders had planned to rendezvous in Plymouth the night of June 9. There "they expected to receive considerable reinforcements from up and down the [Roanoke] river. . . . Some were offered county money to join, other[s] clothes and arms to go to Virginia to help the blacks there to fight the whites." In Washington County on the south side of Albemarle Sound a "rumpus" resulted in the shooting of "6 or 7 blacks . . . on their way to Williamston," also on the Roanoke. As reconstructed by white interrogators, the plot included caching guns and ammunition in the swamps, and crafting other weapons such as clubs with nails driven through them. On the night of the uprising the insurgents were to form into companies under their captains, "go to every man's house, set fire to it, kill the men and boys over 6 or 7 years of age; the women over a certain age, both black and white were to share the same fate; the young and handsome of the whites they were to keep for themselves, and the young ones of their own colour were to be spared for waiters." The slave Bob explained that the rebels had intended to divide up the lands among themselves. Moses, who asserted "he would be no mans Slave," had pledged to take one particular white girl as his "wife." Thomas Blount, a former congressman and leading slaveholder, understood "that when all the white men were killed the Black men were to take their places, have their wives, &c. &c."[61]

One could easily overstate the insurgents' plans to take white wives, to murder all women (black and white) over a certain age, and to spare a few black women as servants. White fantasies about Negro sexuality were of-

[60]A letter, supposedly written by a Negro conspirator, is in the Bertie County Slave Papers, 1744-1815. The letter, though badly faded, is obviously the one cited in the *Raleigh Reg.*'s account of the insurrection.
[61]*Raleigh Reg.*, June 22, July 27, 1802; Charles Pettigrew to Ebenezer Pettigrew, June 21, 1802, in Sarah McCulloh Lemmon, ed., *The Pettigrew Papers*, I (Raleigh, N.C., 1971), 287-288; Thomas Blount to John Gray Blount, June 28, 1802, in William H. Masterson, ed., *The John Gray Blount Papers*, III (Raleigh, N.C., 1965), 516-517. See also Nathaniel Blount to Charles Pettigrew, May 4, 1802, in Lemmon, ed., *Pettigrew Papers*, I, 283.

ten at the center of insurrection scares. The image of sexually aggressive Negroes reflected white anxiety and guilt about the treatment of black women. In times of interracial crisis white men were quick to impute to others their own sexual aggressiveness. Despite numerous rumors to the contrary in North America and the West Indies throughout the eighteenth century, there is no evidence of rebel slaves seizing white women for their own use.[62] In the North Carolina plot, blacks expressly stated that they were fighting "against the white people to obtain their liberty." Moreover, black women played key roles in the conspiracy, from organizing meetings to passing messages, so it seems unlikely that they would have agreed to their own systematic extermination or reenslavement.

Even so, it is always difficult to separate black intentions from white hysteria in such situations. There is little doubt that an insurrection plot, centered in Bertie County, existed. The plot was certainly known to blacks in adjoining counties such as Hertford and Martin, but how well coordinated the conspiracy was beyond those boundaries is impossible to determine. It is clear, however, that an insurrection mania possessed whites. Besides the eleven slaves hanged in Bertie, the toll in other counties included four in Camden, two in Currituck, two in Martin, and one each in Perquimans, Hertford, Washington, Edgecombe, and Halifax. Another two dozen slaves were executed in Virginia, where a similar insurrection scare existed in 1802. By all accounts, eastern North Carolina was in an uproar during the spring and summer. The county militias were out in force, visiting plantations, keeping "nearly every negro man . . . under guard," and seizing suspected rebels (especially those who could read and write) against their masters' wishes. More than one hundred Negroes were jailed in Martin County alone. One episode illustrates particularly well the hysteria engulfing eastern North Carolina. A rumor swept Winton in Hertford County that Windsor in Bertie County had been attacked and burned by rebelling slaves. The town council dispatched a messenger to ascertain the truth of the report. On the way he met a rider from Windsor who had been sent to Winton for the same purpose.[63]

In Martin County the white hysteria that led to the incarceration of over one hundred blacks subsided as cooler heads prevailed. Dispassionate ob-

[62]Jordan, *White over Black*, 150-153; Allan Kulikoff, "The Origins of Afro-American Society in Tidewater Maryland and Virginia, 1700 to 1790," *WMQ*, 3d Ser., XXXV (1978), 239-240.

[63]*Raleigh Reg.*, July 6, 1802. Two companion papers on the North Carolina and Virginia slave insurrection scares were delivered at the 1977 meeting of the Organization of American Historians in Atlanta, Ga. Scott Strickland in "The 'Great Revival' and Insurrectionary Fears: North Carolina, 1801-1802," focused on the white community's reaction to the religious revival and its impact on race relations. Bertram Wyatt-Brown in "Slave Insurrection Scares as Southern Witchhunts: The Case of Virginia, 1802," totally discounted any revolt in the Old Dominion. Both viewed the insurrection scares as a means of solidifying the white community and setting boundaries for permissible slave behavior. See also Thomas C. Parramore, "The Great Slave Conspiracy," *The State*, XXXIX (Aug. 15, 1971), 7-10, 19.

servers like "J.R." admitted that some people had credited the wildest reports of slave insurgency while others dismissed the most sober evidence. He hinted that some planters did not want their slaves implicated in the plot for financial reasons. He also reported that Martin County magistrates kept compliant and militant slaves in separate jails. A county committee of inquiry then examined the suspects individually, beginning with the youngest. The interrogators told the younger slaves that they had been implicated and that they would receive lenient treatment if they confessed. In this way some twenty-five or thirty were questioned without the lash. However, the "old ones and chiefs amongst them, were true and faithful to their trust; not one of them would acknowledge at first that he knew anything of the plot." Tight-lipped rebels would give "no information until whiped." The coerced confessions "agreed perfectly with the evidence of the others, that never received a stroke." Ultimately, only two of the conspirators in Martin County were hanged. The others "received a very severe reprimand, and were made sensible to the folly and danger of their attempt; after which every one was chastised, more or less, according to his previous bad or good conduct, and ordered home."[64]

The fear of Negro insurgencies in the eighteenth century, as in other periods of southern history, provided the impetus for reasserting social control and unifying the white populace. In such instances, racial conflict resolved certain tensions and reestablished stability by eliminating causes of fragmentation among whites. Antagonists in one setting (politics, religion, economics) became allies in another.[65] Janet Schaw had witnessed the same phenomenon in Wilmington in 1775 when loyalists joined whigs to suppress an expected slave insurrection.

The insurrection scare of 1802 in North Carolina climaxed three decades of heightening conflict between blacks and whites. The Revolutionary War, with its severe strains and disruptive impact on society, left a legacy of unstable racial patterns in which blacks and whites struggled to define their places and roles in postwar society. Afro-Americans, buoyed by rising hopes of freedom, developed a greater cohesiveness and took collective measures to oppose the slaveholders' regime. Whites attempted to maintain their authority in the face of restive slaves, religious egalitarians, and a few slaveholders who wished to improve the slave's lot even as they perpetuated slavery. Violence between blacks and whites signaled society's internal tensions, but it also served a political function—as a form of resistance among blacks and as a means of social control among whites.

Slave rebelliousness had always carried within it the seeds of political protest, but the Revolution provided the social and ideological conditions necessary to galvanize blacks into collective resistance and to create a new

[64]A letter by "J.R." appeared in the *Raleigh Reg.*, July 27, 1802.
[65]A cogent article examining this process in another time and place is Dan T. Carter, "The Anatomy of Fear: The Christmas Day Insurrection Scare of 1865," *Jour. So. Hist.*, XLII (1976), 345-364.
[66][Tucker], *Letter . . . On The Subject Of The Late Conspiracy*, 7.

sense of community among slaves. St. George Tucker recognized this revolutionary process when he identified the difference between those slaves who ran off to the British in 1775 and those who joined Gabriel Prosser in 1800. At the beginning of the Revolution, he observed, slaves had "fought [for] freedom merely as a good; now they also claim it as a right."[66]

RESISTANCE TO SLAVERY

George M. Fredrickson and Christopher Lasch

THE ISSUES INVOLVED IN THE STUDY of "resistance" to slavery are badly in need of clarification. The problem, one would suppose, is not whether the plantation slave was happy with his lot but whether he actively resisted it. But even this initial clarification does not come easily. Too many writers have assumed that the problem of resistance consists mainly of deciding whether slaves were docile or discontented and whether their masters were cruel or kind. In this respect and in others, as Stanley Elkins noted several years ago, the discussion of slavery has locked itself into the terms of an old debate.[1] The pro-slavery stereotype of the contented slave, which was taken over without much conceptual refinement by U. B. Phillips and others, has been attacked by recent historians in language much the same as that employed by the abolitionists more than a hundred years ago, according to which slaves hated bondage and longed to be free. "That they had no understanding of freedom," Kenneth Stampp argues, ". . . is hard to believe." A few pages later, and without any intervening evidence, Stampp progresses from this cautious thought to a fullblown statement of the case for "resistance." "Slave resistance, whether bold and persistent or mild and sporadic, created for all slaveholders a serious problem of discipline." He concludes, in a burst of rhetoric, that "the record of slave resistance forms a chapter in the story of the endless struggle to give dignity to human life."[2]

It should be apparent that the traditional terms of reference, on either side of the dispute, are not sufficiently precise to serve as instruments of analysis. One of the faults of Phillips' work is his consistent failure to distinguish between cruelty and coercion. By compiling instances of the kindness and benevolence of masters, Phillips proved to his own satisfaction that slavery was a mild and permissive institution, the primary function of which was not so much to produce a marketable surplus as to ease the accommodation of the lower race into the culture of the higher. The critics of Phillips have tried to meet him on his own ground. Where he compiled lists of indul-

---

[1] Stanley Elkins, *Slavery: A Problem in American Institutional and Intellectual Life* (Chicago, 1959), Ch. I.

[2] Kenneth Stampp, *The Peculiar Institution* (New York, 1956), pp. 88, 91.

gences and benefactions, they have assembled lists of atrocities. Both methods suffer from the same defect: they attempt to solve a conceptual problem—what did slavery do to the slave—by accumulating quantitative evidence. Both methods assert that plantations conformed to one of two patterns, terror or indulgence, and then seek to prove these assertions by accumulating evidence from plantation diaries, manuals of discipline, letters and other traditional sources for the study of slavery. But for every instance of physical cruelty on the one side an enterprising historian can find an instance of indulgence on the other. The only conclusion that one can legitimately draw from this debate is that great variations in treatment existed from plantation to plantation. (But as we shall see, this conclusion, barren in itself, can be made to yield important results if one knows how to use it.)

Even if we could make valid generalizations about the severity of the regime, these statements would not automatically answer the question of whether or not widespread resistance took place. If we are to accept the testimony of Frederick Douglass, resistance was more likely to result from indulgence and rising expectations than from brutalizing severity.[3] A recent study of the geographical distribution of authentic slave revolts shows that most of them occurred in cities and in areas of slavebreeding and diversified agriculture, where, according to all accounts, the regime was more indulgent than in the productive plantation districts of the Cotton Kingdom.[4] Open resistance cannot be inferred from the extreme physical cruelty of the slave system, even if the system's cruelty could be demonstrated statistically.

II

There is the further question of what constitutes resistance. When Kenneth Stampp uses the term he means much more than open and flagrant defiance of the system. To him resistance is all noncooperation on the part of the slaves. And it cannot be denied that the annals of slavery abound in examples of this kind of behavior. Slaves avoided work by pretending to be sick or by inventing a hundred other plausible pretexts. They worked so inefficiently as to give rise to the suspicion that they were deliberately sabotaging the crop. They stole from their masters without compunction, a fact which gave rise to the complaint that slaves had no moral sense, but which is better interpreted as evidence of a double standard—cheating the master

[3] Frederick Douglass, *The Narrative of the Life of Frederick Douglass, An American Slave* (Cambridge, 1960), pp. 132-133.
[4] Martin D. de B. Kilson, "Towards Freedom: An Analysis of Slave Revolts in the United States," *Phylon*, XXV (1964), 179-183.

while dealing honorably with other slaves. Nor was this all. Their grievances or frustrations led at times to the willful destruction of the master's property by destroying tools, mistreating animals, and setting fire to plantation buildings. Less frequently, they took the ultimate step of violent attack on the master himself. Perhaps the most common form of obvious noncooperation was running away; every large plantation had its share of fugitives.[5]

The question which inevitably arises, as Stampp piles up incident after incident in order to show that slaves were "a troublesome property," is whether this pattern of noncooperation constitutes resistance. Resistance is a political concept. Political activity, in the strictest sense, is organized collective action which aims at affecting the distribution of power in a community; more broadly, it might be said to consist of any activity, either of individuals or of groups, which is designed to create a consciousness of collective interest, such consciousness being the prerequisite for effective action in the realm of power. Organized resistance is of course only one form of political action. Others include interest-group politics; coalitions of interest groups organized as factions or parties; reform movements; or, at an international level, diplomacy and war. In total institutions, however, conventional politics are necessarily nonexistent.[6] Politics, if they exist at all, must take the form of resistance: collective action designed to subvert the system, to facilitate and regularize escape from it; or, at the very least, to force important changes in it.

Among despised and downtrodden people in general, the most rudimentary form of political action is violence; sporadic and usually short-lived outbursts of destruction, based on a common sense of outrage and sometimes inspired by a millennialistic ideology. Peasant revolts, all over the world, have usually conformed to this type.[7] In total institutions, prison riots are perhaps the nearest equivalent. In American slavery, the few documented slave rebellions fall into the same pattern.[8] What makes these upheavals political at all is that

[5] Stampp, *Peculiar Institution*, Ch. III.

[6] Total institutions are distinguished not by the absolute power of the authorities—a definition which, as will become clear, prejudges an important issue—but by the fact that they are self-contained, so that every detail of life is regulated in accordance with the dominant purpose of the institution. Whether that purpose is defined as healing, punishment, forced labor, or (in the case of the concentration camps) terror, all total institutions are set up in such a way as to preclude any form of politics based on consent.

[7] See E. J. Hobsbawm, *Primitive Rebels: Studies in Archaic Forms of Social Movement in the 19th and 20th Centuries* (Manchester, 1959); Norman Cohn, *The Pursuit of the Millennium* (New York, 1957).

[8] Nat Turner's rebellion in 1831, the only significant slave uprising in the period 1820-1860 that got beyond the plotting stage, would seem to be com-

they rest on some sense, however primitive, of collective victimization. They require, moreover, at least a minimum of organization and planning. What makes them rudimentary is that they do not aim so much at changing the balance of power as at giving expression on the one hand to apocalyptic visions of retribution, and on the other to an immediate thirst for vengeance directed more at particular individuals than at larger systems of authority. In the one case, the sense of grievance finds an outlet in indiscriminate violence (as against Jews); in the other, it attaches itself to a particular embodiment of authority (as in prisons, where a specific departure from established routine may set off a strike or riot demanding the authority's dismissal and a return to the previous regime). But in neither case does collective action rest on a realistic perception of the institutional structure as a whole and the collective interest of its victims in subverting it. That explains why such outbreaks of violence tend to subside very quickly, leaving the exploitive structure intact. Underground resistance to the Nazis in western Europe, on the other hand, precisely because it expressed itself in an organized underground instead of in futile outbreaks of indiscriminate violence, had a continuous existence which testifies to the highly political character of its objectives.

It is easy to show that Negro slaves did not always cooperate with the system of slavery. It is another matter to prove that noncooperation amounted to political resistance. Malingering may have reflected no more than a disinclination to work, especially when the rewards were so meager. Likewise, what is taken for sabotage may have originated in apathy and indifference. Acts of violence are subject to varying interpretations. If there is something undeniably political about an organized, premeditated rebellion, an isolated act of violence could arise from a purely personal grievance. Even the motive of flight is obscure: was it an impulse, prompted by some special and immediate affront, or was it desertion, a sort of separate peace? These acts in themselves tell us very little. We begin to understand them only when we understand the conceptual distinction between resistance and noncooperation; and even then, we still feel the need of a more general set of conceptions, derived from recorded experience, to which slavery—an unrecorded experience, except from the masters' point of view—can be compared; some general model which will enable us to grasp imaginatively the system as a whole.

parable to a millennialist peasants' revolt. Turner was a preacher who, according to his own testimony, received the visitation of a spirit commanding him to "fight against the serpent, for the time was fast approaching when the first should be last and the last should be first." Quoted in Herbert Aptheker, *American Negro Slave Revolts* (New York, 1943), p. 296. See also Aptheker, *Nat Turner's Slave Rebellion* (New York, 1966).

III

Only the testimony of the slaves could tell us, once and for all, whether slaves resisted slavery. In the absence of their testimony, it is tempting to resort to analogies. Indeed it is almost impossible to avoid them. Those who condemn analogies, pretending to argue from the documentary evidence alone, delude themselves. Resistance to slavery cannot be established (any more than any other general conception of the institution can be established) without making an implicit analogy between Negro slavery and the struggles of free men, in our own time, "to give dignity to human life" by resisting oppression. The question, in the case of slavery, is not whether historians should argue from analogy but whether they are willing to make their analogies explicit.

Stanley Elkins compares slavery to the Nazi concentration camps and concludes that the effect of slavery was to break down the slave's adult personality and to reduce him to a state of infantile dependence, comparable to the condition observed by survivors of the concentration camps. In evaluating this particular analogy, we are entitled to ask how well it explains what we actually know about slavery. In one respect, it explains too much. It explains the fact that there were no slave rebellions in the United States comparable to those which took place in Latin America, but it also rules out the possibility of non-cooperation. Elkins' analogy suggests a state of internalized dependency that does not fit the facts of widespread intransigence, insubordination, and mischief-making. Stampp may not adequately explain this pattern of behavior, but he convinces us that it existed. Elkins is open to criticism on empirical grounds for failing to take into account a vast amount of evidence that does not fit his theory of slave behavior. Many of Elkins' critics, however, have not concerned themselves with the substance of his analogy. Raising neither empirical nor theoretical objections against it, they have seized on its mere existence as a means of discrediting Elkins' work. He should rather be congratulated for having made the analogy explicit, thereby introducing into the study of slavery the kinds of questions that modern studies of total institutions have dealt with far more systematically than conventional studies of slavery.

Elkins was careful to emphasize the limits of the comparison. He did not argue that the plantation resembled a concentration camp with respect to intentions or motives; "even 'cruelty,' " he added, "was not indispensable as an item in my equation." His "essentially limited purpose" in bringing the two institutions together was to show the psychological effects of closed systems of control; and the objections to the analogy may after all derive not from the analogy itself but from a tendency, among Elkins' critics, to take it too literally. As Elkins observes, the "very vividness and particularity [of analogies] are coercive: they are almost too concrete. One's impulse is thus to reach for extremes. The thing is either taken whole hog . . .; or it is rejected out of hand on the ground that not all of the parts fit." It is precisely because all the parts don't fit that an analogy is an analogy rather than a literal correspondence, and it ought to be enough, therefore, if just one of the parts demonstrably fits.[9]

The real objection to Elkins' analogy is not that analogies in themselves are pernicious but that there is no compelling theoretical reason, in this case, to stop with one. The concentration camp is only one of many total institutions with which slavery might have been compared; a total institution being defined, in Erving Goffman's words, as "a place of residence and work where a large number of like-situated individuals, cut off from the wider society for an appreciable period of time, together lead an enclosed, formally administered round of life."[10] An excellent example—the one, indeed, that springs immediately to mind—is the prison, "providing," Goffman says, that "we appreciate that what is prison-like about prisons is found in institutions whose members have broken no laws."[11] In several respects, prisons, especially penitentiaries, are more analogous to plantation slavery than concentration camps. Prisons are not, like the concentration camps, designed as experiments in deliberate dehumanization, although they often have dehumanizing effects; in this respect the motive behind the system more nearly approximates that of slavery than of the concentration camp. More important, the problem of control is more nearly analogous. The disproportion between the authority of the guards and the impotence of the inmates is not absolute, as it was at Dachau and Buchenwald, but subject, as it seems to have been under slavery, to a number of variables—the temperament of the guard or master, the composition of the prisoners or slaves, the immediate history of the institutions involved.

Prison officials, like slaveowners and overseers, face a constant problem of noncooperation. "Far from being omnipotent rulers who have crushed all signs of rebellion against their regime, the custodians are engaged in a continuous struggle to maintain order—and it is a struggle in which the custodians frequently fail."[12] This situation occurs, according to the sociologist Gresham Sykes, because although the

[9] Elkins, *Slavery*, pp. 104, 226.
[10] Erving Goffman, *Asylums: Essays on the Social Situation of Mental Patients and Other Inmates* (Garden City, 1961; Chicago, 1962), p. xiii.
[11] *Ibid.*
[12] Gresham M. Sykes, *The Society of Captives: A Study of a Maximum Security Prison* (Princeton, 1958), p. 42.

custodians enjoy an absolute monopoly of the means of violence, their enormous power does not rest on authority; that is, on "a rightful or legitimate effort to exercise control," which inspires in the governed an internalized sense of obligation to obey. In the absence of a sense of duty among the prisoners, the guards have to rely on a system of rewards, incentives, punishments, and coercion. But none of these methods can be carried too far without reaching dangerous extremes of laxity or demoralization. As in most total institutions—the concentration camp being a conspicuous exception—rigid standards of discipline tend to give way before the need to keep things running smoothly without undue effort on the part of the custodians. An absolute monopoly of violence can be used to achieve a state of total terror, but it cannot persuade men to work at their jobs or move "more than 1,200 inmates through the mess hall in a routine and orderly fashion."[13] The result, in the maximum-security prison, is a system of compromises, an uneasy give-and-take which gives prisoners a limited leverage within the system. To the extent that this adjustment limits the power of the guards, a corruption of authority takes place.[14]

Plantation literature produces numerous parallels. We can read the masters' incessant and heartfelt complaints about the laziness, the inefficiency, and the intractibility of slaves; the difficulty of getting them to work; the difficulty of enlisting their cooperation in any activity that had to be sustained over a period of time. We can read about the system of rewards and punishments, spelled out by the master in such detail, the significance of which, we can now see, was that it had had to be resorted to precisely in the degree to which a sense of internalized obedience had failed. We see the same limitation on terror and physical coercion as has been observed in the prison; for even less than the prison authorities could the planter tolerate the demoralization resulting from an excess of violence. We can even see the same "corruption of authority" in the fact that illicit slave behavior, especially minor theft, was often tolerated by the masters in order to avoid unnecessary friction.

One of the most curious features of the "society of captives," as described by Sykes is this: that while most of the prisoners recognize the legitimacy of their imprisonment and the controls to which they are subjected,. they lack any internalized sense of obligation to obey them. "The bond between recognition of the legitimacy of control and the sense of duty has been torn apart."[15] This fact about prisons makes it possible to understand a puzzling feature of the contemporary literature on slavery, which neither the model of submission nor that

[13] *Ibid.*, p. 49.   [14] *Ibid.*, pp. 52-58.   [15] *Ibid.*, p. 46.

of resistance explains—the curious contradiction between the difficulty of discipline and the slaves' professed devotion to their masters. Those who argue that the slaves resisted slavery have to explain away their devotion as pure hypocrisy. But it is possible to accept it as sincere without endorsing the opposite view—even in the sophisticated form in which it has been cast by Stanley Elkins—that slaves were children. The sociology of total institutions provides a theory with which to reconcile the contradiction. "The custodial institution," Sykes argues, "is valuable for a theory of human behavior because it makes us realize that men need not be motivated to conform to a regime which they define as rightful."[16] It is theoretically possible, in short, that slaves could have accepted the legitimacy of their masters' authority without feeling any sense of obligation to obey it. The evidence of the masters themselves makes this conclusion seem not only possible but highly probable. Logic, moreover, supports this view. For how could a system that rigorously defined the Negro slave not merely as an inferior but as an alien, a separate order of being, inspire him with the sense of belonging on which internalized obedience necessarily has to rest?

IV

It might be argued, however, that slaves developed a sense of obedience by default, having had no taste of life outside slavery which would have made them dissatisfied, by contrast, with their treatment as slaves. It might be argued that the convict's dissatisfaction with prison conditions and the insubordination that results derives from his sense of the outside world and the satisfactions it normally provides; and that such a perspective must have been lacking on the plantation. Elkins, in denying the possibility of any sort of accommodation to slavery short of the complete assimilation of the master's authority by the slave, contends that a consciously defensive posture could not exist, given the total authority of the master and the lack of "alternative forces for moral and psychological orientation."[17] This objection loses its force, however, if it can be shown that the slave did in fact have chances to develop independent standards of personal satisfaction and fair treatment within the system of slavery itself. Such standards would have made possible a hedonistic strategy of accommodation, and in cases where such a strategy failed, strong feelings of personal grievance.

It is true that the plantation sealed itself off from the world, depriving the slave of nearly every influence that would have lifted him out of himself into a larger awareness of slavery as an oppressive social system which, by its very nature, denied him normal satisfac-

16 *Ibid.*, p. 48.   17 Elkins, *Slavery*, p. 133n.

tion. In order to understand why slaves did not, as Elkins suggests, become totally submissive and ready to accept any form of cruelty and humiliation, it is necessary to focus on an aspect of slavery which has been almost totally ignored in discussion of slave personality. The typical slave, although born into slavery, was not likely to spend his entire life, or indeed any considerable part of it, under a single regime. The slave child could anticipate many changes of situation. It would appear likely, from what we know of the extent of the slave trade, that most slaves changed hands at least once in their lives; slave narratives and recollections suggest that it was not at all uncommon for a single slave to belong to several masters in the course of his lifetime of servitude. In addition, the prevalence of slave-hiring, especially in the upper South, meant that many slaves experienced a temporary change of regime. Even if a slave remained on the same plantation, things could change drastically, as the result of death and the accession of an heir, or from a change of overseer (especially significant in cases of absentee ownership).[18] Given the wide variation in standards of treatment and management techniques—a variation which, we suggested earlier, seems the one inescapable conclusion to be drawn from the traditional scholarship on the management of slaves—we are left with a situation that must have had important psychological implications. An individual slave might—like Harriet Beecher Stowe's Uncle Tom—experience slavery both at its mildest and at its harshest. He might be sold from an indulgent master to a cruel one or vice versa. He might go from a farm where he maintained a close and intimate relationship with his master to a huge impersonal "factory in the fields," where his actual master would be only a dim presence. These changes in situation led many slaves to develop standards of their own about how they ought to be treated and even to diffuse these standards among the stationary slave population. By comparing his less onerous lot under a previous master to his present hard one, a slave could develop a real sense of grievance and communicate it to

[18] Frederic Bancroft, in *Slave Trading in the Old South* (New York, 1959), concludes (pp. 382-406) that more than 700,000 slaves were transported from the upper South to the cotton kingdom in the years 1830-1860, and that most went by way of the slave trade. He also estimates (p. 405) that in the decade 1850-1860 an annual average of approximately 140,000 slaves were sold, interstate or *intra-state*, or hired out by their masters. This meant that one slave in twenty-five changed his *de facto* master in a given year. When we add to these regular exchanges the informal transfers that went on within families, we get some idea of the instability which characterized the slave's situation in an expansive and dynamic agricultural economy. The way slaves were sometimes shuttled about is reflected in several of the slave narratives, especially Frederick Douglass, *Narrative*; Solomon Northrop, *Twelve Years a Slave* (Auburn, Buffalo, and London, 1853); and [Charles Ball] *Fifty Years in Chains: Or the Life of an American Slave* (New York, 1858).

others.[19] Similarly, slaves were quick to take advantage of any new leniency or laxity in control.[20] Hence it is quite possible to account for widespread noncooperation among slaves as resulting from a rudimentary sense of justice acquired entirely within the system of slavery

[19] Positive evidence of this development of internal standards and of the vacillation between contentment and dissatisfaction to which it gave rise is as difficult to find as evidence on any other aspect of slave psychology. As we have indicated, adequate records of personal slave response simply do not exist. There is, however, some indication of this process in the slave narratives and recollections. One of the most revealing of the slave narratives is Charles Ball, *Fifty Years in Chains.* Ball's account seems truer than most to the reality of slavery because, unlike most fugitives, he escaped from servitude at an age when it was difficult for him to acquire new habits of thought from his free status and association with abolitionists. Ball recounts the common experience of being sold from the upper South with its relatively mild and permissive regime into the more rigorous plantation slavery farther south. Upon his arrival on a large South Carolina cotton plantation, Ball, who was from Maryland, makes the acquaintance of a slave from northern Virginia who tells him what he can now expect. "He gave me such an account of the suffering of the slaves, on the cotton and indigo plantations—of whom I now regarded myself as one— that I was unable to sleep this night." (pp. 103-104.) Later, he describes himself as "far from the place of my nativity, in a land of strangers, with no one to care for me beyond the care that a master bestows upon his ox . . ." (p. 115). The regime is indeed a harsh one, and he feels very dissatisfied, except on Sunday when he is taken up by the general hilarity that prevails in the slave quarters on the holiday. Eventually, however, he experiences a temporary improvement in his situation when he is given to his master's new son-in-law, who seems kindly and permissive. In a remarkable description of slave hedonism, Ball recalls his state of mind. "I now felt assured that all my troubles in this world were ended, and that, in future, I might look forward to a life of happiness and ease, for I did not consider labor any hardship, if I was well provided with good food and clothes, and my other wants properly regarded." (p. 266.) This is too good to last, however; and Ball's new master dies, leaving him in the hands of another man, "of whom, when I considered the part of the country from whence he came, which had always been represented to me as distinguished for the cruelty with which slaves were treated, I had no reason to expect much that was good." (pp. 271-272.) His new master turns out to be much less harsh than anticipated, but the master's wife, a woman with sadistic tendencies, takes a positive dislike to Ball and resents her husband's paternal attitude toward him. When the master dies, Ball recognizes his situation as intolerable and resolves upon flight. (p. 307.) Ball's narrative reveals the way in which a slave could evaluate his changes of condition by standards of comfort and accommodation derived from experience within the system itself. In desperate situations, this evaluation could lead to extreme forms of noncooperation.

Despite the fact that he was recalling his experience after having escaped from slavery and, presumably, after coming under the influence of northern antislavery sentiment, Ball's general attitude remained remarkably accommodationist, at least in respect to slavery at its best. In a revealing passage, he notes that the typical slave lacks a real sense of identity of interest with his master. is jealous of his prerogatives, and steals from him without qualms. Yet, Ball concludes, there "is in fact, a mutual dependence between the master and his slave. The former could not acquire anything without the labor of the latter, and the latter would always remain in poverty without the judgment of the former in directing labor to a definite and profitable result." (p. 219.)

[20] See Stampp, *Peculiar Institution,* pp. 104-108.

itself. These standards would have served the same function as the standards convicts bring from the outside world into the prison. At the same time it is necessary to insist once again that they give rise to a pattern of intransigence which is hedonistic rather than political, accommodationist rather than revolutionary.

If this picture of slave motivation is less morally sublime than contemporary liberals and radicals would like, it should not be construed as constituting, in any sense, a moral judgment on the Negro slave. Sporadic noncooperation within a broad framework of accommodation was the natural and inevitable response to plantation slavery. It should go without saying that white men born into the same system would have acted in the same way. Indeed, this is the way they have been observed to act in modern situations analogous to slavery. In total institutions, the conditions for sustained resistance are generally wanting—a fact that is insufficiently appreciated by those armchair moralists who like to make judgments at a safe distance about the possibilities of resistance to totalitarianism. Rebellions and mutinies "seem to be the exception," Erving Goffman observes, "not the rule." Group loyalty is very tenuous, even though "the expectation that group loyalty should prevail forms part of the inmate culture and underlies the hostility accorded to those who break inmate solidarity."[21]

Instead of banding together, inmates of total institutions typically pursue various personal strategies of accommodation. Goffman describes four lines of adaptation, but it is important to note that although these are analytically distinguishable, "the same inmate will employ different personal lines of adaptation at different phases in his moral career and may even alternate among different tacks at the same time." "Situational withdrawal," a fatalistic apathy, is the condition into which many inmates of concentration camps rapidly descended, with disastrous psychic consequences to themselves; it undoubtedly took its toll among slaves newly arrived from Africa during the colonial period. "Colonization," which in some cases can be regarded as another type of institutional neurosis, rests on a conscious decision that life in the institution is preferable to life in the outside

[21] Goffman, Asylums, pp. 18-19. Cf. Donald Clemmer, The Prison Community (New York, 1958), pp. 297-298: "The prisoner's world is an atomized world. . . . There are no definite communal objectives. There is no consensus for a common goal. The inmates' conflict with officialdom and opposition toward society is only slightly greater in degree than conflict and opposition among themselves. Trickery and dishonesty overshadow sympathy and cooperation. . . . It is a world of 'I,' 'me,' and 'mine,' rather than 'ours,' 'theirs,' and 'his.'" Clemmer adds, p. 293: "Such collective action of protest as does arise, comes out of an immediate situation in which they themselves are involved, and not as protest to an idea."

world. Colonization, in turn, must be distinguished from "conversion," the inmate's internalization of the view of himself held by those in power. In Negro slavery, this is the "Sambo" role and is accompanied, as in the concentration camp, by an infantile sense of dependence. Colonization, on the other hand, would apply to the very small number of slaves who agreed to reenslavement after a period as free Negroes.[22]

The fourth type of accommodation is "intransigence," which should not be confused with resistance. The latter presupposes a sense of solidarity and an underground organization of inmates. Intransigence is a personal strategy of survival, and although it can sometimes help to sustain a high morale, it can just as easily lead to futile and even self-destructive acts of defiance. In slavery, there was a substantial minority who were written off by their masters as chronic troublemakers, "bad niggers," and an even larger group who indulged in occasional insubordination. It is precisely the pervasiveness of "intransigence" that made slaves, like convicts, so difficult to manage, leading to the corruption of authority analyzed above. But as we have already tried to show, there is nothing about intransigence that precludes a partial acceptance of the values of the institution. In fact, Goffman observes that the most defiant of inmates are paradoxically those who are most completely caught up in the daily round of institutional life. "Sustained rejection of a total institution often requires sustained orientation to its formal organization, and hence, paradoxically, a deep kind of involvement in the establishment."[23] The same immersion in the institutional routine that makes some inmates so easy to manage makes other peculiarly sensitive to disruptions of the routine, jealous of their "rights" under the system. Indeed, periods of intransigence can alternate, in the same person, with colonization, conversion, and even with periods of withdrawal.

The concentration camp was unique among total institutions in confronting the typical prisoner with a choice between situational withdrawal, which meant death, and conversion, which, in the absence of alternatives, came to dominate the personality as a fully internalized role. In other total institutions, however, all four roles can be played to some extent, and "few inmates seem to pursue any one of them

---

[22] Colonization, while uncommon among slaves, is frequently encountered in prisons and particularly in mental institutions. The high rate of recidivism among convicts and the frequency with which mental patients are sent back to asylums reflect not simply a relapse into a former sickness which the institution did not cure, but in many cases, a sickness which the institution itself created —an institutional neurosis which has its own peculiar characteristics, the most outstanding of which is the inability to function outside systems of total control.
[23] Goffman, Asylums, p. 62.

very far. In most total institutions most inmates take the tack of what some of them call 'playing it cool.' This involves a somewhat opportunistic combination of secondary adjustments, conversion, colonization, and loyalty to the inmate group, so that the inmate will have a maximum chance, in the particular circumstances, of eventually getting out physically and psychologically undamaged."[24] The slave had no real prospect of "getting out," but unless he was infantilized—a hypothesis that now seems quite untenable—he had a powerful stake in psychic survival. He had every reason to play it cool; and what is more, slavery gave him plenty of opportunities.

But the most compelling consideration in favor of this interpretation of slavery is that the very ways in which slavery differed from other total institutions would have actually reinforced and stabilized the pattern of opportunistic response that we have described. The most obvious objection to an analogy between slavery and the prison, the mental hospital, or any other institution of this kind is that slaves for the most part were born into slavery rather than coming in from the outside as adults; nor did most of them have any hope of getting out. We have answered these objections in various ways, but before leaving the matter we should point out that there is, in fact, a class of people in modern asylums—a minority, to be sure—who spend the better part of their lives in institutions of one kind or another. "Lower class mental hospital patients," for instance, "who have lived all their previous lives in orphanages, reformatories, and jails," are people whose experience in this respect approximates the slave's, especially the slave who served a series of masters. As a result of their continuous confinement, such patients have developed a kind of institutional personality. But they are not, as one might expect, Sambos—genuine converts to the institutional view of themselves. Quite the contrary; these people are the master-opportunists, for whom "no particular scheme of adaptation need be carried very far."[25] They have "perfected their adaptive techniques," experience having taught them a supreme versatility; and they are therefore likely to play it cool with more success than those brought in from the outside and incarcerated for the first time. These are the virtuosos of the system, neither docile nor rebellious, who spend their lives in skillful and somewhat cynical attempts to beat the system at its own game.

V

There is a passage in Frederick Douglass' *Narrative* that suggests how difficult it was even for an ex-slave—an unusually perceptive observer, in this case—to understand his former victimization without

[24] *Ibid.*, pp. 64-65.   [25] *Ibid.*, pp. 65-66.

resorting to categories derived from experiences quite alien to slavery, categories that reflected the consciousness not of the slaves themselves but, in one way or another, the consciousness of the master-class. Douglass described how eagerly the slaves on Colonel Lloyd's Maryland plantations vied for the privilege of running errands to the Great House Farm, the master's residence and home plantation. The slaves "regarded it as evidence of great confidence reposed in them by the overseers; and it was on this account, as well as a constant desire to be out of the field from under the driver's lash, that they esteemed it a high privilege, one worth careful living for. He was called the smartest and most trusty fellow, who had this honor conferred upon him the most frequently."

Then follows a passage of unusual vividness and poignancy:

The slaves selected to go to the Great House Farm, for the monthly allowance for themselves and their fellow-slaves, were peculiarly enthusiastic. While on their way, they would make the dense old woods, for miles around, reverberate with their wild songs, revealing at once the highest joy and the deepest sadness. . . . They would sometimes sing the most pathetic sentiment in the most rapturous tone, and the most rapturous sentiment in the most pathetic tone. Into all of their songs they would manage to weave something of the Great House Farm. Especially would they do this, when leaving home. They would then sing most exultingly the following words:—
    'I am going away to the Great House Farm!
        O, yea! O, yea! O!'
This they would sing, as a chorus, to words which to many would seem unmeaning jargon, but which, nevertheless, were full of meaning to themselves. I have sometimes thought that the mere hearing of those songs would do more to impress some minds with the horrible character of slavery, than the reading of whole volumes of philosophy on the subject could do.

But as these passages so clearly show, the "horrible character of slavery" did not lie, as the abolitionists tended to think, in the deprivations to which the slaves were forcibly subjected—deprivations which, resenting, they resisted with whatever means came to hand—but in the degree to which the slaves (even in their "intransigence") inevitably identified themselves with the system that bound and confined them, lending themselves to their own degradation. In vying for favors they "sought as diligently to please their overseers," Douglass says, "as the office-seekers in the political parties seek to please and deceive the people."[26]

Even more revealing are the reflections that follow. "I did not, when a slave, understand the deep meaning of those rude and apparently incoherent songs. I was myself within the circle; so that I neither

[26] Douglass, *Narrative*, pp. 35-37.

saw nor heard as those without might see and hear." It was only from without that the slave songs revealed themselves as "the prayer and complaint of souls boiling over with the bitterest anguish"— anguish, it should be noted, which expressed itself disjointedly, "the most pathetic sentiment" being set to "the most rapturous tone." It was only from without that the "dehumanizing character of slavery" showed itself precisely in the slave's incapacity to resist; but this perception, once gained, immediately distorted the reality to which it was applied. Douglass slides imperceptibly from these unforgettable evocations of slavery to an abolitionist polemic. It is a great mistake, he argued, to listen to slaves' songs "as evidence of their contentment and happiness." On the contrary, "slaves sing most when they are most unhappy." Yet the slaves whose "wild songs" he has just described were those who were "peculiarly enthusiastic," by his own account, to be sent to the Great House Farm, and who sang "exultingly" along the way. The ambiguity of the reality begins to fade when seen through the filter of liberal humanitarianism, and whereas the songs revealed "at once the highest joy and the deepest sadness," in Douglass' own words, as an abolitionist he feels it necessary to insist that "crying for joy, and singing for joy, were alike uncommon to me while in the jaws of slavery."[27]

If the abolitionist lens distorted the "horrible character" of slavery, the picture of the docile and apparently contented bondsman was no more faithful to the reality it purported to depict. But this should not surprise us. It is not often that men understand, or even truly see, those whom in charity they would uplift. How much less often do they understand those they exploit?

[27] *Ibid.*, pp. 37-38.

REBELLIOUSNESS AND DOCILITY
IN THE NEGRO SLAVE: A Critique
of the Elkins Thesis

Eugene D. Genovese

DESPITE THE HOSTILE RECEPTION given by historians to Stanley M. Elkins' *Slavery: A Problem in American Institutional and Intellectual Life*,[1] it has established itself as one of the most influential historical essays of our generation. Although Elkins ranges widely, we may restrict ourselves to his most important contribution, the theory of slave personality, and bypass other questions, such as his dubious theory of uncontrolled capitalism in the South. His psychological model would fit comfortably into other social theories and may, up to a point, be analytically isolated.

Elkins asserts that the Sambo stereotype arose only in the United States. He attempts to explain this allegedly unique personality type by constructing a social analysis that contrasts a totalitarian plantation South with a feudal Latin America in which church, state, and plantation balanced one another. To relate this ostensible difference in social structure to the formation of slave personality he invokes an analogy to Nazi concentration camps to demonstrate the possibility of mass infantilization and proceeds to apply three theories of personality: (1) the Freudian, which relates the growth of a personality to the existence of a father figure and which accounts for the identification of a tyrannized child with a tyrannical father; (2) Sullivan's theory of "significant others," which relates the growth of a personality to its interaction with individuals who hold or seem to hold power

[1] Stanley M. Elkins, *Slavery: A Problem in American Institutional and Intellectual Life* (Chicago, 1959). For a brief critique of the book as a whole see Genovese, "Problems in Nineteenth-Century American History," *Science & Society*, XXV (1961). This present paper shall, so far as possible, be limited to questions of method and assumption. A much shorter version was read to the Association for the Study of Negro Life and History, Baltimore, Maryland, Oct., 1966, where it was incisively criticized by Professor Willie Lee Rose of the University of Virginia. Mrs. Rose was also kind enough to read and criticize the first draft of this longer version. I do not know whether or not my revisions will satisfy her, but I am certain that the paper is much better as a result of her efforts.

293

over its fortunes; and (3) role theory, which relates the growth of a personality to the number and kinds of roles it can play.[2] Elkins assumes that Sambo existed only in the United States and that our task is to explain his unique appearance in the Old South. I propose to show, on the contrary, that Sambo existed wherever slavery existed, that he nonetheless could turn into a rebel, and that our main task is to discover the conditions under which the personality pattern could become inverted and a seemingly docile slave could suddenly turn fierce.

Elkins asserts that the United States alone produced the Sambo stereotype—"the perpetual child incapable of maturity." He does not, as so many of his critics insist, equate childishness with docility, although he carelessly gives such an impression. Rather, he equates it with dependence and, with a subtlety that seems to elude his detractors, skillfully accounts for most forms of day-to-day resistance. His thesis, as will be shown later, is objectionable not because it fails to account for hostile behavior, but because it proves too much and encompasses more forms of behavior than can usefully be managed under a single rubric.

Elkins' assumption that the existence of a stereotype proves the reality behind it will not stand critical examination either as psychological theory or as historical fact. As psychological theory, it is at least open to question. John Harding and his collaborators have argued that stereotypes, under certain conditions, may in fact be without foundation;[3] this side of the problem may be left to specialists and need not alter the main lines of the argument. Historically, Sambo was emerging in the United States at the same time he was emerging in the French colonies. Negroes, if we would believe the French planters, were childlike, docile, helpless creatures up until the very moment they rose and slaughtered the whites. Accordingly, I have a sporting proposition for Elkins. Let us substitute French Saint-Domingue for the United States and apply his logic. We find a Sambo stereotype and a weak tradition of rebellion. True, there was a century of maroon activity, but only the efforts of Mackandal constituted a genuine revolt. Those efforts were, in the words of C. L. R. James, "the only hint of an organized attempt at revolt during the hundred years preceding the French Revolution."[4] Boukman's revolt ought properly to be regarded as the first phase of the great revolution of 1791 rather than

[2] Elkins, *Slavery*, pp. 115-133 and the literature cited therein.
[3] John Harding, *et al.*, "Prejudice and Ethnic Relations," *Handbook of Social Psychology*, Gardner Lindzey (ed.) (Cambridge, 1954, II, 1021-1062, esp. 1024.
[4] C. L. R. James, *The Black Jacobins: Toussaint L'Ouverture and the San Domingo Revolution* (Vintage ed., New York, 1963), p. 21.

a separate action. In short, when the island suddenly exploded in the greatest slave revolution in history, nothing lay behind it but Sambo and a few hints. Now, let us rewrite history by having the French Jacobins take power and abolish slavery in 1790, instead of 1794. With the aid of that accident the slaves would have been freed as the result of the vicissitudes of Jacobin-Girondist factionalism and not by their own efforts. We would then today be reading a Haitian Elkins whose task would be to explain the extraordinary docility of the country's blacks. As the rewriting of history goes, this excursion requires little effort and ought to make us aware of how suddenly a seemingly docile, or at least adjusted, people can rise in violence. It would be much safer to assume that dangerous and strong currents run beneath that docility and adjustment.

Reaching further back into history, we find an identification of Negroes, including Africans, with a Sambo-like figure. As early as the fourteenth century—and there is no reason to believe that it began that late—so learned and sophisticated a scholar as Ibn Khaldun could write:

Negroes are in general characterized by levity, excitability, and great emotionalism. They are found eager to dance whenever they hear a melody. They are everywhere described as stupid. . . . The Negro nations are, as a rule, submissive to slavery, because (Negroes) have little (that is essentially) human and have attributes that are quite similar to those of dumb animals.[5]

In 1764, in Portugal, a pamphlet on the slavery question in the form of a dialogue has a Brazilian slaveowning mine operator say: "I have always observed that in Brazil the Negroes are treated worse than animals. . . . Yet, withal the blacks endure this." The conclusion drawn was that this submissiveness proved inferiority.[6]

Sambo appears throughout Brazilian history, especially during the nineteenth century. In the 1830's the ideologues of Brazilian slavery, significantly under strong French influence, assured planters that the black was a "man-child" with a maximum mental development equivalent to that of a white adolescent. This and similar views were widespread among planters, particularly in the highly commercialized

[5] Ibn Khaldun, The Muqaddimah (tr. Franz Rosenthal; New York, 1958), I, 174, 301; the parentheses were inserted by the translator for technical reasons. David Brion Davis maintains that as Muslims extended their hegemony over Africa, they came to regard black Africans as fit only for slavery: The Problem of Slavery in Western Culture (Ithaca, 1966), p. 50. Cf. Basil Davidson, Black Mother (Boston, 1961), pp. xvii, 7, 45, 92-93 for Sambo's appearance in Africa.
[6] C. R. Boxer (ed.), "Negro Slavery in Brazil" [trans. of Nova e Curiosa Relacao (1764)], Race, V (1964), 43.

southern coffee region.[7] Brazilian sociologists and historians accepted this stereotype well into the twentieth century. Euclides da Cunha, in his masterpiece, *Rebellion in the Backlands*, described the Negro as "a powerful organism, given to an extreme humility, without the Indian's rebelliousness."[8] Oliveira Lima, in his pioneering comparative history of Brazil and Spanish and Anglo-Saxon America, described the Negro as an especially subservient element.[9] Joao Pandía Calógeras, in his long standard *History of Brazil*, wrote:

The Negro element in general revealed a perpetual good humor, a childish and expansive joy, a delight in the slightest incidentals of life. . . . Filled with the joy of youth, a ray of sunshine illumined his childlike soul. Sensitive, worthy of confidence, devoted to those who treated him well, capable of being led in any direction by affection and kind words, the Negro helped to temper the primitive harshness of the Portuguese colonists.[10]

One of the leading interpretations in Brazil today regards the blacks as having been subjected to a regime designed to produce alienation and the destruction of the personality by means of the exercise of the arbitrary power of the master. The account given in Kenneth M. Stampp's *The Peculiar Institution* of the efforts to produce a perfect slave has a close parallel in Octavio Ianni's *As Metamorfoses do Escravo*, which analyzes southern Brazil during the nineteenth century.[11]

[7] Stanley J. Stein, *Vassouras: A Brazilian Coffee County, 1850-1900* (Cambridge, Mass., 1957), p. 133.

[8] Euclides da Cunha, *Rebellion in the Backlands (Os Sertoes)* (trans. Samuel Putnam; Chicago, 1944), p. 71; for a critical review of some of this literature see Arthur Ramos, *The Negro in Brazil* (Washington, 1939), pp. 22-24.

[9] Manoel de Oliveira Lima, *The Evolution of Brazil Compared with That of Spanish and Anglo-Saxon America* (Stanford, 1914), p. 122.

[10] Joao Pandía Calógeras, *A History of Brazil* (Chapel Hill, 1939), p. 29. Even today, when Negroes face discrimination in Brazil, whites insist that it is a result of their own incapacities and sense of inferiority. See Fernando Henrique Cardoso and Octavio Ianni, *Côr e mobilidade em Florianópolis* (Sao Paulo, 1964), p. 231.

[11] Kenneth M. Stampp, *The Peculiar Institution* (New York, 1956), p. 148: "Here, then, was the way to produce the perfect slave: accustom him to rigid discipline, demand from him unconditional submission, impress upon him his innate inferiority, develop in him a paralyzing fear of white men, train him to adopt the master's code of good behavior, and instill in him a sense of complete dependence. This at least was the goal."

Octavio Ianni, *As Metamorfoses do Escravo* (Sao Paulo, 1962), pp. 134-135: "Essential to the full functioning of the regime [was] a rigorous, drastic system of control over the social behavior of the enslaved laborer; . . . mechanisms of socialization appropriate to the dominant social strata . . .; the impossibility of vertical social mobility; . . . rules of conduct ordered according to a standard of rigid obedience of the Negroes in front of white men, whether masters or not."

See also Fernando Henrique Cardoso, *Capitalismo e Escravidao no Brasil Meridional* (Sao Paulo, 1962), pp. 312-313. Davis follows Ianni and others and speaks of Brazilian slaves as having been reduced "to a state of psychic

Nor did Sambo absent himself from Spanish America. The traditional advocacy of Indian freedom often went together with a defense
of Negro slavery based on an alleged inferiority that suggests a Sambo
stereotype.[12] In 1816, Simón Bolívar wrote to General Jean Marión of
Haiti:

I have proclaimed the absolute emancipation of the slaves. The tyranny
of the Spaniards has reduced them to such a state of stupidity and instilled in their souls such a great sense of terror that they have lost even
the desire to be free!! Many of them would have followed the Spaniards
or have embarked on British vessels [whose owners] have sold them in
,neighboring colonies.[13]

Elkins cites evidence that the Spanish regarded the Indians as docile
and the Negroes as difficult to control, but evidence also exists that
shows the reverse. The view of the Indian or Negro as docile or rebellious varied greatly with time, place, and circumstance.[14] Sidney
Mintz, with one one eye on Cuba and Puerto Rico and the other eye on
Brazil, has suggested that, regardless of institutional safeguards, the
more commercialized the slave system the more it tended to produce
dehumanization. This thesis needs considerable refinement but is at
least as suggestive as Elkins' attempt to construct a purely institutional
interpretation.[15]

On close inspection the Sambo personality turns out to be neither
more nor less than the slavish personality; wherever slavery has existed, Sambo has also.[16] "Throughout history," David Brion Davis has
written, "it has been said that slaves, though occasionally as loyal and
faithful as good dogs, were for the most part lazy, irresponsible, cunning, rebellious, untrustworthy, and sexually promiscuous."[17] Only the
element of rebelliousness does not seem to fit Sambo, but on reflec-

---

shock, of flat apathy and depression, which was common enough in Brazil to
acquire the special name of banzo." Problem of Slavery, p. 238; cf. Ramos, Negro in Brazil, pp. 22, 135-136.

[12] Davis, Problem of Slavery, p. 171.

[13] Selected Writings of Bolívar (New York, 1951), I, 131.

[14] For an interpretation of the Spanish slave law as holding Negroes to be an
especially revolutionary people see Augustín Alcalá y Henke, Esclavitud de
los negros en la América espanola (Madrid, 1919), p. 51. For a view of Brazilian Indians that sounds much like Sambo see the comments of the famous Dutch
sea captain, Dierck de Ruiter, as reported in C. R. Boxer, Salvador de Sá and the
Struggle for Brazil and Angola (London, 1952), p. 20.

[15] Sidney Mintz, review of Elkins' Slavery, American Anthropologist, LXIII
(1961), 585.

[16] "Slavery is determined 'pas par l'obeissance, ni par rudesse des labeurs,
mais par le statu d'instrument et la réduction de l'homme a l'etat de chose.'"
François Perroux, La Coexistence pacifique, as quoted by Herbert Marcuse, One-
Dimensional Man: Studies in the Ideology of Advanced Industrial Society (Boston, 1964), pp. 32-33.

[17] Davis, Problem of Slavery, pp. 59-60.

tion, even that does. Sambo, being a child, could be easily controlled but if not handled properly, would revert to barbarous ways. Davis demonstrates that by the fifth century B.C. many Greeks had come to regard the submission of barbarians to despotic and absolute rulers as proof of inferiority.[18] By the end of the eighteenth century, America and Europe widely accepted the image of the dehumanized ˎblack slave, and even Reynal believed that crime and indolence would inevitably follow emancipation.[19]

Sambo has a much longer pedigree and a much wider range than Elkins appreciates. Audrey I. Richards, in 1939, noted the widespread existence of "fatal resignation" among primitive peoples in Africa and suggested that their psychological and physical sluggishness might be attributable in a large part to poor diet and severe malnutrition.[20] Josué de Castro, former head of the United Nations Food and Agriculture Organization, has made the same point about Braziliah slaves and about people in underdeveloped countries in general.[21] As Jean-Paul Sartre has suggested, "Beaten, under-nourished, ill, terrified— but only up to a certain point—he has, whether he's black, yellow, or white, always the same traits of character: he's a sly-boots, a lazy-bones, and a thief, who lives on nothing and who understands only violence."[22] By constructing a single-factor analysis and erroneously isolating the personality structure of the southern slave, Elkins has obscured many other possible lines of inquiry. We do not as yet have a comparative analysis of slave diets in the United States, Brazil, and the West Indies, although it might tell us a great deal about personality patterns.

It is generally believed that Elkins merely repeated Tannenbaum when he declared Sambo to be a native of the Old South; in fact, the assertion is, for better or worse, entirely his own. I would not dwell on this point were it not that I cannot imagine Tannenbaum's taking so one-sided a view. I intend no disrespect to Elkins by this observation, for, as a matter of fact, his single-mindedness, even when misguided, has helped him to expose problems others have missed entirely. Elkins' greatest weakness, nonetheless, is his inability to accept the principle of contradiction, to realize that all historical phenomena must be regarded as constituting a process of becoming, and that, therefore, the other-sidedness of the most totalitarian conditions may in fact repre-

---

[18] Ibid., pp. 66-67.
[19] Ibid., p. 420.
[20] Audrey I. Richards, Land, Labour and Diet in Northern Rhodesia: An Economic Study of the Bemba Tribe (London, 1939), p. 400.
[21] Josué de Castro, The Geography of Hunger (Boston, 1952), passim.
[22] Jean-Paul Sartre, preface to Frantz Fanon, The Wretched of the Earth (New York, 1965), p. 14.

sent the unfolding of their negation. If Sambo were merely Sambo, then Elkins must explain how an overseer could publicly defend his class, without challenge, for having "to punish and keep in order the negroes, at the risk of his life."[23]

Elkins recognizes a wide range of institutional factors as having contributed to the contrast between the Latin and Anglo-Saxon slave systems, but he places special emphasis on the system of law in relation to the structure and policies of Church and Crown.[24] Although in this way Elkins follows Tannenbaum, he necessarily must go well beyond him, and therein lies his greatest difficulty. Tannenbaum's well-known thesis need not be reviewed here, but we might profitably recall his suggestive comment on *Las Siete Partidas:*

Las Siete Partidas was formed within the Christian doctrine, and the slave had a body of law, protective of him as a human being, which was already there when the Negro arrived and had been elaborated long before he came upon the scene.[25]

The essential point of Tannenbaum's contrast between this legal tradition and that of the Anglo-Saxon lies in its bearing on the problem of emancipation. Whereas the Hispanic tradition favored and encouraged it, the Anglo-Saxon blocked it.[26] So long as a general contrast can be demonstrated, Tannenbaum's thesis obtains, for he is primarily concerned with the social setting into which the Negro plunged upon emancipation. His thesis, therefore, can absorb criticism such as that of Arnold A. Sio, who argues that the Romans assimilated the rights of their slaves to property despite a legal code which respected the moral personality of the slave. Sio finds evidence of a similar tendency in Latin as well as Anglo-Saxon America.[27] Tannenbaum's thesis would fall only if the tendency were equally strong everywhere; but obviously it was not.[28] Elkins, however, cannot absorb such quali-

[23] Quoted from the *Southern Cultivator,* VII (Sept., 1849), 140, by William K. Scarborough, "The Southern Plantation Overseer: A Re-evaluation," *Agricultural History,* XXXVIII (1964), 16.
[24] See his explicit summary statement, "Culture Contacts and Negro Slavery," *Proceedings of the American Philosophical Society,* CVII (1963), 107-110, esp. p. 107.
[25] Frank Tannenbaum, *Slave & Citizen: The Negro in the Americas* (New York, 1946), p. 48.
[26] *Ibid.,* pp. 65, 69, and *passim.*
[27] Arnold A. Sio, "Interpretations of Slavery: The Slave Status in the Americas," *Comparative Studies in Society and History,* VII (1965), 303, 308. For a fresh consideration of the problem of slave law in the islands see Elsa V. Goveia, "The West Indian Slave Laws in the Eighteenth Century," *Revista de Ciencias Sociales* (1960), 75-105.
[28] Marvin Harris has counterposed an economic viewpoint to Tannenbaum's. Despite considerable exaggeration and one-sidedness, he does demonstrate the partial applicability of an institutional approach. For a critical analysis of Harris' polemic and the literature it touches see Genovese, "Materialism and

fications, for he necessarily must demonstrate the uniqueness of the southern pattern as well as the absoluteness of the contrast with Latin America. If the contrast could be reduced to a matter of degree, then we should be left with more American than Latin American Sambos, but Elkins' notion of a special American personality pattern and problem would fall.

Elkins, like Tannenbaum, ignores the French slave colonies, but nowhere was the gap between law and practice so startling. The *Code Noir* of 1685 set a high standard of humanity and attempted to guarantee the slaves certain minimal rights and protection. It was treated with contempt in the French West Indies, especially when the islands began to ride the sugar boom. It is enough to quote a governor of Martinique, one of the men charged with the enforcement of these laws: "I have reached the stage of believing firmly that one must treat the Negroes as one treats beasts."[29] On the eve of the Haitian Revolution probably not one of the protective articles of the *Code Noir* was being enforced.[30]

Elkins offers Brazil as a counterpoint to the Old South and invokes the Iberian legal tradition, together with the power of Church and Crown. Yet, even Gilberto Freyre, on whom Elkins relies so heavily, writes of the widespread murders of slaves by enraged masters.[31] As late as the nineteenth century, slaves were being whipped to death in the presence of all hands. The law might say what it would, but the *fazendeiros* controlled the police apparatus and supported the doctors who falsified the death certificates.[32] The measures designed to prevent wanton killing of slaves do not seem to have been better in Latin American than in Anglo-Saxon America.[33] If Brazilian slaves went to the police to complain about unjust or illegally excessive punishment,

---

Idealism in the History of Negro Slavery in the Americas," *Journal of Social History*, forthcoming.

The experience of the Dutch demonstrates how much religious and national attitudes gave way before the necessities of colonial life. The Dutch experience in Surinam, New Netherland, Brazil, etc. varied enormously. See, e.g., C. R. Boxer, *The Dutch in Brazil* (Oxford, 1957), esp. p. 75; Edgar J. McManus, *A History of Negro Slavery in New York* (New York, 1966), Ch. I.

[29] Quoted by James, *Black Jacobins*, p. 17.

[30] *Ibid.*, p. 56; Davis, *Problem of Slavery*, p. 254 and the literature cited therein.

[31] Gilberto Freyre, *The Masters and the Slaves: A Study in the Development of Brazilian Civilization* (2nd English Language ed., rev.; New York, 1956), p. xxxix.

[32] Stein, *Vassouras*, p. 136.

[33] See, e.g., the discussion of the law of 1797 in Antigua in Elsa V. Goveia, *Slave Society in the British Leeward Islands at the End of the Eighteenth Century* (New Haven, 1966), p. 191.

the police would, in Freyre's words, give them a double dose.[34] If the law mattered much, we need to know the reason for the repeated re-enactment of legislation to protect slaves. The famous Rio Branco Law of 1871, for example, granted slaves rights they were supposed to have enjoyed for centuries, and these too remained largely unrespected.

The Portuguese Crown could legislate in any manner it wished, and so later could the Emperor of Brazil; local power resided with the *fazendeiros*, as the emissaries of the Crown learned soon enough. We may imagine conditions in the first three centuries of colonization from Freyre's succinct comment on conditions in the middle of the nine-teenth century: "The power of the great planters was indeed feudalis-tic, their patriarchalism being hardly restricted by civil laws."[35] Not until that time did a strong central government arise to challenge ef-fectively the great planters.[36] That the contrast with the Old South might have been the reverse of what Elkins thinks is suggested by the diary of an ex-Confederate who fled to Brazil after the war. George S. Barnsley, formerly a Georgia planter and Confederate army surgeon, complained as late as 1904 of the lack of government and the preva-lence of virtually feudal conditions.[37]

Las Siete Partidas constituted a theoretical work and standard of values, the importance of which ought not to be minimized, but it had little to do with the actual practice on which Elkins' thesis depends.[38] The kind of protection that transcended the theoretical and might have conditioned decisively the personality development of the slave population as a whole probably did not appear until the *Real Cédula* of 1789. As Davis suggests, "There are many indications, moreover, that Spanish planters paid little attention to the law."[39]

Elkins assumes that the strongly centralized Spanish state could and did prevail over the planters. No doubt it did in matters of prime importance to its survival and income. In most matters, notwithstand-ing its best efforts at institutional control, the planters continued to have their way on their own estates. The Spanish court promulgated

[34] Gilberto Freyre, *The Mansions and the Shanties: The Making of Modern Brazil* (New York, 1963), p. 226.
[35] Gilberto Freyre, "Social Life in Brazil in the Middle of the Nineteenth Century," *Hispanic American Historical Review*, V (1922), 597-628; see also, Freyre, *Masters*, pp. xxxiii, 24, 42; *New World in the Tropics: The Culture of Modern Brazil* (New York; Vintage ed., 1963), p. 69.
[36] Alan A. Manchester describes 1848 as the turning point. See *British Pre-Eminence in Brazil* (Chapel Hill, 1933), pp. 261-262.
[37] George S. Barnsley MS Notebook in the Southern Historical Collection, University of North Carolina, Chapel Hill.
[38] For a penetrating discussion of these two sides of *Las Siete Partidas* see Davis, *Problem of Slavery*, pp. 102-105.
[39] *Ibid.*, p. 240.

humane legislation to protect the natives of the Canary Islands, but attempts at enforcement so far from home proved futile. The problem swelled enormously when transferred to the West Indies, not to mention to the mainland.[40] The fate of the protective features of the Laws of Burgos (1512) and of similar legislation is well known.[41] The British and other foreigners who did business in Spanish America ridiculed the mass of laws and the clumsy administrative apparatus designed to enforce them. As the agent of the South Sea Company at Jamaica noted in 1736, he who wants to deal illegally with the Spanish officials needs only the cash necessary to bribe them.[42] The lot of the slaves could, under such conditions, hardly reflect other than the disposition of the masters. A case study by Jaime Jaramillo Uribe of the judicial system of New Grenada shows that even the reform laws of the eighteenth century could not reach down into the plantations to protect the slaves.[43]

Much of Elkins' treatment of Spanish law deals with Cuba and flows from the work of Herbert Klein.[44] Without attempting a close examination of the intricacies of the Cuban case, we ought to note that it presents a striking picture of a bitter struggle between planters and state officials. The planters, there too, usually won the day. The liberal Governor Concha finally admitted that the resistance of the slaveowners to government intervention was justified by the necessity for controlling the blacks and avoiding any ambiguity in authority. In 1845 the government did seriously challenge the masters' power, but the uproar proved so great that the militant officials had to be removed.[45]

The fate of the law during the sugar boom requires more attention than Elkins and Klein have given it. In its earlier phases Cuban slavery was exceptionally mild and fit much of Elkins' schema. When the Haitian Revolution removed the Caribbean's leading sugar producer from the world market, Cuba entered into a period of wild expansion and prosperity. The status of the slave declined accordingly. The old

---

[40] Arthur Percival Newton, *The European Nations in the West Indies, 1493-1688* (London, 1933), p. 3.

[41] For a useful recent summary discussion of the literature see Harris, *Patterns of Race*, pp. 18-20.

[42] Cf., Arthur S. Aiton, "The Asiento Treaty as Reflected in the Papers of Lord Shelburne," *Hispanic American Historical Review*, VIII, (1928), 167-177, esp. p. 167.

[43] Jaime Jaramillo Uribe, "Esclavos y Senores en la sociedad colombiana del siglo XVIII," *Anuario colombiano de historia social y de cultura*, I (1963), 1-22.

[44] Herbert Klein, "Anglicanism, Catholicism and the Negro," *Comparative Studies in Society and History*, VIII (1966), 295-327; *Slavery in the Americas: A Comparative Study of Cuba and Virginia* (Chicago, 1967).

[45] See H. H. S. Aimes, *A History of Slavery in Cuba, 1511 to 1868* (New York, 1907), pp. 150-151, 175-177.

institutional arrangements did not disappear, but their bearing on the life of the great mass of slaves became minimal or nonexistent.[46]

The legal and political structure of Spanish America in general and of Cuba in particular helped ease the way to freedom by providing a setting in which the slave might be abused brutally but retained a significant degree of manhood in the eyes of society. For Tannenbaum's purpose, this distinction establishes the argument: the slave was abused as a slave but only incidentally as a Negro. The master might rule with absolute authority, but only because he could get away with it, not because it was, by the standards of his own class, church, and society, just and proper. Tannenbaum and Freyre do make too much of this argument. The persistence and depth of racial discrimination and prejudice in twentieth-century Brazil and Cuba ought to remind us that the enslavement of one race by another must generate racist doctrines among all social classes as well as the intelligentsia. Qualitative and quantitative distinctions nonetheless obtain, and Tannenbaum's argument requires correction and greater specificity, not rejection. For Elkins, Tannenbaum's distinction, however qualified, is not enough. If, as seems likely, the great majority of the slaves labored under such absolutism, theoretical or not, their personalities would have been shaped in response to conditions equivalent to those he describes for the United States.

In the United States, as in the British West Indies and everywhere else, custom and conventional moral standards had greater force than the law, as Ulrich B. Phillips long ago argued. Just as the vast range of rights granted the slaves in Latin America usually proved unenforceable in a society in which power was largely concentrated in local planter oligarchies, so in Anglo-Saxon America the quasi-absolute power of the master was tempered by the prevailing ethos. Tannenbaum, and especially Elkins, go much too far in denying that English and American law recognized the moral personality of the slave. As Davis has demonstrated, the double nature of the slave as thing and man had to be, and in one way or another was, recognized in law and custom by every slave society since ancient times. As a result, every southern planter knew intuitively the limits of his power, as imposed by the prevailing standards of decency. If he exceeded those limits, he might not suffer punishment at law and might even be strong enough to prevent his being ostracized by disapproving neigh-

---

[46] On this point see Sidney Mintz, foreword to Ramiro Guerra y Sánchez, *Sugar and Society in the Caribbean* (New Haven, 1964), and his review of Elkins' book in the *American Anthropologist*, LXIII (1961), 579-587. Klein, Tannenbaum and Elkins make much of the practice of *coartación*. For a critical assessment see Davis, *Problem of Slavery*, pp. 266-267.

bors. For these reasons historians have dismissed community pressure as a factor. In doing so, they err badly, for the point is not at all what happened to a violator of convention but the extent to which the overwhelming majority of slaveholders internalized conventional values. In this respect the legal structures of Brazil and the United States were important in conditioning those conventional values. Once again, the difference between the two cases suffices for Tannenbaum's thesis but not for Elkins'—which depends entirely on the experience of absolute power by the slave.

Elkins follows Tannenbaum in ascribing a special role to the Catholic Church in the development of Ibero-American slave societies. The Church defended the moral personality of the slave from a position of independent institutional strength, whereas in the Anglo-Saxon world the separation of church and state, the bourgeois notion of property rights, and the divisions within the religious community largely excluded the churches from the field of master-slave relations. The religious as well as the legal structure helped generate a particular climate of moral opinion into which the Negro could fit as a free man. The difference in structure and result satisfies Tannenbaum's argument; it does not satisfy Elkins' argument, which turns on the specific role played by the priesthood in the life of the slave.

Since Brazil, as the largest Catholic slaveholding country, ought properly to serve as a test case, we might profitably begin with a consideration of developments in Angola, which supplied a large part of its slaves. The clergy, including Jesuits and Dominicans, participated in every horror associated with the slave trade; there is little evidence of its having played a mediating role.[47] By the middle of the seventeenth century Catholic proselytism in the Congo and Angola had spent its force. Contemporary Catholic sources admitted that much of the failure was due to the greed of the clergy in pursuing slave-trade profits and to the generally venal character of priests, secular officials, and laymen.[48] The governor of Angola, the troops, the bishop, and the entire staff of civil and ecclesiastical officials drew their salaries from the direct and indirect proceeds of the slave trade. The Holy House of Mercy [Misericordia] at Luanda, as well as the Municipal Council [Camara] lived off the trade. Since the Junta das missoēs, the chief missionary agency, was supported by these proceeds we need not be surprised that it accomplished little.[49]

[47] Boxer, Salvador de Sá, p. 279.
[48] C. R. Boxer, Race Relations in the Portuguese Colonial Empire, 1415-1825 (Oxford, 1963), pp. 7-8, 11-12, 21.
[49] C. R. Boxer, Portuguese Society in the Tropics: The Municipal Councils of Goa, Macao, Bahia, and Luanda, 1510-1800 (1965), pp. 131-132, Davidson, Black Mother, p. 158.

In Brazil itself the decisive questions concern the number, character, and relative independence of the priests.[50] We have little data on numbers, but in the mid-twentieth century, Brazil, with a population of fifty million, of whom 95 per cent were nominal Catholics, had, according to Vianna Moog, only six thousand priests.[51] We may, nonetheless, assume for a moment that a high ratio of priests to slaves existed. There is good reason to believe that a significant percentage of the priests who ventured to the colonies had questionable characters and that many of good character succumbed to the indolence, violence, and corruption that marked their isolated, quasi-frontier environment. It is no insult to the Church to affirm this state of affairs, for the Church has had to struggle for centuries to raise the quality of its priests and to maintain high standards of performance. Like other institutions of this world it has consisted of men with all the weaknesses of men, and in the difficult circumstances of colonial life the adherence of its men to the high standards of the Church Militant proved erratic and uncertain.

Even if we grant the Brazilian clergy a higher quality than it probably deserved, we confront the question of its relationship to the master class. The local chaplain depended on and deferred to the planter he served more than he depended on his bishop. The Brazilian Church never achieved the strength and cohesion of the Church in Spanish America. The typical sugar planter, in Freyre's words, "though a devout Catholic, was a sort of Philip II in regard to the Church: he considered himself more powerful than the bishops or abbots." Under these conditions the interposition of priest between master and slave was probably little more significant than the interposition of the mistress on a plantation in Mississippi. The analogy assumes particular force when we consider that, increasingly, the Brazilian priesthood was recruited from the local aristocracy.[52] In coffee-growing southern Brazil, in which slavery centered during the nineteenth century, few priests resided on plantations at all and visits were possibly less common than in the United States. The large number of

[50] Elkins certainly errs in ascribing a protective role to the Jesuits, whose efforts on behalf of the Indians were not repeated with the Negroes. Jesuit treatment of those Negroes within their reach does not constitute one of the more glorious chapters in the history of the order. The literature is extensive; for a good, brief discussion see Joao Dornas Filho, *A Escravidao no Brasil* (Rio de Janeiro, 1939), p. 105.

[51] Vianna Moog, *Bandeirantes and Pioneers* (New York, 1964), p. 209. Cf., Percy Alvin Martin, "Slavery and Abolition in Brazil," *Hispanic American Historical Review*, XIII (1933), 168: "On most plantations the spiritual life of the slaves received scant attention. Priests were found only on the larger estates."

[52] Freyre, *New World in the Tropics*, pp. 70-71, 87-88; *Mansions*, p. 244.

Africans imported during 1830-1850 received little attention from the Church.[53]

The situation in Spanish America worked out more favorably for Elkins' argument because the Church there came much closer to that independence and crusading spirit which has been attributed to it. Even so, the ruthless exploitation of Indians and Negroes by large sections of the clergy is well documented. The position of the Church as a whole, taken over centuries, demonstrates its growing subservience to state and secular power in respects that were decisive for Elkins' purposes. The bulls of Popes and the decrees of kings proved inadequate to temper the rule of the great planters of the New World, although they did play a role in shaping their moral consciousness.[54] In Cuba the clergy acted more boldly and, according to Klein, had a numerical strength adequate to its tasks. However, the effective interposition of even the Cuban clergy during the sugar boom of the nineteenth century has yet to be demonstrated, and if it were to be, Cuba would stand as an exception to the rule.

That more Brazilian and Cuban slaves attended religious services than did southern is by no means certain, the law to the contrary notwithstanding. That the Catholic clergy of Latin America interposed itself more often and more effectively than the Protestant clergy of the South cannot be denied. On balance, Tannenbaum's case is proven by the ability of the Catholic Church to help shape the ethos of slave society and the relative inability of the Protestant to do the same. But Elkins' case falls, for the difference in the potentialities for and especially the realities of personal interposition remained a matter of degree.

Despite the efforts of law and Church in Latin America it is quite possible that as high or higher a percentage of southern slaves lived in stable family units than did Latin American. The force of custom and sentiment generally prevailed over the force of law or institutional interference. In Brazil, as in the Caribbean, male slaves greatly outnumbered female; in the United States the sexes were numerically equal. This factor alone, which derived primarily from economic and technological conditions, encouraged greater family stability in the United States and therefore casts great doubt on Elkins' thesis. To the extent that participation in a stable family life encouraged the development of a mature personality, the slaves of the South probably fared no worse than others. Elkins argues that the Latin American families could not be broken up because of Church and state restrictions. In fact, they often were broken up in open defiance of both.

53 Stein, Vassouras, pp. 196-199.
54 Cf., Rene Maunier, The Sociology of Colonies (London, n.d.), I, 293-294.

The greatest guarantee against sale existed not where the law forbade it, but where economic conditions reduced the necessity. The attendant argument that Latin American slaves could function in the roles of fathers and mothers, whereas southern slaves could not, is altogether arbitrary. The feeling of security within the family depended on custom and circumstance, not law, and a great number of southern slaves worked for masters whose economic position and paternalistic attitudes provided a reasonable guarantee against separate sales. In any case, all slaves in all societies faced similar problems. When a slaveowner beat or raped a slave woman in Brazil or Cuba, her husband was quite as helpless as any black man in Mississippi. The duties, responsibilities, and privileges of fatherhood were, in practice, little different from one place to another.

The point of Elkins' controversial concentration camp analogy is not altogether clear. Sometimes he seems to wish to demonstrate only the possibility of mass infantilization, but if this were all he intended, he could have done so briefly and without risking the hostile reaction he brought down on himself. At other times he seems to intend the analogy as a direct device. Although he denies saying that slavery was a concentration camp or even "like" a concentration camp, he does refer to concentration camps as perverted patriarchies and extreme forms of slavery; he finds in them the same total power he believes to have existed on the southern plantations. In the first, restricted, sense the analogy, used suggestively, has its point, for it suggests the ultimate limits of the slave experience. In the second, and broader, sense it offers little and is generally misleading. Unfortunately, Elkins sometimes exaggerates and confuses his device, which only demonstrates the limiting case, with the historical reality of slavery. His elaborate discussion of detachment offers clues but is dangerously misleading. The process did not differ for slaves bound for different parts of the New World; only the post-shock experience of the slave regimes differed, so that we are led right back to those regimes. No doubt Elkins makes a good point when he cites concentration camp and slave trade evidence to show that many participants were spiritually broken by the process, but he overlooks the contribution of newly imported Africans to slave disorders. Everywhere in the Americas a correlation existed between concentrations of African-born slaves and the outbreak of revolts. The evidence indicates that creole slaves were generally more adjusted to enslavement than those who had undergone the shock and detachment processes from Africa to America.[55]

The fundamental differences between the concentration camp and

[55] Elkins seems troubled by this—see p. 102—but he does not pursue it. K.

plantation experience may be gleaned from a brief consideration of
some of the points made in Bruno Bettelheim's study, on which Elkins
relies heavily.[56] Prisoners received inadequate clothing and food in
order to test their reaction to extremities of inclement weather and
their ability to work while acutely hungry. Slaves received clothing
and food designed to provide at least minimum comfort. Slaves suffered from dietary deficiencies and hidden hungers, but rarely from
outright malnutrition. In direct contrast to prisoners, slaves normally
did not work outdoors in the rain or extreme cold; usually, they were
deliberately ordered to stay indoors. Pneumonia and other diseases
killed too many slaves every winter for planters not to take every precaution to guard their health. Therein lay the crucial differences:
prisoners might be kept alive for experimental purposes, but slaves
received treatment designed to grant them long life. Prisoners often
did useless work as part of a deliberate program to destroy their personality; slaves did, and knew they did, the productive work necessary for their own sustenance. Prisoners were forbidden to talk to each
other much of the day and had virtually no privacy and no social life.
Slaves maintained a many-sided social life, which received considerable encouragement from their masters. The Gestapo deliberately set
out to deny the individuality of prisoners or to distinguish among
them. Planters and overseers made every effort to take full account
of slave individuality and even to encourage it up to a point. Prisoners
were deliberately subjected to torture and arbitrary punishment; those
who followed orders endured the same indignities and blows as those
who did not. Slaves, despite considerable arbitrariness in the system,
generally had the option of currying favor and avoiding punishment.
As Hannah Arendt has so perceptively observed: "Under conditions
of total terror not even fear can any longer serve as an advisor of how
to behave, because terror chooses its victims without reference to individual actions or thoughts, exclusively in accordance with the ob-

---

Onwuka Dike points out that Guineans brought to the trading depots of the
Niger Delta had already been prepared psychologically for slavery by the religious indoctrination accompanying the cult of the Aro oracle. See "The Question of Sambo: A Report of the Ninth Newberry Library Conference on Ameri-
can Studies," Newberry Library Bulletin, V (1958), 27 and Dike's Trade and
Politics in the Niger Delta, 1830-1885 (Oxford, 1956), Ch. II.
    56 Bruno Bettelheim, "Individual and Mass Behavior in Extreme Situations,"
Journal of Abnormal and Social Psychology, XXXVIII (1943), 417-452. On the
general problem of the concentration camp analogy see the remarks of Daniel
Boorstin as reported in the Newberry Library Bulletin, V (1958), 14-40 and
Earle E. Thorpe, "Chattel Slavery & Concentration Camps," Negro History
Bulletin, XXV (1962), 171-176. Unfortunately, Mr. Thorpe's thoughtful piece
is marred by a clumsy discussion of the problem of wearing a mask before white
men.

jective necessity of the natural or historical process."[57] Concentration camp prisoners changed work groups and barracks regularly and could not develop attachments. Slaves had families and friends, often for a lifetime. The Gestapo had no interest in indoctrinating prisoners. They demanded obedience, not loyalty. Masters wanted and took great pains to secure the loyalty and ideological adherence of their slaves. In general, the slave plantation was a social system, full of joys and sorrows and a fair degree of security, notwithstanding great harshness and even brutality, whereas the concentration camp was a particularly vicious death-cell. They shared a strong degree of authoritarianism, but so does the army or a revolutionary party, or even a family unit.

With these criticisms of data we may turn to Elkin's discussion of personality theory. His use of Sullivan's theory of "significant others" breaks down because of his erroneous notion of the absolute power of the master. In theory the master's power over the slave in the United States was close to absolute; so in theory was the power of Louis XIV over the French. In practice, the plantation represented a series of compromises between whites and blacks. Elkins' inability to see the slaves as active forces capable of tempering the authority of the master leads him into a one-sided appraisal.[58]

According to Elkins, the Latin American slave could relate meaningfully to the friar on the slave ship; the confessor who made the plantation rounds; the zealous Jesuit who especially defended the sanctity of the family; the local magistrate who had to contend with the Crown's official protector of the slaves; and any informer who could expect to collect one-third of the fines. In general, it would not be unfair to say that, notwithstanding all these institutional niceties, the Latin American slaveowners, especially the Brazilian, ruled their plantations as despotically as any southerner. Priest, magistrate, and anyone careless enough to risk his life to play the informer came under the iron grip of the plantation owners' enormous local power.

Various other persons did affect meaningfully the lives of slaves in all systems. The plantation mistress often acted to soften her husband's rule. The overseer did not always precisely reflect the master's temperament and wishes, and slaves demonstrated great skill in playing the one against the other. The Negro driver often affected their

[57] Hannah Arendt, "Ideology and Terror: A Novel Form of Government," *Review of Politics*, XV (1953), 314. I am indebted to Professor Daniel Walden of the Pennsylvania State University for calling this illuminating article to my attention and for suggesting its relevance to the subject at hand.

[58] For a perceptive and well-balanced discussion of this side of plantation life see Clement Eaton, *The Growth of Southern Civilization* (New York, 1961), p. 74 and *passim*.

lives more directly than anyone else and had considerable authority to make their lives easy or miserable. Slaves who found it difficult to adjust to a master's whims or who feared punishment often ran to some other planter in the neighborhood to ask for his intercession, which they received more often than not. Elkins ignores these and other people because they had no lawful right to intervene; but they did have the power of persuasion in a world of human beings with human reactions. To the vast majority of slaves in all systems, the power of the master approached the absolute and yet was tempered by many human relationships and sensibilities. To the extent that slavery, in all societies, restricted the number of "significant others," it may well have contributed toward the formation of a slavish personality, but Latin America differed from the South only in permitting a somewhat larger minority to transcend that effect.

Similar objections may be made with reference to the application of role theory. The Latin American slave could ordinarily no more act the part of a husband or father than could the southern. The typical field hand had roughly the same degree of prestige and authority in his own cabin in all societies. Legal right to property did not make most Latin American slaves property owners in any meaningful sense, and many southern slaves were de facto property owners of the same kind. The theoretical right of the one and the mere privilege of the other did not present a great practical difference, for the attitude of the master was decisive in both cases. For Tannenbaum's social analysis the significance of the difference stands; for Elkins' psychological analysis it does not.

The theory of personality that Elkins seems to slight, but uses to greatest advantage, is the Freudian, perhaps because it offers a simple direct insight quite apart from its more technical formulations. We do not need an elaborate psychological theory to help us understand the emergence of the slaveowner as a father figure. As the source of all privileges, gifts, and necessaries, he loomed as a great benefactor, even when he simultaneously functioned as a great oppressor. Slaves, forced into dependence on their master, viewed him with awe and identified their interests and even their wills with his. Elkins' analogy with concentration camp prisoners who began to imitate their SS guards indicates the extreme case of this tendency. All exploited classes manifest something of this tendency—the more servile the class the stronger the tendency. It is what many contemporary observers, including runaway slaves and abolitionists, meant when they spoke of the reduction of the slave to a groveling creature without initiative and a sense of self-reliance. Elkins, using Freudian insight, has transformed this observation into the politically relevant suggestion that the slave actually learned to see himself through his master's eyes.

Elkins has often been criticized for failing to realize that slaves usually acted as expected while they retained inner reservations, but he did recognize this possibility in his discussion of a "broad belt of indeterminacy" between playing a role and becoming the role you always play. The criticism seems to me to miss the point. The existence of such reservations might weaken the notion of total infantilization but would not touch the less extreme notion of a dependent, emasculated personality. The clever slave outwitted his master at least partly because he was supposed to. Masters enjoyed the game: it strengthened their sense of superiority, confirmed the slaves' dependence, and provided a sense of pride in having so clever a man-child. On the slave's side it made him a devilishly delightful fellow but hardly a man. The main point against Elkins here is the same as elsewhere —when he is sound he describes not a southern slave but a slave; not a distinctly southern Sambo personality but a slavish personality.[59]

Elkins' general argument contains a fundamental flaw, which, when uncovered, exposes all the empirical difficulties under review. In his model a regime of total power produces a Sambo personality. Confronted by the undeniable existence of exceptions, he pleads first things first and waives them aside as statistically insignificant. Even if we were to agree that they were statistically insignificant, we are left with a serious problem. Elkins did not construct a model to determine probabilities; he constructed a deterministic model, which he cannot drop suddenly to suit his convenience. The notion of "total power" loses force and usefulness and indeed approaches absurdity in a world of probabilities and alternatives. If Elkins were to retreat from this notion and consequently from his determinism, he could not simply make an adjustment in his model; he would have to begin, as we must, from different premises, although without necessarily sacrificing his remarkable insights and suggestions. If the basic personality pattern arose from the nature of the regime, so did the deviant patterns. It would be absurd to argue that a regime could be sufficiently complex to generate two or more such patterns and yet sufficiently simple to generate them in mutual isolation. The regime threw up all the patterns at once, whatever the proportions, and the root of every deviation lay in the same social structure that gave us Sambo.

This range of patterns arose from the disparity between the plantations and farms, between resident owners and absentees, and above all

59 Brazilian slaves saw their masters as patriarchs and, in Freyre's words, "almighty figures." Freyre, *Mansions*, p. 234. See also Celso Furtado, *The Economic Growth of Brazil* (Berkeley, 1963), pp. 153-154.

between the foibles and sensibilities of one master and another. They arose, too, within every slaveholding unit from the impossibility of absolute power—from the qualities, perhaps inherited, of the particular personalities of slaves as individuals; from the inconsistencies in the human behavior of the severest masters; from the room that even a slave plantation provides for breathing, laughing, crying, and combining acquiescence and protest in a single thought, expression, and action. Even modern totalitarian regimes, self-consciously armed with unprecedented weapons of terror, must face that opposition inherent in the human spirit to which Miss Arendt draws attention. The freedom of man cannot be denied even by totalitarian rulers, "for this freedom—irrelevant and arbitrary as they may deem it—is identical with the fact that men are being born and that therefore each of them *is* a new beginning, begins, in a sense, the world anew."[60] We need not pretend to understand adequately that remarkable process of spiritual regeneration which repeatedly unfolds before our eyes. The evidence extends throughout history, including the history of our own day; its special forms and content, not its existence, constitute our problem. Miss Arendt therefore concludes her analysis of terror wisely: "Every end in history necessarily contains a new beginning. . . . Beginning, before it becomes a historical event, is the supreme capacity of man; politically, it is identical with man's freedom. . . . This beginning is guaranteed by each new birth; it is indeed every man."[61]

Sambo himself had to be a product of a contradictory environment, all sides of which he necessarily internalized. Sambo, in short, was Sambo only up to the moment that the psychological balance was jarred from within or without; he might then well have become Nat Turner, for every element antithetical to his being a Sambo resided in his nature. "Total power" and "Sambo" may serve a useful purpose in a theoretical model as a rough approximation to a complex reality, provided that we do not confuse the model with the reality itself. Neither slavery nor slaves can be treated as pure categories, free of the contradictions, tensions, and potentialities that characterize all human experience.

Elkins, in committing himself to these absolutist notions, overlooks the evidence from his own concentration camp analogy. Bettelheim notes that even the most accommodating, servile, and broken-spirited prisoners sometimes suddenly defied the Gestapo with great courage. Eugen Kogon devotes considerable space in his *Theory and Practice of Hell* to the development and maintenance of resistance within the

[60] Arendt, *Review of Politics*, XV (1953), 312.
[61] *Ibid.*, 327.

camps.[62] In a similar way the most docile field slaves or the most trusted house slaves might, and often did, suddenly rise up in some act of unprecedented violence. This transformation will surprise us only if we confuse our theoretical model with the reality it ought to help us to understand.

Elkins has not described to us the personality of the southern slave, nor, by contrast, of the Latin American slave; he has instead demonstrated the limiting case of the slavish personality. Every slave system contained a powerful tendency to generate Sambos, but every system generated countervailing forces. Elkins, following Tannenbaum, might properly argue that differences in tradition, religion, and law guaranteed differences in the strength of those countervailing forces; he cannot prove and dare not assume that any system lacked them.

Elkins accounts for such forms of deviant behavior as lying, stealing, and shirking by absorbing them within the general framework of childish response. He is by no means completely wrong in doing so, for very often the form of a particular act of hostility degraded the slave as much as it irritated the master. Elkins' approach is not so much wrong as it is of limited usefulness. Once we pass beyond the insight that the form of rebelliousness might itself reveal accommodation, we cannot go much further. If all behavior short of armed revolt can be subsumed within the framework of childishness and dependence, then that formulation clearly embraces too much. Our historical problem is to explain how and under what conditions accommodation yields to resistance, and we therefore need a framework sufficiently flexible to permit distinctions between accommodating behavior that, however slightly, suggests a process of transformation into opposite qualities; such a framework must, moreover, be able to account for both tendencies within a single human being and even within a single act.

It has become something of a fashion in the adolescent recesses of our profession to bury troublesome authors and their work under a heap of carping general and specific complaints; it is no part of my purpose to join in the fun. Elkins' book has raised the study of southern slavery to a far higher level than ever before, and it has done so at a moment when the subject seemed about to be drowned in a sea of moral indignation. It has demonstrated forcefully the remarkable uses to which psychology can be put in historical inquiry. It has brought to the surface the relationship between the slave past and a wide range of current problems flowing from that past. These are extraor-

[62] Bettelheim, *Journal of Abnormal and Social Psychology*, XXXVIII (1943), 451; Eugen Kogon, *The Theory and Practice of Hell* (New York, 1950), esp. Chs. XX, XXXI.

dinary achievements. To advance in the direction Elkins has pointed out, however, we shall first have to abandon most of his ground. We cannot simply replace his psychological model with a better one; we must recognize that all psychological models may only be used suggestively for flashes of insight or as aids in forming hypotheses and that they cannot substitute for empirical investigation. As the distinguished anthropologist, Max Gluckman, has observed, respect for psychology as a discipline requiring a high degree of training in the acquisition and interpretation of data forces us to bypass psychological analyses whenever possible.[63] Or, to put it another way, if we are to profit fully from Elkins' boldness, we shall have to retreat from it and try to solve the problems he raises by the more orthodox procedures of historical research.

[63] Max Gluckman, *Order and Rebellion in Tribal Africa* (New York, 1963), pp. 2-3.

314

178

SEYMOUR L. GROSS
University of Detroit

EILEEN BENDER
University of Notre Dame

History, Politics and Literature:
The Myth of Nat Turner

UP UNTIL A FEW YEARS AGO NAT TURNER AS A FIGURE OF HISTORY WAS
not known to many Americans, although there is evidence that the name of
"old Prophet Nat" had been kept alive in black oral tradition. But with the
publication of William Styron's *The Confessions of Nat Turner* in 1967,
and the sensational and far-reaching reaction to the novel by much of the
black intelligentsia, the relative obscurity of this leader of a slave rebellion in 19th century Virginia is itself a thing of the past. Now he belongs
to all of us. But it will be the intention of this essay to show that he belongs
to us as he has always belonged to those who used him—as a myth, as an
imagined configuration of convictions, dreams, hopes and fears. This is as
true of the insanely religious fanatic of Thomas Gray's *The Confessions of
Nat Turner* in 1831 as it is of the Black Power militant of Addison Gayle's
"Nat Turner vs. Black Nationalists" in 1968, in which the meaning of
Turner's life is seen to "negate the absurd and nonsensical philosophy of
Martin Luther King."[1]
   The rhetoric of accusation and vilification with which black writers and
critics have responded to Styron's novel, of which *William Styron's Nat
Turner: Ten Black Writers Respond* is but the most formal,[2] has many of
the unpleasant intellectual characteristics of party discipline carried over
into literary studies. It is reminiscent not only of the vulgar Marxist
criticism of the 1930s but, ironically, of the deliberately mounted attacks on
Uncle Tom's Cabin in the white South of the 1850s as well. With the
notable exceptions of John Hope Franklin and James Baldwin, those black
critics whose initial reaction to Styron's novel was favorable, Poppy Can-

[1]*Liberator*, 8 (Feb. 1968), 6.
[2]John Henrik Clarke, ed. (Boston: Beacon Press, 1968).

non White and Gertrude Wilson, for example, found it incumbent upon them to recant.[3]

Much of the black criticism of *The Confessions of Nat Turner* has taken the form of tactical insult of its author and distortions of the novel: Styron is "an unreconstructed southern racist" suffering from "moral senility," who deliberately "dehumanizes every black person in the book" for the criminal purpose of legitimatizing "all of [the white] myths and prejudices about the American black man"—and so on.[4] Like the white schoolchildren in South Carolina at the turn of the century who had to take an oath never to read *Uncle Tom's Cabin* because there was no truth in Mrs. Stowe, present-day blacks are being similarly assured that they can safely despise Mr. Styron's book without having to read it. One index of how successful this programmatic onslaught has been is the fate of the motion picture based on the book. According to Styron, "irrational" and "intentionally false" charges by black militants that the book was racist so intimidated 20th Century-Fox that it severed Styron's connection with the film. As of now, the movie is "shelved."[5]

A less dramatic but perhaps more disturbing result of the war on *The Confessions* is to be found in the case of Ralph Ellison. Ellison, as all who have followed his career know, has always been his own man in cultural and literary matters concerning the Negro in America and has written what many readers think to be the most powerful treatment of the black experience in our country. Nor has he escaped abuse for this stance ("I am known as a bastard by certain of my militant friends because I am not what they call a part of the Movement"). It is therefore distressing to note that Ellison has recently admitted that "after the controversy I deliberately did not read [*The Confessions of Nat Turner*]," although he seems to have read *Ten Black Writers*.[6] Surely this is an evasion; and if such a man as Ralph Ellison is evading, then it would seem as if, indeed, the black campaign against Styron's novel has had just about complete success. After asserting that Styron "invited the kind of attack he received," Stephen E. Henderson, with evident satisfaction, concludes, "one can be fairly certain that the next white writer will think twice before presuming to interpret the Black Experience."[7]

One of the essays in *Ten Black Writers* is entitled "You've Taken My

[3]White's columns are in the Nov. 25 and Dec. 9, 1967, issues of the *New York Amsterdam News*, Wilson's in the Oct. 21 and Dec. 30, 1967, issues of the same newspaper.
[4]The quotations are respectively from pp. 56, 72, viii and 34 of *Ten Black Writers.*
[5]Detroit *Free Press* (UPI), Mar. 13, 1970.
[6]Ralph Ellison, William Styron, Robert Penn Warren, C. Vann Woodward, "The Uses of History in Fiction," *Southern Literary Journal*, I (Spring 1969), 74, 87.
[7]Mercer Cook and Stephen E. Henderson, *The Militant Black Writer* (Madison: Univ. of Wisconsin Press, 1969), p. 74.

Nat and Gone." The "My" in this title—as throughout the volume—is meant to refer to the "real," the "true," the "historical" Nat Turner, the meaning of whose life Styron has deliberately attempted "to steal." For these black critics, there is neither ambiguity nor haziness nor complexity in the figure of Nat Turner. *They* know him—know him not merely as a racial symbol but as an historical fact. And the historical fact which Styron has "distorted," "manipulated," "rejected," "emasculated" is the "true story" of an authentic militant hero and revolutionist, a 19th century version of H. Rap Brown or Stokely Carmichael.[8] Now this may indeed be the truth of the matter, but how do these 20th century critics think they know this? They know this, they tell us, because *history* has told them so. And what is this history? It is, for the most part, the 1831 *Confessions* ("the basic historical document"), the full text of which is appended to the volume to serve, presumably, as a starkly historical repudiation of the "vile racist myth" of Styron's "faked confessions." Although some reservations about Gray's pamphlet are voiced (most particularly by John Killens), and some other 19th century historical writings are referred to, it is "the astringent report of Lawyer Gray," as Vincent Harding puts it (p. 29), which is for these black writers the basis of "the real history." "It should be noted," remarks Lerone Bennett, "that Nat Turner was served better in many instances by Thomas Gray, the avowed racist, than by William Styron, the avowed liberal" (p. 5). "Gray . . . gives [Turner] to history, unrepentant, courageous, sure of his act and his eventual vindication" (p. 16). This needs some looking at.

The year 1831 is a highly significant one in the annals of American Negro history. In January of that year, William Lloyd Garrison began publication of *The Liberator*, an abolitionist newspaper considered so dangerous that the Georgia legislature offered a reward for his capture. In his first issue, Garrison presented his readers with this piece of melodramatic emancipatory rhetoric:

> Wo if it come with storm, and blood, and fire,
> When midnight darkness veils the earth and sky!
> So to the innocent babe—the guilty sire—
> Mother and daughter—friends of kindred tie!
> Stranger and citizen alike shall die![9]

Seven months later, as if to prove Garrison's verse prophetic, a grandly

---

[*] The connection between Turner and Carmichael or Brown is made throughout the book, sometimes explicitly (e.g., pp. ix, 32, 36), sometimes implicitly by reference to present-day Black Power advocates. A 1968 anthology of militant writings, *The Black Power Revolt*, includes a section from Gray's *Confessions*.

[9] Quoted by W. P. Garrison, *William Lloyd Garrison* (New York: Century, 1885), I, 229.

mad or a madly grand slave—which, we shall perhaps never know—named Nat Turner led a band of some sixty Negroes in a bloody massacre of some fifty-five whites, mostly women and children, in Southampton, Virginia. Some of the rebels lost their lives battling federal and state troops, some were deported, some were hanged. Others were let off because they were considered mere dupes of Turner, thereby obviating the injustice of punishing the "innocent" owners of only semi-guilty property. Turner himself escaped capture for about ten weeks; he was tried on November 5, 1831, and hanged six days later, but not before he presumably gave an account of himself, "fully and voluntarily," to one Thomas R. Gray, who had it published in Baltimore in an edition of thousands of copies as *The Confessions of Nat Turner, The Leader of the Late Insurrection in Southampton, Va.* (1831).[10] Although, according to Gray, Turner had killed but one person, Margaret Whitehead, he was universally considered by whites as the sole "author of their misfortune." According to a later account, William Drewry's *The Southampton Insurrection* (1900), Turner's body was skinned by physicians and a spiritual progenitor of the Bitch of Buchenwald had a purse made from part of the hide.[11]

There had been slave unrest before 1831, most frequently expressed in individual rebellion or escape, a phenomenon which southern psychology handled by attributing it to a disease—"drapetomania," from the Greek words meaning "runaway slave" and "insanity." Then, too, there were two large-scale revolts led by Gabriel Prosser in 1800 and Denmark Vesey in 1822, both, however, aborted through betrayal by one or more of the leader's black followers. Nevertheless, despite their failure, both insurrections contributed to the shattering of the relative tranquility with which white Southerners customarily contemplated their peculiar institution, a tranquility in no small part dependent upon a conspiracy of silence. During the Denmark Vesey scare, for example a Charleston lady wrote that 2500 whites were under arms but cautioned her correspondent that "it is a subject not to be mentioned . . . say nothing about it."[12] Governor Monroe of Virginia writing President Jefferson of the Prosser revolt calls it "unquestionably the most serious and formidable conspiracy we have ever known of the kind," and says that he tried to keep it "secret" for as long as he could.[13] But it was the success of the Turner insurrection, Prosser and

[10]All quotations from Gray's *Confessions* are from a facsimile copy of the 1831 edition in the William L. Clements Library of the University of Michigan.

[11]This grisly fact is supported by John Cromwell, whose 1920 article reports that "there still lives a Virginian who has a piece of [Turner's] skin which was tanned." ("The Aftermath of Nat Turner's Insurrection," *Journal of Negro History*, 5 [1920], 218.)

[12]Quoted by T. W. Higginson, "Gabriel's Defeat," *Atlantic Monthly*, 10 (1862), 337–45.

[13]S. M. Hamilton, ed., *Writings of James Monroe* (New York: G. P. Putnam's, 1898–1903), III, 201. The letter is dated Sept. 5, 1800.

Vesey's contemplated murders accomplished, which broke the secret and unleashed a widespread fear of a general servile war. That slaves would rise up in the night to butcher their masters in what George Fitzhugh was to characterize as "civilized and virtuous" Virginia, where "negroes . . . love their master and his family, and the attachment is reciprocated,"[14] this could hardly help causing a shock of horrified bewilderment to pass through the mind of the white South. Here, then, were the materials for a crisis in the stereotyped white perception of the slave-master relationship. The place was not Mississippi or Arkansas where mind-and-body-killing practices could drive slaves to the measures of despair. "No one has dreamed of any such event happening in any part of Virginia," the astonished Richmond *Enquirer* lamented two days after the revolt.[15] Nor was the slave himself, even by his own admission, ill-treated. How, then, could it have happened?

It would be difficult to exaggerate the psychic toll which the Turner massacre exacted from the southern mind. As is evidenced in the ritualistic desecration of Turner's body, the event had cut through to the lower layers of the psyche where the nightmares are transacted. The Richmond *Enquirer* quotes one reader as saying "there it is, the dark and growing evil at our doors. . . . What is to be done? Oh! My God, I do not know, but something must be done."[16] A contemporary in Richmond wonders if the Turner rebellion might not "excite those to insurrection that never thought of such a thing before." A southern lady judges the situation to be "like a smothered volcano," is afraid "that death in the most horrid form threatens us," and asserts that some have already "become deranged from apprehension since the South Hampton affair." A Virginian writes a friend in Ohio: "These insurrections have alarmed my wife so as really to endanger her health, and I have not slept without anxiety in three months. Our nights are sometimes spent listening to noises. A corn song, a hog call, has often been a subject of nervous terror, and a cat, in the dining room, will banish sleep for the night."[17]

Considering the psychological investment that the white Southerner had made in a life based upon the institution of slavery, it is not surprising that when confronted with an event that cried out for a reassessment of the presiding assumptions upon which that institution was based, he turned in wrath toward combating the effects, and in righteousness toward preventing

[14]*Cannibals All!* (rpr. Cambridge: Harvard Univ. Press, 1960), p. 200.
[15]Quoted by Herbert Aptheker, *Nat Turner's Slave Rebellion* (New York: Grove Press, 1968), p. 58.
[16]Quoted in C. G. Sellers Jr., "The Travail of Slavery," *American Negro Slavery*, A. Weinstein and F. O. Gatell, eds. (New York: Oxford Univ. Press, 1968), p. 179.
[17]Aptheker, pp. 59–60.

its recurrence, rather than in doubt toward scrutinizing its causes. Vigilante committees were hurriedly formed to kill and terrorize Negroes and state legislatures met in emergency sessions to pass laws which would further inhibit the freedom of slaves and discourage manumission. "We have," one Virginia lawmaker affirmed, "closed every avenue by which light might enter their minds. If you could extinguish the capacity to see the light, our work would be completed: they would then be on a level with the beasts of the field, and we should be safe."[18] This is precisely the specific moral that Thomas Gray was to draw from the Turner insurrection: "It is calculated . . . to demonstrate the policy of our laws in restraint of this class of our population, and to induce all those entrusted with their execution, as well as our citizens generally, to see that they are strictly and rigidly enforced."

The attacks on Styron's novel generally take it for granted that Thomas R. Gray was not much more than a recorder of Turner's words and that therefore his *Confessions* is a reasonably reliable source for our knowledge of Turner and his motives. Aptheker, for example, uses Gray's pamphlet as the base in reality from which to attack Styron's novel as a "consequential distortion" of the truth.[19] Our impression, however, is that Gray was anything but a blank-faced scrivener; that he was, on the contrary, a very shrewd man who knew precisely what he was doing and why; and that his pamphlet is a political document in the most basic sense of the word.

We ought, first of all, to remind ourselves just how much of the pamphlet, despite its title, is Gray's. It is Gray who structures the work so that Turner's words are sandwiched between his own interpretation of the event and his horrified eyeball-to-eyeball confrontation with the black murderer; it is Gray who decides when to quote and when to paraphrase; it is Gray who ends the document with the lists of murdered whites and sentenced Negroes. Moreover, it is also well to remember that we have only Gray's word for it that the section of the pamphlet entitled "Confession" is in fact the "faithful record" of Turner's statement "with little or no variation." It is certainly true that a lot of effort went into authenticating the document—some might feel too much. Five Justices of the Peace certified that the confession was read to Turner who acknowledged it "to be full, free, and voluntary," and then the county clerk certified the judges. But considering Turner's position at the time ("covered with chains") and what we know of eliciting confessions from prisoners, one can be pardoned for not accepting all the legal paraphernalia as prima-facie evidence of the authenticity

---

[18]Quoted in W. L. Katz, *Eyewitness: The Negro in American History* (New York: Pitman, 1967), p. 104.

[19]"Styron's Nat Turner . . . A Note on the History," *Nation*, 205 (Oct. 16, 1967), 375–76.

of the *Confession*, especially when certain internal evidences, which we will come to in a moment, also lend themselves to doubt.

Gray's pamphlet is an exercise in reassurance—on two levels. Most explicitly, it attempts to lay to rest the "thousand idle, exaggerated and mischievous reports" which had so "greatly excited the public mind." Because the specter of a mass uprising of slaves had been somewhere back in the shadows of the white Southerner's mind ever since the successful revolt in Haiti in the 1790s, rumors inflated the extent of the uprising in Southampton to frightening proportions. Accordingly, Gray assures his readers that the insurrection was purely "local," and that Turner's "designs" were "confided but to a few, and these in his immediate vicinity." Gray tells us that when he questioned Turner about an insurrection occurring in North Carolina about the same time, "he denied any knowledge of it. . . ."[20] What Gray calls "the first instance in our history of an open rebellion of the slaves" has proved to be a purely parochial phenomenon.

More interesting, however, is the way the pamphlet confronts what Gray recognizes as the deeper psychic disturbance inherent in the "conspiracy." Although Gray usually keeps the level of his discourse safely above the sinister with such psychologically innocuous phrases as "public curiosity," he is keenly aware of the "deep impression" that Turner's rebellion has made "not only upon the minds of the community where this fearful tragedy was wrought, but throughout every portion of our country, in which this population [slaves] is to be found."[21] He knows that unless he can satisfactorily explain (or, rather, reassuringly explain away) "the origin and progress of this dreadful conspiracy, and the motives which influence[d] its diabolical actors," his pamphlet will have failed in one of its essential purposes—the removal of "doubts and conjectures from the public mind."

With the word "diabolical" Gray signals his primary strategy—a deliberate attempt to depict Turner as a possessed, deluded, religious maniac so as to short-circuit any disturbing thoughts about the institution of slavery which might tend to issue from the insurrection. *Ferocious, dark, remorseless, corrupted, warped, perverted, fiendlike, inhuman*—these adjectives thread Gray's framing remarks and point the direction of his characteriza-

---

[20]What Gray is probably referring to is the *report* of an extensive slave conspiracy in eastern North Carolina in early October 1831. (See Hugh T. Lefler, ed., *North Carolina History Told by Contemporaries* [Chapel Hill: Univ. of North Carolina Press, 1934], p. 265.)

[21]An example of the perturbation caused by the Turner insurrection was the reaction in Murfreesboro, North Carolina, as reported by the Baltimore *Gazette* (Nov. 16, 1831): "Fear was seen in every face, women pale and terror stricken, children crying for protection, men fearful and full of foreboding, but determined to be ready for the worst." (Stephen B. Weeks, "The Slave Insurrection in Virginia," *Magazine of American History*, 25 [1891], 456.)

tion. The "fearful tragedy," Gray assures his white contemporaries, "was not instigated by motives of revenge or sudden anger" against slaveholders. It was rather the result of a "bewildered and over-wrought mind" in whose "dark recesses" religious enthusiasm had turned to homicidal mania. "Fiendish," "inhuman," "hellish," the massacre was, but only in the sense that it emanated from "a mind . . . endeavoring to grapple with things beyond its reach." Religion "bewildered and confounded, and finally corrupted" Turner's naturally intelligent mind until he was left outside the pale of humanity, "a complete fanatic." How else, Gray asks, can we explain that of all the insurrectionists only Turner made no attempt "to exculpate himself," but frankly and without remorse acknowledged his monstrous acts?

Gray has looked into the pit, but it is, after all, he assures his readers, a psychologically manageable one. Gray has attempted to make his readers feel what we feel when we read in a newspaper that a man has killed his entire family because God had commanded him to do so. We may be appalled but we are not involved. Murder for passion or money or freedom— these are capable of implicating us as social creatures, or individuals, because we can identify with such murders humanly. But religious madness leaves us safely on the outside: nothing we do or do not do can affect it.[22] What we are suggesting, then, is that even as Gray recounts the ghastly details of the massacre, he is supplying his readers with the means for removing it from the structure of the slave-master relationship. The white man's self-fulfilling prophecy—his selective inattention to all aspects of slavery save those which reenforced his stereotyped response—has been left intact.

The self-portrait which emerges from the section of the pamphlet entitled "Confession" dovetails with the "argument" in Gray's framework. It breaks into two almost equally discrete parts: a rhetorically pressured account of the origin and progress of Turner's communion with supernatural forces, followed by a matter-of-fact resumé of the massacre. The contrast between the passionate sense of divine election and the dispassionate murder of human beings is, as we are certain it was intended to be, grotesque.

As a child of three or four, Turner astounded his family by relating events which occurred before he was born. The mysterious ease with which he learned to read (he had no recollection of learning the alphabet) and his capacity for knowing of things even before he learned they existed, convinced Nat that he was not like other men. His superior knowledge ("perfected by Divine inspiration") set him above and apart from the other

[22]"The case of Nat Turner warns us [that] no black man ought to be permitted to turn a preacher. . . . the law must be enforced—or the tragedy of Southampton appeals to us in vain" (Richmond *Enquirer*, Apr. 30, 1832).

slaves, who looked to him for leadership. But having discovered himself "to be great," he must appear so: "[I] therefore studiously avoided mixing in society, and wrapped myself in mystery, devoting my time to fasting and prayer—" One day at prayer the "Spirit" spoke to him, saying "Seek ye the kingdom of Heaven and all things shall be added unto you." (When Gray asked him what he meant by "Spirit," Turner replied, "The Spirit that spoke to the prophets in former days.") After two more years of prayer, the Spirit spoke to him again and "fully confirmed [him] in the impression" that he "was ordained for some great purpose in the hands of the Almighty." At this point, Turner, knowing the influence he had over his fellow slaves, who attributed his wisdom to "the communion of the spirit," began to prepare them for "the great promise that had been made to [him]." In 1825, Turner's destiny was made manifest in another vision: he saw white and black spirits locked in mortal combat in the sky, from which blood flowed in streams while the sun darkened and thunder rolled through the heavens. "Such is your luck," he heard a voice say, "such you are called to see, and let it come rough or smooth, you must surely bare [sic] it." He withdrew even further into solitude until one day a voice promised him that it would be given to him to know the whole nature of the cosmos: "the knowledge of the elements, the revolution of the planets, the operation of tides, and changes of the seasons." Turner then sought even more strenuously the state of "true holiness," and when he was made "perfect," he saw the light from Christ's hands stretched across the skies. He prayed for certainty and in answer he discovered blood upon the leaves, which, in "hieroglyphic characters," represented the figures he had seen in the heavens. The Holy Ghost revealed himself to Turner and explained that the blood which Christ had shed on earth had ascended to heaven and was now returning to earth—"the great day of judgment was at hand." On May 12, 1828, the Spirit again appeared to Turner, telling him to prepare to fight the "Serpent," for the day when the last shall be first was approaching. (At this point Gray asked him if he felt himself now mistaken, to which Turner replied: "Was not Christ crucified [?]") The sign which the Spirit had promised appeared in February 1830, in the form of an eclipse of the sun, and Turner communicated "the great work laid out for me to do" to four of his most trusted fellow slaves. They hoped to begin "the work of death" on July 4, 1831, but were unable to arrive at a suitable plan; when another sign appeared in August, they delayed no longer.

It may be objected at this point that Turner's charisma is not so unusual since it was the customary practice of 19th century Negro rebels against slavery to relate their advocacy of rebellion to Christian morality and biblical precedent. But a comparison of Turner's "explanation" with, for example, the use made of Christian ethics and teminology in Frederick

Douglass' *Narrative* (1845) or David Walker's *Appeal* (1829) shows a difference of such degree as to be a difference in kind. Whereas Turner unequivocally asserts the literal presence of supernatural phenomena in his life, Douglass only quietly indicates his faith in Providence, of which the following remark is typical: "I may be deemed superstitious, and even egotistical, in regarding this event [his being sent to Baltimore] as a special interposition of divine Providence in my favor. But I should be false to the earliest sentiments of my soul, if I suppressed the opinion."²³ And whereas Turner locates the command "to begin the work of death" in divine signs specially communicated to him, Walker evokes divine sanction for his holy crusade more as metaphor than as fact: "The man who would not fight under our Lord and Master, Jesus Christ, in the glorious and heavenly cause of freedom and God— . . . ought to be kept with all of his children or family, in slavery, or in chains. . . ."²⁴ Douglass exhibits the modulated faith of a Christian in the rectitude of his cause; Walker accommodates the rhetorical force of a readily available analogy to his political intention. But Turner—the Turner of Gray's pamphlet—is simply God-mad.

The mystical origin of the insurrection covers about five pages; the progress of the revolt and Turner's capture about six. Whereas the first part, as we have already suggested, is primarily directed toward discounting any socio-political implications in Turner's actions, the second both substantiates the religious madness of the leader and justifies the repressive measures which resulted from "this unparalled and inhuman massacre." This section conveys the impression that only a man whose connection with humanity has been totally severed could recount murder in such chillingly prosaic terms. Each death is flatly stated as a statistical fact, without so much as a hint of emotional involvement. "The murder of this family, five in number, was the work of a moment"; "there was a little infant sleeping in a cradle, that was forgotten, until . . . Henry and Will returned and killed it"; "we entered, and murdered Mrs. Reese in her bed"; "Will immediately killed Mrs. Turner, with one blow of his axe"; "I struck her several blows over the head, but . . . the sword was dull"; "they . . . had not been idle; all the family were already murdered"; "I killed her by a blow on the head, with a fence rail"; "Having murdered Mrs. Waller and ten children, we started for Mr. William Williams'— [and] killed him and two little boys that were there."

If these are indeed Turner's words, then he has given us a devastatingly effective self-portrait of a man who, through a sense of divine mission, has

²³*Narrative of the Life of Frederick Douglass* (rpr. Cambridge: Harvard Univ. Press, 1967), p. 56.
²⁴Milton Meltzer, ed., *In Their Own Words: A History of the American Negro* (New York: Thomas Y. Crowell, 1967), I, 26.

rendered himself unavailable to normal human feelings. Gray, however, seems not to have trusted wholly to this technique. His editorial prompting is not only evident in interspersed parentheses (which the careless reader might take for Turner's), but can perhaps also be discerned in several remarks supposedly made by Turner. For example, in the opening paragraph of the "Confession" Turner says that his early childhood "laid the ground work of that enthusiasm, which has terminated so fatally to many, both white and black, and for which I am about to atone at the gallows." Since Turner was convinced of the supernatural support of his insurrection, we would hardly expect him to characterize his religious commitment as "enthusiasm" since by the 19th century the term had only derogatory connotations, as is clear from Gray's later use of the word. Moreover, how can we possibly reconcile the idea of his having to "atone" for his "enthusiasm" with his response to Gray's query concerning Turner's feelings of guilt —"Was not Christ crucified?" *Atone* implies a sense of personal wrongdoing; the identification with Christ implies rectitude and holy sacrifice. They are scarcely reconcilable.

Other places in the *Confessions* betray additional signs of Gray's editorial hand. Considering Turner's rhetorically matter-of-fact method of recounting the murders, it is jarring to come upon stock locutions which italicize in the manner of sentimental fiction. It is difficult to conceive of Turner speaking of sending Richard Whitehead "to an untimely death," or crying out "Vain hope!" in response to a door shut by a white family against the invaders, or declaiming that Mrs. Reese's "son awoke, but it was only to sleep the sleep of death." Equally unbelievable is Turner's gothicized self-portrait of himself as viewing "the mangled bodies ... in silent satisfaction" or searching for "more victims to gratify our thirst for blood." The real Nat Turner, or even the Nat Turner who cold-bloodedly narrates the details of the slaughter, may indeed have *felt* something like this, but the language is as clearly Gray's as is its intention.

Near the end of the pamphlet Gray quotes the sentencing speech of the presiding judge in which Jeremiah Cobb remarks to Turner, "Your only justification is, that you were led away by fanaticism." And therein, Gray makes clear, is the central explanation. "It has been said," Gray earlier commented, "he was ignorant and cowardly, and that his object was to murder and rob for the purpose of obtaining money to make his escape." He was neither ignorant nor cowardly—a stereotype the white Southerner could identify—nor did he kill for money with which to escape, Gray replies. The truth, dramatically embodied, Gray gives his readers in that last glimpse of the two of them sitting in "the condemned hole" of the prison: "The calm, deliberate composure with which he spoke of his late deeds and intentions, the expression of his fiend-like face when excited by enthusiasm, still bearing the stains of the blood of helpless innocence about him; clothed with rags and covered with chains; yet daring to raise his manacled hands to heaven, with a spirit soaring above the attributes of man; I looked on him and my blood curdled." Driven by God-madness beyond all human definition, even that of the black human, Nat Turner has soared beyond the problem of slavery. Gray, then, despite recalcitrant materials, managed to do the job which John Calhoun demanded of Southerners—"We must satisfy the consciences, we must allay the fears, of our own people. We must satisfy them that slavery is of itself right . . . that it is not an evil, moral or political."[25]

It may be, as Aptheker says, that Gray's 1831 pamphlet must be the main source for our understanding of the Turner revolt—though we have already indicated our reservations—but its place in the 19th century creation of a Turner legend is far from unambiguous. It is to be expected that around its relatively meager details would swirl an enlarging body of folkloristic matter such as predictably accompanies any event of shocking magnitude, especially when, as is the case with the *Confessions*, the account does not satisfy one's imaginative sense of the drama. Such matter almost immediately achieved the status of fact in Samuel Warner's rumor-ridden and "almost wholly inaccurate"[26] *Authentic and impartial narrative of the tragical scene which was witnessed in Southampton County* . . . (1831). Then, to further complicate matters, subsequent reprintings of Gray's *Confessions* silently deleted significant portions of Gray's framework and/or, with equal silence, added spurious portions to it. An 1861 reprint, for example (as well as the version in the November 1859 issue of the *Anglo-African Magazine*), inserts, after Cobb's sentencing speech, a section entitled THE EXECUTION, an account of Turner's last moments.

—Nat Turner was executed according to sentence, on Friday, the 11th of November, 1831, at Jerusalem, between the hours of 10 A.M. and 2 P.M. He exhibited the utmost composure throughout the whole ceremony; and, although assured that he might, if he thought proper, address the immense crowd assembled on the occasion, declined availing himself of the privilege; and, being asked if he had any further confessions to make, replied that he had nothing more than he had communicated; and told the sheriff in a firm voice, that he was ready. Not a limb or muscle was observed to move. His body, after death, was given over to the surgeons for dissection.[27]

This material was to be used repeatedly by pro-Turner writers as if its source were the original Gray pamphlet.

[25]Quoted in Katz, p. 104.   [26]Aptheker, p. 116.
[27]*The Confessions of Nat Turner* (1861) (rpr. Miami: Mnemosyne, 1969), p. 12; *The Anglo-African Magazine*, 1 (rpr. New York: Arno, 1968), 396.

It is perhaps impossible by now to unscramble all but the most salient facts of the Turner insurrection from the legendizing matter which has been spun around it, to, in Louis Rubin's words, "reconstruct anything resembling the real Nat Turner. . . ."[28] What is of interest, then, is how these "facts" were used by subsequent writers. The bloody fiend with his manacled hands raised blasphemously to heaven gave the proslavery mentality its basic image of the demonized alien; but the very power of the portrait, aided by additional materials, evoked for opposing points of view moral shapes quite the reverse of what Gray intended.

Thomas Gray's interpretation of Nat Turner had a long life in the South. Turner's kind master coupled with the rebel's imagined communion with the supernatural made the motiveless malevolence explanation all but irresistible. Perhaps, as several scholars have suggested, Poe's nightmare vision of white men trapped in a fiendish black world—the Tsalal episode of *Arthur Gordon Pym* (1837–38)—takes its motive force from the southern view of Turner's insurrection. Under the mask of kindness of disposition and docile accommodation, the blacks lure the white men into a wholesale slaughter, literally tearing them to pieces in "brute rage." These blacks, Pym relates in horror, "for whom we entertained such inordinate feelings of esteem," were, in reality, "the most wicked, hypocritical, vindictive, bloodthirsty race of men upon the face of the globe." More directly, John Esten Cooke in his *Virginia: A History of the People* (1884) asserts that "Turner's motives remain unknown." The "plausible theory," he goes on, that Turner reacted to "cruelty is not supported by the facts." It is, says Cooke, the simple case of "a negro of feeble person [i.e. mind]" being driven mad by "passions and superstitions," the result of which was "a frenzied desire to shed blood, without further aims."[29] Even as late as 1941, a writer for the Virginia WPA saw the Southampton debacle as "an orgy of butchery" brought into bloody being by a religious maniac who had "exhorted into frenzy" his fellow-slaves.[30]

The only change of note rung on the Gray thesis was the accusation, utterly predictable and without any foundation in fact, that Abolitionist propaganda had driven over the brink a mind already unbalanced by superstition. In his "The Morals of Slavery . . ." William Gilmore Simms attributed the Southampton insurrection to "the secret workings of the abolitionists,"[31] and W. S. Drewry found abolitionist incitation a useful explanation for an event which seemed to him rationally opaque—a well-

[28]"William Styron and Human Bondage: *The Confessions of Nat Turner*," *Hollins Critic*, 4 (Dec. 1967), 6.
[29](New York: Houghton, Mifflin, 1884), p. 487.
[30]*Virginia: A Guide to the Old Dominion* (New York: Oxford Univ. Press, 1941), p. 473.
[31]*The Pro-Slavery Argument* (Charleston: Walker, Richards, 1852), p. 223.

treated slave leading a murderous insurrection.[32] Something of the same thing is to be seen in *The Old Dominion; or, The Southampton Massacre* (1856) by G. P. R. James, an Englishman whose four years' residence in Virginia as consul at Norfolk evidently made him sympathetic—at least partially—to the southern view of Turner. Sir Richard Conway, the hero, has inherited a plantation close to the one on which Turner is a slave. His first meeting with Turner jars his conception of the Negro as a happy-go-lucky child of nature utterly devoid of intellect. Sir Richard is initially impressed by Turner's apparent metaphysical cast of mind, although Turner's idiotic laugh upon catching a fish gives the Englishman pause. In subsequent meetings Sir Richard acknowledges that Turner is a superior specimen, but that even he has "almost all the peculiar weaknesses of the African race"; he is cunning, superstitious, conceited and, as Sir Richard discerns, capable of ruthless cruelty. The real villain in the piece, however, is a nefarious northern abolitionist, the Reverend Mr. M'Grubber, who duplicitously incites Turner to his disastrous insurrection and is given his just deserts when he becomes the first man Turner kills. "I have come to the conclusion"—says Sir Richard's "acute friend"—"that the abolitionists are the very worst enemies of the slaves themselves."

Of far greater interest are the responses in the north to Gray's proslavery apology. Unwittingly, the *Confessions*, directly or indirectly, set in motion a process of reverse mythologization by giving the antislavery intellectuals a romantic symbol which they could recreate in terms of their own most passionate convictions. Although the emphases vary, these writers changed Turner's purpose, his motivation, the quality of his mind, the character of his religion, even his appearance. The maniac became messiah; the Black Beast became the Black John Brown; mad murder became moral symbol.

When the nonresistant abolitionist William Lloyd Garrison read Gray's pamphlet, he acidly remarked that a bounty should be put on Gray's head, for his pamphlet would "hasten other insurrections," a method of emancipation to which he was strongly opposed. Mrs. Stowe also read the pamphlet as creating a slave-hero; but because she saw slavery as primarily a religious problem, her response to Gray's Turner was not Garrison's. That Turner had aligned himself with the Savior—"Was not Christ crucified?"—was for Mrs. Stowe the decisive fact. In *Dred* (1856), to which she appended the *Confessions*, presumably for the purpose of authenticating her portrait, the title character, although nominally the son of Denmark Vesey, is really Nat Turner. Like Gray's Turner, Dred has learned to read with mysterious ease, has seen bloody "hieroglyphics" on the leaves and the crucified Christ in the heavens, and is consumed by his sense of an apoc-

[32]William S. Drewry, *The Southampton Insurrection* (Washington: Neal, 1900), *passim.*

alyptic destiny. But the proslavery Turner is, of course, turned 180 degrees
—from a "warped and perverted" demon to a sacrificial prophet of emancipation. "Nat Turner—they killed him," Dred exclaims, "but the fear of
him almost drove them to set free their slaves! . . . Die? Why not die? Christ
was crucified."

When Thomas Wentworth Higginson, a brave champion of the black
man's rights, turned his attention to "Nat Turner's Insurrection" in 1861,[33]
he did so with something more than a scholarly interest in his subject. His
sources were contemporary newspaper accounts, "legends" and what he
calls "a small pamphlet, containing the main features of the outbreak"
(not Gray's, he admits). His essay, however, is an imaginative construct as
well, for it was Higginson's intention to contour a portrait which would
validate his claim that "beside the actual Nat Turner," Mrs. Stowe's "Dred
seems dim and melodramatic."

Higginson's Nat Turner suffers the indignities and injustices of slavery.
He has a wife whom he cannot protect from sexual "outrage," scars on his
body which may have come from white hands, and a band of blacks that
"had been systematically brutalized from childhood" and who "had seen
their wives and sisters habitually polluted" by white ravishers. More important, Prophet Nat has the strength of character that comes of rectitude,
such as had John Brown, to whom he is compared. He confesses his crimes
but pleads not guilty; meets his death "with perfect composure," signaling
the sheriff "in a firm voice that he was ready"; and at his execution "not a
limb nor a muscle was observed to move." (The source for these facts, it
will be noted, is the passage which was later spuriously added to Gray's
Confessions.)

But what is most significant in Higginson's portrait is his handling of
the mystical pronouncements of Gray's Turner. Higginson acknowledges
them, to be sure, quoting whole passages. As "religious hallucinations,"
he remarks casually, they are "as genuine as the average of such things,
and are very well expressed." As Higginson begins to deploy them, however, it becomes clear that he views them as rhetorical strategies for revealing the intensity of Turner's commitment to freedom for his people, a
commitment so passionate that it needed the vocabulary of apocalypticism
to be adequately exposed. Even Thomas Gray, in Higginson's reading,
when vouchsafed a symbolic glimpse into "the heart of this extraordinary
man . . . who devoted himself soul and body to the cause of his race" (in the
manacled hands to heaven scene), rose, despite himself, "into a sort of bewildered enthusiasm." It was no religious fanatic, then, who fell like an
"earthquake on the doomed community around—and who . . . took the life

[33]*Atlantic Monthly*, 8 (1861), 173–87.

of man, woman, and child, without a throb of compunction, a word of exultation, or an act of superfluous outrage." It was, rather, in Higginson's final words, "a symbol of retribution triumphant."

Two years earlier, the preface to a heavily edited reprint of Gray's *Confessions* in the *Anglo-African Magazine* for 1859 made a somewhat different use of the Turner insurrection. "Emancipation must come, and soon," the black writer pronounced, and in only two ways could it be effected—the way of John Brown or the way of Nat Turner. Whereas John Brown believed that emancipation could be accomplished without blood by making the two races equal, "Nat Turner's terrible logic could only see the enfranchisement of one race compassed by the extirpation of the other." Had the order of events been reversed, the writer went on to say, "had Nat Turner been in John Brown's place . . . the soil of Virginia and Maryland and the far South, would by this time be drenched in blood." If John Brown's method of emancipation be not soon adopted, "then Nat Turner's will be by the enslaved South." Here Turner is neither maniac nor messiah, religious fanatic nor symbol of retribution. His insurrection is seen, rather, as the inevitable recoil to historical injustice, which, if not soon obviated in a rational manner, will leave the American slave with no choice other than Turner's "wild and sanguinary course." Which shall it be, the editorial concludes, Brown's way of reason or Turner's way of mass bloodletting? (p. 356).

William Wells Brown, who himself had at one time been a slave, devoted sixteen pages of his *The Black Man, His Antecedents, His Genius, and His Achievements* (1863) to Nat Turner,[34] almost half of them direct quotation from some version of Gray's pamphlet. Brown clearly had a fertile imagination: at one time or another he put forward three different autobiographical versions of his parentage and childhood. His novelistic bent (he was the author of *Clotel*) served him well in his dramatization of the progress of Nat Turner from a child "of an amiable disposition" to the gloomy man who "was never known to smile," thus fleshing out those "private . . . wrongs" which Higginson said we could never know. Detailed anecdotes, minutely observed settings, and long speeches give the impression that Brown was there (as a novelist is "there") and bring Turner much closer to the reader than he is in Higginson's account. Brown gives no sources for his sketch except for Gray, who, he says, "had known Nat from boyhood," thus perhaps implying that Gray is the source for Brown's stories of Turner's childhood, which he is not.

It is in the context of the southern view of the Southampton insurrectionist that Brown's opening assertion that "the American people are not

[34](Repr. New York: Arno, 1969), pp. 59–75.

prepared to do justice" to Turner is to be understood. Accordingly, Brown sets out to trace the "circumstances" which changed an intelligent young slave of "kind and docile" disposition into one who was wracked with "the most intense hatred [for] the white race." Brown begins with two as-the-twig-is-bent incidents. When still a boy, Turner was "severely flogged" by two "patrolers," Whitlock and Mull, for being off his master's plantation without a pass; a few months later, a gang of white boys cruelly pelted Nat, who had "no right to retaliate," with snowballs. No Sambo, Nat responds to these incidents with a burning desire for revenge. With Tom Sawyer-cleverness, Nat tricks the two patrolers into an accident, Mull suffering a dislocated shoulder and a severely lacerated face, and Whitlock a broken wrist and a bashed head; a concealed Nat repays the gang of boys for their snowballs with accurately hurled rocks. Both incidents, as Brown-the-novelist shapes them, not only serve as motivating factors but also as symbolic prophecies of the central action of Turner's life, thereby contributing significantly to that sense of wholeness and continuity in his subject's life which all mythicized figures must possess.

Growing ill-treatment causes Nat to withdraw more and more into himself and into communion with his visions. "Being hired out to cruel masters" (in Gray, "placed under an overseer"), Nat runs away for thirty days but returns, his only explanation being the biblical injunction "Return to your earthly master, for he who knoweth his Master's will, and doeth it not, shall be beaten with many stripes." (Brown omits the rest of the quotation which in Gray concludes with "and thus have I chastened you.") The final meeting before the insurrection takes place in a "wild and romantic" swampland "upon which human feet seldom trod, on account of its having been the place where a slave had been tortured to death by a slow fire. . . ." Turner's final speech, which is "quoted" directly, certainly attempts to normalize the insurrection. It concludes: "Remember that we do not go forth for the sake of blood and carnage, but it is necessary that in the commencement of this revolution all the whites we meet should die, *until we shall have an army strong enough to carry on the war upon a Christian basis* [emphasis added]. Remember that ours is not a war for robbery and to satisfy our passions; it is a struggle for freedom. Ours must be deeds, not words. Then let's away to the scene of action." Then follows the account of the progress of the insurrection from Gray, and Nat's conduct at his execution from the interpolated paragraph already referred to.

An interesting addition to the legend is Brown's expanded characterization of Will, who here functions as a contrast to Turner. In Gray, all we learn of Will is that he joined the conspiracy without invitation, was willing to die for freedom and earned the title of "executioner" for his work during the slaughter. In Brown, however, Will joins the revolt "as much to satisfy revenge, as for the liberty he saw in the dim distance." His scarred body and face, testimony to his intractableness (he "scorned the idea of taking his master's name"), and the memory of "a dear and beloved wife sold to the negro trader" turn him into the most "bloodthirsty and revengeful" of the insurrectionists. His dying words were, "Bury my axe with me," because, Brown explains, Will "religiously believed that in the next world the blacks would have a contest with the whites, and that he would need his axe." Here, then, we can see how some of the religious madness of the proslavery image of Turner has been shifted to one of his lieutenants.[35]

Brown concludes his portrait with a conscious attempt to evoke Turner's mythic status—and a warning. Turner had predicted that the sun would refuse to shine at his death, and so it was that Southampton suffered the most "boisterous" storm in its history on the day of his execution. He is dead but his acts "live in the hearts of his race, on every cotton, sugar, and rice plantation at the South." For the present generation of slaves there is magic in his name and a belief that in another insurrection "Nat Turner will appear and take command." In the midst of the crisis of the Civil War, in which "the negro is an important item," all eyes are "turned towards the south, looking for another Nat Turner." And this should curdle the blood of the slave-holding states as Turner himself had curdled the blood of Thomas Gray, for "a negro insurrection, in the present excited state of the nation, would not receive the condemnation that it did in 1831."

Brown's omissions are of interest and worth speculating upon. He omits Turner's identification of himself with Christ (from Gray) perhaps because it smacked too much of religious mania; he makes no mention of the baptizing of the white man, Etheldred T. Brantley (also from Gray), perhaps because it would jar the black-white antithesis he works with— there are no good white men in the sketch; and he does not acknowledge the wife Higginson says Turner had (Brown had read Higginson's essay) because he may have felt that such a human connection would have destroyed his portrait of a lonely, isolated figure enveloped in "a gloom and melancholy that disappeared only with his life," one married solely to a desire for "freedom for his race."

The Nat Turner in George Washington Williams' magisterial *History of the Negro Race in America* (1883)[36] is essentially that of Wells Brown, much of which he quotes and paraphrases. The same items are omitted and

---

[35] It is interesting to compare the characterization of Will here with Brown's characterization of one Picquilo in his earlier account of the Turner insurrection. In *Clotel* (1853), Brown speaks of Picquilo (who is nowhere else mentioned in the literature of the revolt), as "one of the leaders of the Southampton insurrection"; this figure, from "one of the barbarous tribes in Africa," of "stern and savage countenance," "from revenge imbrued his hands in the blood of all the whites he could meet" (*Clotel* [rpr. New York: Arno, 1968], pp. 59-60).

[36] (Rpr. New York: Arno, 1968), II, 85-90.

the portrait is similarly directed toward presenting a "Black John Brown," whose image "is carved on the fleshy tablets of four million hearts," although because legal slavery was no more, Williams does not add the threat of further insurrections. Williams' contribution to the evolving image of Turner resides primarily in the extent to which he regularizes Turner's religion, making him even less of a religious freak than he was in Brown (who considered Turner's visions "wild" and the man himself, at least partially, though not crucially, "a victim of his own fanaticism"). Williams who was himself, amongst an impressive variety of accomplishments, a Baptist minister, considers Turner "a Christian and a *man*." Nat's early background made a religious emphasis inevitable. His parents, though unlettered, were very pious people, the father a preacher and the mother "a mother in Israel." From a very early age Nat was "set apart to the Gospel ministry by his father, the church, and visiting preachers." Turner's orthodoxy is revealed in his severe denunciations of such pagan practices as " 'conjuring,' 'gufering,' and fortune telling." It is to his well-meaning mother that Nat owed his sense of mission: "she would sing to him snatches of wild rapturous songs and repeat portions of prophecies she had learned from the preachers of the times." To these exciting tales the impressionable youngster "listened with reverence and awe, and believed every thing his mother said." His grandmother, too, "a very old and superstitious person [Brown called her "ignorant"] encouraged him in his dreams." His death is a set-piece of Christian sentimentalism: "He died like a man, bravely, calmly, looking into eternity, made radiant by a faith that never faltered."

By the time Turner comes to William J. Simmons' massive biographical dictionary, *Men of Mark* (1887),[37] all mention of the bizarre aspects of Turner's religion has disappeared. Turner is now a Baptist preacher ordained by his father; his eyes "shone with the brightness of diamonds" whenever "he spoke of the Scriptures or the wrongs of his race." On Sundays he would come to the plantations to preach to the slaves and then go back to the mountains "to brood over the condition of his burdened people." Naturally, Simmons remarks (with justice), some racists have tried to demean this "Spartacus of the Negro race" by calling "him a religious fanatic." "When men of other nations have arisen and used whatever means they had at their command to liberate their people, it has been called heroism; with the Negro it is brutality." Simmons' clear-eyed "bold emancipator" has come as far from Gray's "gloomy fanatic" as it is possible to come: the counter-myth is complete. Simmons' most imaginative addition is his expansion of the story of Turner's having run away for thirty days.

[37](Rpr. New York: Arno, 1968), pp. 1035-39.

Where before Turner simply leaves, here he strikes the slave-breaker to the ground and leaves him tied in ropes.[38]

As we hope the above survey makes clear, Styron's novelistic attempt, in his words, "to re-create and bring alive that dim and prodigious black man" is not, as hostility would have it, a "libelous" deviation from history into myth. It is, rather, very much a part of a tradition. Styron has "used" Nat Turner as Gray, Higginson, Wells Brown and, indeed, the accusing critics themselves have used him—reading into him, and out of him, those usable truths which seemed to him to coalesce about the image he was contemplating. Styron's hostile critics may not like what his imaginative search has turned up; they may even in the free country which is literary study denigrate his motives and try to deny him the right to his subject. But they can scarcely attack his "meditation on history" from some supposedly unassailable rampart of historicity. There is no such lofty redoubt from which to hurl down upon the head of the author of *The Confessions of Nat Turner* a barrage of shattering historical facts with the killing aim these ten black critics imagine they possess, as the following examples will illustrate.[39]

"In real history," says John A. Williams, "Will was almost as patient and self-possessed as Turner" (p. 48). Mike Thelwell strenuously takes exception, as does Aptheker, to Styron's depiction of Will as a bestial, hate-ravished, scarred-up "half-nigger, half-beast" (Williams' words—p. 88). It is quite true, as Thelwell contends, that the Will in Gray does not suggest dementia or frenzy. It is difficult, however, to see the efficient killer whom the Turner in Gray refers to as "the executioner" as being "patient," if Gray's pamphlet is what Williams means by "real history." But more to the point, William Wells Brown (whom Thelwell quotes approvingly, though he calls him James Wells Brown and cites the wrong book) tells us that Will, a battleground of physical and mental scars, has indeed been driven nearly mad by his life under slavery. Brown's Will joined the in-

---

[38]Until the appearance of Styron's novel and the critical recoil it occasioned, the 20th century added little to the image of Nat Turner. Two plays—Randolph Edmonds' *Nat Turner* (1934) and Paul Peters' *Nat Turner* (1944)—are well intentioned but essentially unimaginative treatments of the Black Moses. Daniel Panger's novel, *Ol' Prophet Nat* (1947), to which we make reference further on in the text, is a rather pedestrian fictionalizing of Higginson's essay, which is its primary source. Those 20th century black historians who have devoted some attention to Turner's insurrection—Carter Woodson, E. Franklin Frazier, Saunders Redding, Benjamin Quarles and John Hope Franklin, for example—have stayed pretty close to the slim historical record, content to describe what happened in objective terms.

[39]We address ourselves only to criticisms of the novel premised on Styron's purported historical distortions of the facts. Objections to style or other formalistic matters, psychological credibility or wholly "made-up" characters or situations, we have mostly passed over as lying outside the focus of this study, although not, of course, as lying outside legitimate areas of defense.

surrection "as much to satisfy revenge, as for the liberty he saw in the dim distance"—which is to say more immediately for revenge than for freedom. Having been tormented beyond endurance, Will turns out to be the most "unfeeling of the insurrectionists," the most "bloodthirsty and revengeful" of the conspirators, and his dying wish to be buried with his axe so as to be ready for the race war in the after life is a moving revelation of hatred becoming psychotic. If the accounts of Will in William Wells Brown and George Washington Williams (they are similar) are historical (and Thelwell says "Mr. Brown ... was, after all, writing history not fiction"), then Styron's Will is equally so. If they are not, then Brown and Williams also deserve the "racist" label for having turned Will into a "black beast stereotype." Considering the little we learn of Will from Gray's pamphlet, Thelwell's view of Will as an "archetypal destroyer" is quite as "imaginative" as Styron's portrait of him as a slavery-maddened killer.

The outraged critical objection to the form which Will's desire for revenge takes in Styron's novel—murder and rape are twisted in his mind into a single cathartic act—is admittedly more problematic. No sexual incidents seem to have occurred during the insurrection, and Styron depicts none. The absence of sexual molestation seemed remarkable enough to later commentators to be worth noting. Higginson, for example—who is approvingly cited by various of the critics on other historical matters—mentions a report that some of the conspirators "were resolved on taking white women for wives, but were overruled by Nat Turner." "If so," he goes on to say, "he is the only American slave-leader of whom we know certainly that he rose above the ordinary level of slave vengeance..." (p. 176). Considering the well-documented fact that servile vengeance (and not just black) often takes the form of murder and sexual outrage, and that Higginson gives us some reason for believing that the Turner insurrection was not *wholly* eccentric in this regard, then Styron's decision to characterize Will as he did is not an utter historical "perversion," as has been asserted, although there is no *biographical* justification for the portrait. With the exception of Turner himself, no other conspirator is so individuated in the historical record as is Will; his ferocity made him the logical choice to act out an authentic modality of slave life, without which the depiction of that wretchedly peculiar institution would be that much the more incomplete. In this connection it is instructive to glance at Arna Bontemps' *Black Thunder* (1936), the novel which has been repeatedly flung in Styron's face as an example of how a slave-revolt novel should be written.

The sexual undertone of Gabriel Prosser's revolt reverberates effectively all through *Black Thunder*. Bontemps' handling of the one murder in the insurrection is a splendid dramatization of what Harold Cruse in *The Crisis of the Negro Intellectual* has described as "that racial drama of love and hate between slave and master, bound together in the purgatory of plantations." As Criddle, one of the insurrectionists, crouches outside a white farmhouse, he derives "an unaccountable pleasure from the thought of thrusting [his scythe-sword] through the pale young female that stood looking into the darkness.... Yet she looked flower-like and beautiful to him there.... She reminded him of a certain indentured white girl in town, a girl who made free with slaves.... That wasn't the kind of cutting he was up against tonight, though. Yet and still, there *were* similarities.... He held his sword arm tense; the scythe blade rose, stiffened, stiffened and remained erect. 'I'm going to start in right here, me.' "[40] Such explicit use of sexual imagery to crisscross and complicate the desire for murder during an insurrection by a black novelist in no way vitiates black critical enthusiasm for this "tremendous and perceptive novel." But when one of these critics contemplates a similarly imaged scene of sex and death in Styron's work, he contemptuously dismisses it with, "it looks as if nigger-beast has struck again" (p. 89).

Styron assigns Turner's education to his white master, but the critics insist that he was taught by his parents, citing the 1831 *Confessions* as evidence; they interpret this transfer as part of Styron's plot to create, as Bennett puts it, "a proper ADC slave family" (p. 9). Aptheker, who likewise sees Styron working in terms of "the so-called Moynihan thesis," puts the matter squarely: "Turner tells us that his parents taught him to read—though he adds that he has no memory of just how early this occurred" ("A Note on the History," p. 375). This is not *quite* what the pamphlet says. First of all, "Turner" does not tell us that his parents taught him to read. In that part of the *Confessions* in which he is presumably speaking in his own voice he says, "the manner in which I learned to read and write ... had great influence on my mind, as I acquired it with the most perfect ease, so much so that I have no recollection whatever of learning the alphabet." Moreover, his parents could hardly have taught him because when he demonstrated his ability, it was "to the astonishment of the family." It is *Gray*, speaking in his own voice, who later, in corroborating Turner's literacy, adds parenthetically "(it was taught him by his parents)." The matter, then, is not as unambiguous as these critics would lead us to believe. It is interesting to note, in this connection, that none of the later sympathetic accounts of Turner ascribe his learning to read to his parents, evidently preferring the more romantic explanation. When William Wells Brown, for example, quotes the passage in which Gray's paren-

[40](Rpr. Boston: Beacon Press, 1968), pp. 90-92.

thesis appears, he drops it out without a sign, having already chosen to go with the averred legend that "a full knowledge of the alphabet came to him in a single night" (pp. 72, 61). Only the proslavery accounts—those which had a vested interest in emphasizing the dangers of slave literacy—ascribed Turner's education to his parents.

There is nothing particularly "corrupt" historically about Styron's having rejected both explanations—the familial and the mystical—and having chosen to have Turner taught to read by a white master. After all, that prototypical slave-rebel, Frederick Douglass (whose autobiographical writings are one of the "sources" of Styron's novel), was similarly served by a white owner. The rejection of the mystical explanation is part of Styron's intention—which, as we have seen, was *the* intention of the 19th century pro-Turnerites—to eliminate Turner's most fanatic face, that religious warrior-freak who, Gray and Cooke knew, would be hard for the slaveholder or racist to recognize. This led him to omit as well the descriptions of Turner "praying at the plow," the bizarre "hieroglyphic characters ... in blood," the manacled-hands-to-heaven scene in which Turner becomes "a spirit soaring above the attributes of man," and the literal identification of himself with Christ—which Mrs. Stowe found so apt but which the later black historians downgraded. Since Styron intended a representationally human victim of the tragedy of slavery, the critical accusation that he refused "to confront the man who talked to God and who heard God order the destruction of the enemies of God and man" (p. 12) could hardly strike him as telling. It may be, as Bennet asserts, that Turner's visions "are obviously genuine [since] Thomas Gray was hardly up to inventions of that order" (p. 5), but it is interesting to note that in the preface to the 1968 reprint of *Black Thunder* Arna Bontemps tells us that one of the reasons he chose *not* to write on the Turner insurrection "was the business of Nat's 'visions' and 'dreams.'" Not quite knowing how to take this "trance-like mumbo jumbo," and, like Styron, distrusting Gray, he turned to Gabriel Prosser, for "freedom was a less complicated affair in his case" (pp. xii–xiii).

Styron's decision to have Samuel Turner teach his intelligent slave to read, although without specific justification in the historical record, is part of his intention to expose one aspect of the relationship of the well-meaning slaveholder to the institution of slavery. That is, it functions in the service of revealing that well-validated historical insight which Styron in the novel calls "the central madness of nigger existence": that the more humanely the slave was treated the more he rebelled against the inhumanity of his condition. Samuel Turner, the benevolent slaveholder, it will be remembered, is the only man for whom Turner felt a gaggingly intense personal hatred, and who, more than anyone else in the novel, impelled Turner to his final decision to make white blood flow "in a foaming sacrament." The truth of this apparently paradoxical insight was first testified to by Frederick Douglass, who repeatedly asserted that kind treatment intensified rather than lessened the slave's desire for freedom. Higginson, remarking on "the extreme felicity of [Turner's] position as a slave" (in Gray, Turner acknowledged that his last owner "was to me a kind master [of whose treatment] I had no cause to complain") also pointed to the paradox that "in all insurrections, the standing wonder seems to be that the slaves most trusted and best used should be most involved" (p. 186). It is therefore puzzling in the extreme to discover that these critics, for whom Gray, Douglass and Higginson are historically valid touchstones (Higginson and Douglass are repeatedly cited), consider this aspect of Styron's novel another instance of his lack of historical understanding "of the psychology which makes slaves rise up and cut their oppressors' throats from ear to ear." For Charles Hamilton, such a portrayal denies Turner "his basic revolutionary temperament" and shows "Styron join[ing] that school of thought which believes that the kinder you treat the subjects, the more likely they are to rebel" (p. 76). And Loyle Hairston reads the slaveowner's kindness in the novel as Styron's attempt to show how "benign" the peculiar institution was, to prove that Turner's insurrection was only "the vengeful ingratitude of a literate, pampered slave for his benevolent masters, an ingratitude which turns, unprovoked, into hatred and murder" (p. 67). This not only demonstrates a lack of knowledge of the historical tradition in which Styron is working, but a penchant for malicious misreading as well.[41]

Among the other "historical discrepancies" of which Styron is accused is his handling of Turner's grandmother and his omission of Turner's reputed wife.[42] In Gray, Turner says of his grandmother only that she encouraged him in his sense of special destiny and that he was "much attached" to her. Later accounts either drop her or characterize her as "ignorant" or "superstitious" (Brown and Williams), part of that fundamentalistic religious ambience which helps to explain Turner's "belief that

[41] The ubiquitous association of Styron with the views of U. B. Phillips throughout *Ten Black Writers* is a depressing example of how when politics is in possession of a reader he can make himself believe anything he wants to, even to the point of fantasy.

[42] The accusation in *Ten Black Writers* that "Styron has eliminated thè troublesome black father" (p. 9) and that Turner "has no knowledge of his father" (p. 82) needs little to rebut it. It is simply not true. What is significant about Turner's father is that he was a proud man, who, when slapped by his owner, escaped into freedom for good. This action has left a decisive mark on Turner's memory and consciousness and is part of his evolving rebelliousness. That the father's escape takes place in the novel before Nat's birth rather than, as the legend has it, after, would seem to make no difference since even the child who was alive when it happened would have to think of it as an adult before its meaning would emerge for him.

he had seen visions, and received communications direct from God." Since Styron de-emphasized this aspect of the received legend, Turner's grandmother (even in memory) functions in a quite different historical way. In one of the most moving scenes in *The Confessions of Nat Turner*, Nat at age thirteen thinks of his grandmother dead at thirteen, as he stands gazing at the decaying orthography of the Negro cemetery. Destroyed by a Christian civilization, Turner's grandmother lies in a grave marked by a monument of poignant irony:

"TIG"
AET. 13
BORN AN
HEATHEN
DIED BAP-
TISED IN CHRIST
A.D. 1782
R.I.P.

Turner has never laid eyes on his grandmother, though he has "heard about her and her kind"; in his mind's eye he can see the pregnant, terrified Coromontee child-woman, paralyzed at the approach of her white owner, who to her was "white, white as bone or skulls or deadwood, whiter than those ancestral ghosts that prowl the African night," and who she believes is about to eat her. Having been "driven crazy by her baffling captivity," she tries to tear to pieces her newborn baby, Nat's mother, and dies in a stupor a few days later, having refused to eat. Why should Thelwell, who knows something of the history of slavery, be so contemptuous of this portrait of, as he snidely puts it, "a mute, catatonic, culturally shocked Coromontee wench" (p. 83)? True enough, there is no historical source, narrowly construed, for the portrait; but, typologically, it is unassailably historical, and, more important, its presence in the novel makes the evil of human bondage reverberate in a far wider historical context than it would if it were limited to just the actual life of the protagonist.

In making Turner derive from a Coromontee (we do not know from which tribe or tribes he actually derived), Styron has placed his insurrectionist in the tradition of African rebellion. For, as he would know from his reading of Mannix and Cowley's *Black Cargoes*, the Coromontees were the most frequent leaders of slave mutinies. The Jamaica House of Assembly, for example, in describing a series of slave revolts in the mid-18th century, reported that "all these disturbances ... have been planned and conducted by the Coromantin Negroes who are distinguished from their brethren by the ... martial ferocity of their dispositions."[43] Moreover, the shocked response of Nat's grandmother is not historically absurd. Many Africans believed that the white men were malevolent spirits who planned to eat them. Oloudah Equiano (or Gustavus Vassa), who was enslaved about the time of Nat's grandmother and who was also sold to a Virginia planter, tells in his memoirs of the terror he experienced at first encountering his white captors. Their strange complexions and language terrified Oloudah into believing that he had fallen "into a world of bad spirits"; and when he saw the boiling copper cauldron on ship and the chained slaves in a state of dejection, he was convinced that he was "to be eaten by those white men with horrible looks," and, "quite overpowered with horror and anguish," he fainted away on the deck.[44] Other slaves, less resilient than Oloudah, suffered the fate of Nat's grandmother, as witness this contemporary account: "Many of the slaves we transport ... to America are prepossessed with the opinion that they are carried like sheep to the slaughter and that the Europeans are fond of their flesh; which notion so far prevails with some as to make them fall into a deep melancholy and to refuse all sustenance, tho' never so much compelled and even beaten to oblige them to take some nourishment; notwithstanding all which they will starve to death."[45]

Stryron makes no mention of Turner's having a wife. This omission particularly infuriates the black critics because, as they see it, it is part and parcel of the white novelist's plot to depict Turner as a brute nigger lusting only after white women. Drawing upon Higginson (who probably got it from Warner's highly questionable pamphlet), they uniformly assert that the real Turner had a slave wife, the unequivocal evidence for which Stryon deliberately ignored in pursuit of his "project" to destroy "the vitals of the historical personage named Nat Turner" (pp. vii, 11, 20, 40, 63). "Why is not the author," Alvin Poussaint asks pointedly, "able to 'imagine' that Nat Turner had a young, feminine, beautiful, and courageous black woman who stood by his side throughout his heroic plan to revolt against slavery!?" (p. 21). One might begin by answering that the very source which Poussaint cites as evidence for the existence of such a woman (Higginson, p. 174), says that "Nat Turner's young wife was a slave [who] belonged to a different master from himself," so that it would have been rather difficult for her to be by his side all through the lengthy planning

[43]Daniel P. Mannix and Malcolm Cowley, *Black Cargoes: A History of the Atlantic Slave Trade* (New York: Viking Press, 1965), p. 17.

[44]*The Interesting Narrative of the Life of Oloudah Equiano, or Gustavus Vassa The African.* Written by Himself (1791), excerpted in Meltzer, ed., *In Their Own Words*, I, 3-4.

[45]*Black Cargoes*, pp. 48-49. Cf. also pp. 85-86.

stages for the insurrection. More apposite, however, is why if Turner had a wife did he not mention her in Gray? He mentions the rest of his family. (Given our position on Gray's document, we could argue that the presence of an emotional motivation for the revolt—the splitting up of families—would militate against Gray's portrait of motiveless malignity; but these critics take the document rather straight, so they cannot avail themselves of such an explanation.) Anna Mary Wells' explanation for Turner's failure to mention his wife in Gray's *Confessions* as an attempt "to spare her further suffering" is extremely far-fetched since it assumes that Turner believed that no one knew he had a wife, which, considering the composition and size of the society in which Turner lived, is rather unlikely. Miss Wells may have had this explanation suggested to her by Daniel Panger's novel, *Ol' Prophet Nat* (1967), in which Nat doesn't write the name of his wife in his diary (found by the narrator in a present-day junk shop) for fear that "the raging white men might blame her for some part in my doings." And finally, if, as Miss Wells says, at the time Higginson wrote the existence of Nat Turner's wife "had then never been questioned,"[46] then why did William Wells Brown, two years later, make no mention of her, especially since the ripping apart of husbands and wives was one of his explanations for the insurrection? Nor did any of the other 19th century black historians mention her. Even Aptheker, who formulated the pattern for the critical attacks-from-history, omits the detail of a wife from his catalogue of Styron's historical "distortions." All this is to say, then, that Turner may indeed have had a wife, but there is no reasonable way to assert it as an unequivocal fact and then to use it as evidence of Styron's racist imagination.[47]

The charge of total historical irresponsibility has also been leveled at Styron in the matter of slaves helping to put down the Turner insurrection. For Aptheker, the references in the novel "to masters arming loyal

[46]Miss Wells' remarks appear in "An Exchange on 'Nat Turner'" (*New York Review of Books*, Nov. 7, 1968, p. 31), an exchange of letters between several black writers and Eugene Genovese, whose "The Nat Turner Case" (*New York Review of Books*, Sept. 12, 1968, pp. 34–37) attacked the "ferocity and hysteria" of *Ten Black Writers*.

[47]It is interesting to consider the black writers' claim that Styron has "reduced history to sex," comparing his view of an intense, celibate revolutionary with Bontemps' Gabriel in *Black Thunder*. Gabriel has just such a black woman by his side as Poussaint wanted for Turner—the "tempestuous" Juba. "She sat astride Araby's bare back, her fragmentary skirt curled about her waist, her naked thighs flashing above the riding boots . . . and felt the warm body of the colt straining between her clinched knees" (p. 80); "She could still feel Araby twitching and fretting between her clinched knees. Lordy, that colt. . . . Almost as much fun as a man, that half-wild Araby" (p. 114). One can easily guess what Styron would have been accused of had he depicted the "courageous black woman" who stood by Turner's side in these terms!

slaves to resist the rebels are made up of whole cloth; there is no evidence of this whatsoever . . . " ("A Note on the History," p. 376). Thelwell concurs: "Mr. Styron, contrary to any historical evidence, has Turner's ultimate defeat coming as a result of the actions of loyal slaves who fought in defense of their beleved masters" (p. 90). This is too unequivocally put. But first, to set the record straight, Styron does not attribute Turner's *ultimate* defeat to the loyal slaves: his Turner says only that "the black man had caused my defeat *just as surely as* the white" (italics mine); moreover, there is no indication in the novel that the slaves fight their racial brothers out of love for their masters: we are told that they fight with "passion and fury," which need hardly imply love but only repressed assertiveness which welcomes any kind of outlet, even the tragic one of slave killing slave.

A lack of black solidarity, although not encountered with the frequency that a proslavery mythology would have had us believe, is nevertheless one of the sad facts of history. According to the black social historian E. Franklin Frazier, "faithful house-servants were often bound . . . to their masters by close emotional ties and common interests" and "in Jamaica and Brazil, where Negro revolts were generally more successful [than in the United States], it was always a faithful slave who revealed a conspiracy."[48] Both the Prosser and Vesey plots were, as already remarked, betrayed by loyal blacks. William Wells Brown tells us in his *Narrative* that "twenty-one years in slavery had taught me that there were traitors, even among colored people,"[49] and the escaping hero of his *Clotel* of 1853 acts out the lesson his author learned in life by not daring to "go amongst even his colored associates for fear of being betrayed" (p. 227). In Gray, Turner tells us that although he begged two Negroes to conceal him from the whites, he knew from their responses that "they would betray me."

At the slightest rumor of an uprising, John Hope Franklin has written, "All whites—loyal Negroes, too—were expected to do their share to prevent death and destruction from stalking through the land. . . ."[50] Although there is no justification for the "great numbers" that are mentioned in the novel,[51] there is also no justification for the allegation that Styron has made up the situation out of whole cloth, "contrary to any

---

[48]*The Negro in the United States* (New York: Macmillan, 1949), p. 91.
[49]*Narrative of William Wells Brown, A Fugitive Slave* (Boston: Anti-slavery office, 1847), pp. 95–96.
[50]"Slavery and the Martial South," *Journal of Negro History*, 37 (1952), 42.
[51]In an interview in the *New York Times Magazine* the week after his novel's publication, Styron admitted that there was no historical fact behind his image of "Negroes in great numbers with rifles and muskets . . . firing back at us"; in creating that episode, he claims, he was sensing what might lie between the lines of Turner's recorded agony.

historical evidence." Higginson, in recounting a touching story of a slave who had saved his master's life during the insurrection and then asked to be killed because he could no longer live in bondage, remarks that the master must be one Dr. Blunt—"his being the only plantation where slaves were reported as . . . defending their masters" (p. 181). Brown tells something of the same story but in his version the master is one Captain Harris. Whether this indicates another plantation on which slaves helped their masters or whether it is the same story with a different cast of characters, it is impossible to tell. At any rate, buried in the records of the 1832 Virginia legislature is this partial corroboration of Higginson: "The Assembly received five petitions on the part of persons who had lost eight slaves in the suppression of the Insurrection, praying that they might receive the value of their negroes. More justifiable was the petition for compensation for a slave killed while actually in arms in defense of Dr. Blunt's house."[52]

Several other alleged historical discrepancies deserve at least brief attention. John Killens wonders "why did not Styron use Walker's *Appeal* as part of Turner's motivation?" "Surely," Killens thinks, "Nat had read and been inspired, yes, inflamed by David Walker's *Appeal . . . to the Colored Citizens of the World But in Particular and very Expressly to those of the United States*," and concludes that Styron was trying to give the impression that there was very little unrest among the slaves and that therefore Turner "was some kind of freak" among his brother slaves (p. 41). The kind of motivation Killens wants, as we have already seen, was that suggested by several proslavery writers on Turner, but is without historical foundation. Aptheker, after surveying the possibilities of a literary stimulus, concludes, "The fact is that never has an iota of evidence been submitted to show any abolitionist propaganda, of the Walker, Garrison, or milder type, had any connection whatsoever with bringing on the Turner revolt" (*Nat Turner's Slave Rebellion*, p. 42). Killens also objects to Turner's comparing himself to Napoleon in the novel ("Lord, how I strove to drive the idea of a nigger Napoleon into their ignorant minds!")—"why did not Nat think to inspire them with an example of black militancy in the person of black Toussaint . . .?" (p. 42). Comparisons to the white John Brown are ubiquitous in the pro-Turner literature, but to Toussaint L'Ouverture not at all. There is no more evidence for believing that Turner was influenced by Napoleon than by

---

[52]Quoted in T. M. Whitfield, *Slavery Agitation in Virginia, 1829-1832* (Baltimore: Johns Hopkins Press, 1930), p. 123. Panger in *Ol' Prophet Nat* has "ten or more" of Dr. Blunt's slaves firing back at Turner's band: they had been beaten so often that they had become "willing beasts." Being fired upon by black men leaves the insurrectionists "shaken, our spirits badly dampened" (pp. 151-52).

Walker or L'Ouverture, but Wells Brown did at least find an analogy between Turner and Napoleon (p. 59). There is, at any rate, an unsuspected irony in Killens' approval of Gabriel Prosser's having compared himself to George Washington in contrast to Styron's Turner having compared himself to Napoleon: a Virginia slaveholder as model seems even less appropriate than the French "man of destiny" (pp. 39, 43).

One of the more astonishing moments in Gray's pamphlet is Turner's story of having converted and baptized a sinful white man, Etheldred T. Brantley. Of Brantley personally we know almost nothing, except what we can reconstruct imaginatively from between the lines.

> About this time I told these things [the coming Day of Judgment] to a white man, (Etheldred T. Brantley) on whom it had a wonderful effect—and he ceased from his wickedness, and was attacked immediately with a cutaneous eruption, and blood oozed from the pores of his skin, and after praying and fasting nine days, he was healed, and the Spirit appeared to me again, and said, as the Saviour had been baptised so should we be also—and when the white people would not let us be baptised by the church, we went down into the water together, in the sight of many who reviled us, and were baptised by the Spirit—After this I rejoiced greatly, and gave thanks to God.

Higginson adds only the fact that Brantley was "poor"—as of course he must have been; the later 19th century commentators drop him.

Styron portrays Brantley as an impoverished, physically repulsive, ignorant homosexual, whose pleading presence fills Turner with "pity and disgust." But it is just because Brantley is so agonized, so hopeless, so enslaved by nature and circumstances, almost—Turner thinks—"as wretched and forsaken as the lowest Negro," that Turner agrees to "save" him. Styron follows Gray in the matters of Brantley's ghastly dermatological eruptions, the unsuccessful attempt to have the baptism take place in a church, the sacramental immersion in a natural body of water, and the outraged response of the crowd of whites who watch the baptism. Brantley's "wickedness" Styron concretizes into drunkenness and sexual deviationism. Thelwell and Harding consider Styron's portrait as "demeaning" Nat Turner, as "diminishing [his] power," since only "a pariah-like" white man is shown as being "drawn to Nat Turner's religious teachings," only a "degenerate. . . . is shown associating with slaves on anything that looks like simple human terms" (pp. 27, 87).

Therefore, when the critics condemn Styron's portrait as having no justification in the historical record, they can mean only the form that Brantley's "wickedness" takes in the novel. Yet Thelwell himself admits that Turner's baptizing a white man was "an event unprecedented in Tidewater Virginia of the time." What then must have been the depths of self-loathing and shame that drove a white man, even the most wretched of poor whites, to seek the help of what he would have thought of as a nigger preacher rather than some religious of his own color? Perhaps, too, something of Brantley's moral state can be induced from the suddenness and severity of his dermatitis, which, in Gray, sounds suspiciously psychosomatic. Brantley's physical affliction, if indeed it is psychological in origin, would be consonant with some guilt far more terrible than a merely generalized feeling of sinfulness or just drunkenness. It is precisely because Panger's Brantley is only a drunkard in *Ol' Prophet Nat* (with a consumptive wife and sickly children) that the entire interlude is so unconvincing. The encounter is handled so casually that even the baptism comes off without the presence of reviling spectators. We shall never of course know if Brantley's wickedness was pederasty, as Styron has it; but surely it, or something like it, is needed to explain the extraordinary behavior of Etheldred T. Brantley. But perhaps the truth, as we suspect, is that the objection is not so much to the characterization of Brantley as it is to the fact that Turner warns him of the coming holocaust. Nat Turner in Styron's novel finds himself the victim of his own humanity: he cannot do to whites what whites have done to blacks—reduce them all to an abstraction. For these critics, however, this is a betrayal of the historical Nat Turner, who, in their view, was committed to a revolutionary ethic that made no distinctions. It hardly needs to be pointed out, however, that even in "the basic historical document," Gray's pamphlet, Turner does treat a white man with a kindness that betokens a certain vulnerability to humane considerations.

It seems clear to us that the widely disseminated charge, believed even by some critics whose interest in *The Confessions of Nat Turner* is not politically motivated,[53] that Styron is guilty of distorting the facts of history is itself not supported by the facts. It has been the intention of this essay to try to free Styron's novel from the coffle of propagandistic criticism masquerading as historicity so that its achievement can be more justly evaluated. For us, that achievement is appreciable—and not only because as the great black historian of slavery Benjamin Quarles has suggested, in Styron's "pages Turner emerges as the man he must have been in real life. . . ."[54] Of greater importance is the fact that Styron's literary imagination, working with the fragments of a dynamic legend—

[53]Richard Gilman, for example, in support of his literary attack on Styron's handling of Turner's sexual desire, remarks with unjustifiable certainty, "he was in fact married, which Styron ignores" ("Nat Turner Revisited," *New Republic*, 158 [Apr. 27, 1968], 26).

[54]*Social Studies*, 59 (Nov. 1968), 280. In addition to John Hope Franklin and Benjamin Quarles, a third black historian, Saunders Redding, also finds *The Confessions of Nat Turner* "very perceptive and true" (*American Scholar*, 37 [1968], 542). In contrast to these three professional historians, Darwin Turner, a black English professor, dismisses the novel as the product of Styron's "sick and bigoted fancies" (*Journal of Negro History*, 53 [1968], 185).

which is all there is—has brought to life truths of the national ordeal of slavery which reverberate from 1831 to the present. Our survey of Nat Turner in the American imagination from Thomas Gray to William Styron has led us to believe that at least in this instance Macaulay's dictum should be reversed: History begins in the essay and ends in the novel.

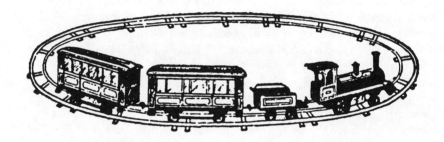

AMERICA'S RESPONSE TO THE SLAVE REVOLT IN HAITI, 1791-1806

Donald R. Hickey

The slave revolt in French St. Domingue in the 1790s cast a long shadow over the history of the New World.* Most of the great powers in Europe had slave-based colonies in the Caribbean, and the United States had a sizable servile population within its own borders. It was in the interest of each of these powers to suppress the revolt, and to prevent the contagion of rebellion from spreading to other slaves in the New World. Yet this shared interest was offset by the desire of each power to engross the trade of the colony, and to gain strategic advantages over its rivals in the tense climate of the French revolutionary and Napoleonic wars. Because of these countervailing influences, the policies adopted by the Atlantic powers toward the black rebels and their former masters fluctuated considerably.

Although slavery was a sectional issue in the United States, the slave revolt in St. Domingue[1] divided Americans more along party than sectional lines. The Federalists controlled American foreign policy in the 1790s, and while at first they favored the French planters, they subsequently aided the black rebels. When the Jeffersonian Republicans took office in 1801, they gradually reversed the pro-rebel policy. The culmination of this reversal was

Mr. Hickey is a member of the Department of History at Wayne State College in Wayne, Nebraska, and editor of *The Midwest Review*.

*An earlier version of this paper was presented at the annual SHEAR meeting in Urbana, Illinois, on July 18, 1980. For helpful criticism of earlier drafts, the author is indebted to Jerry Martin, Robert McColley, and Reginald Horsman. The author would also like to thank Timothy Matthewson and James Broussard for sharing their research on this subject.

[1] St. Domingue was variously called San Domingo, Santo Domingo, St. Domingo, and Haiti.

JOURNAL OF THE EARLY REPUBLIC, 2 (Winter 1982). © 1982 Society for Historians of the Early American Republic.

the adoption of a law in 1806 that prohibited all trade with the ex-slaves. The Federalists vigorously opposed this law, but without effect. The trade ban crystallized American opposition to the blacks and laid the foundation for a hostile policy that endured until the Civil War.

St. Domingue had once been known as "the pearl of the Antilles." It was situated on the western end of the island of Hispaniola, which the natives called Haiti. Columbus had discovered this island on his first voyage to America in 1492. While the Spanish developed the eastern portion into the colony of Santo Domingo, the French developed the western part into Saint Domingue. The French colony grew rapidly and quickly outstripped its neighbor. By 1789 it was the largest colony in the Caribbean, with a population of some 40,000 whites, 28,000 free blacks and mulattoes, and 452,000 slaves. It was also the richest colony in the region. By 1791 it was the world's leading producer of sugar (177,000,000 pounds annually) and coffee (74,000,000 pounds annually), and it accounted for half the slaves in the Caribbean. Some of the colony's planters amassed huge fortunes and spent half the year in Paris, where "rich as a Creole" was a common expression. French officials prized the colony highly not only because its cheap tropical produce won markets in North America and Europe, but also because trade with the colony gave employment to so many of France's seafaring subjects. On the eve of the French Revolution, trade with St. Domingue accounted for a third of France's external commerce, employing 1,282 ships manned by some fifteen thousand sailors.[2]

In spite of British and French navigation laws, American merchants tapped into this lucrative trade in the eighteenth century. The trade flourished even more in the 1780s after America had shaken off the shackles of Britain's navigation system and France

---

[2] Thomas O. Ott, The Haitian Revolution, 1789-1804 (Knoxville 1973), 3, 5, 53; H. P. Davis, Black Democracy: The Story of Haiti (rev. ed., New York 1936), 24-25; Rayford W. Logan, The Diplomatic Relations of the United States with Haiti, 1776-1891 (Chapel Hill 1941), 3; Ludwell L. Montague, Haiti and the United States, 1714-1938 (Durham 1940), 5; John H. Coatsworth, "American Trade with European Colonies in the Caribbean and South America, 1790-1812," William and Mary Quarterly, 24 (April 1967), 245; Timothy M. Matthewson, "George Washington's Policy toward the Haitian Revolution," Diplomatic History, 3 (Summer 1979), 322; Timothy M. Matthewson, "The Crisis of the Sugar Colonies: The Founding Fathers and the Haitian Revolution," unpublished ms., 1.

had opened several ports in the colony to American ships and broadened the list of foodstuffs that could be imported. The Franco-American consular treaty of 1788 further facilitated the trade. By 1790, some five hundred ships were employed in this trade, and St. Domingue stood second only to Great Britain in the foreign commerce of the United States. By this time St. Domingue supplied the United States with practically all the sugar and molasses it imported. In return, France's West Indian colonies (of which St. Domingue was by far the most important) took 16 percent of American exports, including 23 percent of the flour exported from the United States, 73 percent of the livestock, 77 percent of the processed beef, 63 percent of the dried fish, and 80 percent of the pickled fish.[3]

St. Domingue's wealth, however, rested on a soft foundation. The colony had a long history of unruliness, and beneath the surface there was considerable discontent. Neither the free people of color nor the slaves were happy with their condition, and the whites were sharply divided along class lines. In 1791, when the French Revolution was eroding authority in both the mother country and the colony, the slaves in the North Plain rose in revolt, killing their masters and burning their plantations. The revolt soon spread to other parts of the island until the entire colony was engulfed by flames. At first the leader of the revolt was one Boukman, an enormous black man who used the medium of voodoo to spread revolutionary ideals. Boukman soon perished and was succeeded by Toussaint Louverture, a gifted ex-slave who had loyally provided for the safety of his master's family before joining the revolt in late 1791. Toussaint quickly forged the blacks into an effective fighting force and soon demonstrated an intuitive grasp of both the science of war and the art of diplomacy.

The vicious civil war that ensued was extraordinarily complex as the various racial and social groups in the colony repeatedly made and broke alliances with one another in the pursuit of

---

[3] T. Lothrop Stoddard, *The French Revolution in San Domingo* (Boston 1914), 18; Coatsworth, "American Trade with European Colonies," 245-247; Logan, *Diplomatic Relations*, 6-7; Montague, *Haiti and the United States*, 32; Matthewson, "Crisis of the Sugar Colonies," 21. The governor of St. Domingue sometimes went far beyond his authority to facilitate trade with America. See Thomas Jefferson to George Washington, Jan. 4, 1792, in Paul L. Ford, ed., *The Writings of Thomas Jefferson* (10 vols., New York 1892-1899), V, 419; and Stoddard, *French Revolution in San Domingo*, 76.

victory. French commissioners dispatched from the motherland tried to end the fighting in 1793 by proclaiming the freedom of all slaves, a step ratified by the French National Convention the following year when it abolished slavery throughout the empire. This decision was never accepted by the planters and was later reversed by Napoleon. The bloody contest on the island continued.[4]

Britain and France each sought to restore order and establish control over St. Domingue by sending huge armies to the island. In each case, the troops suffered enormous casualties, partly from rebel fire but even more from the virulent effects of tropical diseases such as malaria and yellow fever. Great Britain, unwilling to pass up an opportunity to seize so rich a prize from her ancient foe, occupied the colony from 1793 to 1798. As of 1796, the British officially put their losses at seventy-five hundred men, but their actual losses in the campaign were probably three times this number. The French occupied the island in 1802-1803 and fared even worse, losing fifty thousand killed, many of whom were experienced veterans from Europe — the flower of Napoleon's army. The losses suffered by the resident population were even greater. Most of the whites and mulattoes were killed or driven off the island, and more than half the black population perished. In all, the total number of people killed in St. Domingue from 1791 to 1803 must have exceeded three hundred thousand.[5]

When news of the slave revolt reached the United States, the first impulse of the Federalist administration was to aid the white planters. Between September 1791 and June 1793, George Washington's government advanced French whites in St. Domingue $726,000 drawn against America's revolutionary war debt to France. The United States government sold the planters arms and ammunition, and American merchants kept them supplied with food. Some resident Americans fought alongside the planters, and on occasion so too did visiting American sailors. The official government aid, however, came to an end in 1793 when the

---

[4] The history of the revolt can be followed in Ott, *Haitian Revolution*; Stoddard, *French Revolution in San Domingo*; Davis, *Black Democracy*; and C. L. R. James, *The Black Jacobins: Toussaint L'Ouverture and the San Domingo Revolution* (rev. ed., New York 1963).

[5] Ott, *Haitian Revolution*, 182, 186; Davis, *Black Democracy*, 74, 86; Matthewson, "Crisis of the Sugar Colonies," 141, 145; Sir John Fortescue, *A History of the British Army* (13 vols., London 1910-1930), IV, 565.

planter regime in the colony collapsed and the blacks established control over most of the island.[6]

The end of white hegemony in St. Domingue did not mean an end to commercial profits. On the contrary, American merchants simply made their contracts with the British occupation force and later with the black rebels and their mulatto allies. Hence trade with the colony continued to grow. American exports to the French West Indies, which stood at $3,200,000 in 1790, rose to $5,000,000 in 1793, and to $8,400,000 in 1796. By 1797, there were reportedly six hundred ships engaged in the trade with St. Domingue, and American exports to the colony were valued at more than $5,000,000.[7]

As relations with France deteriorated after the United States signed the Jay Treaty with England in 1794, many Federalists saw the independence of St. Domingue as a means of guaranteeing commercial profits and striking a blow at French power in the New World.[8] Timothy Pickering, who served as secretary of state from 1795 to 1800, believed that Toussaint was "a prudent and judicious man possessing the general confidence of the people of all colours." Pickering favored collaborating with Toussaint and was an early advocate of independence for St. Domingue. "Nothing is more clear," he wrote in 1799, "than, if left to themselves, that the Blacks of St. Domingo will be incomparably less dangerous than if they remain the subjects of France .... France with an army of those black troops might conquer all the British Isles [in the Caribbean] and put in jeopardy our Southern States."[9]

---

[6] Matthewson, "George Washington's Policy," 321, 325, 327, 332-333, 335; Matthewson, "Crisis of the Sugar Colonies," 56, 76. The American government continued to provide aid to those planters who fled to the United States. See *Annals of Congress*, 3d Cong., 1st sess., 1417-1418.

[7] Logan, *Diplomatic Relations*, 60; Montague, *Haiti and the United States*, 47n; Matthewson, "Crisis of the Sugar Colonies," 76, 106.

[8] President John Adams, however, disagreed. See Adams to Timothy Pickering, Apr. 17, 1799, in Charles F. Adams, ed., *The Works of John Adams* (10 vols., Boston 1850-1856), VIII, 634.

[9] Pickering to William Smith, Feb. 13, 1799, Pickering Papers, reel 10 (Massachusetts Historical Society); Pickering to Smith, May 5, 1799, *ibid.*, reel 11; Charles C. Tansill, *The United States and Santo Domingo, 1798-1873: A Chapter in Caribbean Diplomacy* (Baltimore 1938), 33-34, 52-53; Pickering to Rufus King, Mar. 12, 1799, in Charles R. King, ed., *The Life and Correspondence of Rufus King* (6 vols., New York 1894-1900), II, 557.

According to Pickering, southern Federalists in Congress shared this view. Of the danger posed by France, he said, "the Southern Members were convinced, and therefore cordially concurred in the policy of the Independence of St. D., if T[oussain]t and his followers will it. Mr. [Jacob] Read [of South Carolina] was the only exception to this opinion, and his opinions are sometimes unaccountable." That southern Federalists preferred independence was confirmed by Thomas Pinckney of South Carolina, the man who had negotiated the Spanish treaty of 1795 and had been the Federalist candidate for the vice presidency the following year. In a congressional speech delivered in 1799, Pinckney asserted that "it would be more for the safety of the Southern States to have that island independent, than under the Government of France, either in time of peace or war."[10]

With the outbreak of the Quasi-War with France in 1798, Congress banned all trade with the French empire. Later that year Toussaint, desperate for provisions and munitions, sent a special envoy to the United States to seek a renewal of trade. In exchange, the black dictator offered to suppress privateers that were using his ports to prey upon American commerce. The administration welcomed this proposal, and Congress responded by passing a law that authorized the president to reopen trade with "any island, port, or place" belonging to France if he considered it in the best interest of the United States to do so. This provision, which was known as "Toussaint's clause," divided Congress along party lines as Federalists (northerners and southerners alike) supported the measure and Republicans opposed it.[11]

Working in close harmony with the British, who wanted a share of the trade, Pickering sent Edward Stevens to St. Domingue to open discussions. Since Congress had made no appropriation for the mission, Pickering authorized the envoy to take a cargo of

---

[10] King, ed., *Life and Correspondence of Rufus King*, II, 557-558; speech of Thomas Pinckney, Jan. 23, 1799, *Annals of Congress*, 5th Cong., 3d sess., 2766-2767.

[11] Timothy Pickering to Rufus King, Dec. 15, 1798, and Pickering to Edward Stevens, Dec. 16, 1803, Pickering Papers, reels 14, 37; *Annals of Congress*, 5th Cong., 3d sess., 2212, 2214, 2791-2792, 3795-3798; Tansill, *United States and Santo Domingo*, 15; Alexander DeConde, *The Quasi-War: The Politics and Diplomacy of the Undeclared War with France, 1797-1801* (New York 1966), 135.

provisions to defray his costs.[12] Stevens soon reached an agreement with Toussaint, and President John Adams issued a proclamation formally reopening trade with St. Domingue as of August 1, 1799. As a result, American commerce with the colony — which had never entirely ceased — once again flourished. Toussaint took advantage of the renewal of trade to buy large quantities of provisions and arms. Indeed, so essential did this trade become to the black rebels that they began referring to Americans as "the good whites."[13]

The American navy had already been dispatched to the Caribbean to suppress French privateers and to protect American commercial interests. Even before trade with St. Domingue had been officially reopened, Toussaint showed his good faith by allowing these armed American vessels to use his ports while denying this privilege to the French. The American navy subsequently made the island one of its principal bases in the Quasi-War. The navy also helped Toussaint defeat his domestic foe, Benoît Joseph Rigaud, a mulatto who was closely tied to France and whose privateers were preying on American commerce. In late 1799 the navy transported Toussaint's troops to the southern front, established a blockade of Rigaud's ports, and bombarded his position. Early the next year the navy again helped Toussaint by supporting his troops and attacking Rigaud's ships. By the time the Federalists left office in early 1801, Rigaud had been routed and Toussaint's power on the island was at least momentarily secure.[14]

---

[12] This generated a good deal of criticism, especially from Republican merchants who resented Stevens' opportunity to make a profit on trade that was still officially banned. See Benjamin Stoddert to Timothy Pickering, Mar. 8, 1799, Pickering Papers, reel 24; Bernard C. Steiner, *The Life and Correspondence of James McHenry, Secretary of War under Washington and Adams* (Cleveland 1907), 420.

[13] Oliver Wolcott to John Adams, [Nov. 1799], in George Gibbs, *Memoirs of the Administrations of Washington and John Adams, Edited from the Papers of Oliver Wolcott, Secretary of the Treasury* (2 vols., New York 1846), II, 300, 303; Edward Stevens to Timothy Pickering, May 3, May 23, 1799, in "Letters of Toussaint Louverture and of Edward Stevens, 1798-1800," *American Historical Review*, 16 (Oct. 1910), 68-70, 72; Tansill, *United States and Santo Domingo*, 31-71; Ott, *Haitian Revolution*, 132; Stoddard, *French Revolution in San Domingo*, 290; James, *Black Jacobins*, 262; Bradford Perkins, *The First Rapprochement: England and the United States, 1795-1805* (Philadelphia 1955), 106-111; Henry Adams, "Napoleon I. at St. Domingo," *Historical Essays* (New York 1891), 140.

[14] Edward Stevens to Timothy Pickering, May 3, 1799, in "Letters of Toussaint and Stevens," 71: Tansill, *United States and Santo Domingo*, 70, 73; Ott,

The Republicans shared neither the Federalists' fear of French power in the New World nor their enthusiasm for the colonial trade. They had opposed both the independence of St. Domingue and the establishment of such close ties with the black rebels. As early as 1791, when whites still controlled the colony, Jefferson had warned several representatives from the island that independence was neither "desirable" nor "attainable" and that it increased the danger that the island would fall under the dominion of another power — presumably Great Britain. In an address before Congress in 1799, Albert Gallatin also argued against independence for St. Domingue. "Toussaint's clause" would encourage the natives to declare independence, which would be "extremely injurious to the interests of the United States." The ex-slaves, he warned, would "continue to live, as heretofore, by plunder and depredations" and would endanger American commerce in the Caribbean and the social order of the southern states.[15]

Jefferson, like other Republicans, shared Gallatin's view of "Toussaint's clause." The object of this measure, he said, "as is charged by the one party and *admitted* by the other, is to facilitate the separation of the island from France." Jefferson believed that "Toussaint's clause," coupled with the stationing of American warships around the island, would be "a circumstance of high aggravation" to France and would "probably be more than the [French] Directory will bear." Moreover, calling Toussaint and his followers "cannibals," he expressed fear that "black crews, & supercargoes & missionaries" from St. Domingue would cause trouble in the southern states. "If this combustion can be introduced among us under any veil whatever," he concluded, "we have to fear it."[16]

Haitian Revolution, 110, 113-114; Logan, *Diplomatic Relations*, 101-110; DeConde, *Quasi-War*, 128, 208; Gardner W. Allen, *Our Naval War with France* (Boston 1909), 115-116, 180-181, 188, 205-206.

[15] Jefferson to William Short, Nov. 24, 1791, in Andrew A. Lipscomb and Albert E. Bergh, eds., *The Writings of Thomas Jefferson* (20 vols., Washington 1903-1905), VIII, 261; speech of Albert Gallatin, Jan. 22, 1799, *Annals of Congress*, 5th Cong., 3d sess., 2751-2752.

[16] Jefferson to James Monroe, Jan. 23, 1799, and Jefferson to James Madison, Feb. 5, 1799, in Lipscomb and Bergh, eds., *Writings of Thomas Jefferson*, X, 73, 95; Jefferson to John Page, Jan. 24, 1799, in Ford, *Writings of Thomas Jefferson*, VII, 323; George F. Tyson, Jr., ed., *Toussaint L'Ouverture* (Englewood Cliffs 1973), 93; Jefferson to Madison, Feb. 12, 1799, in Ford, *Writings of Thomas Jefferson*, VII, 349.

After taking office in 1801, Jefferson quietly suspended official relations with the black rebels by accrediting the new consul on the island to Port Cap Français (instead of to the black government) and by depriving the consul of any diplomatic powers. The following July the French chargé d'affaires in Washington, Louis Pichon, asked for assistance in restoring white rule to the colony and the president replied that if France first made peace with England, "then nothing would be easier than to furnish your army and fleet with everything, and to reduce Toussaint to starvation." Jefferson was not yet ready to halt trade with the colony, fearing that he might offend public opinion. Nonetheless, the administration was determined not to allow this trade to disrupt Franco-American relations. As Secretary of State James Madison put it, "The United States would withdraw from Saint-Domingue rather than hurt relations with France."[17]

The Republicans' position on St. Domingue was put to a test after France failed to subdue the blacks in 1802-1803. Although French officials seized Toussaint by treachery in 1802 and shipped him to a dungeon in the mother country, he was succeeded by Jean Jacques Dessalines who proclaimed the Republic of Haiti in late 1803. French officials driven from Haiti retired to Spanish St. Domingue and to Cuba, from which they issued a host of commissions to French and Spanish privateers. Although these vessels were authorized to seize only ships trading with Haiti, they indiscriminately seized American vessels throughout the Caribbean, splitting their booty with conniving French and Spanish officials. American merchantmen responded by arming for defense and, in several cases, fighting off marauding privateers. In late 1804 a flotilla armed with eighty cannon departed for Haiti from New York City with a cargo that included contraband of war. This venture proved highly successful, and at a public dinner held to celebrate the armada's return a toast was offered to the new Haitian republic.[18]

---

[17] Tansill, United States and Santo Domingo, 80-81; Ott, Haitian Revolution, 120; De Conde, Quasi-War, 314-315; Carl L. Lokke, "Jefferson and the Leclerc Expedition," American Historical Review, 33 (Jan. 1928), 324.

[18] Littleton W. Tasewell to Madison, April 28, 1804, Madison Papers, reel 8 (Library of Congress); P. Sisson, Mahlon Bennet, and James Ross, Jr., to George Barnewall, July 26, 1804, in American State Papers: Foreign Relations, II, 608; Memorial of Philadelphia Chamber of Commerce, in Philadelphia United States'

England and France both lodged protests against the armed trade. The British minister, Anthony Merry, complained that American vessels were carrying contraband to Britain's enemies and that they might resist lawful search by British cruisers. Merry called on the United States to suppress these "illegal proceedings." The protests from French officials were sharper. Pichon accused American merchants of arming vessels "to support, by force, a traffic contrary to the law of nations, and to repel the efforts which the cruisers of the French republic are authorized to make, in order to prevent it." The *chargé d'affaires* said the merchants were carrying on "a private and piratical war against a Power with which the United States are at peace," and threatened reprisals if the warfare continued.[19]

Republican leaders were receptive to these protests. Madison recognized that with the evacuation of the French and Dessalines' declaration of independence, American trade with Haiti fell under "some delicate considerations." The administration had no objection to suppressing the trade in contraband goods. "With respect to articles for War," Madison said, "it is probably the interest of all nations that they should be kept out of hands likely to make so bad a use of them. It is clear at the same time that the United States are bound by the law of Nations to nothing further than to leave their offending Citizens to the consequences of an illicit trade."[20]

The trade in non-contraband goods was another matter. The administration believed that France had no right to enforce restrictions against this trade on the high seas, but could do so only in ports that were directly under her control or in a state of blockade. Since France could neither control nor blockade Haiti's ports, she could not interfere with the trade. Robert R. Livingston, the

---

Gazette, Dec. 14, 1804; New York *Evening Post*, reprinted in Philadelphia *United States' Gazette*, Jan. 14, 1805; Logan, *Diplomatic Relations*, 162, 170; Stoddard, *French Revolution in San Domingo*, 349; Irving Brant, *James Madison* (6 vols., Indianapolis and New York 1941-1961), IV, 180-183; Henry Adams, *History of the United States during the Administrations of Jefferson and Madison* (9 vols., New York 1889-1891), III, 87-88.

    [19] Merry to Madison, Aug. 31, 1804, in *American State Papers: Foreign Relations*, II, 607; Pichon to Madison, May 7, 1804, *ibid.*

    [20] Madison to Robert R. Livingston, Jan. 31, 1804, U.S. Department of State, Diplomatic Instructions, Series M-77, reel 1 (National Archives); Madison to Livingston, Mar. 31, 1804, *ibid.*

American minister in Paris, told the French minister of foreign affairs, Talleyrand, that this trade benefited France anyway because it prevented Haiti from falling into Great Britain's commercial orbit or sinking into barbarism.[21]

Livingston protested against "the depredations committed upon the Commerce of the United States by French Privateers," and suggested a convention to put trade with the French West Indies on "a just & reasonable footing." In exchange for the right to trade freely in innocent goods, the United States was willing to adopt legislation for suppressing the arms trade. France, however, responded that free trade would be granted only for "a pecuniary equivalent." The United States rejected this proposal, and although it continued to press for an agreement on its own terms, France remained adamant.[22]

Even without a *quid pro quo* from France, President Jefferson was anxious to resolve the Haitian trade problem. He had no love for the Haitians and no desire to become embroiled with the great powers over trade with the island. Moreover, as a southerner he was anxious to minimize any contact with the ex-slaves. In the summer of 1804, the administration considered asking the judiciary if it could require armed American vessels to give bond not to misuse their weapons. But there was no suitable case pending before the courts and no assurance that the judges would support the administration. In October Jefferson told John Quincy Adams that he was determined to suppress trade with Haiti altogether. In his opening message to Congress the following month, he presented France's view of the problem by asserting that American merchants were arming vessels "to force a commerce into certain ports and countries in defiance of the laws of those countries." He said the United States could not permit its citizens "to wage private war," and he recommended that Congress take remedial action.[23]

---

[21] Madison to Livingston, Jan. 31, 1804, *ibid*; Livingston to Talleyrand, June 25, 1804, U.S. Department of State, Dispatches from United States Ministers to France, Series M-34, reel 12 (National Archives).

[22] *Ibid.*; Madison to John Armstrong, June 6, 1805, Diplomatic Instructions, M-77, reel 1; Madison to Armstrong, Nov. 10, 1804, Mar. 5, 1805, and Mar. 15, 1806, *ibid*.

[23] Albert Gallatin to Jefferson, June 7, 1804, in Henry Adams, ed., *The Writings of Albert Gallatin* (3 vols., Philadelphia 1879), I, 194-196; Madison to

Shortly thereafter, on November 23, 1804, Boston Republican
William Eustis introduced a bill in the House to regulate the clear-
ance of armed vessels.[24] The following month the president's son-
in-law, John W. Eppes, moved to prohibit vessels from arming altogether unless they were headed for the piratical Mediterranean or
Orient. "We are informed," he said, "that armed vessels sailing to
the West Indies are sold, with their arms and ammunition, to a
class of people it is the interest of the United States to depress and
keep down." This motion was opposed by several commercial Republicans, who argued that the armaments were essential to
protect merchantmen from depredations in the Caribbean.
William McCreery said that Baltimore insurers alone had suffered
almost half a million dollars in losses from the recent seizures in
the West Indies. The motion was defeated, and the House passed
an amended version of the original bill despite opposition of both
northern and southern Federalists. The Senate greatly weakened
the bill and then passed it with the Federalists again in
opposition.[25]

The measure had been treated roughly in both houses of Congress. As one Federalist newspaper put it, the bill had been
"bandied about from house to house and from committee to
committee" and had "excited no little speculation and a more than
ordinary share of ridicule in every part of the country." The
version originally passed by the House provided for punishing
ships (instead of their owners and masters), and one Senate version
required shipowners and masters to obey "the laws of nations."
Even before the bill got out of the House, it was so greatly altered
that a Republican newspaper conceded that "the opponents of the
bill had nearly gained their object." And this version was watered

Armstrong, July 15, 1804, in Diplomatic Instructions, M-77, reel 1; Charles F.
Adams, ed., *Memoirs of John Quincy Adams* (12 vols., Philadelphia 1874-1877), I,
314; Jefferson to Congress, Nov. 8, 1804, *Annals of Congress*, 8th Cong., 2d sess.,
11.
 [24] *Annals of Congress*, 8th Cong., 2d sess., 698, 722-723.
 [25] Speech of John W. Eppes, Dec. 13, 1804, *Annals of Congress*, 8th Cong., 2d
sess., 813; speeches of William Eustis, Joseph Clay, and William McCreery, Dec.
13, 1804, *ibid.*, 814-818; *ibid.*, 820, 861-862, 63-64; William Branch Giles to
Madison [early 1806], Madison Papers, reel 9; Timothy Pickering to Rufus King,
Feb. 24, 1805, in King, ed., *Life and Correspondence of Rufus King*, IV, 442; Hartford *Connecticut Courant*, Feb. 13, 1805.

down even more by the Senate. As finally enacted, the bill merely prohibited armed vessels trading in the Caribbean from selling their weapons or using them for any but defensive purposes. The measure did not meet Jefferson's objections nor did it satisfy the French, who would settle for nothing less than the commercial isolation of Haiti in the hope of forcing the blacks back into the French fold.[26]

The Federalists in Congress had unanimously opposed this bill, and they were supported by Federalist newspapers across the country. With the Philadelphia *United States' Gazette* leading the way, Federalist papers printed and reprinted articles (particularly from the *Gazette*) opposing any attempt to limit the trade. Newspapers in the North were especially vigorous in upholding the independence of Haiti and America's right to trade with her. One Boston newspaper even compared the Haitians' experience to America's own. "Their case," said the *Centinel*, "is not dissimilar to that of the people of the United States in 1778-1800." Few southern organs would go this far, but they too defended the independence of Haiti and opposed any restrictions on the trade. The only exception was the Norfolk *Publick Ledger*, whose editor thought there were "many reasons of policy, and perhaps of justice" for not countenancing "the trade with the ports of St. Domingo in the possession of the blacks."[27]

The new law did not seriously interfere with the Haitian trade in either innocent or contraband goods. Even with insurance rates approaching forty percent, American merchants could still make a

---

[26] Philadelphia *United States' Gazette*, Feb. 11, Jan. 29, Feb. 26, 1805; Frederick-Town *Herald*, Dec. 29, 1804; Philadelphia *Aurora*, reprinted in Boston *Columbian Centinel*, Dec. 26, 1804; *Annals of Congress*, 8th Cong., 2d sess., 1698-1699.

[27] Philadelphia *United States' Gazette*, Nov. 3, 23, Dec. 7, 1804; New York *Evening Post*, Nov. 16, 30, 1804; Boston *Columbian Centinel*, Nov. 17, Dec. 8, 19, 1804, Jan. 9, 12, 1805; Boston *New England Palladium*, Jan. 1, 1805; Hartford *Connecticut Courant*, Dec. 24, 26, 1804, Jan. 9, 1805; Boston *Columbian Centinel*, Dec. 8, 1804; Charleston *Courier*, Jan. 26, Mar. 2, 1805; Raleigh *Minerva*, Dec. 31, 1804; Alexandria *Daily Advertiser*, Nov. 13, 22, 1804, Jan. 26, 1805; Richmond *Virginia Gazette*, Dec. 19, 1804; Halifax *North-Carolina Journal*, Jan. 7, 28, 1805; Martinsburg *Berkeley Intelligencer*, Jan. 11, 1805; Frederick-Town *Herald*, Dec. 22, 1804, Jan. 5, Feb. 23, 1805; Norfolk *Gazette and Publick Ledger*, Nov. 26, 1804. Senator Samuel White of Delaware also compared the Haitian revolt to the American Revolution. See his speech of Feb. 20, 1806, *Annals of Congress*, 9th Cong., 1st sess., 125.

profit. A decree issued by Louis Ferrand, the commander in chief of the French forces stationed at Spanish St. Domingo, indicated that American merchants interpreted the law loosely or simply ignored it. Ferrand claimed that "several of the most respectable mercantile houses of New York, Philadelphia, Baltimore, &c. have, for a long time past, kept up a continued intercourse with the revolted blacks, and have habitually supplied them with every sort of provisions and warlike stores." Ferrand said one armed American vessel, the *Jane* of Baltimore, had forcefully resisted a French privateer and was taken only "after a bloody engagement." The French commander named three other American vessels — and claimed there were several more — that "are not only engaged in that execrable commerce, but actually transport the arms and ammunition of Dessaline's [sic] army from one port to another, thereby becoming the auxiliaries of the black rebels against France."[28]

In the summer of 1805 the French renewed their diplomatic offensive against the Haitian trade. On August 10, Napoleon told Talleyrand that "it is shameful in the Americans . . . to take part in a commerce so scandalous" and that "it is time for this thing to stop." In a message to the American minister, Talleyrand called on the United States to "interdict every private adventure, which, under any pretext or designation whatever, may be destined to the ports of St. Domingo occupied by the rebels." A week later Talleyrand renewed his plea for an end to the trade. American merchants, he complained, had entered into new contracts with Dessalines to provide not only supplies but also munitions of war. The French government, he added, considered all vessels trading with the blacks lawful prize. The French minister in Washington, Louis Turreau, delivered similar protests.[29]

Jefferson, already sympathetic to French aims, now had an additional reason for cooperating — the prospect of acquiring the Spanish Floridas. Administration officials had long coveted the Floridas and had tried unsuccessfully to use some spoliation claims

---

[28] Philadelphia *Aurora*, Jan. 23, 1806; decree of Louis Ferrand, June 6, 1805, in *American State Papers: Foreign Relations*, II, 728-729.

[29] Napoleon to Talleyrand, Aug. 10, 1805, in Adams, *History of the United States*, III, 89; Talleyrand to John Armstrong [summer 1805], in *American State Papers: Foreign Relations*, II, 727; Talleyrand to Armstrong, Aug. 16, 1805, *ibid.*; Turreau to Madison, Oct. 14, 1805, and Jan. 3, 1806, *ibid.*, 725-726.

to pry them loose from Spain. French officials had earlier indicated an interest in mediating the transfer of the Floridas to the United States if the price were right. In the summer of 1805 the French government renewed its proposal, and at a cabinet meeting held in November, Jefferson's administration decided to accept the offer. The negotiations were likely to be delicate, however, and it was important not to alienate France on the Haitian question.[30]

Having failed to secure a strong measure against Haiti from the previous Congress, Jefferson remained in the background this time. Instead, it was Senator George Logan of Pennsylvania who headed the drive to cut off trade with the black republic. Logan was a genuine pacifist. He opposed any action that was likely to cause trouble with the great powers — or in the southern states. In 1798 he had traveled to France in an effort to avert war with that nation, an act which prompted Congress to pass the so-called Logan law outlawing private diplomatic missions. In early 1805, to avoid a renewal of trouble with France, he had tried unsuccessfully to introduce a bill in the Senate to suspend all trade with Haiti.[31]

On December 20, 1805, Logan again asked the Senate for permission to introduce his bill. He claimed the law passed the previous session was "a deception" that neither complied with the president's wishes nor met the objections of the British and French ministers. Logan said the trade with Haiti violated the law of nations and the Franco-American Convention of 1800. "Whilst we are anxious to have our own national rights respected," he asked, "is it honorable to violate the rights of a friendly Power with whom we are at peace? or is it sound policy to cherish the black population of St. Domingo whilst we have a similar population in our Southern States?" When Federalists later asked Logan how the trade ban could be enforced, he replied that he had no intention of actually putting an end to the Haitian trade. He merely wanted a

---

[30] Adams, *History of the United States*, III, 70-79, 103-108; Isaac J. Cox, *The West Florida Controversy, 1798-1813: A Study in American Diplomacy* (Baltimore 1918), 102-138, 227-265; Madison to John Armstrong and James Bowdoin, Mar. 13, 1806, Diplomatic Instructions, M-77, reel 1.

[31] Frederick B. Tolles, *George Logan of Philadelphia* (New York 1953), 247, 257, 261-262; *Annals of Congress*, 8th Cong., 2d sess., 65.

law that would satisfy the French and serve notice on American merchants that they traded with Haiti at their own risk.[32]

After considerable debate, the Senate voted overwhelmingly to give Logan leave to introduce his bill. The Senate also asked the president to turn over copies of the complaints lodged by the French government against the Haitian trade. Although Delaware Federalist James A. Bayard suggested that the Senate seek the administration's official response to these complaints, his proposal was rejected. Republican Samuel Latham Mitchill of New York claimed that this resolution was defeated because it was known "that Mr. Madison's answer contained a vindication of our right to trade to that island — & that if it was produced it would have a powerful tendency to prevent the passing of the bill."[33] The Senate subsequently approved the bill by a party vote of 21-8, with all the Federalists in opposition. According to Federalist William Plumer, "several of the Senators from the southern States declared that almost the only reason that reconciled them to the bill was the fatal influence that the independence of the Haytians would have on their own slaves."[34]

When the bill was received in the House, southern Republicans rose in its defense. John W. Eppes, who was living with the president, said: "We are called on by a nation friendly to us to put a stop to this infamous and nefarious traffic. It is time to do it; let us pass the bill at once." With the French minister sitting in the gallery, the bill was hustled through the House despite Federalist objections. It received final approval by a vote of 93-26, with Federalists from both sides of the Mason-Dixon Line in opposition. In its final form, the bill prohibited anyone residing in the United States from trading with any part of Haiti "not in possession, and under the acknowledged Government of France."

---

[32] Speech of George Logan, Dec. 20, 1805, *Annals of Congress*, 9th Cong., 1st sess., 26-29; Adams, ed., *Memoirs of John Quincy Adams*, I, 383; Everett S. Brown, ed., *William Plumer's Memorandum of Proceedings in the United States Senate, 1803-1807* (New York 1923), 387.

[33] *Annals of Congress*, 9th Cong., 1st sess., 30-38, 40-43, 47, 52, 75-76, 84-85; Brown, ed., *William Plumer's Memorandum*, 414. The Madison letter referred to here could not be found. The relevant volume of Department of State records has been lost.

[34] *Annals of Congress*, 9th Cong., 1st sess., 138; Brown, ed., *William Plumer's Memorandum*, 435.

Merchants had to give bond to obey the law, and violators forfeited both ship and cargo.[35]

As the bill was being hurried through Congress, Pickering (now a member of the Senate) took alarm. Fearful that the branch of trade he had so carefully cultivated during the Quasi-War would be suppressed, he took the extraordinary step of sending an appeal directly to the president. In a vigorous and lengthy letter, Pickering called on Jefferson to oppose the bill. Suggesting that the ex-slaves were guilty of nothing more than having a dark skin, Pickering insisted "that the Haytians, tho' declared revolted subjects of France, are in actual possession of independence; that they are engaged in a civil war; and therefore that those powers who intend to maintain their neutrality, are bound to act towards them with impartiality." Pickering claimed that suspending trade with Haiti would put American lives and property on the island in jeopardy, and expose American shipping throughout the Caribbean to retaliation from Haitian-based privateers. He also warned against abandoning this commerce "at the *nod*, at the *insolent demand* of the minister of France . . . . One act of submission," he said, "begets further unwarrantable demands; and every subsequent compliance still further debases the nation, blunts the sense of national honour, and sinks the spirit of the people."[36]

All this, of course, was hardly calculated to move Jefferson. But even the most tactful of letters probably would have failed, given the government's determination to end the trade. Although the administration told France that the new measure went "beyond the obligation of the United States under the law of nations," it presented a somewhat different view to Congress. The year before, when the arms embargo was under consideration, Secretary of the Treasury Albert Gallatin had outlined the government's position (after consulting Madison) in a lengthy letter to Samuel Latham Mitchill. Gallatin argued that "San Domingo is a French colony, recognized as such by the United States and by

---

[35] Speech of John W. Eppes, Feb. 24, 1806, *Annals of Congress*, 9th Cong., 1st sess., 499; dispatch from Washington reprinted from Albany *Gazette* in Boston *New England Palladium*, Mar. 14, 1806; *Annals of Congress*, 9th Cong., 1st sess., 516, 1228-1229.

[36] Pickering to Jefferson, Feb. 24, 1806, Jefferson Papers, reel 35 (Library of Congress).

every European nation, a colony in a state of rebellion against the mother-country." Trade with Haiti was therefore "altogether illegal." Neither the justice of the rebels' cause, Gallatin declared, nor the fact that they controlled the colony had any bearing on the case. Under the circumstances, the United States had only two choices: "either continue to acknowledge the supremacy of the nation over its rebellious province or colony, and therefore submit to its laws and regulations respecting the commerce with such province or colony, or acknowledge, at the risk or rather with the certainty of a war, the independence of the rebellious province or colony."[37]

In accordance with administration policy, Jefferson signed the new measure into law on February 28, 1806. The trade ban was renewed in 1807 and expired on April 25, 1808. Trade with Haiti continued to be prohibited under the embargo and the non-intercourse act, since the administration still viewed the black republic as a French colony. Thus it was not until the spring of 1810 that trade with Haiti was once again legal. In spite of these restrictions, some American supplies reached Haiti anyway, carried either in foreign ships or in American ships operating clandestinely. But the trade never reached its earlier proportions: the island's economic base had deteriorated too much for that.[38]

The Haitian trade ban did not live up to the hopes and fears of contemporaries. It did not force the blacks to resume their allegiance to France (as Napoleon had wished), it did not lead to the American acquisition of the Floridas (as Jefferson had hoped), and it did not undermine American independence or cause the loss of American property and lives in the Caribbean (as Pickering had feared). Even so it was a significant benchmark in Haitian-American relations because it firmly established American hostility toward the black republic. Although other nations extended diplomatic recognition to Haiti, the United States refused to take

---

[37] Madison to John Armstrong, Mar. 15, 1806, Diplomatic Instructions, M-77, reel 1; Gallatin to Mitchill, Jan. 3, 1805, in Adams, ed., *Writings of Albert Gallatin*, I, 219-226.

[38] *Annals of Congress*, 9th Cong., 1st sess., 1229; *ibid.*, 9th Cong., 2d sess., 1262; Jefferson to Gallatin, Jan. 12, 1807, in Lipscomb and Bergh, eds., *Writings of Thomas Jefferson*, XI, 134; speech of Edward St. Loe Livermore, June 26, 1809, *Annals of Congress*, 11th Cong., 1st sess., 445; Logan, *Diplomatic Relations*, 181, 183.

this step until 1862. The triumph of Jefferson's Haitian policy fixed the course of Haitian-American relations for more than half a century.

Runaway Slaves and the Slave Communities in South Carolina, 1799 to 1830

Michael P. Johnson

RUNAWAY slaves pose an important problem for interpretations of the character of slave communities in the United States. Although slaves ran away for many different reasons, all runaways engaged in a dramatic form of resistance: they deprived their masters of control over their labor, at least for a time. The typical runaway was a young man who absconded alone.[1] Slaves often gave runaways moral and material support, but most slave women and older men were restrained from running away alone by their familial obligations and community bonds.[2] However, the same community ties that had to be severed to run away alone could and did strengthen slaves of both sexes and a wide range of ages to run away together, in groups. These groups exemplified the bonds of affection, loyalty, and trust that knit the larger slave community and gave collective expression to the spirit of resistance.

This article analyzes advertisements for groups of runaway slaves that appeared in the Charleston, South Carolina, newspapers from 1799 to

Mr. Johnson is a member of the Department of History at the University of California, Irvine. He wishes to thank Ira Berlin, Jonathan M. Wiener, Carl N. Degler, Mark D. Kaplanoff, Stanley L. Engerman, and Michael Craton for critical readings of drafts of this article. The research was supported, in part, by a fellowship from the American Council of Learned Societies.

[1] For example, in a study of 2,002 runaway slaves, Daniel E. Meaders found that "the average runaway slave was male, single, between the ages of eighteen and thirty, and had usually belonged to no less than two owners" ("South Carolina Fugitives as Viewed Through Local Colonial Newspapers with Emphasis on Runaway Notices, 1732-1801," *Journal of Negro History*. LX [1975], 292). For similar conclusions see Peter H. Wood, *Black Majority: Negroes in Colonial South Carolina from 1670 through the Stono Rebellion* (New York, 1974), 241; Gerald W. Mullin, *Flight and Rebellion: Slave Resistance in Eighteenth-Century Virginia* (New York, 1972), 40; John Donald Duncan, "Servitude and Slavery in Colonial South Carolina, 1660-1776" (Ph.D. diss., Emory University, 1972), 529-587; and Lathan Algerna Windley, "A Profile of Runaway Slaves in Virginia and South Carolina from 1730 through 1787" (Ph.D. diss., University of Iowa, 1974), 63-79.

[2] John W. Blassingame, *The Slave Community: Plantation Life in the Antebellum South*, rev. ed. (New York, 1979), 198; Herbert G. Gutman, *The Black Family in Slavery and Freedom, 1750-1925* (New York, 1976), 264-270; Eugene D. Genovese, *Roll, Jordan, Roll: The World the Slaves Made* (New York, 1974), 452-453, 657.

1830.[3] Every issue of the Charleston *Courier* and the *City Gazette and Daily Advertiser* was surveyed, and each advertisement for a group of runaway slaves was collected.[4] A group is defined as two or more slaves who ran away together. Over the entire thirty-two-year period, advertisements appeared for 351 groups, comprising a total of 983 slaves.[5] In general, the advertisements indicate that South Carolina contained two distinct slave communities, an urban community and a rural plantation community; that relationships formed and tested in the day-to-day experience of work and family life structured these communities; that both communities nurtured a spirit of collective resistance, despite their different orientations toward white society and culture; and that the reopening of the African slave trade between 1804 and 1807, and the incorporation of large numbers of African-born blacks into the existing slave communities, invigorated collective acts of resistance.[6]

[3] For other discussions of groups of runaways see Blassingame, *Slave Community*, 206-209; Gutman, *Black Family*, 262-263; Genovese, *Roll, Jordan, Roll*, 656-657; Mullin, *Flight and Rebellion*, 43; Kenneth M. Stampp, *The Peculiar Institution: Slavery in the Ante-Bellum South* (New York, 1956), 111; and Duncan, "Servitude and Slavery in S.C.," 567.

[4] For the period before publication of the *Courier* in 1803, all the advertisements are taken from the *Gazette*. To establish a base line before the African trade was reopened, I chose 1799 because a continuous run of the *Gazette* is available for that year but not earlier in the 1790s. From 1803 through 1830, advertisements were collected from both the *Courier* and the *Gazette*, with the exception of eight years for which the *Gaz.* (title varies) is not extant: 1806, 1807, 1809 (*City Gazette and Daily Advertiser*); 1811, 1812, 1819 (*City Gazette and Commercial Advertiser*); 1822, 1826 (*City Gazette and Commercial Daily Advertiser*). I chose 1830 as a convenient ending date because two decades seemed to be an adequate period for assessing the impact of the reopening of the African trade on groups of runaways, and because after 1830 the content of advertisements might be expected to be more rigorously censored, with a wary eye on sectional politics and the growing abolitionist movement. The advertisements ran for widely varying lengths of time. I have cited individual advertisements on or soon after the date of first publication. Since the purpose of this study is to examine the nature of the bonds among slaves in groups of runaways, I did not collect advertisements for single runaways, nor have I attempted to determine the proportion of all runaway advertisements that were for groups. Duncan has found that group runaways made up 30% of the slaves who ran away between 1732 and 1752 ("Servitude and Slavery in S.C.," 567).

[5] Obviously, many South Carolina slaves who ran away between 1799 and 1830 never appeared in newspaper advertisements. Since it is impossible to discover how many slaves ran away in groups—as distinct from the number of advertisements for groups of runaways—the advertisements furnish no reliable way to generalize about all groups. It is far less hazardous to use evidence of the bonds among slaves in advertised groups of runaways as a guide to some of the strongest and most important bonds within the general slave community.

[6] Ira Berlin has emphasized the distinctive character of the two South Carolina slave communities in "Time, Space, and the Evolution of Afro-American Society

For purposes of analysis, groups that absconded from rural plantations were separated from those that ran away from the city. Each group was also assigned to one of three categories, according to the type of bonds among slaves in the group. Groups in which all members belonged to the same family are termed *family groups*. Groups that included at least two members of the same family and at least one other (apparently) unrelated member are defined as *community groups*. Groups whose members were not related by family, at least as far as can be ascertained from the advertisements, are labeled *work groups*. (See Table I.) Obviously, the assignment of groups to these categories depends completely on the information contained in the advertisements. If a master was unaware of kin ties among members of a group of runaways, or if he knew of a kin relationship but did not mention it in his advertisement, a group that should have been categorized as a family group has been miscategorized as a work or community group. The assignment of groups to the work and community categories is consistent with the evidence contained in the advertisements. Evidence discussed below makes clear that many of the groups *defined* as work groups *were* work groups, that the same is true of community groups, and that the three types of groups as *defined* were in fact *different*. The names of the three categories were chosen to emphasize what appear to be the principal characteristics of the groups they contain. A more precise though less connotative set of category names would be *no kin* (work groups), *some kin* (community groups), and *all kin* (family groups). However, the names of the categories are not as important as the possible failure of the advertisements to mention kin ties that actually existed among group members. We have no way to determine the frequency of such relationships. When they did exist, it was probably not uncommon for masters to fail to mention them, especially when the relationships extended beyond a slave's immediate family. Therefore, the significance of kinship is almost certainly understated in the following analysis.

Prudence dictated small groups; the dangers of betrayal, detection, and capture increased with the size of the group. Most (70 percent) of the advertised groups included only two slaves. For convenience, these will be called "small" groups. "Large" groups of three or more slaves included half of the slaves in all the groups.[7] Groups containing family members were much more common among the large groups; work groups predominated

in British Mainland North America," *American Historical Review*. LXXXV (1980), 44-78.

[7] By "half of the slaves" I mean half of the 983 slaves in all the advertised groups of runaways. I do not, of course, mean half of all slaves who ran away or half of all slaves in South Carolina. I have avoided using the clumsy construction, "slaves in all the advertised groups of runaways," each time I refer to all or some of the slaves in these groups. When I refer to slaves other than those in the advertised groups, I have sought to do so explicitly and unambiguously.

TABLE I
SUMMARY OF ADVERTISEMENTS FOR GROUPS OF
RUNAWAY SLAVES IN SOUTH CAROLINA, 1799 TO 1830

Group Types	Rural	Number of Groups Urban	Total
Work	146	70	216
Small	104	62	166
Large	42	8	50
Family	63	50	113
Small	40	41	81
Large	23	9	32
Community	14	8	22
Totals	223	128	351
		Number of Slaves	
Work	371	172	543
Small	208	124	332
Large	163	48	211
Family	171	115	286
Small	80	82	162
Large	91	33	124
Community	117	37	154
Totals	659	324	983

among the small groups. Specifically, work groups accounted for two-thirds of the small groups; family and community groups made up a majority (52 percent) of the large groups. This simple relationship between the size and type of groups suggests the relative importance of family ties and hints that kinship complemented work relationships to incorporate non-kin into groups of slaves who braved the risks of taking off together.

The general relationship between kinship and group size holds true for both rural and urban groups, as Figure 1 illustrates. At first glance, there are two important differences between urban and rural groups: a larger fraction of urban groups included family members; large groups were more common among rural groups. Despite these differences, nearly identical proportions of all the slaves in the large groups were in groups that contained family members: 56 percent for the rural groups and 59 percent for the urban groups. The rural groups in Figure 2 clearly exhibit the relationship between group size and type. As the size of the groups

FIGURE 1. Number of groups by size, type and location

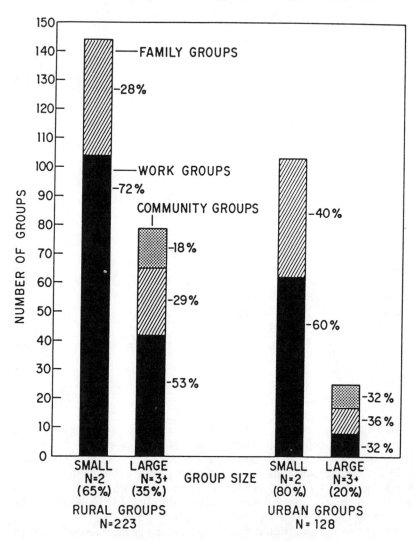

increased, kin ties became more common among group members. In the largest groups, kinship was less the exclusive determinant of group membership than a nucleus of loyalty and strength around which non-kin could cluster. The predominance of work groups among all the groups of runaways is evidence that the most common relationship among slaves—one between non-kin who worked together—could be similar to kinship in fostering the mutual respect necessary for a dangerous cooperative act. Likewise, the frequency of kin ties among slaves in the large groups

FIGURE 2. Larger groups by size, type and location

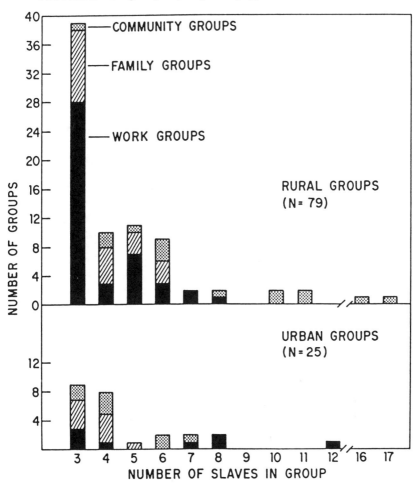

suggests that as the possible cross-currents of disloyalty increased, so did the significance of kinship in annealing the group. A closer look at intra-group relationships reveals how the routines of work and family life shaped the circumstances in which these slaves identified with each other.

In Charleston, blacks and whites were in constant contact.[8] Loading and unloading ships, working as tradesmen in shops throughout the city,

[8] For more detailed discussions of urban slavery see Ulrich Bonnell Phillips, "The Slave Labor Problem in the Charleston District," *Political Science Quarterly*, XXII (1907), 416-439; Leonard Price Stavisky, "The Negro Artisan in the South Atlantic States, 1800-1860: A Study of Status and Economic Opportunity with

thronging the markets, carrying and huckstering goods through the streets, and above all attending to domestic chores in hundreds of white households, slaves were forced to learn what whites wanted. Most of the time, whites demanded obedience from slaves and would not tolerate slackness or impudence. But as slaves worked in the city, they learned far more than obedience.

The pronounced sexual division of labor in Charleston meant that the comradeship of work tended to develop bonds among slaves of the same sex. Most of the slaves in the shops and on the wharves were men, as were 85 percent of the slaves in the urban work groups. Three-quarters of the urban work groups were composed exclusively of men, another 8 percent included only women, and the rest contained both sexes. Almost all (94 percent) of the members of the large work groups were men. Most of the men in the all-male groups were skilled tradesmen.[9] Presumably, they worked together. Certainly, the runaways Anthony and Renty, "known about town as excellent Carpenters," were work mates, as were Jack and Edmund, both "Blacksmiths by trade," or the eight ropemakers who absconded from a ropewalk, or men like Primus and Scipio who were hired out as laborers.[10] Although men in some of the other groups did not have the same trades, they probably came to know one another at work. The carpenter Polydore probably worked with his runaway companion John, a bricklayer, as did the coachman Sam who ran off with Jemy, a blacksmith, or the sawyer Gorey who left with Sam, a laborer, or the three coopers who took off with a blacksmith.[11] The work of these skilled tradesmen brought them together under circumstances that allowed them to come to know and trust one another. The twelve ship carpenters who "went off in a boat" were building more than boats as they worked together.[12]

The tradesmen's relative freedom of movement in the city contrasted with the constant white supervision house servants endured. That may be why only one of the urban work groups included two men who were identified as house servants, although the relatively small number of male

---

Special Reference to Charleston" (Ph.D. diss., Columbia University, 1958); Richard C. Wade, *Slavery in the Cities: The South, 1820-1860* (New York, 1964); and Robert S. Starobin, *Industrial Slavery in the Old South* (New York, 1970).

[9] Fifty-eight percent of the 53 exclusively male urban work groups included one or more slaves whose occupation is specifically mentioned in the advertisement. Twenty of the 46 advertisements for all-male groups of two give the occupations of both slaves. The occupations of two or more slaves are mentioned for 5 of the 7 large all-male groups. Of all the slaves in these all-male groups, 54% (74/137) are mentioned as having a specific occupation.

[10] *Courier*, May 17, 1820; *Gaz.*, May 12, 1815; *Courier*, Apr. 29, 1818; *Gaz.*, June 18, 1801.

[11] *Courier*, May 9, 1807; *Gaz.*, Apr. 30, 1804; *Courier*, Apr. 6, 1819, Nov. 7, 1815.

[12] *Courier*, Oct. 4, 1821.

house servants was probably also a factor.[13] Some of the men whose occupations are not mentioned in the advertisements may have been house servants, but most of them were probably common laborers who were hired out.[14] The work these men did was more like that of tradesmen in requiring them to move about in the city and in providing a certain distance from white supervision. Among the advertisements that contain no occupational information, four mention that the slaves were well known in the city.

Most of the slave women in Charleston worked as domestic servants. Only two of the twenty-five women in the urban work groups were specifically identified as house servants, but many of the others probably were, too.[15] Their duties of marketing, washing, and running errands occasionally took them outside the white household and brought them into contact with other slaves. That may have been how Delia, a cook who was hired out, came to know her runaway companion Bob, or how Tena became acquainted with her runaway partner Jim, a sailor in the Georgetown trade, or how Diana cooperated with Peter, a carter.[16] Eight of the women were described as well known in the city, suggesting that their daily activities brought them into contact with whites and blacks outside their masters' households. But domestic work allowed women fewer opportunities than men for socializing free from the supervision of whites. Such occasions were important for the runaways Betty and Sue, "so well known for many years as vendors of Oysters and Shrimps," and for Stepney's companion Matty, who sold milk in the city.[17] On the whole, however, slave women's work in white households made it more difficult and dangerous for them to run away with co-workers.

Slaves in the urban work groups understood white expectations, and the advertisements make clear that masters expected runaways to exploit their understanding. Nineteen of the twenty-two advertisements (86 percent) that mention the verbal or social skills of the runaways identify slaves like the cooper Jack, "a very plausible fellow, and very smart in answering any person who will interrogate him," or the carter Peter, "a sly, subtle, cunning fellow, of smooth speech," who "has duped some people by his fair words and got off from them some time ago."[18] Only one tradesman was said to have had a speech impediment of any sort—the carpenter

[13] For the group see *Gaz.*, Apr. 13, 1808. In all, only 4 of the 147 men (3%) in the urban work groups are identified as house servants.
[14] Since the attributes of a tradesman or a house servant would make a runaway more recognizable, masters presumably made a point of noting occupations in such cases.
[15] *Gaz.*, Apr. 7, 1814; *Courier*, Nov. 19, 1821.
[16] *Courier*, Nov. 19, 1821; *Gaz.*, June 12, 1816; *Courier*, Apr. 4, 1807.
[17] *Courier*, Dec. 3, 1824; *Gaz.*, Apr. 16, 1801.
[18] *Courier*, Nov. 7, 1815, Apr. 4, 1807. These slaves did not exhibit the stuttering that Mullin found associated with the "assimilated's divided self and cultural marginality" (*Flight and Rebellion*, 98-103, quotation on p. 98). For a

Renty, who was "disposed to talk much, stutters a little when he speaks, and a great deal when suddenly addressed."[19] Slaves who were not identified as tradesmen were also said to be "very sensible," like Phil, or, like Absolom and Cyrus, "very artful."[20] In general, the work these slaves did in the city gave them an education in white ways which they used to develop, as was said of the carpenter January, "a smooth way" in dealing with whites.[21]

By running away with their co-workers, these slaves demonstrated that their knowledge of white language and culture did not lead them to identify with whites. The skills, knowledge, and experience that made them valuable also made them refractory. Running away was not the only sign of their rebelliousness: Cato had "a few recent scars on his shins, having had fore legs [irons]"; the "active artful wench," Eddy, had "a mark over her right eye from a whip"; and the two "notorious offenders" Frank and Charles, both ship carpenters, each "for their misbehavior have an iron on one of their legs."[22] By turning toward the culture of whites, urban slaves who ran away with their co-workers did not turn their backs on each other.

Slaves in urban family groups turned toward one another in different ways. Women predominated in the urban family groups. In fact, three-quarters of all the women in urban runaway groups were in family groups. Seventy-nine percent of the adults in urban family groups were women, more than two-thirds of them mothers who ran away with their children.[23] By far the most common group was a mother and her child; a mother and one or more of her children made up 74 percent of all the urban family groups.[24] Fathers, in contrast, were included in only two groups.[25]

One might suppose that slave mothers ran away with their children simply because the children were completely dependent upon them, but

skeptical discussion of evidence of speech patterns in runaway advertisements see Blassingame, *Slave Community*, 203-206.

[19] *Courier*, May 17, 1820.

[20] *Gaz.*, June 15, 1825, July 5, 1813. Seven of the 20 urban work groups of two men with no mentioned occupations contained such men.

[21] Two groups contained slaves who had become dangerously well educated: the blacksmith Andrew's companion Robin was a bricklayer, "a smart likely fellow [who] reads and writes English tolerably well" (*Courier*, Jan. 11, 1808); Betty's companion Bob "can write, and by forging a pass may induce a belief that he is a free man" (*Gaz.*, Apr. 17, 1805).

[22] *Gaz.*, Aug. 23, 1799, Sept. 6, 1803, Apr. 5, 1805.

[23] Of the 59 women 10 years or older in these groups, 41 (69%) were mothers.

[24] Of the 41 groups of two, 29 (71%) comprised a mother and her child. Six of the 9 large groups included a mother and children, and 2 others included a grandmother, mother, and one or more children.

[25] One group comprised a father and child; another, a father, mother, and two children. *Gaz.*, May 8, 1818, July 26, 1799. Two groups contained two sisters; one group was made up of two brothers; and eight groups comprised a man and wife.

such an explanation is discounted by the ages of the children. Only a fifth of the mother-child groups included children two years old or younger.[26] Rachel's six-month-old daughter Sally was probably still nursing, and Violet's twenty-month-old son Dennis was still a toddler, as was Venus's two-year-old Jim.[27] But 42 percent of the mother-child groups included children between three and eight years old, like Sanite's six-year-old son George or Betsey's seven-year-old daughter Henny.[28] The remaining 37 percent of the groups included children aged nine or older. The mean age of the children in these groups was sixteen; that of the mothers, forty-one. Nancy, for example, was forty-five when she ran away with her son Robin, twenty-five; Venus, forty, was accompanied by her daughter Betty, twenty; the "elderly Negro wench" Chloe ran away with her daughter Nelly and her grandchild; Flora took off with her infant daughter Cate, her adult daughter Daphne, and her grandchild, Daphne's sixteen-month-old infant.[29] Many of the children in the urban family groups were old enough to help plan and execute the getaway.

Only a third of the mothers in these family groups were identified as having worked out in the city or as having a specific job that took them beyond the confines of the white household.[30] Four of the mothers worked out as washerwomen. Among them, Adeline was "well known as a washer, having been accustomed to washing at the fresh water Ponds," and Mary was "well known about the city as a washer woman, particularly on board vessels."[31] Three others were marketwomen: Dye, for example, was "accustomed to attend at market daily [and] is well known throughout it," and Matilda was "well known as a seller of cakes in the city, for several years, and has sat for some time on the Bay, near the New Market."[32] Most of the rest of the mothers probably worked as house servants, although the advertisements do not say so.

Urban slave women were as well educated as slave men in the ways of whites. A fifth of the urban family groups included women who were unusually skillful at negotiating encounters with whites, like Fanny, who was "very plausible . . . and will no doubt endeavor to pass herself off as a free person," or the sisters Patty and Phillis, who were described as "very

[26] For the 39 groups that included children, 6 advertisements (15%) do not mention the ages of the children. Of the 33 groups for which the childen's ages are given, 7 (21%) included children aged two or younger.
[27] *Courier*, Dec. 5, 1822; *Gaz.*, May 12, 1815, Jan. 14, 1805.
[28] *Gaz.*, Feb. 2, 1828; *Courier*, Dec. 13, 1824. The mean age of the children in these groups was 6, that of the mothers, 28, which was the same as for the mothers of younger children.
[29] *Gaz.*, Dec. 22, 1814, Oct. 22, 1799; *Courier*, Jan. 29, 1817; *Gaz.*, Dec. 17, 1817.
[30] This was true of 12 of the 35 mothers (34%).
[31] *Gaz.*, June 11, 1817; *Courier*, Mar. 24, 1810.
[32] *Gaz.*, June 11, 1817; *Courier*, June 27, 1811.

sensible and capable of telling plausible stories."[33] Given the frequent contact between slave women and whites, however, it is surprising that more of the women were not singled out as plausible, artful, or smart.[34] The reason probably has less to do with the social and verbal skills of slave women than with the expectations of whites. As domestic servants, most slave women confronted whites in a work setting where they were supposed to be deferential and compliant. Expecting deference, perhaps whites did not often think they were being manipulated by their house servants' plausibility and therefore did not mention it in their advertisements. While the advertisements are silent about the social skills of most of the women, only three women are identified as exhibiting any uneasiness in the presence of whites.[35] Yet an easy familiarity with the expectations of whites did not translate simply or automatically into accommodation, as demonstrated by the actions of all the women in the runaway groups and most dramatically by Dinah, who ran away with her nine-year-old son Adam, even though she "had on when she went off . . . an iron on her right leg [and was] much marked in the face by the whip."[36]

The sexual division of labor in the city probably explains the absence of fathers from the urban family groups. The majority of slaves in Charleston were women, some 56 percent in 1830. Some had husbands who also worked in the city, but many did not. Nine of the urban family groups comprised a husband and wife, like the marketwoman Sally and her husband Will, a coachman; or Daphney and Jacob, a drayman; or Amarita, who was hired out, and Billy, "who used to attend his late master's store in King Street for several years."[37] Yet only one of these groups included children, and only one other group included a father and child.[38] The reason fathers were absent from the urban family groups is probably not that the bond between slave men and their families was weak but that it had been disrupted by masters. The husbands of many of the women who worked in Charleston probably remained on plantations in the country. Even when both husband and wife worked in the city, the sexual division of labor meant that they rarely worked together. Masters' careful selection of the slaves they wanted to have with them in the city may also explain why most (77 percent) of the urban family groups included only one child,

---

[33] Eleven of the 50 urban family groups (22%) contained adult women described as plausible, artful, smart, or well spoken. For the groups cited in the text see *Courier*, June 4, 1824, and *Gaz.*, Aug. 4, 1801.

[34] Only one of the women whose occupation is identified was said to be plausible or artful. Thirty-one percent of the urban work groups had members described in this way.

[35] One woman "when questioned closely appears to stammer much in her speech." Two other women had "a downcast look when spoken to." There are no other reports of speech difficulties or obvious discomfort in the presence of whites. *Gaz.*, Mar. 14, 1803, Aug. 5, 1817; *Courier*, Dec. 13, 1824.

[36] *Gaz.*, Jan. 6, 1808.

[37] *Ibid.*, Oct. 1, 1823, Nov. 15, 1803; *Courier*, Nov. 1, 1825.

[38] *Gaz.*, July 26, 1799, May 18, 1818.

even though the mothers were old enough to have had several children. The distinctive character of urban work had at least as much to do with the kinds of family bonds represented among the urban runaways as did the inherent strength of the bonds between family members.

More than nine out of ten slaves in South Carolina lived on the rice and sea-island cotton plantations along the coast or on the short-staple cotton plantations throughout the upcountry.[39] As cotton cultivation spread across the state at the turn of the century, the proportion of slaves in the population rose steadily from 43 percent in 1790 to 55 percent in 1830.[40] Whites had only tenuous control over the culture of the slaves. While the urban slave community was oriented toward whites by the character of urban work, the rural slave community was structured by the work of plantation agriculture and was oriented toward the Afro-American culture of the quarters.

Most country slaves were field hands. Accordingly, the proportion of slaves in rural work groups who were identified in the advertisements as having a specific occupation was much smaller (under half) than among the urban work groups.[41] Two groups contained field hands who certainly worked together: Bob, who "knows something of cropping and works eagerly with his hoe," and his runaway companion Hardtimes, who "ploughs well"; and Abraham, a fifty-six-year-old "field hand, and cooper by trade," who took off with Fortune, fifty, "a field hand, and by trade a carpenter."[42] Field hands like these men predominated among runaways, as among rural slaves generally.

Most field hands worked in gangs under the supervision of a white owner or overseer or a black driver. Although the task system was common on the rice plantations of the low country, even there slaves were often organized into gangs for specific chores. In contrast to the organization of urban work, plantation labor brought together large numbers of slaves. Working in larger groups, rural slaves also ran away in larger groups. Forty-four percent of the slaves in rural work groups ran away in

[39] Between 1790 and 1830, the proportion of the state's slaves who lived in Charleston dropped from 8% to 6%.
[40] The cotton boom was accompanied by an exodus of whites from the state. Between 1800 and 1830, the white population of South Carolina grew at only about 1/5 of the rate of the lower South as a whole. See the convenient statistical tables in Ira Berlin, *Slaves Without Masters: The Free Negro in the Antebellum South* (New York, 1974), 400-403.
[41] Advertisements for 29% of the 104 rural work groups of two slaves mention the occupation of at least one slave; 16% note the jobs of both. The corresponding figures for the small urban work groups are 57% and 43%. For the 42 large rural work groups, 24% of the advertisements mention the occupation of at least one slave, compared to 63% of the large urban work groups. Advertisements for only 7% of the large rural work groups specify the jobs of two or more slaves, compared to half of the large urban groups.
[42] *Gaz.*, Jan. 21, 1803; *Courier*, Mar. 30, 1826.

groups of three or more, compared to 28 percent of the urban slaves.[43] The large rural work groups also reflected the heterogeneous age and sexual composition of the plantation work gangs.

Unlike the urban groups, almost half (47 percent) of the large rural work groups contained slaves whose ages were fifteen or more years apart, such as September, twenty-four, Sandy, twenty-nine, and Simon, fifty-two; or William and Prince, both about thirty, and Bob, about fifty; or the young woman Doll and her companions Charles, about thirty-five, and Sanders, fifty-eight.[44] Similarly, since slave men and women often worked together as field hands, women were much more commonly included in rural work groups. Almost a third of the large rural work groups contained both men and women, while none of the large urban groups did.[45] As men and women like Dick, Jack, and Betty, or Bob, London, and Lucy, or Joe, Moses, Amy, and Doll worked together in the fields, they cultivated the spirit of collective resistance.[46]

The distinctive features of rural work were also apparent among the slaves whose occupations are mentioned in the advertisements. Some were common laborers on canals, like Robin and Wauney, who had worked together "six or seven years last past in the service of the Santee Canal Company."[47] Others, like the six men who ran away from a brickyard, were involved in manufacturing.[48] Tradesmen, almost all of them carpenters, accounted for 35 percent of the rural work groups for which the occupation of one or more slaves is specified.[49] Five of these groups contained two carpenters, who almost certainly worked together. But skilled slaves on plantations were less likely than their urban counterparts to work exclusively with other skilled slaves. That may explain why seven groups were composed of one carpenter and one or more other slaves whose jobs were not mentioned, like Griffin, "a good plain carpenter," and his companion Jack, or the carpenter Prince and his fellow runaways Flora, Pender, Musa, and Bob.[50]

[43] Likewise, 29% of the rural work groups were large groups, compared to 11% of the urban work groups.

[44] *Gaz.*, June 10, 1804, Oct. 30, 1817, May 3, 1804. The median and mean ages of the 167 men in the rural work groups whose ages are given a numerical value were 25 and 28; those of the 24 women whose ages are listed were 30 and 32. Nine of the 19 large groups that included two or more slaves whose ages are mentioned contained slaves whose ages were 15 or more years apart. This was true of only 20% of the urban work groups.

[45] Twenty-nine percent of the large rural work groups and 13% of the small groups contained both sexes. Sixteen percent of the small urban work groups included a man and a woman.

[46] *Courier*, Dec. 10, 1828; *Gaz.*, Feb. 2, 1818, Oct. 8, 1803.

[47] *Gaz.*, Mar. 14, 1800.

[48] *Courier*, July 17, 1824.

[49] Fourteen of the work groups included skilled tradesmen. In addition to the carpenters, one group included two bricklayers, another a barber who had worked in Charleston.

[50] *Gaz.*, Mar. 30, 1803, July 29, 1799.

Boatmen possessed even more typically rural skills. Numerous slaves manned the craft that moved along South Carolina's rivers and coastal waterways. Boatmen were included in a third of the rural work groups for which a slave's occupation was identified.[51] Harry and Tom, for example, were "accustomed to the river and are considered prime Boat Hands"; Bob and Bartlett "have both been accustomed to boating, and have been trained to that occupation"; and Tinco and Sam were "employed in the three-masted boat Beaufort Packet," Tinco as the patroon, the person in charge.[52] The skill, initiative, and responsibility the boatmen exercised as they passed between rural and urban slave communities gave them experience they could put to work for themselves. The master of the three "good boat hands" Peter, Primus, and Scipio reported that they had "walked away from their work at the plantation to play in town," where they were well known.[53] Although a few field hands periodically worked in the city, boat hands enjoyed unique opportunities to draw upon their contacts among slaves in the countryside and the city.[54]

In the country as in the city, most house servants were women who lived in or near the white household. Yet only 2 of the 146 rural work groups contained women whom the advertisements identify as house servants: Daphney, the companion of Joe and Sue, was "brought up in the house from a child as an attendant and seamstress," and Peter's companion Hannah, who was "handy about the house and [was] a pastry cook."[55] The house servants in the other 7 rural groups in which servants were mentioned were all men, like Carolina and Cyrus, both "accustomed to wait in the house."[56] The underrepresentation of female house servants suggests the distance that separated the daily work of house servants and field hands, and the difficulty of bridging that distance. It may have been more common for men who worked in the house to work periodically outside the house with other slaves. That may help explain how Charles, "well known as a waiting man," came to run away with Bristol, "a field hand," or how Sandy, a cook, Simon, a gardener, and September, "a field negro," plotted their getaway.[57]

---

[51] Boatmen were included in 13 of the 40 groups.

[52] *Courier*, July 28, 1824; *Gaz.*, Apr. 20, 1808; *Courier*, Aug. 3, 1820. Five of the groups included two boatmen; the rest included one boatman along with other slaves whose occupations were not specified.

[53] *Gaz.*, Mar. 17, 1802.

[54] Eleven of the rural work groups that included slaves whose occupations were not mentioned contained one or more slaves who were said to be well known in the city. That was true of all the slaves in five of the groups and of one in the other six groups.

[55] *Gaz.*, May 20, 1803, Feb. 25, 1803.

[56] In all, the 9 groups containing house servants accounted for 23% of the 40 rural work groups that contained slaves whose occupations were mentioned. *Ibid.*, July 3, 1799.

[57] *Ibid.*, Sept. 3, 1802, June 10, 1804.

Field hands had relatively few chances to develop confidence in their ability to manipulate the expectations of whites. Skilled slaves, of course, had more opportunities than field hands and apparently took advantage of them. The carpenter George, for example, "speaks with great confidence and very good English, is very artful and will probably obtain a pass"; Griffin, another carpenter, "when spoken to speaks with a great deal of assurance [and is] very sensible and artful."[58] But even among rural tradesmen, speech difficulties were nearly twice as common as they were in the city.[59] Typical of such tradesmen were the carpenter David, who "stammers very much when he speaks," and the laborer Robin, who "when frightened or confused . . . stammers in his speech."[60] Among the rural slaves whose occupations are not identified, speech difficulties were extremely common. Three-quarters of those whose speech is mentioned did not speak what their masters identified as good English, like Jim, who "stammers when spoken to," or Joe, who "speaks very much Broken," or Daniel, who "has a difficulty of speech."[61] In general, rural slaves were less at ease with whites, less certain they could exploit what whites would recognize as plausibility. The behavior of Cato, who "when questioned shews great uneasiness and keeps his fingers in constant motion," betrayed the anxiety many rural slaves felt in the presence of whites.[62]

Whites expected plantation slaves to be submissive, to approach them hat in hand. Some slaves obligingly responded, like Andrew, who "has a humble submissive way when he speaks, but is an arch, subtle fellow," or the young man with a "rather stupid look" who, "when spoken to by a white person, has a remarkable down look, but is very artful and plausible in his speech," or Charles, who "speaks very bad English, but is artful enough to pass for a free man."[63] But above all, the stuttering, the down looks, and the sulkiness that the masters of rural runaways commonly

---

[58] *Ibid.*, Feb. 11, 1804, Mar. 30, 1803. Three rural groups contained slaves who could read, and two of these slaves could also write.

[59] Among the members of rural work groups containing slaves whose occupations are identified were 23 slaves whose speech is described. Nine of these slaves (39%) were said to have noticeable speech difficulties. Only 4 (22%) of the 22 urban slaves whose speech is mentioned had even the most minimal impediment.

[60] *Ibid.*, Nov. 28, 1823, Mar. 14, 1800.

[61] *Courier*, Jan. 18, 1822; *Gaz.*, Dec. 18, 1802; *Courier.* Feb. 1, 1825. Among the members of rural work groups containing slaves whose occupations were not mentioned were 59 slaves whose speech was described. Thirty-two of these slaves (54%) were said to stammer, stutter, or speak English poorly; another 12 (20%) were said to speak English tolerably. Although many of these slaves were Africans, the distinction between rural and urban slaves was not confined to newly imported Africans. When they are excluded from the count, 61% of the remaining slaves (20/33) are found to have exhibited impediments in encounters with whites.

[62] *Gaz.*, Nov. 8, 1799.

[63] *Courier*, June 18, 1807; *Gaz.*, Aug. 5, 1799, May 3, 1804.

noted arose from a plantation slave community that identified white culture with the whip.[64]

While some slaves disguised their hostility with appropriate submissive behavior, others were openly rebellious. Ten of the rural work groups contained slaves who had been punished for recalcitrance. Ross, for example, "has the print of the whip on her breast and arms"; Scipio was "considerably marked with the cowskin," as were Daniel, whose "back [is] very much scarified by the whip," and Billy, who bore "the marks of a severe correction upon his back and his ears are trimmed by taking off the top rim [and he] limps when he walks."[65] Five other slaves ran away with irons on: Lymerick "had an iron on one of his legs when he went away," as did Frank and Pompey; Abraham "had on when he absconded irons on each leg," and Lander "had an iron about his neck."[66] Urban slaves were less likely to be openly defiant, more likely to appear to be accommodating. Among plantation slaves there was less artifice, more open hostility.

Kinship structured the groups of almost half (44 percent) of the rural runaways. A quarter of the slaves were in family groups; another fifth were in community groups. A majority of the slaves in the family groups ran away in groups of three or more, almost twice the proportion in large urban family groups and a fifth more than in the rural work groups.[67] The mean size of the rural family groups was 4.0; the mean of the rural community groups was 8.4.[68] The mean size of all the rural groups that included kin (3.7) was about half again as large as that of all the urban groups including kin (2.6) or that of all the rural work groups (2.5).

The character of the rural family groups differed strikingly from that of their urban counterparts. The most common rural family group comprised a slave husband and wife, often accompanied by one or more children; 57 percent included slaves like Cuffee and his wife Molly, or Quaco and his wife Deler, or Hector and Careful, or Frank, Charlotte, and their children,

[64] Eugene D. Genovese wisely cautions against attempting "to construct a depth psychology of strangers long since dead." But he concludes that "the stuttering, stammering, and downcast looks before white men betrayed not only fear but smoldering anger and resentment" (*Roll, Jordan, Roll*, 647). See also Blassingame, *Slave Community*, 203-206.

[65] *Gaz.*, Feb. 21, 1800, Sept. 17, 1818, Aug. 19, 1805; *Courier*, Aug. 30, 1810.

[66] *Gaz.*, July 3, 1799, May 11, 1808, May 21, 1817, Oct. 12, 1808, Aug. 6, 1803.

[67] Fifty-three percent of the slaves in rural family groups were in large groups, compared to 29% of slaves in urban family groups. Forty-four percent of the slaves in rural work groups were in large groups.

[68] The mean size of the large rural work groups was 3.9, that of the large urban family groups, 3.7. The mean of all the rural family groups was 2.7, that of all the urban family groups, 2.3. The mean of the urban community groups was 4.6.

Morris, Eliza, Lydia, and Rosabelle.[69] A husband and wife are found in only 18 percent of the urban family groups. The contrast is even sharper with the rural community groups, in which three-quarters of the slaves were in groups that included one or more couples, like the group of seventeen composed of March, Mingo, Jack, Paul, Harry, Hess, Sarey, Amey and her son Sam, Jim, his wife Lizzy, and their six children.[70] In fact, 62 percent of all the rural family groups contained a slave husband or father, impressive testimony to the strength and authority of slave men in rural families.

The vast majority of slaves in the rural family and community groups were field hands—or so we may conclude from the fact that 87 percent of those old enough to work had no occupation specified in the advertisements.[71] The same was true of 95 percent of the slaves in the rural community groups. Tradesmen, boatmen, and house servants were represented among the family and community groups as husbands and fathers— like Job, a carpenter who ran away with his wife Lydia and their two daughters Sylvia and Rebecca; or Bungy, a patroon who took off with his wife Monomia and their children Adam and Tinah—or as mothers, like Rose, who was "very ingenious and understands sewing, knitting, spinning, weaving, washing, cooking, &c.," and who absconded with her daughter Hester.[72] But far more typical of the slaves in the rural family groups were Bella's husband Dan, who was "accustomed to all kinds of field work," or Peggy's husband David, who had been a driver for many years, or the group of ten slaves comprising Sue, Harry, Dye, Sarah, Big June, Manuel, Driver Tom, his wife Binah, and their two children.[73] The daily routines of plantation life tended to engage family members in common endeavors, allowing kinship to reinforce ties between co-workers. The day-to-day significance of the interaction of kinship and work is suggested by the contrast in the sexual composition of the rural groups. Only 17 percent of the rural work groups included both men and women, compared to 95 percent of the rural family groups and 86 percent of the rural community groups.

Above all, as Herbert G. Gutman has demonstrated, the slave family was the agency through which slaves created, transmitted, and recreated their culture.[74] In the family, slaves of one generation educated those of the next. The ages of the parents and children in the rural family groups indicate the salience of parental authority. The median age of the children

[69] Fifty-five percent of the small groups were composed of a husband and wife, and 61% of the large groups were composed of a couple and one or more children.

[70] *Gaz.*, Feb. 26, 1810.

[71] Of the 119 slaves 9 years or older in the rural family groups, occupations are mentioned for 15.

[72] *Gaz.*, Mar. 29, 1816; *Courier*, Mar. 3, 1828; *Gaz.*, Nov. 22, 1816.

[73] *Gaz.*, Aug. 9, 1816, Jan. 1, 1802; *Courier*, Aug. 10, 1830.

[74] Gutman, *Black Family*, 185-229, 327-360, *passim*.

was nine; a quarter of them were fifteen or older.[75] The fathers' median age was forty; that of mothers, thirty-five.[76] The slaves in the father-mother-child(ren) groups—like Bob, "an old man," his wife Rose, "an old woman," their son David, twenty-six, and their daughters Betty and Lydia, twenty-four and thirty—had developed over the years a strong cultural unit that nurtured its members and kept alive the mutual respect on which cooperative resistance was based.[77] More dramatic examples of the links between generations were Jacob, forty, his wife Eve, thirty-five, and their two-year-old twins who ran away with Eve's mother Delia and her son Sammy, fourteen; or Bella, an "aged wench with a crooked leg," who ran away with her daughter and her grandchildren, Cato, twelve, Rhina, ten, and Hector, five.[78] Additional evidence of parental authority is the almost complete absence of family or community groups composed of siblings without parents. Only 2 of the rural family groups (3 percent) contained siblings without parents, and there were only 9 of this type among the 135 rural and urban family and community groups.[79] This suggests that in the absence of parental authority, siblings were more or less like co-workers, or, to put it differently, co-workers were more or less like brothers and sisters.

Slaves in the family and community groups shared the general orientation of rural slaves toward the culture of the quarters. The advertisements mention nothing about the speech or behavior patterns of nearly nine-tenths of the slaves in these groups.[80] Among the rest were some who were skilled in relations with whites, like Charles and his wife June, both "very plausible and artful, the fellow in particular";[81] but more characteris-

[75] The advertisements give ages for 28 of the 31 children in the father-mother-children groups. A quarter of them were under age 2; 54% were 9 or older. In the mother-children groups, ages are noted for 17 of the 19 children; they were somewhat younger, with a median age of 6 and a mean of 8. In all the rural family groups, few children were toddlers. Most were old enough to work alongside their parents in the fields.

[76] Ages are given for 9 of the 14 fathers in the father-mother-children groups; their mean age was 42. Eleven of the 14 mothers have their ages specified; their mean age was 38. The mean age of the mothers in the mother-children groups was 33, the median 30, for the 8 of 12 whose ages are noted. Among the husband-wife groups, the ages of 18 husbands and 14 wives are specified; they had the same median and mean ages, 30 and 33.

[77] *Courier*, Apr. 17, 1815.

[78] *Gaz.*, July 10, 1817, Feb. 7, 1801.

[79] There were seven groups that included two brothers, two groups that included two sisters. Of course, it is possible that advertisements did not mention sibling relationships that actually existed.

[80] The speech of only 15 of the 119 adult slaves (13%) in the family groups is mentioned. Eight were said to speak well or plausibly; seven had impediments.

[81] *Gaz.*, July 16, 1800. Indeed, slaves in four of the family groups caused their masters to speculate that they would attempt to pass for free.

tic were those whose speech or behavior betrayed their discomfort in the presence of whites, like Daphney's husband Simon, who "when spoken to appears much alarmed, and has a wild look," or Nelly's husband Sam, who "if closely interrogated forms a bad tale, and when intimidated, has an impediment in his speech."[82]

More significant evidence of rural slaves' reliance on the cultural resources of the quarters were the activities of two community groups that operated as maroons. Robin and Carolina, two boat hands, along with John, Sambo, Israel, and Frederick, were thought by their owner to be with Sancho, "harbored in the woods, adjoining Mrs. Brandt's settlement, through the people and boats belonging to which, they all, including Ned and Sancho communicate it is supposed with town."[83] Another group of sixteen runaways was reported to "have been living together in the woods." Jemmy, Adam, Keating, Eleck, Owen, John, Isaac, Susey, Dolly, two women named Chloe, and five children were "not only supported by the people of the adjoining Plantations," their master noted, "but pick black moss, make baskets, and take them to the City in boats" for sale.[84] The activities of these slaves left few doubts about their determination and collective self-reliance.

From 1804 through 1807 about 40,000 Africans were legally imported into South Carolina.[85] Some of these slaves were sold out of the state, but the many who remained were a significant fraction of South Carolina's 165,000 slaves.[86] As the African-born slaves were incorporated into the state's slave communities, as they became acculturated, they made a distinctive contribution to the kinds of groups slaves formed to run away.[87]

Evidence from the advertisements suggests that in the initial phase of acculturation the Africans drew largely upon their own human and cultural

[82] Courier, May 16, 1822; Gaz., May 3, 1817.

[83] Gaz., Apr. 28, 1804. On maroons see Eugene D. Genovese, From Rebellion to Revolution: Afro-American Slave Revolts in the Making of the Modern World (Baton Rouge, La., 1979), 51-81.

[84] Courier, May 28, 1825.

[85] On New Year's day, 1808, the Courier reported that 39,310 slaves had been imported since 1804. See also Patrick S. Brady, "The Slave Trade and Sectionalism in South Carolina, 1787-1808," Journal of Southern History, XXXVIII (1972), 601-620.

[86] Brady has estimated a net immigration of about 10,000 slaves between 1800 and 1810 ("Slave Trade," Jour. So. Hist., XXXVIII [1972], 601-620). Unfortunately, the net increase has no necessary bearing on the fraction of the newly imported Africans who remained in the state.

[87] For an introduction to the vast literature on acculturation see Berlin, "Time, Space, and Evolution of Afro-Am. Soc.," AHR, LXXXV (1980), 45; Monica Schuler, "Afro-American Slave Culture," Historical Reflections/Reflexions Historiques, VI (1979), 121-137, with commentaries by Mary Karasch, Richard Price, and Edward Kamau Brathwaite, ibid., 138-155; Allan Kulikoff, "The Origins of Afro-

resources. As they learned the terms of their servitude, many refused to accept them. Some were overcome with despair, like the "new African man slave, belonging to Mr. Fordham, blacksmith, who . . . hanged himself in the course of the . . . night, from the shop window fronting Black's Wharf, with a small piece of cord."[88] Others resisted by "wandering away" or "straying" from their purchasers.[89] Most of the Africans were taken out of the city and put to work on rural plantations. Some simply walked away, like the two "New Negro men of the Congo nation" who "strayed" from their plantation "with their names (Samson and Paul) and that of their owner on a bit of card, suspended from their necks."[90]

In this first phase of acculturation, Africans tended to run away in each other's company. Between 1804 and 1809, two-thirds of the groups that contained Africans contained only Africans.[91] Typical were the six "new Negroe men" who were "unable to speak the English language," some of whom were "very much marked in the face"; "they will answer," their master noted, "to the names of February, March, September, October, November, and December." These men apparently considered slavery no more integral to their lives than their new names. Their master, John Bee Holmes, "earnestly requested that they may be treated kindly by any person meeting them" because "it is highly probable that they thought they could go back to their own country."[92] Holmes asked that they be returned to his plantation on Goose Creek.

On plantations, at work and in the quarters, Africans became acquainted with creole slaves and with their culture. Soon after the slave trade was reopened, Africans and creoles began to cooperate in runaway groups. In 1805, for example, Dinah, a twenty-eight-year-old country-born woman, ran away from a plantation on the Ashley River with two "new negro men" who could "speak little English and know not their owner's name"— Blacksmith and the thirty-year-old Sambo, a man "of grave countenance" who "writes the Arabic language."[93] As the process of acculturation represented by Dinah, Blacksmith, and Sambo continued, the proportion of runaway groups that contained both Africans and creoles more than doubled, from 29 percent of all groups containing Africans between 1803 and 1809, to 63 percent between 1810 to 1819, to 71 percent between 1820 and 1830.

American Society in Tidewater Maryland and Virginia, 1700 to 1790," *William and Mary Quarterly*, 3d Ser., XXXV (1978), 226-259; and Mullin, *Flight and Rebellion*, 34-82.

[88] *Courier*, Jan. 7, 1807.
[89] See, for example, *ibid.*, July 21, 1807, and Jan. 5, 1808.
[90] *Gaz.*, May 21, 1804.
[91] Twenty-four groups contained Africans; they represented 36% of all the advertised groups in this period. Seventy-one percent of these groups contained only Africans.
[92] *Gaz.*, Apr. 9, 1804.
[93] *Courier*, Feb. 7, 1805.

TABLE II
ENGLISH SKILLS OF AFRICAN-BORN SLAVES IN RUNAWAY GROUPS

	Percent of African-born Slaves Who Were Said to Speak English			
	Poorly	Tolerably	Well	Number Mentioned
1799-1803	100			6
1804-1809	89	11		46
1810-1819	33	33	33	15
1820-1830	8		92	12

An important part of the Africans' acculturation was their increasing fluency in English. At first, as Table II shows, none of the African-born slaves in the runaway groups was said to speak English well, and 89 percent of them spoke it poorly or not at all, like Caesar, the companion of three other Africans, Cadley, Kissary, and Baryarran, who "cannot speak English, but has a very pleasant countenance when spoken to."[94] Only a few slaves like Cuffee, Purgerson, and Tom were said to "speak English tolerably well."[95] After the slave trade closed, the English skills of the African-born runaways improved impressively, and by the 1820s more than 90 percent were like the nine men and two women, "most of them African born," all of whom "speak the English language very well," who took their master's "Long Boat, with sails, oars, &c., and it is supposed they proceeded to sea."[96] In fact, the temporal distribution of groups containing Africans suggests that they were becoming culturally unidentifiable to whites by the 1820s: between 1804 and 1809, 36 percent of all the runaway groups contained one or more Africans; between 1810 and 1819 the proportion declined to 20 percent and then to 7 percent between 1820 and 1830. But as the Africans learned the English language from their fellow slaves, they also taught some lessons of their own.

African-born slaves contributed to the increasing number of slaves who ran away in community groups. As Table III shows, before 1810 most slaves ran away in groups that did not include kin; thereafter, the pattern reversed. The proportion who ran away in community groups more than doubled in the two decades following the closing of the African trade. This pattern was most pronounced among rural groups, as Table IV demonstrates. After 1810, the proportion of rural slaves who ran away in community groups was almost twice that of urban slaves. Africans were more frequently included in community groups than in the contemporaneous work or family groups. As Table V illustrates, Africans figured in half or more of the rural community groups between 1804 and 1819. As Africans became less visible to whites in the 1820s, they were less

[94] *Gaz.*, Apr. 26, 1808.
[95] *Courier*, June 11, 1806.
[96] *Gaz.*, Mar. 9, 1821.

TABLE III
PERCENTAGE OF SLAVES BY GROUP TYPES AND
TIME PERIODS

| | Groups | | | No. of |
	Work	Family	Community	Slaves
1799-1803	66	34		228
1804-1809	75	15	10	171
1810-1819	44	35	21	277
1820-1830	47	28	25	307

TABLE IV
PERCENTAGE OF RURAL AND URBAN SLAVES BY
GROUP TYPES AND TIME PERIOD

| | Rural Groups | | | No. of |
	Work	Family	Community	Slaves
1799-1803	71	29		168
1804-1809	78	14	8	114
1810-1819	43	31	26	159
1820-1830	44	26	30	218
1799-1830	56	26	18	659
	Urban Groups			
1799-1803	53	47		60
1804-1809	68	18	14	57
1810-1819	45	41	14	118
1820-1830	54	33	13	89
1799-1830	53	35	11	324

frequently noted in the advertisements. However, their influence probably continued to be felt, since the proportion of slaves who ran away in
community groups in the 1820s was higher than ever. In general, evidence
from the advertisements suggests that acculturation in the fields and
quarters linked Africans and creoles in runaway groups that included kin
and non-kin.

An additional index of the Africans' influence on the slave communities
is that groups that included Africans tended to be larger than those that
did not. Table VI shows that in the early stages of acculturation, groups
with Africans were only slightly larger than those without. As accultura-

TABLE V
PERCENTAGE OF RURAL AND URBAN GROUPS
CONTAINING AFRICAN-BORN SLAVES

	Work	Rural Groups Family	Community
1799-1803	6	0	
1804-1809	45	14	50
1810-1819	21	16	60
1820-1830	8	0	14
1799-1830	21	6	36
		Urban Groups	
1799-1803	0	0	
1804-1809	21	0	0
1810-1819	26	5	33
1820-1830	6	8	33
1799-1830	13	4	25

Zeroes indicate that the groups in these categories contained no African-born slaves. Blanks indicate that no urban or rural community groups existed.

TABLE VI
MEAN SIZE OF GROUPS WITH AND WITHOUT
AFRICAN-BORN SLAVES

	Mean Number of Slaves in Group		Number of Groups	
	With Africans	Without Africans	With Africans	Without Africans
1799-1803	3.3	2.5	3	89
1804-1809	2.9	2.4	24	43
1810-1819	4.2	2.6	18	76
1820-1830	4.1	3.1	7	90
1799-1830	3.5	2.7	53	298

tion continued in the decades after 1810, the average size of groups with Africans jumped from 2.9 to 4.2, considerably larger than the groups without Africans, which averaged 2.6. Nonetheless, the average size of the latter continued to increase, hinting that acculturation did indeed work both ways.

During the first third of the nineteenth century, advertisements appeared for almost a thousand slaves who ran away in the company of one or more of their co-workers or family members. Some of them took advantage of the special opportunities available to skilled tradesmen or those who worked out. But most were field hands and common laborers, ordinary men, women, and children who depended on their wives, husbands, fathers, mothers, and friends for the strength and cooperation necessary to run away in a group. In the city, they commonly used their knowledge of white culture for their own ends. In the country, they turned more toward the culture of the quarters and its emphasis on kinship. When large numbers of African-born slaves were incorporated into the creole communities they apparently invigorated a spirit of collective resistance and Afro-American identity. Although the slaves who appeared in the advertisements composed only a tiny fraction of all the slaves in the state, the same bonds that strengthened the runaway groups probably helped most other slaves to endure.

'THAT DISPOSITION TO THEFT, WITH WHICH THEY HAVE BEEN BRANDED': MORAL ECONOMY, SLAVE MANAGEMENT, AND THE LAW

That disposition to theft, with which [slaves] have been branded, must be ascribed to their situation, and not to any depravity of the moral sense. The man in whose favor no laws of property exist, probably feels himself less bound to respect those made in favor of others. When arguing for ourselves, we lay it down as fundamental, that laws, to be just, must give reciprocation of right; that without this, they are mere arbitrary rules, founded in force, and not in conscience, and it is a problem which I give to the master to solve, whether the religious precepts against the violation of property were not framed for him as well as his slave? and whether the slave may not justifiably take a little from one who has taken all from him, as he may slay one who would slay him?

-Thomas Jefferson

By now it is safe to say that we are past a historiography of American slavery that accepts slaves as docile, brutalized and unresisting chattel. Most recent works on slavery have portrayed resistance as an integral part of any picture of antebellum plantation life. An obsolete racist historiography characterized forms of resistance – malingering, stealing, arson, violence – as functions of inherent racial characteristics, thereby ratifying and justifying the explanations of slave discontent offered by slaveowners themselves.[1] Since then historians have tried to describe resistance in a manner that treats slaves as an oppressed people seeking to make their plight more bearable or to reject their status all together. This essay will examine one particular form of resistance to slavery, theft of property, in the belief that existing discussions do not adequately or systematically explain its causes, its consequences, or its meaning for slaves and slaveowners.

Theft made an appearance in some of the earliest revisionist historiography, most notably in Kenneth Stampp's *The Peculiar Institution*.[2] Stampp treated theft by slaves sympathetically, regarding it as a clear sign of slave discontent based on an autonomous and rebellious moral code. By stealing, "slaves did not...repudiate law and morality: rather they formulated legal and moral codes of their own."[3] Stampp pointed out that most masters assumed such dishonest behavior to be nothing more than an inherent trait of blacks. But the slaves made a clear distinction between the legitimate "taking" of property from whites and the reprehensible "stealing" from their fellow slaves.[4]

Amending Stampp's legitimation of slave resistance, Eugene Genovese has argued for more complex dialectical implications of such behavior. Although theft certainly should be seen as a form of "day-to-day resistance" to slavery, Genovese maintained that it contained some profoundly negative elements as well. He argued that theft could weaken slave morality and dignity; it may have challenged the moral code and authority of the planters, but it could not offer a counter-hegemonic morality because many slaves "had to have mixed feelings and to experience some degradation" when they stole. Such "mixed feelings" were the result of the contradiction between the slaves' Christian sense of morality – for Genovese, one of their most basic sources of moral and personal strength – and their desire or need to steal.[5]

More recently Lawrence Levine and Edward Ayers have discussed the ambiguity of slave theft in a similar manner, but have explained the contradiction between morality and behavior with the help of "neutralization" theory.[6] Both Levine and Ayers draw on the work of criminologists Gresham Sykes and David Matza, who argue that the deviant often recognizes the "moral validity of the dominant normative system" even when he or she breaks its laws or codes. Neutralization thus emotionally and mentally aids the delinquent in the commission of immoral or illegal acts, but more importantly, also serves to implicitly ratify the dominant normative system, instead of constructing "moral imperatives, values or attitudes in direct contradiction to those of the dominant society."[7]

Thus, in exploring the relationship of theft and folklore, Lawrence Levine points to a set of "situational" values created around theft. Citing the work of Sykes and Matza, Levine argues that when theft was a necessary tactic of survival, the slaves' "practical set of values. . . were used to neutralize" the countervailing normative values of their culture and religion, making it "possible for slaves to rationalize their need to lie, cheat and steal." Thus slaves were able to steal without creating a counter-morality, and the resulting tension between "universal morality and everyday needs for survival" was mediated by folktales. Edward Ayers' view of theft in Vengeance and Justice rests on similar assumptions. Ayers agrees with Genovese that many slaves felt degraded by theft, in particular because of their religious values, and concludes that theft failed to create alternative values. The function of theft as a "neutralizing" moral category is thus, according to Ayers, "evidence both of humankind's capacity for righteousness in the face of adversity and of the force of a hegemonic morality." Furthermore, such tensions about crime supposedly "underlie any society in which one class suffers at the hands of another;" consequently, theft left oppression "untouched and unchallenged." Ayers also cites Sykes and Matza in defense of this position.[8]

This functionalist assumption that "deviancy" and its accompanying rationales are constructed so as to reproduce a social equilibrium flattens historical models of slave resistance. The notion that the contradiction between slave behavior and slave morality was resolved in favor of stasis should be rejected. Plantation theft and the ideologies surrounding it were part of the sustained struggle between master and slave to define the parameters of power. Historians can focus on the many forms this struggle took and the varied ideological terrain on which it was fought, rather than its alleged functional tendency toward equilibrium or "neutral" moral ambiguities.

The critique of Sykes and Matza offered by Marxist criminologists provides a helpful theoretical framework for a revised approach. Neutralization theory, according to its Marxist critics, ignores structures of power and forms of struggle against oppression in societies based on class (or race) domination. Thus neutralization is not a "technique," as Sykes and Matza would have it, but a mystification, because the "cultural options available [to the oppressed]...in an inequitable...society are designed to make opposition look like neutralizations rather than the critique of the frustrated and deprived." To depict delinquent acts as simply the neutral negation of societal norms avoids the essential ideological and material significance of theft: the fact that "the mass of delinquents are literally involved in the practice of redistributing private property."[9]

Similarly, theft by slaves can be understood as a form of behavior with economic and ideological, as well as moral, implications. Theft impinged upon the relationship between masters and slaves in a number of important ways, and at a number of different levels. If theft was a focus of tension on the plantation, that tension is not found in the slaves' attempts to forge a contradictory neutralizing morality, but in the struggle between slaves and masters to define conflicting notions of authority, property and customary rights. Far from fitting into a static model of paternalist master-slave relations, theft served as a potential means with which slaves could redefine and extend the bounds of paternalism. By looking closely at the actual practice of theft, and the different implications it held for slaves and their masters, we can locate a crucial pressure point of class-conflict which threatened the slaveowners' hegemony in the ideological and economic spheres of the antebellum South.

Such an argument obviously risks overstating both the significance and prevalence of theft, and may overlook the degree to which such behavior was incidental and at times purely mischievous or malicious. Nor should one pretend against the evidence that all slaves stole all of the time. Yet I think it is possible to demonstrate that in one of the most widespread slave "crimes," the theft of food,[10] we can discern a moral economy rooted, at the least threatening level, in a struggle over the control of the slaves' diet, and at the most threatening level, in conflicting claims of economic rights to agricultural production. In the former instance of moral economy, the pilfering of food to supplement the plantation diet demonstrated a low level of conflict over the master's power and authority to distribute and restrict food; in the latter, the systematic theft of plantation foodstuffs and goods for exchange beyond the bounds of the plantation indicated an incipient class-conflict over the forms the slave economy would take and the claims to its profits.

By "moral economy" I mean the notion that an oppressed group or class develops an autonomous conception of their economic and social rights, essentially drawing a line across which the ruling class cannot legitimately step. These customary rights and traditional practices arise from the experience and culture of a class or group, and become defined as a set of expectations which must be adhered to by rulers and ruled alike if class power is to remain stable and unchallenged. This theory was developed by E.P. Thompson and other British labor historians with reference to the plight of the English laboring poor in the face of economic transformations and changing social relationships during the eighteenth century. In particular, the term "moral economy" applies to actions such as food riots, smuggling, poaching, insistence on foraging and grazing rights, and of course, the theft of production materials to protest the rationalization and increased alienation of the work process. Each of these activities consisted of the assertion of rights to certain "just" economic practices in the face of ruling-class attempts to redefine or erode these rights, usually by use of the law. In all of these cases the behavior defined by the law or those in authority as "criminal" was popularly legitimated by the participants and those who shared their grievances at the community level.[11]

It is important to note the relevance this concept has for Genovese's treatment of slavery. The existence of moral economy is predicated upon the fact that the ruling class traditionally permits the exercise of customary economic rights – similar to the workings of Genovese's "paternalism," and clearly exemplified by slave provision grounds.[12] It is only when the existence of these rights appears to challenge the hegemony of the ruling class, or blocks a reconsolidation of their power in new economic relationships, that a struggle ensues. The dominant class then attempts to restrict the sphere of legitimate autonomous "plebian" behavior, often with the mask of neutrality and apparent legitimacy offered by the power of the law, while the dominated class insists more vigorously – and now "illegally" – on the continued existence of their rights. Thus it is surprising that Genovese places the dialectic of theft primarily within the slave quarters, rather than locating it in a conflict between slave and master over customary rights. Theft in Southern slave society was similar to the "social crime" of eighteenth-century England; it represented the slave's insistence on receiving his or her due from the master, both in terms of diet and the right to the products of labor. As such, theft fits firmly within Genovese's conception of a constant give and take between master and slave. Theft was a testing of the limits of paternalism, the claiming and reclaiming of economic rights by the slave, and the ultimate defense of what was seen by slaves as granted and legitimate. And when theft was combined with slave participation in an interracial market network, when slaves moved from moral economy to actual economy, they more directly challenged the class relations of the South and their masters' hegemony within those relations. At that point the dialectic of moral economy and the law was set into motion.[13]

Even as masters struggled with their slaves over the limits to economic autonomy and the forms the slaves' economic identity would take, they constantly sought to contain such struggles within the less threatening realm of management and morality. For the slaves, however, participation in exchange relations and their claims to property based on the belief (found by Olmsted as a justification for stealing) that "the result of labor belongs of right to the laborer"[14] had far greater implications. For while few slaves were willing to gainsay their right to steal food when they were hungry, the bolder step of stealing in order to participate in market transactions rested on a stronger consciousness of counter-morality and an inherent right to economic autonomy, and thus represented a greater threat to the slave system. As Lawrence McDonnell has pointed out,

> few incidents of slave life rivalled market relations for political and psychological meaning. Commodity exchange and property accumulation...exposed and transformed real relations between master and slave.... When slaves bought, sold and bartered, produced, accumulated...consumed [and, I would add, stole] property they claimed as their own, central questions of power, community and humanity arose.[15]

Significantly, when the planters recognized the threat posed by theft for the purpose of exchange they shifted from a reliance on private slave management techniques to dependence on the coercive, public power of the law.

An examination of slave narratives, autobiographies, letters and testimony provides a sense of the conditions under which theft occurred, how slaves understood and justified it, and their perceptions of their masters' reactions.[16] From these sources it is clear that the primary target of appropriation was food; at least this is all ex-slaves' memories will admit to. Historians have shown that the slaves' diet was objectively deficient in providing slaves with enough sustenance to reproduce their labor.[17] The constant experience of hunger led inevitably to a systematic pilfering of the smokehouse, corn-crib, chicken coop, and melon-patch as slaves sought to supplant their meager diet in quantity and quality.[18] Slaves themselves had a clear articulation of the relationship between theft and diet, and had no hesitation about laying the blame with their masters. "Po' nigger had to steal back dar in slav'y eben to git 'nuff to eat...ef it hadn't been fo' [whites] nigger wouldn't know nothin' bout stealin,'" claimed one ex-slave.[19] Ex-slaves also explained theft with specific reference to the rations they received from their masters, often stressing the lack of quality and variety of the food provided, as well as its insufficient quantity. Rosa Barnwell, an ex-slave, wrote a letter to the Liberator in 1862, describing the rations on her plantation as a weekly "allowance" of a peck of corn and half a peck of sweet potato. She added that slaves "were never allowed a piece of meat, unless they should take sometimes a hog on their own account."[20]

Many others recalled chickens and hogs as frequently stolen items, arguing that such stock appeared plentiful on the plantation, but was rarely provided as food by their masters. Slaves were fed "rat meat, jowls and heads and jaws," according to Benjamin Johnson, while they were acutely aware of the meat hanging in the smokehouse.[21] Another ex-slave recalled that he had plenty of food, but no chicken unless it was stolen.[22] "I used to steal some chickens 'cause we didn't have enough to eat," confessed another, "and I didn't think I done wrong, 'cause the place was full of 'em."[23] The combination of the drive of hunger and a sharp awareness of the plenty around them made the "taking" of food understandable and justifiable behavior for many slaves.

Some ex-slaves went further in justifying these supplements to their diet, arguing beyond the terms of necessity that "we sho' earned what we et."[24] The recognition of the right to materially reproduce their own labor could also justify the theft of food in the name of property as well as compensation for labor. Louisa Gause, an ex-slave, regarded the food allowance on the plantation not as a gift, but as an exchange for labor; the master never "give [slaves] nothin' widout dey work to get it en dat been dey portion." Acknowledging that this "portion" often was augmented by pilfered melons and corn, she observed that "if [a slave] did [steal], he never take nothin' but what been belong to him."[25]

The response by masters to constant pilfering was twofold: brutal punishment and experiments with management techniques which might discourage theft. Most ex-slaves recalled the punishments. Many descriptions of theft found in the slave narratives and testimony are followed by references to the whippings received by those slaves unlucky enough to be caught.[26] One ex-slave testified to the effectiveness of brutality, describing the beating and salting she remembered as the punishment for stealing a pig. "When dey get through wid you, wou wouldn't want to steal no mo'. . . if you see a pig a mile off you'd feel like runnin' from 'im."[27] Nevertheless, such punishment could hardly overcome the hunger that drove many slaves to steal. "[Whipping] was easier to stand when the stomach was full," recalled Robert Falls.[28]

Some slaveowners actually recognized that a full stomach might indeed prevent the need to whip slaves for stealing, since "[l]iberally and plentifully fed [slaves] will not be urged, by a hungry longing for meat, to steal their masters' hogs, sheep and poultry," according to one self-acknowledged expert on slave management.[29] This strategy would supposedly improve the "moral character" of slaves,[30] rather than simply provide them with an adequate diet without the pain of whipping. In any event, the prudent master allowed his slaves an abundant supply of food, even if this was rationalized in terms of the slaves' "natural" fondness for excess. "They will steal if they are not well fed, and the very best remedy for hog stealing is to give the rogues plenty to eat," concluded one planter.[31]

The most astute slaveowners understood what their slaves were well aware of: theft for nutritive purposes was a matter of both economic necessity and right. "There are many farmers who feed their negro sparingly, believing that it is economy and that they will save by it," wrote John F. Thompkins, a North Carolina planter and doctor, "but such is not the fact. . . the negro will have [food], and he is sure to steal it generally from his master, believing that he has a right to do so; and pray, who is there to dispute this right?"[32] "Let 'em have rice! My rice – my nigger!" was one mistress's response to the pilfering of grain on her plantation, recalled an ex-slave.[33] A correct relationship of diet and labor was in the final economic interest of the slaveholder, who owned the laborer, his or her labor power, and the food necessary to reproduce that labor.

For the slaves, however, the theft of food was not just a matter of diet. The struggle to control and define the right to sustenance was also a question of power. The appropriation of food was a gesture of the control wielded by slaves over compensation for their labor, their role as provider for a family, and even their identity as individuals able to participate in exchange relations. Food became a salient symbol of power in slave folktales, for as Charles Joyner points out in his book *Down by the Riverside*, "the trickster [in Afro-American folktales] found his greatest satisfaction not in the mere possession of food, but in *taking* it from the more powerful animals" (emphasis in the original).[34] So too could the slave assert a claim to increasing the quality and quantity of his consumption by taking food from his master. Both Joyner and Lawrence Levine emphasize the ambivalence of many of the trickster tales, particularly because of their supposed role in "neutralizing" the potential moral contradictions of theft. Yet both agree that the tales also provided "tactical lessons" in theft, and linked food acquisition to guile and forms of power and resistance available to slaves.[35] Folktales told by ex-slaves and collected by Elsie Clew Parsons in the 1920s on the South Carolina Sea Islands demonstrate the important links between theft, food and power. Trickery is used by "Ber Rabbit" in numerous instances not only to steal livestock from men, but to lay the blame on others or cheat his accomplices, so he can distribute the food to his own family or sweetheart.[36] The slave narratives ratify the importance of theft both as a source of status and authority for the male thief and as a means for parents to provide extra food for their children, thus reaffirming their ability and right to feed their family over the countervailing attempt at control of slave diets asserted by the master.[37] Thus, despite the frequent rationalizations made by ex-slaves to white interviewers that they had stolen because "you had to steal" in order to eat,[38] the act of taking food from the slaveowner embodied conflict between slave and master, as the thief sought to assert autonomy and power in confrontation with the master's constant attempts to define and control the relationship between his animate and inanimate property.

This conflict broadens beyond the scope of a struggle over diet if we begin to look further at theft as a specific form of resistance to slavery. The stealing of food was often closely related to forms of social solidarity in the slave quarters, as well as individual acts of rebellion, such as running away. As Gilbert Osofsky points out, although hungry slaves stole food, "others undoubtedly also found thieving satisfying as a form of aggression and revenge" against their masters.[39] Furthermore, slaveowners were perpetually plagued by what one historian has called a "conspiracy of silence," as slaves aided one another in frequent raids on their masters' livestock.[40] The theft of food thus acquired a "social value within the slave community" as well as a dietary one, as slaves demonstrated their guile and skill and maintained fellowship by sharing the spoils of raids.[41] One ex-slave described the custom on his plantation of a number of slaves stealing a hog on Saturday night for their Sunday barbecue – a social event which was in lieu of churchgoing. "As none o' our gang didn't have no 'ligion, us never felt no scruples bout not getting de 'cue ready fo' Sunday," he explained, adding that when asked by their master where they had been on Sunday, the slaves claimed that they had gone to church.[42]

Such solidarity was often extended to runaway slaves who stole food from plantations as their sole means of survival. During his visit to the South, Olmsted found that many slaves ran away temporarily and hid in the woods or swamplands. He observed, correctly, the "[runaways] cannot obtain means of supporting life without coming often...to steal from the plantations."[43] Hearing a burglary case, the Supreme Court of North Carolina noted that "[runaways] as a class, have a known propensity to steal."[44] And the slave narratives recount many instances of runaways and maroons who stole food from neighboring plantations, often with the connivance of those who remained enslaved.[45] Escaped slaves living in the woods would sneak back to their old quarters when they ran low on provisions, and a friend would often supply food from the master's smokehouse. "This was not considered stealing," observed Pierce Cody, an ex-slave;[46] though in abetting a runaway it was a clear and conscious form of resistance to bondage and a sign of solidarity with those who dared to defy the master's right to own them.

Theft as a "violation of dominant white norms and values," as Philip Schwarz has put it, also played a role in more direct forms of resistance and rebellion. Gabriel Prosser, the slave who led a rebellion in Virginia in 1800, had been caught hogstealing the year before, and had subsequently assaulted the overseer who had apprehended him. In stealing, slaves overcame the constant admonitions against theft, and thus challenged the system of slave control by demonstrating a "knowledge and willingness to test [their] white masters' limitations [on behavior]."[47] Depending on the context, such testing and resistance could blossom into a consciousness of outright revolt against enslavement. This process was most succinctly described by Frederick Douglass, who justified theft from his master, or any other slaveholder, on the grounds that he was "the slave of society at large." Since slaveholding society as a total system robbed the slave of his "rightful liberty, and of the just reward of [his or her] labor," the slave had a right to plunder whatever he or she could from that society; "and...such taking is not stealing in any just sense of that word," concluded Douglass.[48]

Yet Douglass did not detach his rhetoric of rights, liberty and labor from what he called the "clear apprehension of the claims of morality."[49] If few slaves could make what Edward Ayers has called the leap from theft to "class-consciousness," as Douglass did,[50] many nonetheless found their religious beliefs in accord with their defense of thievery. Thus slaves articulated their consciousness of theft in moral terms, often in the context of their religion, their masters' sanctimonious and self-serving exhortations against stealing, and the contradiction between the two that they easily discovered in their masters' own behavior.

Whites attempted to use the social force of religion to inculcate a morality in slaves that could serve as a barrier to theft. White preachers routinely admonished slaves not to steal from their masters — though it appears that few slaves were convinced by their words.[51] An ex-slave recalled that the "preacher man would git up dere en tell us 'Now you min' yo Marster en Missis en don steal fum dem.' "[52] Olmsted quotes a Southern bishop reminding the slaves in his congregation that "when you are idle and neglectful of your masters' business, when you steal, and waste, and hurt of their substance [these are] faults against God himself."[53]

Yet slaves were able to come to very different conclusions about theft than those advocated by their masters, the teachings of white religion, or the institution of the church, by drawing on their own religious beliefs and by observing the irreligious behavior of their owners. One highly religious slave, a church member and prayer leader, argued to his master's face that he could take the food he worked for when he wanted because "the Bible says a man has a right to the sweat of his own eyebrows."[54] Olmsted recounted the story of a slave who stole her mistress's jewelry, wore it to church, and when confronted, defended herself by saying that "ole Aunt Ann says it alles right for us poor colored people to 'popiate whatever of de white folks' blessins de Lord puts in our way."[55] "Religion never was designed/To make our pleasure less," quoted Josiah Henson, an escaped slave. In Henson's view, far from being a moral transgression, theft was positively chivalric, especially when carried out by a male thief who could steal a chicken to "carry to some poor overworked black fair one, to whom it was at once food, luxury and medecine." "I felt good, moral, heroic," asserted Henson in referring to his role as plantation thief, "[and] I esteemed it as among the best of my deeds."[56] Despite the didactic purpose of Henson's autobiography, the construction of a counter-morality of theft that was reinforced (rather than neutralized or contradicted) by religious and moral beliefs, is evident.

Frederick Douglass noted the moral emptiness of his master's religious sanctions against stealing, when he observed the hypocrisy of his master and mistress in prayer while he and his fellow slaves were forced by hunger to steal.[57] Other slaves were able to reject white standards of morality and religion by witnessing their master's behavior and finding it wanting in piety and dignity. The ex-slave Henry Johnson remembered being preached to by whites not to steal from his master, and then pointed out that his master had used his slaves to steal his neighbors' livestock. At night, on the master's orders, the slaves would round up the cattle, kill them, dress them and store the meat in their master's smokehouse. When the Justice of the Peace arrived at the plantation the next day, Johnson's master offered to let him search the slave quarters, reassuring him that "my niggers don't steal." "Sure we didn't have nothin' didn't belong to us," recalled Johnson, "but de boss had plenty." The contradictions of such moral hypocrisy were plain to slaves: "[d]en dey tell us, don't steal," Johnson bitterly concluded.[58]

Henry Bibb, an escaped slave, confronted his former master directly with these contradictions. In a letter to his ex-master, Albert Sibley, Bibb wrote: "you call yourself a christian...but you compelled me to cheat, lie and steal from your neighbours. You have often made me drive sheep and hogs which you knew to be the property of your neighbour." Bibb lashed out at the hypocrisy of "a Methodist class leader, stealing and slaughtering his neighbours' sheep and hogs," and concluded that slaves could and would have no confidence or faith in a morality imposed by a "sheep stealing and man robbing religion."[59] Thus by developing a consciousness of the self-serving character of the religious and moral doctrines preached by their masters, slaves were able to justify theft as behavior which did not come into conflict with their own values. To the contrary, theft could be integrated into a coherent counter-morality opposed to that of the master class, undermining the slaveowners' claims to moral and ideological, as well as economic, superiority.

Nevertheless, the slaveowners themselves rarely recognized the contradictions of their moral poses; they persisted in viewing the "depredations" of their slaves through the lens of the moral strictures on which their ideology and authority were based. Rare was the master who recognized the slave's "right" to steal, who understood the economic implications of the connection between theft and diet, or who perceived theft as a form of economic or proto-political resistance to slavery. Far more often theft by slaves was regarded by slaveowners as a *moral* problem, explained by the inherent racial tendencies of the African race, and approached as a problem of slave management in the moral and religious sphere.

Noting that black church members often had to be disciplined for theft, the Reverend C.C. Jones concluded that "they are proverbially thieves...[this is] the character of slaves in all ages, whatever their nation or color." (Jones appeared equivocal in his racism however, having just previously written that "[blacks] bear this character [of theivery] in Africa" — was it the condition of slavery, or their "nation and color" that led black slaves to steal?)[60] In fact, many slaveowners demonstrated uncertainty about what moral standards actually could be applied to their slaves. T.C. Law, a South Carolina planter, wrote in his "Report on Management of Slaves" that slaves must be regarded as "human beings – morally accountable" for their acts. Nevertheless, he was unable to make this belief consistent with his racism, for he went on in the same report to argue that

> the negro race are almost universally deceptive...It is inculcated in them from the cradle, by their parents, to deceive, to lie and steal from their owners – and I verrily [sic] believe many of them think it no harm.[61]

Other writings by slaveholders on slave management affirmed that in the case of theft slaves did not "know the difference between right and wrong," and that without supervision "a cunning fellow will help himself to a bushel of corn."[62]

Yet the same writer did not fail to recognize that the slaves had a moral code of their own, "learned from observation of superiors," and based on opposition to the master. A slave who steals "will never be informed upon by his fellow laborers," observed this slaveholder, "for an informer, in [the slaves'] eyes, is held in greater detestation than the most notorious thief."[63] The Reverend C.C. Jones, in The Religious Instruction of the Negroes in the United States quoted another slaveowner who at once insisted that slaves had no moral scruples and yet described a distinct counter-morality of thievery: "[t]o steal and not be detected is a merit among [slaves]...And the vice which they hold in the greatest abhorrence is that of telling upon one another," he complained. Yet somehow this was indicative of the fact that "there seems to be an almost entire absence of moral principle" among slaves.[64]

A reconciliation of this contradiction of dual morality was sought in "correct" religious instruction. Slaveowners quickly found that this offered no solution, since even the most devout slaves were often caught stealing. This was explained by the influence of the black preacher, who was "the most consumate villain and hypocrite on the [plantation]" who held "a kind of magical sway over the minds and opinions of the rest [of the slaves]," and who "steals his master's pigs and is still an object commanding the peculiar regard of Heaven." With this example, "why may not his disciples" also easily reconcile their appropriations with their religious beliefs, wondered a frustrated planter.[65] Another observer noted that on his plantation religious meetings actually led to problems with theft. Though his slaves appeared to be very devout this did not deter their "depredations" – killing hogs and sheep, stealing potatoes. This master too discovered to his dismay that "the coloured preachers were the greatest and most active thieves."[66]

Despite these obstacles, some masters still retained their faith that their slaves' "moral character" could be "molded." "If you distrust them, and treat them as thieves, they will become ones," argued one planter. But if you "induce them to think...that they are not unworthy of some confidence" they will be made honest – an odd and contradictory response to be expected from chattel that supposedly had no moral sense.[67] Slaveowners persisted in these contradictory attitudes because by relegating "depredations" to the moral sphere they dismissed any of their own consciousness of resistance or opposition to their claims to economic power and property rights in the slave. Instead, slaveholders' perception of theft could reinforce both their racial attitudes and their paternalist sentiments, and help them treat the slave as a child who misbehaved solely because of his lack of moral sense.

It proved impossible, however, for slaveowners to contain their management strategies and preventative measures against theft solely within the moral realm. Theft was clearly an economic problem on the plantation as well as a social one; the constant pilfering of goods disrupted the plantation production system, and eroded the social control of slave labor that made such a system possible and profitable.[68] The management advice for planters found in Southern agricultural journals such as the *Southern Agriculturalist* and the *Farmers Register* dealt as often with the practical methods of protecting plantation property from appropriation by slaves as it did with the contradictory attempts to instill a moral code in beings whose economic identity was defined by the amoral terms reserved for chattel. This shift from moral to economic management techniques was often a response to planters' inability to keep the problem of theft within the bounds of their own plantation.

One major concern of planters was that hungry or malcontent slaves might not restrict theft to their own master's plantation, but would be tempted to make "predatory excursions upon his neighbors."[69] Such behavior could immensely complicate the question of theft, for it would move it beyond the sphere of paternalism and master-slave relations, and impinge upon issues of property and authority in the more open context of Southern society, rather than the closed and more easily controlled realm of the plantation. In such cases management would have to give way to the law, which was needed to "resolve disputes that crossed plantation lines."[70] Accordingly, laws in Southern states explicitly made masters responsible for thefts committed on other plantations by their slaves.[71] In order to avoid opening slave theft to the complex social disequilibrium generated by the insertion of the legal system into the master-slave relation,[72] management strategies were directed at keeping illicit property transfers within the bounds of the plantation. If this succeeded, at its worst theft could be reintegrated into the plantation economy through the relations of reciprocity, compensation, labor and property − Douglass' notion of shifting property from one "tub" owned by the master, the corn-crib, to another, the slave's stomach and labor power.[73]

Planters were anxious to keep such behavior within the realm of their control, for their peers held them "morally responsible" for the crimes "into which their slaves are led, or driven, by [the owner's] negligence or mismanagement."[74] Well organized plantation management and distribution of food, and the prevention of slave access to sources of economic autonomy − a market or barter network outside of the plantation, for example − would hinder theft.[75] Such isolation of the slave and his economic identity depended on the inviolability of the plantation as an economic and social space. Paradoxically, this might include the protection of the "property rights" of slaves from "ill treatment" by "maintaining what of right belongs to them," according to planter T.C. Law. Yet this must be done with recognition of the fact that "by interfering on [the slaves'] behalf we may encourage them unintentionally in depredating on others;" thus slaves must be punished for "any interference with that which belongs to neighbours."[76]

Such management techniques, judiciously blending vigilance against theft with the recognition of some "rights" accorded slaves, contained inevitable contradictions. If attempting to "mold" a morality that would counter an impetus to thievery forced slaveowners to recognize the slave's moral identity – as much as they may have misrecognized it – more purely practical forms of theft prevention acknowledged slaves' autonomous economic identity, as beings who attempted to influence or determine the compensation received for their labor, or who even participated in exchange relations within and beyond the boundaries of the plantation. The tensions evident in the desire to keep slaves inoculated from outside temptations to theft, to protect the plantation as the realm of the master's unmediated economic, social and moral power, and to control within that space the relationship of animate and inanimate property, most clearly emerged in managerial debates over slave provision grounds and market participation.

Although earlier historiography explained the readiness to steal by the fact that "nothing can give the slave respect for property rights, since he had no property and could get none"[77] more recent studies have clearly demonstrated many instance of a quasi-right to a "peculium" – land on which the slave could grow produce and raise stock for his own use – granted by economy-minded masters.[78] The extent and limits of this customary right, its function as either an incentive or disincentive to theft, and its relationship to an economic network outside of the master-slave nexus, were widely discussed in Southern agricultural journals. T.C. Law, for example, recommended that slaves should be allowed to raise a crop on their own time, and even sell it to their master, for "this practice enables the master to detect theft. . . as he is better able to judge of the quantity each would probably make from the ground cultivated."[79] Permitting such economic autonomy while enforcing careful supervision would protect the master's property. One Alabama planter calculated this strategy of control in careful agricultural terms, informing his readers that he let his slaves work their own patches of land and bought their produce, but that he "generally plant[ed] corn on it [rather than cotton], because I think [slaves] are less liable to be tempted to steal to add to its bulk." This prudent master recognized that theft by slaves was rational economic behavior; cotton, being worth more per pound than corn, was a more logical and profitable target for appropriation than corn.[80]

The theory behind these strategies was that if slaves were kept industrious for themselves when not laboring for their master, they would become aware of "the advantages of holding property." With "a stocked poultry house, a small crop advancing, a canoe in the making, or a few tubs [of butter?] unsold" slaves would supposedly stay out of mischief.[81] Slaveowners did not give up their arbitrary power over slaves, but in efforts to prevent theft they recognized them as economic beings in a manner sharply at odds with their identity as chattel.

Not all slaveowners agreed with this method of theft prevention, however. There was a widespread belief among planters that the economic autonomy and customary rights inherent in the provision grounds aided and encouraged the slave in his attempts to pilfer his master's moveable property. On Louisiana sugar plantations, for instance, it was explained to Frederick Law Olmsted, there was a different "philosophy" about provision grounds. Slaves were occasionally allowed to cultivate their own patches of produce, but it was generally discouraged "because the produce thus obtained is made to cover much plundering of their master's crops, and of his live stock."[82] Such efforts by slaves to supplement their own crops with the master's property, or to disguise their pilferings with their "legitimate" production of surplus food, appeared to be rational economic behavior, with a close relationship to slave access to a market and forms of exchange. One planter insisted in the pages of the *Southern Agriculturalist* that it was essential to prohibit the slaves' independent cotton planting. Since slaves were lazy and unproductive — presumably even when working for themselves — they would make up for the deficiency in their own crops by stealing part of the day's cotton pickings from their master, raiding the gin-house, rifling the cotton bales, or even making off with whole bales[!]. And where was all this pilfered cotton disposed of? In trade of course, exchanged by the slaves for cheap whisky. Apparently independent growing of cotton could set a precedent for independent barter in slave-owned cotton as well, encouraging theft for trade.[83]

Thus theft did not just encourage the slaves to seek exchange relations outside of the plantation context; this process was reciprocal, since access to the market itself increased a temptation to theft. As one planter put it, "where there are no receptacles [for stolen cotton] there will be no deposits."[84] Corn, cotton and rice were all "standing temptations, provided a market be at hand, and [the slaves] can sell or barter them with impunity," according to the Reverend C.C. Jones, who here seemed to recognize the economic, rather than moral — or amoral — impetus to steal. Such thefts varied from county to county "in exact proportion as the market for plunder varies," Jones claimed.[85] A planter writing in the *Southern Agriculturalist* claimed that he did not allow his slaves to sell anything without his permission, for if they were allowed to freely participate in exchange relations "a spirit of trafficing[sic] is at once created." Once this condition of exchange existed, he maintained, "a negro would never be content to sell only what he raises of either corn, poultry or the like; but he would sell part of his [food] allowance also, and would be tempted to commit robberies to obtain things to sell."[86] In the view of many slaveholders, theft and slave market participation were inseparable issues of slave management.

Clearly one of the "advantages of holding property" recognized by the slaves themselves was the right and opportunity to exchange what they produced for other goods. Some masters who permitted provision grounds approached this problem by keeping such economic behavior within the bounds of the plantation, preventing access to an exterior market network. Buying the surplus produce from their own slaves, trading them other goods — such as tobacco — or setting up a plantation "store" where slaves could purchase goods on credit or with the surplus they had earned, were the most popular methods of economic control.[87] A letter from an overseer to the *Southern Agriculturalist*, noting that "negroes should be in no instance permitted to trade, except with their masters," suggested that plantation owners should keep a stock of what the slaves would want to buy elsewhere, and then "trade" it to the slaves for "corn and such things as they have to sell," thus assuring that the slaves would be "put out of the way of the temptation to roguery."[88] Olmsted, during his visit to a South Carolina rice plantation, discovered that "Mr. X [the plantation owner]...allows his

servants [i.e., slaves] no excuse for dealing with [unscrupulous shopkeepers]."
Instead, the master purchased everything that his slaves wanted to sell, giving
them a "high price," according to Olmsted. What he could not use was resold,
containing such transactions among free whites. His slaves would then take
"credit" for their produce, and could purchase items from the "plantation store."
This system prevented slaves from dealing with "grog-shops" in their exchange
relationships. "Mr. X" even owed his own slaves over $500, Olmsted remarked
incredulously.[89] Thus with careful management techniques, the system of
paternalism was able to absorb even the independent slave economy, re-
integrating it into a quasi-market on the plantation itself. This served to blunt
the threat of theft, yet simultaneously gave the slaves some economic autonomy,
implicitly recognizing their ability and right to labor for their own profit.

One advantage of this system was the master's ability to control the
commodities which slaves could exchange their produce for, most notably limiting
their access to liquor. If the master allowed his slaves to raise their own crops
but did not help them find a buyer or purchase their goods himself, the slaves
would search for a market elsewhere themselves. In the eyes of slaveholders this
was a grave problem not only because of its connection to theft or the scope
of economic activity it permitted, but because such trade "leads to one of the
greatest evils attending the management of negroes — the trafficking with persons
who will furnish them with liquor."[90]

The generalized fear of planters was that a combination of an available market
for produce and the bartering of liquor to slaves would lead to the multiple
problems of increased theft, labor and management disruption on the plantation,
and local disorder.

> It is a fact well known to thousands dwelling in towns and villages, and to every
> keeper of a road shop, [that] these lazy [slaves] will not only plunder their masters,
> but deprive themselves and their children, of the necessaries of life

because they will sell their own food and "anything upon which they can lay their
hands" for liquor, lamented one slaveholder.[91] Olmsted too noted the close
connections between independent slave food production, the market, liquor and
theft. On the South Carolina rice plantation he visited, Olmsted observed that
each slave family was permitted land on which they could grow their own produce
for sale. The only restriction on their participation in a market economy was
a ban on trading for liquor. Yet Olmsted pointed out that this injunction was
impossible to enforce, and that "grog shops, at which stolen goods are bought
from the slaves, and poisonous liquors. . . are clandestinely sold to them have
become an established evil [in South Carolina]."[92]

For Southerners, this "established evil" threatened slave society and economy
in a number of ways. Slave participation in a market led to theft and drained
agricultural profit and production; it hurt the masters' slave property and
diminished slaves' productive capability (liquor disrupted plantation labor control
and discipline); it undermined the masters' economic authority and power; and
it led to collusion between slaves and non-slaveholding whites in depredations
against slaveowners' property. This latter consequence of trade with slaves could
challenge the racial and class systems on which antebellum Southern society

was based. Olmsted quotes an article from the Charleston *Standard* decrying the "abominable practice of trading with slaves, [which] is not only taking our produce from us, but injuring our slave property;" an injury, Olmsted pointed out, directly attributable to "grog shops," and furnishing much fuel in the region for a prohibition campaign. Significantly, however, the *Standard* did not lay the blame for this state of affairs on the usual evils of the laziness, drunkeness or inherent thievery of the slaves, but on the fact that "negroes will steal and trade as long as white persons hold out to them the temptation to steal and bring to them [their masters' goods]."[93] A planter writing in the *Farmers Register* also drew out the dangerous implications of this clandestine relationship between blacks and whites. He argued that "intercourse, trading and dealing with slaves is probably an evil which has done more mischief. . .to the morals of *both* slaves and free people. . .than any other cause" (emphasis added), and that this was the result of slaves trading with "white people of unexceptional character" – that is, non-slaveholders.[94]

Daniel Hundley, in his book, *Social Relations in Our Southern States*, made these fears even more explicit. Grog-shop keepers in the South – usually non-slaveowning whites – were able to make a large profit at the slaveowners' expense because they were "surrounded by thieving blacks, who are always glad to exchange their master's meal, their mistress' poultry, or the neighbor's pigs for a bottle [of liquor]." The ultimate danger of such commerce, according to Hundley, was that a "real sympathy between the slaves and the groggery-keepers" would arise, thus exacerbating the constant tensions of race and class that underlay any autonomous slave activity outside of the bounds of the master's paternalism and the plantation sphere of control.[95] When slaves and non-slaveholders interacted in exchange relations the ideological structures of race and class in slave society were undermined. At these moments, when their authority was no longer sufficiently maintained by management techniques, the planters would often turn to the legal system in order to reassert their threatened hegemony.[96]

This process can be historically mapped in the struggle between moral economy and the law that took place in the South Carolina lowcountry between the seventeenth and nineteenth centuries. Some forms of the slave "underground economy" as it developed in the lowcountry demonstrate the emergence of a moral economy and offer an example of the roles theft, the market and the law played in the struggle between masters and slaves. Peter Wood, in his book *Black Majority*, notes that during the colonial period economic control of the slaves on the South Carolina rice coast was exercised informally. As a result, there existed widespread autonomous slave participation in the local economy. But as control over the slaves and the demands of a more regimented and integrated production system increased, the more flexible and open slave economic practices became problematic for slaveowners. Wood argues that South Carolina slave statutes in the colonial period "reveal a gradual movement toward forced dependence, with slaves being allowed to manage fewer things for their own use or profit and masters being required to provide more," thus "curtailing black [economic] initiative." Once slaves found that they were "restricted in what they could produce on their own and sell, [they] increasingly took to selling goods

which were legally the [slaveowner's]." Thus theft and the slave economy were
intimately linked; "appropriating" white property became a form of resistance
to slavery, and from such practices a dialectic of moral economy and the law
emerged.

> As the slaves' relative status deteriorated and their opportunities became more
> circumscribed, they resorted increasingly to the dangerous practice of simply taking
> what they needed . . . or were denied, and then using it or trading it as suited their
> purposes,

according to Wood. And as the market flow in stolen goods steadily increased
the slaveowners took steps – both within the scope of their authority on the
plantation and with the power of the law – to block this commerce. Yet "the
more the Negro community was explicitly prohibited from earning, purchasing
and possessing goods, the more respectable, justifiable and necessary such
clandestine activity would become as an economic way of life."[97] Although he
does not use the term, Wood here has described a perfect parallel to the moral
economy detected by historians of eighteenth-century Britain – a form of
resistance perhaps found in most societies undergoing transformations in methods
of labor control and exploitation.

Despite the early attempts by slaveowners to limit slave economic autonomy
and prevent the growth of a market for stolen goods, such activities continued
well into the nineteenth century. As Philip Morgan has shown, lowcountry slaves
were given a certain measure of control over their time and labor, since rice
cultivation was based on the task system. The slaves used this autonomy to raise
crops and stock, and barter goods in the market, thus coming to own property.
Morgan argues that this widespread "internal economy," still prevalent in the
nineteenth century, provided slaves with autonomy, initiative and decision-
making power in the economic sphere, and thus was a significant aspect of the
slave experience and community in coastal South Carolina.[98]

Yet there were strong elements of tension and struggle inherent in these
economic practices; slaveowners were willing to acquiesce in this form of economy
only up to a certain point. The "internal economy" was also a moral economy
based on resistance to the restrictions placed on economic behavior, and carried
out through theft as well as sanctioned forms of production and exchange. Ben
Horry, an ex-slave from South Carolina, described one form such an
underground economy might take. Horry recalled that "rice been money dem
day and time [during slavery]. . . . My father love he liquor. That take money.
He aint have no money but he have the rice barn key and rice been money."
He then went on to recount how his father crafted a mortar, stole a pestle from
his master, and threshed the pilfered rice on his own time, preparing it for market.
He would then take it to town and clandestinely sell it independently of his
master's transactions. "With the money he get when he sell that rice, he buy
liquor," concluded Horry.[99] This was exactly the sort of economic behavior that
slaveowners most desperately sought to control, without success. Much of the
lowcountry slave economic activity Morgan describes – particularly that
involving the market – not only was frowned upon by masters, but was actually
illegal in South Carolina by the mid-nineteenth century.[100] Autonomous slave

production and exchange within the plantation may have been readily sanctioned, but the formation of a market beyond the plantation threatened the master's power. This explains the constant use of management techniques to prevent slave access to the market and, perhaps more significantly, the repeated attempts on the part of the slaveholding class to pass and enforce statutes restricting the slaves' "internal economy" and forbidding other whites to trade with slaves.

In South Carolina these statutes initially appeared, as Wood points out, in order to restrict the scope of economic activities available to slaves.[101] The statute passed in 1740, "An Act for the better Ordering and Governing of Negroes and other Slaves in this Province [South Carolina]," prohibited slaves from buying and selling goods in Charleston without express permission from their master. Punishment was prescribed for the slaves, but no charges were levelled against the white merchants who did business with them. Furthermore, it was made illegal for slaves to keep canoes, raise stock, or own anything else that might encourage bartering, because this would provide "an opportunity of receiving and concealing stolen goods."[102] As Howell Henry pointed out in *Police Control of the Slave in South Carolina*, the statute of 1740 and early laws like it were "enacted more with a view to reaching and punishing the slave than punishing the white man who became his accomplice by trading with him."[103]

It is significant, however, that when Henry, who was concerned with the police control of *slaves*, turned to a discussion of laws against trade, he argued that "the slave from his inherent racial thieving tendencies would take the risk of a whipping so long as there was someone who would lend his aid by becoming the purchaser of his stolen goods."[104] Slaveowners soon realized that if the power of the law was to be effectively used to prevent slave participation in the market it would have to be directed against the merchants who readily bought the masters' pilfered property. This would have the added advantage of throwing the weight of the law onto the non-slaveholders and away from the slaveowners' property, that is, their slaves. This strategy would also allow slaveholders to fall back on management techniques when possible, and thus avoid applying the law to master-slave relations. The law would only be invoked when slave behavior pushed struggles and disputes beyond the basic and necessarily unmediated relationship between a master and his chattel.

Accordingly, in 1796 the South Carolina General Assembly passed "An Act more effectually to prevent Shopkeepers, Traders and Others, from dealing with Slaves having no Tickets from their Owners." This act was designed to prevent slaves from engaging in trade "to the prejudice of their owners." Any purchase from a slave of corn, rice, bacon, flour, tobacco, indigo and a host of other basic goods was made illegal if the slave did not have a written and signed permit from his master. Shopkeepers who did trade with unauthorized slave barterers would be fined up to $200.[105] Thus the law recognized and prosecuted the economic collusion, rooted in theft, between non-slaveholding whites and slaves, in order to combat the threat this relationship posed to the property of the slaveholding class.

Apparently the act of 1796 did not do much to deter the traffic in stolen goods, because in 1817 another act was passed to increase the penalties against whites who traded illegally with slaves. The act stated that the previous imposition of a $200 fine had been "insufficient" and ineffective. The new law raised the fine to $1000 and added a potential jail sentence of up to one year. Furthermore, because of difficulties encountered in gathering evidence to prosecute such cases, shopkeepers were required to retain the slave's permission ticket after trading with him or her, and produce it if accused of making illegal transactions. If unable to show the ticket for an exchange with a slave, the shopkeeper was liable for prosecution. Thus the burden of proof in such cases was shifted to the non-slaveholding class.[106]

In 1834, as the problem of illicit trade continued to plague slaveowners, a new law prohibiting the purchase of any goods from a slave "with or without a permit" was passed. The rules of evidence of illegal transactions were tightened still further; if a slave was seen entering a shop with some goods and then left without them, or if he came out of a shop carrying something he had not taken in, this alone was proof that the shopkeeper had engaged in illegal trade with the slave.[107] Nowhere in any of the acts of 1796, 1817 or 1834 were the penalties for slaves specified, increased or amended beyond those prescribed in 1740. In fact, the legal system approached the matter of the slaves' participation in illegal trading only to tighten up loopholes through which white merchants tried to slip – loopholes created by the courts' confusion about the relationship between punishment for whites and slaves found guilty of the same offense. This was done by making it clear that however the law might be applied – or not applied – to slaves, the whites in collusion with them would be punished.[108] Of course slaveowners would preserve their plantation-based authority to punish, without the help of the law, the slave who participated in illegal trade. After all, as the editor of the *Southern Agriculturalist* pointed out, "[the South's] refinement in the police and over legislation are ill adapted to the structure of Negro society."[109]

If legal relations intervened in the master-slave relationship this sharply raised the contradiction of the dual slave identity as person and property, the very contradiction planters were attempting to circumvent in their management strategies.[110] Consequently, the law was only applied when slave economic behavior – "legal" or "illegal" – stretched beyond the boundaries of the plantation and the limits of paternalism.[111] The "crime" of theft was dealt with whenever possible by the summary justice of the plantation, thus denying or disguising the radical economic and political implications of the moral economy of stealing as a form of resistance to slavery and an imposed slave identity. But when theft or the forms of exchange linked to it entered social and racial terrain normally denied to slaves – the white-dominated market – the law was brought to bear against both races. In the official legal sphere, on the ocassions that slaves did appear in the criminal dockets of the South Carolina courts it was often for the crime of "unlawful trafficking" in stolen goods, not the crime of theft itself.[112]

The creation of statutes designed to prevent unchecked economic exchange between slaves and non-slaveholders indicated a concern both with theft and with shifting or ambiguous Southern class relations. When theft was linked to a market economy that undercut the slaveowners' economic hegemony, the law and the contradictions it raised moved to the forefront of economic and ideological questions posed by the existence of a slave moral economy. For when slaves participated in exchange relations, they did not only "transform real relations between master and slave,"[113] but also transformed their relations with the class of non-slaveholding whites. This is what made the link between theft and exchange so economically and ideologically threatening to slaveowners, and spurred them to augment their paternalistic and direct power with the law, a mechanism of power which could be applied to class relations beyond the plantation. When management strategies failed to prevent theft and clandestine slave participation in the market, and particularly when such behavior impinged upon class relations among whites and race relations between slaves and non-slaveholders, disclosing competing claims to the fruits of the slave-based economy, the law was mobilized in the slaveowners' favor.

But law in a slave society was fraught with difficulties of its own. Even though shifting legal sanctions to the whites who traded with slaves permitted the slaveholders to avoid the contradictions of applying the law to their own chattel, enforcement of these sanctions was a constant problem once slave theft entered an economy exterior to the plantation. Plantation owners found it frustratingly difficult to use the law to protect their property. Olmsted noted that "the nuisance of petty traders dealing with the negroes, and inducing them to pilfer" was very hard to detect and punish. One planter confided to Olmsted that the "law rather protects [the traders and thieves] than us," because slaves were often the only available witnesses to illegal transactions, and the law barred their testimony from court. "The law which prevents the reception of the evidence of a negro in the courts, here strikes back, with a most annoying force, upon the dominant power itself," Olmsted wryly remarked. "We can never get [the traders] punished, except we go beyond or against the law ourselves," concluded the exasperated planter.[114]

As a result, some planters "organized an association" to bring white offenders to trial, according to Olmsted, and Howell Henry wrote that "vigilance committees were forced to compass the evil of negro trading by lawful prosecution if possible, and by extra-legal methods if necessary."[115] Extra-legal methods were called for because of the difficulties planters had in obtaining convictions, even when they were able to catch the traders red-handed. Examining the records of South Carolina district courts in the period 1817-1860, Henry showed that conviction rates for trading with slaves ranged from 20% to 48%; in no district, then, did even half of these cases result in convictions.[116] Olmsted offered an interesting explanation for this state of affairs, one which casts light on Southern class relations of the period. "It is almost impossible, in a community of which so large a proportion [of whites] is poor and degraded, to have a jury sufficiently honest and intelligent to permit the law to be executed," he argued.[117] Thus, unable to contain the problem of theft within the scope of their plantation authority, and wary of the contradictions and expense of applying the legal system to their slave property, planters had to wrangle with the class tensions inherent in the narrow field of Southern democracy. The jury system could institute a moral economy of its own, one which might have sanctioned the collusion of slaves and the white non-slaveholding class in the redistribution of the slaveowners' property.

To circumvent these obstacles, planters often resorted to a form of entrapment in order to root out the shopkeepers who acted as magnets for pilfered goods. Because of the legal disputes this raised, such cases found their way into the appeals courts, where Southern judges explicitly defined the role the law would play in preventing this form of property redistribution. In *State v. Anone*, a slaveowner gave his slave a bag of corn to sell to the shopkeeper Anone, but purposely neglected to give his slave a permission ticket. Anone was then convicted of trading illegally with the slave. The appeals court upheld the conviction, ruling that this method of entrapment did not legalize trading, and was in fact an excellent "means of detecting persons who notoriously trade with slaves."[118] Justice Richardson of the South Carolina Court of Appeals, referring to the act of 1817, clearly articulated the slaveholders' views on the independent slave economy:

> The evident object of [the act of 1817] is to prevent any trading whatever with a slave. For this purpose, at least, a slave can have no property.... [T]he act of 1817 will embrace every instance of selling to, buying from, or bartering with a slave having no license.[119]

In a similar case in North Carolina, Judge Ruffin of the North Carolina Supreme Court broadened the slaveowners' arguments against trading with slaves. He noted that economically autonomous slaves could cause problems, because "one of the evils of trading with slaves is the temptation to them to leave their owner's service, and, breaking their natural rest, to become night walkers and vagabonds." Furthermore, the purpose of restrictions on trading with slaves, according to Ruffin, was *not* just to protect slaveholders' property, "but also to protect the community from such dealings with those persons, as may probably induce [slaves] to commit depredations upon others as well as their owners, and render their detection difficult." Since the law in North Carolina requiring permission tickets (as in South Carolina) would "facilitate the discovery of any petty thefts by slaves by the readier tracing of their dealings," such threats to the community could be more readily controlled, to the benefit of the white caste across class lines. As contradictory as it was, the law, when properly manipulated and articulated, could serve to disrupt the outlets for slave moral economy, and ratify racial hegemony by obscuring, rather than disclosing, class tensions among whites.[120]

Both privately and publicly, in the form of slave management and legal codes and practice, slaveowners articulated strategies for dealing with slave theft that by necessity recognized it for what it was – economic, not moral, behavior. However slaveholders tried to understand theft, however hard they attempted to contain it within the sphere of morality, and thus racial rather than class relations, the slaves' insistence on their economic rights – both those granted by custom and those taken by stealth – forced their masters to respond in ways that precipitated struggle for authority and control. This struggle was initially over the shape of master-slave relations, but, when sharpened by interracial exchange relations, also could undermine the slaveholders' hegemony and class position within Southern society as a whole. The slaves themselves recognized these dynamics, perhaps more clearly than their masters, and structured *their* understanding of theft around a moral economy which could offer them economic autonomy and dignity and lay claim to the appropriated product of their labor. Theft thus was a form of resistance to slavery and an assertion of economic rights that slaveowners ultimately were unable to dismiss or discourage. Slaves used theft to reject, not accommodate to, their condition of slavery.

University of Pennsylvania   Alex Lichtenstein
Philadelphia, PA 19104

FOOTNOTES

1. See, for example, James B. Sellers, *Slavery in Alabama* (University, AL, 1950), p. 255. The author claims that it is "hard to understand" why slaves would commit arson: "Perhaps the impulse to burn was an expression of their child-like minds, their desire to 'get even' with someone who offended them," he speculates.

2. Kenneth Stampp, *The Peculiar Institution* (New York, 1956).

3. Ibid., p. 25.

4. Ibid., pp. 126-27.

5. Eugene D. Genovese, *Roll, Jordan, Roll* (New York, 1972), pp. 599-609, especially p. 609.

6. Lawrence Levine, *Black Culture and Black Consciousness: Afro-American Folk Thought From Slavery to Freedom.* (New York, 1977); Edward L. Ayers, *Vengeance and Justice: Crime and Punishment in the Nineteenth-Century American South* (Oxford, 1984).

7. Gresham Sykes and David Matza, "Techniques of Neutralization: A Theory of Delinquency," *American Sociological Review* 22 (December, 1957): 664-70.

8. Levine, *Black Culture and Black Consciousness*, pp. 123, 465 n10; Ayers, *Vengeance and Justice*, pp. 130, 314 n59.
   As Sykes and Matza tell us, such "situational" values "represent tangential or glancing blows at the dominant normative system rather than the creation of an opposing ideology." "Techniques of Neutralization," p. 669.

9. Ian Taylor, Paul Walton, and Jock Young, *The New Criminology: For a Social Theory of Deviance* (New York, n.d.), pp. 184-87.

10. Michael S. Hindus, *Prison and Plantation: Crime, Justice and Authority in Massachusetts and South Carolina, 1767-1878* (Chapel Hill, 1980), p. 140, concludes that "by far the most common [slave] crime was theft," which comprised 34.6% of slave prosecutions in two South Carolina districts for theft. Marion J. Russell, "American Slave Discontent in the Records of the High Courts," *Journal of Negro History* 31 (October 1946): 432, demonstrates that "goods" and meat were the two most common items stolen by slaves. See also, U.B. Phillips, "Slave Crime in Virginia," *American Historical Review* 20 (1912): 336-40, and Alice A. Bauer and Raymond H. Bauer, "Day-to-Day Resistance to Slavery," *Journal of Negro History* 27 (1942): 388-419, for further evidence of food theft. See also Philip Schwarz, *Twice Condemned: Slaves and the Criminal Laws of Virginia, 1705-1865* (Baton Rouge, 1988), for a statistical compilation of theft incidents in Virginia. Schwarz's figures indicate that while slave crime varied over time and place, theft was always the most frequent violation of law, and food was the most frequently stolen item. Schwarz's conclusions about theft as resistance to slavery are close to my own. Schwarz, pp. 98-110, 170-78, 232-33, and Tables 13, 18, 19, 31.

11. See the essays in Douglas Hay, et. al., *Albion's Fatal Tree* (New York, 1975) and E.P. Thompson, *Whigs and Hunters: The Origins of the Black Act* (New York, 1975) for poaching, smuggling, and illegal foraging in eighteenth-century England as examples of moral economy. John Rule, *The Experience of Labour in Eighteenth-Century Industry* (London, 1981) and Craig Becker, "Property in the Workplace: Labor, Capital and Crime in the Eighteenth-Century British Woolen and Worsted Industry," *Virginia Law Review* 69 (November 1983): 1487-1515, apply this theory to the theft of production materials in the workplace. The term "moral economy" was coined by E.P. Thompson, in his groundbreaking article "The Moral Economy of the English Crowd in the Eighteenth Century," *Past and Present* 50 (1971): 76-136.

For a more contemporary – and perhaps more relevant – use of this concept, the work of James C. Scott on the Southeast Asian peasantry is indispensable. See James C. Scott, *The Moral Economy of the Peasant: Rebellion and Subsistence in Southeast Asia* (New Haven, 1976); Scott, *Weapons of the Weak: Everyday Forms of Peasant Resistance* (New Haven, 1985).

Marvin L. Michael Kay and Lorin Lee Cary have applied the idea of moral economy to slavery in their article "They are Indeed the Constant Plague of Their Tyrants': Slave Defence of a Moral Economy in Colonial North Carolina, 1748-1772," *Slavery and Abolition* 6 (December, 1985): 37-56.

12. On slave provision grounds see Genovese, *Roll Jordan, Roll*, pp. 535-40. Also see note 78 below.

13. James' Scott's work on "everyday forms of peasant resistance" in Southeast Asia has helped me clarify my view of theft as a non-accommodating form of resistance. Scott, *The Moral Economy of the Peasant*; Scott, *Weapons of the Weak*. For the most condensed articulation of his position, see James Scott, "Everyday Forms of Peasant Resistance," *Journal of Peasant Studies* 13 (1986): 5-35. Scott argues that in rural Malaysia theft represents "a constant process of testing and renegotiation of production relations between classes." He goes on to say that while "rural theft by itself is unremarkable....[w]hen such theft takes on the dimensions of a struggle in which property rights are being contested...it may become an essential element of any careful analysis of class relations." He notes that the intentionality and "self-interest" of such class actions are rooted in "the often defensive effort to mitigate or defeat appropriation," and that this is a universal form of resistance by dominated classes. Referring to Genovese's contention that " 'day to day resistance to slavery' generally implied accommodation and made no sense except on the assumption of an accepted status quo the norm of which, as perceived or defined by the slaves, had been violated," Scott says: "This position...fundamentally misconstrues the very basis of the economic and political struggle conducted daily by subordinate classes...in repressive settings." Genovese, *Roll, Jordan, Roll*, p. 598; Scott, "Everyday Forms of Peasant Resistance," pp. 18-19, 24, 27.

14. Frederick Law Olmsted, *A Journey in the Seaboard Slave States, with Remarks on their Economy* (New York, 1968 [1856]), p. 117.

15. Lawrence T. McDonnell, "Money Knows No Master: Market Relations and the American Slave Community," in Winfred B. Moore and Joseph F. Tripp, eds., *Developing Dixie: Modernization in a Traditional Society* (Westport, CT, forthcoming). See also Sidney Mintz, "Slavery and the Rise of Peasantries," *Historical Reflections/Reflexions Historiques* 6 (Summer 1979): 240-41 for a similar analysis of the effect of slave market participation.

16. George P. Rawick, ed., *The American Slave: A Composite Autobiography*, 31 vols. (Westport, CT, 1972-77); Charles L. Purdue, Jr., Thomas E. Barten, and Robert K. Phillips, eds., *Weevils in the Wheat: Interviews with Virginia Ex-Slaves* (Bloomington, 1980); and John W. Blassingame, ed., *Slave Testimony: Two Centuries of Letters, Speeches, Interviews and Autobiographies* (Baton Rouge, 1977) proved the most useful in this regard.

17. Eugene D. Genovese, *The Political Economy of Slavery* (New York, 1968), pp. 44-46; Kenneth Kiple and Virginia Himmelstein King, *Another Dimension to the Black Diaspora: Diet Disease and Racism* (Cambridge, 1981).

18. Stampp, *Peculiar Institution*, p. 286.

19. Perdue, Barten, and Phillips, *Weevils in the Wheat*, pp. 244-45.

20. Blassingame, *Slave Testimony*, p. 698.

21. Norman R. Yetman, *Life Under the 'Peculiar Institution': Selections from the Slave Narrative Collection* (Huntington, N.Y., 1976), p. 178.

22. Rawick, *The American Slave*, supp. 1, vol. 8 (3)MS: 939.

23. Ibid., vol. 4 (2)TX: 1181.

24. Ibid.

25. Rawick, *The American Slave*, vol. 2 (2)SC: 110.

26. See Blassingame, *Slave Testimony*, pp. 275, 698, 567-68; Rawick, *The American Slave*, supp. 1, vol. 16MS: 246; Perdue, Barten, and Phillips, *Weevils in the Wheat*, pp. 57, 124.

27. Perdue, Barten, and Phillips, *Weevils in the Wheat*, pp. 266-67.

28. Yetman, *Slave Narrative Collection*, p. 116.

29. "Remarks on Overseers and the Proper Treatment of Slaves," *Farmers Register* 5 (1837): 302.

30. Ibid.

31. H.C., "On the Management of Negroes – Addressed to the Farmers and Planters of Virginia," *Southern Agriculturalist* 7 (July 1834): 370.

32. John F. Thompkins, "The Management of Negroes," *Farmers Journal* 2 (May 1853): 52-54.

33. Rawick, *The American Slave*, vol. 3 (4)SC: 317.

34. Charles Joyner, *Down by the Riverside: A South Carolina Slave Community* (Urbana, 1984), p. 177.

35. Ibid., p. 194; Levine, *Black Culture and Black Consciousness*, pp. 125-30.

36. Elsie Clew Parsons, *Folk-Lore of the Sea Islands, South Carolina* (Cambridge, MA, 1923), pp. 30 (tale #17), 32 (tale #19), 145 (tale #170), are good examples.

37. Perdue, Barten and Phillips, *Weevils in the Wheat*, p. 201; Rawick, *The American Slave*, supp. 1, vol. 8 (3)MS: 1216.

38. Perdue, Barten and Phillips, *Weevils in the Wheat*, p. 124.

39. Gilbert Osofsky, ed., *Puttin' on Ole Massa: The Slave Narratives of Henry Bibb, William Wells Brown, and Solomon Northup* (New York, 1968), p. 25.

40. John B. Boles, *Black Southerners, 1619-1869* (Lexington, KY, 1984), p. 91.

41. Philip J. Schwarz, "Gabriel's Challenge: Slaves and Crime in Late Eighteenth-Century Virginia," *Virginia Magazine of History and Biography* 90 (July 1982): 296.

42. Rawick, *The American Slave*, vol. 2 (1)SC: 2-3.

43. Olmsted, *Journey in the Slave States*, p. 160.

44. State v. Bill (a slave), 6 Jones NC 36 (Dec. 1858).

45. Rawick, *The American Slave*, vol. 12 (1)GA: 199; ibid., vol. 3 (4)SC: 113, ibid., supp. 1, vol. 6 (1)MS: 58; Perdue, Barten and Phillipps, *Weevils in the Wheat*, pp. 63, 78, 117, 125.

46. Rawick, *The American Slave*, vol. 12 (1)GA: 199.

47. Schwarz, "Gabriel's Challenge," p. 305.

48. Frederick Douglass, *My Bondage and My Freedom* (New York, 1855), pp. 189-91.

49. Ibid.

50. Ayers, *Vengeance and Justice*, p. 131.

51. See Boles, *Black Southerners*, pp. 161, 165; Ayers, *Vengeance and Justice*, p. 125; Rawick, *The American Slave*, vol. 12 (2)GA: 15; ibid., vol. 12 (1)GA: 195, for examples and evidence of slave skepticism about white preaching.

52. Rawick, *The American Slave*, vol. 16 (6)TN: 6.

53. Olmsted, *Journey in the Slave States*, pp. 118-19.

54. This conversation was recorded in "Report on Management of Slaves-Duty of Overseers and Employers," a draft of a report that planter Thomas C. Law planned to present to his local agricultural society. Thomas C. Law Papers, Plantation Records, Series A, Part 2, Reel 7, South Caroliniana Library, Columbia, SC, p. 936.

55. Olmsted, *Journey in the Slave States*, pp. 116-17.

56. Josiah Henson, *Father Henson's Story of His Own Life* (Boston, 1858), pp. 21-22.

57. Douglass, *My Bondage*, pp. 189-90.

58. Yetman, *Slave Narrative Collection*, pp. 182-83.

59. Blassingame, *Slave Testimony*, p. 53.

60. Charles C. Jones, *The Religious Instruction of the Negroes in the United States* (Savannah, 1842), pp. 131, 135.

61. Thomas C. Law, "Report on Management," Thomas C. Law Papers, Plantation Records, Series A, Part 2, reel 7, p. 936.

62. "Remarks on Overseers and the Proper Treatment of Slaves," *Farmers Register* 5 (1837): 302.

63. Ibid.

64. Jones, *Religious Instruction*, p. 144.

65. James O. Breeden, *Advice Among Masters: The Ideal in Slave Management in the Old South* (Westport, CT, 1980), p. 230.

66. N. Herbemont, "On the Moral Discipline and Treatment of Slaves," *Southern Agriculturalist* 9 (Feb. 1836): 71.

67. "Remarks on Overseers and the Proper Treatment of Slaves," p. 302.

68. Philip Schwarz shows that in Virginia prosecutions of slaves for theft surpassed all other charges. Schwarz, *Twice Condemned*, pp. 106, 232, and Tables 3-4. Given slaveowners' reluctance to apply the law to their chattel such court records vastly understate the frequency of theft, as Schwarz notes.

69. "Remarks on Overseers and the Proper Treatment of Slaves," p. 302.

70. Hindus, *Prison and Plantation*, p. 139.

71. For example, a North Carolina statute mandated;

> In case any slave who shall appear not to have been properly clothed and fed, shall be convicted of stealing any corn, cattle, hogs, or other goods whatsoever, from any person not the owner of such slave, such injured person may maintain an action in the case, against the possessor of such slave, for his damages.

North Carolina Revised Code of 1855 (Raleigh, 1856), chap. 107, sec. 27. See *The Statutes at Large of South Carolina*, vol. 7 (Columbia, 1840), p. 374, for a similar law.

72. Mark V. Tushnet, *The American Law of Slavery: Considerations of Humanity and Interest* (Princeton, 1981) offers a compelling interpretation of the antebellum Southern legal system, arguing that it required an often untenable balance between "law" and "sentiment." The slaves' dual identity as property and persons was embedded in this primary contradiction of law and slavery.

73. Douglass, *My Bondage*, p. 190.

74. ["A Southerner"], "Dieting etc. of Negroes," *Southern Agriculturalist* 9 (October 1836): 520. As noted above, slaveowners were also held *legally* responsible for their slaves' "predatory excursions;" the moral and legal spheres so assiduously separated for their chattel were conflated in the case of slaveholder behavior.

75. Ibid.

76. Thomas C. Law, "Report on Management," pp. 937-38.

77. Joe G. Taylor, *Negro Slavery in Louisiana* (Baton Rouge, 1963), p. 204.

78. For discussions of the "peculium" or "provision grounds" see Orlando Patterson, *Slavery and Social Death* (Cambridge, MA, 1982), pp. 182-84; Philip D. Morgan, "The Ownership of Property by Slaves in the mid-Nineteenth-Century Low Country," *Journal of Southern History* 49 (August 1983): 399-420; Sidney Mintz, *Caribbean Transformations* (Baltimore, 1974), pp. 146-56; Mintz, "Slavery and Peasantries;" Joyner, *Down by the Riverside*, p. 130; Boles, *Black Southerners*, p. 89.

79. Law, "Report on Management," p. 937.

80. Francis Boykin, "Management of Negroes," *Southern Field and Fireside* 1 (June 1860): 406. See also [A Practical Planter], "Observations on the Management of Negroes," *Southern Agriculturalist* 5 (April 1832): 182, in which a planter observed that corn was frequently stolen but was heavier for the money received than cotton, and thus entailed more risk and more work for less profit to the thief. Thus more incentive to produce, rather than steal, followed from the independent planting of corn by the slaves. This was supposedly better for their "moral condition" than planting cotton on their own time.

81. R. King, Jr., "On the Management of the Butler Estate, and the Cultivation of Sugar Cane" [Letter to William Washington], *Southern Agriculturalist* 1 (December 1828): 525-28.

82. Olmsted, *Journey in the Slave States*, p. 689.

83. ["A Practical Planter"], "Observations on the Management of Negroes," p. 182.

84. Ibid.

85. Jones, *Religious Instruction*, pp. 135, 145. Jones also noted that free blacks, "who derived their chief subsistence from slaves," often provided the market for stolen food: Ibid., p. 145.

86. "On the Management of Slaves," *Southern Agriculturalist* 6 (June 1833): 285-86. See also "Management of Negroes Upon Southern Estates," *DeBow's Review* 10 (June 1851): 621-27.

87. Letter to the editor from B. McBride, *Southern Agriculturalist* 3 (May 1830): 239; King, "Management of the Butler Estate," p. 529; ["An Overseer"], "On the Conduct and Management of Overseers, Drivers and Slaves," *Southern Agriculturalist* 9 (May 1836): 230; "On the Management of Negroes," *Southern Cabinet* 1 (May 1840): 279.

88. ["An Overseer"], "On the Conduct and Management of Overseers," p. 230.

89. Olmsted, *Journey in the Slave States*, pp. 442-43.

90. "On the Management of Negroes," p. 279.

91. ["A Southerner"], "Dieting etc.," p. 518.

92. Olmsted, *Journey in the Slave States*, p. 439.

93. Ibid., p. 441.

94. Charles Woodson, "On the Management of Slaves," *Farmers Register* 2 (1836): 248.

95. Daniel R. Hundley, *Social Relations of Our Southern States* (Baton Rouge, 1979 [New York, 1860]), pp. 228-30.

96. Jonathan Weiner has demonstrated that this conflict persisted into the postbellum period, when planters advocated "sunset laws" to prevent their sharecroppers from trading with black belt merchants. Jonathan Weiner, *Social Origins of the New South: Alabama, 1865-1885* (Baton Rouge, 1978), pp. 94-96.

97. Peter Wood, *Black Majority: Negroes in Colonial South Carolina from 1670 through the Stono Rebellion* (New York, 1974), pp. 209-11, 217.

98. Morgan, "Ownership of Property." Morgan explicitly compares these conditions to Sidney Mintz's description of the "proto-peasant" semi-autonomous slave economy of the Caribbean. See Mintz, *Caribbean Transformations*, pp. 180-213; Mintz, "Rise of Peasantries." For a similar analysis of the Georgia rice coast see Thomas Armstrong, "From Task Labor to Free Labor: The Transition along Georgia's Rice Coast, 1820-1880," *Georgia Historical Quarterly* 64 (Winter 1980): 432-47. Armstrong notes that in the spare time provided by the task system slaves were able to "produce items for cash sale in local markets that . . . were outside of the control of the planter," p. 436.

99. Rawick, *The American Slave*, vol. 3 (4)SC: 310.

100. Another historian of the South Carolina lowcountry, Charles Joyner, is aware of the

tensions emobdied in the moral economy of independent slave production, but argues that slaveowners were willing to flaunt the law and let their slaves raise crops for sale on the market. According to Joyner, this system prevailed because "the planters perceived such social relations to be positive incentives to slaves." Yet Joyner too overlooks the degree of ambivalence masters felt about their slaves' economic autonomy; he ignores the slaveowners' fear that market participation contributed to theft and does not mention their consequent desperate efforts to limit this economic activity. Joyner, *Down by the Riverside*, p. 129. These tensions are in contrast to the Caribbean situation portrayed by Mintz, in which market participation posed a much less serious threat to slaveowners. Perhaps this was due to the relative absence of caste and class frictions between slaves and non-slaveholding whites, the latter being a negligible class in the Caribbean. See Mintz, *Caribbean Transformations*, pp. 180-213.

101. Wood, *Black Majority*, p. 111.

102. *The Statutes at Large of South Carolina*, vol. 7 (Columbia, 1849), law no. 670, secs. 30, 31, 34, 35, pp. 407-09.

103. Howell Henry, *The Police Control of the Slave in South Carolina* (New York, 1968 [1914]), p. 81.

104. Ibid. It is unclear if the "inherent racial theiving tendencies" are Henry's view, or one he attributes to antebellum whites.

105. *Acts of the General Assembly of South Carolina*, vol. 2 (Columbia, 1808), p. 91.

106. "An Act to Increase the Penalties which are now, by Law, inflicted on Persons who deal or trade with Negro Slaves, without a License or Ticket from their Master or Owner," *Statutes of South Carolina* pp. 454-55.

107. "An Act to amend the Laws in relation to Salves and Free Persons of Color," sec. 5, ibid., p. 469. North Carolina had a battery of similar laws prohibiting trade with slaves; e.g. "An act to prevent thefts and robberies by slaves, free negores and mulattoes," *Laws of the State of North Carolina* (Raleigh, 1821), chap. 267, pp. 562-64.

108. Confusion arose when slaves were caught stealing and were prosecuted for petty larceny, since the receiver of their stolen goods could not be charged under any existing statute as an accessory to petty larceny, because this was only a misdemeanor. Further tensions occurred when a white was indicted for trading with slaves, or receiving stolen goods, because the "principal," i.e. the slave, had to be charged as well — exactly what slaveholders hoped to avoid. An act passed in 1829 clearly demarcated the indictments which could be brought against white participants in clandestine exchange relations. See "An Act to Punish the Receiver of Stolen Goods," *Acts and Resolutions of the General Assembly of South Carolina* (Columbia, 1830), chap. 19, p. 40. See also State v. Wright, 4 McCord SC 358 (1827); State v. Hardy Counsil, 1 Harper SC 53 (1823); State v. Taylor, 2 Bailey SC 40 (1831), for the relevant South Carolina case law.

109. [The Editor], "Account of an Agricultural Excursion Made into the South of Georgia in the Winter of 1832," *Southern Agriculturalist* 6 (Nov. 1833): 576.

110. See Tushnet, *American Law of Slavery*.

111. Hindus, *Prison and Plantation*, p. 140.

112. Henry, *Police Control of the Slave*, p. 79.

113. McDonnell, "Money Knows No Master."

114. Olmsted, *Journey in the Slave States*, pp. 674-75.

440   journal of social history

115. Ibid., p. 440; Henry, *Police Control of the Slave*, p. 89.

116. Henry, *Police Control of the Slave*, pp. 86-87.

117. Olmsted, *Journey in the Slave States*, p. 440.

118. State v. Francis Anone, 2 Nott and McCord SC 28 (1819).

119. Ibid.: 29.

120. State v. James Hart, 4 Iredell NC 248-49 (1844).

SLAVERY IN MICROCOSM: A CONSPIRACY SCARE IN COLONIAL SOUTH CAROLINA

Philip D. Morgan
Institute of Early American History and Culture

George D. Terry
University of South Carolina

Just before the middle of the eighteenth century British North American colonies experienced a rash of slave conspiracies and fears of conspiracies. From then to the mid-1770s, and perhaps even to the 1790s, American society was free from such fears and occurrences.[1] In 1749, in an area of South Carolina served by the eastern branch of the Cooper River, a conspiracy came to light that was potentially of more moment than the Stono revolt of ten years earlier. One hundred four slaves and sixteen lower-class whites were implicated by name; the South Carolina Council interrogated twenty-three slaves and seven whites at length, and minutes of the cross-examinations took approximately eighty pages of the council's journal.[2] The plot was taken seriously.

This investigation will pursue three objectives: to explore the facts of the case, particularly the role of the planter whose slaves were at the heart of the supposed conspiracy; to illumine aspects of the slave

---

1. Even Herbert Aptheker, who is inclined to take a rumor for a revolt, notes "a marked decline of organized rebellious activity on the part of the Negro slaves" in the generation after 1750, *American Negro Slave Revolts* (New York, 1969, 1st pub., 1943), 196. The two major conspiracies to occur before mid-century were those of South Carolina in 1739 and New York in 1741. For a recognition of this pattern and for a more detailed and insightful discussion of these two revolts and the conspiracy scares of the 1790s, see Winthrop D. Jordan, *White Over Black: American Attitudes Toward the Negro, 1550-1812* (Chapel Hill, 1968), 110-122 and 391-99.

2. The investigations began on January 24, 1749 and were completed two weeks later, on February 7. Their recording begins on page 47 and, with other business intervening, ends on page 168 of Council Journal no. 17, Part 1 (subsequently referred to as CJ no. 17), which is to be found in the South Carolina Department of Archives and History (subsequently, SCDAH). In fact, there are three copies of this Journal: a fair copy and duplicate in the SCDAH and a manuscript version in the Public Record Office in London. Spelling and punctuation varies slightly from one to the other. All citations are taken from the fair copy in the SCDAH.

The term "lower class white" is a shorthand term which the authors readily admit to be definitionally imprecise. Four were boatmen, four were artisans, and Springer was both an artisan and overseer. That only one left an inventory suggests their personal property was modest; and, in his case, one James Mathews, a weaver, whose estate was appraised in 1750, no slaves were listed and his estate was indeed modest. See inventory of James Mathews, June 11, 1750, Inventory Book B, 285-286, SCDAH.

The majority of the planters mentioned in the Council investigations resided in the parish of St. Thomas and St. Dennis, although some lived in the parish of St. John's Berkeley and a few in that of St. James' Goose Creek.

experience in post-Stono South Carolina;[3] and to offer glimpses into a plantation society dynamics by asking how such a potentially explosive incident was contained.

* * *

Slaves belonging to James Akin, a planter residing in the parish of St. Thomas and St. Dennis, were the most deeply involved in the alleged conspiracy. Its prime mover, according to both Akin and his slaves, was James Springer, who became an overseer on one of Akin's outlying plantations in December 1747. Springer reportedly attempted to recruit a band of conspirators from lower class whites and Cooper River slaves. He left for Maryland in the spring of 1748, but a number of meetings in the summer of that year were, so it was claimed, the occasion for renewed plotting. In the fall, Akin's Joe, the "head man" in the conspiracy, so one slave asserted, was executed for a barn-burning incident committed three years earlier.[4] This was said to have proved only a temporary set back, for more meetings were believed to have been held over the Christmas holidays and in early January, at which time Akin became aware of the conspiracy and notified the authorities.

The aims of the plot were not distinctive. Indeed, one historian has claimed that black creole conspirators invariably tended to direct "their elaborate schemes and ambitions at the whites' forts and port towns," as these slaves apparently did. Thus Akin's Agrippa referred to conversations about escaping to the Spaniards in St. Augustine but not before setting Charlestown and its magazine on fire and killing as many whites as possible. Similarly, Akin's Sambo claimed that after the magazine had been blown up, and "the People in Town" killed, "the Negroes in the Country were to kill the White People up the

---

3. We have in mind the conclusion to a recent book on the black experience in early South Carolina which characterized the Stono uprising "as a turning-point in the history of South Carolina's black population": Peter Wood, *Black Majority: Negroes in Colonial South Carolina* (New York, 1974), 308. Did a "new social equilibrium" emerge after 1739 that "was based upon a heightened degree of white repression and a reduced amount of black autonomy"? This cannot be the place to explore that question fully. Nevertheless, the lack of concern that South Carolina's executive displayed toward the slave mobility and the familiarity between slaves and lower-class whites manifest in this incident, some ten years after the Stono revolt, might lead us to query Wood's conclusion. A much more extensive analysis is necessary to buttress what can only be a mild query at this point.
4. CJ no. 17, 49. James Akin received £200 compensation for Joe. See R. Nicholas Olsberg, ed., *Journal of South Carolina Commons House of Assembly, 23 April 1750—31 August 1751* (Columbia, 1974), 42.

Path."[5] A more significant feature was the key role said to have been played by white agitators who utilized a variety of arguments to motivate the blacks. According to James Akin, his slaves had reported that whites tried to arouse their resentment against the hardships of slave life by asking "how they could be Satisfied with Eating Homminy, Potatoes and such Victuals and . . . how they could work in the Sun without Shirts." Others made threats: two whites supposedly told Akin's Tony that if he and his acquaintances "would not go with them they might stay and be damned for they had enough would go with them and them that would not should be served the same sauce with the White People." A more idealistic alternative might be advanced: "if they would go with him," Springer asserted, according to Akin's Susannah, "he would undertake to carry them off where they should live as well as White People." Both Akin and one of his slaves reported use of another argument, that baptism led to freedom.[6]

The testimony of respectable white neighbors of Akin's adds a strange twist to the story. Dr. William Bruce, of the parish of St. Thomas and St. Dennis, claimed to know more about the conspiracy than anybody else. He drew attention to Akin's testimony at Joe's trial (for barn burning): Akin's slave Kate had been implicated, and Akin had promised to transport her and her children out of the province. From this, Bruce deduced that the conspiracy was nothing more than an ingenious ruse to avoid transporting Kate, for Akin "had a greater value for the said Wench and her Children than for his own Wife and Children."[7] In other words, the plot was an elaborate fraud

---

5. Whether slave conspiracies, which were directed at towns, were necessarily dominated by creoles, is a moot point but, for this suggestion, see M. Mullin, "British Caribbean and North American Slaves in an Era of War and Resolution, 1775-1807," in Jeffrey J. Crow and Larry E. Tise, eds., *The Southern Experience in the American Revolution* (Chapel Hill, 1978), 239. For Agrippa's and Sambo's testimony, see CJ no. 17, 47 and 63.

6. Ibid., 121, 62, 64. Akin's slave George (who was later to preface his confession to the Governor with the claim, "Sir I am now in your presence, my Master tells me that you are head of the Country. It is true I am not a white Man, but I have a soul as well as others, and I believe there is a Heaven and a Devil," ibid., 99) related how Springer had told Akin's slaves that "if they would go with him, they should be Baptized as the white People are . . . ," ibid., 72; and Akin also mentioned that Springer had told them that in the country he came from "the Blacks there were baptized and went to Church that the Black fellows married White Women and the Black Women married to Whitemen and that the Whites and Blacks are all one . . . , ibid., 121. See Jordan, *White Over Black*, 180-187 for a detailed discussion of this pervasive fear among whites of the link between baptism and freedom.

7. CJ no. 17, 95. One wonders whether such behavior ran in the family: James Akin's son, also named James and also a planter in the same parish, manumitted three

by which Kate, and the other slave witnesses who had divulged it, would be set free by the government, receive a gratuity, and thereby become immune from transportation. This interpretation gained credence when two of Akin's slaves confessed that they had been party to a fabrication. George, supported by Tony, explained that "the two Mustee Wenches frequently carried Falsehoods to their Master and that he was very apt to give Credit to what they said & always examined the Negroes upon the truth of it, and punished them if they did not say as these Wenches said."[8] Here, the implication is less that Akin had initiated the fraud than that he had been duped, but then it is open to question how willingly he accepted the deception. The two "Mustee Wenches" are not identified, but it would seem likely that they were Kate and Susannah. Kate and Susannah, along with Susie and Robin, were sentenced to transportation for fabricating this "plot."[9]

Other witnesses inclined to the view that Akin was deceived, rather than that he was an instigator of deception, but those witnesses were Akin's sister, Mary Russell, and her daughter, and his brother, Thomas. Furthermore, Mary's deposition was ambiguous, for she stated that Akin's plantation had been "in continual distraction" for a number of years and that "of late her Brother seems to her not right in his Sences." She also mentioned that, when she recently visited the plantation, Kate had voluntarily held to the story but that Susannah and another female slave did so only under duress. The implication is that Akin had whipped them to make them keep to the story, and that he and Kate wanted it to be believed.[10] In fact, Kate was the

---

mulatto children in his will. They were to be apprenticed, supported out of the estate, and receive £1,000 each on reaching adulthood. It seems virtually certain that these were his own children; no other children were mentioned in the will. See Will Book WW, 1780-1783, 97-98, SCDAH. Incidentally, James Akin I's mother had manumitted a mulatto man in 1745; see Will Book FF, 353, SCDAH.

8. Ibid., 100. There is a striking pattern to these confessions: when these two slaves were brought before the man whom they conceived to be the "head of the Country," as George put it, they fully confessed and claimed to be telling the truth; other slaves similarly changed their testimony when appearing before the Governor.

9. Susannah was a house servant, the wife of "headman" Joe, and was acknowledged by the Council to be "a Sincible Wench," ibid., 64; we may presume therefore that she was one of the "mustee Wenches." And, especially if Dr. Bruce's allegations were true, we might safely assume Kate to be the other. The only other possible candidate was Susie or Sue, who was the third female slave reckoned to be a party to the conspiracy's fabrication, but less is known about her for she was never brought before the Council.

10. CJ no. 17, 117-119, for the depositions of Mary Russell Senior and Junior; ibid., 92, for Thomas Akin's testimony. The lack of harmony between master and slave on James Akin's plantation was evident even to the end of his life. In his will, he men-

only principal collaborator who refused to retract her story. Moreover, the members of the Council were aware that Akin's characterization of Robin had radically altered: at Joe's trial he was a villain; now Akin was presenting him as a reliable and upstanding slave. Similarly, when Agrippa claimed that Susannah, Kate, Susie, and Robin had constructed the "conspiracy," he also noted that Akin had charged him to keep to *this* story.[11] Finally, one tantalizing and inconclusive piece of evidence points to Akin's involvement: in the list of slaves, made by the appraisers of Akin's estate in 1758, is found a slave called Kate valued at £300. This list contains no Susannah, no Susie, no Robin. Is it possible that Akin avoided transporting his favorite slave after all?[12]

What can we conclude about the bare facts of the case? Skepticism certainly seems in order when we recall that two of the alleged chief conspirators—James Springer and Akin's Joe—were conveniently unavailable for comment by the time the story was leaked. The wilder accusations of a concerted plan to storm the town and kill large numbers of whites may well be without foundation. On the other hand, blacks may well have speculated about such things and were apparently aware of the arguments lower class whites might employ to incite them to revolt. Nor would it be surprising if nonslaveholding whites encouraged slaves to run away, or at least were guilty of reckless talk along these lines. Most important, what the investigations reveal about slave meetings, the movement of slaves and their famil-

---

tioned that his sister had wished to bequeath a slave to his son but he pointed out that the slave had "Behaved in a very Idle and Villanous Manner Since he hath been in my Care & Possession during the great Part of which time There hath been a Necessity to Either Confine or keep him in a Chain," and the slave was sold. He also expressed a wish that any troublesome slave should be sold before his children reached the age of twenty-one. Will of James Akin, October 22, 1758, Will Book, 1757-1760, 132, SCDAH.

11. CJ no. 17, 146 and 147.

12. Inventory of James Akin, December 8, 1758, Inventory Book T, 118-123, SCDAH. Akin, by all conventional criteria, was a pillar of respectability. He served as a representative in the South Carolina lower house from September 15, 1742 to May 25, 1745. [See J. H. Easterby, ed., *Journal of South Carolina Commons House of Assembly, September 14, 1742—January 27, 1744* (Columbia, 1954) and *Journal of South Carolina Commons House of Assembly, February 20, 1744—May 25, 1745* (Columbia, 1955)]. In 1744 he was paid £1,545 by the government for supplying cedar posts to be used in constructing fortifications (*ibid.,* 123). He remained a Justice of the Peace for Berkeley county throughout the 1740s and early 1750s [see, for example, J. H. Easterby, ed., *Journal of South Carolina Commons House of Assembly, March 28, 1749—March 19, 1750* (Columbia, 1962), 45 and R. Nicholas Olsberg, ed., *Journal of South Carolina Commons House of Assembly, April 23, 1750—August 31, 1751* (Columbia, 1974), 213]. He also owned fifty-nine slaves at death. See also Walter B. Edgar and N. Louise Bailey, eds., *Biographical Directory of the South Carolina House of Representatives* (Columbia, 1977), Volume II, 27-28.

iarity with lower class whites, can largely be taken to be accurate, for there is too much independent corroboration, as we hope to show, to disbelieve them. Even James Akin's wife, for example, who was skeptical about the evidence of active plotting, still maintained that "some white People had tampered with their Negroes particularly Simmons and Wade for she had heard that the latter . . . used to come to their Plantation in the night time and on Sundays without coming to the House."[13] The nature of Akin's motivation and the depth of his personal involvement must, it seems, remain obscure, but it should now be clear that one historian's judgment, that Akin "very obviously had" been duped by his slaves, is at least questionable.[14]

*   *   *

If the very fact of the conspiracy, its origins, and its extent are shrouded in mystery, the investigation is significant from a number of other points of view. First, when viewed in a wider perspective, it can reveal much about slave life. As Elinor Miller and Eugene Genovese have noted, "the slave experience itself, analyzed locally and in depth" is absent from most of the literature on plantation life.[15] One hundred and four slaves belonging to thirty different masters were named as slave after slave pointed an accusing finger; this represents only five per cent of the 2,062 slaves who were reported for the parish of St. Thomas and St. Dennis two years later, but it is still an impressively large number.[16] Of these one hundred and four, only nine were females. We know that the adult sex ratios of slaves belonging to nineteen Cooper River planters (out of the thirty who had slaves implicated in this conspiracy) were not markedly imbalanced: 124 males per 100 females.[17] Why, then, were so few women mentioned? If slaves, perhaps intimidated under cross-examination, were simply

---

13. CJ no. 17, 116.
14. Jordan, *White Over Black*, 121-122.
15. Elinor Miller and Eugene D. Genovese, eds., *Plantation, Town and County: Essays on the Local History of American Slave Society* (Urbana, 1974), 161.
16. Very few tax returns survive for colonial South Carolina parishes. In the case of the parish of St. Thomas, we are fortunate to have an abstract of a return of 1751. In that year, the churchwardens placed an advertisement in the newspaper stating that the collectors of the Poor Tax had returned 70,265 acres, 2,062 slaves and £21,366 at interest for the parish: *South Carolina Gazette* (subsequently, *SCG*), August 26, 1751, Stephen Hartley and Andrew Hazell, Churchwardens.
17. Twelve of the nineteen inventories were reported between 1750 and 1755. The adult sex ratio of all South Carolina inventories, drawn up between 1745 and 1749, was 159 males per 100 females. See Philip Morgan, "The Development of Slave Culture in Eighteenth Century Plantation America" (Ph.D. dissertation, University College London, 1977), 289-290.

casting about for likely candidates as co-conspirators, we might expect them to name passing boatmen or skilled slaves, prominent in the
neighborhood: both groups were predominantly male.[18] If the conspiracy is accorded greater validity, we might expect that those acting
with bravado with lower class whites would be men rather than
women. Certainly, men seem to have dominated the various dancing
and drinking sessions referred to in a number of independent slave
testimonies. On the other hand, although few female slaves were mentioned, a number of those who were wielded considerable influence:
indeed, three of the four arch-conspirators of fabricators were
women. Their influence was such that on one Monday "twenty slaves
came Voluntarily and Confessed" a plot, as Mrs. Akin testified.[19] By
juxtaposing, then, the dominance of males in the testimonies and the
relatively equal sex ratios in the broader society, we are led to consider the sexual divisions inherent in certain situations and in certain
slave roles.

If the sexual divisions in lowcountry slave society were perhaps
more complex than we might have imagined, one elementary and un-
complicated fact about slave life is revealed by the slave testimonies:
most slaves, it would seem, lived in separate houses or huts. Akin's
Agrippa, for example, was asked "what Negro House at Colonel
Vanderdussens he was in. He answered in Pompeys . . ."; Thomas
Broughton's Scipio "owned that he had been at several of his [i.e.
James Akin's] Negro Houses and had Eat and Drank there"; the
houses of Akin's Susannah, Kate and Will are all individually mentioned; and Quash's Guy noted that Akin's Joe called at his house for
water.[20] Indeed, questions are immediately raised about the size of
such houses: Drake's patroon, Tony, casually mentioned sleeping at
the house of Samuel Wragg's Negro overseer, Kingroad, with three
other slaves; and Agrippa said that in Pompey's house one afternoon
were "Pompey and his Wife with a good many other Negroes."[21] No

---

18. Runaway boatmen listed in colonial newspapers and watermen listed in colonial
inventories were always male. Of the 1,271 skilled slaves found among inventoried
South Carolina estates for the period 1730-1779, only 12% were female. See Morgan,
"The Development of Slave Culture," 102-104.
19. CJ no. 17, 115-116. The sexual division that is evident in certain slave roles is a
topic worthy of further exploration. Lawrence Levine, for example, has noticed the
small role that women played in slave folk tales, " 'Some Go Up and Some Go Down':
The Meaning of the Slave Trickster," in Stanley Elkins and Eric McKitrick, eds., *The
Hofstadter Aegis: A Memorial* (New York, 1974), 109-110.
20. CJ no. 17, 60, 60, 65, 86, 87, 98.
21. Ibid., 79-80 and 60. There is little information on the size of slave houses. Josiah
Smith suggested to George Austin that six "double" houses, 32 feet by 16 feet, be built
for twelve families, "some of whom are now pretty large" on Austin's Peedee planta-

reference to barracks or dormitories for single slaves has been uncovered in any of the colonial South Carolina material searched.[22] The significance of separate dwellings was emphasized by Springer in his attempt to open up a rift between Akin and his slaves: he claimed that Akin's slaves "had too much liberty in living in separate houses & advised [Akin] to have one House of a considerable length built that his Slaves might lodge together in it in order to be more restrain'd and kept from Stealing and Concealing their theft." Since Springer came from and returned to Maryland where barrack-like buildings for slaves were more common, his prior familiarity with such arrangements may well have prompted this suggestion.[23]

If a prosaic, humdrum and everyday feature of slave life can be culled from the investigations into the alleged conspiracy, rather more qualitative insights are provided. For example, although the Council Journal rarely noted direct speech, something of the flavor of slave language filters through. The way slaves reckoned time is occasionally reported: Agrippa referred to a time "in the beginning of this Winter before the Potatoes were all dug in"; Kent, belonging to Thomas Broughton, said he last saw Captain Shubrick's Diamond "in the time of the last great Snow"; Captain Walker's Cyrus said he had not been at Akin's landing "since Mrs. Trott's death"; Akin's slave, George, claimed to have seen Drake's Scipio at his master's plantation "about the time of digging Potatoes"; and Drake's Tony asserted that "he had not been at Mr. Akin's Plantation since the Yellow Fever was in Town last Summer."[24] The direct, earthy nature of

---

tion. Rather fortuitously, the inventory of that plantation survives, taken three years later. The plantation included 111 slaves and indeed some of the two-parent families were "pretty large," ranging from four to twelve slaves. The twelve largest families had an average size of 5.7 and the average size of all two-parent and single-parent families with children, was 4.8. If it is assumed, then, that an average of five people were to be found in a family dwelling, then there would be approximately forty-five square feet of sleeping space per person. See Josiah Smith to George Austin, June 17, 1771, Josiah Smith Letterbook, Southern Historical Collection, University of North Carolina; inventory of George Austin, December 6, 1774, Inventory Book AA, 42-51, SCDAH.

22. This statement is based largely on a reading of all the descriptions of plantations offered for sale in eighteenth century South Carolina newspapers.

23. CJ no. 17, 121. That plantations in the Chesapeake region often furnished barrack-like buildings for their slaves, see Morgan, "The Development of Slave Culture," 51-53.

24. CJ no. 17, 49, 60, 70, 83, 79. Incidentally, Mrs. Trott's death must have made some impact for Thomas Akin's Ammon mentioned it as the last time he had been at the "Haigen," ibid., 160. Gerald W. Mullin has found similar examples of traditional time reckoning in colonial Virginia fugitive slave advertisements. See his *Flight and Rebellion: Slave Resistance in Eighteenth-Century Virginia* (New York, 1972), 45-46 and Eugene D. Genovese has discussed the persistence of this way of conceiving time in *Roll, Jordan, Roll: The World the Slaves Made* (New York, 1974), 289-294.

slave language can occassionally be heard: Thomas Broughton's Kent mentioned that he had last seen Vanderdussen's Pompey "at a distance as he came down the River and Called to him how do you"; James Akin's George said that Abraham Wade was constantly prodding them to revolt or that he "kept dogging of them."[25]

Status within the slave community, as perceived by the slaves themselves, can also be glimpsed: for example, the two "headmen" most referred to by other slaves were Akin's Joe, a boatman, and Dr. William Bruce's Scipio, whose occupation was not indicated. "Negro Overseers" (for this is how they were described, not "drivers"), of whom six were mentioned, figure less prominently in the testimony of Cooper River slaves than some women, boatmen, and field hands. As with many preindustrial communities, age-stratification seems to have been particularly important: Akin's Tony noted "that as he was a Young fellow he kept out in the Yard (at Mr. Vanderdussen's plantation), where they were playing on the Bangio for most part," whereas the old men talked in one of the slave houses.[26] If slaves could defer to the aged and to the unskilled, this suggests that status, as slaves defined it, did not necessarily accord with status, as their masters defined it.

Tony's comment raises another insight: according to the latest authority, this is the earliest reference to a banjo yet found for the North American mainland. (It occurs twice: Vanderdussen's Pompey also referred to it when he said that the slaves at his master's yard "had not any particular Talk, but only played on the Bangio"). A banjo is, of course, an Afro-American musical instrument (with direct African antecedents) and its early presence in the lowcountry slave community provides a clue to the acculturative process in that community. Another insight into that process concerns the magical beliefs held by South Carolina slaves. James Akin relayed to the Council information his slaves had given him of meetings in late December 1748, where Landgrave Morton's Hector was reported to have said, "let the fire kindle as fast as it will, he will Engage by his obias to stiffle and put it

---

25. CJ no. 17, 71 and 72.
26. Ibid., 101. As for occupational status, one particularly wonders about the role of overseer Will on James Akin's plantation. George noted that when Will tried to tell Akin that "there was no truth in all that Story" so ardently propagated by the "two Mustee Wenches" and so willingly believed by Akin, he received a wound for his pains when his master threw an axe at him, CJ no. 17, 100. Mrs. Akin confirmed that her husband had struck Will, ibid., 116. Incidentally, Will was the most valuable slave (at £450) listed in James Akin's inventory, December 8, 1758, Inventory Book T, 118-123; whereas Scipio was only valued at £250 in the inventory of Dr. William Bruce, May 26, 1752, Inventory Book R (1), 426-431, SCDAH.

out." This is the first reference to *obeah* on the North American mainland that has so far been uncovered, although there are substantive parallels between eighteenth century Jamaican and American slave magical practices. What this fragment of evidence suggests is that South Carolina slaves possessed a closer connection, in terms of their belief systems, to West Indian slaves than has hitherto been detected; this is confirmed by roughly contemporaneous references to the presence of banjos in the slave communities of Jamaica and the lowcountry.[27]

Brief but suggestive glimpses into the experience of South Carolina slaves at mid-century are thus revealed. However, the detailed Council investigations allow a more systematic analysis of one facet of slave life, namely the mobility of Cooper River slaves and the relationships thereby established. In the summer of 1748 an expedition to fetch oyster shells allowed nine slaves from Akin's plantation (in two boats) to rendezvous with four slave boatmen belonging to Captain Broughton at Colonel Vanderdussen's plantation. All parties acknowledged that Vanderdussen's Negro overseer, Pompey, and his wife had entertained these slaves in their house, plying them with food and with musical diversion.[28] On another occasion, a number of James Akin's slaves travelled up the Cooper River to its head, where Thomas Akin's plantation was situated. Along the way, various slaves belonging to separate plantations were notified of the gathering, and that night, apart from the Akin brothers' slaves, Tom-Paine, the overseer of Edward Harleston's plantation, George belonging to Mr. Hasell, Tom and others belonging to Mr. Ball, Tom belonging to Thomas Wright, and Guy, the overseer of Mr. Quash's plantation, were present. There was no dispute about this meeting: Thomas

---

27. CJ no. 17, 70 and 139. For corroboration that this is the first reference to a North American Banjo (by twenty-five years) and for the three references to banjos in mid-eighteenth century Jamaica, see Dena J. Epstein, *Sinful Tunes and Spirituals: Black Folk Music to the Civil War* (Urbana, 1977), 33-34 and Appendix II. As for the other "first," obeah can be spelled obi. Orlando Patterson's definition of Jamaican obeah—as "essentially a type of sorcery which largely involved harming others at the request of clients, by the use of charms, poisons, and shadow-catching. It was an individual practice, performed by a professional who was paid by his clients."—comes close to describing the practices found in colonial America. See his *The Sociology of Slavery* (Rutherford, 1969), 188. For substantive parallels between Jamaican and American magical practices, see Morgan, "The Development of Slave Culture," 391-393. Hector was valued at £300 in the inventory of Landgrave John Morton, January 9, 1752, Inventory Book R (1), 285-289, SCDAH.
28. This meeting is described most fully by Akin's Agrippa, Broughton's Kent and Scipio, and Vanderdussen's Pompey. See CJ no. 17, 47-48, 59-60 and 70-71. Pompey Sr., a "driver", aged fifty-years old and valued at £180, was listed in the inventory of Alexander Vanderdussen, April 4, 1758, Inventory Book T, 1-3, SCDAH.

Akin's Ammon freely admitted it and named those present, but said, "they came only to see him & no harm was spoke."[29] At a subsequent meeting at Irish Town, the same slaves were present, but were complemented by Mr. Quash's Jack and Hannah, Mr. Roche's Tony, Frank, Horatio, Grace, Sharper, Cuffey and Toby, Mr. Bonnoist's Jamie and at least another fifteen more, according to Negro Guy the overseer, who freely admitted this meeting.[30]

These gatherings, and many less specific ones which were alleged to have taken place at a later date, are significant in suggesting the degree and range of movement open to slaves. For example, the oyster expedition of summer 1748 saw nine slaves from Akinfield plantation travel about eleven miles to Colonel Vanderdussen's plantation; they were "overtook" by a boat, with four slaves, from Captain Thomas Broughton's plantation which was about twenty miles from Vanderdussen's plantation.[31] Another jaunt, already mentioned, took some of James Akin's slaves to his brother's plantation, "Master Tomeys" as the slaves called it. One can follow their progress clearly; the sequence in which various plantations are mentioned tallies with a reconstruction of plantation locations along the Cooper River. As Agrippa relates it, Akin's slaves first passed Bonneau's ferry where they met with one of Edward Harleston's slaves; they then stopped at "Mr. Hazell's Landing" (John Hasell of Longwood), "Mr. Baals Landing" (Elias Ball of Kensington) and "Mr. Hughers Landing" (Daniel Huger of Limerick). Residences were situated "½ a mile, a mile and two miles distant from each other."[32] Following the course of the river, the trip was about fifteen miles. They had set out on a Sunday afternoon, apparently in two canoes, and reached Thomas Akin's plantation at the head of the Cooper River "soon after dark." Unfortunately, we do not know how many hands were propelling these canoes, but the speed and extent of such mobility is suggestive.

---

29. CJ no. 17, 160.
30. Ibid., 97-98.
31. All mileages refer to straight-line measurements taken along the river's course; if actual distances (taking into account the twists and turns of the river) are required, then mileages might have to be doubled. Fairly precise locations were established for twenty-one of the thirty plantations mentioned in the cross-examinations (although dotted lines indicate particularly approximate cadastral boundaries). The map was constructed from the following sources: H.A.M. Smith Map Collection, South Carolina Historical Society; McCrady Plat Collection, SCDAH; the *South Carolina Historical Magazine,* passim.; Colonial Plats, SCDAH; Gailliard and Gailliard, Map of Berkeley County, South Carolina, 1900-1960; and John B. Irving, *A Day on the Cooper River* (Columbia, 1969).
32. CJ no. 17, 49; Brian Hunt to the Secretary, May 6, 1728, A21, 98, SPG archives, London.

Certainly, such mobility begins to "transform the picture of an imprisoned slave labouring unit on each plantation, with only internal social relationships, into a much more open affair."[33]

This mobility was not just the privilege of specialist boatmen: for example, of those attending at Irish-Town, only Thomas Wright's Tom, and Joe and Agrippa belonging to James Akin, can be identified as boatmen. Out of the hundred and four slaves named, only twenty-three, just over one-fifth, were boatmen. This is still a sizeable proportion and, as many of these boatmen belonged to all-slave crews with a black patroon in command (five patroons were named), the potential for information to be relayed from plantation to plantation and for slave actions to be coordinated was obvious. Testimony from one black patroon, Drake's Tony, gives a rare insight into the self-reliant, independent lives such skilled slaves led, and deserves to be quoted in full:

[Last Saturday] he got to Mr. Wraggs Plantation at Dacon . . . he carried a Letter from Mr. Wragg to his Overseer there which he delivered to him at three oclock in the afternoon that they took in eight or ten Barrils of Rice that Night that he slep't on Saturday night at Samuel Wraggs Plantation in the House of Kingroad his Negro Overseer that he went to Mr. Samuel Wraggs to carry some things to one Mrs. Smiths who was not at home, that on Sundays night he Slept at Mr. Joseph Wraggs in the House of Gibby his Negro Overseer that Jemmey Scipio and Worster commonly goes with him in the Boat, being asked how long it was since he had been at Mr. Akins Plantation, answered that he had not been at Mr. Akins Plantation since the Yellow Fever was in Town last Summer but knew most of their Negroes and had been frequently before that at his Plantation, being asked when he loaded his Boat, said he finished Loading his Boat last Tuesday about Noon and then set away for Town.[34]

It seems from this account that these boatmen occupied a black world, spending days away from their base among fellow slave crew-

33. Peter Laslett, *Family Life and Illicit Love in Earlier Generations* (Cambridge, 1977), 252. A knowledgeable canoeist informs us that between two and four miles per hour would be well within the capacity of even a two-man canoe (and it seems that at least eight of James Akin's slaves made the trip to the head of the Cooper River); a trip of between fifteen and thirty miles with periodic stops could therefore be accomplished in an afternoon and summer evening.
34. CJ no. 17, 78-79. The five patroons were Broughton's Kent, Drake's Tony, Walker's Cyrus, Cordes' Porter and Shubrick's Diamond.

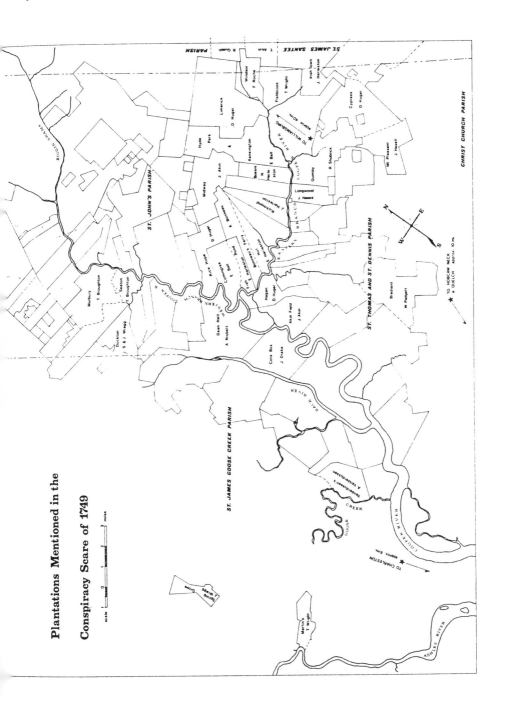

Plantations Mentioned in the

Conspiracy Scare of 1749

men, being sustained by the slaves of plantations at which they called. This pattern continued. Thirteen years later the parishioners of St. Thomas and St. Dennis composed an open letter to the *South Carolina Gazette* pointing out that "divers boats plying there having only slaves that go in them by which all manner of pilfering was facilitated." The sense of independence and self-reliance that being a boatman undoubtedly fostered probably accounts for the prominence of this group among South Carolina's runaways. Watermen formed one-quarter of the total skilled runaways that were advertised in the pages of the *Gazette* between 1732 and 1783 (192 out of a total of 772); the same group comprised only nine per cent of the skilled slaves found among inventoried estates for the same period (110 out of a total of 1,271).[35] Captain Shubrick inadvertently confirms this view. He came before the Council on the 27th of January and informed them that Diamond, his patroon, had gone "up Cooper River" on the 26th and was "believed at Hughers Landing." He expected him to be down by Saturday, the twenty-eighth of January. Diamond did not make himself available until the following Friday, the 3rd of February, and his owner called Diamond "a great Rogue." Perhaps James Akin himself had concluded that boatmen were more trouble than they were worth, since he ordered the executors of his will to "Sell all my Cannoes and not to keep any one Canoe at my Estate."[36]

If opportunities for mobility were afforded field slaves as well as boatmen, what sort of relationships did they form as a result? Slaves visited their relations: Joe visited his brother Ammon; Scipio, belonging to Dr. Bruce, was seen with his brother Jack, belonging to Mrs. Naylor; Mr. Drake's Tony took a wife who belonged to Mr. Nesbitt and who had formerly been the wife of James Akin's George. Much mobility had a recreational purpose: Quash's Guy mentioned that so many Negroes had gathered at Irish-Town because "Mr. Wrights Tom being a Fiddler he and the rest met there to play and dance,"

35. *SCG.* April 3, 1762, several of the inhabitants of the parish of St. Thomas. The information concerning skilled slaves found in inventories, and skilled runaways found in newspaper advertisements, is taken from Morgan "The Development of Slave Culture," 102-104. Some of the residents of St. Thomas' parish were personally familiar with this aspect of boatman behavior. Dr. William Bruce, for example, advertised for one of his slaves, an Angolan, who wore a "sailor's oznabrug frock," had previously been harboured by the Boatswain of the *Rose*, and was thought to have "a mind to go to sea," *SCG,* November 26, 1744. Thomas Wright reported three cases of absenteeism from his pettiaugar between 1742 and 1744, *SCG,* March 20, 1742, June 11, 1744, and December 24, 1744.
36. CJ no. 17, 58; will of James Akin, October 22, 1758, Will Book, 1757-1760, 132, SCDAH.

and Ball's Tom mentioned that they "Eat and drank together . . . [and] only played and Laughed."[37] In addition, slaves engaged in trade among themselves. Ammon planted rice "himself in his own time and by his Masters allowance and leave": what could be more natural than that he should then want to sell some of his produce to his brother? Similarly, Ball's Tom gave, as his reason for travelling to Akin's plantation on one occasion, the fact that a man there "owed him some money."[38] And, finally, friendships were forged, acquaintances made and favors tendered: two of Broughton's boatmen knew Vanderdussen's overseer, Pompey, because they "had once saved him from drowning in a Boat coming down to Town with Pease"; and Akin's George remembered Drake's Scipio because he had once given him provisions. The long list of acquaintances cited by some slaves should raise doubts about the stereotyped picture of self-sufficient, self-contained plantations with little or no contact between the residents.[39]

Furthermore, one should not neglect the obvious fact that acquaintances can soon become enemies. The cohesion of the slave community has perhaps been assumed rather than explored by many recent historians: certainly, the evidence, at least for the eighteenth century, is by no means one-sided. Slaves themselves were just as aware as whites of the distinctions to be made between them. Ethnic divisions were obviously more evident in the colonial period: Akin's Susannah,

---

37. CJ no. 17, 98 and 80. Whether Tom, the "Fiddler," was a more acculturated slave than the anonymous "bangio"-player at Vanderdussen's plantation, must remain a mystery. For slave "fiddlers," see Epstein, *Sinful Tunes and Spirituals*, particularly 112-117. Many of the runaways advertised in colonial newspapers were said to be "visiting" and, in many cases, they were visiting relations. See, for example, Mullin, *Flight and Rebellion*, 106-108 and Philip D. Morgan, "Less marrons de la Caroline du sud: luer signification pour la culture des esclaves," *Annales, Économies, Sociétés, Civilisations* (forthcoming). One illustration of this "visiting" is worthy of mention for its concerns some slaves of Andrew Quelch, who lived at Hobcaw and who had two slaves implicated in the conspiracy. He died in 1753 and his slaves were sold in August of that year. Some six weeks after the sale, an advertisement was placed on behalf of Isaac Nicholls of Stono pointing out that a family of slaves (husband, wife and three children), bought from Quelch, had run away and were thought to be about Hobcaw or in Charlestown; a month later, Humphrey Sommers reported that a slave he had bought from Quelch had run off and was thought to "be harboured on Hobcaw Neck"; finally, another week later, Mary Beckerman advertised for Chloe, also formerly belonging to Quelch, who was "supposed to be harboured at Hobcaw Neck." These slaves were presumably mobile enough to build up ties in the locale which were hard to sever. See *SCG*, September 24, 1753, Christopher Gadsen; *ibid.*, October 29, 1753, Humphrey Sommers; *ibid.*, November 5, 1753, Mary Beckerman.
38. CJ no. 17, 160 and 80.
39. *Ibid.*, 71 and 83. Agrippa, for example, named thirty-two slaves belonging to seventeen separate masters.

for example, referred to "a sensible Angola fellow and another ordinary Negro with him."[40] Color and racial origin were not neglected
by slaves: Akin's Robin described "a Tall Mustee with a Gun and
Cutlass, and a lusty Yellow· Fellow at there Meeting."[41] Acculturative differences also divided slaves. Leadership might reside with the
unacculturated but deference had to be shown those familiar with
white ways—such seems to be the implication of Akin's claim that his
slaves had informed him that "many of the Headmen of the Slaves
. . . did consult & agree to Engage as many of the Cleverest Slaves as
they could to provide Provisions to serve them to Runaway. . . ."
However, we have it on authority from one acculturated slave that a
lack of acculturation was not easily forgiven: Drake's Scipio was
overheard telling a fellow waterman that "he Scipio, knew how to go
before Gentlemen, for he had waited before on his Master in the
Council Chamber, and was used to it, but Kent was a Fool and did
not know how to Talk before White People, and if he had not stood
by and Pinched him, he would have told all & blown them."[42] Even
the camaraderie of the boatmen was a fragile bond, it would seem.
Divisions were undoubtedly fostered by whites; and the dominating
and overwhelming fact of oppression must have strained any cohesion
slaves might attain. The lack of cohesion is underlined by Agrippa's
report that the conspirators had allegedly "agreed to Murder all the
Negroes that would not join with them in leaving the Province."
Furthermore, under interrogation, slave might turn on slave: Nisbett's
Somerset informed the Council, no doubt with some bitterness, that

---

40. *Ibid.*, 83. Ethnic animosity amongst Latin American slaves was often remarked
upon by contemporaries. See for example, Frederick P. Bowser, *The African Slave in
Colonial Peru 1524-1650* (Stanford, 1974), 179-183. Obviously, North American slavery
varied a great deal from its Latin American equivalents; but when it is remembered that
approximately two-thirds of the slave population in South Carolina at mid-century were
Africans, then the potential for parallels should not be lightly dismissed. See Morgan,
"The Development of Slave Culture," 301-302. There is fragmentary evidence that
ethnic divisions were important: Alexander Garden, for example, noted that within the
"Whole Body of Slaves" there are "so many various Ages, Nations, Languages,"
Alexander Garden to the Secretary, May 6, 1740, B7, 235, SPG archives. Similarly, an
owner, advertising for an Angolan runaway, pointed out that, "as there is abundance of
Negroes in this Province of that Nation, he may chance to be harbour'd among some of
them," *SCG*, August 13, 1737, Isaac Porcher.
41. CJ no. 17, 66. Reference has already been made to Akin's "two Mustee
Wenches" and Susannah herself implicated a mustee and a "yellow fellow" belonging
to Mr. Warnock, ibid., 65.
42. Ibid., 131 and 98. An SPG missionary noticed that acculturation separated
slaves, for when some were baptised, he reported, "all other slaves do laugh at 'em and
render 'em worse and worse," Rev. James Gignilliat to the secretary, May 28, 1710,
A5, 119, SPG archives. Kent was valued at £240 in the inventory of Thomas
Broughton, February 10, 1752, Inventory Book R (1), 339-342.

"he knew Susanna and all Akins Negroes to be great Lyars . . .";
Susannah had threatened revenge on Thomas Akin's Ammon because
the latter had informed his master of her theft of a sheet.[43] However,
the more significant generalization would be that some of these divisions seem internally generated rather than externally imposed.

* * *

Divisiveness in plantation societies was not, of course, confined
solely to the slave community. White society, especially in the eighteenth century, was neither monolithic nor homogeneous. Gerald
Mullin, for example, has drawn attention to a considerable number of
"ill-disposed" whites who "entertained" blacks in eighteenth century
Virginia. David Brion Davis, in an aside, has put in a plea for the
history of these "independent and irreverent fraternisers" to be
told.[44] Obviously, this cannot be the place to do that. However, at
least by pointing to one graphic illustration of the role lower class
whites could play in a slave community, the potential of such a history should be self-evident. This applies particularly to an example
taken from the South Carolina low country where the conditions were
hardly propitious for such contact, in contrast to Virginia, where a
dispersed slave population and a large white population made fraternization more likely.

One parallel that seems to hold for both colonies concerns white
boatmen who were probably the most "irreverent fraternizers" of all.
Of the sixteen lower class whites who were cited as having contact
with the slaves, at least four were boatmen. Agrippa mentioned that
one or two white men out of Thomas Wright's boat used to come to
his master's plantation to consult with the Negroes; and at another
January meeting there were several whites in sailor's dress, so it was
claimed. The two whites in Wright's boat were later identified: William Followsby was never brought before the Council, but Lawrence

43. CJ no. 17, 48, 150, and 160. For a further discussion of divisions within the
slave community, see Morgan, "The Development of Slave Culture," 385-388. Sir
Alexander Nisbett's Somerset was probably well known throughout the Cooper River
area. In 1754 he was valued at £800—one of the most valuable slaves listed in any
inventory in the early 1750s—in the inventory of Sir Alexander Nisbett, February 26,
1754, Inventory Book R (2), 164-167, SCDAH. An advertisement placed in 1760, testifies to his renown: a young woman named Sue ran away from a plantation near the
Quarter House and, the advertisement continued, as she was "purchased from Sir Alexander Nisbett, deceased, it is apprehended she may be harboured by SOMERSET
her father, or some other of the Negroes at Coatbaw plantation . . . ," SCG, February
9, 1760, James Michie.
44. Mullin, Flight and Rebellion, 112-116; David Brion Davis, The Problem of Slavery in the Age of Revolution 1770-1823 (Ithaca, 1975), 279.

Kelly, an illiterate Irishman who had been in the province fifteen years and came most recently from Pennsylvania, was interrogated. He admitted to being at Akin's plantation on a number of occasions, and he was obviously antagonistic towards Akin who, he claimed, had "ruined him" two or three times previously. According to Akin, Kelly had been seeking an overseer's post and presumably Akin had refused him one. The other boatman interrogated at length by the Council was George Nicholas, the patroon of Mr. Drake's boat. He informed the Council of his recent itinerary and it must have been clear that, through his familiarity with a large number of plantations and the close working conditions with his three slave crew members, he had access to large numbers of slaves.[45]

A certain equality of living standards between these two groups may have fostered feelings of fellowship; but, as is all too clear, this same fact often spurred on the whites to put as much distance between themselves and the slaves as possible. Put another way, hostility towards the Negro served to identify non-slaveholders with the planter class; and proximity of estate allowed for few paternalistic feelings. There was also a more direct reason for hostility, namely, the threat posed by the slaves to those whites' very livelihood. It is significant that in 1744, white patroons complained of "several Planters and others in this Province, who did order, permit and appoint their Negro Slaves to be constantly employed to go as Masters or Patroons of their Pettiaugars or small Vessels without any white Man on board to take any Charge or Care of such Vessels, which hindered the Petitioners from being constantly employed here."[46] Perhaps Kelly was looking for an overseer's position for this very reason. The ambivalence inherent in the lower class white's attitude towards the slave was, it would seem, recognized by the slaves. Kelly's fellowship

---

45. The testimony of Kelly and Nicholas can be found in CJ no. 17, 84-85 and 77 respectively. An intensive search of local records has failed to reveal information concerning Lawrence Kelly or the fourth boatman interviewed by the Council—John Gainer, patroon of Mr. Wragg's boat. However, in October 1749, William Followsby (occasionally spelled Follinsby) bought 1410 acres of land in the parish of St. James Santee from Jonathan Drake (who had nine slaves implicated in the conspiracy, four of which were interrogated), Land Memorials 10: 515-516, SCDAH. George Nicholas is mentioned in a number of land transactions in Berkeley county and Williamsburg township in the 1730s—Charlestown Deeds R: 210, P: 211, R: 77; Land Grants 42: 103 and Z, pt. 1: 253, SCDAH.
46. J. H. Easterby, ed., *Journal of South Carolina Commons House of Assembly, September 14, 1742–January 27, 1744* (Columbia, 1954), 556. No doubt, planters on occasion behaved generously towards nonslaveholders; thus, James Akin released William Followsby, cited as a possible conspirator in this case, from a debt of £277, will of James Akin, October 22, 1758, Will Book, 1757-1760, 132, SCDAH.

with the slaves had certain limits as Robin's testimony makes evident: he "teazed them from time to time to do it, and told them to keep it secret and not to mention it, for if they did he would swear against them, and that a White Mans word would go further than a Negroes."[47] Slaves were probably always aware of the bounds to which interracial fraternization could extend. Indeed, as much hostility may have been directed by slaves towards lower class whites as vice-versa (as Genovese has remarked, it was probably the slaves who coined the term "poor white trash"). Akin's Joe, for example, "at his Death Blamed Simmons, and the other white Men for all he had done, and laid his Death to them . . .''; and Susannah mentioned that "since the affair was talked of, one Donilly had frightened them & told them they had now brought Death upon themselves."[48]

Furthermore, what might be taken for poor white subversion may have been much more self-serving. Surely this is the implication of a reported conversation between Akin's slaves and Kelly. He had told them that "Akin had good Negroes but did not know how to use them, but if he had them He would know better and told them they had better leave him. . . ." Indeed, before the conspiracy even came to light, Abraham Wade had been "committed to Goal by Col. Lejeau upon suspicion of enticing some of Mr. Akins Negroes to run off this Province with him." Akin's Robin testified that Simmons "had often mentioned carrying them away to Mariland, Antigua or to the Spaniards" and when Springer left for Maryland, it was claimed that he tried to engage some of "Quashes Cleverest Slaves" to desert.[49] We can probably assume that this form of instigation to run away was not an act of altruism on the part of lower class whites. Moreover, overseers have often been portrayed as men in the middle with their positions constantly being undermined from both above and from below; but occasionally, they could put this tenuous position to some use. Springer, for example, would insinuate to Akin that his "Principal slaves were very idle and did little or nothing" and, at the same time, tell the slaves that Akin had "been cursing & damning them for very idle fellows."[50]

---

47. CJ no. 17, 65.

48. Genovese, *Roll, Jordan, Roll,* 22; CJ no. 17, 65 and 65.

49. CJ no. 17, 84; ibid., 51; ibid., 65 and 124. One hundred and thirteen colonial South Carolina runaways were advertised as running away with whites: see Morgan, "The Development of Slave Culture," 230. In 1754, James McCrannell, a labourer of St. John's parish, Berkely county, was sentenced to death (later, pardoned) for attempting to make off with three slaves, Records of the Secretary of the Province, June 6, 1754, KK, 20-21, SCDAH.

50. CJ no. 17, 121, See Genovese, *Roll, Jordan, Roll,* 12-22, for a discussion of the

The proximity of estate that engendered much hostility between slave and lower class white could also facilitate the development of mutual sympathies and shared bonds. One such bond was that of trade. Akin's Susannah claimed that "Simmons had promised Joe a Cow, and Kelly had promised him a Barrow to keep all Secret." Kelly himself confirmed that he had fulfilled his promise although, naturally, he put a different construction on the exchange: "being asked whether he gave Joe a Barrow, answered in the affirmative, being asked what he gave it him for, said it was for a Deers Skin and upon no other account. . . . " Akin's George reckoned that "Kelley borrowed a Gun of him and Joe, which he did not bring back to them and when they went for it he bid them set down gave them Rum" and tried to make them run away.[51] In fact, drinking sessions between these two groups—slaves referred to this as being "treated"—were common. Akin informed the Council that his wife had seen Springer "take a bottle of Rum and drink to Some of [his] slaves and they have taken the Bottle from him and pledged him by drinkg and She has known the said Springer to give them Rum many times and that in one forenoon the said Springer in company with Kelley; John Jones & Richard King drank & gave to the Deponents Slaves Two Gallons of Rum." On another occasion, Springer gave Joe a key to a case in Akin's house, sent him to Susannah, Joe's wife, and one of Akin's house servants, so that she could open the case and bring them rum. Dram shops where whites retailed liquor to slaves were a constant complaint of the Charlestown establishment, but clearly liquor was also available to rural slaves.[52] One final example of a shared bond

overseer's position. The most comprehensive treatment of the overseer is to be found in William K. Scarborough, *The Overseer: Plantation Management in the Old South* (Baton Rouge, 1966).

51. CJ no. 17, 64; ibid., 85; ibid., 84. Interracial trading especially between nonslaveholding whites and slaves elicited much comment and no little legislation. For example, hawkers and peddlers proved such a menace that in 1738 a law was passed licensing their activities. The preamble noted they had "travelled from town to town, and from one plantation to another, both by land and water, exposing to sale rum, sugar, and other goods, wares and merchandises, and taken in payment therefor, from negroes and other slaves, hogs, fowls, rice, corn and other produce, to the great prejudice of the planters their masters," Thomas Cooper and David J. McCord, eds., *The Statutes at Large of South Carolina,* 10 vols. (Columbia, 1836-1841), III, 487.

52. CJ no. 17, 122. For references to Charlestown "Dram-Shops," see South Carolina Council Journal, April 29, 1745, SCDAH; *SCG,* June 2, 1766 and *SCG & CJ,* May 17, 1768, Grand Jury Presentments. That liquor was available to rural slaves, see, for example, the Orangeburgh District Grand Jury's complaint against the owners of the "many Small Tippling Houses along the Public Roads" who "often deal clandestinely with Slaves," *SCG,* November 26, 1772, Orangeburgh District Grand Jury Presentments. John Jones seems to have been a resident of Craven county, as a number of

between lower class whites and slaves comes not from the Council investigations but from local records: it is a striking case and can be considered relevant because it concerns one of the slaves of Captain Thomas Broughton, who had both Kent and Scipio interrogated by the Council. Broughton possessed a mulatto slave, Elizabeth, who "by the consent & approbation of the said Thomas Broughton did intermarry with one Henry Clusteny by whom she had Issue one Daughter cux Elizabeth . . . For her good & faithful services, the request of Elizabeth, the desire of her husband, Thomas promised to set her, her daughter, & her future issue free." This, Nathaniel Broughton, Thomas' brother, did after his brother's death. That Clusteny, whom we can probably safely assume to be a lower class white, could marry a slave, is testimony indeed to the mutual sympathies that could arise between these two groups.[53]

If there is evidence of mutual sympathies and bonds, this is, of course, only what the planter class suspected and feared. One basis for the divisions within the white community seems to be evident from this case: transient nonslaveholders—those whose commitment to a locale could be questioned, as presumably was the case with boatmen and newcomers—were the most feared. James Springer apparently arrived in South Carolina in 1747, and left in the spring of the following year. In fact, Springer is reported to have mentioned the initial hostility that he encountered when first arriving in South Carolina: "he had Endeavored to take Lodgings for about three Months . . . but the People of this Country appeared very shy in Lodging of Strangers." Richard Simmons left the parish of St. Thomas and St. Dennis in the summer of 1748. Precipitate departures probably aroused suspicions as presumably did sudden arrivals. Thus, Thomas Russ, a New Englander, who only entered the province on January 4, 1749, and who tried to find employment with James Akin as a shoemaker, found himself put under arrest and interrogated. In the case of others, there was, coincidentally perhaps, a connection

---

land plats were registered by him in the Welsh Tract in the 1740s and 1750s—Land plats 4: 192, 197, 202, 503, and 5: 391. See also Royal Grants 3: 584 and 586 and Charlestown Deeds OO: 312, SCDAH. A number of land transactions are reported for a Richard King in the same county in the mid-1760s—Land Plats 17: 478, Royal Grants 15: 361 and Land Memorials 9: 370, SCDAH.

53. Records of the Secretary of the Province, October 19, 1754, KK, 290-291, SCDAH. The only reference to a Henry Clusteny that we have been able to find, although not resolving the issue of his race, certainly suggests that he was white. In 1738 an advertisement in the newspaper simply noted that a runaway slave had been captured at Mrs. Child's plantation at Strawberry (in the Cooper River area) by "Henry Clastany": *SCG,* October 12, 1738, Charlestown Gaol.

with Williamsburg township, some forty miles from the parish of St. Thomas. John Atholl was, in fact, a resident of the township, although he was a frequent visitor at John McGovan's house in the Cooper River area; Edward Donilly, although apparently a confirmed resident of the parish of St. Thomas, was a son-in-law to John Bordline of Williamsburg; and John Mathews, the weaver, was recommended to James Akin's employ by Mr. Rae, the Presbyterian minister in Williamsburg. Furthermore, in 1750, the year of his death, Mathews had returned to Williamsburg. Whatever the truth of slave allegations about these whites, it is not surprising that suspicions centered on such men.[54]

*   *   *

Despite all the evidence of interracial contact and slave mobility, the Council finally decided that the notion of a well-planned and considered conspiracy, involving both whites and blacks, was without foundation. Indeed, Winthrop Jordan has characterized the Council's investigations as a most "sober and realistic handling of a potentially explosive incident."[55] Certainly, no orgy of hangings concluded the Council's work: the extent of the retribution was to order the transportation of four slaves. However, earlier in the proceedings, the Council had directed that no boat be allowed to pass Fort Johnson on any pretense whatsoever (despite the hardship this caused some planters) and had issued letters to commanders of militia regiments to prevent all slave meetings "and secure all persons suspected of any dangerous designs against the Peace of the Province." Furthermore, early in the investigation, news "of a most horrible Insurrection in tended by the Negroes there which was providentially discover'd before any mischief done" even reached Henry Laurens, who was in London at the time. Moreover, in their concluding remarks, the

---

54. CJ no. 17, 121. The information on Springer, Simmons, Russ, Atholl and Mathews is in part derived from CJ no. 17, 50-125. In addition, see the land grant of 50 acres to John Atholl in Williamsburg township, dated 27 May 1741, Land Grants 42: 51, SCDAH; the will of John Mathews, c1750, Will Book 1740-1760, 130, SCDAH. The Donilly mentioned by Akin's Susannah was probably Edward Donilly. Edward Donilly, Jr. received 200 acres in the parish of St. Thomas from his father in 1733, Land Memorials 2: 121, SCDAH; he was a collector of the parish poor tax in 1751, SCG, August 26, 1751; and he is mentioned in the will of John Bordline of Williamsburg, c1745, Will Book, 1740-1760, 38, SCDAH. Gregory Stiverson kindly searched all the likely Maryland indexes for a James Springer but was unable to find such a name. However, he informed us that Springer is a common Pennsylvania name, especially in the counties bordering Maryland, and one wonders whether Springer originally came from Pennsylvania, like Kelly, and returned there via Maryland.
55. Jordan, *White Over Black*, 122.

Council warned the prominent planters of the area to keep a "strict
Eye over their Slaves" for it was obvious that such a plan was "feasible."[56] Crucial to the Council's assessment of the evidence was undoubtedly the opinion of a number of respectable residents of the parish. From Mr. Stones to Mary Russell, from Dr. William Bruce to
Francis Simmons, the residents of the parish of St. Thomas testified
that they could see no grounds for a conspiracy. In fact, Francis
Simmons, whose barn had burned down in the fall of 1748, admitted
that he did at first "suspect his own Negroes were guilty of setting the
said Barn on fire," but had since changed his mind.[57] In the face of
such calm appraisals of the situation, the Council was no doubt impressed. Conversely, Akin certainly seemed to be suffering from
undue hysteria, especially when he related how in November he took
his gun and toured his plantation, only to notice that he was being
followed by a slave boy. Akin caught the boy who had been "lurking
and Creeping" after him and questioned him as to why he had been
"watching him in so private a manner and gave him a few whips with
a very small Twig." The boy confessed, Akin reported, that his
mother had him spy on Akin to see if he discovered the hiding-place
of some runaways.[58]

A fine line had to be drawn in slave societies, with regard to a
possible slave revolt, between an attitude of realism, even complacency on the one hand, and a justifiable fear bordering on hysteria on
the other. In this particular case, whether the Council's realism can
be attributed solely to the internal inconsistencies in the evidence
presented to them is at least questionable. Other conspiracies, no less
well founded, had resulted in hangings if only to serve as warnings to
potentially rebellious slaves. Jordan's explanation is that such realism
came "easily to a people who were committed beyond recall to slav-

56. CJ no. 17, 69; Philip Hamer and George C. Rogers, eds., *The Papers of Henry Laurens*, 7 vols. (Columbia, 1968-), I, 229; CJ no. 17, 167-168. One interesting sidelight on the intensity with which the Council pursued this investigation is suggested by a claim originally viewed as excessive by the South Carolina lower house, "for Candles for the use of the Council Chamber . . . [which] was occasioned by extraordinary Acci-
dents, viz., the Examination of Mr. Akin &c . . . ," " J. H. Easterby, ed., *Journal of South Carolina Commons House of Assembly, March 28, 1749—March 19, 1750* (Col-
umbia, 1962), 145.
57. CJ no. 17, 119. All these white depositions can be found on ps. 117-119.
58. Ibid., 129-130. Akin himself was told that two slaves belonging to Thomas Rose, a St. James' Goose Creek resident, were part of the runaway band (one of whom, named James, a mustee, had a long beard and was armed). According to Akin, they "had a Hutt in Mr. Nesbitts Cedar Swamp, . . . they had a Cannoe [and] . . . they cut some Pine Poles to set the Cannoe in the Creek . . . ," ibid., 143.

ery as a way of life, and knew it."[59] One might push this line of reasoning further and argue that South Carolinians at mid-century realized that they were committed to a slavery which involved runaways and talk of running away, which involved considerable slave mobility and communal autonomy, and which inevitably brought lower class whites and blacks into close contact. Perhaps it was for this reason that, once the spectre of full-scale rebellion had been ruled out, other rather less troubling issues could be lost from view. For example, at one point, the Council addressed itself to the question that had been "insinuated" to them, namely "that Mr. James Akin has put these stories in the heads of his Negroes, and has at some times terrified them by threats to say so and so, at other times has promised them rewards to induce them to declare these matters," but they did not fully investigate the charge. Nor did they pursue another question they posed for themselves: had Akin "expressed any Enmity or ill will . . . to any of the said Gentlemen" whose slaves were accused?[60] Instead, they simply accepted the testimony of two slaves—George and Tony—that four other slaves belonging to Akin had constructed the whole elaborate story. If this were so, it shows, for example, a rather striking awareness on the part of blacks of the language and argument lower class whites might employ; and it does not even bear on the extent of slave mobility and their fraternization with lower class whites which was independently attested.

At this point, we might wonder whether Jordan's explanation can be totally satisfactory. After all, a commitment to slavery did not always rule out hysteria or necessarily induce realism. It may be that slave conspiracy scares require much more wide-ranging explanations. That they tended to be particularly numerous in the early 1740s and 1790s inevitably raises questions about the role of political and social tensions, economic disorders and religious upheavals, in rendering whites susceptible to another form of disorder—black re-

---

59. Jordan, *White Over Black*, 122. Witness the exemplary hangings carried out in South Carolina in 1740; Aptheker, *American Negro Slave Revolts*, 189-190. Indeed, Governor Glen noted how "happy it was, that it was brought before me, for I think it *certain* that had it come before an Inferior Magestrate, numbers of Innocent persons must have suffered," [our emphasis], CJ no. 17, 166.
60. CJ no. 17, 96. Kelly reported an exchange between himself and James Akin that is difficult to interpret. It may point to the eccentricity of Akin; it may also illustrate the South Carolinians' realization that they were committed to a slavery which involved threats of running away. One of the hands belonging to the boat bringing Kelly (and James Akin) to Charlestown said, according to Kelly, "that they would run away to Augustine, upon which Mr. Akin winked at him [i.e. Kelly], and that he said, they might go and be damned," ibid., 85.

volt. Could it be that this scare of 1749 could be viewed more dispassionately because, for instance, the religious excitement associated with the Great Awakening was subsiding and the economic prospects of the colony looked brighter than the preceding years of recession? Perhaps also a study of the neighborhoods of particular slave scares may prove instructive: could it be that, like witchcraft accusations, slave scares reflect, as much as anything else, tensions between neighbors—a point tentatively glimpsed during the Council investigation in this case? In other words, slave scares may arise as much from tensions within the white community as from conspiratorial designs within that of the blacks.[61]

This frustratingly inconclusive, local incident can be too easily dismissed, especially by those searching for evidence of overt slave resistance. The facts of the case are certainly too ambiguous to permit such a Promethean, such an heroic interpretation. And yet if the existence of the slave conspiracy is denied, one is left pondering upon either the subtle and well-informed stratagems of some of Akin's slaves or the even more surprising alliance of Akin and one of his female slaves. Such myopic musings, however fascinating, will not carry us very far, it may be thought; on the other hand, an indication, however fragmentary, of the range and variety of human relationships possible not only between masters and slaves, but among the enslaved themselves, seems consolation enough. If more were needed, we might refer to our aim to make this small event speak, even if *sotto voce*, to larger issues—issues such as the nature of the slave experience in post-Stono South Carolina, the tortured relations of lower class whites and blacks, and the origins of slave conspiracy scares—in making this, in other words, an attempt to study slavery in microcosm.

---

61. This suggestion can only be regarded as a pointer to much-needed further research. However, see the works cited in Peter H. Wood, " 'I Did the Best I Could for My Day': The Study of Early Black History during the Second Reconstruction, 1960 to 1976," *William and Mary Quarterly*, XXXV (1978), 217-218 and footnote 108. For the role of friction between close neighbors in witchcraft scares, see Alan Macfarlane, *Witchcraft in Tudor and Stuart England* (London, 1970), 168-177; and for friction between more distant neighbors, see Paul Boyer and Stephen Nissenbaum, *Salem Possessed: The Social Origins of Witchcraft* (Cambridge, 1974), 33-36, 92-103 and passim.

The Political Significance of
Slave Resistance
by James Oakes

When W.E.B. DuBois wrote that it was 'the black worker. . . who brought
civil war in America,' historians had yet to undertake the extraordinary
studies of slavery that would eventually transform our understanding of all
American history. Since then, scholars have discovered among the slaves a
pattern of 'day-to-day resistance' which promises to give meaning and
substance to DuBois's characteristically astute observation. Slaves engaged
in a variety of acts designed to ease their burdens and frustrate the masters'
wills. They broke tools, feigned illness, deliberately malingered, 'stole'
food, and manipulated the tensions between master and overseer. When
pressed, the slaves took up more active forms of resistance: they became
'saucy', ran away, struck the overseer or even the master, and on rare
occasions committed arson or joined in organized rebellions. And
throughout the slave community a tradition of solidarity sustained and
justified individual and collective acts of resistance.[1]

What has yet to be demonstrated is the political significance of slave
resistance, and there are several reasons for this. Despite the methodological and theoretical sophistication of the field, the ways in which social
tensions were translated into political issues are still not well understood.
Indeed, few historians have even attempted to trace the connections
between everyday resistance and politics. Many scholars remain fixated on
an artificial separation of morality from expediency in political analysis, as
if 'morality' itself were not grounded in specific historical circumstances.
But perhaps the most serious obstacle to further understanding has been
the systematic disregard for the institutional political context of slavery
and the sectional crisis.

It hardly needs to be said that slaves did not influence American politics with their votes, petitions, speeches, and editorials. Slaves could affect the political system only by intruding themselves into it as outsiders. But this simple observation points up some of the fundamental paradoxes of western slavery — paradoxes that reveal how and under what circumstances slave resistance could become politically significant. That slaves were social 'outsiders' in the Old South is no surprise; on the contrary, it places them squarely within a long tradition in western history extending back at least to Ancient Greece. The degree to which slaves were socially and political outcast varied enormously from one slave society to another, as did the consequences of their status. But their fundamental status as outsiders has been one of the few constants in the history of western slavery. (Moslem and African slavery did not always conform to this pattern, and were distinct in several other ways as well.) To be a slave was to be socially and politically ostracized. This was true no matter how important slave labor was to the political and social system, and regardless of the fact that slaves often claimed an ancient ancestry in the land of their bondage. As M. I. Finely writes: 'In principle the slave is an outsider, a "barbarian", and that sets him apart from all the other forms of involuntary labour known to history.'[2]

For all their variety, therefore, slave societies have consistently tended to produce dehumanizing cultural stereotypes that justified the slaves' exclusion from the social mainstream. In the minds of virtually every master class in history, slaves were somehow different 'by nature,' and often sub-human or animal-like. In a notorious passage in *The Politics*, Aristotle declared that 'a slave is a sort of living piece of property. . . The use made of slaves hardly differs at all from that of tame animals: they both help with their bodies to supply our essential needs. It is nature's purpose therefore to make the bodies of free men to differ from those of slaves. . .'[3]

The American South was no exception. Southern masters went to extraordinary lengths to define the slaves as social outcasts in their very midst. At their disposal in this effort was a powerful cultural construct commonly known as 'race'. A peculiar congeries of prejudices and stereotypes, 'race' eventually became the most important ideological weapon in the struggle to distinguish free Southerners, most of whom traced their ancestry to western Europe, from enslaved Southerners who virtually always traced their origins to sub-saharan Africa. The slaveholders at once inherited, refined, and finally helped transform these prejudices into an ideology of pseudo-scientific racism that served as the primary justification for the enslavement of four million 'outsiders'. In the nineteenth century racism provided an artificial but nonetheless effective cultural barrier between masters and slaves who by that time were speaking the same language and praying to the same God.[4]

In the South, as in the ancient world, there was an underlying political purpose to the racist ideology. Though slavery historians are quite familiar with Aristotle's thinking, few have recognized that the philosopher's assertion of a natural physical distinction between slaves and free men served chiefly to introduce a proposition about the nature of citizenship and the polity. While the bodies of slaves were 'strong enough to be used for necessary tasks,' he argued, the bodies of free men were 'well suited for the life of a citizen of a state, a life which is in turn divided between the requirements of war and peace.' What was true of classical Athens was true of antebellum Mississippi: citizenship and slavery were incompatable. The difference was the specific racial gloss white men gave to their arguments about the basis of American democracy. As one Virginian declared in 1850, 'this Anglo-Saxon race of people in the United States of America are the only people ever formed by the hand of God, that are capable of self-government.' If such remarks were commonplace, that is precisely why they were significant. By defining slaves according to 'race' and simultaneously espousing a 'racial' criterion for political self-government, the slaveholders simply fitted themselves into a long-established western tradition.[5]

The implications of this political tradition have scarcely been appreciated. Because slaves were defined as outsiders, slave societies have been marked by a formal separation of the political institutions from the social structure. Accordingly, the political structures of slave societies have not reflexively mirrored the intrinsic tyranny of the master-slave relationship but have been shaped instead by the institutional inheritance and social relations of the non-slave populations — the 'insiders'. This is why slave societies have flourished in a variety of political formations: the autocracy of the Roman Empire, the royal bureaucracies of Spanish-America, and the representative democracies of Periclean Athens and the Old South. One of the few political systems with which slavery was generally incompatible was feudalism, and the reasons for this are instructive. In medieval Europe, the social and political hierarchies were fused into a single structure, and the prevailing ideology reflected that fusion. In theory, seigneurialism incorporated the lowliest serf into an explicitly hierarchical but 'organically' unified society. By contrast, slaves were culturally and politically ostra.ised, and slavery was formally separated from the political structures. Thus the famous paradox of 'slavery and freedom' rested less on what slavery did to the political structure than on what it did not do.[6]

This does not mean that slavery had no effect on politics. On the contrary, the formal separation of slavery from the polity was simply the institutional context for the actual relationship between politics and society in the Old South. But that context was critical, for it defined the points at which slave resistance was likely to intrude into politics and the specific mechanisms through which the larger society reacted to those intrusions. In short, the relationship between slavery and the institutional political arrangements determined the limits as well as the potential consequences of slave resistance.

Any analysis of the political significnace of slave resistance in the United States must therefore begin from the recognition that the political structures within which slavery was embedded were not determined by slavery itself. Rather, 'slave law' in the United States was but one part of a much larger and more powerful body of Anglo-American law. As a legal entity, the master-slave relationship was defined by slave codes passed in representative legislatures, protected by state constitutions, and interpreted by local and national judiciaries. Yet not one of those political structures was determined by or dependent upon slavery. Quite the reverse: the slaveholders' legal survival depended on political institutions that slavery did not create, and in the end this put the master class at a fatal disadvantage.[7]

The slaveholders' domination of the liberal political institutions of the Old South had the paradoxical effect of legitimizing the very political structures that would ultimately be used to destroy slavery. Rather than repudiate the principle of 'checks and balances', the tradition of mass-based representative government, or the concept of judicial review, the slaveholders clung to them as the source of their political authority. *Within* the liberal structures, slaveholders assumed different tactical positions on such issues as property qualifications or legislative reapportionment. But when the political system which had long preserved their power instead became a threat to their power, no one seriously considered the establishment of a titled nobility or the reintroduction of primogeniture and entail, much less the abolition of representative assemblies. Thus, having exercised its authority through the liberal polity, the Old South's ruling class was forced to endure the fatal consequences of the contradiction between slavery and freedom.

Where slave law began from the premise that the slave had no political, civil, or legal rights whatsoever, Anglo-American law began from the premise that certain basic rights were universal and inalienable. The totality of the master-slave relationship notwithstanding, some slaves would always engage in acts of resistance that were beyond the master's control, and often beyond the master's purview. When that happened – when slaves disturbed the lives of the 'insiders' – they found themselves in a political universe whose assumptions were antithetical to those of slavery. At that point slave resistance began to influence American politics.

It should not be assumed that the 'conflict of laws' was entirely sectional in nature. Even within the southern states slave resistance pushed beyond the boundaries of the master-slave relationship and created troublesome legal problems for slaveholders, lawmakers, and judges. By the late antebellum decades, for example, every southern state had outlawed the murder of an unresisting slave. But the enforcement of such laws inevitably raised excruciating questions: Who would determine whether a slave was or was not resisting? If slaves were the only witnesses, as was often the case, could they testify against their master or any other white man? If murder was illegal, did slaves have any rights of self-defense? And how were such questions to be decided when a free man other than the master was one of the parties to a dispute? Slave law alone had no answers to such questions. And so in such cases the determination was made in courts whose rules of procedure rested on principles that were antagonistic to the very nature of slavery: the right to trial by jury of one's peers, the right of self-defense, the right to swear on oath, to bear witness, or to face one's accusers. At the very least, this represented a theoretical threat to the master's authority. Over time, acts of resistance that brought slaves into southern courts began to transform a theoretical possibility into a legal reality.[8]

In most cases, however, the relationship between politics and slave resistance was less straightforward, though no less significant. Consider the politically explosive issue of slavery's expansionism. To what extent was the dramatic westward movement of the slave economy spurred on by the economic consequences of unmotivated and resistant slave labor, or by the need for borders that denied a safe haven to fugitive slaves? Viewed from this perspective, many of the central events of nineteenth-century American history — the Seminole War, the annexation of Florida, the Mexican War, and ultimately the Civil War itself — cannot be fully understood without reference to slave resistance. Yet because slaves influenced the polity indirectly, as outsiders, the debate over slavery rarely centered on slave resistance as such. Instead, most Northerners focused their rhetorical gaze on the most visible consequences of slave resistance: the South's relative economic underdevelopment (which many abolitionists interpreted as the product of resentful labor) and slavery's dangerously expansionistic tendencies. But it does not follow that slavery itself, and the resistance that was part of it, were not the 'real' issue. The question was how and where slavery and slave resistance intruded, given the specific relationship between slavery and the polity that had developed in the United States.

Once we recognize that the political influence of slave resistance was manifested indirectly and through the specific governmental institutions of nineteenth-century America, we can begin to appreciate the slaves' capacity to slowly undermine the essential political component of the masters' authority. To examine this pattern in a preliminary way, the remainder of this essay is deliberately confined to a single subject: fugitive slaves and their impact on the sectional crisis. As slave resistance went, running away was a modest but consequential act. Its political significance could be direct — as in the fugitive slave crisis — or indirect, as when abolitionists used escapes for propoganda purposes. And in some contexts, as we shall see, the political significance of running away could reach revolutionary proportions. The larger point, however, is that slave resistance contributed in substantive ways to the crisis that severed the United States and eventually brought slavery to an end in America.

* * *

Resistance was essential to abolitionist propaganda, even though the slaves themselves were often far removed from the immediate circumstances. Thus Theodore Dwight Weld's famous anti-slavery tract, *American Slavery as it Is*, could hardly have been written had the slaves been a compliant and tractable workforce. Weld's polemical effe₁ t was achieved by his documentary style: a deceptively straightforward litany of fugitive slave advertisements, many of them gruesome in the details of physical abuse and mutilation. Since slaveholders were not a particularly barbaric people, it is safe to assume that the brutality Weld exposed was less a function of sadistic masters than of resisting slaves. Nor was Weld's polemical effect diminished by arguments that his evidence was selective. The point is that he could never have made his selections had there been no fugitive slaves with their identifying scars.[9]

Propagandists used slave resistance in more subtle ways to make their political points. One need not have been an abolitionist to sympathize with Harriet Beecher Stowe's Eliza as she crossed the perilously icy waters of the Ohio River in a desperate effort to keep her child from being sold away. Yet how many readers who held their breath until Eliza's escape was secure could temper their sympathies with the knowledge that in crossing that river Eliza was committing a crime for which she could legally be killed, or that those who assisted the slave mother in her effort to save her child were liable to federal prosecution under the terms of the Fugitive Slave Act of 1850? Stowe's genius lay precisely in her ability to evoke a sympathetic response to criminal acts of resistance.[10]

Stowe's point was made all the more effective by the fact that Eliza was clearly not a habitually rebellious slave, that she was motivated by no overpowering desire for freedom nor by a festering hatred of her master. Instead, Stowe demonstrated that the master-slave relationship inescapably pitted Eliza against her owner in spite of the warm feelings each had for the other. Eliza's motives did not change the fact that her behaviour directly thwarted her master's will, violated state and federal law, and still won the sympathies of hundreds of thousands of Northern readers. When Abraham Lincoln greeted Stowe as 'the little lady who made this big war,' he might just as easily have blamed the Civil War on the author's sympathetic character, the slave Eliza.

Clearly the abolitionists were quintessential pragmatists in the use they made of slave resistance, and this alone should give historians pause before they distinguish the 'moral' from the 'pragmatic' arguments against slavery. All moral crusades, including abolitionism, are grounded in the specific social and political conflicts that define an entire society. Slave resistance exposed those conflicts, and the abolitionists' crusade played on them constantly. At the same time arguments that were ostensibly based on 'expediency' were inescapably moral in their assumptions. To attack the South for its economic backwardness or its undue political influence was to assume a moral preference for a society in which labor was free and in which slaveholders, as slaveholders, had little or no political clout. As the political influence of slave resistance became more consequential, the North/South conflict showed up in public discourse in a variety of forms: as materialistic defenses of Northern economic superiority, as moralistic attacks on Southern sinfulness, and even as racist fears of the spread of black slaves. But in an important sense such distinctions are largely moot. For to define the sectional conflict by its rhetorical manifestations is to miss the fundamental social tensions that provoked the rhetoric to begin with.

Runaways themselves contributed immeasurably to the propaganda war throughout the decades that preceded secession. Fugitive slave narratives are well known − and sometimes criticized − for their formulaic quality: the slave too often seethes under the weight of his or her oppression. Gradually, the slave's determination to be free becomes all consuming. There are unsuccessful escapes, but recapture only strengthens the determination. And finally, often unexpectedly, an opportunity arises, and the dramatic climax is reached. The slave escapes and, once secure, works tirelessly to advance the cause of freedom for all slaves − beginning with a published autobiography. Such narratives were indeed formulaic, which is precisely why they were so effective. By pressing the issue in the most categorical terms of slavery and freedom, runaways helped transform the simple act of escape into a politically explosive fugitive slave controversy.[11]

But even if their exploitation of slave resistance made more enemies than friends for the abolitionists, some kind of fugitive slave crisis would have been difficult to avoid. At the heart of the controversy rested a 'conflict of laws' that could have political significance only if slaves actually ran away. Where northern law presumed that black people were free and so granted them certain basic civil rights, southern law presumed them slaves. To protect northern free blacks from kidnapping by fugitive slave catchers, northern states established legal procedures for determining whether or not a slaveholders' claim of ownership was valid. These 'Personal Liberty Laws' necessarily extended the presumption of freedom to fugitive slaves, flatly contradicting southern law. They thereby created a potential for sectional conflict every time a slave set foot on northern soil. Nor could such conflicts be confined to relations between individual states, for the United States Constitution and the Fugitive Slave Act of 1793 together guaranteed slaveholders the right of 'recaption'.[12]

So long as no slave ever set foot in a free state, this conflict of laws was a matter of mere theoretical interest. Indeed, the Personal Liberty Laws posed no direct threat to slavery, for while they may have discouraged some masters from claiming their runaways, the laws never prevented a single fugitive slave from being returned to the South once a master's claim was validated. By the 1850s runaways had become a major source of sectional antagonism *solely* because of the political conflict they both exposed and provoked. Far more directly than abolitionist propaganda, fugitive slaves forced both the North and South into ever hardening defenses of their conflicting social structures.[13]

The North's extension of the Somerset principle posed a more direct threat to slavery than did the legal protection of fugitives. As originally enunciated in England by Lord Mansfield :n 1772, the Somerset principle extended to slaves certain protections against arbitrary seizure by masters. But as interpreted by many contemporaries, the Somerset principle held that in the absence of positive laws establishing slavery, all persons standing on English – and perhaps American – soil were presumed to be free. Massachusetts jurists invoked this interpretation of the principle a few years after it was declared, and it was subsequently adopted by other northern states as sectional tensions increased. The Somerset principle held out the prospect of freedom to anyone who set foot in the North, including slaves who were merely in transit with their owncrs. By contrast, the Personal Liberty Laws simply established procedures regulating the capture of fugitive slaves, but they could do little more than delay the eventual return of runaways. Like the Personal Liberty Laws, however, the Somerset principle was more significant for its political consequences than for the number of slaves it could possibly free. When Dred and Harriet Scott rested their famed lawsuit on the claim that they had once resided on free soil with their master, the political threat proved far more consequential than the prospect of two slaves being emancipated. Yet for all the outrage that the Supreme Court's decision provoked in the North, Chief Justice Taney's opinion rested on a fairly straightforward assertion of Aristotelian principles: black people were slaves by nature and as such could not be citizens.[14]

Dred Scott's case was only one of a climactic series of incidents that had politicized the issue of slavery to the point where sectional animosities gave way to Civil War. And in many of those cases the precipitating action was taken by slaves who claimed their freedom, sometimes without militant intentions. Margaret Morgan simply assumed her freedom to move from Maryland to York County, Pennsylvania. This put her putative owners in a precarious legal position after they recaptured the slave and returned her to the South. For in so doing they violated Pennsylvania laws against kidnapping and found themselves tied up in a lawsuit that went all the way to the Supreme Court. And while the captors won their case in *Prigg v. Pennsylvania*, the precedent they established subsequently proved more useful to abolitionists than to slaveholders. By contrast, George Latimer ran away claiming a former master had promised him freedom but with full knowledge that his claim was in dispute. Regardless of his motives, however, the controversy generated by Latimer's escape led directly to the passage of the Massachusetts Personal Liberty Law of 1843.[15]

As numerous historians have argued, the consequences of slave resistance intensified whenever the divisions in white society were most severe. But the lines of influence ran in two directions. Political controversy gave heightened significance to slave resistance, but slave resistance often generated political controversy to begin with. There may be no way to tell whether the insurrection panics of the 1850s were based on a rising level of slave resistance or a rising tide of white paranoia. But we can say with certainty that as the conflict between North and South intensified, acts of slave resistance had increasingly disruptive effects. This was also true within the South, where the class conflict between slaveholders and nonslaveholders was always subtly but powerfully influenced by the pervasive fear of servile insurrection. Simply keeping the slaves outside the polity entailed strenuous efforts to maintain the unity of those on the inside. In practical terms, this meant that slaveholders were repeatedly forced to accede to the non-slaveholders' demands for democratic reform. And on more than a few occasions, reformers explicitly invoked the spectre of servile insurrection to press their cause. When class tensions reached new heights in the 1850s, so did the fear of slave revolt. And where political tensions gave way to armed conflict, as they did during the War for Independence and the Civil War, there was a very real upsurge of resistance. This pattern of slaves taking advantage of disunity among whites constitutes one of the most important themes in the history of slave resistance.

Perhaps even more important, though certainly less appreciated, was the subtle but powerful way in which slave resistance redefined the issues in the sectional crisis. The racism of white Northerners and their widespread animosity toward abolitionists are well established. But slaves who ran away or sued for freedom did not compel Northerners to repudiate their racism, to support abolition, or even to interfere in the Southern slave system. Rather, such cases required Northerners to decide whether they were willing to jeopardize their own liberties by re-enslaving those who claimed their freedom without observing the minimal rights of due process. Many Northerners who were perfectly prepared to defend the masters' right to own slaves were increasingly unprepared to let the slaveholders exercise their privileges as masters at the expense of northern liberties and safeguards.

This is not to say that acts of resistance were the precipitating cause of every major controversy in the sectional crisis. It is to say that slave resistance played a powerful role in shaping the general climate in which such controversies took place. Over the long run the political consequences of slave resistance were cumulative, and they were greatest during the Civil War itself.

All of the generalizations drawn from the discussion of the prewar significance of slave resistance were confirmed by the wartime experience. Once again, acts of resistance mattered more than individual motives. The significance of those acts was derived in large measure from the intensity of the divisions in white society, and those divisions were in turn intensified by the acts themselves. And more clearly than ever, the most significant political consequence of slave resistance was that it shifted the terms of the debate in a way that ultimately served the interests of the slaves over their masters.

And yet the situation after 1860 was without precedent. White society in the South was only tenuously united in defense of the Confederacy, while northern and southern whites had literally come to arms. Wars of this sort make for strange bedfellows, and a significant number of slaves appear to have understood this situation from the start. With so many hostile groups vying for supremacy, a tacit coalition formed between the Union Army, the Lincoln administration, and the slaves. No one ever signed a treaty or announced a pact. But within months of Lincoln's inauguration, almost as soon as the fighting began, slave resistance was forcing the North to establish a policy to deal with the 'problem' of fugitive slaves. And as that policy developed, always pushed along by further evidence of the slaves' willingness to resist, the Lincoln administration backed into a pro-emancipation stance.

'I have no purpose, directly or indirectly, to interfere with slavery in the states where it exists,' Lincoln insisted in his inaugural address in the spring of 1861. 'I believe I have no lawful right to do so, and I have no inclination to do so.' Yet within two years Lincoln issued his famous Emancipation Proclamation, and at the time of his death two years later Lincoln was lobbying for the thirteenth amendment abolishing slavery. It is important to understand that Abraham Lincoln was prepared to back into this position. His roots in the Republican Party and his often-stated conviction that slavery was a political, economic, and moral evil made him more responsive than most Democrats and many Republicans to the pressure to adopt a pro-emancipation policy. But Lincoln was quite sincere in his inaugural address. All the evidence suggests that when he assumed the presidency Lincoln really had no intention of advocating emancipation. What caused him to change his mind?[16]

Clearly there were pressures emanating from within the North, particularly from the abolitionists whose moral stock rose to record levels after the South seceded. And there was concern about which way Europe would go if the North could produce no better justification for its crusade than the sanctity of the Union. But the most direct and irresistable pressure came from the slaves who behaved pretty much as they always had. They ran away. Only now the circumstances were different and so the consequences were different also. Indeed, if running away had significant political consequences before the Civil War, it would not be exaggerating to say that during the war escapes took on revolutionary significance. The slaves did not organize guerrilla bands, slink into the homes of their former masters and slit their throats. They formed no 'Sons of Liberty'; no revolutionary cells. But if slave resistance contributed in important ways to emancipation — as the evidence suggests it did — and if emancipation was a revolutionary transformation — as it clearly was — then slave resistance, under the conditions of Civil War, had not only political but revolutionary significance.

Not every slave struck out for freedom. Some actually protected their masters in wartime. But such behaviour is common to revolutionary situations. Neither the Loyalists in the War for Independence, the white Russians during the Bolshevik Revolution, nor the Nationalists of the Chinese Revolution, diminish the reality of those revolutions any more than did faithful slaves diminish the consequences of resistance. When the war was over the faithful slaves were free along with all the others. Clearly, enough slaves had acted so that by 1865 a war that Confederates fought to save slavery and that the North entered only to preserve the Union nevertheless ended with emancipation.

This was in many ways the logical outcome of 'day-to-day resistance', for it was accomplished in large part by thousands of small acts of defiance whose cumulative consequences were immense. From the moment the secession crisis erupted, slaves across the South began to 'talk' of their freedom and showed extraordinary interest in the course of the war. House servants listened in on white conversations and reported the news to field hands in the slave quarters. Slaves hid under beds listening to whites read newspapers aloud; they climbed trees to overhear dinner party conversations. One illiterate slave memorized the letters her master spelled out in her presence hoping she would not understand, but she later had the letters translated in the quarters. Every neighbourhood had one or two literate slaves who got hold of a newspaper to spread reports of the war effort along what slaves called the 'grapevine telegraph'.[17]

Early on southern whites learned that the approach of the Union Army meant more than occupation or physical devastation. As Union troops moved through the South, tens of thousands of slaves left their farms and plantations — long before there was any emancipation policy. Runaways were rarely organized and were therefore difficult to control. Slaves often knew the swamps and forests better than their owners, and so defections were both unpredictable and often impossible to stop.[18]

As early as May of 1861, within weeks of Lincoln's inauguration, the problem of runaway slaves was already occupying the attention of Union commanders. From eastern Virginia, General Benjamin Butler wrote his superiors on May 27 that 'the question in regard to slave property is becoming one of very serious magnitude.' Slaves were running to Butler's encampments from Confederate lines, and they were arriving in whole families. Since the Confederates were using slaves to fortify their own positions, Butler obviously could not send the fugitives back. 'As a military question it would seem to be a measure of necessity' to deprive 'the masters of their services', Butler explained. Would it not be better to put willing slaves to work for the Union Army? But this posed another dilemma. 'As a political question and a question of humanity, can I receive the services of a father and a mother and not take the children?' Thus within weeks of the war's outbreak slaves running to Union lines had presented the military with an unprecedented choice: either send able-bodied men and women back to the enemy, or make a conscious decision to harbor fugitive slaves. What would have been unconstitutional six months earlier had already become what Butler labelled a 'measure of necessity.'[19]

By midsummer of the first year of war, when the problem of fugitives was already overwhelming, the United States Congress responded to the Confederacy's use of slave labor by enacting the first Confiscation Act. In it, the Congress declared that any master who allowed the use of his slave property to support the Confederacy would forfeit the right to that property. By itself, however, the Confiscation Act had a paradoxical quality that would later provoke criticism of the Emancipation Proclamation: Since the Act applied only to those areas under Confederate control, the Union was in no position to enforce it.[20] Nevertheless, the law's revolutionary implications outraged its opponents. 'Are we in a condition now', Senator John J. Crittenden asked, 'to hazard this momentous, irritating, agitating, revolutionary question?' What gave the Confiscation Act its 'revolutionary' character was the fact that, implicitly but inescapably, it depended for its effect on the actions of the slaves themselves. Most of the slaves actually freed by its provisions were those who ran away.[21]

This had become clear only a few days before Congress passed the law. By late July thousands of slaves had fled to Union lines, and Butler — who had declared in May that fugitives should be held as 'contrabands' of war — was now compelled to apply his decision to huge numbers of runaways. But drawing the line at fugitives who had worked on Confederate defenses was impractical, Butler pointed out. That would not solve the problem of what to do about women and children. Moreover, all fugitives by definition had deprived the masters of at least some of the subsistence necessary to sustain their rebellion. Butler would therefore draw a wider net: 'In a loyal state I would put down a servile insurrection', he said. 'In a state of rebellion I would confiscate that which was used to oppose my arms'. With those words Butler made it clear why men such as Crittenden saw the Confiscation Act as intrinsically revolutionary. For a policy of 'confiscation' was close to what Butler implied it was: the refusal to suppress a servile insurrection.[22]

This far the Lincoln administration was still unwilling to go. The property rights of loyal masters had to be protected, wrote Simon Cameron, Lincoln's Secretary of War. But because it was logistically impossible and militarily undesirable to return any fugitives, Cameron instructed Butler to keep a careful record so that '(a)fter tranquility shall have been restored,' Congress could provide 'a just compensation to loyal masters'. Lincoln's own qualms surfaced a few weeks later. On August 30, 1861, General John C. Fremont declared martial law in the area around St. Louis, Missouri, and included in his order a provision that the slaves of rebel masters 'are hereby declared free men'. Lincoln insisted that this provision went well beyond the language and intent of the Confiscation Act, and he required the general to modify his order accordingly. Lincoln subsequently fired Secretary of War Cameron for, among other things, circulating in December, 1861, a proposal to emancipate and arm the slaves. The following May another Union commander in lowcountry South Carolina, General David Hunter, began issuing certificates of freedom to the thousands of fugitive slaves who were fleeing into Union held territories. Once again President Lincoln countermanded the order.[23]

Determined to press further than the President, Congress again took the initiative in early 1862. After a bitter debate the legislators passed a law abolishing slavery in the District of Columbia. Lincoln made no secret of his misgivings about the law, and only after intense pressure from northern blacks did he finally sign it. The slaves in surrounding Maryland had far fewer qualms; they immediately abandoned their owners in huge numbers, flocking into Washington, D.C., to gain their freedom.[24]

Responding to the willingness of thousands of slave to run for freedom if given the opportunity, and to Lincoln's repeated frustration of the actions of Union officers, Congress enacted a second Confiscation Act in July, 1862. In effect, the statute resolved the fugitive slave problem along the lines established by Generals Fremont and Hunter by promising freedom to all slaves held by rebel masters.[25]

Thus, well before the preliminary Emancipation Proclamation was issued, runaway slaves had created political crises for whites in both the North and South. Once behind Union lines the slaves' mere presence edged the Union closer toward an emancipation policy. The fact that so many fugitives were already separated from their masters and were under the purview of the Union Army meant that Northerners had to decide not whether to free the southern slaves but what to do with those who had already escaped. The choice was no longer emancipation or not, but re-enslavement or not. For Northerners, these were two very different issues, reminiscent of the situation in the 1850's when whites who were unprepared to interfere with slavery were nevertheless unwilling to allow slave catchers to interfere with northern civil rights laws. Ten years later slave runaways pushed the North toward an emancipationist policy by once again changing the terms of the debate. If most whites were unprepared to accept a general emancipation, neither were they prepared to re-enslave fugitives, especially those who labored for Union victory. Thus a bill passed by Congress on the same day as the second Confiscation Act promised freedom to slaves who served in the militia, as well as to their wives and children. By actively pursuing their own freedom, slaves made it easier for northern whites to support such policies.

Lincoln acknowledged all of this in strikingly explicit language. Having signed the second Confiscation Act, Lincoln returned it to Congress along with reservations he had put in writing before the bill's passage. He argued that while Congress had no legal right to emancipate slaves, it did have the right to transfer ownership of the slaves to the federal government. At that point, Lincoln noted, 'the question for Congress in regard to them is, "shall they be made free or sold to new masters?"' But having forced that question onto Congress, the 'forfeited slaves' also limited the answers available to the government. 'Indeed', Lincoln added, 'I do not believe it will be physically possible for the General Government to return persons so circumstanced to actual slavery. I believe there would be physical resistance to it which could neither be turned aside by argument nor driven away by force.'[26]

Southern whites were no less aware of the problems created by runaway slaves. They understood that the mobilization of a huge proportion of whites in the military was possible only because black slaves were doing the work at home. Thus runaways clearly threatened the Confederate war effort. To halt the flight of slaves, the Confederate government exempted from the draft one able-bodied male on all plantations with twenty slaves or more, so long as they hired a replacement draftee. But the cure proved worse than the disease. For while it did little or nothing to halt the flood of fugitives and refugees, it provoked enormous resentment among southern whites, many of whom saw the planters' exemption as class bias pure and simple. Thus the problem of slave resistance further weakened the Confederacy by reinforcing the resentment of slaveless whites.[27]

Lincoln finally accepted the military necessity of emancipation once he recognized that tens of thousands of fugitives could simultaneously strengthen the Northern war effort and weaken the Confederacy internally. Yet even Lincoln's final Emancipation Proclamation of 1 January, 1863, depended on the slaves for its full effect. The Proclamation has been criticized by historians, as it was by contemporaries, for freeing only those slaves who were beyond the control of the Union Army. Indeed, Lincoln was attacked for tacitly rewarding loyal masters by allowing them to keep their slaves.

But this criticism hardly diminishes the Proclamation's importance. At the point it was issued it must have been clear to everyone that fugitives *would* give the proclamation real meaning by running to Union lines, or that slaves would enthusiastically accept their freedom as the Union Army advanced through the South. When the British made a similar offer to slaves in the South during the American Revolution, King George III was roundly assailed – even by Thomas Jefferson in the Declaration of Independence – for having 'excited domestic insurrections against us'.

While no one in the Lincoln administration was prepared to say as much, the Emancipation Proclamation did almost exactly the same thing.[28]

Indeed, Frederick Douglass's memoirs suggest that Lincoln fully understood that the force of the Emancipation Proclamation rested on its ability to encourage the massive desertion of the slaves. In a meeting with Douglass shortly after the Proclamation was issued, Lincoln inquired 'as to the means most desirable to be employed outside the army to induce the slaves in the rebel states to come within the federal lines'. The spectacle of an American president encouraging domestic insurrection is sufficiently rare to justify extended quotation from Douglass's account of the event:[29]

> The increasing opposition to the war, in the North, and the mad cry against it, because it was being made an abolition war, alarmed Mr. Lincoln, and made him apprehensive that a peace might be forced upon him which would leave still in slavery all who had not come within our lines. What he wanted was to make the proclamation as effective as possible in the event of such a peace. He said, in a regretful tone, 'The slaves are not coming so rapidly and so numerously to us as I had hoped.' I replied that the slaveholders knew how to keep such things from their slaves, and probably very few knew of his proclamation. 'Well', he said, 'I want you to set about devising some means of making them acquainted with it, and for bringing them into our lines.'

Eventually, large numbers of slaves did learn of the Proclamation and did use it as a pretext for claiming their freedom, regardless of its geographic limitations. Even in areas exempted by the document slaves took advantage of the presence of the Union Army and simply assumed their freedom on the day the proclamation was issued. Despite the fact that Norfolk, Virginia, was exempted, for example, 4,000 slaves celebrated their freedom with a parade and a festival when the Proclamation was issued. Much the same thing happened in New Orleans, which was also under Union control and as such technically untouched by the Proclamation. In lowcountry South Carolina thousands of contrabands had lived as if free ever since General Hunter had acted two years earlier, despite Lincoln's revocation of the general's order. With the Proclamation, they celebrated what they interpreted as official recognition of their status as free people.[30]

In countless areas outside Union control slaves got word of the Proclamation and assumed their freedom as soon as it was safe to do so. More and more slaves ran to Union lines as soon as the Army approached. Slaveholders reported widespread insolence and intransigence among their slaves. As historian Bell Wiley concluded, 'disorder and unfaithfulness on the part of the Negroes were far more common than post-war commentators have usually admitted.'[31]

From disorder and running away, slave resistance escalated into organized and disciplined attacks on the Confederacy under the auspices of the Union Army. Northerners initially resisted the idea of black troops, and white Southerners were naturally horrified by it. But many blacks were clearly anxious to fight, and pressured for the right to do so. Northern acquiscence required no diminution of white racism. On the contrary, blacks who wanted to fight actually benefitted from the argument that black soldiers might as well replace white ones. And the miserable conditions fugitives sometimes experienced in contraband camps only enhanced the determination of many slaves to 'oin the Union Army. And join they did, for while the Emancipation Proclamation finally allowed blacks to enlist, they were never drafted. Within a year 50,000 blacks had served and by war's end 179,000 had enlisted, nearly three-fourths of them from the South. They made up nine percent of the Union Army. Another 9,000 blacks enlisted in the Union navy.[32]

With the enlistment of freed slaves into the Union Army the line between resistance and revolution all but faded into irrelevance. We may never know how many slaveholders died, directly or indirectly, because of the 134,111 southern blacks who put on blue uniforms and joined the war against their former masters. If black troops were too often relegated to garrison duty, how many white troops were thereby freed for battle service? One thing is clear: the combined effects of fugitive slaves and black troops proved devastating to the slaveholders' cause. Numbers alone suggest the dimensions of the upheaval. Rough estimates put the proportion of slaves liberated by the war – either by running away or by assuming their freedom with the arrival or the Union Army – at twenty percent, or between 800,000 and 900,000 blacks. Yet when historians tabulate their balance sheets comparing the relative strengths and weaknesses of the Union and the Confederacy, they rarely consider this internal collapse of the southern social structure. The most intense resistance to the war effort in the North did not begin to match the social revolution that was destroying the Confederacy from within: yeomen deserted in increasing numbers as the war dragged on; the slaveholders themselves resisted the sacrifices demanded by their wartime governments; and when 'the moment of truth' arrived the slaves reduced to bitter ashes every prewar declaration of their unswerving loyalty.

But sheer numbers do not establish the significance of slave resistance, nor do they account for the slaves' success. Two important circumstances contributed to the outcome. First, the intrinsic contradictions between the law of slavery and the law of freedom gave the slaves an exploitable opportunity that might not have existed in a different political system. In a theoretically perfect slave society, there was no law beyond the master's whip. But the slaves were human beings, no matter what the law said, and this alone precluded the possibility that a 'perfect' society based on chattel slavery could ever exist. Every time an act of human resistance brought a piece of property before the law, the anomaly of slavery in a free society was exposed. Repeated exposure, even in small doses, weakened the system until legal contradiction gave way to military conflict.

Second, no law of history required the North to assume the pro-emancipationist stance it finally adopted. When Roman bondsmen took advantage of civil war during the last years of the Republic, Augustus suppressed the rebellion by crucifying 6,000 slaves and putting 20,000 more to work in his own navy. In addition, as he later boasted, 'I captured about 30,000 slaves who had escaped from their masters and taken up arms against the republic, and I handed them over to their masters for punishment.' Clearly it matters that the Republican Party would not do the same thing after 1861, just as it matters that the Lincoln administration acted as it did in response to the problem of fugitive slaves. The 'alliance' between the Union forces and the slaves may have been tacit and the circumstances unique, but the pattern was by no means historically anomalous. The American revolutionaries had once taken advantage of indispensible French support and the Bolsheviks would later take advantage of the immense disruption of the Great War. So too did the slaves take advantage of the crisis of the Union, a crisis they had helped provoke. In so doing they demonstrated the political significance of their long and courageous tradition of day-to-day resistance.[33]

NOTES

For their comments and suggestions, I would like to thank Deborah Bohr, Paul Finkelman, Anthony Grafton, William Jordan, Stanley Katz, Louis Masur, James McPherson, Reid Mitchell, Kenneth Stampp, Lawrence Stone, and Sean Wilentz.

1   W. E. Burghardt DuBois, *Black Reconstruction in America*, New York, 1935, p. 15.
The literature on slave resistance is immense, but among the most important studies are: Raymond A. Bauer and Alice H. Bauer, 'Day to Day Resistance to Slavery', *Journal of Negro History* 27, 1942, pp. 388–419; Herbert Aptheker, *American Negro Slave Revolts*, New York, 1943; Kenneth M. Stampp, *The Peculiar Institution: Slavery in the Ante-Bellum South*, New York, 1956; Sterling Stuckey, 'Through the Prism of Folklore', *Massachusetts Review* vol. 9, 1968; John Blassingame, *The Slave Community*, New York, 1972; Gerald W. Mullin, *Flight and Rebellion: Slave Resistance in Eighteenth-Century Virginia*, New York, 1972; Peter Wood, *Black Majority: Negroes in Colonial South Carolina from 1670 through the Stono Rebellion*, New York, 1974; George P. Rawick, *From Sunup to Sundown: The Making of the Black Community*, Westport, Conn., 1972; Leslie Howard Owens, *This Species of Property: Slave Life and Culture in the Old South*, New York, 1976; Albert J. Raboteau, *Slave Religion: The 'Invisible Institution' in the Antebellum South*, New York, 1978; Paul Escott, *Slavery Remembered: A Record of Twentienth-Century Slave Narratives*, Chapel Hill, N.C., 1979; Deborah Gray White, *Ar'nt I A Woman: Female Slaves in the Plantation South*, New York, 1985.
Eugene D. Genovese, *Roll, Jordan, Roll: The World the Slaves Made*, New York, 1974, pp. 597–598, argues that 'day-to-day resistance to slavery' generally implied accommodation and that it was 'at best prepolitical and at worst apolitical'. Lawrence W. Levine, *Black Culture and Black Consciousness*, New York, 1977, p. 54, disputes the legitimacy of the political standard.
2   The quotation is from M. I. Finley, *Aspects of Antiquity: Discoveries and Controversies*, New York, 1968, p. 157. See also, M. I. Finley, *Ancient Slavery and Modern Ideology*, New York, 1980, pp. 93–122; Orlando Patterson, *Slavery and Social Death: A*

Comprehensive Study, Cambridge, Mass., 1982; William D. Phillips, Jr., *Slavery from Roman Times to the Early Transatlantic Trade*, Minneapolis, 1985, p. 6.

3 Aristotle, *The Politics*, translated by T. A. Sinclair, revised by Trevor J. Saunders New York, 1981, pp. 64—5, 69.

4 Winthrop D. Jordan, *White Over Black: American Attitudes Toward the Negro, 1550—1812*, Chapel Hill, 1968, traces the transformation of hostile prejudices into racism. George Fredrickson, *The Black Image in the White Mind*, New York, 1972, sees a later dating for the transformation.

5 Finley, *Ancient Slavery*, 118; Aristotle, *The Politics*, 69.

6 On the relation between slavery and the state in Ancient Rome see Chris Wickham, 'The Other Transition: From the Ancient World to Feudalism', *Past and Present*, vol. 103, May, 1984, pp. 3—36. For the structure of government in colonial Spanish-America, the classic study by C. H. Haring, *The Spanish Empire in America*, New York, 1947, is still useful. On the feudal state, see Joseph Strayer's elegant introduction to *Feudalism*, New York, 1965. On the social relations and ideology of feudalism, the starting point is Marc Bloch, *Feudal Society* trans. by L. A. Manyon Chicago, 1961. A new view of the relationship between politics and society emerged out of the 'internalist' interpretation of feudalism's decline, beginning with Maurice Dobb, *Studies in the Development of Capitalism*, New York, 1947, pp. 33—82, which was followed by a major exchange in *Science and Society*, subsequently published as Paul M. Sweezy, et al, *The Transition from Feudalism to Capitalism: A Symposium*, New York: third printing, 1967. For an insightful critique by a scholar sympathetic to the internalist position, see Robert Brenner, 'Dobb on the transition from feudalism to capitalism,' *Cambridge Journal of Economics*, vol. 2, 1978, pp. 121—140. Brenner's own important reformulation of the internalist argument, and the equally important exchange it provoked, has been published as Brenner, et al, *The Brenner Debate*, Cambridge, 1985. But the most important case studies include those by Rodney Hilton, cited extensively by Brenner, along with Guy Bois, *The Crisis of Feudalism: Economy and Society in Eastern Normandy c. 1300—1500*, Cambridge, 1984, and Witold Kula's brilliant, *Economic Theory of the Feudal System: Toward a Model of the Polish Economy, 1500—1800*, London, 1976, trans. Lawrence Garnier.

The paradox of slavery and freedom is examined in M. I. Finley, *The Ancient Greeks*, New York, 1963, p. 46, and in more detail in M. I. Finley, *Economy and Society in Ancient Greece*, Brent D. Shaw and Richard P. Saller, (eds.,) New York, 1981, 97—115. The literature on America is vast, but see in particular Edmund S. Morgan, *American Slavery, American Freedom: The Ordeal of Colonial Virginia*, New York, 1975.

7 For a different but perceptive view of slave law, see Mark Tushnet, *The American Law of Slavery, 1810—1860: Considerations of Humanity and Interest*, Princeton, 1981.

8 The tensions intrinsic to the concept of 'human property' have been explored by numerous scholars, but see especially David Brion Davis, *The Problem of Slavery in Western Culture*, Ithaca, N.Y., 1966; and Genovese, *Roll, Jordan, Roll*, part 1.

9 (Theodore Dwight Weld), *American Slavery as it Is: Testimony of a Thousand Witnesses*, New York, 1839.

10 Harriet Beecher Stowe, *Uncle Tom's Cabin*, 1852.

11 On the value of slave autobiographies, see Blassingame, *Slave Community*, revised and enlarged ed., 1979, pp. 367—382.

12 Thomas D. Morris, *Free Men All: The Personal Liberty Laws of the North, 1780—1861*, Baltimore, 1974.

13 Stanley W. Campbell, *The Slave Catchers: Enforcement of the Fugitive Slave Law, 1850—1860*, Chapel Hill, N.C., 1968, 1970, pp. 49—95.

14 William M. Wiecek, *The Sources of Antislavery Constitutionalism in America, 1760—1848*, Ithaca, N.Y., 1977, pp. 20—39; Paul Finkelman, *An Imperfect Union: Slavery, Federalism, and Comity* Chapel Hill, 1981; Don E. Fehrenbacher, *The Dred Scott Case: Its Significance in American Law and Politics* New York, 1978.

15 Paul Finkelman, '*Prigg v. Pennsylvania* and Northern State Courts: Anti-Slavery Uses of a Pro-Slavery Decision', *Civil War History* vol. 25, 1979, pp. 5—35; Paul Finkelman, *Slavery in the Courtroom: An Annotated Bibliography of American Cases*, Washington, D.C., 1985, pp. 60—64.

16 Roy P. Basler, ed., *The Collected Works of Abraham Lincoln*, 9 vols., New Brunswick, N. J., 1953—1955, vol. IV, pp. 263.

17 Benjamin Quarles, *The Negro in the Civil War*, Boston, 1953, pp. 42—55; John Hope

Franklin, *The Emancipation Proclamation*, New York, 1963; Leon F. Litwack, *Been in the Storm So Long*, New York, 1979, pp. 3–63.

18 Bell Irvin Wiley, *The Plain People of the Confederacy*, Baton Rouge, La., 1944, pp. 70–104; James M. McPherson, *The Negro's Civil War*, New York, 1965, pp. 19–36, 55–68; Quarles, *Negro in the Civil War*, pp. 57–77; Litwack, *Been in the Storm So Long*, pp. 104–166.

19 *New York Times*, 2 June, 1861; Robert Engs, *Freedom's First Generation: Black Hampton, Virginia, 1861–1890* Philadelphia, 1979, 18–22.

20 *U. S. Statutes*, XII, 319.

21 *Congressional Globe*, 37th Cong., 1st sess., (1861) 222–223.

22 *War of the Rebellion: A Compilation of the Official Records of the Union and Confederate Armies*, Washington, D.C., 1880–1901, Ser. 1, vol. 2, p. 649; Frank Moore (ed.), *The Rebellion Record*, vol. II, New York, 1861, pp. 437–38.

23 Moore, ed., (Rebellion Record), II, 493; Basler (ed.), *Collected Works*, vol. IV, p. 506 and vol. V, pp. 222–224.

24 Barbara J. Fields, *Slavery and Freedom on the Middle Ground: Maryland during the Nineteenth Century*, New Haven, Conn., 1985, pp. 108–112.

25 Edward McPherson (ed.), *The Political History of the United States During the Great Rebellion*, New York, 1864, pp. 196–7.

26 *Ibid.*, p. 198.

27 Georgia L. Tatum, *Disloyalty in the Confederacy* Chapel Hill, N.C., 1934; Stephen Ambrose, 'Yeomen Discontent in the Confederacy', *Civil War History* vol. 8 1962, pp. 259–268.

28 The classic critique of the Proclamation is Richard Hofstadter, *American Political Tradition*, New York, 1948, pp. 131–132. Details of the slaves' reaction to the British offer of emancipation during the American Revolution are presented in Benjamin Quarles, *The Negro in the American Revolution* Chapel Hill, N.C., 1961, pp. 19–32, pp. 111–181.

29 Frederick Douglass, *Life and times of Frederick Douglass* rev. ed., 1892: reprinted London, 1962, p. 358.

30 Franklin, *Emancipation Proclamation*, pp. 100–103, pp. 108–112.

31 *Ibid*, pp. 120–123, pp. 132–133; Quarles, *Negro in the Civil War*, pp. 163–82; Bell Irvin Wiley, *Southern Negroes, 1861–1865*, New Haven, 1938, p. 83.

32 For a different view of the significance of northern racism, see Louis S. Gerteis, *From Contraband to Freedman: Federal Policy Toward Southern Blacks, 1861–1861*, Westport, Conn., 1973. On black troops, see Dudley Taylor Cornish, *The Sable Arm: Negro Troops in the Union Army, 1861–1865*, 1956: New York, 1966; Litwack, *Been In the Storm So Long*, 65–103. See also the major documentary collections on the black military experience and emancipation published under the general editorship of Ira Berlin, *Freedom: A Documentary History* 2 vols., New York, 1983, 1985.

33 Finley, *Ancient Slavery and Modern Ideology*, 110; Finley, *Economy and Society in Ancient Greece*, pp. 104–111.

4

MAKING MISSISSIPPI SAFE FOR SLAVERY: THE INSURRECTIONARY PANIC OF 1835

Laurence Shore

Anxiety over the possibility of slave insurrection made southern slaveholders a particularly troubled ruling class. Unwilling to live in a state of "military preparation," slaveholders preferred a regime based upon the consent—not the coercion—of the enslaved. Such a regime was rife with slaveholders' uneasiness about whether slaves were really consenting. A rumor about some alleged slave unhappiness could swiftly fan ever-present white tension into hysteria, provoking white communities to perform ritual executions. But bloodbaths led to uneasiness about violating democratic values. The tormented white community then swung back to "normality" —relaxed discipline, calling slaves family friends, 'and pretending that the friends consented. Historians, placing these tensions at the center of their analysis, have conventionally interpreted insurrection panics as a classic example of the anxiety facing Americans who would be slaveholders and republicans too.[1]

But this explanation does not suffice. It fails to take into account that in white minds blacks constituted only half of a problem that straddled the color line. The threat of black insurrection generated another threat, one that cut to the heart of white society: the possibility that all whites would not stand together to suppress a black uprising. White southerners were not only unsure of their slaves' "blackness," but also suffered doubts over their own

328

"whiteness." Work associations between whites and blacks and interracial sexual unions constantly reminded whites of fissures in the color line.[2]

In many major North American insurrecton panics whites were implicated as conspirators in alleged black plots. Some 20 whites, together with 161 blacks, stood accused of conspiracy to burn New York City and murder its white inhabitants in the "Great Negro Plot" in 1741. Confessions of slaves implicated in Gabriel Prosser's conspiracy to overtake Richmond (1800) suggested that white Frenchmen helped devise the insurrectionary plan. During the height of the Denmark Vesey panic in Charleston (1822), Anna Hayes Johnson, daughter of United States Supreme Court Justice William Johnson, wrote to her cousin, "I blush to own that it [the conspiracy] has been traced to the whites for this day one or two white men have been taken up and the proofs are so strong as to hang them." In his study of the Christmas Day inssurrection scare of 1865, Dan T. Carter found considerable evidence of white fears concerning dangerous actions of "nonconformist white southerners." An abundance of episodes of this type led many whites in slaveholding communities to lose confidence in their ability to maintain solidarity among themselves.[3]

One such episode has been conventionally interpreted as an example of "popular frenzy" that erupted when a stimulus was applied to the "current of uneasiness in Southern society." The insurrection panic of 1835 in west-central Mississippi, according to Clement Eaton, grew out of a rumor that a gang of outlaws had organized a servile revolt. "Mob violence reigned supreme" as "pathologically fearful" Mississippians hanged "more than a dozen negroes" and five white men ("nearly all . . . of Northern birth").[4] Edwin Miles, in a more detailed coverage of the panic, shows how the "reign of terror" in Mississippi contributed to "hostility in the South towards the abolitionist crusade." Although Miles notes that white men were implicated in the insurrection plot, his primary focus is the external threat—the aggressive campaign of the American Anti-Slavery Society—that white southerners perceived.[5]

But what makes this panic of crucial importance is the stark form in which tensions *within* the white community were manifested. At least six whites were hanged; at least seven were flogged and banished from the state; and one was shot and killed as he attempted to arrest a prominent slaveholder on the charge of complicity in the alleged insurrection plot. This panic represented, in the course of southern history, the most extreme direction in which white anxiety over lack of cohesion within white communities would lead.[6]

When insurrection rumors circulated in June 1835, white Mississippians in Madison and Hinds counties established various precautions—they formed patrols and prepared to defend their families against attack. But when later reports implicated local whites as insurrectionary leaders and included details of slaves' lust for white women, anxiety escalated into panic. The panic peaked when the immediate black threat had already been eliminated. In an observer's words:

> It is no longer the negroes, but white man against white man. The Mississippians are ruining their own State. By their own high-handed and violent measures, they are giving a magnitude and terror to the contemplated insurrection which it otherwise never could have gained.[7]

Use of "high-handed and violent measures" against other whites led to feelings of guilt. By subjecting members of their own community to coercion, whites exhibited—to themselves and to the nation—an even more blatant example of their failure to act as republicans. Indeed, in the panic's aftermath citizens of Madison County felt compelled to issue a pamphlet justifying their actions. Conveniently for these citizens, the opportunity arose to blame "outsiders" (outlaws and abolitionists) as instigators of the alleged insurrection. This rationalization provided Mississippians and southerners with little psychological comfort, but perhaps enough to enable them to cope with a profound conflict of values.[8]

In the mid-1830s a cotton boom rapidly changed the character of west-central Mississippi. Although the west-central counties had constituted the state's most vigorously growing area in the 1820s, small farms—not plantations—predominated until the boom of the

1830s.[9] Thus, white society was being transformed in precisely the way U. B. Phillips outlined it: "The tide of small farmers advancing toward the frontier" was followed by a "tide of planters" seeking new openings for their capital.[10] Abundant opportunity for enrichment also enabled many small producers to maintain or increase holdings.[11] In addition, the "tide of planters" carried in many men interested in exploiting new southwestern wealth in any way possible, the "straw men" that Joseph Glover Baldwin depicted so well in his *Flush Times of Alabama and Mississippi*.[12]

One measure of stability in plantation societies is the slave to free population ratio. By this measure, the unstable nature of west-central Mississippi plantation society during the 1830s is strikingly apparent. Population figures for Hinds and Madison counties indicate a large and rapid influx of slaves: in 1830 slaves were 39 percent of the total population of Hinds and Madison; by 1840 they increased to 69 percent.[13] In 1835 the spirit of speculation was particularly intense. Between the brief financial downturn of 1834 and the crash of 1837, easy acquisition of credit enhanced investment opportunities in land and slaves.[14]

Despite the opening of new land further north in Mississippi (ceded by Choctaws and Chickasaws in 1830 and 1832), the fertile soil of Hinds and Madison remained in heavy demand by speculators and planters from eastern slave states. Hinds County, in particular, attracted more "respectable" investors. In 1834 a correspondent for the Jackson *Mississippian* noted: "I know of no county in the state where land is sought with so much avidity as it is in Hinds at the present time."[15] In addition to navigable streams and an ideal environment for cotton, Hinds offered "good society." The earliest established county in west-central Mississippi, Hinds contained many schools, many churches, and four growing towns. Although its land area was occasionally reduced—in 1829, for example, representatives of Madison County managed to "steal" townships from Hinds through legislative maneuvering—Hinds remained prosperous and politically powerful. Two of its four towns had statewide significance: Jackson, the state capital, and Clinton, one of the state's land office sites. A temperance society boasting 100 members in 1834, a college with 180 male and female students, and two "brick churches" (Methodist and Presbyterian) for a population of 700 endowed Clinton with a reputation as the cultural center of Mississippi.[16]

In Madison County, however, "good society" was not developing. No other county in Mississippi contained as much fertile cotton land as Madison. But opportunity to gain large profits proved more compelling to investors than opportunity to build "an interesting state of society." Conversion to cotton fields and slave quarters, together with a high rate of absentee ownership, left few whites, few schools, few churches. In 1834, a correspondent for the *Mississippian* reported "that many respectable citizens of the county, seeing the course which things are taking, are leaving it in despair and seeking homes elsewhere."[17] Among the county's four small towns, Livingston (population 200) was barely maintaining its existence. The transfer of the county seat from Livingston to Canton deprived Livingston of the possibility of becoming "a village of some consequence," although its inhabitants still endeavored to sustain their town.[18]

Though the character of the counties contrasted, social transformation made both Madison and Hinds counties ripe for an insurrection scare. Faced with an influx of "unfamiliar" slaves, and with Nat Turner's 1831 revolt fresh in memory, whites were highly attentive to potential dangers. Significantly, this transformation occurred during a period of national expansion and crisis. Leonard L. Richards has shown that from 1833 to 1838 was a peak period of mob violence in the nation. Economic dislocation, abolitionist fervor, and antiabolitionist response coincided. By 1835, moreover, the "positive good" proslavery argument had yet to triumph throughout the South. Whites not only remembered Nat Turner, but also recollected the aftermath of Turner's revolt: Virginians in the state legislature nearly abolished slavery in their state. White southerners saw their fundamental social institution challenged by other white southerners.[19]

Institutions such as churches, schools, and temperance societies could ease such conflicts between whites because they could foster consent, disseminate "proper" values and thereby aid development of community solidarity. As we have seen, Hinds County contained an institutional framework that Madison lacked. Clinton and Livingston epitomized this contrast. It is therefore not surprising that these towns manifested divergent patterns of behavior during the insurrection panic. Clinton citizens could be more confident of white unity within their community; accordingly, the Clinton "committee of vigilance" did not hang any whites and eventually reacted against the fervor of Livingston citizens in the insurrection scare of 1835. Madison County was the "main focus of excitement," not least because it lacked previously established instruments of voluntary control over its white citizens—particularly those on the outskirts of the community.[20]

Given the time and place, a rumor of potential slave insurrection was not something to be dismissed without full investigation. Thus, when Madam Latham, an extensive slaveholder in Beatie's Bluff, a community near Livingston in Madison County, reported hearing from a slave of an impending black uprising, concern escalated. Rumor of insurrection circulated throughout the county, and in the village of Livingston a large "meeting of the citizens" convened on Saturday, 27 June, to discuss precautions against attack. Colonel Hardin D. Runnels, a relative of Governor Hiram G. Runnels, chaired the meeting, during which patrols and committees of investigation were appointed and a further meeting scheduled for 30 June.[21]

At the 30 June meeting in Livingston, William Johnson, a local planter, informed citizens that his driver, "a negro man in whom he had confidence," had discovered that one of Johnson's elderly slaves knew about a "rising of the blacks." The old slave's information came from Peter, one of Ruel Blake's six slaves.[22] Blake, destined to be a key figure in the panic, was a cotton gin maker and carpenter; he had resided in Madison County about six years. Noted for his industriousness, he had accumulated all six slaves and property in Livingston worth $150 since he had moved to the county.[23]

Johnson's old slave, who was brought into town, denied the existence of a slave conspiracy and was subsequently whipped. Livingston citizens' liberal use of the lash eventually produced what they wanted to hear: the old slave "confessed" that an insurrection was planned, though he did not provide any details. Nothing at all was learned about the alleged conspiracy from an "examination" of Peter. Both slaves were remanded to jail for the night.[24]

In the course of the examination of Peter, the first sign of division within the white community appeared. Many Livingston citizens felt that Blake, a man of impressive physical stature, was not whipping his slave in earnest. When other citizens, led by William Johnson, tried to make a better job of it, Blake interfered, and a fight ensued between Blake and Johnson. The fight was as much between two conceptions of how much coercion a slaveholder must use under such circumstances as between two men. The next morning, Blake, accused of being "soft" on slaves, fled Livingston on horseback, only to return a week later under circumstances even less pleasant than when he had departed.[25]

Citizens of Beatie's Bluff, still having failed to uncover any concrete details of the intended insurrection, met on 1 July to discuss the matter further. Jesse Mabry, a resident of the Bluff area, examined the Latham slave girls. They confirmed the rumor spread by Madam Latham. Another resident then claimed to have overheard two other slaves, Joe and Weaver (a preacher), conversing about an insurrection. As preachers were "generally considered to be the greatest scoundrels among negroes," citizens of the Bluff wasted no time in investigating this accusation. Mabry led a committee of three to question these slaves. After extended "examination," Joe stated that one of Mabry's slaves (Sam, a carpenter) had informed him of a "negro rising" to kill all whites on 4 July. White men were at the head of the insurrection—the only names that Joe could remember were Ruel Blake, Dr. Joshua Cotton, and Dr. William Saunders. Joe also implicated slaves as ringleaders: Weaver, Russell (also a preacher), and Sam. Insurrectionary strategy was as follows: beginning on 4 July, slaves in the Beatie's Bluff area would massacre whites in their homes and would then obtain ammunition from storehouses in the Bluff. Proceeding to Livingston, slaves would gain strength, recruiting and sacking as they traveled. From Livingston, the burgeoning slave army would murder its way through Vernon (another town in Madison County), Clinton, and Natchez. Finally, they would make a stand at "Devil's Punch Bowl," an area near Natchez.[26]

Although Weaver was "put under the lash," he called Joe a liar and refused to confess. The examiners released Joe from custody and questioned Russell at a neighboring plantation. Prolonged punishment resulted in a full statement by Russell, "in all particulars, precisely like the one made by Joe." Apparently satisfied with its investigative work, the committee transacted no further business until the next day.[27]

At Livingston on 1 July, local officials arrested Joshua Cotton, a "steam doctor." A medical fad of the 1820s and 1830s, steam doctoring (based on the principle that "inward heat" produced from vapor baths and herb preparations was the best treatment for illness) was a convenient profession for "straw men" in the Southwest. The occupation itself was slightly disreputable, and the men who practiced it were inevitably on the fringes of the community.[28]

The previous day, William Saunders, a fellow steam doctor, had accused Cotton of slave-stealing. Saunders's charge and "other evidence of his bad character" led to Cotton's arrest on 1 July. He was discharged the same day. It is unclear whether the new disclosures from Beatie's Bluff were available to Livingston citizens at the time of Cotton's discharge, "but Saunders having left town, and no evidence being offered at his examination sufficient to justify the citizens in detaining him," Cotton was released. He went to stay at his father-in-law's house in Hinds County. That day ended with the only available white suspect enjoying his freedom.[29]

The account thus far raises many questions and is subject to various interpretations. The first question is the truth of a confession provoked by the searing use of a whip. As the editor of the Nashville *Banner* would later speculate, slaves under torture probably answered according to obvious wishes of excited white interrogators.[30] Another question concerns implication of whites. Again, excited interrogators could have provided names to which a black man might be forced to nod his assent. As we will see, actions of Cotton and Saunders had previously raised doubts about their racial fidelities. Ruel Blake, by not vigorously whipping his slave, had revealed that in a time of crisis he was unwilling to perform duties incumbent upon all slaveholders. Still, at this point in the growing crisis, Thomas Hudnal, one of Madison County's largest slaveholders, had provided Blake with the horse on which he fled Livingston. Anxiety over possible white involvement had not yet escalated into panic.[31]

Of course, an insurrectionary conspiracy could have really existed, whether or not organized by whites. But if a conspiracy did exist, slaves, after seeing precautions taken by whites, were probably—and justifiably—reluctant to enact their plans. In the judgment of one white observer: "So soon as the contemplated scheme was discovered, and the ringleaders arrested, we were safe."[32] But rising tension within white communities could not be reduced without a clear example to slaves and to whites of the power and purity of "whiteness"—even if purity had to be achieved through purgation.

On 2 July investigations continued at Beatie's Bluff. Mabry, after whipping a slave named Jim, elicited another confession. Jim corroborated Joe's statement and implicated more white men by name, including one who was present at his examination (Angus Donovan). Jim also raised the ultimate red flag: he announced that the rebels' intention was:

. . . to slay all the whites, except some of the most beautiful women, whom they intended to keep as wives; said that these white men had told them that they might do so, and that he had already picked out one for himself; and that he and his wife had already had a quarrel in consequence of his having told her his intention.[33]

Another slave (Bachus) corroborated Jim's statement, confirming slaves' desire for white wives. That was enough for the examiners. Jim, Weaver, Russell, Sam, and Bachus were hanged.[34]

Before this news reached Livingston, Saunders was in the town jail. Traveling to Vicksburg, Saunders met a man to whom he allegedly stated that Cotton was the leader of the insurrection plot. His fellow traveler arrested Saunders and delivered him to Livingston citizens. Saunder's statement led to the rearrest of Cotton, who was brought back to Livingston the same night. After news of Jim's confession and the executions at Beatie's Bluff circulated in the county, suspense turned into unbearable tension. The two slaves belonging to William Johnson and Ruel Blake were summarily hanged by a mob in Livingston.[35] As justification for this and subsequent disregard of civil authority, Livingston citizens later pointed to the sexual horror: "Already had many of the slaves marked out many of the victims of their lust or revenge; and no time to convince them of the fatal attempts of their rash enterprise was to be lost."[36] But execution of slaves would not suffice:

It was not believed that the execution of a few negroes, unknown and obscure, would have the effect of frightening their *white* associates from an attempt to perpetrate horrid designs; which *association* was fully established by the confessions of the accused and other circumstances."[37]

"Respectable" white citizens felt, however, that summary hangings of whites would be as inadequate a solution as appeal to civil authority. Normal democratic procedures were infeasible because all known slave conspirators were dead and black testimony was inadmissable in any event. But lynch law entailed the problem of "wresting and restraining those wild sallies of passion . . . of an enraged people." Furthermore, the "parties implicated" deserved "something like a *trial*, if not *formal*, at least *substantial*." Citizens therefore called a general assembly of the community for 9:00 A.M. the next morning to decide upon a course of action.[38]

For the rest of the evening of 2 July, Cotton, Saunders, Donovan (conveyed from the Bluff), Albe Dean (a white man implicated by Saunders), James Mitchell, a white blacksmith, and about fifteen slaves were all imprisoned. Patrols worked the countryside the entire night, and "discipline" was maintained within the town. The citizens of Canton, twelve miles from Livingston and also in Madison County, had already filled their jail with alleged white and black conspirators.[39]

Jail, after all, was the only place for men accused of insurrection and therefore assumed to condone miscegenation. Jim's confession, however "true," seemed "truest" to whites when it suggested that black insurrectionaries wanted white wives. Harriet Martineau, writing about her travels in Alabama and Mississippi in spring 1835, revealed why white males had cause to shudder. "Licentious masters," she noted, deprived black men of wives and therefore provoked blacks' "desire to retaliate."[40] The Livingston pamphlet indicated how closely related the threats of insurrection and miscegenation were in the minds of whites by "calling for every manly energy" in the defense of all that "we hold most dear in this world."⁴¹ Throughout west-central Mississippi, precautions taken during the panic reflected this need to exhibit "manly energy": "The women and children are stowed away in the largest house the place affords every night, and the men, with arms, guard the town [Mississippi Springs in Hinds County]."⁴²

Mississippi whites were not anxious solely about black males violating the color line. Most "licentious masters" could (covertly) cross the color line without raising suspicions about their racial loyalty. But some white men conducted their sexual liaisons with black women in such a way as to raise suspicions. White men without white families to protect, overtly cohabiting with their own or—even more in defiance of the color line—somebody else's slaves, did not qualify as defenders of what southern men "held most dear in this world."

At 9:00 A.M. on 3 July, more than 160 "respectable citizens" met in Livingston to formulate a clearly defined defense against the black and white menace. Dr. Joseph J. Pugh, apparently a "regular" physician, proposed organization of a "committee of safety," consisting of thirteen freeholders invested with power to investigate and punish any persons, white or black, found aiding or exciting slaves to revolt. Citizens pledged to support this committee against all personal and pecuniary liability. They resolved that the committee, meeting daily from 9:00 A.M. to 4:00 P.M., could act either according to the "law of the Land" or to its discretion. With selection of thirteen men "conspicuous for wealth and intelligence" and appointment of "search guards," the committee began conducting "trials."⁴³

Although Livingston was the focus of the panic, similarly composed and empowered "vigilance committees" supplanted normal forms of law throughout west-central Mississippi, particularly in Madison and, to a lesser extent, Hinds, counties. In Canton, for example, 3 July also marked the beginning of the temporary reign of a committee of vigilance. Various patrols busily brought blacks and whites into Canton to be tried by appointed citizens. The

Canton committee, like that in Livingston, evinced as much concern over white involvement as over black involvement in the alleged conspiracy."

The trials of Joshua Cotton and William Saunders—and untold numbers of hangings of slaves—occupied attention in Livingston on 3 July. According to the Livingston pamphlet, citizens presented the following information at the trials. Cotton, a native of New England, had emigrated to Mississippi a year earlier. He had initially settled in Hinds, where he soon married. He had then moved to Livingston where he set up shop as a steam doctor. Livingston citizens disliked him, as he had "no social intercourse" with them and was considered a swindler. Saunders again inculpated his partner, charging that Cotton had often used the pretext of "hunting horses" in order to gain opportunities to converse with slaves and "make converts to his [rebellious] propositions, which he could not do by being a steam-doctor." Citizens claiming to have seen Cotton "skulking around" plantations of Livingston, Vernon, and Beatie's Bluff "confirmed" Saunders's charge. Finally, a slave from Beatie's Bluff was brought to Livingston and identified Cotton as a conspirator."

Saunders, a native of Tennessee, had emigrated to Mississippi in autumn 1834, becoming an overseer near Livingston. But he was soon fired from this job ("his deportment was such as to induce his employer to discharge him"), and joined Cotton's steam-doctor practice. Saunders established a new residence in a boardinghouse in Hinds, but "his conduct was of such equivocal character" that his landlord eventually evicted him. The landlord provided details to the Livingston committee "which went to show that Saunders was a fit instrument for such an enterprize [sic]" as leading a slave conspiracy." After leaving Hinds, Saunders "was seen lurking about the neighborhood of Livingston." Other citizens provided, according to the Livingston pamphlet, abundant proof of Saunders's "general bad character.""

Even their southern ties provided little safeguard against suspicion. Neither Cotton nor Saunders was thought to be an abolitionist. Both, in fact, had established residences in Mississippi. Cotton may have been of northern birth, but his wife was a Missis-

sippi resident and his partner was not only of southern birth but
had held that most southern of occupations—plantation overseer.
In a phrase pregnant with unintended meaning, the editor of the
Jackson *Mississippian* would later refer to Cotton and Saunders as
"men who stood fair in society."[48] Both men, however, were
outside the purview of the white community. Cotton had no
"social intercourse" with Livingston citizens. Saunders, as evidence quoted above suggests, behaved in such a morally corrupt
manner that other whites questioned his fidelity to the color line.
Both men also held the dubious occupation of steam doctoring. In
a time of crisis, their "deviances" became more important than
their whiteness, and they were regarded as serious threats tc white
society.

On 4 July Livingston and neighboring towns resembled armed
camps. The committee of safety convicted Cotton and Saunders
and sentenced them to hang. Urged to name white accomplices,
Cotton acquiesced, stating he would confess completely if he were
not hanged immediately. At this point, Cotton wrote and signed
a confession. He claimed to be a member of John Murrell's clan
of outlaws, a group of whites intent on exciting black insurrection
not for the purpose of liberation, but to plunder white communities
from Maryland to Louisiana. Murrell, a notorious outlaw of the
Natchez Trace, had been captured in 1834 and would spend the
next ten years of his life in a Tennessee penitentiary. And in spring,
1835, his captor, Virgil Stewart, published a pamphlet detailing
Murrell's life and crimes, one crime being a projected slave insurrection for Christmas Day 1835.[49]

It is impossible to know whether the alleged Murrell conspiracy
existed. Furthermore, if such a conspiracy did exist, Cotton's involvement would still be open to question. One thing, however,
can be safely asserted: until Cotton mentioned Murrell in his confession, no reference to Murrell's "mystic clan" had had any
impact on origins and development of the panic. In fact, no copy of
Stewart's pamphlet could even be obtained in Madison or Hinds
until late July or early August 1835. Before Cotton referred to
Murrell's clan, Stewart's pamphlet was considered a joke wherever it was distributed.[50]

Why, then, did Cotton choose to emphasize his connection with Murrell? And why did Madison County whites increasingly rely on the alleged Murrell connection to explain the panic? As for Cotton, he probably had a twofold purpose. First, he wanted to buy time for himself. And second, he wanted to wrench his soon-to-be executioners into an even more twisted state of anxiety. To buy time Cotton had to do more than mention Murrell—he had to provide names of coconspirators. He cleverly implicated more people on the fringe of the white community. That he was doing nothing more than naming names is supported by evidence that many people he implicated were discharged after their trials.[51]

Neither element of Cotton's purpose was fulfilled. The committee refused to allow him more time to make additional disclosures, possibly fearing that Cotton, given more time, would implicate "respectable citizens." And, though Cotton succeeded in intensifying the panic by declaring that an organized band of white outlaws was operating in the heart of white communities, he ultimately provided Mississippians and southerners with a defense for their actions. A band of outlaws was comparable to a band of "abolitionist fanatics." Mississippians and southerners could later claim that Tennessee outlaws had actually invaded their society just as abolitionist outsiders threatened to invade. They could thereby divert attention from their doubts over racial loyalties of members of their own slaveholding society. An obvious early example of this "diversion" process appeared in the New Orleans *True American* (13 July 1835), where Cotton and Saunders were identified as "two itinerant abolitionist preachers."[52]

Livingston citizens celebrated the fourth of July with afternoon hangings of nine blacks and two whites. Cotton, before he was "swung off," did nothing to allay white anxiety. He confirmed that part of the insurrection plot involved blacks taking a "few chosen females" as wives, and he warned the populace to "Beware of tonight and tomorrow night." Saunders, declaring his innocence to the end, also tried to frighten Livingston citizens by implying that spies of the "clan" had infiltrated the very crowd that was about to hang him. Finally, Cotton and Saunders were hanged. The committee of safety then adjourned until Monday 6 July, claiming

341

that patrols needed time to capture the more than fifty whites implicated by Cotton and Saunders.⁵³

While patrol squads delivered suspected whites to jail (seventeen or eighteen were in Livingston by the evening of 5 July),⁵⁴ citizens of Madison and Hinds maintained their sense of "dreadful alarm." Men expected "every moment to be burned up or have our throats cut by the negroes."⁵⁵ And, almost every account of the panic mentions the "great distress among the women."⁵⁶ One observer noted that the populace, "breathing fury and vengeance, are up for blood—they have tasted some, and God alone knows where they will stop."⁵⁷ The governor, however, did not intercede: "No minister of the law has attempted to stay a course of procedure which threatens the property, the lives and respectability of citizens."⁵⁸

On the morning of 6 July the Livingston committee of safety renewed trials. The Livingston pamphlet, significantly, mentions only two trials—Albe Dean's and Lee Smith's—for this day. But numerous other trials and activities occurred. The "official" account of Dean's trial is a revealing statement about why certain cases were emphasized.⁵⁹

A native of Connecticut, Dean had emigrated to Livingston in 1833 and initially worked as a maker of washing machines. After becoming acquainted with Cotton, Dean abandoned his business, settled in Hinds, and became a steam doctor with "Cotton, Saunders, and Company." In addition to gaining a reputation for dishonesty, Dean was known for associating with blacks and for persuading masters not to whip runaways; he was "soft" in the manner of Ruel Blake about using coercion to maintain control of slaves. At his trial citizens accused him of "prowling about" plantations near Vernon, Beatie's Bluff, and Livingston. Implicated by Cotton, Saunders, and slaves, Dean was convicted and hanged two days later.⁶⁰

The 6 July Livingston public meeting also sentenced John Gregory, seventy-two years old and a citizen of Mississippi for at least five years, to fifty lashes and perpetual banishment from the state. A fifty-year-old man received a sentence similar to Gregory's, incurring one hundred additional lashes. It is unclear whether

Cotton had implicated these men and what positions they held in the white community. But in the case of Lee Smith, definitely implicated by Cotton and also tried and punished on 6 July, his position in the white community is clearer.[61]

A native of Tennessee and a resident of Hinds since at least 1824, Smith was a small farmer. In 1831 he acquired his first slave and by 1835 enlarged his holdings to four slaves. By summer 1835, however, he apparently turned to steam-doctoring to pay off heavy debts. Thus, despite Smith's long residence and his slaveholding status, Cotton's accusation and Smith's work as a steam doctor qualified him for the sentence of flogging and banishment by Livingston's committee. After his discharge from Livingston, Smith's own neighbors arrested and "slicked" him, a punishment whereby "the prisoner is stripped naked, laid on his belly, his hands and feet fastened to four pegs; [and] he receives the stripes from different hands."[62]

The most likely interpretation of this incident is that Smith, by failing to pay his debts and by assuming the occupation of steam doctor, had angered many "respectable citizens." A slaveholder, residing in the area for at least eleven years, could hardly have been considered an insurgent unless his precarious financial position as an insider and his flirtation with steam-doctoring outsiders had made him a candidate for disloyalty. This slight "deviance" had exploded—in white minds—into a potentially devastating threat to slavery. Anxiety over white conspiratorial involvement was so great that slaveholders like Smith and Ruel Blake, who revealed adherence to a less stringent code of slave treatment, were thought to be enemies of slavery.

The most dramatic example of tensions within the white community occurred on 6-7 July, when a band of vigilante "Regulators" from Madison attacked Patrick Sharkey, a prominent slaveholder who resided in Hinds. It all began 6 July when the Livingston committee dispatched a party of horsemen under command of Hiram Perkins to arrest two young white men named Rawson (or Ransom), residents of Hinds and neighbors of Sharkey. Again, Cotton had implicated men on the fringe of the white community: "As the Ransom family was of the poor farmer class, these young men had been picking cotton on the Birdsong plantation with Mr. Birdsong's slaves."[63] Perkin's squad captured the Rawsons, but Sharkey (who "after long acquaintance thought highly of them")[64] and James Kilborn, another Hinds slaveholder, ordered their release. Sharkey and Kilborn explained their actions in a letter to the governor (7 July).

Yesterday we were called upon to examine three white men taken up in this neighborhood by a company of armed men from Madison county. On examination we believed that two of them ought to be discharged and one taken before a justice of the peace for further examination. A confusion ensued—all talked—none reasoned—and the Madison men finally broke off and left the prisoners who of course deliberately walked away.[65]

On 7 July Perkins reported Sharkey's acquittal of the Rawsons to citizens of Livingston, "which excited the greatest indignation against Sharkey, and the suspicion of many that he was an accomplice." This reaction developed despite knowledge of Sharkey's long residence in the area, his wealth in slaves and land, and his family connections—Sharkey's cousin (William L. Sharkey) was chief justice of the Mississippi Supreme Court. Livingston citizens demanded a "scrutiny of the motives which influenced" Sharkey to rescue the Rawsons. The committee of safety, more interested in the Rawsons, reinforced Perkins's party and simply ordered the "recapture of the Rawsons at all hazards."[66]

Sharkey was aware of the impending assault and appealed to Governor Runnels to take steps to end vigilante activity. He asserted that no one stood "in any further fear of negros." But the outbreak of "lawless passions of man" would soon lead to the reign of "confusion and desolation" unless the governor issued a "proclamation . . . commanding all illegal tribunals to desolve [sic]" and "all unlawful bands under the name of Regulators to dispurce [sic]."[67] Governor Runnels chose, at this time, not to act. In fact, he would wait until 13 July before issuing any such "proclamation." Family considerations undoubtedly influenced his inaction: though Runnels was a resident of Hinds, he had many relatives in Madison—a few of whom were deeply involved in vigilance committee activities. Indeed, the governor's nephew was a member of Perkins's "Regulators."⁶¹

In regarding Sharkey as a threat to slavery, Livingston citizens clearly had lost any semblance of a rational perspective; in leading the attack on Sharkey, Perkins lost his life. Sharkey prepared for Perkins's attempt to arrest him by taking his family and a supply of firearms to an outbuilding near his home: "At night, fires were kindled around this house, no lights admitted inside." Perkins led his horsemen to the outbuilding and then made the mistake of passing in front of a window. He received a wound "which proved mortal the next day." Perkins's squad returned the fire, and shattered Sharkey's right hand. But Sharkey continued his defense, firing pistols with his left hand. He wounded Robert Hodge, Jr., in the thigh, and he narrowly missed killing Hiram Reynolds (the governor's nephew), the bullet "cutting the collar of his coat." Perkins's squad then retreated, and Sharkey and his family made their escape.⁶⁹

Perkins's rash action on the night of 7 July can be explained in two ways. Perkins may have had a personal vendetta against Sharkey. In their encounter on 6 July, Sharkey, who enjoyed controversies, may well have humiliated Perkins. Recapture of the Rawsons, in this case, signified recapture of lost honor. But Perkins's financial and social background suggests a second reason for his zealous and blind leadership. From 1827-1831, as a resident of Hinds, Perkins owned no slaves and little, if any, land. At some point in the early 1830s, he moved to Madison County but remained a small producer (in 1834 he owned only one slave). By the time of the panic, however, Perkins had greatly augmented his wealth; he owned nine slaves and 160 acres of first-class land. Thus, the threat of insurrection came at a time when Perkins was just beginning to enjoy the fruits of slavery, and when he was undoubtedly trying to establish firmly his newly won status in'the community. Concern over protection of new wealth and status— as well as slighted honor—probably brought Perkins to the point of his attack on Sharkey. Whatever the personal motives of Perkins and Sharkey, their confrontation underscored differences between the slave societies of Hinds and Madison. Sharkey's effort to use democratic procedures to investigate innocent whites reflected Hinds County's stronger institutional framework and its "respectability." Madison, the county devoid of institutions and "good society," clearly supported Perkins's effort to use lynch justice to purge those so "soft" as to cling to impotent democratic procedures.[70]

The morning of 8 July, Sharkey managed to get to Clinton ". . . and proposed to throw himself under the protection of the committee there sitting, being certain that if dragged to Madison in the existing temper of the popular mind there he should never get home again alive."[71] But Sharkey was not yet out of danger. In Hinds as in Madison, committees of safety had arraigned and tried many slaveholders. Sharkey appealed to his cousin, the chief justice, to defend him before the Clinton committee. Judge Sharkey, according to Henry Foote (at that time a lawyer residing in Clinton), made a masterly speech in which he conceded the powerlessness of the courts and appealed directly to the intelligence of the committee: "he showed the gross absurdity of the charge of *complicity* which had been preferred" and urged the "committee to protect the citizens of their own county from trial beyond its confines."[72]

A group of Madison citizens present at Sharkey's trial demanded custody of him, desiring to take him to Livingston. But the chief justice had swayed the Hinds committee; they declared Patrick Sharkey innocent of "complicity," freed him, and "declared their determination to protect him against all further molestation."[73] This ruling did not, however, end the Sharkey episode. In an observer's words, "Madison folks now swear they will have him; people of Hinds are resolved to defend him. Should an attack be made, a civil war must ensue. When I left Hinds, the citizens were arming and rallying in his defense."[74]

George Wyche, a neighbor of Sharkey, appealed to Governor Runnels to issue a proclamation that would remove the government of Madison County from the "hands of the Mob": "The danger from the slaves vanished at the detection of the conspiracy and another danger has taken place more formidable than that."[75]

Civil war did not ensue. Madison whites did not press the

Sharkey matter. For they had confronted an impassable limit to their desire to purge the white community. An open battle with other white slaveholders—provoked by doubts over a prominent slaveholder's loyalty to slavery—simply could not be justified. At least some Madison whites in positions of authority must have recognized that such an extreme step could have led to annihilation of slave society.[76]

While Sharkey fought for his life, other whites continued to lose their lives in Livingston. On 7 July, Angus Donovan, a trader and boatman from Kentucky, was tried and convicted. Citizens accused him of intimacy with blacks and noted his bad character:

Donovan's conduct was so very extraordinary and suspicious after he commenced boarding with Moss [a citizen of Livingston] as to induce . . . the neighborhood to watch his movements. He was repeatedly found in the negro cabins, enjoying himself in negro society.[77]

Before the panic a few Livingston citizens had even asked Donovan to leave Mississippi. With this "evidence," in addition to previous implications, the committee condemned Donovan to hang the next day.[78]

Donovan appealed to lawyer Henry Foote, who agreed to try to intercede with the committee. Foote later described the scene as he entered Livingston the next morning:

I saw a large multitude convened, composed almost altogether of excited white citizens, to most of whom I was personally well known. I dared not name my business to anyone, for had I done so there was not much probability that I should have ever returned to my own home again.

Foote believed that Donovan was innocent and tried to save him with the following interrogation:

You are a *white* man; you say that you have a wife and children at home whom you love dearly . . . now tell me, I beseech you, were you to witness a bloody conflict between the slaves of this country and the white people, on which side would you be?

347

Donovan's response, "Certainly, sir, I should be on the side of my own color," and Foote's efforts were futile. Donovan was hanged alongside Albe Dean that afternoon.[9]

Other whites had more successful trials on 7 July. The committee acquitted Mitchell, a blacksmith, and banished four others. The Livingston pamphlet contains trial accounts for two of these four. In the case of William Benson, a day-laborer who worked for Ruel Blake, even Livingston citizens admitted that evidence was thin. Although slaves implicated Benson, the committee judged him to be more a fool than a conspirator and therefore merely banished him. The committee considered Lunsford Barnes an ignorant but hard-working youth, and doled out the same punishment. Livingston citizens also noted that "other evidence was before the committee which did not add anything to his [Barnes's] good character."[10]

Given Livingston citizens' intense excitement and the committee's inclination to condemn on the basis of thin evidence, it is remarkable that more accused men did not lose their lives. The cases discussed above suggest that evidence of any sort was difficult to obtain. Decisions to banish also indicate that the committee was as concerned about future safety as about punishment: it would not suffice to whip a white man and allow him to remain if his obedience to the color line would always be in doubt.

Banishment, however, was not decided upon for Ruel Blake. A search guard arrested Blake in Vicksburg (Warren County) and conveyed him to Livingston on 8 July. Angered citizens almost hanged Blake immediately. But the committee's authority prevailed, and he stood trial.[11]

The Livingston pamphlet describes Blake as being almost aloof from white society, "oftener seen among negroes." As a cotton gin maker he became acquainted with slaves on most of the large plantations.[12] A more trustworthy account of proceedings at Livingston describes Blake as "totally destitute of principle or morality."[13] It should be remembered that Blake first got into trouble by protecting his implicated slave from being whipped. Blake's climactic case, then, highlights elements operative all along: someone outside the purview of white society becomes, in time of crisis, an object of suspicion. Thus, despite his status as a slaveholder, and his protestation of innocence even as he stood upon the scaffold, Blake hanged on 10 July. But before he hanged, Blake arranged for the emancipation of his slaves after his death— further evidence that he was "soft" on slavery.[14]

The final major incident of the panic occurred, appropriately, in Livingston. On 15 July the Earl brothers, William and John, whom Cotton had implicated, were brought to Livingston from Vicksburg. Though accounts conflict, a group of "unauthorized" Vicksburg citizens apparently captured the Earls and took them to Livingston. Their ostensible purpose was to acquire testimony unavailable in Vicksburg. But the Earls' captors also realized that they could not try the Earls in Vicksburg and protect themselves from "personal or pecuniary injury." Livingston provided this protection as well as a good chance for winning a conviction.[15]

The committee, however, did not have the opportunity to convict William Earl; he died the night before his trial. According to the Livingston pamphlet, William hanged himself in jail. This may be accurate. But the pamphlet fails to mention that a group of Livingston citizens (encouraged by a committee member) tortured William Earl before jailing him:

. . . in addition to the whipping, he was laid upon the ground stark naked with his back up, and a large cat caught by the tail and dragged to and fro . . . until his back was well-scratched (as they term it) and then dropped over his back hot sealing wax!—and this done all to extort confessions from a prisoner.[16]

Upon hearing of this cruelty, another group of Vicksburg citizens decided to bring the Earls back to Warren County for trial. Too late to save William, they did manage to remove John.[17]

The Earl incident marked the end of the panic. A few slaves were executed later in the summer, but no more whites were "swung off."[18] Perhaps no more whites were suspected. More likely, Livingston whites realized, as they realized in the Sharkey affair, that tyranny over whites was dissolving the color line. In the treatment of William Earl, whites saw another white being treated as if he were black. "However guilty they [the Earls] may be," one man wrote, "we are bound to ask, if this be cruel for savages, how much more cruel for free-born Americans!"⁸⁹ By punishing Earl so cruelly, Madison County whites were no longer saving white supremacy. Instead, they were destroying distinction of color. The purging had gone too far. "Respectable" citizens recognized this danger and undoubtedly acted to end extralegal actions. This community simply had to find "normal" legal procedures to contain its anxieties.

Thus it comes as no surprise that the insurrection panic of 1835 made slavery the overriding issue for the first time in "normal" Mississippi politics. It provoked the 1836 session of the state legislature to embrace officially the "positive good" argument.⁹⁰ It also launched the career of one politician and ended the career of another. Franklin E. Plummer, whose previous political victories had stemmed in large part from his appeal to Mississippi's small farmers of the piney woods area, was defeated for a seat in the United States Senate. After the summer of 1835, nonslaveholding politicians had to convince cotton planters that they were "true" to slavery. Plummer, a nonslaveholder, could not overcome the charge that he held antislavery views. In Congress, in 1834, Plummer had denounced slaveholders, claiming that many "have as little regard for the rights of the people as for their own negroes."⁹¹ Such statements carried more weight than Plummer's lukewarm support for the actions of citizens of Madison County during the insurrection panic.⁹²

Robert J. Walker, on the other hand, won the Senate seat by convincing the electorate that he was "safer" to represent them in the Senate "if the slave question, as regards the District of Columbia, is really to be agitated in Congress."⁹³ Walker enjoyed the fortunate circumstance of having bought a cotton plantation in Madison County a few months before the panic. This purchase enabled him to campaign as a cotton planter who held the same interests as slaveholders in Mississippi. Indeed, Walker pressed the issue of insurrection. He frequently claimed that the Whigs under Henry Clay deliberately fostered servile revolt.⁹⁴

Walker's ascent, then, marked a new era in Mississippi politics:

the effort to deal with anxiety over "questionable" whites entered a new and more "democratic" phase. Whites such as Plummer, supposedly "soft" on slavery, could be controlled by charges of "disloyalty"—a technique that enabled Mississippians and southerners to walk the tightrope between consent and coercion more successfully than did lynch justice. Furthermore, Mississippians could no longer afford to indulge in forms of frontier vigilantism if they wanted to avoid harsh criticism from northerners and southerners dedicated to the principle of "a fair trial and full investigation."[5]

Foreseeing more "legitimate" means of dealing with anxiety, the editor of the Jackson *Mississippian* urged potential emigrants to Mississippi not to hesitate:

Property and life here are as safe as in any of the States where slavery exists, and recent occurrences should not prevent emigration to our State, or deter capitalists from investing their funds in our Stocks . . . our negroes, uninfluenced by base and designing men, are as orderly and obedient as the negroes of any State in the Union."[6]

The qualification, "uninfluenced by base and designing men," was the editor's small concession to the existence of a white enemy that did not reside in the North. As we have seen, citizens of west-central Mississippi exaggerated the threat posed by this internal enemy; in certain cases, they imagined white enemies where none at all existed. But these perceptions are not incomprehensible. A slaveholder had to live with the knowledge that there was no defense against the midnight attack during which slaves could rape white females and massacre white males before the white community could aid his family. He reasoned that slaves would not commit the individual massacre if they recognized that collective white power prevented massacre beyond a single household."[7] There was always, however, his ineradicable anxiety over racial loyalties of fellow whites. There were, after all, men who lived on the fringes of white society, who practiced such "disreputable" professions as steam-doctoring, who enjoyed such "disreputable" pleasures as interracial sex, and who entertained such "disreputable" ideas as freeing or not whipping their slaves. A county like Madison had no institutions to influence these men to consent to becoming more "reputable": and coercing whites made white democracy no longer reputable at all. No wonder that southern slaveholders, as the Mississippi panic so cogently indicates, lived in their own special age of anxiety.

Notes

1. For slaveholders' anxieties see, among others, Harvey Wish, "American Slave Insurrections Before 1861," *Journal of Negro History* 22 (July 1937): 299-320; Kenneth M. Stampp, *The Peculiar Institution: Slavery in the Antebellum South* (New York, 1956); Richard C. Wade, "The Vesey Plot: A Reconsideration," *Journal of Southern History* 30 (May 1964): 143-61; Charles B. Dew, "Black Ironworkers and the Slave Insurrection Panic of 1856," *Journal of Southern History* 41 (August 1975): 321-38. In 1833, Governor Robert Y. Hayne of South Carolina declared: "A state of military preparation must always be with us a state of perfect domestic security. A period of profound peace and consequent apathy may expose us to the danger of domestic insurrection." Quoted in Wish, "American Slave Insurrections Before 1861," p. 306.

2. See Winthrop D. Jordan, *White Over Black; American Attitudes Toward the Negro, 1550-1812* (Chapel Hill, 1968) for a discussion of the blurred color line. Many historians have noted alleged involvement of whites in certain alleged insurrections, but few have gone any further than making the observation. One who tried to do so is James H. Johnston, "The Participation of White Men in Virginia Negro Insurrections," *Journal of Negro History* 16 (April 1931): 158-67.

3. The standard source for the New York panic is Daniel Horsmanden, *The New York Conspiracy* (1810; reprint ed., Boston, 1971). For the Gabriel conspiracy, see the documents in Willie Lee Rose, ed., *A Documentary History of Slavery in North America* (New York, 1976), pp. 107-114. The Anna H. Johnson letter is in Robert S. Starobin, ed., *Denmark Vesey: The Slave Conspiracy of 1822* (Englewood Cliffs, N.J., 1970), p. 72. Also see Dan T. Carter, "The Christmas Day Insurrection Scare of 1865," *Journal of Southern History* 42 (August 1976): 345-64.

4. Clement Eaton, *Freedom of Thought in the Old South* (Durham, N.C., 1940), pp. 95-117.

5. Edwin A. Miles, "The Mississippi Slave Insurrection Scare of 1835," *Journal of Negro History* 32 (January 1957): 48-60.

6. It is difficult to determine accurately numbers of hangings and banishments. Figures must be culled from a pamphlet (see note 8), newspaper editorials and twelve letters written by various participants in or observers of the panic. Extracts of these letters were reprinted in many newspapers, northern as well as southern.

7. Washington *United States Telegraph*, 5 August 1835. This letter was postmarked Vicksburg, 12 July 1835, and was initially sent by a "gentleman" in Vicksburg to his friend in Lexington, Kentucky.

8. Thomas Shackelford, ed., *Proceedings of the Citizens of Madison County, Mississippi, at Livingston, in July, 1835, In Relation to the Trial and Punishment of Several Individuals Implicated in a Contemplated Insurrection in This State* (Jackson, 1836). A copy of this pamphlet (hereafter cited as the Livingston pamphlet) is reprinted in H. R. Howard, comp., *The History of Virgil A. Stewart . . .* (New York, 1836). Subsequent page citations refer to the Howard volume. In their indignant letter of 28 August 1835, to R. G. Williams, antislavery publisher of New York, Clinton (Hinds County) citizens revealed how eagerly this rationalization was embraced. See *United States Telegraph*, 24 Sept. 1835.

9. Edwin A. Miles, *Jacksonian Democracy in Mississippi* (Chapel Hill, N.C., 1960), pp. 1-120; Charles S. Sydnor, *Slavery in Mississippi* (New York, 1933), pp. 164-67, 181-202.

10. U. B. Phillips, "The Origin and Growth of the Southern Black Belts," in E. D. Genovese, ed., *The Slave Economy of the Old South* (Baton Rouge, 1968), p. 97. This essay was initially published in 1906 (*American Historical Review*).

11. Ibid., pp. 110-11.

12. Joseph G. Baldwin, *The Flush Times of Alabama and Mississippi* (1853; reprint ed., New York, 1957), pp. 34-63.

13. Lewis C. Gray, *History of Agriculture in the Southern United States,* vol. 2 (Washington, D.C., 1933), p. 903. See also Table 4.1.

14. Miles, *Jacksonian Democracy*, pp. 117-19; H. S. Ruff, "The History of Hinds County, Mississippi, Before 1860" (M.A. thesis, Duke University, 1934), pp. 36-58; Sydnor, *Slavery in Mississippi*, pp. 164-67.

15. Jackson *Mississippian*, 24 January 1834.

16. Jackson *Mississippian*, 24 January and 28 February 1834; Ruff, "The History of Hinds County," pp. 1-75; E. O. Rowland, *History of Hinds County, Mississippi, 1821-1922* (Jackson, 1922); Shirley Faucette, "Clinton—Yesterday," *Journal of Mississippi History*, 40 (August 1978): 215-30; J. H. Ingraham, *The Southwest By A Yankee*, vol. 2 (New York, 1835), 166-68.

17. Jackson *Mississippian*, 14 March 1834.

Table 4.1

POPULATION FIGURES FOR HINDS AND MADISON COUNTIES,
MISSISSIPPI, 1830-1840

Hinds County

Year	Total Whites	Males	Females	FCP	Total Slaves	Males	Females	WPOLLS	Land Value ($)
1830	5,419	2,967	2,452	14	3,212	1,604	1,608		
1833				7	4,390			1,464	134,655
1835				7	5,354			1,259	148,827
1840	6,878	3,892	2,986	45	12,275	6,317	5,958		

Madison County

1830	2,781	1,547	1,234	25	2,169	1,111	1,058		
1833				2	3,217			689	127,823
1835				2	4,904			658	196,900
1836				1	6,171			678	233,646
1840	3,986	2,269	1,717	11	11,533	5,801	5,732		

SOURCE: U.S., Census Bureau, *Fifth Census* and *Sixth Census*; Mississippi Department of Archives and History, *Personal Tax Rolls* (Record Group 29); Records of the States of
the United States, *Journal of the State Senate of Mississippi.*

FCP = Free Colored Persons
WPOLLS = White Polls

Population in Madison grew faster and "blacker" (see Table 4.2).

Table 4.2

GROWTH RATE OF MADISON AND HINDS COUNTIES, 1830-1840

Madison		Hinds	
432 %	Growth rate, slaves	282 %	Growth rate, slaves
43	Growth rate, whites	27	Growth rate, whites
214	Growth rate, total	122	Growth rate, total

18. Ibid.
19. Leonard L. Richards, *'Gentlemen of Property and Standing': Anti-
Abolition Mobs in Jacksonian America* (New York, 1970), pp. 14-62; J. H.
Johnston, *Race Relations in Virginia and Miscegenation in the South*
(Amherst, Mass., 1970), pp. 98-105.

20. H. S. Foote, *Casket of Reminiscences* (Washington, D.C., 1874), p. 253; Clinton (Miss.) *Gazette*, 11, July 1835, indicates that all suspected whites brought before the Clinton committee of vigilance had been discharged.

21. Livingston pamphlet, pp. 221-25.

22. Ibid., p. 225.

23. *United States Telegraph*, 6 October 1835; Mississippi Department of Archives and History, *Personal Tax Rolls—Madison County*. Blake had started with nothing. In 1830 he owned one slave; by 1833 he still owned one slave. But by 1834 his holdings had increased to four slaves.

24. Livingston pamphlet, p. 225-27.

25. Ibid., p. 253; *United States Telegraph*, 8 August 1835.

26. Livingston pamphlet, pp. 228-32.

27. Ibid.

28. Ibid., pp. 238-39; Dumas Malone, ed., *Dictionary of American Biography* (New York, 1935), pp. 488-89; Foote, *Casket of Reminiscences*, pp. 249-59; *United States Telegraph*, 6 October 1835.

29. Livingston pamphlet, pp. 238-39.

30. Nashville *National Banner*, 24 July 1835.

31. Livingston pamphlet, p. 254.

32. Nashville *National Banner*, 7 August 1835 (extract from a letter postmarked Vicksburg, 12 July 1835).

33. Livingston pamphlet, p. 232.

34. Ibid.

35. Ibid., pp. 232-34, 239-40.

36. Ibid., p. 223.

37. Ibid., p. 234.

38. Ibid., pp. 234-35.

39. Ibid., pp. 246-49; *United States Telegraph*, 6 October 1835; Alexandria (Va.) *Gazette*, 28 July 1835 (extract from a letter postmarked Canton, 3 July 1835).

40. Harriet Martineau, *Society in America*, 2 vols. (New York, 1837), 2: 118-20.

41. Livingston pamphlet, p. 222.

42. Alexandria *Gazette*, 29 July 1835 (extract from a letter postmarked Mississippi Springs, 7 July 1835).

43. See Table 4.3. Livingston pamphlet, pp. 235-36; *United States Telegraph*, 6 October 1835; Richmond *Enquirer*, 14 August 1835; Miles, "The Mississippi Slave Insurrection Scare of 1835," pp. 50-51; Mississippi Department of Archives and History, *Personal Tax Rolls* (Record Group 29).

Table 4.3

THE LIVINGSTON COMMITTEE OF THIRTEEN

	1834		1835	
	Slaves	Acres of Land	Slaves	Acres of Land
Hardin D. Runnels	33	844	39	844
Thomas Hudnal, Sr.	118	2,700	130	3,000
Israel Spencer	26	?	42	160
Sack P. Gee	8	320	15	1,100
M. D. Mitchell	4	80	5	80
Nelson Taylor	20	160	24	?
Robert Hodge, Sr.	9	560	22	560
John Simmons	42	1,100	56	1,100
James Grafton	26	400	116	640
Charles Smith	18	240	18	240
D. W. Haley	17	320	30	320
Jesse Mabry	?	?	?	?
William Wade	42	1,042	71	1,680

NOTE: Runnels, Gee, Wade, Grafton, Hodge, Hudnal, Haley, and Smith were all Madison residents since at least 1830. Spencer was a Mississippi resident since at least 1831. Mitchell was a Madison resident since at least 1833. I have no further information on Taylor, Simmons, and Mabry.

44. Foote, *Casket of Reminiscences*, pp. 247-59; Alexandria *Gazette*, 28 July 1835 (extract from a letter postmarked Clinton, 5 July 1835); Alexandria *Gazette*, 28 July 1835 (extract from a letter postmarked Canton, 3 July 1835).
45. Livingston pamphlet, pp. 238-46.
46. Ibid.
47. Ibid.
48. Jackson *Mississippian*, 7 August 1835. Also see Alexandria *Gazette*, 4 August 1835.
49. *National Intelligencer*, 27 and 28 July 1835 (extracts from letters postmarked Clinton, 5 July 1835, and Carson Grove, 9 July 1835); Livingston pamphlet, pp. 238-44; Stewart's pamphlet is reprinted in Howard, *The History of Virgil A. Stewart*. See J. F. H. Claiborne, *Life and Correspondence of John A. Quitman* (New York, 1860), vol. 1, p. 139, for a statement of the position that Stewart fabricated the details of an insurrection conspiracy in order to enrich himself.
50. Jackson *Mississippian*, 7 August 1835: "We have not been able to obtain a copy of the 'Western Land Pirate,' but from what we have

learned, it discloses the history and mysteries of one of the most daring and extensive schemes of robbery that has ever been set on foot in this or any other country." Also see *Niles' Register*, 8 August 1835.

51. Livingston pamphlet, p. 243; Alexandria *Gazette*, 29 July 1835 (reprint of an extract from a letter that originally appeared in the Natchez *Courier*, 10 July 1835). Also see Alexandria *Gazette*, 30 July 1835 (extract from a letter postmarked Carson Grove, 9 July 1835). These accounts suggest that Cotton implicated more than fifty whites; of this number, at least seventeen were arrested and examined. Probably not more than eight hanged.

52. New Orleans *True American*, 13 July 1835. Also see *United States Telegraph*, 24 September and 6 October 1835, and Clinton *Gazette*, 11 July 1835.

53. Livingston pamphlet, pp. 237-46; *United States Telegraph*, 6 October 1835; Alexandria *Gazette*, 28-30 July 1835 (extracts from three letters: Clinton, 5 July; Carson Grove, 9 July; Jackson, 8 July).

54. Alexandria *Gazette*, 30 July 1835 (extract from a letter postmarked Carson Grove, 9 July 1835).

55. Nashville *National Banner*, 15 July 1835 (extract from a letter sent by "a gentleman of respectability" in Hinds to a merchant in Nashville).

56. See for example, Nashville *National Banner*, 15 July 1835; *United States Telegraph*, 6 October 1835; Alexandria *Gazette*, 29 July 1835.

57. Nashville *National Banner*, 7 August 1835 (extract from a letter postmarked Vicksburg, 12 July 1835).

58. Ibid.

59. Livingston pamphlet, pp. 246-48. Letter-writers who provided "*Officious* and *gratuitous* information" to the public displeased Madison citizens.

60. Ibid.

61. *United States Telegraph*, 6 October 1835; Richmond *Enquirer*, 14 August 1835; Livingston pamphlet, pp. 255-56.

62. Miss. Dept. of Arch. and Hist., *Personal Tax Rolls* (Record Group 29); *Fifth Census* of the United States; Richmond *Enquirer*, 14 August 1835; Livingston pamphlet, pp. 255-56; *United States Telegraph*, 8 August 1835; Clinton *Gazette*, 12 September 1835.

63. George C. Osborn, "Plantation Life in Central Mississippi as Revealed in the Clay Sharkey Papers," *Journal of Mississippi History* 3 (October 1941): 277-78.

64. *United States Telegraph*, 6 October 1835.

65. Sharkey and Kilborn to Hiram G. Runnels, Fleetwood, Hinds

County, 7 July 1835. Record Group 27, Mississippi Department of Archives and History.

66. *United States Telegraph*, 6 October 1835. Also see Richmond *Enquirer*, 14 August 1835, and Foote, *Casket of Reminiscences*, pp. 259-61.

67. Sharkey and Kilborn to Runnels, 7 July 1835.

68. Richmond *Enquirer*, 14 August 1835; Jonathan Daniels, *The Devil's Backbone: The Story of the Natchez Trace* (New York, 1962), pp. 244-45.

69. *United States Telegraph*, 6 October 1835; Alexandria *Gazette*, 30 July 1835 (extract from a letter postmarked Carson Grove, 9 July 1835).

70. G. C. Osborn, "Plantation Life in Central Mississippi," pp. 277-78; *Personal Tax Rolls*, Mississippi Department of Archives and History; U.S. Census Bureau, *Fifth Census*.

71. Foote, *Casket of Reminiscences*, p. 260.

72. H. S. Foote, *The Bench and Bar of the South and Southwest* (St. Louis, 1876), p. 68; Foote, *Casket of Reminiscences*, p. 261.

73. Foote, *Casket of Reminiscences*, p. 261. Foote also notes: "After this I instituted in the name of the injured Sharkey, a suit for damages, and recovered $10,000."

74. Nashville *National Banner*, 7 August 1835 (extract from a letter postmarked Vicksburg, 12 July 1835).

75. Wyche to Runnels, Fleetwood, Hinds County, 8 July 1835. Record Group 27, Mississippi Department of Archives and History.

76. A reconciliation of some sort between Livingston and Clinton must have been achieved by July 10 because the July 11 issue of the Clinton *Gazette* praises the Livingston community for its "utmost order" and the Livingston committee for the "calmness and dignity" of its proceedings. The *Gazette* omits the Sharkey episode in its account of the "horrible conspiracy." The Livingston pamphlets also omits the Sharkey episode.

77. Livingston pamphlet, pp. 248-52.

78. Ibid.

79. Foote, *Casket of Reminiscences*, pp. 253-55. Also see *United States Telegraph*, 6 October 1835.

80. Livingston pamphlet, pp. 256-57. Also see *United States Telegraph*, 6 October 1835.

81. Livingston pamphlet, pp. 252-55; *United States Telegraph*, 6 October 1835.

82. Ibid.

83. *United States Telegraph*, 6 October 1835.

84. Ibid.

85. See Natchez *Courier*, 7 August 1835, and Vicksburg *Register*, 17

September 1835, for accounts that place Livingston citizens in a good light. Livingston pamphlet, pp. 257-59, contains a section on the Earls. For a different and—in my opinion—more reliable account, see Vicksburg *Register*, 13 August 1835, and also see *United States Telegraph*, 6 October 1835.

86. Vicksburg *Register*, 13 August 1835.

87. Ibid.

88. The final execution was apparently in September 1835. A "notorious negro" belonging to Captain Hudnal had escaped during the panic and was not captured until September. See Niles' *Register*, 31 October 1835.

89. Vicksburg *Register*, 13 August 1835.

90. For the panic's impact on state politics, see Miles, *Jacksonian Democracy*, pp. 125-26; J. P. Shenton, "The Compleat Politician: The Life of Robert John Walker" (Ph.D. diss., Columbia University, 1954), pp. 1-22; Shenton, *Robert John Walker: A Politician From Jackson to Lincoln* (New York, 1961), pp. 1-30; Miles, "Franklin E. Plummer: Piney Woods Spokesman of the Jackson Era," *Journal of Mississippi History* 14 (January 1952): 2-34; *Journal of the State Senate of Mississippi* (January 1836), Records of the States of the United States.

91. Miles, "Franklin Plummer," p. 34.

92. Columbus (Miss.) *Argus*, 6 October 1835.

93. Jackson *Mississippian*, 18 September 1835.

94. Shenton, *Robert John Walker*, pp. 1-2.

95. Shenton, "The Compleat Politician," pp. 21-22; Livingston pamphlet; Jackson *Mississippian*, 14 August 1835, blamed northern abolitionists for the "recent attempted insurrection." For an example of criticism of "mob law," see Nashville *National Banner*, 24 July 1835. For similarities between vigilantism in Mississippi and frontier areas, see R. M. Brown, "The American Vigilante Tradition," in H. D. Graham and T. R. Gurr, eds., *Violence in America*, 2 vols. (Washington D.C., 1969), 1: 121-169.

96. Jackson *Mississippian*, 17 July 1835.

97. On slaveholders' fear of the midnight attack see Nashville *National Banner*, 24 July 1835; *U.S. Telegraph*, 1 December 1835; (Natchez) *Mississippi Free Trader*, 28 August 1844 (letters written by General Felix Huston in 1833 and 1835 reprinted). In August 1835, Huston, referring to the July panic, declared that "if one family had been murdered, one female violated by that unhallowed union of white and black desperadoes, no man in the State who held abolition principles or who took abolition papers would have escaped—they would have perished to a man."

Rebels and Sambos: The Search for the Negro's Personality in Slavery

By Kenneth M. Stampp

I think it is safe to say that no historical scholar has ever been altogether satisfied with his sources. Whatever the subject of his investigation, whether he is concerned with the remote or recent past, the available records never tell him all he would like to know—never permit more than a partial reconstruction of any historical event. Under the best of circumstances the historian is obliged to write about men he has never known from scattered, fragmentary, and often censored records that leave many crucial questions unanswered.

Historians who investigate the subject of slavery in the antebellum South confront this problem in one of its more exasperating forms; and they find it most acute when they inquire, as some have done in recent years, about the behavior of slaves, about their relationships with the master class, and about their personalities. There are, to be sure, problems of conceptualization as well as of research, for explanations of broad patterns of slave behavior, if such exist, must be based on one or another theory of personality development. Nevertheless, whatever methodological or conceptual strategies a historian may devise, his search for answers to questions concerning slave behavior and personality must begin with the accumulation of a reasonable amount of empirical data. It is this urgent need for data that introduces at the outset the problem of limited sources.

What we know about slaves and their masters we have learned mostly from the business records, diaries, letters, memoirs, and autobiographies of slaveholders; from travelers' observations; from contemporary newspapers and periodicals; and from various government documents, including court records. Direct evidence from the slaves themselves is hopelessly inadequate. Well over 90

Mr. Stampp is Morrison Professor of American History at the University of California in Berkeley. The paper in a slightly abridged form was read on November 11, 1970, at a general session of the annual meeting of the Southern Historical Association at Louisville, Kentucky.

percent of them were illiterate, and even the small literate minority seldom found an opportunity to write or speak with candor. Travelers in the South occasionally interviewed slaves; in the 1850s Benjamin Drew, a white New England abolitionist, interviewed a group of fugitives who had settled in Canada;[1] and a few ex-slaves left autobiographies of varying quality. But I know of not a single slave diary; and letters written by slaves are rare. For more than sixty years after emancipation, no one made a systematic attempt to record the narratives of former slaves. Three belated efforts in the 1920s and 1930s appear to have come too late to be of much value to historians, though the narratives are of considerable interest to folklorists.[2] Historians have no doubt failed to make as much use of the Negro's oral tradition of songs and folklore as they should; but this material, as a source for slavery, also presents problems. Among other things, the songs and folklore are ever changing; and, since the collections were made for the most part after slavery, we can seldom be sure that what they contain are true expressions of the slaves.[3]

Inevitably, then, our knowledge of the life and behavior of American Negroes in slavery comes mainly from the testimony of white observers. The letters written by slaves were usually written to white men; the slave autobiographies were often dictated to and written by white men; and the early collections of slave songs and folklore were put together by white men, who may well have missed the nuances in this often subtle material. In short, the ubiquitous white man, as master, editor, traveler, politician, and amanuensis, stands forever between slave and historian, telling the historian how the slave was treated, how he behaved, what he thought, and what sort of personality he had. However imagi-

---

[1] Drew, The Refugee: or the Narratives of Fugitive Slaves in Canada (Boston, 1856).

[2] John B. Cade, "Out of the Mouths of Ex-Slaves," Journal of Negro History, XX (July 1935), 294–337; Fisk University Social Science Institute, Unwritten History of Slavery (Nashville, 1945); Benjamin A. Botkin, ed., Lay My Burden Down (Chicago, 1945). See also Norman R. Yetman, "The Background of the Slave Narrative Collection," American Quarterly, XIX (Fall 1967), 534–53. My evaluation of these collections of slave narratives is based on the above published extracts. A careful study of the more than two thousand narratives collected by the Federal Writer's Project in the 1930s may lead to a more favorable assessment of their historical value.

[3] A good case for the value of this material is presented in Lawrence W. Levine, "Slave Songs and Slave Consciousness: An Exploration in Neglected Sources," in Tamara Hareven, ed., Anonymous Americans (New York, 1971), 99–130. See also Sterling Stuckey, "Through the Prism of Folklore: Black Ethos in Slavery," Massachusetts Review, IX (Summer 1968), 417–37.

native the historian may be, he will always have trouble breaking through this barrier, and he will always be handicapped by the paucity of firsthand testimony from the slaves themselves.

This being the case, it is hardly surprising that historians who have studied the behavior and personality of the Negro in slavery have failed to agree on the meaning of the evidence and have left many problems unsolved. Indeed, two of the books that address themselves directly and explicitly to this problem—Herbert Aptheker's *American Negro Slave Revolts*[4] and Stanley M. Elkins's *Slavery*[5]—arrive at opposite conclusions. Aptheker, whose purpose is to depict "in realistic terms the response of the American Negro to his bondage," found "that discontent and rebelliousness were not only exceedingly common, but, indeed, characteristic of American Negro slaves."[6] Elkins, focusing more narrowly on plantation field hands, suggests that characteristically they were not rebels but Sambos, with personalities very much as they were described in southern lore:

Sambo, the typical ' plantation slave, was docile but irresponsible, loyal but lazy, humble but chronically given to lying and stealing; his behavior was full of infantile silliness and his talk inflated with childish exaggeration. His relationship with his master was one of utter dependence and childlike attachment: it was indeed this childlike quality that was the very key to his being.[7]

These two portraits of the southern slave, one as the discontented rebel, the other as the passive Sambo, are worth examining, because together they define the two extremes—the outer limits—of possible slave behavior.

Of the two portraits, Aptheker's is the easier to evaluate. From his empirical research, mostly in newspapers and government documents, he claims to have uncovered approximately 250 revolts and conspiracies, each involving a minimum of ten slaves and having the winning of freedom as its apparent goal.[8] He makes no attempt to explain slave behavior with any personality theory; but implicit throughout the book is an assumption that when a mass of people are as brutally exploited as the southern slaves, discontent and rebelliousness against the ruling class are bound to be endemic.

[4] Aptheker, *American Negro Slave Revolts* (New York, 1943).
[5] Elkins, *Slavery: A Problem in American Institutional and Intellectual Life* (2d ed., Chicago and London, 1968).
[6] Aptheker, *Slave Revolts*, 374.
[7] Elkins, *Slavery*, 82.
[8] Aptheker, *Slave Revolts*, 162.

We are indebted to Aptheker for providing a useful corrective to the view, still prevalent when his book was published in 1943, that the slaves were almost uniformly contented. He presents detailed accounts of a few rebellions and of a number of authentic conspiracies; but above all he shows how persistent the *fear* of rebellion was among white southerners and how frequently insurrection panics drove them to near hysteria. However, the book has three major shortcomings. First, it fails to use sources critically; second, it argues beyond the evidence; and, third, it does not distinguish between slave discontent, which was probably widespread, and slave rebelliousness, which was only sporadic and always local. A more accurate title for this book would be *American Negro Slave Revolts, Conspiracies, and Rumors of Conspiracies*, for it is the last of these things that most of the book is really about.

An example of Aptheker's misinterpretation of his data can be found in the twelve pages devoted to the years 1835–1842, which follow a chapter on the Nat Turner Rebellion. He begins by declaring that "The year 1835 witnessed the reopening of this never-long interrupted drama of the organized struggle of an enslaved people to throw off their yoke." Then, presenting his evidence year by year, he tells us of rumors that "began to fly around," of plots that "were overheard," of reports of "what appears to have been a bona filde conspiracy," and of whisperings of "large-scale conspiracies." Aptheker then relates that after 1842 the "remainder of the forties were relatively quiet years." But his own evidence indicates that in the history of slave insurrections, except for the usual budget of rumors and alarms, the year 1835–1842 were also quiet ones.[9] Clearly, though revealing much about the anxieties of white masters, he has failed to establish his thesis that rebelliousness was characteristic of American Negro slaves.

Elkins, in a decidedly more influential counterhypothesis, offers the placid and contented Sambo as the typical plantation slave. He is concerned almost entirely with describing and explaining Sambo's personality and behavior rather than with offering empirical evidence of his existence. He disposes of the problem of evidence in two sentences: "The picture [of Sambo] has far too many circumstantial details, its hues have been stroked in by too many different brushes, for it be denounced as counterfeit. Too much folk-knowledge, too much plantation literature, too much of the Negro's own lore, have gone into its making to entitle one

[9] *Ibid.*, 325–36.

in good conscience to condemn it as 'conspiracy.' " Beyond this, at several points, Elkins simply tells his readers that the widespread existence of Sambo "will be assumed," or will be "taken for granted," and then proceeds to his explanation.[10]

Since the Elkins thesis is familiar, I will only summarize the three chief points of his strategy, which are (1) his use of comparative history, (2) his use of personality theory, and (3) his use of analogy. Elkins argues, first of all, that the Negro with a Sambo-type personality was not a universal product of slavery in the Americas but, because of certain unique conditions, a peculiar product of slavery in the United States. The principal differences between North American and Latin American slavery, he believes, were the latter's relatively greater flexibility and openness, the far greater opportunities it gave the Negro to escape into free society, and the presence of not one but several centers of authority: church and state as well as slave master. In the antebellum South slavery grew unchecked by church or state; its form was dictated by the needs of the planter capitalists; and state laws treated the slave essentially as property, thus depriving him of his identity as a human being. Southern slavery operated as a "closed system" in which the slaves had only limited contacts with free society and little hope of becoming part of it. It was this closed system that produced Sambo.[11]

Second, to explain how southern slavery had this devastating effect on the Negro, Elkins utilizes some of the literature on personality theory. Using Freud, he points to the impossibility of a "meaningful relationship between fathers and sons" and to the difficulty of becoming a man without "acceptable male models to pattern yourself after."[12] But he relies chiefly on a blend of certain aspects of the interpersonal theory of Harry Stack Sullivan and of role psychology. Sullivan maintains that personality can be studied only as it manifests itself in interpersonal relations,[13] and he stresses the manner in which personality is formed in relationships with so-called "significant others"—that is, with those in positions of authority or otherwise capable of enhancing or endangering one's security. Out of anxiety concerning the attitudes of these significant others a person learns to behave in ways that

[10] Elkins, *Slavery*, 84–86, 88–89.
[11] *Ibid.*, 81–82, 84, 134–37.
[12] *Ibid.*, 130, 242.
[13] Sullivan defines personality as "the relatively enduring pattern of recurrent interpersonal situations which characterize a human life." *The Interpersonal Theory of Psychiatry* (New York, 1953), 111.

meet their expectations. Eventually, some of this behavior is internalized and becomes part of the personality. Role psychology emphasizes the roles, or models of behavior, that are extended to individuals throughout their lives by organizations, or by groups, or by society at large.[14] There are rewards for playing the expected role well and penalties for playing it badly or not at all. How well an individual plays a role depends in part on his skill, on his motivation, on his "role knowledge," and on "role clarity," the last requiring a condition of general agreement about proper behavior. The more clearly a role is defined the better it is likely to be performed, and the greater its impact is likely to be on the personality of the performer. Thus, it may be that to some degree one's personality consists of the roles one plays.

Applying these ideas to the southern plantation slave, the Elkins hypothesis runs something like this: In a closed system from which there was virtually no escape, the master, whose authority was absolute, who dispensed rewards and punishments, was the only significant other in the slave's life. The master defined the slave's role, provided him with a clear and simple script, judged his performance, and rewarded him according to its quality. The result was Sambo, the perpetually dependent, irresponsible child. Elkins does not claim that Sambo was the universal slave personality, for he recognizes that there were "a great profusion of individual types." A "significant number," including house servants, skilled craftsmen, slaves who hired their own time, slave foremen, and those who lived in single families on small farms managed "to escape the full impact of the system and its coercions upon personality." For these slaves "there was a margin of space denied to the majority . . . ," and few of them took on the character of Sambo. But of the mass of field hands on large and small plantations, though Elkins recognizes that some did not fit the classic Sambo type, it is clearly his intention to suggest that Sambo embraced the majority.[15]

Finally, to illuminate certain aspects of southern slavery, Elkins resorts to the analogy of the Nazi concentration camp. He warns that an analogy must not be taken literally, for things that are analogous are not identical. His purpose is to examine two

[14] "A role is a cluster of traits (or pattern of behavior) which serves as the culturally normal or modal solution to recurrent, usually social problems peculiar to a particular status or position in society." David C. McClelland, *Personality* (New York, 1951), 293. See also Eugene L. and Ruth E. Hartley, *Fundamentals of Social Psychology* (New York, 1952), 485–86.

[15] Elkins, *Slavery*, 86–87, 137–38.

situations which, in spite of their "vast dissimilarities," contain "mechanisms that are metaphorically comparable and analytically interchangeable." In this analogy the mechanism was "the infantilizing tendencies of absolute power."[16] Elkins sees a rough similarity between the Sambo produced by slavery on the southern plantation and the human product of the concentration camp, whose experiences often led to personality disintegration, infantilization, and even a tendency to look on SS guards in a childlike way as father figures.

Both the master of the plantation and the commander of the concentration camp were the sole significant others in the lives of the people under their control. Both could mete out punishment or grant protection, while the slaves and inmates were reduced to complete dependence. "A working adjustment to either system," Elkins concludes, "required a childlike conformity . . ."; the crucial factor

was the simple "closedness" of the system, in which all lines of authority descended from the master . . . . The individual, consequently, for his very psychic security, had to picture his master in some way as the "good father," even when, as in the concentration camp, it made no sense at all. But why should it not have made sense for many a simple plantation Negro whose master did exhibit, in all the ways that could be expected, the features of the good father who was really "good"? If the concentration camp could produce in two or three years the result that it did, one wonders how much more pervasive must have been those attitudes, expectations, and values which had, certainly, their benevolent side and which were accepted and transmitted over generations.[17]

It is no small tribute to Elkins's achievement that his essay should have provided the focus for virtually all scholarly discussion of slave personality for the past decade and that a volume of commentary, with a response from Elkins, has recently been published.[18] I doubt that any future historian of slavery will fail to recognize Sambo as an authentic personality type among the slaves on southern plantations. More generally, Elkins has contrib-

[16] *Ibid.*, 104, 225.
[17] *Ibid.*, 128–30.
[18] Ann Lane, ed., *The Debate over* Slavery: *Stanley Elkins and His Critics* (Urbana, Ill., 1971). In his response, except for one important point mentioned in note 34 below, Elkins concedes very little to his critics. Therefore, since he has neither changed his position significantly nor added any supporting empirical evidence, my comments on his use of analogy, his use of personality theory, and his view of the life of plantation slaves are as relevant to the new essay as to the old.

uted much to arousing interest in the problem of slave personality and to making historians aware of the possibility of dealing with the problem through an interdisciplinary approach. On the other hand, I believe that the discussion has been rather too much preoccupied with his hypothesis; that, in consequence, we have made little additional progress during the past decade; and that the time has come for renewed investigation. Elkins, after all, intended his essay to be the start of a new approach, suggestive rather than definitive; and, accordingly, he left plenty of work for others to do. Moreover, his essay contains a number of flaws, which give the remaining work a special urgency.

Because of their fascination with the essay's methodology and conceptualization, many scholars seem to have overlooked its lack of empirical evidence—its bland assumption that the prevalence of Sambo on the plantations can be taken for granted. The concentration-camp analogy, of course, proves nothing; at most, Elkins can argue that *if* the typical plantation slave was a Sambo, the literature on the camps might suggest an explanation of *why* he was a Sambo.[19] Elkins, as I have noted, takes Sambo for granted because Sambo appears so prominently in antebellum plantation literature. But most of this literature was written by white men, and much of it is in defense of slavery. To accept it at face value would be only slightly more justifiable than to accept at face value a body of literature on the concentration camps written not by former inmates and competent scholars, such as Bruno Bettelheim, but by the SS guards. Moreover, the public testimony of white witnesses does not by any means invariably support the Elkins hypothesis, for contemporary writers often speak of the resourcefulness and guile of Negroes, and numerous essays on the governing of slaves warn masters never to trust them.[20] Elkins is certainly mistaken when he asserts that the prevalence of Sambo was part of the Negro's own lore. Neither the slave narratives nor

[19] It is unlikely that Elkins thought of his analogy as more than an explanation. Yet he creates a small ambiguity by labeling one of the sections of Appendix A (p. 225) "*Analogy as evidence.*"

[20] Winthrop D. Jordan has called my attention to an important question about when Sambo first began to appear prominently in southern plantation literature. He was not the typical slave depicted in the seventeenth and eighteenth centuries. In those earlier years the slave was more often thought of as a dangerous element in the population—a threat to the peace and safety of the English colonies. Of course, it is possible that the Negro's personality had changed by the nineteenth century, when Sambo first became important in southern literature; but there may have been a connection between the appearance of Sambo and the growing moral attack on slavery. Sambo was always one of the proslavery writers' major arguments for keeping the Negro in bondage.

the Negro's oral tradition give validity to Sambo as the typical plantation slave; rather, their emphasis is on the slave dissemblers and the ways in which they deceived their masters.

In an essay on sources, Elkins explains why he did not use manuscript plantation records, which constitute the private testimony of the white slaveholders. Manuscripts, he writes, "are useful principally on questions of health and maintenance, and they have already been worked over with great care and thoroughness by eminent scholars."[21] But the plantation manuscripts are in fact quite valuable for the study of slave personality, and even information on maintenance and health (including mental health) is decidedly relevant. If the manuscripts have been worked over by other scholars, that is really of little help to Elkins, because no one has used them for precisely his purpose and with his hypothesis in mind. He offers no explanation for his failure to examine other sources, especially newpapers, with their extremely revealing fugitive-slave advertisements, and contemporary periodicals, with their countless essays on the management of slaves and their descriptions of slave behavior. As a result, Elkins is obliged in the end to offer corroborating testimony from sources such as John Pendleton Kennedy's *Swallow Barn* (1832), where we learn that the slave had "the helplessness of a child—without foresight, without faculty of contrivance, without thrift of any kind"; and from Edward Pollard's *Black Diamonds Gathered in the Darkey Homes of the South* (1859), which assures us that "The Negro . . . in his true nature, is always a boy, let him be ever so old . . . ." "Few Southern writers," Elkins concludes, "failed to describe with obvious fondness . . . the perpetual good humor that seemed to mark the Negro character, the good humor of an everlasting childhood."[22]

David C. McClelland, one of Elkins's authorities on personality, devotes two chapters of his book to the problems of collecting and interpreting data. In one of them, McClelland observes that an individual's personality may change "as he changes or as the scientist's insights improve."[23] This is an important point, for the accumulation of an ample supply of data is often the beginning

[21] Elkins, *Slavery*, 224.

[22] *Ibid.*, 131–32. It hardly needs to be said that Elkins does not endorse the racist implications of these statements. He uses them merely to illustrate the Sambo character that slavery allegedly forced on the Negro in the South. Still, it is worth noting that, except for the racist overtones, his description of the plantation slave is almost identical with that found in the writings of Ulrich B. Phillips.

[23] McClelland, *Personality*, 70.

of improved insight. Eugene D. Genovese, after paying tribute to Elkins's achievement, reminds us "that all psychological models may only be used suggestively for flashes of insight or as aids in forming hypotheses and that they cannot substitute for empirical investigation."[24]

The remaining shortcomings of the Elkins essay concern its conceptual and methodological strategies and its apparent misunderstanding of the life of plantation slaves. Several critics have already questioned Elkins's comparative approach, particularly his exaggerated notion of the success of church and state in Latin America in protecting the slave's humanity. They have also demonstrated that Sambo was not a unique product of North American slavery, for he appeared in Brazil, in the French colonies, and in Spanish America as well. "On close inspection," writes Genovese, "the Sambo personality turns out to be neither more nor less than the slavish personality; wherever slavery has existed, Sambo has also."[25] Since the antebellum South did not actually produce a distinct slave personality, the explanation for Sambo may be sought not there alone but everywhere in the Western World.

Elkins's concentration-camp analogy, as I will try to demonstrate, may help to illuminate the condition of one small group of plantation slaves, but it is of little value as an aid to understanding Sambo. He would be quite justified in using his analogy for limited purposes, provided, first, that he could establish a controlling mechanism that is in truth "analytically interchangeable," and, second, that the obvious and admitted elements of dissimilarity between slavery and the concentration camps did not themselves have an important bearing on the formation of personality. To Elkins, the "shock and detachment" experience of adult camp inmates—an experience that slaves born into the system did not endure—was less crucial to personality than adjusting to "the requirements of a 'closed system' of absolute authority."[26]

However, Elkins dismisses far too easily certain vital elements of dissimilarity that did have a profound impact on adult per-

[24] Genovese, "Rebelliousness and Docility in the Negro Slave: A Critique of the Elkins Thesis," *Civil War History*, XIII (December 1967), 314.

[25] *Ibid.*, especially 295–98; quote on page 297. See also David B. Davis, *The Problem of Slavery in Western Culture* (Ithaca, 1966), especially Chap. VIII; Carl N. Degler, "Slavery in Brazil and the United States: An Essay in Comparative History," *American Historical Review*, LXXV (April 1970), 1004–28; Marvin Harris, *Patterns of Race in the Americas* (New York, 1964), 65–78.

[26] Elkins, *Slavery*, 229.

sonality, and first among them is the systematic policy of terror
and brutality in the concentration camps. Slaves were rarely
treated as cruelly as camp inmates. The realities of slavery
dawned on them gradually over a period of years, while the realities of the concentration camp hit the inmates with one stunning
and often disintegrating blow. Moreover, plantation slavery was
a rational institution; it had a logic and purpose that was utterly
missing in the camps, where life, with its total unpredictability,
had about it a nightmarish quality. The extermination policy
eventually adopted in the camps destroyed all belief in the value
of human life. Everybody in the camps, as Bettelheim observed,
"was convinced that his chances for survival were very slim; therefore to preserve himself as an individual seemed pointless."[27] It
was this hopelessness, rather than the absolute authority of one
significant other, that explains the phenomenon of inmates
walking without resistance to the gas chambers. Slavery, though
its influence on personality was severe, still afforded its victims
something a good deal closer to normal life, and therefore it did
not ordinarily have anything like as shattering an impact on personality as did the concentration camps.

The most momentous difference between the two institutions
is evident in the fact that only about 700,000 out of nearly eight
million inmates survived the camps. Elkins declares that he is
necessarily concerned only with the survivors, but among those
he thus eliminates from consideration are nearly all who in some
manner resisted the system and whose personalities were not
crushed by it.[28] To establish a comparable situation in slavery,
one would have to imagine that the system had become vastly
more brutal in the 1850s and that, in consequence, only 400,000
rather than four million slaves were alive in 1860, the rest having
been murdered by their masters for resistance or rules infractions,
or in medical experiments, or as victims of a Negro extermination
policy. One could hardly argue seriously that such a profound
change in the nature of slavery—in terms of the slave's expecta-

[27] Bettelheim, The Informed Heart (Glencoe, Ill., 1960), 138. For statements of
the crucial differences between slavery and the concentration camps see Genovese,
"Rebelliousness and Docility in the Negro Slave," 308–309; and Earle E. Thorpe,
"Chattel Slavery and Concentration Camps," Negro History Bulletin, XXV (May
1962), 173.

[28] The literature on the camps indicates that there was resistance, but such
behavior is not taken into account in Elkins's essay. See especially Eugen Kogon,
The Theory and Practice of Hell (New York, 1950). See also Genovese, "Rebelliousness and Docility in the Negro Slave," 312–13; Thorpe, "Chattel Slavery and
Concentration Camps," 175.

tions of survival—would have had no significant impact on personality. Nor would one then want to limit a study of slave personality to the cringing 400,000 survivors. It would appear, therefore, that absolute power was not the controlling mechanism as much as the manner in which the power was used.

Turning finally to the theoretical foundation of the Elkins essay, the important question is whether personality theory, when applied to the available data, points unmistakably to Sambo as the typical plantation slave. This does not seem to be the case, for there are important aspects of the theories that Elkins uses, together with much data, that suggest other plausible hypotheses.[29] In addition, personality theory contains more than a few ambiguities. For example, role psychology does not provide a clear answer to the question of whether the Sambo role played by many plantation slaves was internalized and became part of their personalities, or whether it was a form of conscious hypocrisy, a mere accommodation to the system. David McClelland asserts that the roles an individual plays are part of his knowledge "and therefore part of his personality."[30] But Ralph Linton thinks that playing a role proves nothing about an individual's personality, "except that he has normal learning ability." The psychologist must be able "to penetrate behind the façade of social conformity and cultural uniformity to reach the authentic individual."[31] Two recent writers on role theory, Theodore R. Sarbin

[29] Since psychologists cannot agree on a definition of personality, the literature gives the historian plenty of latitude. One psychologist compiled a list of almost fifty definitions of personality. Calvin S. Hall and Gardner Lindzey, *Theories of Personality* (New York, 1957), 7–10. Though I am not here considering the personality theories that Elkins does not use, I do question whether he was justified in making so little use of Freud, especially Freud's emphasis on the molding of the child's superego through experiences with the parents. Elkins explains why he thinks that Freud is not very useful in understanding the impact of the concentration camps on personality, but he never explains adequately why he thinks that Freudian concepts would not help us to understand the personality of the slave. While on the subject of what Elkins has neglected, I must note his failure to use the decidedly relevant writings of Erik H. Erikson on the problem of identity.

[30] McClelland, *Personality*, 296. See also Hartley and Hartley, *Fundamentals of Social Psychology*, 509–11. However, it is important to note that those who relate roles to personality are usually writing about children and the role the parents prescribe. In the case of the slave child, it was the mother or the father or a slave nurse, not the master, who taught the child a role in his early years. The master's direct involvement in child training did not usually begin until the child was old enough to perform some chores—say, at the age of seven or eight. By that time a large part of the child's personality had been formed. In the early formative years the master was not so much the one who prescribed a role as he was an object whom the child was taught to cope with in one way or another.

[31] Ralph Linton, *The Cultural Background of Personality* (New York, 1945), 26.

and Vernon L. Allen, illustrating a new trend, hardly touch on the matter of role and personality. They are far more interested in the interaction between role and social identity, and they state explicitly that they "are not using 'social identity' and 'self' as synonyms. Selfhood . . . embodies more residuals of behavior than those generated through role enactment."[32]

At times Elkins approaches this problem warily, suggesting only that the roles an individual plays are internalized to "an extent," or that "deliberate" role-playing and "natural" role-playing grade into each other "with considerable subtlety." Returning to the problem in an appendix, Elkins again refuses to generalize: "The main thing I would settle for would be the existence of a broad belt of indeterminacy between 'mere acting' and the 'true self'"; to the extent that they "grade into one another" it seems "permissible to speak of Sambo as a personality 'type.'"[33]

These cautious statements are hardly disputable, but they do not represent the tone of the essay as a whole. The clear inference to be drawn from Elkins's comparison of North American and Latin American slavery, from his introduction of the concentration-camp analogy, and from his use of personality theory is that Sambo was not a dissembler but a distinct personality type and the typical plantation slave. Indeed, in one footnote, Elkins explicitly rejects the possibility that the Sambo role was only a form of conscious accommodation. Not until after emancipation, he insists, did the Negro's "moral and psychological orientation" permit the development of "the essentially intermediate technique of accommodation . . . as a protective device beneath which a more independent personality might develop."[34]

Yet the theory of role psychology, when applied to the information we have concerning the life and behavior of plantation slaves, provides plenty of room for personalities other than Sambo. This theory, which stresses the importance of "role clarity," holds that adequate role performance will be unlikely if there is uncertainty concerning the nature of an appropriate role. In addition, role conflict occurs when a person finds himself occupying more than

[32] Sarbin and Allen, "Role Theory," in Gardner Lindzey and Elliot Aronson, eds., *The Handbook of Social Psychology* (2d ed., 5 vols., Reading, Mass., 1968–1969), I, especially 550–57; quote on page 554.

[33] Elkins, *Slavery*, 86n, 125, 227–28.

[34] *Ibid.*, 132n–33n. In his recent essay Elkins claims that his statement about "a broad belt of indeterminacy between 'mere acting' and the 'true self'" expresses the position he had taken in the original essay. Lane, ed., *The Debate over Slavery*, 359. However, in my opinion, this claim represents a shift in his basic position rather than an accurate statement of his original point of view.

one status at a given time, each requiring different behavior, or when there is more than one source of advice about how a role is properly played. Conflicting obligations or conflicting expectations may lead to a personal crisis and to difficulty in playing any role successfully.[35] These were problems that troubled plantation slaves in their daily lives—problems whose psychic strains they resolved in ways that varied with their individual natures and experiences.

Harry Stack Sullivan's model of interpersonal relationships, when fully utilized, also provides theoretical support for a variety of plantation slave personalities. Sullivan describes a highly complex and subtle interplay between an individual and the significant others in his life. One side of it—the side that Elkins explores —is the anxiety that helps to mold an individual's personality as he behaves in certain ways to meet the expectations of authority figures. But there is another side, which involves the conscious manipulation of significant others to the individual's own advantage. By the time a child is ready for school, Sullivan observes, he has "evolved techniques" for handling his parents "with only a modicum of pain"; he now encounters other adults "who have to be managed."[36] In addition to manipulation, there is still another and less fortunate way that a person deals with tendencies in his personality that are strongly disapproved by his significant others. These tendencies are neither lost nor resolved but simply "dissociated from personal awareness." In the process of dissociation they are "excluded from the self" and become part of the "extraself." But the tendencies still remain an integral part of the personality, manifesting "themselves in actions, activities, of which the person himself remains quite unaware."[37]

Sullivan's concept of dissociation describes a condition which, at a certain point, may lead to serious psychic problems. Generally speaking, he believes that the "healthy development of personality is inversely proportionate to the amount, to the number, of tendencies which have come to exist in dissociation."[38] In Elkins's conceptualization we encounter the significant other of Sullivan's

[35] McClelland, *Personality*, 316–18; Hartley and Hartley, *Fundamentals of Social Psychology*, 521–32; Sarbin and Allen, "Role Theory," 540–44.
[36] Sullivan, *Conceptions of Modern Psychiatry* (Washington, 1947), 18. Speaking of the child and his relations with his parents, Sullivan notes the child's "realistic appreciation of a necessity and a human development of devices to meet the necessity. . . . that marvelous human thing, great adaptive possibilities applied successfully to a situation." *Ibid.,* 19–20.
[37] *Ibid.,* 13, 21–22.
[38] *Ibid.,* 22.

interpersonal theory but not the phenomena of manipulation and dissociation; yet all three concepts are relevant to the problem of slave personality.

I believe that a historian utilizing the available evidence on slave behavior and master-slave relationships and taking account of all aspects of the personality theories used by Elkins will be forced to abandon his hypothesis that Sambo was the typical plantation slave. Several historians have already briefly suggested other possibilities,[39] and at present several have more ambitious projects under way. The following is my own sketch of an alternative to the Elkins hypothesis.

I would begin by accepting Elkins's description of southern slavery as a closed system from which few escaped and in which the slaves had only limited contacts with free society; his emphasis on the dehumanizing tendencies of slavery (though not in North America alone); his belief that the system had built into it powerful pressures toward dependent, infantilized, emasculated personalities;[40] and his conception of the master as a formidable significant other in the life of nearly every slave—partly an object of fear, partly a Freudian father figure. But I would reject his assertions that the master's power was absolute; that he was the only significant other in the lives of his slaves; that he was the sole author of the role, or roles, they played; and that southern slaves were almost totally dehumanized. Finally, I would suggest that plantation slaves encountered significant others in their own families and communities; that dissembling, manipulation, dissociation, role conflict, and lack of role clarity were important ingredients of slave behavior; and that plantation life enabled most slaves to develop independent personalities—indeed, provided room for the development of a considerable range of personality types.

In his concentration-camp analogy Elkins observes that a small minority of the inmates, who held minor administrative jobs, was

[39] Genovese, "Rebelliousness and Docility in the Negro Slave," 293–314; Genovese, "American Slaves and Their History," New York Review of Books, December 3, 1970, pp. 34–43; George M. Fredrickson and Christopher Lasch, "Resistance to Slavery," Civil War History, XIII (December 1967), 315–29; Levine, "Slave Songs and Slave Consciousness," 99–130; Willie Lee Rose, "Childhood in Bondage," unpublished paper read at the annual meeting of the Organization of American Historians, Los Angeles, April 1970. I have suggested other possibilities in Chapters III and VIII of The Peculiar Institution: Slavery in the Ante-Bellum South (New York, 1956).

[40] My study of slavery also called attention to these pressures: "Ideally [slavery] was the relationship of parent and child. . . . The system was in its essence a process of infantilization . . . ." Stampp, Peculiar Institution, 327.

able to escape the full impact of the system on personality. This minority could engage in petty underground activities, such as stealing blankets, getting medicine from the camp hospital, and negotiating black-market arrangements with the guards. These activities turned out to be crucial for the fortunate prisoner's psychological balance. For him the SS was not the only significant other, and the role of the child was not the only one open to him—he was able to do things that had meaning in adult terms.[41]

If these trivial activities could preserve the psychic balance of camp inmates, then the plantations afforded the great mass of field hands infinitely greater opportunities to preserve theirs. Though plantation slaves were exposed to influences that encouraged childlike dependency and produced emasculated personalities, the system nevertheless permitted them a degree of semiautonomous community life and the opportunity to do many things that had meaning in adult terms. They lived in their own separate quarters where they could escape the constant scrutiny of their masters. Unlike the slaves on the sugar and coffee plantations of Brazil and Cuba, where men outnumbered women by as much as three to one, those on the plantations of the Old South could experience something like a normal sex life, because the sexes were usually evenly divided. Though slave marriages had no legal support and families were ever in danger of being broken up by sales, southern slaves nevertheless lived in family groups more often than those on the commercialized plantations of Latin America. In fact, it was customary for them to live in family groups.[42]

Slave families, because of their relative lack of economic significance, their instability, and the father's severely restricted role, may well have been less important in the lives of slaves than the broader plantation slave communities. The latter provided opportunities for self-expression in their celebrations of holidays, in their music and folklore, and in other aspects of community life. Historians have perhaps viewed religion among plantation slaves too much in terms of the nonreligious uses to which it was put. We know that masters used religious indoctrination as a

---

[41] Elkins, *Slavery*, 134–35. I suspect that the ability of these petty administrators to escape the full impact of the terror and brutality of the camps was even more crucial to their psychological balance.

[42] In her unpublished paper, "Childhood in Bondage," Willie Lee Rose argues that historians have underestimated the importance of the slave family, especially the role of the father in raising children. See also Genovese, "American Slaves and Their History," 37–38.

means of control and that slaves found in their religious services subtle ways of protesting their condition. But there were other and deeper ways in which religion served them. It provided a system of beliefs that comforted and sustained them in their bondage, and it afforded additional means of self-expression that helped them retain their psychic balance. I do not believe that a truly autonomous Afro-American subculture developed in slavery days, but some of the ingredients for one were certainly there.

Both the family and the community provided plantation slaves with roles other than that defined by the master, and with significant others besides the master. For the very young child the mother, not the master, was the significant other in the sense that Sullivan uses this concept. Though the near impossibility of fathers acting as true authority figures was of great psychic importance, meaningful relationships did sometimes exist between fathers and sons. As the child grew, the master's role as a significant other became increasingly vital, but he was always in competition with significant others in the slave community: with husbands, wives, fathers, and mothers; with religious leaders; with strong male models, some of whom may even on occasion have served as substitute father figures;[43] with slaves believed to possess mystical powers; and with those whose wisdom was respected. Few planters had any illusions about being the only authority figures on their estates; as one of them noted, there were always slaves who held "a kind of magical sway over the minds and opinions of the rest."[44]

In his community, in the presence of these significant others, the slave could play a role decidedly different from the one prescribed by his master. This situation often led to the psychologically important problem of role conflict. An obvious illustration is the dilemma of a slave being questioned by his master concerning the whereabouts of a fugitive. Here the rules of proper conduct that the master tried to instill in him came in conflict with the values of his community. If we can trust the testimony of the masters themselves, community values usually triumphed, even though punishment might be the consequence.

Was there any sense in which the master's power was really

[43] In discussing the problem that boys without fathers have in learning the male role, Eugene and Ruth Hartley note that the situation changes quickly when such boys find other opportunities to observe the male role: "They learn from their playmates and from any adult males with whom they come into repeated contact." *Fundamentals of Social Psychology*, 504.
[44] *Southern Cultivator*, IX (1851), 85.

absolute? Only in the sense that if a master killed a slave by overwork, or by cruel punishment, or in a fit of rage, it was nearly impossible to convict him in a court of law. But southern state laws did not themselves give the master absolute power over his slaves, for the laws recognized their humanity and attempted to control the degree of punishment that might be inflicted, the amount of labor that could be required, and the care that was to be provided. Where the laws failed, the master might be restrained by his own moral standards or by those of the white community. If law and custom were not enough, he was still confronted by the fact that, unlike the inmates of a concentration camp, his slaves had monetary value and a clear purpose—to toil in his fields—and therefore had bargaining power. The master got work out of his slaves by coercion, by threats, by promises of rewards, by flattery, and by a dozen other devices he knew of. But if he were prudent, he knew that it was not wise to push slaves too far—to work them too long, punish them too severely or too often, or make too many threats. Slaves had their own standards of fair play and their own ways of enforcing them.[45] The relationship between master and slave was not one in which absolute power rested on one side and total helplessness on the other; rather, the relationship was one of everlasting tensions, punctuated by occasional conflicts between combatants using different weapons.

If the master had the *de facto* power of life and death over his slaves, the slaves knew that he was most unlikely to use it. They knew that rules infractions and certain forms of resistance did not ordinarily lead to death but to milder and often quite bearable forms of punishment, or to sale to another master, or, on occasion, to no penalty at all. In the conflicts between masters and slaves, the masters or their overseers sometimes suffered defeat, and the resulting collapse of discipline led inflexibly to economic disaster. To read the essays "On the Management of Negroes" that frequently appeared in southern periodicals is to appreciate the practical limits of the master's power. Clearly, for the slave, as he responded to the problems of his existence, the choices open to him were a good deal more complex than a simple one between life and death.

Role psychology, as those who have written on the subject ob-

---

[45] Fredrickson and Lasch, in "Resistance to Slavery," 322–25, suggest that slaves developed their own standards of fair play through their varying experiences with different masters and overseers.

serve, tempts one to view the whole problem metaphorically as drama.[46] But in slavery the theatrical situation was seldom one in which the master wrote the script and the slaves played their roles and read their lines precisely as their master had written them. The instructions masters gave to their overseers, which describe the qualities they hoped to develop in their slaves, suggest something quite different. Significantly, the model slave described in these instructions is not Sambo but a personality far more complicated. Masters wanted their slaves, like Sambo, to be docile, humble, and dependent; but they also wanted them to be diligent, responsible, and resourceful—in short, as Earle E. Thorpe has noted, "to give a very efficient and adult-like performance."[47] The slaves in turn had to find ways to resolve the obviously incongruent role expectations of their masters, and many of them responded as persons troubled with this or other forms of role conflict often do. They resorted to lying and deceit.

Eugene Genovese, in an otherwise valuable essay on slave personality, is not very perceptive when he argues that slaves who tricked their masters, rather than coping with problems of role conflict and role definition, were merely playing a game which the masters enjoyed and had themselves written into the script.[48] True, a master might occasionally be amused when a house servant outwitted him, but there is scant evidence that he enjoyed this "game" when played by field hands. This was certainly not in the script, and masters frequently expressed their anger or perplexity at the "untrustworthiness" of Negroes. Their appreciation of the slave trickster was confined mostly to their public defenses of slavery and to sentimental plantation literature. In private they were seldom amused.

Plantation field hands, finding no escape from slavery but plenty of elbow room within it, usually managed to preserve their individuality and therefore revealed a considerable variety of personality types. Among the types, there were, to be sure, genuine Sambos who seemed to have internalized much of the role, for some slaves simply lacked the psychic strength to withstand

[46] "Role, a term borrowed directly from the theater, is a metaphor intended to denote that conduct adheres to certain 'parts' (or positions) rather than to the players who read or recite them." Sarbin and Allen, "Role Theory," 489, 547–50.
[47] Thorpe, "Chattel Slavery and Concentration Camps," 174–75. This is an excellent example of one kind of role conflict—the kind that results when an authority figure holds "simultaneous contradictory expectations for one role." Sarbin and Allen, "Role Theory," 540.
[48] Genovese, "Rebelliousness and Docility in the Negro Slave," 310–11.

the infantilizing pressures of the system. They looked on the master as a father figure, accepted his values, identified with him, and perhaps even viewed themselves through his eyes.

We may assume that the slave who internalized the Sambo role did accept his master as his only significant other and that he was relatively untroubled by the problem of role conflict. But he must have been sorely disturbed by the psychic process of dissociation—that is, exclusion from the self of disapproved personality tendencies, which then become part of what Sullivan calls the "extra-self." Such dissociated tendencies, we must remember, still remain part of the personality; and, therefore, Sambo was Sambo only up to a point—in Genovese's words, "up to the moment that the psychological balance was jarred from within or without . . . ."[49] Plantation records often reveal the astonishment of masters when slaves, who had long given evidence of Sambo personalities, suddenly behaved in disturbingly un-Sambo ways.

Another personality type was evident on certain large plantations, especially on those of absentee owners in new areas of the Southwest, where labor was sometimes exploited ruthlessly and punishments were brutal. This type displayed none of the silliness of Sambo, none of his childlike attachment to master or overseer; rather, he was profoundly apathetic, full of depression and gloom, and seemingly less hostile than indifferent toward the white man who controlled him. One slaveholder observed that slaves subjected to overwork and cruel punishments were likely to fall "into a state of impassivity" and to become "insensible and indifferent to punishment, or even to life . . . ."[50] These brutalized slaves had their counterparts on Latin American plantations, where extreme cruelty produced in some a state of psychic shock manifested in apathy and depression. In colonial Brazil this condition was sufficiently common to be given a special name: *banzo*.[51] It is this condition that seems to be analogous to the concentration camps, where life had lost its meaning, and to prisons and asylums, where "situational withdrawal" is a form of institutional adaptation.[52]

More numerous among plantation personalities were the men

---

[49] *Ibid.*, 312.

[50] *De Bow's Review*, XXV (July 1858), 51.

[51] Davis, *Problem of Slavery*, 238.

[52] See Fredrickson and Lasch, "Resistance to Slavery," 325–27, and their sources for behavior in total institutions, especially Erving Goffman, *Asylums: Essays on the Social Situation of Mental Patients and Other Inmates* (Garden City, N. Y., 1961).

and women with sufficient strength of character to escape the emasculating tendencies of the system, a group whose size Elkins seriously underestimates. These slaves were not only not Sambos, but they did not *act* like Sambos—their behavior was in no respect infantile. Though observing all the niceties of interracial etiquette, they maintained considerable dignity even in their relations with their masters. Judging from plantation diaries, masters often treated slaves of this kind with genuine respect and seldom made the mistake of regarding them as children. Slaves such as these were not troublemakers; they were rarely intransigent as long as what was asked of them and provided for them was reasonable by their standards. They worked well and efficiently and showed considerable initiative and self-reliance. They tended to be fatalistic about their lot, expected little of life, and found their satisfaction in the religious and social activities of the slave communities. No doubt their psychic balance and their relative tranquillity was sometimes disturbed by a certain amount of role conflict; and they could hardly have escaped the phenomenon of dissociation described by Sullivan.

Herbert Aptheker's rebels must also be included among those whose personalities were far removed from the traditional Sambo. I would not limit these to the organizers of or participants in rebellions, for their number was very small.[53] Rather, I would include all who were never reconciled to the system and engaged in various acts of resistance: running away, arson, the damaging of crops and tools, and sometimes even assaults on masters, overseers, or other whites. Needless to say, it is often impossible to distinguish conscious resistance from the unconscious carelessness and indifference of slaves, but the evidence of genuine resistance is clear enough in some cases.[54] Genovese argues that the slaves did not develop a genuine revolutionary tradition, that

[53] For persuasive explanations of why there were relatively few insurrections in the antebellum South see Degler, "Slavery in Brazil and the United States," 1013–16; Eugene D. Genovese, "The Legacy of Slavery and the Roots of Black Nationalism," *Studies on the Left*, VI (November-December 1966), 4–6. I believe that a major factor contributing to the larger number of insurrections in Brazil was the imbalance of the sexes on the plantations, whereas most southern slaves lived in family groups. The presence of a large number of young men without women and the absence of the stabilizing influence of the family on Brazilian plantations were bound to create a condition highly conducive to rebellions.

[54] See Raymond A. and Alice H. Bauer, "Day to Day Resistance to Slavery," *Journal of Negro History*, XXVII (October 1942), 388–419; Stampp, *Peculiar Institution*, Chap. III; Vincent Harding, "Religion and Resistance Among Antebellum Negroes, 1800–1860," in August Meier and Elliott Rudwick, eds., *The Making of Black America* (2 vols., New York, 1969), I, 179–97.

their acts of resistance were usually nihilistic, and that at best they came out of slavery with a tradition of recalcitrance—"of undirected, misdirected or naively directed violence." George M. Fredrickson and Christopher Lasch object even to calling the acts of slave rebels "resistance" and insist that it was only "intransigence." They define the former as organized, purposeful political action, the latter as mere "personal strategy of survival" which can easily lead to "futile and even self-destructive acts of defiance."[55] Surely, little that was done by the rebels could form the basis for a revolutionary tradition or satisfy so narrow a definition of resistance; but these were rebels, nonetheless, who never internalized the masters' standards of good conduct and never dissociated from their conscious selves all the disapproved tendencies of their personalities.

All of these slaves types, with myriad individual variations, were recognizable on the plantations. But I believe that the personalities of most slaves are less easily classified, because their behavior when observed by whites was usually that of conscious accommodators. They played the role of Sambo with varying degrees of skill and consistency,[56] but, in contrast to the authentic Sambos, most characteristics of the role did not become part of their true personalities. For them the Sambo routine was a form of "ritual acting"—that is, they went through the motions of the role, but with a rather low degree of personal involvement.[57]

Several aspects of role theory support this hypothesis. One assumption of this theory is that the average normal person plays not one but several roles, and often two or more simultaneously. To think of the slave as playing but one role—that of Sambo—is to assume that he responded to a single social situation, which was clearly not the case. Moreover, when a role performance is demanded primarily in terms of the pains and penalties for nonperformance, as it was on the typical plantation supervised by an overseer and run as a business enterprise, the role is likely to be enacted with little conviction and minimal personal involvement. The Sambo role doubtless was performed more convincingly and with more feeling in a paternalistic situation. Finally, the extent to which a given role makes an impact on the self depends on its

[55] Genovese, "The Legacy of Slavery," 7–11 (quote on page 9); Fredrickson and Lasch, "Resistance to Slavery," 317, 326.
[56] Sarbin and Allen note the great qualitative differences in role performance among individuals: "One person may enact a role convincingly and skillfully, while another may be inept." "Role Theory," 514.
[57] Ibid., 492–96; Hartley and Hartley, Fundamentals of Social Psychology, 493.

"preemptiveness"—on how much of a person's time is spent playing the role.[58] Therefore, one must ask how preemptive the Sambo role actually was. During the week the plantation field hand spent most of his waking hours as an agricultural worker, planting, cultivating, or harvesting, and the demand on him was for a responsible adult performance. He spent evenings and holidays in the slave community playing a variety of roles, only occasionally being observed by master or overseer. The one occasion that called for the Sambo role was that of a direct contact with a member of the white race, when the Negro was forced to acknowledge in some way not only that he was a slave but that he belonged to a degraded caste. However, for the average field hand such contacts were brief and relatively infrequent; therefore the pressures on him most of the time were to play roles other than Sambo.

In short, most plantation slaves avoided the internalization of Sambo, first, because they were able to play different roles in their communities; second, because the Sambo role was not unduly preemptive; third, because masters were not the only significant others in the lives of slaves; fourth, because slaves found abundant opportunities to behave in ways that had meaning in adult terms; and, last, because conditions on the average plantation were not so brutal that they were destroyed as human beings. In consequence, slaves could use the essentially external Sambo role, in Elkins's words, "as a protective device beneath which a more independent personality might develop."[59] Those who consciously and purposefully acted the part of Sambo, thereby reducing sources of friction and putting limits on what would normally be expected of them, were in no sense being childish or infantile; rather, their behavior was rational, meaningful, and mature.

In an essay based on studies of other total institutions, George Fredrickson and Christopher Lasch suggest that conditions in prisons and asylums are more analogous to slavery than conditions in concentration camps. They note that the inmates of such institutions do not usually internalize a sense of obligation to obey their rules and accept their values. In the case of slavery, they conclude, "a system that rigorously defined the Negro slave not merely as an inferior but as an alien, a separate order of be-

[58] Sarbin and Allen, "Role Theory," 491, 496–97, 535; Hartley and Hartley, *Fundamentals of Social Psychology*, 498.
[59] Elkins, *Slavery*, 133n.

383

ing," could hardly have instilled in him "the sense of belonging on which internalized obedience necessarily has to rest."[60]

However, I think there is a better approach to understanding the personalities of plantation slaves than that provided by either of these analogies. Much more can be learned from a study of ex-slaves and their descendants in the rural South in the decades after Reconstruction, when, for all practical purposes, the system was still a closed one from which few escaped, and when powerful forces again generated tendencies toward emasculated personalities. Now their humanity was assaulted and their race denigrated by the most extreme forms of prejudice, segregation, and discrimination; and they felt strong pressures, both subtle and crude, to internalize the white man's opinion of them. After emancipation there was still a white landlord to serve as a counterpart to the slaveowner as a significant other. More important, the whole white community now became, collectively, a significant other, imposing a subservient and dependent role on the Negro and enforcing an etiquette of race relations with sanctions equal to those available to masters in slavery days. Yet, most Negroes, as in slavery days, found ways of maintaining a degree of psychic balance. Through their churches, their music, and a great variety of organized social activities, they gradually developed a semi-autonomous Afro-American subculture; in their communities and families they responded to their own significant others; and in their mature years they had a variety of adult roles to play, even though whites persisted in calling black men boys and black women girls.

In circumstances whose psychic impact had many parallels to slavery, Negroes once more resorted to conscious accommodation. The investigations of twentieth-century social scientists provide much evidence that most post-Reconstruction Negroes did not internalize the Sambo role they played before the white community. For example, in the 1930s, John Dollard observed that the southern Negro played two roles:

one that he is forced to play with white people and one the "real Negro" as he appears in his dealings with his own people. What the white southern people see who "know their Negroes" is the role that they have forced the Negro to accept, his caste role. . . . It is perhaps this fact which often makes Negroes seem so deceptive to white people; apparently our white caste wishes the Negro to have only one

[60] Fredrickson and Lasch, "Resistance to Slavery," 320–23.

social personality, his caste role, and to *be* this with utter complete-ness.[61]

The testimony of post-Reconstruction Negroes themselves, espe-cially in their music and folklore, also suggests a prevalent pat-tern of conscious accommodation.[62]

Similarly, the slaves, in their scattered records, and the mas-ters, in their private papers and published essays on the manage-ment of Negroes, indicate that conscious accommodation was a widespread behavior pattern on the antebellum plantations. Whatever the masters may have said about the loyal, childlike "darky" in their public defenses of slavery, the dissembling pseudo-Sambo was the most common reality that confronted them in their daily lives. As one planter wrote: "The most general defect in the character of the Negro, is hypocrisy; and this hy-pocrisy frequently makes him pretend to more ignorance than he possesses; and if the master treats him as a fool, he will be sure to act the fool's part. This is a very convenient trait, as it frequently serves as an apology for awkwardness and neglect of duty."[63]

However, the fact that some masters saw through the Sambo act, as this one did, suggests that slave accommodators may often have missed their lines. Playing this intricate role could never have been easy, and it may have caused even the most skilled of them serious psychic problems, especially if there was a basic incongruence between the self and this role.[64] I suspect that many had profound difficulties with role conflict, as the weaker characters who internalized the Sambo role suffered from dis-sociation. Those who study slave personality would be well ad-vised to watch for signs of character disorders in these seemingly gay dissemblers. I want to point again, as I did in *The Peculiar Institution*, to the astonishing frequency of speech problems among slaves. Time after time, owners advertising for runaways reported that a slave "stutters very much," "stammers very much,"

[61] Dollard, *Caste and Class in a Southern Town* (3d ed., Garden City, N. Y., 1957), 257–59.

[62] See, for example, Lawrence W. Levine, "The Concept of the New Negro and the Realities of Black Culture," in Nathan I. Huggins, Martin Kilson, and Daniel M. Fox, eds., *Key Issues in the Afro-American Experience* (2 vols., New York and other cities, 1971), II, 125–47.

[63] *Farmer's Register*, V (May 1837), 32. For an excellent analysis of "Quashee," the Jamaican counterpart of Sambo, and of the degree to which he was a conscious role-player, see Orlando Patterson, *The Sociology of Slavery: An Analysis of the Origins, Development and Structure of Negro Slave Society in Jamaica* (London, 1967), 174–81.

[64] Sarbin and Allen, "Role Theory," 524.

"speaks quickly and with an anxious expression of countenance," or is "easily confused when spoken to."[65] Such data are open to several interpretations, but one respectable theory suggests that speech impediments are symptoms of buried hostility. Dr. Murry Snyder of the Speech Rehabilitation Institute of New York City believes that "Underneath the cloak of inhibition and mild manner, the stutterer often seethes with anger."[66] In the case of slaves, speech problems may also have been a manifestation of role conflict or of incompatibility between self and role.

The art of conscious accommodation, along with all its psychic consequences, is one of the skills that Negroes carried with them from slavery to freedom. Accommodation continued to be a part of life for many of them, especially in the rural South, for another century. Being obliged to wear the mask of Sambo, whatever they may have been inside, doubtless they were, as in slavery days, troubled to an extraordinary degree by the problem of role conflict. To escape this problem seems to be one of the aims of the present black revolution, for the search for black identity is in part a search for role clarity. To end the dissembling, to be all of a piece, to force the white community to accept them as they really are, not as it so long wanted to see them, is quite obviously one determined goal of the new generation of blacks.

[65] One must, of course, ask whether runaways were not exceptional slaves with special psychic problems. I do not think that this was the case, because many kinds of slaves ran away for a variety of reasons. But this is a matter that requires further investigation.

[66] *Time,* XCVI (August 24, 1970), 42. See also Sarbin and Allen, "Role Theory," 527.

The Vesey Plot: A Reconsideration

By RICHARD C. WADE

ON MAY 25, 1822, TWO SLAVES STOOD ALONGSIDE THE FISH WHARF IN Charleston harbor chatting idly about the ships that lay at anchor nearby. William Paul asked Devany Prioleau if he knew that "something serious is about to take place." Then, more precisely, he said that "many of us are determined to right ourselves" and "shake off our bondage." Devany had not heard of the plot. "Astonished and horror struck," he quickly broke off the conversation and hurried away.[1] After a few agitated days he confided the news to a free Negro, George Pencil, and asked what to do. Pencil told him to tell his owner. On May 30 at three o'clock Devany gave the fateful information to Mrs. Prioleau.[2]

Two hours later the Mayor of Charleston called the city council into extraordinary session. The police picked up both Devany and William; officials began an intensive inquiry. For a week they kept William in solitary confinement in the "black hole of the Work-House," interrogating him every day. Finally he gave them the names of Mingo Harth and Peter Poyas. These Negroes were questioned but disclosed nothing. In fact, they "behaved with so much composure and coolness, and treated the charges . . . with

[1] Lionel H. Kennedy and Thomas Parker, *An Official Report of the Trials of Sundry Negroes, Charged with an Attempt to Raise an Insurrection in the State of South-Carolina: Preceded by an Introduction and Narrative; and in an Appendix, a Report of the Trials of Four White Persons, on Indictments for Attempting to Excite the Slaves to Insurrection. Prepared and Published at the Request of the Court* (Charleston, 1822), 50.

[2] A postscript to the publication revised this original version slightly, asserting that Devany told his young master before he did Pencil, but the free Negro advised him to go directly to his master. Since Mr. Prioleau was not available he told Mrs. Prioleau. The editor concluded that this added information "places the fidelity of the slave . . . on much higher ground." *Official Report*, "Extracts," 4. The state rewarded both Devany and Pencil with a $50 annuity for life. In 1837, when Devany turned seventy, the state raised it to $150. Memorial of the City Council of Charleston to the Senate of South Carolina, 1822 (South Carolina Archives Division); Petition of Peter Devany for Increase of Annual Bounty Conferred upon Him by the Act of Assembly, Anno Domini, 1822 for Meritorious Services in the Disturbances of That Year, October, 1837 (South Carolina Archives Division). Devany had also been manumitted for his role in uncovering the plot.

MR. WADE is professor of history in the University of Chicago.

so much levity" that the officials were "completely deceived" and released them both.[3] Later William implicated others, but they too claimed no knowledge. The authorities were further baffled when Ned Bennett, a slave of Governor Thomas Bennett of South Carolina, came in voluntarily to clear himself of suspicion.[4]

Having turned up nothing—but suspicious of everything—the Mayor strengthened his patrols, armed his men for extensive action, and waited. On June 14 the break came. Another slave corroborated William Paul's testimony, disclosing that the uprising originally set for July 2 was now moved up to June 16. For the first time the public knew that danger threatened. A strong guard surrounded the city; the police appeared in force. Still nothing happened. On June 16, ten slaves were arrested; and, two days later, a hastily assembled court of freeholders began hearing secret testimony. On June 21 the police brought in Denmark Vesey. And eleven days later, on July 2, the bodies of Vesey and five other Negroes swung from the gallows at the edge of town.

The uprising now seemed quashed. But, as word of it spread in the city, public shock turned into hysteria. No master could be sure his bondsmen were not involved; whites who owned no slaves had little more assurance. Every Negro became a possible enemy, indeed assassin; every action by a black could be construed as a prelude to violence. Since slaves lived in the same yard with their masters, it was not even possible to lock out the intruder.

As the terror spread, so too did the presumed magnitude of the conspiracy. The letters of Ana Hayes Johnson, daughter of a respected judge and a niece of the Governor, describe the fears and rumors that were current. "Their plans were simply these," she wrote late in June: "They were to set fire to the town and while the whites were endeavoring to put it out they were to commence their horrid depredations." Then in more detail: "It seems that the Governor, Intendant [i.e. Mayor], and my poor father were to have been the first victims—the men and Black women were to have been indiscriminately murdered—& we poor devils were to have been removed to fill their—Harams—horrible—I have a very beautiful cousin who was set apart for the wife or more properly, the 'light of the Haram' of one of their chiefs."[5]

[3] Official Report, 51.
[4] Ibid., 3ff.
[5] Ana Hayes Johnson to Elizabeth E. W. Haywood, Charleston, June 23, 1822, in Ernest Haywood Papers (Southern Historical Collection, University of North Carolina Library).

Panic gripped the colored community, too, after the execution. As more and more blacks disappeared into prison, as rumors widened, and as the newspapers announced new arrests, the alarm deepened. Was someone informing on his neighbor? Had the police picked up so many that some had to be housed in a nearby county? Were white irregulars about to take things in their own hands because the court was too slow? In the awful uncertainty the Negroes found an uneasy unity. Most of those questioned by municipal officials professed no knowledge of any plot; others wore armbands of crepe in mourning for the dead until officials forbade demonstrations of sympathy.[6]

Outwardly, the normal deference to whites increased. "There was a wonderful degree of politeness shown to us," a white recalled, "bows and politeness, and—give way for the gentlemen and ladies, met you at every turn and corner."[7] Before long the crisis waned. The first six executions seemed to have ripped the heart out of the rebellion. "We thought it was ended," Miss Johnson wrote on July 18; "the court had been dismissed and the town was again sinking into its wonted security when information was given that another attempt would be made." The tip came from a Negro who later became a key witness. The court reassembled, the patrol returned to its stations, and more Negroes were jailed.

A new excitement swept the city, and the court, working rapidly, ordered more executions. "In all probability the executed will not end under 100," Miss Johnson estimated, and others asserted that "even should there be 500 executed there would still be enough" conspirators to pull off the scheme. "How far the mischief has extended heaven only knows," she lamented fearfully.[8] A later letter reported morbid details: "22 unfortunate wretches were at one fatal moment sent to render their account, 29 had been sentenced but 7 had their sentences commuted to perpetual banishment—but on Tuesday 6 more are to be executed . . . gracious heavens to what will all this lead . . . and I am told that there are an awful number yet to be tried." Miss Johnson had more knowledge than most, but she could observe on the street that "there is a look of horror in every countenance." "I wish I could act for myself," she added; "I would not stay in this city

---

[6] A Colored American, *The Late Contemplated Insurrection in Charleston, S. C., with the Execution of Thirty-Six of the Patriots, Etc.* (New York, 1850), 7.

[7] Charleston *Southern Patriot and Commercial Advertiser*, September 12, 1822.

[8] Ana Hayes Johnson to Elizabeth E. W. Haywood, Charleston, July 18, 1822, in Ernest Haywood Papers.

another day . . . my feelings have been so lacerated of late that I can hardly speak or act."[9]

From the beginning municipal authorities had been no less frightened, but they were compelled to act. The five freeholders who comprised the court appointed on June 18 were chosen because they possessed "in an eminent degree the confidence of the community." The tribunal quickly drew up its rules: no slave could be tried without the presence of his owner or the owner's counsel; "the testimony of one witness unsupported by additional evidence, or by circumstances, should lead to no conviction of a *capital* nature"; witnesses would confront the accused except "where testimony was given under a solemn pledge that the name . . . would not be divulged" because the judges feared the informant might be "murdered by the blacks"; a master or free Negro could have counsel if asked for, and "the statements of defenses of the accused should be heard, in every case, and they be permitted themselves to examine any witness they thought proper."[10] The freeholders worked in complete secrecy because of the "peculiar nature of the investigations" and because "it was also morally certain that no coloured witness would have ventured to incur the resentment of his comrades, by voluntarily disclosing his testimony in a public court."[11]

During its sittings, from the first outbreak in June until July 26, the court heard over 130 cases.[12] It divided the conspirators into two groups. The first comprised those "who exhibited energy and activity"; they were executed. The other included those "who did little (if any more) than yield their acquiescence to the proposal to enter the plot"; they were deported. The judges later confided to the Governor that the distinction did not wholly meet the facts, but "the terror of example we thought would be sufficiently operative by the number of criminals sentenced to death" that "without any injury to the community . . . a measure might be adopted . . . which would save the necessity of more numerous executions than policy required."[13]

[9] Ana Hayes Johnson to Elizabeth E. W. Haywood, Charleston, July 27, 1822, *ibid.*

[10] *Official Report,* vi.

[11] *Ibid.,* iii, vii.

[12] The court sat in "arduous session for five weeks and three days" and probably had some contact with more than this number. *Southern Patriot and Commercial Advertiser,* July 27, 1822.

[13] L. Kennedy, Thomas Parker, William Drayton, Nathaniel Heyward, J. R. Pringle, H. Deos, and Robert J. Turnbull to Governor Thomas Bennett, July 24, 1822 (South Carolina Archives Division).

The court found it difficult to get conclusive evidence. Vesey and the first five went to the gallows without confessing—indeed asserting their innocence. During the second trial, however, three men under the sentence of death implicated, under a promise of leniency, scores of other blacks. In asking the Governor to pardon Monday Gell, Charles Drayton, and Harry Haig, the judges described the conditions of their testimony: "Under the impression that they could ultimately have their lives spared they made . . . disclosures not only important in the detection of the general plan of the conspiracy but enabling the court to convict a number of principal offenders." Like "the terror of example," the officials wanted deportation in place of the hangman so that "negroes should know that even their principal advisers and ringleaders cannot be confided in and that under the temptations of exemption from capital punishment they will betray the common cause."[14]

Despite the difficulty of acquiring sufficient evidence, the court moved energetically and decisively. Of the 131 picked up, 35 were executed, 31 transported, 27 tried and acquitted, and 38 questioned but discharged.[15] Throughout July the gallows was kept busy. On "the Line," which separated the city from the Neck, the neighborhood numbly watched the public display.

Most of the condemned died without admitting guilt, and some with almost defiant contempt. Bacchus Hammett, who had "confessed," "went to the gallows *laughing and bidding his acquaintances in the streets* 'good bye;' on being hung, owing to some mismanagement in the fall of the trap, he was not thrown off, but the board canted, he slipped; yet he was so hardened that he *threw himself forward, and as he swung back he lifted his feet, so that he might not touch the board!*"[16] Others were dispatched more expertly, and the bodies left to dangle for hours to make certain that no colored resident could mistake the point of the punishment.

Constable Belknap, the executioner, later complained that the frequency of the hangings had caused him great "personal inconvenience" and had "deranged" his "private business." At the height of the crisis he had spent "all his time and services" in the

---

[14] Petition for the Pardon of Monday Gell, Charles Drayton, and Harry Haig to the Governor of South Carolina, July 24, 1822 (South Carolina Archives Division).
[15] *Official Report*, 183.
[16] Bacchus, the Slave of Benjamin Hammett, Confession, in William and Benjamin Hammett Papers (Duke University Library).

"call of the public, both by night and by day, in assisting at the preparation of the Gallows, the digging of the graves and various other offices connected with the execution."[17] The city's budget too felt the strain. In December the council asked the state to reimburse it for the unusual expenses surrounding the plot and trial. The bill came to $2,284.84¼, including costs of confinement, a payment of $200 to "Col. Prioleau's man Peter for secret services rendered," and the expenses of "erecting a Gallows" and procuring "carts to carry the criminals to the place of execution."[18]

A second court, which included Robert Y. Hayne and Joel Poinsett, was appointed August 1 "for the trial of sundry persons of color, apprehended for attempting to raise an insurrection."[19] Though it sat only a week, it sentenced one man to death and directed six others to be transported out of the state. These new cases, however, were connected with the events of May and June.[20]

As the court wound up its grim business, the city tried to recover something of its old composure. In the second week of August the *Courier* closed the books on the episode. "The legal investigations of crime have ceased. The melancholy requisitions of Justice, as painful to those who inflicted, as to those who suffered them, have been complied with; and an awful but a necessary, and, it is hoped, an effectual example has been afforded to deter from further occasions of offense and punishment."[21] The editor then called on the council for a day of thanksgiving to God for "his preserving care" and because "he has watched and guarded the tranquillity of our city" and "endowed our magistrates with firmness and wisdom, rendered necessary by an alarming crisis."[22]

This brief narrative includes the essential facts about the Vesey uprising generally accepted by historians today. The standard source is a long pamphlet containing the court's record of the

---

[17] Petition of B. Belknap of the City of Charleston to the Senate and House of Representatives, November 14, 1822 (South Carolina Archives Division).

[18] Report of the Committee on the Memorial of the City of Charleston, Senate Committee, December 14, 1822 (South Carolina Archives Division).

[19] *Southern Patriot and Commercial Advertiser*, August 2, 1822.

[20] *Ibid.*, August 8, 1822. The prisoner who was executed, William Garner, had earlier escaped from the city. His death brought the total to thirty-six and explains the confusion in secondary sources concerning the precise number of executions. H. M. Henry, *The Police Control of the Slave in South Carolina* (Emory, Va., 1914), 152.

[21] Charleston *Courier*, August 12, 1822.

[22] *Ibid.*, August 24, 1822.

trial, published by the city in 1822 under the title of *An Official Report of the Trials of Sundry Negroes* and edited by two members of the court. This document conveyed a special authenticity because the testimony and confessions purported to be as "originally taken, without even changing the phraseology, which was generally in the very words and by the witnesses." Indeed, the court had instructed the editors *"not to suppress any part of it."*[23] Scholars had few other sources to turn to. Charleston newspapers imposed a nearly perfect blackout on the details of the episode throughout the summer, confining themselves to a simple recording of sentences and executions. And contemporaries left only a few scattered items to help fill out the slight skeleton provided by the council's publication.

Hence, historians accepted the only facts available and drew their accounts from the official record. They did not question the court's findings but rather dwelt on certain aspects of the episode. Some, like Carter G. Woodson and Ulrich B. Phillips, emphasized the extent and precision of the planning.[24] Others centered on the extraordinary quality of the rebels, especially their leader. Dwight Dumond found Denmark Vesey a "brilliant man," familiar with the Bible, and acquainted with the debates in Congress over the admission of Missouri to the Union. He concluded that "few men were better informed . . . in the history of race relations." John Hope Franklin characterized Vesey as "a sensitive, liberty-loving person" who "believed in equality for everyone and resolved to do something for his slave brothers." Still others were impressed with the unity of the Negroes which made the plot possible. Herbert Aptheker, for example, quoted the report of two Negroes who said they "never spoke to any person of color on the subject, or knew of any who had been spoken to by the other leaders, who had withheld his assent."[25]

More important was the broader meaning of the conspiracy. Most authors viewed it in the context of the resistance of Negroes to the institution of slavery. Along with Nat Turner, they placed Denmark Vesey at the head of the list of colored rebels. For some

[23] *Official Report*, iii.
[24] Carter G. Woodson, *The Negro in Our History* (Washington, 1927), 180; Ulrich B. Phillips, "The Slave Labor Problem in the Charleston District," *Political Science Quarterly*, XXII (September 1907), 429-30.
[25] Dwight Lowell Dumond, *Antislavery: The Crusade for Freedom in America* (Ann Arbor, Mich., 1961), 114; John Hope Franklin, *From Slavery to Freedom: A History of American Negroes* (New York, 1956), 210; Herbert Aptheker, *American Negro Slave Revolts* (New York, 1943), 270.

his plot demonstrated the latent urge for freedom that lay beneath the regime of bondage; for others it revealed an ugly layer of hatred and revenge contained only by stringent laws and alert policemen.

But all accepted the official version: that a widespread conspiracy existed and only a last-minute betrayal rescued the city from insurrection and civil war. Whether the author was Negro or white, Northerner or Southerner, opponent of or apologist for slavery, there was no quarrel on this point. Historians who otherwise disagreed on many issues did not question the conventional story. Hence there was little incentive for reappraisal.[26]

Yet, in spite of the apparent agreement of most contemporaries and the consensus of subsequent historians, there is persuasive evidence that no conspiracy in fact existed, or at most that it was a vague and unformulated plan in the minds or on the tongues of a few colored townsmen. No elaborate network had been established in the countryside; no cache of arms lay hidden about the city; no date for an uprising had been set; no underground apparatus, carefully organized and secretly maintained, awaited a signal to fire Charleston and murder the whites. What did exist were strong grievances on one side and deep fears on the other. Combined with a number of somewhat unrelated circumstances, they made it possible for many people, both white and Negro, to believe in the existence of a widespread scheme to overturn the institution of slavery.

The first note of skepticism came from a respected judge, a long-time resident of Charleston. Watching the mounting excitement in June, and privy to the proceedings of the court, he warned in a newspaper letter against the "Melancholy Effect of Popular Excitement." In an oblique parable he recounted an episode "within the recollection of thousands" when a freeholders' court had hastily hanged a slave, Billy, for sounding a false alarm to the patrols by blowing a horn. Although "no evidence was given whatever as to a motive for sounding the horn, and the horn was

---

[26] In a paper delivered to the Southern Historical Association meeting in 1957 Thomas T. Hamilton of the University of Wichita evidently developed some doubts about the case from "irregularities in the trials and testimony." Presumably this skepticism stemmed from a close reading of the text. *Journal of Southern History,* XXIV (February 1958), 71. Standard accounts of the Vesey plot include Anne King Gregorie, "Denmark Vesey," *Dictionary of American Biography,* XIX, 258-59; John Lofton, "Negro Insurrectionist," *Antioch Review,* XVIII (Summer 1958), 183-96; and John M. Lofton, Jr., "Denmark Vesey's Call to Arms," *Journal of Negro History,* XXXIII (October 1948), 395-417.

actually found covered and even filled with cobwebs, they condemned that man to die the next day!" The only testimony had been provided by another slave who "was first whipped severely to extort a confession, and then, with his eyes bound, commanded to prepare for instant death from a sabre" if he would not divulge the needed information. Many of the worthiest men in the area protested and asked for "a more deliberate hearing." It did no good, however. "Billy was hung amidst crowds of execrating spectators," the "popular demand for a victim" being so great that it was doubtful whether even a Governor's pardon could have saved him.[27]

The letter was unsigned, but everyone knew its author was of "commanding authority." Moreover, published at the time of the newspaper blackout, it obviously came from someone close to those involved in the trial. In fact, its author was William Johnson, a judge and brother-in-law of the Governor. His daughter observed that when the article appeared, the freeholders "took up the cudgels, supposing it was a slur at them—guilty conscience you know" and "threatened their anathemas at him." Johnson responded with a pamphlet, which his daughter characterized as asserting the "entire innocence of the slaves" and in which he pointed out that the charge against Billy had been "an attempt to raise an insurrection."[28] The moral could hardly be clearer: he feared the court would bend to the popular hysteria and find guilt where there was none.[29]

His daughter, too, soon took this view. Her letters spanning the two months of the crisis moved from frenzy to skepticism. At the beginning of the trouble she wrote that the conspirators spoke of "rapine and murder" with "the coolness of demons" and that "the plot is computed to be about 30,000—the children were to have been spiked and murdered &c."[30] A few weeks later the tone be-

[27] Charleston *Courier*, June 21, 1822.

[28] Ana Hayes Johnson to Elizabeth E. W. Haywood, Charleston, July 24, 1822, in Ernest Haywood Papers. For the court's reply see Charleston *Courier*, June 29, 1822.

[29] "If it was intended as it would seem to be to make this moral, and the story which accompanies applicable to a supposed existing state of things in our community, . . ." wrote the Mayor [Intendant], "I have only to remark that the *discretion* of the writer is altogether equal to the unjust libel he has insinuated against his Fellow Citizens." The Mayor contended that the measures adopted were taken "in a spirit of the most perfect justice and moderation." *Southern Patriot and Commercial Advertiser*, June 22, 1822.

[30] Ana Hayes Johnson to Elizabeth E. W. Haywood, Charleston, June 23, 1822, in Ernest Haywood Papers.

came more measured, the numbers involved much fewer, and she could "thank God none of our slaves have been found in the plot, though there are twenty of them in the yard."[31]

Still later some deeper doubts crept in. "You know," Miss Johnson wrote, "that the leading characteristic of our state is our impetuosity and ardency of feeling which unavoidably lays them [the people] open to deception and consequently leads them on to error in action." Not much, however, could be done about it: "you might as well attempt to 'fetter tides with silken bands' as to make them listen to reason when under this excitement." Yet she concluded that in a few days "the unfortunate creatures are to be hung—it is most horrible—it makes my blood curdle when I think of it, but they are guilty most certainly."[32] Her final letter mentions no plot at all and is obsessed with "the most awful tragedy in this . . . city that comes within the recollection of man"— the mass executions. "Certainly," she added, the whole affair "will throw our city back at least ten years."[33] By the end, Miss Johnson, if she believed a conspiracy existed at all, thought it surely had not extended far enough to justify the massive retaliation of the courts.

The criticism by Governor Thomas Bennett was much more precise. The court should not have "closed its doors upon the community" in its secret proceedings and "shut out those accidental rays which occasionally illuminate the obscurity." Moreover, he found the testimony gathered by the judges "equivocal, the offspring of treachery or revenge, and the hope of immunity." "Nor should it be less a source of embarassment and concern," he continued, contesting the official version of the city, "that the testimony should be received under pledges of inviolable secrecy" and "that the accused should be convicted, and sentenced to death, without seeing the persons, or hearing the voices of those who testified to their guilt."[34]

The Governor noted particularly that the decisive information came from three witnesses "while they were under the impression

[31] Ana Hayes Johnson to Elizabeth E. W. Haywood, Charleston, July 18, 1822, ibid.

[32] Ana Hayes Johnson to Elizabeth E. W. Haywood, Charleston, July 24, 1822, ibid.

[33] Ana Hayes Johnson to Elizabeth E. W. Haywood, Charleston, July 27, 1822, ibid.

[34] Message of Governor Thomas Bennett to the Senate and House of Representatives of the State of South Carolina, November 28, 1822 (South Carolina Archives Division). The Charleston delegation thought the Governor's message too harsh on the city's handling of the episode. Charleston Mercury, December 18, 1822.

that they would have their life spared." Their testimony not only facilitated "the detection of the general plan of conspiracy, but enabled the court to convict a number of the principal offenders." While questioned "two of them were sometimes closeted together," achieving a uniformity of evidence. In one case William, "the slave of Mr. Palmer," was convicted "exclusively on the testimony of two of the persons under sentence of death." He protested his innocence, claimed he had attended no meetings and had never talked about a plot, and demonstrated his high reputation in many ways. Worse still, Charles Drayton "predicated his claim of escape [from the gallows] on the number of convictions he could make" with his story. "Nothing," Governor Bennett asserted, "could exceed the chilling depravity of this man."

Though the Governor probably believed in a plot of some kind, he could not take the one described by the city very seriously. "It is scarcely possible to imagine one, more crude or imperfect," he said. "They were unprovided with arms," and except for a few pennies that had been subscribed, "no effort was used to procure them." The leaders showed "no confidence in each other"; in fact, they were "in many instances unknown to each other." They had "no definite plans of attack concerted; nor place of rendezvous fixed." Yet the city represented the danger as "mature and within a few hours of consummation."

He went on to say that the idea of an insurrection itself seemed unlikely, although some of the reasons he gave are less convincing. "The liberal and enlightened humanity of our Fellow Citizens, produce many attachments, that operate as checks on the spirit of insubordination." Indeed, there were "unsurmountable obstacles"—the "habitual respect" of the slaves "for an obedience to the authority of their owners; their natural indolence, and want of means and opportunities to form combinations; their characteristic cowardice and treachery, excited by a knowledge of the positive ability of the state to crush in an instant their boldest enterprise." The Governor's view of the episode was plain. "The public mind had been raised to a pitch of excitement" over the rumor of a slave revolt and "sought relief in an exhibition of truth."[35] Instead, the action of the city created further panic and confusion.

A close examination of the published record of the trial tends to confirm the Governor's doubts. Though the testimony seems at first reading to suggest a ripe plan, the important evidence is

[35] Message of Governor Thomas Bennett.

missing at the critical points. For example, the transcript stated that "the whole numbers engaged" were 9,000, "partly from the country and partly from the city." But, it added, "it is true that the witness who had made these assertions did not see the lists [of accomplices] himself; but he heard from one who was in daily communication with Peter, . . . and as Peter wrote a good hand and was active throughout the whole affair, it is impossible to doubt that he had such lists." To be sure, the judges then contended that the larger figure was "greatly exaggerated, and perhaps designedly so."[36] Yet not a single roster of names ever turned up.

If the numbers were conjectural, the extent of the conspiracy was even more so. The report estimated the infected area covered not only the regions around the city but neighboring parishes as well. All through the crisis, however, no one detected any activity in the rural sections.[37] The charge that some of the central figures had acquaintances in the surrounding area was not accompanied by any evidence of complicity. Indeed, one black testified that Pierre Lewis told him "something serious would happen" but that "I was country born, and he was afraid to trust me."[38]

On the matter of weapons the official record reveals the same ambivalence. A blacksmith was supposed to have made some long pikes, six of which a few witnesses claimed existed. But the pikes were never located, thereby forcing the court into a curious logic: "as those six pike heads have not been found, there is no reason for disbelieving the testimony of there hav[ing] been many more made." Later the transcript mentions that "one hundred (pike heads and bayonets) were said to have been made at an early day, and by the 16th June, as many as two or three hundred, and between three and four hundred daggers." And there was still more. "Besides the above mentioned, it was proved that Peter had a sword; that Charles Drayton had a gun & sword; that John Henry had a sword; that Pharo Thompson had a scythe converted into a sword; that Adam Yates had a knife . . . that Monday had a sword"; and that Bacchus Hammett gave a sword and a gun to

[36] *Official Report,* 25-26.
[37] Nonetheless, a prominent planter explained "the orderly conduct of the negroes in any district within 40 miles of Charleston, is no evidence that they were ignorant of the intended attempt. A more orderly gang than my own is not to be found in this state—and one of Denmark Vesey's directives was, that they should assume the most implicit obedience." *Official Report,* 28n-31n. The plot presumably stretched as far as 70 or 80 miles from the city. *Ibid.,* 31.
[38] *Ibid.,* 159.

others. Yet, except for these few individual weapons, no arms cache was uncovered. "To presume that the Insurgents had no arms because none were seized," the judges concluded, "would be drawing an inference in direct opposition to the whole of the evidence."[39] Since the city published the full text of the trial to allay suspicions both in Charleston and in the North that some injustice had been done, the inconclusiveness of the case at the crucial points is significant.[40]

Equally important is the fact that the printed transcript is at odds in both wording and substance with manuscript records of the witnesses. For example, the confessions of Bacchus Hammett and John Enslow, among the few surviving original documents, have been carefully edited in the authorized version. Some passages were omitted; facts not mentioned in the original interrogation were added; even the tone of the narrative was changed with the alterations.[41]

For example, while Bacchus Hammett is reported to have testified: "At Vesey's they wanted to make a collection to make pikes for the country people, but the men had no money,"[42] the manuscript suggests something different: "Denmark told me in March, he was getting arms fast, about 150 to 200 pikes made, and there was a great deal of money placed in his hands for the purpose."[43] Again the *Official Report* lists names of accomplices. "Bellisle Yates I have seen at meetings, and Adam Yates and Napham Yates and Dean Mitchell, and Caesar Smith, and George a Stevidore [*sic*]." It also includes Jack McNeil, Prince Righton, Jerry Cohen. None appear in the original confession.[44]

At some points the manuscript included material not found at all in the printed version. To use but a single instance, the confession of Bacchus is quite explicit on a rebellion in Georgetown which would precede the Charleston uprising. "I also heard them

---

[39] *Ibid.*, 32.
[40] The Washington *Daily National Intelligencer* of August 3, 1822, noted that the Charleston *City Gazette* promised that "a succinct account of the whole transaction shall be given to the world. It will bring to view a scheme of wildness and of wickedness, enough to make us smile at the folly, did we not shudder at the indiscriminate mischief of the plan and its objects. Those (they were but few) who at first thought we had no cause for alarm, must be overwhelmed with conviction to the contrary."
[41] Bacchus, the Slave of Benjamin Hammett, Confession, and The Confession of Mr. Enslow's Boy John, 1822, in William and Benjamin Hammett Papers.
[42] *Official Report*, 146.
[43] Bacchus, the Slave of Benjamin Hammett, Confession, and The Confession of Mr. Enslow's Boy John.
[44] *Official Report*, 146, 7.

say that they were well informed in Georgetown. That they would let the principal Men know the time of the attack, being a short distance from Charleston, would commence a day or two before." The plan was simple. "Kill all the whites between there and Charleston, make their way through the woods and be in time to assist these people in town. It is also said by them that the Population in Georgetown could be killed in one half hour." Yet the city's account contains no mention of this extraordinary dimension of the plot.

The discrepancies seem deliberate since the preface of the pamphlet went to great pains to say that "the whole evidence has been given in each particular case, in the order of its trial, and wherever any additional, or incidental testimony has been disclosed against any criminal subsequently to his conviction, sentence or execution, it has been noticed." "In most cases," the judges contended, "it was as originally taken, without even changing the phraseology" and using "the very words" of the witnesses.[45] Yet these two depositions indicate that little confidence can be placed in the authenticity of the official account.[46]

Strangely, historians have received it less skeptically than some contemporaries. While many newspapers outside the state approved the silence of the Charleston press during the trial, some also looked forward to a "a succinct account of the whole transaction" that had been promised by the court. When it arrived, however, there was disappointment. "We doubt the policy of the present publication," wrote a reader of the Boston *Daily Advertiser*. "If intended to awe the blacks, it would seem the executions and banishments *silently* made, would be more terrible, but if really designed as an appeal, and a justification to the American people and to the world, as to the justice of the sentences, it appears either too much or too little." The "historical part," he concluded, "is too loose."[47]

In fact, the explanation of the whole episode lay in the "historical part." If a genuine conspiracy was lacking, tension between the races was not. In the years before the "plot," several developments had worsened relations that always were uneasy. The

[45] *Ibid.*, iii.
[46] Indeed, a close reading of the report suggests that the object of the trials was not to discover the extent of the plot but rather to awe the Negroes by a show of force. "The object of punishment being effectually attained by these examples, and the ring leaders being convicted," the court explained, "the arrests stopped here." *Ibid.*, 48, 59.
[47] Boston *Daily Advertiser*, October 8, 1822.

census figures conveniently summed up white fears. Officially Negroes outnumbered whites 14,127 to 10,653.[48] During the summer when many families left the city to escape the heat, the colored majority was even larger. Thomas Pinckney, in an extended post-mortem on the grim event, expressed the consequent anxiety. He called the imbalance "the principal encouragement to the late attempt, for without it, mad and wild as they appear to have been, they would not have dared to venture on a contest of force." In a word, numerical superiority was the "*sine qua non* of insurrection."[49]

Numbers alone, however, would not have produced panic. Some rural areas had a higher percentage of slaves than the city without the same alarm. It was the kind of colored population, not its mere predominance, that frightened white leaders. Charleston's Negroes, like urban blacks elsewhere, were a far different lot than their country brothers. They were more advanced, engaged in higher tasks, more literate, more independent, and less servile than those on plantations. Not confined to the field or the big house, many found employment as draymen, porters, fishermen, hucksters, butchers, barbers, carpenters, and even as clerks and bookkeepers. Their work took these slaves away from the constant surveillance of their masters and generated a measure of self-reliance not usually found in the "peculiar institution." Added to this was an urban environment that provided churches, livery stables, cook houses, and grog shops as centers of informal community life.

Even the domestics who comprised the bulk of urban bondsmen in Charleston afforded slight comfort, though they were popularly believed to be loyally attached to the families of their owners.[50] In fact, Pinckney thought them "certainly the most dangerous" because they had an "intimate acquaintance with all circumstances relating to the interior of the dwellings," because of "the confidence reposed in them," and because of "information they unavoidably obtain, from hearing the conversation, and observing the habitual transactions of their owners." Having "the

[48] *Census for 1820, Published by Authority of an Act of Congress, Under the Direction of the Secretary of State* (Washington, 1821), 26.
[49] Achates [Thomas Pinckney], *Reflections Occasioned by the Late Disturbances in Charleston* (Charleston, 1822), 10.
[50] The *Official Report* contained the conventional view. "Few if any domestic servants were spoken to [by the leaders], as *they* were distrusted." *Ibid.*, 26. Pinckney's appraisal of the domestics suggests that he did not wholly trust the analysis of the court even though he believed in the existence of the plot.

amplest means for treacherous bloodshed and devastation," this group would comprise the core of a conspiracy. Yet these slaves, he complained, had been "so pampered" by "indulgencies," even "being taught to read and write," that the "considerable control" embodied in ordinances and state laws had been frustrated by the "weakness of many proprietors."[51]

Nearly all those believed to be ringleaders by the court came from one or another of these areas of colored life. Denmark Vesey, who "stood at the head of this conspiracy" according to the court's report, was a successful carpenter who had bought his freedom with money won in a lottery in 1801. Since he was the only free Negro executed (six others were questioned and dismissed), officials assumed "the idea undoubtedly originated with him" and that he concocted the plot. His house and shop became the rendezvous of the rebels and he the moving genius. For several years before he "disclosed his intentions to anyone," the court declared, "he appears to have been constantly and assiduously engaged in endeavoring to embitter the minds of the coloured population against the white." He "rendered himself perfectly familiar" with the Bible and used whatever parts "he could pervert to his purpose; and would readily quote them, to prove that slavery was contrary to the laws of God." Moreover, he distributed "inflammatory pamphlets" among the bondsmen. He even "sought every opportunity" to "introduce some bold remark on slavery" into conversations with whites while in the presence of other Negroes.[52]

His associates were no less impressive. Monday Gell not only hired his own time but kept a shop on Meeting Street where he made harness; his owner entrusted arms as well as money to him. Governor Bennett once called him "the projector of the plot" and its "most active partisan."[53] Peter Poyas was a "first rate ship carpenter" who had an excellent reputation and the implicit confidence of his master. Two others belonged to the Governor of the state, and one of them tended the family's business when his owner was at the capital. Only Gullah Jack, who claimed to be a sorcerer with mysterious powers, seemed irregular.

[51] Pinckney, *Reflections*, 6-9.
[52] *Official Report*, 17-19. Later in the testimony, however, the court contended that Vesey "enjoyed so much the confidence of the whites, that when he was accused, the charge was not only discredited, but he was not even arrested for several days after, and not until proof of his guilt had become too strong to be doubted." This does not square well with the previous description of years of agitation and bold confrontation with whites.
[53] Message of Governor Thomas Bennett.

White fears fixed on this colored urban elite, on those who managed to "succeed" a little in bondage. To the whites of Charleston, the character of the city's Negro population made an uprising seem possible, indeed, reasonable. The Negroes were, as a group of residents put it, the "most condensed and most intelligent."[54] Moreover, the extent of literacy brought the "powerful operation of the Press" on "their uninformed and easily deluded minds" and, more precisely, made them privy to events outside the city and the South. The example of Santo Domingo, where the blacks had risen successfully against the whites, and the debate over the Missouri Compromise were thought to have "directly or indirectly" heightened the unrest and encouraged insurrectionary activity.[55] In sum, both the quality and the quantity of Charleston slaves rendered the whites uneasy.

The Negroes, too, were edgy, for things had not gone well for them in the preceding months. New state legislation had made manumission more difficult, nearly closing the door on those who hoped to get their freedom either by purchase or the generosity of their masters.[56] Such "uncivilized laws," "A Colored American" recalled, were "a great and intolerable hindrance" to the slaves' "peace and happiness," since some had already made arrangements to buy their liberty.[57]

Another cause of controversy was the closing of an independent Methodist church established for colored people. In this sanctuary many blacks had found both spiritual consolation and brief relief from servitude. When it was closed down in 1821, the Negro community became embittered. Bible-class leaders especially felt aggrieved because it deprived them of one of the few positions of modest status open to bondsmen. The resentment of this articulate group was scarcely a secret. In fact, the city later charged that almost all the ringleaders were connected with this church.[58]

The atmosphere, then, was charged with fears and grievances. No doubt conversations among whites turned often, if hesitantly, to the topic; and certainly in the grog shops, in Negro quarters, and on the job, the slaves talked about their difficulties. The gap

[54] *Southern Patriot and Commercial Advertiser*, August 21, 1822.
[55] Pinckney, *Reflections*, 9.
[56] *Acts and Resolutions of the General Assembly of the State of South-Carolina Passed in December, 1820* (Columbia, 1821), 22-24.
[57] A Colored American, *Late Contemplated Insurrection*, 5.
[58] The church included both slaves and free blacks. Though some accounts emphasize the petition of free Negroes to the legislature for the privilege of conducting their own worship, the report of the trial asserts that nearly all the bondsmen involved also belonged to the African church and that many were class leaders.

between the races was great, calculatedly so, and was quickly filled by gossip and rumor. Blacks heard the whites were going to "thin out" the colored population, that a false alarm would bring out the militia and volunteers to butcher the slaves on the spot, that new restraints were under consideration in city hall and the state legislature. Circulating among the whites were equally hair-raising notions: a servile uprising, the seizure of the city, the carrying off of women after all males had been exterminated.

Under these circumstances anything specific—names, places, target dates—seemed to give substance to the rumor, suggesting that a plot not only existed but was ripe. Prudence dictated preventive action and a withering show of force by the city. Not only the ringleaders but even those remotely connected had to be swiftly seized, tried, and punished. Hence, the chance encounter of Devany Prioleau with William Paul on the wharf on May 25, 1822, with its garbled but ominous portent, set off a chain of events that did not end until thirty-five had been executed, still more deported, and a town frozen in terror for almost a summer.

Thus Charleston stumbled into tragedy. The "plot" was probably never more than loose talk by aggrieved and embittered men. Curiously, its reputation as a full-scale revolt has endured, in part, because both sides in the slavery controversy believed insurrections to be essential to their broader argument. Apologists for the "peculiar institution" contended that the stringent laws against Negroes in the South were needed to protect whites from violence; opponents of slavery asserted that the urge for freedom was so embedded in human nature that none would passively remain enchained. In either event the Denmark Vesey uprising became a convenient illustration of a larger view of bondage. No closer examination seemed necessary. What *both* Aptheker and Phillips could accept as fact, it was assumed, must necessarily be true.

But the very agreement tended to obscure the important reality. For a concerted revolt against slavery was actually less likely in a city than in the countryside. The chances for success anywhere, of course, were never very good, but ordinary circumstances favored a Nat Turner over a Denmark Vesey. The reasons for this are clear. Nowhere, not even in Charleston, did the blacks have the great numerical superiority that was present on many plantations. Moreover, police forces in the towns, large and well organized, constituted a more powerful deterrent than the vigilante patrol system characteristic of places with scattered populations.

And ironically, the urban environment proved inhospitable to conspiracies because it provided a wider latitude to the slave, a measure of independence within bondage, and some relief from the constant surveillance of the master. This comparative freedom deflected the discontent, leading Negroes to try to exploit their modest advantages rather than to organize for desperate measures.

The white community, however, could see only the dangers. The Negroes in Charleston were not only numerous but quite different from the imbruted field hands of the cane and cotton country. Many mastered skills, learned to read and write, joined churches and in every way tried to comport themselves as free men. This was the source of the fear. They seemed capable both of resenting their bondage and organizing an insurrection against it. It was not difficult to translate a few rumors into a widespread conspiracy. Indeed, it was so easy that historians, too, have done so for nearly a century and a half.

THE JOURNAL

OF

NEGRO HISTORY

Vol. XXII—July, 1937—No. 3

AMERICAN SLAVE INSURRECTIONS
BEFORE 1861

The romantic portrayal of *ante-bellum* society on the southern plantation, which depicts the rollicking black against a kindly patriarchal background, has tended to obscure the large element of slave unrest which occasionally shook the whole fabric of the planter's kingdom. Even the abolitionist, eager to capitalize upon such material, could make only vague inferences as to the extent of Negro insurrections in the South. The danger of inducing general panic by spreading news of an insurrection was a particularly potent factor in the maintenance of silence on the topic. Besides, sectional pride, in the face of anti-slavery taunts, prevented the loyal white Southerner from airing the subject of domestic revolt in the press. "Last evening," wrote a lady of Charleston during the Denmark Vesey scare of 1822, "twenty-five hundred of our citizens were under arms to guard our property and lives. But it is a subject not to be mentioned; and unless you hear of it elsewhere, say nothing about it."[1] Consequently, against such a conspiracy of silence the historian encounters unusual difficulties in reconstructing the true picture of slave revolts in the United States.

[1] T. W. Higginson, "Gabriel's Defeat," *The Atlantic Monthly*, X (1862), 337-345.

299

I. THE BACKGROUND OF SLAVE SHIP MUTINIES

Before considering the nature of American slave insurrections, one may obtain a revelatory background by a survey of Negro uprisings upon the ships which carried the blacks from their African home. The horrors of the trade in human chattel have been frequently told and, for the most part, without serious exaggeration. Pious Captain John Hawkins, plying his profession on *The Jesus*, led the enterprising pioneers of the slave business. In time the miserable traffic was rationalized on religious and humanitarian grounds; but generally speaking, the stakes were too high for any indulgence in sentimentality. George Scelle has written a detailed study of the enormous diplomatic factors involved, the constant rivalry for the much prized *assiento*, and the difficult social and administrative problems arising from the unceasing demand for cheap labor.[2]

It is unnecessary to account for slave ship mutinies by overstressing the revolting conditions which prevailed between decks. The desire for liberty was manifest from the very beginning and outbreaks would occur sometimes as the ship was being loaded, or as it sailed down the Gambia River, or along the West African Coast, as well as in the Middle Passage. Most instances of such insurrections seem to have taken place near the West African Coast, off such places as Sierra Leone, Goree, Cape Coast Castle, Cabinde, and Cape Malpas.

Some slave ship captains put their trust in the relative docility of certain African peoples. Captain Theodore Canot, for example, thought that the Negroes from Whydah were "distinguished for humble manners and docility"; yet he experienced a serious outbreak from these lambs. He believed that the Negroes from Benin and Angola were not

[2] George Scelle, *Histoire politique de la traite negriere aux Indes de Castille*, (Paris, 1902), 2 vols. Profits to the slave trader of 600% and 1000% were not unusual. *The Ninth Annual Report of the British and Foreign Anti-Slavery Society*, (London, 1848), 20.

as addicted to revolt as those north of the Gold Coast.[3] Frequent references appear in documentary accounts as to the refractory qualities of the "Coromantees."

The captives displayed a profound dejection and sought many devices to commit suicide. Sometimes they would jump overboard if the crew did not take every precaution to prevent this. Self-imposed starvation was common. One witness, testifying before a parliamentary committee, declared that compulsory feeding was used on every slave ship with which he was familiar.[4] Sick Negroes would refuse medicines, declaring that they wished only to die. Characteristic of many slavers was a "howling melancholy noise" with the women occasionally in hysterics. Sometimes the slaves were convinced that they were to be eaten.[5] The following type of evidence given in parliament appears in other accounts as well:

"Mr. Towne says, that inquiring of the slaves into the cause of these insurrections he has been asked, what business he had to carry them from their own country. They had wives and children whom they wanted to be with."[6]

Despite the most elaborate precautions slave insurrections frequently broke out. Captain James Barbot, writing in 1700, tells of the meticulous daily search made into every corner of the ship for pieces of iron and wood, and for knives. Small arms for the crew were kept in readiness and sentinels stationed at all doorways. Such care he thought was unusual among other slavers, and, as he remarked, "If all those who carry slaves duly observed them (precautions) we should not hear of so many revolts as have hap-

[3] Brantz Mayer, *Adventures of an African Slaver*, (New York, 1928), 265.

[4] *An Abstract of the Evidence Delivered Before a Select Committee of the House of Commons, 1790-91*, (London, 1791), 39.

[5] Elizabeth Donnan, (ed.), *Documents Illustrative of the Slave Trade to America*, (Washington, 1930-5), I, 462-3; hereafter referred to as *D.S.T.*

[6] *An Abstract of the Evidence* ——— 44.

pened.'"⁷ The tense atmosphere which often preceded an
outbreak has been graphically told by Captain Theodore
Canot of the *Estrella*:

"From the beginning there was manifest discontent among the
slaves. . . . A few days after our departure a slave leaped overboard in a fit of passion and another choked himself during the
night. These two suicides in twenty-four hours caused much uneasiness among the officers and induced me to make every preparation for a revolt."⁸

The insurrection itself was a desperate struggle waged
with the courage of despair. Sometimes weapons would
reach the slaves through the female captives who were frequently given comparative freedom on the deck. Naturally,
in the greater number of cases, the revolt was doomed to
failure, and the retribution was swift and terrible. Every
refinement of torture was utilized by the captain, and the
ring leaders, at least, were killed. Captain Harding, for example, borrowed the methods of savagery by compelling the
rebels to eat the heart and liver of a sailor who had been
killed, and hanged a woman leader by her thumbs, whipping and slashing her with knives.⁹ Occasionally the slaves
were successful in overpowering the crew and escaped by
compelling the pilot to direct them homeward.

There is evidence of a special form of insurance to cover
losses arising specifically from insurrections. An insurance
statement of 1776 from Rhode Island, for example, has
this item: "Wresk of Mortality and Insurrection of 220
slaves, Value £9000 Ste'g at 5 per cent is Pr Month =
£37,10s."¹⁰ A Captain's statement of August 11, 1774, contains a request for insurrection insurance.¹¹ In a Negro

⁷ *D.S.T.*, I, 462. It should be added that the cautious Barbot later experienced an insurrection when off Cabinde and overpowered the rebels only
after terrific slaughter. *Ibid*, 457.
⁸ Mayer, *Adventures of an African Slaver*, 264.
⁹ *D.S.T.*, II, 266.
¹⁰ *Ibid.*, III, 325.
¹¹ *Ibid.*, 293.

mutiny case of May 3, 1785, the court awarded payment in conformance with a policy provision for insurrection insurance.[12] Sometimes the captain of a slaver would throw sick Negroes overboard to profit by the insurance payments given in such contingencies.

From the following summary of slave ship revolts based largely on documentary sources, it is evident that such insurrections occurred very frequently, sometimes recurring on the same ship.[13]

Date	*Ship or Captain*
1. August 22, 1699	*The Albion*[14]
2. August, 1700	Captain James Barbot[15]
3. —— 1703	Captain Ralph Ash, *The Tyger*[16]
4. —— 1704	*The Eagle*[17]
5. June, 1717	*The Ann*[18]
6. —— 1721	Captain Harding, *The Robert*[19]
7. —— 1721	Captain Snelgrave, *The Henry*[20]
8. —— 1722	Captain Messervy, *Ferrers*[21]
9. June, 1730	*Little George*[22]
10. Nov. 14, 1730	Captain William Martin, *The Guinea*[23]
11. Dec. 7, 1731	(Glasgow vessel)[24]

[12] Helen H. Catterall, (ed.), *Judicial Cases Concerning American Slavery and the Negro*, (Washington, 1926), I, 19; hereafter referred to as *J.C.N.* For other illustrations of insurrection insurance see *ibid.*, III, 568 and *D.S.T.*, III, 217.

[13] This list of insurrections is undoubtedly far from exhaustive. In a few cases there may even be duplications.

[14] George Francis Dow, *Slave Ships and Slaving*, (Salem, 1927), 83.

[15] *D.S.T.*, I, 463.

[16] *Ibid.*, 5ff.

[17] William Snelgrave, *A New Account of Some Parts of Guinea and the Slave Trade*, (London, 1734), 164.

[18] *D.S.T.*, II, 232.

[19] *Ibid.*, 266.

[20] Snelgrave, *A New Account of—Guinea and the Slave Trade*, 164.

[21] *Ibid.*, 185.

[22] *D.S.T.*, III, 119.

[23] *Ibid.*, II, 397.

[24] *Ibid.*, 431ff.

12. —— 1731	Captain George Scott[25]
13. —— 1731	Captain Jump[26]
14. August, 1732	Captain John Major[27]
15. Feb. 5, 1733	Captain Williams[28]
16. —— 1735	*The Dolphin*[29]
17. March 16, 1737	Captain Japhet Bird, *Prince of Orange*[30]
18. May, 1747	Captain Beers[31]
19. April 14, 1750	*The Ann*[32]
20. May 8, 1750	*King David*[33]
21. May 28, 1750	(Liverpool vessel)[34]
22. —— 1754	Captain Smith, *The Jubilee*[35]
23. Jan. 12, 1759	*The Perfect*[36]
24. —— 1761	Captain Nichols[37]
25. Sept., 1761	Captain Day, *The Thomas*[38]
26. March, 1764	*The Hope*[39]
27. June, 1764	Captain Joseph Muller[40]
28. Winter, 1764	Captain Toman, *Three Friends*[41]
29. Aug. 16, 1764	Captain Faggot, *Extraordinary*[42]
30. Nov. 25, 1765	Captain Rogers[43]
31. —— 1765	Captain Hopkins[44]

[25] Joshua Coffin, *An Account of some of the Principal Slave Insurrections*, (New York, 1860), 14.

[26] *D.S.T.*, III, 37.

[27] *Ibid.*, 42ff.; also Coffin,—*Principal Slave Insurrections*, 14.

[28] *D.S.T.*, II, 410.

[29] Coffin,—*Principal Slave Insurrections*, 14.

[30] *D.S.T.*, II, 460.

[31] *Ibid.*, III, 51; also Coffin,—*Principal Slave Insurrections*, 15.

[32] *D.S.T.*, II, 485-6.

[33] *Ibid.*, 486-7.

[34] *Ibid.*, 485.

[35] Sylvanus Urban, (ed.), *Gentleman's Magazine*, XXIV, (London, 1754), 141.

[36] Edmund B. D'Auvergne, *Human Livestock*, (London, 1933), 73.

[37] Coffin, *Principal Slave Insurrections*, 15; also *D.S.T.*, III, 452.

[38] *Ibid.*, 67-70.

[39] *Ibid.*, 71.

[40] *Ibid.*, 71, 207.

[41] *Ibid.*, 209ff.

[42] *Ibid.*, 2.

[43] *Ibid.*, 201.

[44] *Ibid.*, 213.

32. —— 1773	Captain Gogart, *The Industry*[45]
33. July, 1776	Captain Peleg Clark, *The Phoenix*[46]
34. Nov. 8, 1776	*The Thames*[47]
35. Dec. 8, 1776	Captain Bell[48]
36. Feb., 1785	(Rhode Island vessel)[49]
37. May 3, 1785	(Bristol vessel)[50]
38. Dec., 1787	*The Ruby*[51]
39. April 23, 1789	Captain Fairfield[52]
40. —— 1793	Captain J. B. Cooke, *The Nancy*[53]
41. —— 1793	Captain Joseph Hawkins, *The Charleston*[54]
42. —— 1795	(Boston vessel)[55]
43. June 10, 1796	*The Mary*[56]
44. —— 1797	Captain Thomas Clarke, *The Thames*[57]
45. May, 1797	*The Cadiz Dispatch*[58]
46. Sept., 1797	*The Thomas*[59]
47. April, 1799	*The Thomas*[60]
48. Aug. 2, 1799	*The Trelawney*[61]
49. Feb., 1804	*The Anne*[62]
50. Aug. 1, 1807	Captain Joseph Viale, *The Nancy*[63]
51. March 19, 1808	*The Leander*[64]

[44] *Gentleman's Magazine*, XLIV, 1774, 469.
[45] *D.S.T.*, III, 318.
[47] *Ibid.*, 331.
[48] *Ibid.*, 323.
[49] *Ibid.*, 341.
[50] *J.C.N.*, I, 19.
[51] Dow, *Slave Ships and Slaving*, 175.
[52] *D.S.T.*, III, 82-3.
[53] *Ibid.*, 358-9.
[54] Joseph Hawkins, *A History of a Voyage to the Coast of Africa*, (Philadelphia, 1797), 145-9.
[55] *D.S.T.*, III, 101.
[56] *Ibid.*, 375.
[57] *Ibid.*, II, 665.
[58] *J.C.N.*, I, 22.
[59] D'Auvergne, *Human Livestock*, 73.
[60] *J.C.N.*, I, 22.
[61] *D.S.T.*, II, 644.
[62] *J.C.N.*, I, 25.
[63] *D.S.T.*, III, 394-6; also Dow, *Slave Ships and Slaving*, 272.
[64] *J.C.N.*, II, 292.

52. May 11, 1808	*The Coralline*[65]
53. —— 1829	Captain Theodore Canot, *L'Estrella*[66]
54. June, 1839	Captain Ramon Ferrer, *Amistad*[67]
55. March, 1845	*The Creole*[68]

II. SLAVE INSURRECTIONS IN THE UNITED STATES

The desire for freedom on the part of the African, evidenced by his struggle on the slave ships, did not die in the New World. On the plantations of Latin-America, in the British and French Indies, and finally in the American cotton, rice, and sugar fields, the aspirations of the Negro, blocked by the white master, gave birth to plots and uprisings. The lesson of San Domingo particularly was suggestive to both whites and blacks. Repressive black codes and emergency patrols frequently converted the plantation into an armed camp. Governor Robert Y. Hayne of South Carolina declared to the Assembly in 1833, two years after the Nat Turner Insurrection:

"A state of military preparation must always be with us a state of perfect domestic security. A period of profound peace and consequent apathy may expose us to the danger of domestic insurrection."[69]

Professor Thomas R. Dew, militant apologist of slavery, sought, in an address that year before the Virginia Legislature, to minimize the fears of insurrection:

"This is the evil, after all, let us say what we will, which really operates most powerfully upon the schemers and emancipating philanthropists of those sections where slaves constitute the principal property. . . . We cannot fail to derive the greatest consolation from the fact that although slavery has existed in our country for the last two hundred years, there have been but three attempts

---

[65] Dow, *Slave Ships and Slaving*, 207.
[66] Mayer, *Adventures of an African Slaver*, 264-5.
[67] Coffin, *Principal Slave Insurrections*, 33.
[68] *J.C.N.*, III, 565.
[69] *Message of Governor Robert Y. Hayne to the Senate and House of Representatives of South Carolina*, (Columbia, November 26, 1833).

at insurrection—one in Virginia, one in South Carolina, and we believe, one in Louisiana—and the loss of lives from this cause has not amounted to one hundred persons in all.''[70]

Despite the serious understatement of the number of insurrections, Dew's remarks are actually revelatory of the fears aroused among the planters. A graphic illustration of the cyclic fears of Negro uprisings during the 1830's is afforded by the remarks of several whites of Mississippi in 1859 to Frederick L. Olmsted:

"Where I used to live (Alabama) I remember when I was a boy—must ha' been about twenty years ago—folks was dreadful frightened about the niggers. I remember they built pens in the woods where they could hide and Christmas time they went and got into the pens, fraid the niggers was risin'.''[71]

The speaker's wife added her recollection to this comment:

"I remember the same time where we was in South Carolina, we had all our things put up in bags so we could tote 'em if we heard they was comin' our way.''[72]

Slave outbreaks and plots appeared both North and South during the Colonial period. Sometimes the white indentured servants made common cause with the Negroes against their masters. This was the case in 1663 when a plot of white servants and Negroes was betrayed in Gloucester County, Virginia.[73] The eastern counties of Virginia, where the Negroes were rapidly outnumbering the whites, suffered from repeated scares in 1687, 1709, 1710, 1722, 1723, and 1730.[74] A patrol system was set up in 1726

[70] The Political Register, (Washington, 1833), III, (1833), 823.
[71] Frederick Law Olmsted, A Journey in the Back Country, (New York, 1860), 203.
[72] Ibid.
[73] Ulrich B. Phillips, American Negro Slavery, (New York, 1918), 472.
[74] William P. Palmer, (ed.), Calendar of Virginia State Papers, (Richmond, 1875), I, (1652-1781), 129-130; also James Curtis Ballagh, A History of Slavery in Virginia, (Baltimore, 1902), 79-80; also Coffin, Principal Slave Insurrections, 11.

in parts of the state and later extended. Attempts were made here as elsewhere to check the importation of slaves by high duties.

Two important slave plots, one a serious insurrection, disturbed the peace of New York City in 1712 and 1741. In revenge for ill-treatment by their masters, twenty-three Negroes rose on April 6, 1712, to slaughter the whites and killed nine before they were overwhelmed by a superior force. The retaliation showed an unusual barbarous strain on the part of the whites. Twenty-one Negroes were executed, some were burnt, others hanged, and one broken on the wheel.[75] In 1741 another plot was reported in New York involving both whites and blacks. A white, Hewson (or Hughson), was accused of providing the Negroes with weapons. He and his family were executed; likewise, a Catholic priest was hanged as an accomplice. Thirteen Negro leaders were burnt alive, eighteen hanged, and eighty transported.[76] Popular fears of further insurrections led the New York Assembly to impose a prohibitive tax on the importation of Negroes. This tax, however, was later rescinded by order of the British Commissioner for Trade and Plantations.[77]

The situation in colonial South Carolina was worse than in her sister states. Long before rice and indigo had given way to King Cotton, the early development of the plantation system had yielded bumper crops of slave uprisings and plots. An insurrection, resulting in the deaths of three

[75] Letter of Governor Robert Hunter to the Lords of Trade, in E. B. O'Callaghan, (ed.), *Documents Relative to the Colonial History of the State of New York*, (Albany, 1855), V, (1707-1733), 341-2.

[76] *Gentleman's Magazine*, XI, (1741), 441.

[77] *D.S.T.*, III, 409. Joshua Coffin also reports plots and actual outbreaks in other slaveholding areas in the Northern Colonies. East Boston is said to have experienced a minor uprising in 1638. In 1723, a series of incendiary fires in Boston led the selectmen to suspect a slave plot and the militia was ordered to police the slaves. Another plot was reported in Burlington, Pennsylvania during 1734. Coffin, *Principal Slave Insurrections*, 10, 11, 12.

whites, is reported for May 6, 1720.[78] Ten years later an elaborate plot was discovered in St. John's Parish by a Negro servant of Major Cordes'. This plan was aimed at Charleston, an attack that was to inaugurate a widespread war upon the planters. Under the pretense of conducting a "dancing bout" in the city and in St. Paul's Parish the Negroes gathered together ready to seize the available arms for the attack. At this point the militia descended upon the blacks and killed the greater number, leaving few to escape.[79]

Owing partly to Spanish intrigues the same decade in South Carolina witnessed many more uprisings. An outbreak is reported for November, 1738.[80] The following year, on September 9, the Stono uprising created panic throughout the southeast. About twenty Angola Negroes assembled at Stono under their captain, Tommy, and marched toward Spanish territory, beating drums and endeavoring to attract other slaves. Several whites were killed and a number of houses burnt or plundered. As the "army" paused in a field to dance and sing they were overtaken by the militia and cut down in a pitched battle.[81] The following year an insurrection broke out in Berkeley County.[82] Charleston was threatened repeatedly by slave plots.[83] These reports are confirmed officially in the petition of the South Carolina Assembly to the King on July 26, 1740. Among the grievances of 1739 the Assembly complained of:

[78] Coffin, *Principal Slave Insurrections*, 11.

[79] Edward Clifford Holland, *A Refutation of the Calumnies Circulated Against the Southern and Western States Respecting the Institution and Existence of Slavery*, (Charleston, 1822), 68-9, 81.

[80] Ralph Betts Flander, *Plantation Slavery in Georgia*, (Chapel Hill, 1933), 24.

[81] *Gentleman's Magazine*, X, (1740), 127-8.

[82] See the Constable's bill in the *Magazine of American History*, XXV, (1891), 85-6.

[83] Edward McGrady, *The History of South Carolina Under the Royal Government*, (1719-1776), (New York, 1899), 5.

"*. . . an insurrection of our slaves in which many of the Inhabitants were murdered in a barbarous and cruel manner; and that no sooner quelled than another projected in Charles Town, and a third lately in the very heart of the Settlements, but happily discovered in time enough to be prevented.*"[84]

Repercussions of slave uprisings in South Carolina sometimes affected Georgia as well. This was particularly true in 1738.[85] In 1739 a plot was discovered in Prince George County.[86] To many slaves St. Augustine on Spanish soil seemed a welcome refuge from their masters.

Indications of many other insurrections in the American Colonies may be inferred from the nature of early patrol laws: The South Carolina law of 1704 for example contains a reference in its preamble to recent uprisings in that Colony.[87] In the British and French possessions to the south, particularly in the West Indies, affairs were much worse and put the planter of the North in constant fear of importing rebellious slaves and the contagion of revolt.

In considering the insurrections of the national period, it is at once evident that abolitionist propaganda played a relatively minor role despite the charges of southern politicians after 1831. The genealogy of revolt extends much further back than the organized efforts of anti-slavery advocates. It is true, however, that white men played an important role in many Negro uprisings, frequently furnishing arms, and even leadership, as well as inspiration.[88] The

[84] Appendix to Holland, *A Refutation of the Calumnies*, —, 71. Another plot of December 17, 1765, is mentioned in *D.S.T.*, IV, 415.

[85] Flanders, *Plantation Slavery in Georgia*, 24; similarly, South Carolina's slave plots sometimes required the assistance of North Carolina as in the scare of 1766. William L. Saunders, (ed.), *Colonial Records of North Carolina*, (Raleigh, 1890), VIII, (1769-1771), 559.

[86] Jeffrey R. Brackett, *The Negro in Maryland*, (Baltimore, 1889), 93.

[87] H. M. Henry, *The Police Control of the Slave in South Carolina*, (Vanderbilt University, 1914), 30.

[88] One aspect of this subject is discussed in James Hugo Johnston's article, "The Participation of White Men in Virginia Negro Insurrections," *Journal of Negro History*, XVI, (1931), 158-167.

motives for such assistance varied from philanthropy to unadulterated self-interest. As might be expected, insurrections tended to occur where King Cotton and his allies were most firmly entrenched and the great plantation system established.

Slave unrest seems to have been far greater in Virginia rather than in the states of the Lower South. Conspiracies like those of Gabriel in 1800 and Nat Turner in 1831 attained national notoriety. The Gabriel plot was developed in the greatest secrecy upon the plantation of a harsh slavemaster, Thomas Prosser, several miles from Richmond. Under the leadership of a young slave, Gabriel, and inspired by the examples of San Domingo and the emancipation of the ancient Israelites from Egypt, some eleven hundred slaves had taken an oath to fight for their liberty. Plans were drawn for the seizure of an arsenal and several other strategic buildings of Richmond which would precede a general slaughter of all hostile whites. After the initial successes, it was expected that fifty thousand Negroes would join the standard of revolt. Beyond this point, the arrangements were hazy.[89] A faithful slave however exposed the plot and Governor James Monroe took rapid measures to secure the cooperation of the local authorities and the federal cavalry. Bloodshed was averted by an unprecedented cloudburst on the day set for the conspiracy and the utter demoralization of the undisciplined "army." Writing to his friend, President Jefferson, the Governor declared:

"It (the Gabriel plot) is unquestionably the most serious and formidable conspiracy we have ever known of the kind. While it was possible to keep it secret, which it was till we saw the extent of it, we did so. . . ."[90]

[89] Details of the Gabriel Plot are in the *Calendar of Virginia State Papers*, X, (1808-1835), 140-173, *et passim;* T. W. Higginson, "Gabriel's Defeat," *The Atlantic Monthy*, X, (1862), 337-345; Robert R. Howison, *A History of Virginia*, (Richmond, 1848), II, 390-3.

[90] Monroe to Jefferson, September 15, 1800; S. M. Hamilton, (ed.), *Writings of James Monroe*, (New York, 1893-1903), III, 201. Much of the Gabriel affair can be followed from the letters of Monroe.

With the opening of the slave trials, hysteria swept the South and many innocent blacks were compelled to pay for this with their lives. Rumors of new plots sprang up everywhere much to the distraction of Monroe. The results of the Gabriel incident were significant. An impetus was given to the organization of the American Colonization Society which took definite form in 1816. The slave patrol laws became very stringent, and the example was copied elsewhere in the South. The incipient feeling of sectional diversity received a new impetus.

Between Gabriel's abortive plot and the Nat Turner uprising, several more incidents occurred which disturbed the sleep of Virginians. In January, 1802, Governor Monroe received word of a plot in Nottaway County. Several Negroes suspected of participation were executed.[91] That same year came disclosures of a projected slave uprising in Goochland County aided by eight or ten white men.[92] Several plots were reported in 1808 and 1809 necessitating almost continuous patrol service.[93] The War of 1812 intensified the apprehensions of servile revolt. Petitions for troops and arms came during the summer of 1814 from Caroline County and Lynchburg.[94] Regiments were called out during the war in anticipation of insurrections along the tidewater area. During the spring of 1816 confessions were wrung from slaves concerning an attack upon Fredericksburg and Richmond. The inspiration for this enterprise was attributed to a white military officer, George Boxley. The latter claimed to be the recipient of divine revelations and the instrument of "omnipotence" although he denied any intention of leading an insurrection. His relatives declared that he was insane, but his neighbors in a complaint to the governor showed serious misgivings on this point:

[91] Hamilton, (ed.) *Writings of James Monroe*, III, 328-9.
[92] James H. Johnston, "The Participation of White Men in Virginia Negro Insurrections," 161.
[93] *Calendar of Virginia State Papers*, X, (1808-1835), 31, 62.
[94] *Ibid.*, 367, 388.

"On many occasions he has declared that the distinction between the rich and the poor was too great; that offices were given to wealth than to merit; and seemed to be an advocate for a more leveling system of Government. For many years he has avowed his disapprobation of the slavery of the Negroes and wished they were free."[95]

Boxley was arrested but escaped. About thirty Negroes were sentenced to death or deportation in consequence.

The years preceding the Nat Turner insurrection brought further news of plots discovered. During the middle of July, 1829, the governor received requests for aid from the counties of Mathews, Gloucester, the Isle of Wight and adjacent counties.[96] The ease with which "confessions" were obtained under duress casts doubt upon the reality of such outbreaks, but the reports are indicative of the ever-present fear of attack.

Nat Turner's insurrection of August 21, 1831, at Southhampton, seventy miles from Richmond, raised fears of a general servile war to their highest point. The contemporary accounts of the young slave, Nat, tend to overemphasize his leanings towards mysticism and under-state the background of unrest.[97] As a "leader" or lay preacher, Nat Turner exercised a strong influence over his race. On the fatal August night, he led his followers to the plantations of the whites killing fifty-five before the community could act. The influence of the Southhampton insurrection upon the South was profound. Gradually the statesmen of that section began to reexamine their "peculiar" institution in the rival aspects of humanitarianism, the race problem, and the economic requirements for a cheap labor supply. How the friends of emancipation failed is familiar

[95] *Calendar of Virginia State Papers*, X, 433-6.
[96] *Ibid.*, 567-9.
[97] Thomas Gray, (ed.), *Nat Turner's Confession*, (Richmond, 1832); Samuel Warner, (ed.), *The Authentic and Impartial Narrative of The Tragical Scene of the Twenty Second of August, 1831*, New York, 1831, (A Collection of accounts by eye witnesses); and William Sidney Drewry, *Slave Insurrections in Virginia, 1830-1865*, (Washington, 1900), *passim.*

421

history. The immediate results were also far-reaching. Laws against the free Negro were made more restrictive, the police codes of the slave states were strengthened, and Negro education became more than ever an object of suspicion.[98] Virginia's lucrative business of supplying slaves to the lower South was gradually undermined by the recurrent insurrections. Frederic Bancroft, the historian of the domestic slave trade, has written:

"Believing that as a result of actual or feared insurrections Virginia and other States were taking pains to sell to the traders the most dangerous slaves and criminal free Negroes, Alabama, Mississippi, Louisiana, and other States passed laws forbidding all importations for sale."[99]

Rumors of slave plots continued to disturb Virginia up to the era of emancipation. During 1856, the state, in common with other slaveholding states, shared in the general feeling that a widespread conspiracy, set for December 25, was maturing. Requests for aid came to the Governor from the counties of Fauquier, King and Queen, Culpeper, and Rappahannock; and particularly from the towns of Lynchburg, Petersburg, and Gordonsville.[100] As for John Brown's visionary deed at Harper's Ferry in the autumn of 1859, the aftermath can be easily imagined. The spectre of a general insurrection again haunted the minds of the white citizenry and large patrols were kept in constant service to prevent Negro meetings of all types.[101]

Maryland and North Carolina, although more fortunate than their slave-ridden neighbor, did not escape unscathed.

[98] The immediate results of the Nat Turner affair are summarized in John W. Cromwell's "The Aftermath of Nat Turner's Insurrection," *The Journal of Negro History*, V, (1920), 208-234.

[99] Frederick Bancroft, *Slave-Trading in the Old South*, (Baltimore, 1931), 18.

[100] *Calendar of Virginia State Papers*, XI, (1836-1869), 50. Other rumors of unrest during 1856 came from the towns of Williamsburgh and Alexandria, and from Montgomery County. See Laura A. White, "The South in the 1850's as seen by British Consuls," *The Journal of Southern History*, I, (1935), 44.

[101] Brackett, *The Negro in Maryland*, 97-99.

The news of Nat Turner and John Brown brought panic to the other states. In Maryland, baseless rumors of conspiracies, rather than actual outbreaks, seemed to be the rule. In 1845 a plot was "disclosed" in Charles County, Maryland, and a number of Negroes were subsequently sold out of the state.[102] Ten years later there was general excitement over alleged uprisings in Dorchester, Talbot and Prince George's Counties. Resolutions were adopted at the time by various citizens asking that slaveholders keep their servants at home.[103] The reaction to John Brown's raid of 1859 was more intense than had ever before been experienced over insurrections in Maryland. The newspapers for days were full of nothing else but the Harper's Ferry incident. Large patrols were called out everywhere and talk was general of a concerted uprising of all the slaves in Maryland and Virginia. A martial atmosphere prevailed.[104]

In 1802 an insurrection was reported in Bertie County, North Carolina, necessitating an elaborate patrol system.[105] A decade later, another outbreak in Rockingham County was narrowly averted;[106] and in 1816 further plots were discovered at Tarboro, New Bern, Camden and Hillsboro.[107] Several minor disturbances occurred in 1821 among the

[102] Brackett, *The Negro in Maryland*, 96.

[103] *Ibid.*, 97.

[104] *Ibid.*, 97-99.

[105] John Spencer Bassett, *Slavery in the State of North Carolina*, Johns Hopkins University Studies in Historical and Political Science, XVII, (Baltimore, 1899), 332. The nature of North Carolina laws during 1777-1788 regarding insurrections indicates the keen fears entertained of slave uprisings. One preamble of 1777 begins "- - Whereas the evil and pernicious practice of freeing slaves in this State, ought at this alarming and critical time to be guarded against by every friend and well-wisher to his country - - -." This idea is repeated in the insurrection laws of 1778 and 1788. Walter Clark (ed.), *The State Records of North Carolina*, (Goldsboro, N. C., 1905), XXIV, (1777-1788), 14, 221, 964. The laws regulating manumission were made increasingly stringent for fear of creating a dangerous class of free Negroes.

[106] *Calendar of Virginia State Papers*, X, (1808-1835), 120-2.

[107] A. H. Gordon, "The Struggle of the Negro Slaves for Physical Freedom," *Journal of Negro History*, XIII, (1928), 22-35.

slaves of Bladen, Carteret, Jones, and Onslow Counties.[108]
On October 6, 1831, a Georgia newspaper reported an extensive slave conspiracy in North Carolina with ramifica-
tions in the eastern counties of Duplin, Sampson, Wayne,
New Hanover, Lenoir, Cumberland, and Bladen.[109]

Slave plots in South Carolina during the national period
seem to have been abortive for the most part, but several
of the projects could easily have been uprisings of the first
magnitude. During November, 1797, slave trials in Charleston disclosed a plot to burn the city. Two Negroes were
hanged and three deported.[110] The Camden plot of June,
1816, was a very serious affair and envisaged a concerted
attempt to burn the town and massacre its inhabitants. A
favorite slave reported the plot to his master, Colonel Ches-
nut, who thereupon informed Governor Williams. Six of
the slave leaders were executed and patrol measures were
strengthened.[111]

The outstanding threat of insurrection in the State was
the Denmark Vesey plot of 1822. The leader, Denmark,
was a free Negro of Charleston, a native of St. Thomas in
the West Indies, who had purchased his freedom in 1800
from the proceeds of a lottery prize and had since worked
in the city as a carpenter. He desired to emulate the Negro
leaders of St. Domingo and win the freedom of his people.
Preaching that conditions had become intolerable for the
slave, he urged a war against the slave-holder. A white

[108] Hugh T. Lefler, (ed.), *North Carolina History told by Contemporaries*,
(Chapel Hill, 1934), 265.

[109] Milledgeville (Georgia) *Federal Union*, October 6, 1831, quoted in
ibid.; The repercussion of the Nat Turner insurrection at Murfreesboro,
Hertford County, has been graphically described by an eye witness, "It
was court week and most of our men were twelve miles away at Winton.
Fear was seen in every face, women pale and terror stricken, children crying for protection, men fearful and full of foreboding, but determined to be
ready for the worst." Quoted from the Baltimore *Gazette*, November 16,
1831, by Stephen B. Weeks, "The Slave Insurrection in Virginia," *American Magazine of History*, XXV, (1891), 456.

[110] H. M. Henry, *The Police Patrol of the Slave in South Carolina*, 150.

[111] Holland, *A Refutation of the Calumnies*, —, 75.

man was to purchase guns and powder for his proposed army; Charleston was to be captured and burnt, the shipping of the town seized, and all would sail away for the West Indies to freedom. Again a "faithful slave"—or spy —exposed the plot and severe reprisals were instituted. Thirty-five Negroes were executed and thirty-seven sold out of the state.[112]

Because of the number of free Negroes involved, the Legislature passed an act preventing such persons from entering the state. To avoid, as far as possible, the contagion of abolitionist and kindred ideas, the purchase of slaves was forbidden from the West Indies, Mexico, South America, Europe, and the states north of Maryland. Slaves, who had resided in these forbidden areas, were likewise denied entrance into South Carolina.[113] A Charleston editor, Benjamin Elliott, penned a sharp reply to the Northern accusations of cruelty, by pointing out that New York in the insurrection of 1741 had executed thirty-five and deported eighty-five. He demanded that the Federal Government act under its power to suppress insurrection.[114] In July, 1829, another plot was reported in Georgetown County[115] and in 1831, the year of Nat Turner's attack, one in Laurens County.[116]

Georgia, like South Carolina, was able to avert the worst consequences of repeated slave plots. One was reported in Greene County in 1810;[117] a plan to destroy Atlanta came to light in May, 1819;[118] during 1831, disquieting rumors came

[112] J. Hamilton, (ed.), *An Account of the Late Intended Insurrection* (Boston, 1822) also Holland, *A Refutation of the Calumnies,* —, 77-82; *Niles Register*, XXIII, (1822-3), 9-12.

[113] *An Act of the Legislature of South Carolina Passed at the Session in December to Prevent Free Negroes and Persons of Color from Entering This State*, (Charleston, 1824).

[114] Appendix to Holland, *A Refutation of the Calumnies*, 81.

[115] *J.C.N.*, 340.

[116] Henry, *The Police Control of the Slave in South Carolina*, 153

[117] Flanders, *Plantation Slavery in Georgia*, 274.

[118] *Niles Register*, XVI (1819), 213.

from Milledgeville and Laurens County;[119] four years later, a plot for a general uprising on the Coast was disclosed;[120] in 1851 another plot in Atlanta was reported;[121] and in 1860, similar reports came from Crawford and Brooks Counties.[122]

Florida experienced an uprising in March, 1820, along Talbot Island which was put down by a detachment of federal troops.[123] Another was reported in December, 1856, in Jacksonville.[124] Alabama discovered a plot in January, 1837, believed to have been instigated by a free Negro, M'Donald.[125] Mississippi seems to have been the central area of a widespread slave plot in July, 1835, threatening the entire Cotton Kingdom. Far-reaching plans of revolt had been drawn up by a white, John A. Murrell, who enjoyed a reputation as a Negro kidnapper and land pirate. Ten or fifteen Negroes and a number of whites were hanged for participation in the plot.[126]

Next to Virginia, Louisiana had the greatest difficulty among the southern states in coping with repeated attempts at insurrection. Governor Claiborne of the Mississippi Territory received frequent letters concerning plots in various parts of Louisiana. In 1804, New Orleans seems

[119] Flanders, *Plantation Slavery in Georgia*, 274.

[120] *Niles Register*, XLIX, (1935-6), 172.

[121] Flanders, *Plantation Slavery in Georgia*, 275. Georgia suffered in common with the other southern states during the scare of 1856; White, ''The South in the 1850's as Seen by British Consuls,'' 43.

[122] Flanders, *Plantation Slavery in Georgia*, 275-6, 186. The abolitionists were accused of organizing the slave plots of the thirties and thereafter. One New England abolitionist, Kitchel, who opened a school for Negroes in Tarversville, Twigg County, Georgia, in 1835, was driven out of the community because he was said to have incited the slaves to revolt. *Ibid.*, 275.

[123] *J.C.N.*, III, 327.

[124] James Stirling, *Letters from the Slave States*, (London, 1857), 299.

[125] *J.C.N.*, III, 141. Alabama had two rumors of slave plots reported in 1860, White, ''The South in the 1850's as Seen by British Consuls,'' 47.

[126] *Niles Register*, XLIX, (1835-6), 119; also Elizur Wright, (ed.), *Quarterly Anti-Slavery Magazine*, (New York, 1837), II, 104-11.

to have been threatened.[127] Several months later another alarm came from the plantations at Pointe Coupee.[128] In 1805, the attempt of a Frenchman to teach the doctrine of equality to slaves, led to general fears of an uprising.[129]

An actual outbreak occurred in January, 1811. Beginning from a plantation in the parish of St. John the Baptist, about thirty-six miles above New Orleans, a concerted slave uprising spread along the Mississippi. The Negroes formed disciplined companies to march upon New Orleans to the beating of drums. Their force, estimated to include from 180 to 500 persons, was defeated in a pitched battle with the troops.[130] According to one historian many of those executed were decapitated and their heads placed on poles along the river as an example to others.[131]

Another uprising took place in the same area in March, 1829, causing great alarm before it was suppressed. Two leaders were hanged.[132] Other plots were reported in 1835, 1837, 1840, 1841 and 1842[133] An uprising occurred in August, 1856, at New Iberia.[134]

The situation in Tennessee, Kentucky, and Texas may be briefly summarized. In Tennessee, plots were disclosed during 1831, 1856, and 1857.[135] Kentucky, in December, 1856, hanged several ringleaders of an attempted insurrection at

[127] Dunbar, Rowland, (ed.), *Official Letter Book of W.C.C. Claiborne,* (Jackson, 1917), II, (1801-1816), 337-8.

[128] *Ibid.,* III, (1804-1806), 6.

[129] *Ibid.,* 187.

[130] *Ibid.,* V, (1809-1811), 93-142.

[131] Francois Xavier Martin, *The History of Louisiana,* (New Orleans, 1829), II, 300-301. During the fall of the following year another plot was reported. *J.C.N.,* III, 449.

[132] *Niles Register,* XXVI, (1829), 53.

[133] *Ibid.,* LIII, (1837-8), 129; LX, (1841), 368; LXIII, (1842-3), 212.

[134] V. Alton Moody, *Slavery on the Louisiana Sugar Plantations,* (Univ. of Michigan Press, 1924), 41; also Phillips, *American Negro Slavery,* 486. *J.C.N.,* III, 648.

[135] Caleb P. Patterson, *The Negro in Tennessee,* Univ. of Texas Bulletin No. 225, (Austin, February 1, 1922), 49; *J.C.N.,* II, 565-6; Stirling, *Letters from the Slave States,* 294.

Hopkinsville, in which a white man was involved.[136] That same year, two Negroes were punished by being whipped to death in Texas for an alleged conspiracy at Columbus, Colorado County.[137]

Owing to the nature of such a study any claim to an exhaustive treatment would be mere pretense. An analysis of slave patrol history alone would suggest the existence of far more conspiracies and outbreaks than those already mentioned. It is clear however that *ante-bellum* society of the South suffered from a larger degree of domestic insecurity than the conventional view would indicate. No doubt many Negroes made the required adjustments to slavery, but the romantic picture of careless abandon and contentment fails to be convincing. The struggle of the Negro for his liberty, beginning with those dark days on the slaveship, was far from sporadic in nature, but an ever-recurrent battle waged everywhere with desperate courage against the bonds of his master.

HARVEY WISH

De Paul University

[134] *J. C. N.*, 299.
[137] Frederick Law Olmsted, *A Journey Through Texas*, (New York, 1857), 513-4; Stirling, *Letters From the Slave States*, 300.

The Slave Insurrection Panic of 1856

By HARVEY WISH

In the fall of 1856 a series of startling allegations regarding numerous slave insurrections broke through the habitual reserve maintained on the topic by the Southern press. Wild rumors of an all-embracing slave plot extending from Delaware to Texas, with execution set for Christmas day, spread through the South. Tales were yet unforgotten of Gabriel's "army" attempting to march on Richmond in 1800, of Denmark Vesey's elaborate designs upon Charleston in 1822, of Nat Turner's bloody insurrection at Southampton, Virginia, in 1831, and of the various other plots and outbreaks that characterized American slavery since the days of the early slave ship mutinies.[1] Silence in the press could not stem the recurrent fears of insurrection transmitted by the effective "grapevine" intelligence of the South.

Sectional passions were stirred almost to the bursting point in the year of the Buchanan-Frémont presidential election. The provocative events in "bleeding Kansas," intensified by extremists on both sides, revealed a miniature civil war that was prophetic of worse things to come; the assault on Senator Charles Sumner by Preston Brooks of South Carolina furnished a fresh opportunity for displaying mutual hatreds; abolitionists and Southern extremists vied with each other in "dis-unionist conventions"; and unwittingly the Supreme Court poured oil on these flames in the Dred Scott hearings. New economic factors further complicated the situation as the final months of a boom era brought the price of slaves to high levels, inspiring a proposal by Governor James H.

[1] For a summary of slave plots and slave ship mutinies, see the writer's article, "American Slave Insurrections Before 1861," in *Journal of Negro History* (Lancaster, Pa., Washington, 1916-), XXII (1937), 299-320.

Adams of South Carolina that the foreign slave trade be reopened.[2] Although this suggestion became the target of severe criticisms within the South itself, the Northern press regarded it as a fresh provocation.

Worst of all for the cause of conciliation in the eyes of Northern moderates as well as Southerners appeared the ominous rise of the frankly sectional Republican party in 1856 to a position challenging national control. The presidential candidacy of John C. Frémont, like that of Abraham Lincoln in 1860, lent itself to opponents' charges of hostility to the South and seemed to sanction threats of disunion. Contemporary opinion, with remarkably few exceptions, attributed the revival of slave plots to the excitement wrought by the national election. The New York *Herald* of December 11, 1856, editorializing on the numerous slave plots, declared:

> The simultaneous discovery of similar plots in various localities, remote from each other, can only be accounted for upon the hypothesis of some general delusion lately diffused throughout the South, and acted upon spontaneously here and there, by the negroes themselves. . . . The idea, no doubt, was that with Fremont's election all the negroes of the South would be instantly emancipated or supported from the North in a bloody revolt.

Likewise the Manchester *Guardian* of December 23, observing the American scene, showed an intimate knowledge of the prevailing election excitement in the South:

> The ferment excited in the minds of the masters soon extended itself to the slaves—for all who have lived in slave-holding communities well know how eagerly every scrap of parlor conversation, every excited harangue on the stump, or loud-toned dispute in the streets, is treasured by the negro and made the burden of kitchen comment during the hours of the night.[3]

Early reports of slave plots, partially disregarded before election day, revealed that several Texas counties had organized "Vigilance Com-

---

[2] The rising price of slaves was the subject of considerable newspaper comment in 1856. The firm of Dickinson, Hill, and Company, auctioneers of Richmond, Virginia, declared that the gross amount of their Negro sales for that year had reached the enormous sum of two million dollars and that the total for all Richmond houses was approximately twice that much. A Negro carpenter brought $1,615, and a woman of fifty to sixty years of age sold for $725 cash. New York *Herald*, January 16, 1857.

[3] Editorial reprinted in *ibid.*, January 10, 1857. Frederick Law Olmsted, visiting the Lower South at this time, attributed the insurrections of 1856 to the incendiary remarks

mittees" upon the popular California model to investigate alarming tales of insurrection. A committee at Columbus, Colorado County, in the southeastern part of the state, wrote to the Galveston *News* on September 9 that they had discovered a well-organized plot to murder the entire white population. The slaves had in their possession large quantities of pistols, bowie knives, guns, and ammunition. A fantastic conspiratorial organization existed among them with the significant password, "Leave not a shadow behind." At a late hour of September 6 all were to make a simultaneous effort to kill the whites except for certain favored individuals. Two or more slaves were to be apportioned to each house for this purpose. Afterwards they would capture the horses about Columbus and fight their way to freedom in Mexico. More than two hundred Negroes and the entire Mexican element in the county appeared to be involved. There was no definite proof against the Mexicans although there were certain inferences. One of their number, a certain Frank, was believed to be the instigator of the plot. The committee passed a resolution "forever forbidding any Mexican from coming within the limits of the county." All resident Mexicans were ordered to leave the county within five days and never to return on penalty of death. Two Negroes were whipped to death and three others hanged.[4] From the postmaster at Hallettsville, in adjacent Lavaca County, came the details of a proposed slave revolt under an Ohio abolitionist named Davidson and two others who were to lead the slaves to kill their masters, and to seize all available arms and ammunition for a flight to Mexico. Davidson was captured and confessed to the committee that the plot was planned for October 31.[5] He was given a hundred lashes for his part in the conspiracy.[6] During the panic a statement was issued from Harrison County, on the Louisiana border, that the rumors of insurrec-

made during the presidential election by ambitious Southern politicians who misrepresented the effects of a Frémont victory. *A Journey Through Texas* (New York, 1857), xxiv.

[4] New York *Tribune*, November 1, 1856; Boston *Liberator*, October 3, 1856; Olmsted, *A Journey Through Texas*, 503-504.

[5] Letter of Postmaster Graves of Hallettsville, November 9, 1856, to the Galveston *Civilian*, reprinted in Lexington (Kentucky) *Observer and Reporter*, November 26, 1856.

[6] Maysville (Kentucky) *Eagle*, December 13, 1856.

tion there had been exaggerated. Investigation had shown no evidence of an actual plot.[7] This denial, repeated in many newspapers, preceded any actual news of difficulties in the locality.

The Texas incidents were but a prelude to the more serious slave plots which soon broke out in Tennessee and Kentucky, spreading panic into every Southern state. Robert Bunch, British consul at Charleston, reported to his government upon information learned from private sources that Nashville was the center of a projected servile insurrection involving the surrounding states.[8] On October 29 a Negro girl belonging to G. W. Vandel, an engineer of Fayette County, Tennessee, revealed a plot set for the day of the presidential election when all the able-bodied white men would be away at the polls. After murdering and plundering the remaining citizens the slaves planned to go to Memphis where friends awaited them with arms. They then expected to escape to the free states. Vandel and his wife quickly confirmed this story by eavesdropping upon the slave cabins at night. Next day he had thirty-two slaves arrested and sufficient evidence adduced to commit twenty-three to jail at Somerville. A vigilance committee was hastily formed as the community became aroused. One member wrote to the Memphis *Enquirer*:

Facts were brought to light sufficient to satisfy all present, not only of the guilty intentions of some six or eight of the Negroes arrested, but it was made clear to the minds of thinking men present, that the thing was not confined to this particular neighborhood, but that they expected to act in concert with various others in the surrounding counties and States.[9]

A week later further excitement broke out when twenty-four guns and two kegs of powder were discovered in the possession of slaves at Columbia, Maury County. Similar reports of slave plots came from Frank-

[7] *Ibid.*, December 18, 1856. For similar evidences of unrest in Louisiana and Texas, see James Stirling, *Letters from the Slave States* (London, 1857), 300.

[8] Laura A. White, "The South in the 1850's as Seen by British Consuls," in *Journal of Southern History* (Baton Rouge, 1935-), I (1935), 29-48.

[9] Letter of W. E. Eppes of Fayette County to Col. J. P. Pryor, November 2, 1856, in Boston *Liberator*, November 28, 1856.

lin County. A panic in Perry County resulted in the killing of ten or twelve Negroes by their owners.[10]

Perhaps the most terror-stricken community of the entire South in 1856 comprised Stewart and Montgomery counties, Tennessee, on the western border of Kentucky. Although the combined slave population appeared to be 12,000 while the whites were at least 19,000, at many points the Negroes outnumbered the rest of the community. In the iron district on the Cumberland and Tennessee rivers there were eight to ten thousand slaves employed at the various iron works making charcoal, aiding in mining operations, and tending furnaces under the supervision of a few white overseers. Many of the plants were within several miles of each other, some in sections containing few white inhabitants. In the neighborhood of Louisa Furnace, Montgomery County, a keg of gun powder was found beneath a church. A large collection of arms and ammunition had also been discovered and seized. On the morning of November 21, a Negro, Britton, belonging to S. D. Raimey, was heard arousing the slaves, presumably for an outbreak, but his actual words appeared to have been unintelligible. When Britton resisted an overseer's order to halt he was instantly shot.[11] A white man, who was alleged to have been counseling insurrection at the time of his capture, was imprisoned. The slaves, organized as "generals" and "captains," had, according to their confessions, planned an uprising for Christmas day. They were to march on Clarksville, the county seat, capture the town, plunder its banks, and then flee to the North.[12] A citizen wrote that "The plot is deep laid and embraces the slaves throughout a wide extent of territory, ranging from Kentucky South and West."[13] At Clarksville a strong special patrol was on duty every night; it was reported that every housekeeper was prepared with arms for any emergency. By December 11 the Nashville *Union and American* observed:

[10] Louisville *Journal*, November 9, 1856, quoted in Boston *Liberator*, December 12, 1856; also in Baltimore *Sun*, December 11, 1856.
[11] New York *Herald*, December 12, 1856.
[12] Nashville *Banner*, November 27, 1856, quoted in Boston *Liberator*, December 12, 1856; Maysville *Eagle*, December 6, 1856.
[13] Maysville *Eagle*, December 6, 1856.

"Quite a panic has existed in parts of the State during the last two weeks growing out of some discovered plots for insurrection among the slaves. . . . Let the people of the South watch bad white men who come among us in sheep's clothing."[14] The city council of Clarksville notified the ironmasters and other owners of slaves on December 17 that no visiting slave would be permitted to remain in the town for more than two hours unless accompanied by some "responsible white person" on penalty of twenty lashes.[15] Slaves having their master's written permission were exempted. Other stringent rules designed to regulate the holiday activities of the Negro were laid down to avoid contacts of other slaves with those of Clarksville.

At Dover, chief town in adjacent Stewart County, an intense feeling of panic over reports of slave plots developed during the first week of November. The editor of the *Courrier des Etats Unis,* visiting this area on December 2, found the entire white population including the children armed and organized for defense. A Negro, who had escaped from the Cumberland Iron Works to avoid taking part in a conspiracy, made such revelations as to cause the arrest of nearly eighty slaves, "almost all of whom avowed their complicity in the plot and even gave the most precise details as to the execution of their project."[16] Three whites, former members of the Free Soil party, were arrested on a charge of inciting a riot, then beaten, and driven out of the state; and a Negro abolitionist preacher was arrested. The plot, which had been set for Christmas day, was believed to have contemplated a general massacre of whites, the capture of Dover, and escape to the North. As new confessions were wrung from the slaves, the panic spread from the Cumberland River to the Memphis region. Nineteen Negroes were eventually hanged at Dover.[17] The jails in many of the counties were crowded with suspects and the county courts in each district were quickly assembled

---

[14] Quoted in New York *Tribune,* December 20, 1856.

[15] Baltimore *Sun,* December 18, 1856.

[16] Quoted in *ibid.,* December 13, 1856.

[17] Evansville (Indiana) *Journal,* December 9, 1856, quoted in Boston *Liberator,* December 26, 1856; Baltimore *Sun,* December 15, 1856. A white man, one Hurd, suspected of inciting slaves to rebellion, was captured in Memphis, taken across to Arkansas, and given a thousand lashes. Maysville *Eagle,* January 8, 1857.

to hear the terror-stricken prisoners. Vigilance committees and patrols were appointed for each neighborhood and township. Women and children emigrated to more populous districts. The atmosphere was ripe for the most exaggerated claims of slave uprisings. Sixty slaves belonging to Senator John Bell, then absent from the state, and employed in the Cumberland Iron Works were alleged to have been implicated; nine of these were hanged, four by court process and five by a mob. Bell, reputed to have been a kind master, lost some ten thousand dollars of slave property by the insurrection panic.[18] Twenty-five iron furnaces ceased operations due to the common paralysis. During the prolonged excitement which lasted until January no actual slave outbreak occurred.[19]

On December 10 the Nashville city council increased the slave patrol for day and night duty. Negro schools and Negro preachings were forbidden; all assemblages of Negroes after sundown were likewise prohibited. Free Negroes coming in from other counties and free resident Negroes, "if found in suspicious circumstances," were to be arrested.[20] Nashville experienced many wild rumors regarding anticipated uprisings but investigating committees were unable to discover any definite evidence of such plots. In neighboring Gallatin County, a citizen wrote, "Our town has presented one continuous scene of excitement during the past week."[21] Investigation, he claimed, established the fact of a plot

[18] Dispatch, dated December 16, in New York *Tribune*, December 20, 1856. The *Tribune's* correspondent reported: "The insurrectionary movement in Tennessee obtained more headway than is known to the public—important facts being suppressed in order to check the spread of the contagion." *Ibid.*; Baltimore *Sun*, December 24, 1856.

[19] According to the informants of the New York *Tribune*, the confessions appeared spurious. Actually, a story had been circulated among the slaves "that Col. Fremont with a numerous force to back him, was waiting at the bottom of the Cumberland River for Christmas night to come, when he and his army were to emerge from the river to aid in the deliverance of the slaves. The fact that he was there was proved by the sudden rise in the river, which was insisted upon as being caused by the great number of men and boats collected at the bottom. Believing that Fremont's powder would be dampened, the Blacks attempted to buy up a store of it for him. . . . It does not appear that they expected to do anything for themselves." *Ibid.*, December 20, 1856.

[20] Baltimore *Sun*, December 13, 1856; Boston *Liberator*, December 19, 1856; Maysville *Eagle*, January 8, 1857. The Louisville *Democrat* reported that there was a movement on foot in Tennessee to banish free Negroes beyond the border of the state. Lexington *Observer and Reporter*, January 7, 1857.

[21] Lexington *Observer and Reporter*, December 20, 1856; Baltimore *Sun*, December 18, 1856.

but the extent of organization was not yet determined. Twenty-five to thirty Negroes were arrested and brought before a vigilance committee. The Nashville *Union and American,* accounting for the increasing rumors of slave unrest, commented:

> The recent Presidential canvass has had a deleterious effect on the slave population. The negroes manifested an unusual interest in the result, and attended the political meetings of the whites in large numbers. This is dangerous. The necessity for watchfulness is very great. The slaveholders must anxiously guard, both against the attacks of Northern fanatics, and the insidious wiles of enemies at home.[22]

The Memphis *Visitor* editorialized in similar vein at the beginning of the panic:

> The excitement in reference to the recent reports in regard to a probable servile insurrection is probably greater than is justified by the real state of the case. . . . We have heard [during the political campaign] speakers of both parties use language . . . calculated to inspire *the hope among dissatisfied slaves that with an effort on their own part, they would be free* in the event of the success of the most abused candidate; and *we have seen crowds of negroes at the out-skirts of political assemblages in this city, listening attentively to the efforts of restless demagogues to prove* that the prospects were very fair for the election of Fremont. Was it not supposed that the negroes would take these things home and talk over them with other slaves? . . . If this eternal agitation of the slavery question does not cease we may expect servile insurrections in dead earnest.[23]

The panic spirit soon penetrated across the Kentucky border. A vigilance committee of Lafayette, Christian County, in that state addressed an appeal for military aid to the "Gentlemen of Hopkinsville." "From reliable information we expect an attack from the negroes of the Iron Works on our town tomorrow morning, perhaps tonight. Please come to our assistance."[24] The secretary of the committee appended this information:

> The negroes of Eclipse, Clark, and Lagrange have united and are marching towards Dover and were within eight miles of that place when last heard from.

[22] Quoted in Boston *Liberator,* December 12, 1856.
[23] *Ibid.* The editorial continued: "A lady a few days ago went into her kitchen and gave some directions to the negro cook, who replied with a sneer, 'When Fremont's elected, you'll have to sling them pots yourself.' Now, was not this negro led to believe that Fremont would be elected, by some alarmist on the stump?"
[24] Lexington *Observer and Reporter,* December 10, 1856.

Their intention is to relieve the negroes at Dover, then march to the Rolling Mill, then to the Bellwood Furnace, then through Lafayette on to Hopkinsville and the Ohio River.[25]

At Hopkinsville the correspondent of the Louisville *Courier* heard one phrase on all lips, "The negroes are marching on us!" He noted that the telegraph poles were cut down and communication broken off. About one hundred and fifty armed men left for Lafayette under the command of Captain James Jackson and Sheriff Gowen.[26]

During the first week of December rumors of slave plots spread into Henderson County on the Ohio River where it was believed that the holidays would unloose open revolt upon the whites.[27] Another Christmas plot was disclosed by a Negro boy in Campbellsville, Taylor County, where considerable dissatisfaction had existed among the slaves.[28] Four or five Negroes were arrested and a night patrol organized. At Cadiz, Trigg County, it was alleged that another center of a slave plot had been discovered. A free Negro preacher, Solomon Young, declared to be the "generalissimo" of the plotters and a notorious character, was hanged on December 19. The responsibility for the plot was attributed to "locofoco" orators and newspapers. As excitement blazed, a vigilance committee began wholesale arrests of suspects and a special court session was set for Christmas day.[29] Similar excitement was experienced near Russellville, Logan County, where a Negro, employed in one of the iron works across the border in Tennessee, was whipped to death after remarking that he knew all about the plot but would not tell.[30] Even in

[25] *Ibid.*

[26] *Ibid.* A citizen at Pembroke, Christian County, wrote that Bob Murrell, a Negro at the central mill, had been whipped to death for his part in a plot. He added his forebodings: "I have no doubt but that [the plot] is a universal thing all over the Southern States and that every negro, fifteen years old, either knows of it or is into it; and that the most confidential house servants are the ones to be the most active in the destruction of their own families." Canton (Kentucky) *Dispatch*, December 13, 1856, quoted in Boston *Liberator*, January 16, 1857.

[27] Lexington *Observer and Reporter*, December 10, 1856.

[28] Louisville *Journal*, December 17, 1856, quoted in Baltimore *Sun*, December 19, 1856; Lexington *Observer and Reporter*, December 20, 1856.

[29] Lexington *Observer and Reporter*, December 27, 1856; Baltimore *Sun*, December 20, 1856.

[30] Russellville (Kentucky) *Herald*, December 20, 1856, quoted in Baltimore *Sun*, December 22, 1856; Boston *Liberator*, January 2, 1857.

Carter County, at the extreme northeastern part of Kentucky, alleged slave plotters were being discovered and subjected to severe whippings.[31] At Carrollton, Carroll County, some fifty miles northeast of Louisville on the Ohio River, considerable furor was aroused over the alleged slave plots engineered by the Reverend William Anderson, a colored Methodist preacher, who was also accused of aiding fugitive slaves to escape to the North. After a reward of $600 had been offered for his apprehension, he was captured with documents in his possession implicating "distinguished Northerners." His examination, however, proved disappointingly innocuous and he was discharged.[32] Another exciting Christmas plot involving some two hundred Negroes was discovered in Wyoming, Bath County, in the extreme northeastern portion of Kentucky. Forty Negroes, fully armed, were arrested at a colored festival. Their plan was to assemble all the slaves at White Oak Creek and then to cut their way to Ohio. [33] It was estimated that at least ten or twelve alleged leaders of insurrections had been hanged in six counties of Kentucky and that many more awaiting trial might ultimately share their fate.[34] The Lexington *Observer and Reporter,* a Fillmore organ of the American party, noted closely the panic spirit in Kentucky and elsewhere:

From every quarter of the South we hear of insurrections and rumors of insurrections among the slaves. . . . During the Presidential contest the Democratic party was constantly crying out that Fremont would be elected, and the institution of slavery be overthrown, unless the American party of the South came to their rescue. In this city . . . negroes stood in swarms about the Court House Yard. They heard it proclaimed [by the Democrats] that the Know-Nothing party were aiding Fremont in voting for Fillmore, and that they were his secret friends.[35]

From Tennessee and Kentucky the contagion of fear swept across the Mississippi River into Missouri and Arkansas. Insurrectionary move-

[31] This refers to the plot involving the slaves of William McMinnis, a large planter of Carter County. Boston *Liberator,* January 23, 1857.

[32] Baltimore *Sun,* December 17, 22, 1856.

[33] Mount Sterling (Kentucky) *Whig,* December 26, 1856, quoted in Maysville *Eagle,* December 27, 1856.

[34] Maysville *Eagle,* January 6, 1857. The Mayor of Louisville issued a proclamation that "all slaves will be imprisoned who are found from home after 8 o'clock at night during the holidays." Baltimore *Sun,* December 25, 1856.

[35] Lexington *Observer and Reporter,* December 20, 1856.

ments, originating in Obion County, Tennessee, and Fulton County, Kentucky, were traced to New Madrid and Scott counties in Missouri. Information was received that the slaves of the four counties were planning an uprising for Christmas day. A meeting of anxious citizens was held at New Madrid on December 15 to discuss the situation. After listening to evidence obtained from "the ringleaders and instigators" of the plot, the group appointed vigilance committees to carry out a series of resolutions: Negro meetings were banned and colored ministers forbidden to preach; slaves might not attend public meetings unless accompanied by a master or his agent; the system of "passes" for slaves was carefully circumscribed in application; and missionary efforts among them were to be discontinued.[36] The *Missouri Democrat* of December 4, commenting on the "numberless alarms respecting contemplated risings in the South," stated, "This is assuredly a most lamentable condition for the Slave States for nothing causes such terror upon the plantations as the bare suspicion of these insurrections."[37]

In Arkansas the most specific reports of slave plots came from Union County on the Louisiana border and the eastern county of St. Francis. The conspiracy in Union County was declared to be led by an abolitionist, one Hancock, and several others who were organizing three hundred Negroes for an attack to be made on November 14 at the county seat, El Dorado. After a successful massacre and plunder of the town's inhabitants, the assailants expected to reach Kansas. Although Hancock was immediately captured he proved to be innocent, but admitted knowledge of the particulars of the plot. After his acquittal, he was seized by a mob, taken to the woods, and shot. Another alleged leader, a certain Martin, was declared guilty by the El Dorado court and hanged.[38] A similar panic shook adjacent Ashley County. In St. Francis County a slave revealed a plot set for Christmas day when a band would burn

[36] New Madrid (Missouri) *Times*, quoted in Baltimore *Sun*, November 25, 1856; Boston *Liberator*, December 12, 1856.

[37] Quoted in *Annual Reports of the American Anti-Slavery Society, 1857-1858* (New York, 1859), 78.

[38] Lexington *Observer and Reporter*, October 29, 1856; Boston *Liberator*, December 12, 1856.

Madison and other nearby towns. Three Negroes broke down under a whipping by the local vigilance committee to confess that they were involved.[39] Subsequently, a proposal was made before the Arkansas legislature that all free Negroes be removed from the state, but the measure was defeated.[40]

The Hancock affair of Union County, Arkansas, was presumed to be directly related to plots in northern Louisiana. Amidst the growing panic in that section, planters investigated supposed plots among their slaves but were unable to discover any substance to these fears. In the delta region, however, serious plots were reported, particularly in the parishes of St. Martin, Assumption, and St. Mary. The town of St. Martinville, St. Martin Parish, "was thrown into great commotion" on November 18 by Negro confessions regarding an insurrection planned for Christmas day. The ringleaders, alleged to have been favorite family servants, were imprisoned.[41] At Napoleonville, Assumption Parish, a Negro boy, John, belonging to the planter, F. Robichaux, was punished for his part in a proposed uprising by two months imprisonment, 350 lashes, and the requirement that he wear irons for the ensuing two years.[42] Three white men were imprisoned in St. Mary Parish as ringleaders of a slave plot; Negroes, previously arrested on these charges, were released, with the exception of a free Negro.[43] More alarming news came from the Louisiana correspondent of the New York *Tribune* on December 31: "I have reliable information from New Orleans that within a few days there have been serious troubles among the slaves in Louisiana; and that as many as twenty negroes have been hung; but the newspapers carefully refrain from any mention of the facts." In several Louisiana parishes public meetings were held for the purpose of common consultation regarding precautionary measures. The sale of liquor to slaves was denounced as *prima facie* evidence of seditious in-

---

[39] Memphis *Appeal*, December 30, 1856, quoted in Lexington *Observer and Reporter*, January 7, 1857; Maysville *Eagle*, January 8, 1857.

[40] Lexington *Observer and Reporter*, January 14, 1857.

[41] Baltimore *Sun*, December 4, 1856; Lexington *Observer and Reporter*, December 13, 1856; Maysville *Eagle*, December 2, 1856.

[42] Lexington *Observer and Reporter*, January 7, 1857.

[43] Maysville *Eagle*, December 13, 1856.

tentions.[44] When the long-dreaded holidays passed without an outbreak the planters were visibly relieved. The New Orleans *Picayune* of January 2 remarked confidently:

The holidays have come and passed, and we hear no where of the disturbances among the negro population which, according to rumor, were threatened as likely to take place generally in the South about Christmas. . . . There was never any fear of a concerted attempt to rise, or a general insubordination, nor was full credit given to the details which the telegraph brought us from time to time of alleged attempts at insurrection in various places.[45]

Nevertheless, the editor pointed out that the recent presidential election had been so managed as to awaken hopes of emancipation among the slaves and to encourage the efforts of traveling abolitionists.

None of the Gulf states seemed to have escaped the common panic. In Jackson, Mississippi, the community was aroused on December 21 by confessions of a projected slave uprising and twenty-seven Negroes were jailed. The Mayor called upon all citizens to organize for defense.[46] Subsequent newspaper reports ridiculed the rumors of insurrection as "utterly without foundation."[47] Similar fears, probably unfounded, were experienced in Canton, Mississippi. Within Alabama plots were discovered in Sumter, Marion, and Perry counties; one hundred slaves in all were imprisoned and a white man also appeared to be involved.[48] A sensational report that "a bloody conspiracy is now ripening with a certain class of the population" and set for Christmas day came from Quincy, Gadsden County, Florida, on the southern border of Georgia. The editor of the Jacksonville *Floridian and Journal* suggested on December 6 that the citizens of the state organize an adequate slave patrol ready for any emergency.[49] In Georgia the Athens *Southern Watchman*

---

[44] Boston *Liberator*, December 12, 1856. A slave uprising was reported in New Iberia Parish, Louisiana, during August, 1856. Helen T. Catterall (ed.), *Judicial Cases concerning American Slavery and the Negro*, 5 vols. (Washington, 1926-1937), III, 648.

[45] This item, with minor errors, was quoted in Boston *Liberator*, January 23, 1857.

[46] Baltimore *Sun*, December 29, 1856. A Northern visitor to the Vicksburg area in Mississippi on Christmas day, 1857, experienced the tense excitement of a rumored slave outbreak. A. De Puy Van Buren, *Jottings of a Year's Sojourn in the South* (Battle Creek, Mich., 1859), 121-22.

[47] Maysville *Eagle*, January 8, 1857.

[48] Lexington *Observer and Reporter*, January 7, 1857.

[49] Quoted in New York *Tribune*, December 20, 1856.

of January 1, 1857, noted that "our citizens have generally recovered from the 'fright' into which some of them were thrown by the report that an attempt at insurrection was to be made by the negroes throughout the South during the Christmas holidays." The editor demanded that the legislature of Georgia "abate this nuisance" of free Negroes whose residence, he declared, "was incompatible with the public safety."[50]

Maryland shared the nightmare of revolt with her sister states. During the middle of December slave confessions were elicited regarding a Christmas plot in certain parts of Prince George County. To meet this threat public meetings were held for defense measures.[51] About the same time excitement broke out in Charles County after the arrest of two Negroes alleged to have planned insurrection. Two white men, suspected as promoters of the plot, fled from the state before they were apprehended.[52] Elsewhere in Maryland there were reports of the formation of new slave patrols and renewed vigilance exercised over the movements of the colored population.[53] The Baltimore *American* remarked: "The recent frequency of rumors in regard to slave insurrections has not failed to attract attention. . . . Their coincidence . . . with the late election-agitation is not without matter for grave consideration. . . . The happenings of several of these alarms at widely different points within a short interval is ominous."[54]

With the extension of the panic to Virginia, the insurrection wave completed a full cycle within the Southern states. A plot was discovered at Williamsburg during the early part of December which had originated among a group of discontented slaves. The usual arrests followed and the community once more settled down. A similar story came from Montgomery County.[55] In New Kent County a slave named Beverly,

[50] Ulrich B. Phillips (ed.), *Plantation and Frontier*, in John R. Commons *et al* (eds.), *A Documentary History of American Industrial Society*, I, II (Cleveland, 1910), II, 116.

[51] Baltimore *Sun*, December 27, 1856.

[52] New York *Herald*, December 6, 1856. Charles County, Maryland, had already experienced the panic of insurrection plots in 1845. Jeffrey R. Brackett, *The Negro in Maryland* (Baltimore, 1889), 96.

[53] Baltimore *Sun*, December 13, 1856.

[54] Quoted in Lexington *Observer and Reporter*, December 17, 1856.

[55] Baltimore *Sun*, December 13, 1856.

belonging to Sarah Crump, was declared guilty of inciting an insurrection and condemned to be hanged.[56] In Millwood, Clark County, confessions established a plot of free Negroes and slaves which involved Harper's Ferry—an interesting forerunner of John Brown's historic deed. These Negroes told the court that "they had heard white men and negroes talking [that] if Fremont was elected they would be free, and as they knew he was not, they were prepared to fight for it."[57] The citizens of Alexandria and other parts of Fairfax County seemed to have had an exceptionally severe fright over alleged slave plots. Students of the theological seminary formed a special patrol. The Mayor of Alexandria forbade all Negro meetings and strengthened the pass system. State forces sent by Governor Henry Wise arrested forty Negroes at a festival which subsequently proved to be an innocent affair.[58] The Governor received numerous reports of insurrections contemplated for Christmas day and sent arms upon request to the counties of Fauquier, King and Queen, Culpeper, Rappahannock, and the towns of Lynchburg, Petersburg, and Gordonsville.[59] During the Christmas holidays when many waited for the lightning to strike, citizens of Louisa, Spotsylvania, and Orange counties met to organize a committee to whip and drive off all gypsies, peddlers, sellers of spirits to slaves, and all suspicious itinerants in that section of the country.[60] The Richmond *Examiner* of January 23 published a widely-quoted editorial demanding that the free Negroes of the South be either exiled or enslaved on the ground that they were a constant danger in organizing insurrections and setting a bad example of freedom before dissatisfied slaves.[61] The Richmond *Enquirer*, commenting on the symmetry of the Southern slave plots, made this warning statement: "These are not the wild and visionary projects with which negroes may be disposed to amuse themselves in the most

[56] Fredericksburg (Virginia) *News*, January 15, 1857. This newspaper showed extreme reticence in reporting the panic, confining major items to half-inch notices.

[57] Baltimore *Sun*, December 27, 1856.

[58] *Ibid.*, December 16, 1856; *Virginia Traveller*, December 15, 1856, quoted in Boston *Liberator*, December 19, 1856.

[59] H. W. Flournoy (ed.), *Calendar of Virginia State Papers, 1836-1869* (Richmond, 1893), XI, 50.

[60] Fredericksburg *News*, January 26, 1857.

[61] Quoted in Boston *Liberator*, February 27, 1857.

quiet communities but the maturely prepared, and, in some instances, the partially executed plans of a deliberate and widespread purpose of revolt."[62]

At the North many of the abolitionists chose this opportunity to renew their attacks on the slaveholders. The New York *Herald*, professing sorrow over the insurrection panic, complained, "It is painful to see the apparent gusto with which our nigger-worshipping contemporary of the *Tribune* gloats over the news of projected Southern servile insurrections."[63] The editor also expressed his disdain for Thurlow Weed of the Albany (New York) *Journal* who, he said, "rubs his hands together with something of a chuckle of satisfaction." The *Herald* attributed the plots to the universal notion, propagated by agitators, that Frémont's election would mean the emancipation of the slaves who would then be turned loose on the South to provoke civil war. The New York *Tribune* thundered, "Let the South with her growing insurrections look to it. . . . These last suppressed insurrections grew out of the discussions on Kansas. . . . The manacles of the slave must be stricken off."[64] Extremists like A. J. Grover of Illinois proposed that the Garrison group aid all efforts at insurrection on the ground that "revolution is the only hope of the slave; consequently the quicker it comes, the better."[65] A resolution attributed to Frederick Douglass, the famous ex-slave, then editor of a Frémont paper, read, "Resolved, that while we deeply oppose the necessity of shedding human blood . . . we should rejoice in a successful slave insurrection which would teach slaveholders the wrong and danger involved in the act of slaveholding."[66] Abroad, the Manchester *Guardian* commented on the plight of the South:

We venture to assert that in consequence [of the slavery agitation] more slaves

[62] Quoted in *Annual Reports of the American Anti-Slavery Society, 1857-1858*, p. 77; Caleb P. Patterson, *The Negro in Tennessee*, University of Texas *Bulletin* No. 225 (Austin, 1922), 49. In York District, South Carolina, powder and muskets were found in the possession of the slaves. The community was reported to be arming. Maysville *Eagle*, January 6, 1857.

[63] New York *Herald*, December 11, 1856.

[64] New York *Tribune*, December 13, 1856.

[65] A. J. Grover to William L. Garrison, February 24, 1857, in Boston *Liberator*, March 13, 1857.

[66] Maysville *Eagle*, November 1, 1856.

have been induced to escape from their masters, more desperate resolutions have been put into their heads, and more general insecurity entailed upon that species. of property within the past year than during any five years preceding. . . .[67]

Any evaluation of the sensational events of 1856 must observe certain fundamental cautions. Slave confessions made under duress can scarcely meet the test of complete trustworthiness. Although the thesis of an all-embracing slave plot in the South shows remarkable cohesion on the whole as far as geographic and chronological circumstances are concerned, much can be explained away by a counter-thesis of a panic contagion originating in the unusual political setting of the year. It seems probable, however, that a large number of actual slave plots did exist in 1856. The situation in Kentucky and Tennessee particularly seemed to involve authenticated stories of proposed insurrections. It is also apparent from the news items and editorials of the contemporary press that the year 1856 was exceptional for the large crop of individual slave crimes reported, especially those directed against the life of the master. This fact would suggest a fair amount of reality behind the accounts of slave discontent and plotting. The deep-seated feeling of insecurity characterizing the slaveholder's society evoked such mob reactions as those noted in the accounts of insurrections, imaginary and otherwise, upon any suspicion of Negro insubordination. The South, attributing the slave plots to the inspiration of Northern abolitionists, found an additional reason for the desirability of secession; while the abolitionist element of the North, crediting in full the reports of slave outbreaks, was more convinced than ever that the institution of slavery represented a moral leprosy.

[67] New York *Herald*, January 10, 1857.

Acknowledgments

Wendell G. Addington, "Slave Insurrections in Texas," *Journal of Negro History* 35 (October, 1950): 408–34. Reprinted by permission of the *Journal of Negro History*.

Herbert Aptheker, "American Negro Slave Revolts," *Science and Society* 1 (Summer, 1937): 512–38. Reprinted by permission of *Science and Society*.

Herbert Aptheker, "More on American Negro Slave Revolts," *Science and Society* 2 (Spring, 1938): 386–91. Reprinted by permission of *Science and Society*.

Herbert Aptheker, "Maroons within the Present Limits of the United States," *Journal of Negro History* 24 (1939): 167–84. Reprinted by permission of the *Journal of Negro History*.

Raymond A. Bauer and Alice H. Bauer, "Day to Day Resistance to Slavery," *Journal of Negro History* 27 (October, 1942): 388–419. Reprinted by permission of the *Journal of Negro History*.

Jeffrey J. Crow, "Slave Rebelliousness and Social Conflict in North Carolina, 1775–1802," *William and Mary Quarterly*, 3rd Ser., 37 (January, 1980): 79–102. Reprinted by permission of the *William and Mary Quarterly*.

George M. Fredrickson and Christopher Lasch, "Resistance to Slavery," *Civil War History* 13 (1967): 315–29. Reprinted by permission of *Civil War History*.

Eugene D. Genovese, "Rebelliousness and Docility in the Negro Slave: A Critique of the Elkins Thesis," *Civil War History* 13 (1967): 293–314. Reprinted by permission of *Civil War History*.

Seymour L. Gross and Eileen Bender, "History, Politics, and Literature: The Myth of Nat Turner," *American Quarterly* 33 (1971): 487–518. Reprinted by permission of *American Quarterly*.

Donald R. Hickey, "America's Response to the Slave Revolt in Haiti, 1791–1806," *Journal of the Early Republic* 2 (1982): 361-79. Reprinted by permission of the *Journal of the Early Republic*.

Michael P. Johnson, "Runaway Slaves and the Slave Communities in South Carolina, 1799 to 1830," *William and Mary Quarterly,* 3rd Ser., 38

(1981): 418–41. Reprinted by permission of the *William and Mary Quarterly*.

Alex Lichtenstein, "'That Disposition to Theft, With Which They Have Been Branded': Moral Economy, Slave Management, and the Law," *Journal of Social History* 21 (1988): 413–40. Reprinted by permission of the *Journal of Social History*.

Philip D. Morgan and George D. Terry, "Slavery in Microcosm: A Conspiracy Scare in Colonial South Carolina," *Southern Studies* 21, No. 1 (1982): 121–45. Reprinted by permission of *Southern Studies*.

James Oakes, "The Political Significance of Slave Resistance," *History Workshop*, No. 22 (August, 1986): 89–107. Reprinted by permission of *History Workshop*.

Laurence Shore, "Making Mississippi Safe for Slavery: The Insurrectionary Panic of 1835," in Orville Burton and Robert McMath, Jr., eds., *Class, Conflict and Consensus: Antebellum Southern Community Studies* (1982): 96–127. Reprinted by permission of Greenwood Press.

Kenneth M. Stampp, "Rebels and Sambos: The Search for the Negro's Personality in Slavery," *Journal of Southern History* 37 (1971): 367–92. Reprinted by permission of the *Journal of Southern History*.

Richard C. Wade, "The Vesey Plot: A Reconsideration," *Journal of Southern History* (May, 1964): 143–61. Reprinted by permission of the *Journal of Social History*.

Harvey Wish, "American Slave Insurrections Before 1861," *Journal of Negro History* 22 (1937): 299–320. Reprinted by permission of the *Journal of Negro History*.

Harvey Wish, "The Slave Insurrection Panic of 1856," *Journal of Southern History* 5 (May, 1939): 206–22. Reprinted by permission of the *Journal of Southern History*.